THE SUBURBAN CRISIS

The Suburban Crisis

WHITE AMERICA AND THE WAR ON DRUGS

MATTHEW D. LASSITER

PRINCETON UNIVERSITY PRESS
PRINCETON & OXFORD

Published by Princeton University Press
41 William Street, Princeton, New Jersey 08540
99 Banbury Road, Oxford OX2 6JX

press.princeton.edu

GPSR Authorized Representative: Easy Access System Europe - Mustamäe tee 50, 10621 Tallinn, Estonia, gpsr.requests@easproject.com

First paperback printing, 2026
Paperback ISBN 978-0-691-24894-3
Cloth ISBN 978-0-691-17728-1
ISBN (e-book) 978-0-691-24895-0

British Library Cataloging-in-Publication Data is available

Editorial: Bridget Flannery-McCoy and Alena Chekanov
Production Editorial: Kathleen Cioffi
Jacket/Cover Design: Karl Spurzem
Production: Erin Suydam
Publicity: Kate Hensley and Kathryn Stevens
Copyeditor: Dana Henricks

Jacket/Cover image: *TV Room* by Glasshouse Images / Alamy Stock Photo

This book has been composed in Arno Pro

CONTENTS

ILLUSTRATIONS

TABLES

ABBREVIATIONS

ABA	American Bar Association
ACD	Adjournment in Contemplation of Dismissal
ACLU	American Civil Liberties Union
AMA	American Medical Association
BNDD	Bureau of Narcotics and Dangerous Drugs
CBNE	California Bureau of Narcotic Enforcement
CDOJ	California Department of Justice
CFWC	California Federation of Women's Clubs
CMI	California Marijuana Initiative
CYA	California Youth Authority
DARE	Drug Abuse Research and Education (1967)
DARE	Drug Abuse Resistance Education (1983)
DAWN	Developing Adolescents Without Narcotics
DEA	Drug Enforcement Administration
DOJ	U.S. Department of Justice
FBI	Federal Bureau of Investigation
FBN	Federal Bureau of Narcotics
FDA	Food and Drug Administration
GFWC	General Federation of Women's Clubs
HEW	Department of Health, Education, and Welfare
LACNDDC	Los Angeles County Narcotics and Dangerous Drugs Commission
LACSD	Los Angeles County Sheriff's Department

LACYC	Los Angeles County Youth Committee
LAPD	Los Angeles Police Department
LEAA	Law Enforcement Assistance Administration
LSD	Lysergic Acid Diethylamide
MADD	Mothers Against Drunk Driving
MELO	Marijuana Education for Legalization in Oregon
NACC	New York State Narcotic Addiction Control Commission
NFP	National Federation of Parents for Drug-Free Youth
NHTSA	National Highway Transportation Safety Administration
NIAAA	National Institute on Alcohol Abuse and Alcoholism
NIDA	National Institute on Drug Abuse
NIMH	National Institute of Mental Health
NORML	National Organization for the Reform of Marijuana Laws
NTSB	National Transportation Safety Board
ODALE	Office of Drug Abuse Law Enforcement
ODAP	White House Office of Drug Abuse Policy
PANDAA	Parents' Association to Neutralize Drug & Alcohol Abuse
PCP	Phencyclidine (Phenylcyclohexyl Piperidine)
PRIDE	Parents' Resource Institute for Drug Education
SADD	Students Against Driving Drunk
SDS	Students for a Democratic Society
SFPD	San Francisco Police Department
TCLU	Texas Civil Liberties Union

THE SUBURBAN CRISIS

Introduction

PHILLIP WAS FIFTEEN when he bought the heroin that sent three Black male "pushers" to prison in the first mandatory-minimum sentences handed down under Illinois's punitive new narcotics law in 1951. Jeanne, a twenty-year-old showgirl, was confined in a narcotics hospital when Congress and the national media reconfigured her testimony of seeking out dealers in urban slums into a parable of the inevitable progression from marijuana experimentation to heroin addiction and the tragic fate of prostitution across the color line, the tropes that justified the first federal mandatory-minimum penalties for sale and possession of both drugs in the Boggs Act of 1951. Patricia was sixteen and had recovered in a suburban Los Angeles rehabilitation facility when the media saga of her spiral from marijuana to heroin as a victim of "Mexican pushers" helped propel California's escalating war on narcotics during the early-to-mid 1950s. Linda was an eighteen-year-old from a wealthy Connecticut suburb who frequented the "hippie" drug scene in the East Village when her murder played a key role in redefining the 1967 "Summer of Love" as an urban crisis of runaway daughters and hopeless narcotics addiction. A few years later, an anonymous nineteen-year-old female from a "good family" in San Diego, "hooked on heroin" after smoking pot, became President Richard Nixon's rationale for why the 1970 federal drug legislation needed to toughen punishment for traffickers but reduce marijuana possession to a misdemeanor as leverage to coerce victims into rehabilitation. Lee Ann was a twenty-year-old former cocaine dealer in a New York City addiction center when she became the most prominent casualty of the crack "epidemic" to testify to Congress for the Anti-Drug Abuse Act of 1986, which imposed harsh and inflexible trafficking penalties aimed at inner-city Black areas that corrupted entire metropolitan regions. All of these felony lawbreakers were white, transformed into addict-victims and the poster children for each stage of the escalation of the

American war on drugs through a consensus process that united elected officials, mainstream media, and the discretionary criminal justice system as well.[1]

The millions of white youth who consciously broke the drug laws generally viewed themselves as autonomous actors and as victims primarily of the carceral state and criminal prohibition itself, not as the innocent prey of so-called pushers and the apocryphal marijuana-gateway syndrome. Mary Ann was twenty-three and admitted to smuggling heroin across the Texas-Mexico border when she demanded legalization of all drugs and condemned forcible medical institutionalization, refusing to follow the predetermined racial and gender script of her victim status in testimony as the U.S. Senate toughened mandatory-minimum penalties in the Narcotic Control Act of 1956. Joe was seventeen and adamantly defended the freedom to smoke pot, undeterred by multiple arrests, when the *Los Angeles Times* labeled him a "dope addict" in a 1959 series about Mexican pushers defiling white youth that inspired yet another legislative crusade against marijuana and heroin in California. Paula and Eve were young bohemians in the East Village when they told the U.S. Senate in 1966 that a proposed LSD ban would make "criminals of otherwise law-abiding people" and that their generation would never comply. Frank was nineteen when he received a twenty-year prison sentence for marijuana possession in 1969, and his college classmates forecast a "revolution" if the law enforcement crackdown on the youth counterculture continued. Robert was a high school senior from suburban Virginia in 1970 when he informed a dismayed congressional committee that marijuana and LSD should be legalized immediately as a right of personal freedom, that criminal law could never suppress the teenage market, and that the youth generation violated drug laws as part of a broader political rebellion against the hypocrisy and meaningless of middle-class society. Nicole was a college-bound student from an affluent white suburb speaking on national television when she defended the right of teenagers to break underage drinking laws and engage in harmless recreational use of marijuana and even cocaine, part of the widespread youth rejection of zero-tolerance politics during the 1980s.[2]

State institutions and American political culture have consistently waged the war on drugs through the framework of suburban crisis and positioned white middle-class youth as impossible criminals who must be protected from the illegal drug markets and then shielded from the consequences of their criminalized activities. As a racialized political and cultural category, the white middle-class suburban victim has been as foundational to America's long war on drugs and crime as the nonwhite threats of the foreign trafficker, urban gangster/pusher, and predatory ghetto addict. In drug control politics and in discretionary law enforcement operations, these racial binaries have separated the entangled metropolitan and global drug markets into distinct sectors of innocent and "otherwise law-abiding" victims to be arrested and diverted into rehabilitation, and the "real" criminal villains, who should be targeted through saturation policing and incarcerated for a long time. The modern war on drugs has operated through the reciprocal decriminalization of whiteness and criminalization of blackness and foreignness, grounded in selectively deployed law enforcement and in the discursive framing of idealized suburban spaces and pathologized urban slums and border towns. This racial state-building project escalated through a politics of consensus in modern American history, with bipartisan and overwhelming legislative majorities for every landmark federal policy shift and usually at the state level as well. Liberal and conservative regimes alike have mobilized to subdue narcotics traffickers in urban and international markets, defend middle-class suburban communities from external threats, and figure out how to keep white youth out of prison when they continuously refuse to comply with laws and policies designed for their protection and social control. The racial and spatial logics of the war on drugs reflect not only the bipartisan mandate for urban crime suppression and border interdiction but also the balancing act required to resolve the impossible public policy of criminalizing the social practices of tens of millions of white middle-class Americans.[3]

The imperatives of suburban political culture transformed cyclical "epidemics" of illegal drug use by white middle-class youth into crucial foundations of the American war on drugs and the expansion of the carceral state at three key stages between the 1950s and the 1980s. Each of these developments involved the grassroots mobilization of white suburban networks and interest groups—stories largely untold in the existing scholarship about the war on drugs—and the immediate responsiveness of government officials to their political demands and racial anxieties. Each escalation responded to increasing rates of marijuana smoking among white youth by portraying this criminalized leisure practice as a nationwide emergency, magnified by broader forces perceived to be causing once utopian suburbs to descend into dystopian nightmares. During the 1950s, as mass automobile-based suburbanization intensified mainstream fears about an epidemic of juvenile delinquency among affluent teenagers, the news media hyped a marijuana-to-heroin gateway narrative and middle-class women's groups demanded severe penalties to prevent urban and foreign "pushers" from corrupting white youth who were supposed to be safe in their racially segregated neighborhoods. The U.S. Congress unanimously enacted a series of mandatory-minimum drug control laws that explicitly targeted nonwhite villains while recycling the racist tropes of white female addict-prostitute victims popularized by Commissioner Harry J. Anslinger of the Federal Bureau of Narcotics (FBN). In California, the epicenter of the 1950s war on narcotics, lawmakers under pressure from a sustained grassroots suburban crusade repeatedly toughened mandatory-minimum penalties while carving out discretionary loopholes for "good" youth from "good families." This futile effort to eradicate the middle-class market, by arresting and diverting a subset of lawbreakers into rehabilitation, exacerbated racial and economic inequalities without stemming the steady increase in circulation of both marijuana and illicit pharmaceuticals in LA's white suburbs.[4]

The second key stage of the white suburban front in the war on drugs began in the mid-1960s when the "generation gap" revolt on college campuses embraced marijuana and LSD in the context of the anti–Vietnam War movement and the emergence of a "hippie" counterculture in urban bohemian enclaves. By decade's end, this psychedelic drug revolution had become a widespread phenomenon in the urban and suburban high schools of coastal states and major metropolitan areas, where around half of older teenagers had violated the felony marijuana laws (alongside one-fifth of high school seniors nationwide). The generation gap framework placed these high school and college lawbreakers, many of whom righteously advocated marijuana and LSD legalization, into a political rather than a criminal category—even as law enforcement arrested an unprecedented number of white middle-class youth through a strategy of deterring their recreational drug use while diverting them from prosecution to avoid the stigma of a permanent criminal record. The total failure of this approach led to a bipartisan consensus for drug law reform at the federal and state levels, most notably through the Comprehensive Drug Abuse Prevention and Control Act of 1970, a collaboration between Democratic leaders and the Nixon administration that Congress passed with near unanimity. In addition to escalating penalties for "professional traffickers," justified through sordid tales of suburban teenagers taking the marijuana gateway to heroin addiction, the federal law reduced possession and casual sale of all illegal drugs to a misdemeanor in order to use probation to force violators into rehab. This coercive public health policy led to an extraordinary surge in arrests of white marijuana smokers in the early-to-mid 1970s, which in turn produced vibrant grassroots political movements for legalization or decriminalization in order to protect these "otherwise law-abiding" youth from any encounter with the carceral state. The marijuana decriminalization campaign conspicuously insisted that law enforcement should focus only on the "real criminals" in urban heroin markets.[5]

The third and by far the most racially inequitable phase in the modern drug war began not with crack cocaine in the mid-1980s but eight years earlier, when "parent power" groups started forming in upper-middle-class white suburbs to sound the alarm that marijuana smoking and illegal drinking were skyrocketing among younger teenagers and even middle schoolers. This "parents' movement" portrayed itself as a nonpartisan awakening to save suburban children from the permissive effects of marijuana decriminalization and an alleged mass outbreak of "amotivational syndrome," the unscientific and racialized diagnosis that smoking pot turned college-bound white youth into unproductive slackers emulating ghetto pathologies. The parent power campaign placed the twelve-to-fourteen-year-old stoner at the center of its moral crusade, which resonated during an era of economic recession and pervasive concern about white middle-class family breakdown with mothers working and latchkey children unsupervised. The suburban network coalesced into the National Federation of Parents for Drug-Free Youth (NFP) and powerfully shaped the embrace of zero-tolerance policies by the Carter and Reagan administrations, leading to the federal government's prioritization of the white middle-class "gateway" drugs of marijuana as well as underage drinking even as the urban crack cocaine crisis emerged. In 1986, as the Democratic leaders in Congress engineered passage of the Anti-Drug Abuse Act with near unanimity, the national media and the political system continually highlighted white suburban victims of the new marijuana-to-cocaine gateway scourge in direct juxtaposition with the Black inner-city gangsters who sold the poison. As with the invading pusher, runaway daughter, and gateway-to-heroin tropes of previous decades, the zero-tolerance "Just Say No" campaign of the late 1970s and 1980s played a key role in institutionalizing two interlinked but spatially distinct approaches in the drug war: coercive public health campaigns in white middle-class suburbs and militarized interdiction in nonwhite urban centers, at the border, and in the international arena.[6]

The Suburban Crisis utilizes a comparative case study approach to analyze the dynamic interplay among the local, state, and national levels as well as the real and symbolic interrelationship between cities and suburbs in metropolitan regions. The book integrates the areas of politics, culture, and public policy formation by analyzing the circulation of discourses and meanings that constructed the racialized drug crisis alongside social history investigations of how illegal drug markets, law enforcement, criminalized youth practices, and grassroots activism actually played out on the ground. The goal is to bring together the methods of the "new political history" (linking grassroots political culture and metropolitan political economy to state formation at all levels), a capacious approach to urban history (moving beyond the city-suburb binary for a comprehensive assessment of metropolitan regions), and the insights of cultural studies (tracing how discourse, symbolism, meaning, and imagery circulate and shape popular attitudes, political ideologies, and policy outcomes).[7] The chapters that explore the workings of suburban drug markets and criminal law enforcement include case studies of multiple metropolitan regions and emphasize the ways in which these local processes flowed upward to reshape law, politics, and policy in the state capitals and in the legislative and executive branches of the national government. The chapters that revolve around the major federal escalations of drug control legislation between the 1950s and the 1980s connect the action in Washington to the influence of suburban political formations and interest groups, the circulation of crisis discourses about white middle-class victims in the mass media, and not least the criminalized social practices and resistance politics of youth themselves. This comparative methodology documents the racially and economically divergent outcomes for youth who broke the same laws but lived in different parts of metropolitan regions and also reveals that the escalation, and selective de-escalation, of the war on drugs was a bottom-up and not simply a top-down political process.

The centrality of Southern California to this history and the problem of defining American suburbia with precision are interrelated. California's recurring role as the pacesetter for national drug-war trends rested on a spatial foundation in terms of how law and political culture intersected with the built environment. The sprawling and racially segregated suburbs of metropolitan Los Angeles were close enough to the border for white middle-class youth to drive their cars to Mexico to acquire illegal drugs, and even closer to the unincorporated Mexican American area of East LA that grassroots coalitions and law enforcement blamed for causing the problem. Los Angeles County alone produced more than one-third of all drug arrests nationwide through the mid-1960s, as both the LAPD and the county sheriff's department policed diverse metropolitan landscapes with many white suburban-style neighborhoods inside the city limits and significant nonwhite enclaves in the outlying areas. California enacted its first mandatory-minimum drug law in 1951, before the U.S. Congress passed similar legislation. The state's commitment to tough enforcement and coercive rehabilitation provided the template for subsequent federal drug-war crackdowns and also galvanized the nation's most vibrant marijuana legalization movement.[8] Metropolitan Los Angeles also serves as a microcosm for how "the suburbs" functioned as real and imagined places of normative middle-class whiteness in American political culture, obscuring the considerable heterogeneity of the many diverse communities located outside major U.S. cities. This book's equation of the racialized category of "suburban" with the demographic and sociological category of "white middle-class America" involves both a commitment to exploring the politics of drug and crime control in affluent and segregated suburban areas, and an emphasis on how political culture and public policy conflated and constructed these imagined communities through discourses of crisis and epidemics, pushers and victims, utopia and dystopia, white innocence and its racial and spatial opposites.[9]

The Drug-War Consensus and the Carceral State

The Suburban Crisis reassesses the political history of modern America by analyzing the escalation of the war on drugs from the 1950s onward as a consensus project of racial and carceral state-building shaped by the intertwined policies of punitive law enforcement and coercive public health. The consensus framework illuminates the broadly shared commitment to protecting the white middle-class victim and incapacitating the nonwhite urban and foreign predator through drug control laws and crime control strategies that merged punitive policies of incarceration and involuntary rehabilitation into a comprehensive, discretionary, and inequitable system for the social control of teenagers and young adults. Conventional wisdom and much of the scholarship portrays law enforcement and public health as competing if not opposite approaches—the punitive incarceration crackdown spearheaded by conservative Republicans versus the compassionate rehabilitation agenda championed by liberal Democrats. This book demonstrates that the bipartisan architects of the war on drugs always envisioned the operation of both policies in tandem as coercive mechanisms to control youth subcultures through the broader legal umbrella of criminalization. Liberal and conservative policymakers generally agreed that some combination of criminal sanctions and compulsory rehabilitation should regulate the illicit drug market. Criminalization guaranteed that police, prosecutors, and delinquency agencies would largely manage access to the allegedly benevolent alternative of rehabilitation through a discretionary arrest-and-divert process that utilized the threat of incarceration to coerce select illegal drug users, invariably labeled "addicts" or "abusers." The criminalization consensus marginalized the genuine civil liberties alternative that the state should not arrest citizens for "victimless crimes" and that prohibition itself generated criminogenic outcomes. Almost no elected officials or influential policymakers endorsed the position of millions of Americans, and a subset of medical experts, that government should not harass citizens for drug use at all.[10]

The bipartisan politics of drug-war consensus is clearly evident in the overwhelming and often unanimous congressional support for every major escalation. Landmarks include the federal laws targeting Black and Mexican "pushers" in 1951 and 1956, the misdemeanor reforms designed for white marijuana violators in the 1970 omnibus package, and the arms race of harsher penalties for inner-city crack markets in 1986 and 1988. The common thread is race, not partisanship. The shared ideological commitment was to the project of "political whiteness," defined by scholar Daniel HoSang as a hegemonic framework in American political culture where "no large gulf existed between so-called racial liberalism and racial conservatism."[11] While elected officials often sought partisan advantage by maneuvering to claim credit for "tough" policies, this dynamic should not mask the underlying racial consensus that shaped drug control policymaking.[12] The priorities of federal lawmakers at each stage aligned with the dominant racial tropes circulating in the news media, the political demands of white middle-class constituents, and parallel developments in the state legislatures and the nation's vast criminal justice and juvenile control apparatus. This constellation of forces repeatedly transformed the latest drug crisis into a white middle-class "epidemic" that always "spread" outward from urban centers to invade previously placid suburbs and turn "otherwise law-abiding" teenagers and young adults into addict-victims or impossible criminals. Policing agencies and public health authorities then collaborated on strategies to arrest and redirect these innocent casualties or misguided youth into the rehabilitative arm of the carceral state. While affluent white drug criminals rarely experienced incarceration, a consequence disproportionately imposed on lower-income and nonwhite counterparts, these divergent outcomes resulted not only from the inherently discretionary mechanisms of the criminal legal system but also from the racially discriminatory provisions and loopholes built into crime and drug control policies by design.

A main agenda of *The Suburban Crisis* is to bring the carceral studies scholarship on policing, criminalization, and incarceration into dialogue with the urban/suburban history literature on racial and class inequality, which has generally focused on the relationship between state policies and grassroots politics in housing, education, and urban redevelopment. Historians have extensively documented the federal and municipal programs that created racially segregated metropolitan regions throughout the United States during the post–World War II decades and the recurring mobilization of white homeowners and parents to defend these privileges and boundaries against civil rights challenges. This is a story of the broad middle ground in American political culture and policy formation, not primarily a saga of suburban conservativism and the "rise of the Right," anchored in the construction and reproduction of white racial and class power through the interplay among social movements, bipartisan state actors, and constitutional law.[13] The racialized wars on crime, drugs, and delinquency during the second half of the twentieth century accelerated as part of these larger state processes of inequitable metropolitan development and aggressive white suburban defenses of racial and class segregation. State institutions and both political parties proved as responsive to white middle-class fears and demands regarding drug and crime control policies as they were to the parallel movements to protect affluent suburbs from meaningful civil rights remedies to dismantle metropolitan structures of segregation and inequality in housing and education. In recent years, scholars have produced powerful case studies of how policing and criminalization shaped racial inequality in nonwhite urban neighborhoods—but very little equivalent work on how these processes and state-building projects unfolded in segregated white suburbs.[14] This book demonstrates that suburban interest groups and local political formations decisively shaped the trajectory of the drug war and that its enforcement agenda operated in white areas as well.

My investigation of the racialized consensus at the center of the government wars on drugs, crime, and juvenile delinquency challenges the red versus blue polarization thesis and the liberal-conservative binaries that have distorted understandings of modern U.S. political history writ large. The story told in this book, of the continuous racial and spatial inequalities in the nation's escalating drug war, is definitively not a trajectory of the purported "right turn" or "triumph of conservatism" in American politics. In recent years, the burgeoning literature on the carceral state and its crime and drug control projects has moved beyond the traditional overemphasis on conservative "frontlash" and Republican law-and-order campaigns as the driving forces behind mass incarceration and modern forms of racial inequality.[15] Urban and political historians have demonstrated that liberal policymakers in post-1945 America played pivotal and leading roles in the development of punitive and discriminatory policies, as they did during the Progressive and New Deal eras as well, wielding the power and authority of the state in racialized projects that targeted juvenile delinquency, street crime, narcotics addiction, drug traffickers, and many other socially constructed and criminalized problems.[16] This historiographical focus on the bipartisan origins of the drug and crime wars is a necessary correction to scholarship that fixates principally on the racial backlash projects of law-and-order Republicans during the Richard Nixon and Ronald Reagan eras, depicting liberal policymakers and Democratic politicians as reluctant accomplices who were afraid to seem "soft" when boxed in by right-wing maneuvering and inflamed public opinion. The historical distortion arises, most of all, from imposition of an artificial red-blue binary drawn from the discourses of the two-party system that predesignates policy outcomes as liberal or conservative based on factors such as punitiveness and racial inequality, rather than analyzing them as hybrid political processes shaped by diverse groups of actors from across the spectrum and deep structural forces in the national political culture.[17]

Between the 1950s and the 1980s, the most influential policymakers in the expansion of the war on drugs were white liberals who combined a law-and-order commitment to tough enforcement against urban and border traffickers with an empathetic yet coercive approach that all illegal drug users were "sick people" who suffered from the disease of addiction and other forms of psychological maladjustment. This category of historical actors, designated as "public health liberals" in this book, was not just equally as important as racial conservatives in the development of drug control policy; they were most often the predominant voices, especially because they controlled Congress and key states. "The user is usually the victim, a sick person," believed Senator Thomas Dodd of Connecticut, the Democratic chair of the Subcommittee to Investigate Juvenile Delinquency and lead author of the omnibus 1970 federal drug legislation. "And whether he be a heroin user or a marijuana user, he should be treated as a sick person, not subject to harsh imprisonment." The most prominent public health liberals and Democratic drug warriors—Governor Pat Brown during California's early antinarcotics crusade; the leaders of the Juvenile Delinquency Subcommittee during the 1950s and 1960s; Senator Joseph Biden and urban Black politicians such as Representative Charles Rangel during the heroin and crack cocaine crises—championed get-tough crackdowns against the supply side of the market and advocated mandatory rehabilitation for all illegal drug users, whether they lived in upscale suburbs or urban slums. White liberal lawmakers collaborated closely on crime control with the hardliners in the Federal Bureau of Narcotics and later the Drug Enforcement Administration and subscribed to the prevailing psychiatric interpretation that addiction was part of the "culture of pathology" in poor Black neighborhoods. They differed from racial conservatives mainly in their advocacy of far greater funding for urban social welfare programs and their sympathetic view that nonwhite addicts were also victims who deserved compulsory medicalization rather than imprisonment.[18]

The most striking feature of the drug-war consensus from the 1950s through the 1980s involves the almost complete absence of concern for, or even acknowledgment of, racial discrimination in policing and other aspects of the criminal legal system. Scholars have noted that the arbitrary distinction between crack and powder cocaine in the Anti-Drug Abuse Act of 1986, now infamous for its racist consequences, generated no legislative debate at the time. This only continued the bipartisan pattern established during the first federal and state mandatory-minimum narcotics laws of the 1950s, which urban civil rights organizations and liberal antidelinquency coalitions supported to protect Black communities from "dope pushers." Almost no one with any political influence questioned the statistical "truths" about drug crime that the Federal Bureau of Narcotics, Federal Bureau of Investigation, and their state-level counterparts produced—based on arrest records alone—to demonstrate that a large majority of felons in the illegal market were African American, Mexican American, and Puerto Rican. Except for a few dissident scholars and marginalized radicals, there was virtually no discussion during the passage of any landmark law across these four decades about whether the government statistics on drug-related crime revealed not racial criminality but discriminatory police enforcement in targeted geographic areas. Public health liberals and mainstream civil rights organizations portrayed what everyone (falsely) believed to be much higher rates of drug crime and addiction in poor urban Black neighborhoods as a consequence of racial inequality as well as psychopathology, but they also demanded a get-tough war on traffickers and street dealers and rarely addressed either discretionary law enforcement or the extensive corruption among narcotics police that allowed illegal markets to flourish in certain areas. Scholars have recently debated the policy impact of such punitive "law-and-order" politics in urban Black communities, but the most important takeaway is that white victims just mattered more to the white elected officials in power.[19]

The most structurally racist feature of drug control policy during the 1950s and 1960s, however, was not selective enforcement of marijuana and heroin crimes but rather the statutory exemption of the licit and illicit circulation of corporate-manufactured pharmaceuticals from felony laws. Policymakers in Congress worked closely with federal agencies and the pharmaceutical lobby to create an illegal drug economy that was racially contrived, segregationist in its boundaries, and designed to enhance corporate profits through arbitrary criminalization. Commissioner Harry Anslinger, the powerful director of the Federal Bureau of Narcotics from the 1930s through the early 1960s, consistently claimed that almost all illegal drug felons in the United States were "Negro pushers" and "hoodlum addicts," whereas "normal" white Americans were not susceptible to the criminal culture of this racially demarcated market. Anslinger simultaneously denied that prescription barbiturates and amphetamines were addictive, even though they circulated illicitly in massive quantities and posed far greater public health threats than heroin or marijuana. He promoted corporate self-regulation rather than criminal enforcement for this "medical market," explicitly imagined to be populated by white middle-class Americans. The segregationist agenda of the Federal Bureau of Narcotics had a lasting impact on the racially inequitable structures of drug-war enforcement in metropolitan regions, paralleling the much more well-known apartheid policies of urban redlining and racially restrictive suburban development promoted by the Federal Housing Administration in postwar America. Every major federal and state drug control law during the second half of the twentieth century also had three and not just two purposes: incarceration for racialized suppliers of illegal drugs, protection and rehabilitation of certain consumers recast as their helpless victims, and preservation of the pharmaceutical industry monopoly to sell therapeutic and often addictive pills to a global market while the U.S. government pledged in vain to eliminate illicit competition.[20]

It is crucial to highlight how fundamentally the terminology of the American war on drugs distorted both the social practices of sellers and consumers and the scientific properties of controlled substances, since it is impossible to tell this story without reproducing the loaded language utilized by state actors and profit-seeking media corporations to characterize and criminalize the illegal drug marketplace. The "pusher," the principal villain of the American drug war between the 1950s and the 1980s, was a racialized fiction that transformed market suppliers into evil predators who seduced and destroyed their helpless victims, often through absurd tropes such as handing out free marijuana samples or jabbing needles in the arms of youth to induce heroin addiction. The "addict," a potentially more sympathetic category, often applied indiscriminately to all illegal drug consumers in ways that ignored medical research, conflated recreational users with serious substance abusers, lumped marijuana smokers with heroin "junkies," made wildly inaccurate claims about narcotics-fueled violence and other predatory crimes, and justified police crackdowns on everyone in the criminalized market. "Narcotics" was an unscientific category in federal and state law that encompassed not only heroin and other illegal opioids (sedatives with addictive potential) but also marijuana (a mildly psychoactive and nonaddictive drug) and cocaine (a nonnarcotic stimulant that the FBI combined with heroin in its crime data)—all while drawing artificial legal distinctions that downplayed the hazards of narcotic "medicine" that pharmaceutical companies marketed as nonaddictive miracle drugs and deliberately overproduced to profit from the massive illicit market. "Epidemic" transformed the public health concept of rapid community spread of an infectious disease into the racialized and sensationalized "spread" of any degree of illegal drug use associated with nonwhite urban centers into victimized white middle-class neighborhoods and previously placid suburbs, or the hyped "waves" of violent gang crime and predatory addiction in the ghettos and barrios.

White Drug Crime: Hidden in Plain Sight

The Suburban Crisis explores the trajectory of the war on drugs and the expansion of the carceral state from the essential and atypical vantage point of the tens of millions of impossible criminals in white middle-class America. Most scholarship has focused on how the drug war has long operated as a racial system of social control of African Americans and other nonwhite populations, an extension of the federal and municipal wars on urban street crime and the linchpin of the "new Jim Crow" of mass incarceration. Many studies have convincingly documented the systemic disparities produced by racially and geographically targeted enforcement, with African Americans and Latinos representing two-thirds of incarcerated drug offenders by the end of the twentieth century, even though white Americans constituted a large majority of illegal drug users and dealers and broke the law at identical or often higher rates than nonwhite groups.[21] My excavation of the deep historical roots and broader metropolitan foundations of these contemporary disparities reveals that the exemptions created for white middle-class participants in the criminalized underground drug markets were not merely epiphenomenal but rather constitutive of the expansion of the carceral state. Situated on the real and imagined landscapes of affluent suburbia, white youth have long represented the most sympathetic and innocent victims of the narcotics trade, the most resonant justification for punitive legislation against suppliers, the distinctively illegitimate targets of law enforcement crackdowns, and the chief beneficiaries of public health prevention and rehabilitation programs. The war on drugs has continually flourished and intensified as a bipartisan crusade because politics and culture consistently combine to reproduce the intertwined categories of the racialized urban pusher and foreign trafficker and to elevate the equally racialized suburban victim.

The book begins in the 1950s with enactment of a series of mandatory-minimum narcotics laws in the bellwether state of California and in the U.S. Congress. This starting point provides a longer chronological view and a broader ideological dimension to a national antidrug crusade that expanded rather than emerged with Nixon's 1971 declaration of war on "public enemy number one" and the 1973 Rockefeller Drug Laws targeting Black heroin dealers and addicts in New York City. California's early war on narcotics escalated because of grassroots suburban pressure, not simply top-down elite machinations, and also targeted the "foreign" Mexican threat as much as the urban Black pusher during the postwar decades. White suburban organizations representing more than one million residents mobilized to demand this crackdown on "dope pushers" who allegedly supplied marijuana and heroin to innocent teenagers. The state produced more than half of all drug arrests nationwide from the 1950s through the mid-1960s, and then the number of white middle-class youth detained on marijuana charges began to skyrocket. The close attention to metropolitan Los Angeles and the Southern California region throughout the book provides an unprecedented window into how white suburban drug markets actually operated. White teenagers and young adults in automobile-based suburbs usually acquired illegal drugs by crossing the Mexican border themselves. They distributed and consumed marijuana as well as illicit amphetamines and barbiturates through casual networks based in beachfront areas and other centers of the autonomous youth subculture. The political system and its criminal justice arm responded by devising a complex array of formal and informal policies, building on the total statutory discretion and deep racial and class inequalities of juvenile delinquency controls, to arrest and then channel these white middle-class youth into rehabilitative programs. But California's escalating war on narcotics had negligible effect on either supply or demand, and by the late 1960s between one-third and one-half of white college students and older teenagers in affluent suburbs had broken the felony marijuana law.[22]

The most remarkable and underappreciated feature of the war on drugs in white middle-class America is hidden in plain sight in the annual crime reports published by the Federal Bureau of Investigation and the California Department of Justice. Between the mid-1960s and the late 1970s, the proportion of white Americans arrested on drug charges reached historically high levels and the percentage of apprehensions in the suburbs quadrupled, primarily because of targeted enforcement against surging recreational marijuana use among teenagers and young adults (fig. I.1). By 1973, white Americans accounted for 81 percent of all drug arrests nationwide and 89 percent of juvenile apprehensions, which approximated their population share. This represented an unprecedented intervention by the carceral state as it scaled upward and geographically outward in the quixotic mission to criminalize and control the youth subculture through an enormous increase in marijuana arrests (fig. I.2). The crackdown represented both an interregnum in the longer history of the American war on drugs and an exceptional political experiment, exceeding the scope of alcohol Prohibition enforcement in the 1920s, to utilize criminal law in an attempt to deter white youth from smoking pot and as leverage to coerce their rehabilitation when they refused to comply. Only a small subset of white middle-class lawbreakers ultimately served sentences in prison or jail, and racial disproportionality in drug-war policing and especially incarceration rates of African Americans remained pronounced even during this era, although the combined share of heroin and cocaine arrests did plummet to an all-time low. The need to exercise caution in utilizing the FBI's unreliable and politicized crime data definitely applies, especially because the arrest category illustrates criminalization and discretionary enforcement rather than actual "crime," much less convictions, and also because the white category encompasses most Hispanics. Even still, the mass criminalization of white middle-class marijuana users was an extraordinary development in the U.S. war on drugs.[23]

What actually happened to the millions of white teenagers and young adults arrested for drug violations during the 1960s and 1970s by a criminal legal system designed to leave few official traces of their illegal activities? Excavating the answers to this puzzle is a central goal of *The Suburban Crisis* and a social history investigation that provides insight into the discretionary and discriminatory operations of the criminal justice system and the racial state writ large. In recent years, the "new political history" has been invigorated by

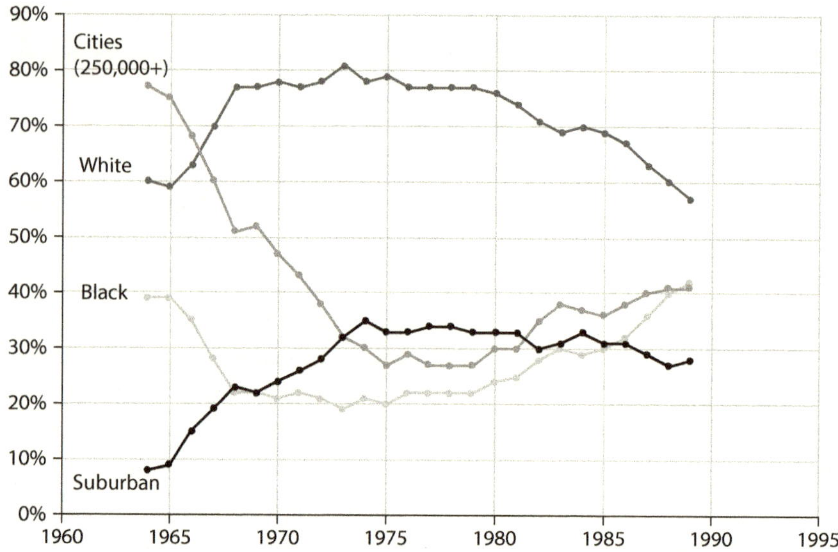

FIGURE I.1. Racial and select geographic characteristics of the population arrested on drug charges in the United States, 1964–89, as a percentage of total arrests in each category. The proportion of white drug arrests rose rapidly during the second half of the 1960s and reached its modern peak, 81% of total drug arrests, in 1973. Suburban drug arrests simultaneously increased from 8% in 1964 to 32% by 1973, while the proportion of drug arrests in the largest cities plummeted. Most of the increase involved marijuana possession arrests of white teenagers and young adults during a ten-year period when the number of drug arrests nationwide increased by 12.7 times (see fig. I.2). The percentage of white arrests remained at a historically high level throughout the 1970s before steadily declining in the 1980s during the racially targeted war on urban crime and crack cocaine. African American drug arrests remained disproportionate relative to population share throughout this era, but at much lower levels during the late 1960s and early 1970s compared to the 1980s, when the percentage of Black arrests nearly doubled. (FBI, *Uniform Crime Reports*, 1964–1989.)

Note: The FBI reported crime data for cities of various sizes, some of which could be classified as "suburbs," and used a different measurement than the U.S. census for the "suburban" category included here. Therefore, this data is not an accurate indicator of the total percentage of drug arrests in the "suburbs" per se, but rather a comparative and rough portrait of the changing percentage of national drug arrests that took place in the largest cities versus the areas that the FBI classified as suburban. Urban or suburban categories also estimated for three years of incomplete data (1978, 1979, 1984). The FBI did not report data on Hispanics separately during this period, except for "ethnic origin" estimates between 1980 and 1986 (see figs. 6.8 and 7.2 for details). The majority of Hispanic arrests are presumably included in the "white" category. The FBI's "racial" data on drug arrests of American Indians and variously defined Asian groups remained below 1% of the total through the 1980s and is not included in this and subsequent graphs for clarity of presentation. The racial breakdown of the U.S. population in the 1970 census was 87.6% white, 11.1% Black, and an estimated 4.5% Hispanic (with overlap between the white and Hispanic categories). The racial breakdown of the U.S. population in the 1980 census was 79.6% white (non-Hispanic), 11.5% Black, and 6.5% Hispanic (when the census began tabulating Hispanics separately). The 1990 census totals were 75.6% white non-Hispanic, 11.8% Black, and 9.0% Hispanic.

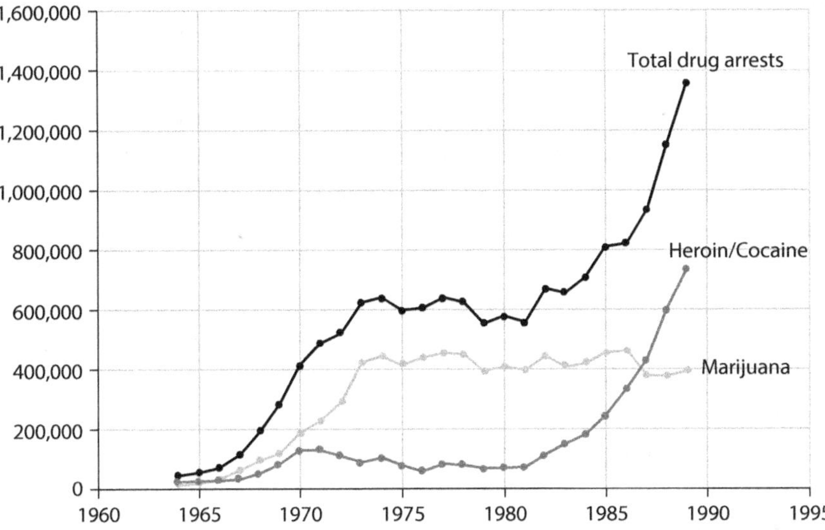

FIGURE I.2. Marijuana and heroin/cocaine arrests as a proportion of total drug arrests in the United States, 1964–89. Marijuana arrests surpassed combined heroin/cocaine arrests in 1966 and nearly tripled as a percentage of total drug arrests between 1964 (26%) and the modern peak in 1976 (72%). The number of marijuana arrests increased by thirty-four times during this thirteen-year period. Annual marijuana arrest totals stabilized in the mid-1970s even as total drug arrests kept climbing, from 49,700 in 1964 to 609,700 in 1976 to 1.36 million by 1989. The proportion of marijuana arrests declined rapidly in the 1980s, from 71% in 1981 to 29% in 1989. During the same decade, combined heroin/cocaine arrests escalated from 12% to 54% of total drug arrests, disproportionately involving African Americans. (FBI, *Uniform Crime Reports*, 1964–1989.)

Note: Heroin/cocaine total approximate for 1965 due to incomplete data. The FBI combined heroin and cocaine arrests in its crime reports because law enforcement agencies historically grouped them together, a legacy of the unscientific "narcotics" category in federal and state laws. Arrest data is also not an indication of actual "crime" but of criminalization, and a substantial percentage of drug arrests did not result in convictions.

exploration of processes of bureaucratic discretion by the state's most local agents. This has broadened state-centered scholarship through engagement with the racial formation–inspired and interdisciplinary cultural studies literature on identity construction and policing of normative boundaries of rights and citizenship. Every scale of governance and regulatory encounter—including border guards, police on the street, juvenile probation officers, prosecutors and judges, immigration agents, health officials—involves the discretionary application of law, the discriminatory distribution of rights and penalties, and the reproduction of categories of normal/deviant and criminalized/decriminalized based on race, gender, sexuality, class, citizenship status, and other variables.[24] In drug and crime control policy, these dynamics illuminate the broader ways in which state institutions, law enforcement agencies, and discourses in media and political culture criminalized nonwhite youth collectively while seeking to control and rehabilitate white middle-class youth. By explicit design, the modern war on drugs updated the Progressive Era outcome that Khalil Muhammad labels the "masking of crime among whites." Close attention to the local level also reveals striking similarities in how discretion operated under both indeterminate ("rehabilitative") and mandatory-minimum ("punitive") sentencing regimes—because constitutional law provided little check on police autonomy, delinquency law authorized almost anything, and prosecutors held nearly absolute power at their bottleneck point.[25]

The heart of this book combines case studies of metropolitan regions with quantitative crime data and evidence scattered across more than seventy-five government and organizational archives to overcome the extensive and deliberate silences regarding how illegal drug markets and discretionary law enforcement actually operated in white middle-class suburbs. White youth who broke the law had every incentive to cover their tracks, but many still gave accounts to academic ethnographers, public health researchers, and journalists who mobilized to explain the shocking phenomenon of mass illegal drug use in American middle-class suburbia and in urban countercultural enclaves. Radicalized teenagers and young adults told their stories as they advocated for drug legalization in underground newspapers, political manifestos, and legislative hearings. Affluent parents of arrested youth often left a paper trail by filing complaints with the ACLU, demanding intervention by elected officials, or fighting charges in the courts. Although law enforcement records are generally closed, police and probation departments frequently provided governors and legislative committees with summaries of enforcement operations as well as detailed internal studies of the discretionary processes of diversion and disposition following arrest. Agencies such as the California Department of Justice published extensive annual reports breaking down aggregate data on drug and delinquency arrests, probation, diversion to rehab, prosecution, and incarceration by categories such as race, gender, and geographic location. Federal agencies funded academic surveys of illegal drug activity among college and high school students as well as multiyear studies of "Drug Abuse in Suburbia" by probation departments that tracked the discretionary disposition process following arrest. These sources reveal the broader patterns for white middle-class youth who encountered a drug-war apparatus that sought to deter, rehabilitate, occasionally confine, and most of all to protect them from their own actions without the stigma of a criminal record.[26]

A fusion of race, class, gender, and geography fundamentally shaped disparate outcomes for youth arrested on drug charges in metropolitan centers. The campaign against teenage use of marijuana initially utilized the existing mechanisms of total statutory discretion in the delinquency control system, which expanded alongside mass suburbanization during the postwar decades. In affluent suburbs, police and delinquency authorities almost always released college-bound youth to the custody of their parents, leaving no official record, in exchange for informal commitments to internal family discipline and often private psychiatric counseling. When this strategy failed to stem the illegal drug culture, police departments intensified profiling of white marijuana users based on age, male gender, and most notably "hippie" appearance. Surging arrests created a quandary for prosecutors and juvenile judges who wanted to deter their felony activities without inconveniencing middle-class futures with a permanent criminal record. Many white youths pled down to alcohol-related violations such as public intoxication or disorderly conduct, and others agreed to enter treatment programs under threat of prosecution, but the criminal justice system simply dismissed a majority of marijuana possession cases by the late 1960s. The futility of this approach of scaring white youth into obeying the law through felony arrests without consequences led to the federal- and state-level misdemeanor possession reforms of the early 1970s. This approach still involved discretionary justice but had considerably harsher outcomes for tens of thousands of recreational pot smokers defined as "sick people" and "drug abusers" and forced through probation into mandatory rehabilitation programs. Growing anger about the carceral state's crackdown on marijuana crimes by "otherwise law-abiding" youth inspired popular campaigns for legalization and decriminalization supported by the ACLU and the interest group NORML, which each operated within "political whiteness" by reserving true victim status in the drug war for these middle-class and suburban Americans.[27]

The suburban zero-tolerance movement that reinvigorated the federal war on marijuana during the late 1970s and 1980s blamed the increase in pot smoking among younger teenagers on the "permissiveness" of decriminalization. But the Carter and Reagan administrations also remained within its racial and spatial boundaries by prioritizing public health policies of prevention and private-sector rehab for white middle-class suburbs while intensifying crime control enforcement against heroin and later cocaine markets in nonwhite urban centers. As the FBI data reveals, the drug-war interregnum came to an end during the militarized assault on urban crack markets following passage of the bipartisan Anti-Drug Abuse Act of 1986, and the arrest proportion of African Americans returned to the level of the early 1960s though at an exponentially greater scale. The illegal use and sale of marijuana by white Americans remained relatively constant throughout the 1980s, and their cocaine law violations increased dramatically, but targeted enforcement in "high-crime" urban areas resulted in proportionately fewer arrests of suburban teenagers and white middle-class adults. At the same time, the embrace of zero-tolerance drug and underage alcohol policies by the federal government and many state and local officials, under pressure from suburban coalitions, including the National Federation of Parents for Drug-Free Youth and Mothers Against Drunk Driving, meant that tens of thousands of white youth continued to be arrested and coerced into rehabilitation for participating in criminalized recreational practices in a mood-altering culture and a drug-dependent society. These white suburban lawbreakers—arbitrarily harassed and often inconvenienced and sometimes institutionalized as the presumed victims of illegal drug markets that they had willingly and often enthusiastically sought out—were certainly not the primary casualties of the carceral state on its road to mass incarceration. But their fates were still intertwined with their urban and nonwhite counterparts as the racially divergent targets of the drug-war consensus in American politics.[28]

Drug control policies and politics in the United States never underwent a macro-level shift from liberal/rehabilitative to conservative/punitive during the second half of the twentieth century, because the consensus framework of criminalization and coercive medicalization always encompassed both. The most fundamental transformation wrought by the bipartisan war on drugs involved the dramatic increase in the scale and punitive capacity of the carceral state and its intertwined apparatus of law enforcement agencies, jails and prisons, and rehabilitation programs. In 1964, the FBI reported fewer than 50,000 drug arrests across the United States; in 1989, the total exceeded 1.3 million. The federal government alone spent $3.8 billion in direct drug-war funding in 1989, more than seventeen times its expenditure in 1969 (adjusted for inflation). Around 66 percent of the 1969 total went to public health and treatment programs, compared to 74 percent for law enforcement after the mid-1980s mobilization against urban cocaine markets. There is no question that U.S. drug control policies became more oriented toward the punishment and incarceration of African Americans in particular during the selective escalation against heroin and cocaine in the 1970s and 1980s, compared to the agenda of public health liberals to arrest and divert nonwhite as well as white "addicts" into involuntary treatment programs during the early stages of the antinarcotics crusade. But deep continuities remained—especially for the impossible drug criminals in white middle-class America—in the discretionary mechanisms through which the criminal legal system sorted its targets into incarceration or rehabilitation based on discriminatory variables of race, class, gender, age, geography, and related categories. After the white arrest share ascended rapidly during the drug-war interregnum, from 59 percent in 1965 to an average of 78 percent throughout the 1970s, it sharply declined to 57 percent by the end of the 1980s. Yet the drug-war escalation meant that the number of white Americans arrested still continued to rise: from around 30,000 in 1964, to 510,000 in 1973, to 776,000 in 1989.[29]

Youth Politics and Social Control

In 1954, a young adult white male incarcerated in the San Quentin prison for a heroin offense wrote a letter informing Governor Goodwin Knight of California that every aspect of the war on narcotics was not only repressive but irrational and counterproductive. The state government had recently declared all-out war on "dope pushers" in the context of media sensationalism about Mexican gangsters supplying marijuana and heroin to white teenagers and an outpouring of demands by middle-class suburban groups for a law enforcement crackdown to protect their children. The governor's imprisoned critic instead insisted that "narcotics should be legalized" and argued that California had embarked on a crusade as unjust and unwinnable as the 18th Amendment that ushered in Prohibition of alcohol in 1920. He defined drug addiction as a symptom of psychological illness, denounced his prior involuntary commitment to the federal narcotics hospital as well as his current confinement, and insisted that "we do not behave any differently than other law-abiding people." He called FBN Commissioner Harry Anslinger a liar and asked why politicians enacted drug laws based on the advice of police agencies rather than medical experts. He said that everyone in the underground market knew that heroin was a sedative painkiller that did not cause violent crimes and that marijuana was a mild drug, neither addictive nor dangerous. He laid out the obvious truth that prohibition itself, not narcotics traffickers, had turned heroin into the most lucrative and "vicious contraband in the world." He described an illegal drug market that flourished because of systemic police corruption even as the U.S. government spent millions of dollars "to make our lives a nightmare" while deceiving the public that the war could be won. The young man concluded: "Is there no humanitarian sensibility of justice left?" It is striking to read a letter from seven decades ago, so far outside the political consensus at the time, that captures almost every critique (except for race) that scholars and activists have subsequently made about the futility and inequity of the war on drugs.[30]

The inability to deter and suppress the criminalized social practices and recreational drug subcultures of white middle-class youth turned out to be an unsolvable problem for the carceral state. The social control and depoliticization of teenagers under the guise of protecting them from danger is deeply embedded in American political culture and public policy, but it does not seem like an exaggeration to conclude that the average juvenile with any experience in the illegal drug scene understood how market supply and demand actually operated with more sophistication than the public rhetoric of almost every elected official in the United States during the second half of the twentieth century. "You can buy heroin almost anywhere," a nineteen-year-old white female from Los Angeles named Barbara explained to the California state legislature in 1958. She proposed legalization through a medically regulated system, similar to prescription painkillers, which would "put the dope peddlers out of business, but no one seems to see it that way." When asked at a 1966 Senate hearing how the "LSD pushers" targeted them, a group of young countercultural activists openly mocked their inquisitors and said that "it is a social thing, really" and "you will have a very hard time finding out." In 1974, a petition from 120 suburban high school students in Orange County, California, informed the state government that "there is no difference" between alcohol and marijuana, and so eighteen-year-olds with the legal right to vote should have the freedom to consume both. By what right did the police "handcuff me, take me to jail and book me as a felon," a young white woman busted for marijuana possession asked Governor Jerry Brown in 1975. She expressed anger and not gratitude that the state of California had diverted her to probation and a six-month treatment program—"making themselves feel good about 'rehabilitating' hardened criminals like myself." Only rarely did political discourse in Washington and the state capitals depict these illegal drug users as they saw themselves, as citizens responsible for their own choices in a wrongly criminalized market.[31]

The overlapping wars on suburban juvenile delinquency and teenage narcotics addiction emerged simultaneously during the 1950s as racialized state projects designed for the social control of all white middle-class youth. The Senate Subcommittee to Investigate Juvenile Delinquency, which is mainly remembered for its campaign against violent imagery in comic books and Hollywood films, played a central role in constructing the crisis of a white middle-class "epidemic" of lawbreaking and dope addiction, and its public health liberals crafted most major federal drug control laws through the early 1970s. Politicians and experts blamed the juvenile delinquency outbreak in white middle-class suburbs on outside invader "dope pushers" as well as the new catch-all explanation of psychological maladjustment, generally attributed to permissive parenting practices and corruptive mass media. Both the external and the internal causes explained how juvenile delinquency and illegal drug markets could have jumped the tracks from the nonwhite urban slums, long pathologized as the socioeconomic locations and racial groups primarily susceptible to criminality. The twin crises then served to justify and reinforce the prevailing racial patterns of comprehensive housing segregation throughout metropolitan America, with state governments and antidelinquency agencies advocating "homogeneous" single-family suburbs as the most effective way to protect "normal" middle-class children from dangerous outside influences. This solution, premised on maternal supervision and community consensus in a suburban utopia of compliant and depoliticized teenagers, inevitably failed because of the autonomous and adventurous actions of adolescents themselves on the automobile-centered metropolitan landscape. In response, state and local agencies expanded the juvenile justice system originally designed to criminalize and "reform" Black and immigrant youth in urban centers in an ambitious law enforcement project to regulate and control white suburban teenagers without formally adjudicating them as delinquents.[32]

The juvenile delinquency system in postwar America was a vast apparatus with a social control agenda based on complete statutory discretion and no fundamental due process rights until the 1967 *Gault* ruling. Its liberal ideology of coercive rehabilitation sorted youth into categories of criminality and noncriminality based on discriminatory risk assessment factors that included race and gender, grades and college aspirations, church attendance, parental income and (perceived) level of involvement, social class, and geographic residence. Police officers, juvenile probation officials, and juvenile court judges made these discretionary assessments at every stage of the process from point of arrest to formal adjudication. A substantial majority of juvenile arrests were for status offenses rather than actual criminal conduct—leading reasons included underage alcohol mischief, "delinquent tendencies," curfew violations, and lack of parental supervision. The juvenile delinquency laws by design were so capacious that almost every adolescent in the United States technically violated them almost every day. The inevitably discretionary and discriminatory enforcement therefore reproduced and intensified the racial and socioeconomic inequalities of the metropolitan landscape and broader society. In affluent white suburbs, police departments and delinquency authorities reprimanded and released most detained youth to the custody of parents and perhaps the promise of private counseling, often even for serious crimes of violence. This system of discretionary criminalization sought to regulate the adolescent subculture of alcohol-related and automobile-based "thrill seeking" without compromising their futures with an official record or committing them to juvenile facilities that overwhelmingly incarcerated lower-income and nonwhite youth. The delinquency control system largely absorbed the first small-scale "epidemic" of white teenage marijuana "addiction" that emerged in the mid-1950s, but the arrival of a mass illegal drug culture in the middle-class suburbs by the late 1960s posed a much more difficult challenge.[33]

The criminal legal system responded to the millions of white teenage rebels who enthusiastically broke drug laws with discretionary procedures that operated differently based on the racial geography of the metropolitan landscape but also discriminated against certain types of youth within segregated suburbs. Between the mid-1960s and mid-1970s, police arrested several million white teenagers and young adults for recreational drug crimes. Law enforcement agencies, first through ad hoc processes and then via statutory revisions, devised an array of strategies inspired by the delinquency control system and the compulsory drug rehabilitation regime to reform many, but not all, of these offenders without the stigma of a permanent record. Suburban jurisdictions punished some youth more harshly based on a combination of gender, political ideology, countercultural style, and economic status. Police generally arrested males but released females without processing, except for "runaways." They profiled longhaired "hippies" and retaliated against political activists, especially students who joined antiwar protests and openly embraced radical causes. They apprehended possession violators in stop-and-search traffic operations and then entrapped their friends and acquaintances in order to catch dealers who were often only casual providers. Undercover squads infiltrated public schools and staked out rock concerts to make mass busts of "narcotics pushers" who typically were either just sharing their stash or were low-level suppliers of marijuana and sometimes LSD and illicit pharmaceuticals. Police departments then subjectively assessed criminality and released many juveniles to their parents, turned a subset over to delinquency agencies that released even more and placed some on informal probation, and adjudicated a fairly small fraction into formal rehabilitation or confinement. Prosecutors and judges often placed young white felony-level dealers on misdemeanor probation, downgraded marijuana possession to public intoxication, and dismissed many charges outright and others pending successful rehabilitation.[34]

The criminalization and interdiction of marijuana moved to the epicenter of the national war on drugs in the late 1960s and remained the most urgent priority for almost two decades because its illegal use by white middle-class teenagers, college students, and young adults posed the greatest symbolic threat to normative suburban values and capitalist ideologies. Why would the United States spend billions of dollars and arrest millions of "otherwise law-abiding" young people for smoking a relatively mild social intoxicant that did not cause addiction or crime (beyond that related to prohibitionist policies) and was demonstrably far less hazardous in a public health sense than legal regulated products such as alcohol, tobacco, and pharmaceuticals? Politically conscious youth constantly demanded to know the answers to these questions, and the reasons are evident enough, even if the explanations provided by authorities were unscientific, contrived, even preposterous. During the 1950s, the Federal Bureau of Narcotics and its political and media allies began to supplant the traditional "reefer madness" mythology, that marijuana triggered violent crimes and sexual depravity by nonwhite hoodlums, with the gateway-to-heroin and pusher-victim tropes that fundamentally mischaracterized how the market operated but proved very effective in generating public and legislative outrage. The gateway-progression thesis also universalized the racial crisis represented by the relatively contained urban narcotics market and, as the Nixon administration understood well, there were not nearly enough heroin addicts alone to mobilize popular support for a nationwide drug war. The direct link between marijuana and the political and countercultural revolts of the 1960s transformed the drug into a symbol of generational rebellion and an alarming explanation for why white middle-class youth were adopting perceived "ghetto" values and behaviors. The diagnosis of mass "amotivational syndrome" that climaxed in the 1980s portrayed marijuana as a direct cause of adolescent insubordination, family breakdown, capitalist nonproductivity, even national decline.[35]

The Power and Permanence of Suburban Crisis

The suburban crisis is a deeply embedded and seemingly permanent structural force in the political culture, state processes, policy formations, and media productions of modern America. My conceptual model of suburban crisis begins with the juxtaposition of the political and cultural discourses surrounding the mythology of the American Dream and reveals that the utopian and dystopian visions of white middle-class suburbia are really flip sides of the same coin. Since the 1950s, the U.S. political system has celebrated—and promised to protect and defend—white suburban families as the heart and soul of the nation, the hardworking and tax-paying and law-abiding heroes of Middle America. For just as long, popular culture has taken a much darker view of what goes on behind the white picket fences and inside the private suburban homes of the idealized nuclear family—a pathological landscape of repression and distress and conflict, of dysfunctional children and shockingly unexpected youth criminality. These powerful and pervasive images and discourses in politics and mass culture have operated to erase the structural forces of metropolitan racial and class segregation by recasting affluent white suburbanites as the innocent victims of their landscapes of psychological trauma and cookie-cutter conformity. Consider the dominant tropes of white suburban victimization—through the framework of male Baby Boomer pseudo-rebellion, illegal alcohol or drug escapism, and psychological repression—that connect Jim Stark drunk and alienated in the middle-class teen delinquency drama *Rebel Without a Cause* (1955), Ben Braddock drunk and drifting through a plastic society in the generation gap touchstone *The Graduate* (1967), culminating in Lester Burnham stoned and miserable amid the affluence and suburban superficiality of *American Beauty* (1999). This ongoing suburban crisis is an evasion of the historical and contemporary policies that created and have reproduced racial segregation and class inequality in modern America, making affluent white families the nation's heroes and victims all at the same time.[36]

The utopian/dystopian framework in the political culture of suburban crisis is recurring and structural, generating policy outcomes through the tropes of white innocence lost, racialized external invasions, and the cyclical "spread" of drug and crime "epidemics" from the inner cities to the middle-class sanctuaries. When the news media and the political system sensationalize the threat of violent predators—a perceived "wave" of drug pusher infiltrations or gang-related crimes or child kidnappings or school shootings—the utopian assurance that "it can't happen here," meaning in a safe and segregated white suburb, collapses into the dystopian nightmare that "it can happen anywhere" and no one in America is safe. In the tragic murder of Polly Klaas, for example, the framework of innocence lost extended not only to the twelve-year-old victim but to the entire suburban town of Petaluma ("where people once believed they were safe") and by extension to all of white middle-class America—directly inspiring the passage of California's "Three Strikes" referendum in 1994 and serving as the Clinton administration's most urgent rationale for the extraordinarily punitive Violent Crime Control and Law Enforcement Act. When the suburban crisis involves the criminal actions of white middle-class teenagers, from the marijuana and delinquency outbreaks of the 1950s through the Columbine school massacre of 1999, the most politically resonant response blames the mass media and other outside villains for corrupting innocent youth by exposing them to drugs and violence, blackness and urban vices. For white females, the most symbolic victim role is the runaway daughter of the suburban crisis, lured from domestic safety into the urban underworld of drugs, prostitution, and racial boundary crossings. There is a direct line from the racist Federal Bureau of Narcotics propaganda about white addict-prostitutes and "Negro pushers" in the 1950s to the war on drugs epic *Traffic* (2000), where the desperate white father rescues sixteen-year-old Caroline from the Black dealer who turned his daughter into a "crack whore," ultimately to be saved in a private rehab center.[37]

The consistent depiction of white suburban youth as the primary victims of the criminal drug markets served simultaneously to politicize them as a moral and racial weapon in American law and culture and to depoliticize them collectively as citizens and autonomous actors deserving of rights, freedoms, and responsibilities. Scholars have produced a rich literature analyzing the racial ideologies and boundaries of "innocent childhood" and the pernicious ways in which crusades to protect "our children" from socially constructed threats and external enemies have advanced punitive policies and propelled the expansion of policing regimes and carceral institutions. Childhood and youth are inherently political categories, deployed constantly by social movements and institutional actors from all across the spectrum, but the dynamic that historically gained the most traction in American culture and policy formation revolves around an endangered innocence that is generally inaccessible to nonwhite counterparts both marginalized and criminalized.[38] It is myopic to view the political and cultural campaigns to protect innocent white childhood as primarily the province of conservative activists, Republican administrations, and the "culture wars" provoked by the religious right. The history of the drug and crime wars in modern America clearly reveals that the discursive and political production of the innocent white child-victim and the endangered white suburb is a structural feature of American political culture—constantly reproduced by state institutions, the corporate media, nonpartisan social formations such as the National Federation of Parents for Drug-Free Youth and the victims' rights movement, and a bipartisan consensus of elected officials competing to lead the way. It is also important to emphasize that while the politics of innocent and victimized childhood has created massive racial and social inequalities and justified punitive policies of selective crime control, the framework of suburban crisis also promotes the depoliticization and social control of white middle-class youth under the guise of their safety and protection.

Despite the drug-war consensus in public policy and the ubiquity of suburban crisis in media and political culture, a large majority of the families in white middle-class American communities were not participants in a mass "moral panic" about dope pushers, urban gangs, or internal outbreaks of drug addiction and teenage delinquency. *The Suburban Crisis* deliberately does not deploy the sociological concept of "moral panic" that many historians have embraced to explain political mobilizations and policy outcomes that are not based in rational fears and statistically likely threats, such as crime "waves" and drug or kidnapping "epidemics" inflamed by media hype and the instrumentalist agendas of law enforcement, elected officials, and interest groups.[39] There is no doubt that state agencies and the mainstream media circulated, and the majority of American adults at various points believed, unscientific nonsense about the properties and health hazards and criminogenic effects of various illegal drugs, as well as racialized mythologies about "pushers" targeting innocent youth and the gateway progression from marijuana experimentation to hopeless addiction. But most white suburban parents were not "panicking" about these threats because most of their teenage children were not participating in any illegal drug market except for marijuana and the normative violation of underage alcohol laws by around 90 percent of juveniles. Instead, the grassroots political crusades and interest groups that escalated the drug war in a series of feedback loops with state and media actors emerged from specific spatial contexts, particularly affluent inner-ring white suburbs located near urban centers. These "moral entrepreneurs" claimed to speak on behalf of all American parents but did not even clearly represent the majority view in their own neighborhoods, which repeatedly led them to decry the "permissiveness" of other middle-class families that seemed tolerant or resigned to the illegal recreational market. Most white parents primarily did not want their children to encounter the criminal justice system, and almost all youth certainly agreed.[40]

The recurring mobilization of public officials and media corporations in response to white middle-class pressure and peril reveals the structural power and political potency of the framework of suburban crisis. The preponderance of evidence in this book about the grassroots activism of suburban antidrug movements and the political resistance of white teenagers and young adults comes from traditional state archives such as the papers of gubernatorial and presidential administrations and the hearings and files of legislative committees. The prominence of white middle-class voices in these sources provides valuable insights into how activist groups and ordinary parents influenced the development of the war on drugs, confirming which American citizens mattered most to lawmakers and policymakers. The correspondence files of California governors contain thousands of letters and petitions from white parents and suburban groups that demanded a tougher war on marijuana and heroin traffickers during the 1950s and 1960s, and hundreds of others who protested the arrest and prosecution of their children or called for addiction treatment instead of incarceration. Between the mid-1960s and the late 1970s, many white teenagers and young adults (and some of their parents) denounced the marijuana enforcement crackdown and urged governors of states such as California, Oregon, and New York to enact legalization or decriminalization. The files of White House officials during the late 1970s and 1980s include extensive records of suburban "parent power" coalitions from across the nation, which they closely tracked. The Carter administration helped create the National Federation of Parents for Drug-Free Youth, and the Reagan White House consulted its leadership constantly while appointing both of his "drug czars" directly from its ranks. Congressional hearings and investigations likewise privileged white suburban activist groups and also provide extensive records of how law enforcement operated in middle-class areas, in addition to the often-silenced perspectives of criminalized youth occasionally given a platform to testify.[41]

The book's opening sections explore the original eruption of suburban crisis through the juvenile narcotics and delinquency epidemics in racially segregated white communities during the 1950s and early 1960s, culminating in the political and generational youth revolt on the college and high school campuses and in the counterculture. The prologue and first chapter, "Pushers and Victims," move back and forth between the state of California and the U.S. Congress to reveal how this racialized binary emerged as a consensus framework that shaped the passage of mandatory-minimum laws against heroin and marijuana and launched discretionary law enforcement campaigns to incapacitate or forcibly rehabilitate participants in the criminalized market. The second chapter, "Suburban Rebels," explores the war on juvenile delinquency and alcohol-related status offenses in the white middle-class suburbs and its direct connections to the campaign to eradicate the illegal adolescent drug subculture of marijuana and illicit pharmaceuticals. This story continues with the emergence of a mass "psychedelic drug culture" of marijuana and LSD use on the college campuses during the mid-to-late 1960s, politically linked to anti-Vietnam War activism and the bohemian counterculture, and its subsequent depoliticization as an urban crisis of runaway white daughters in dangerous "hippie" slums. "Generation Gap," the third chapter, investigates how white suburban drug markets really operated and how local and state law enforcement agencies responded to mass violations of the felony marijuana laws by white middle-class high school students during the second half of the 1960s. This comparative analysis is based on contemporary ethnographic studies of the youth subculture and the records of law enforcement and juvenile delinquency agencies, enabling a multiple case study approach that illuminates the discretionary and discriminatory processes of criminalization and decriminalization in the metropolitan regions of Los Angeles, the San Francisco Bay Area, the New York City suburbs, and greater Washington, DC.

The Nixon administration and public health liberals in Congress nationalized the law enforcement strategies forged in these coastal suburbs in the omnibus federal legislation of 1970, part of the broader consensus behind the racial state-building project to launch a full-blown drug war against urban and border traffickers while arresting and coercing their alleged victims into involuntary treatment programs. Chapter 4, "Public Enemy Number One," reveals how and why the white suburban marijuana crisis moved to the center of the national war on drugs, based not only on the traditional pusher-victim and gateway-to-heroin tropes but also the belief that escalating enforcement would save middle-class youth from "amotivational" lifestyles associated with hippies, ghettos, and capitalist nonproductivity. "Impossible Criminals," the fifth chapter, returns to the local and state levels to explore the explosion of marijuana arrests of white youth in the 1970s and the political rise of legalization and decriminalization crusades to rescue these "otherwise law-abiding" Americans from drug-war jeopardy. Case studies of California, Texas, Oregon, and New York in the era of the Rockefeller Drug Laws demonstrate that the partial decriminalization compromise of the mid-1970s involved a legislative tradeoff that intensified the war on heroin and the "real criminals" in nonwhite urban centers. The final two chapters, "Parent Power" and "Zero Tolerance," chart the ascendance of the suburban antimarijuana movement during the Carter and Reagan administrations and its considerable success in reversing the momentum for decriminalization and reescalating the war on drugs with a priority mission of stopping white teenagers from smoking pot, depicted as the cause of middle-class family breakdown and mass "amotivational syndrome." The parent power coalition also achieved the futile social control policy of raising the national drinking age to twenty-one and ensured that, even during the crack cocaine crisis and its militarized assault on urban centers, federal policymakers remained obsessed with drug prevention and rehab campaigns for affluent white victims.

America's long and never-ending war on drugs is unjust, counterproductive, and unwinnable for many reasons—but a central and underappreciated factor is that most of the white middle-class youth subjected to systems of criminalization and social control for their own safety and protection do not actually want to be saved. The history of the war on drugs reveals what anyone can see and what no politician or policymaker caught up in the bipartisan consensus has been willing to say out loud: it is not possible to eradicate or even meaningfully impede a lucrative consumer market through law enforcement crackdowns and supply-side controls that create the crime and violence that the state duplicitously blames solely on "traffickers" and "pushers" and "addicts." It also is not possible to eradicate the demand side of a criminalized market in a drug-dependent society through zero-tolerance mandates and gateway-to-doom lies, false distinctions between the hazards of legal and illegal products, mass arrests and diversion of some "deserving" victims to involuntary rehabilitation, social control of teenagers in a culture that celebrates freedom and mobility, or any other strategy deployed thus far. In fact, as several sections of this book illustrate, the "responsible use" and "harm reduction" polices endorsed by some public health officials and implemented in a number of suburban communities starting in the 1970s proved far more effective than zero-tolerance authoritarianism and threatened arrest, because they engaged with teenagers as politically conscious citizens who could be trusted to make responsible choices—not all the time, but the same is true of adults as well. The genuine alternative to punitive drug and crime control policies is not a return to the indeterminate sentencing of the "liberal" rehabilitative era, or less racism in the arrest and diversion of sympathetic victims to treatment programs. The civil liberties position that is well outside the drug-war consensus is the end of criminal prohibition for all banned substances and public health challenges, not just for marijuana, and decriminalization of juvenile status offenses as well.[42]

PROLOGUE

Los Angeles, 1950–51

IN APRIL 1950, the Los Angeles media began publicizing a sudden epidemic of drug-fueled crime and random violence by Mexican American youth, labeled "Wolf Packs" and "Rat Packs" in the sensational newspaper headlines. The *Los Angeles Daily News* attributed the reign of terror to "youthful malcontents," who trafficked marijuana and turned into "roving gangs of hoodlums"; "marauding 'wolf pack' youth"; and an "infestation of juvenile rat packs," driving their cars across the metropolitan region on deranged crime sprees. The *Herald Express* warned of "wolf gangs of youthful hoodlums on a rampage," from downtown to the suburbs, with "a gang of eight swarthy" teenagers assaulting and robbing pedestrians and another group pulling a young white man from his car and terrorizing his wife and baby. The *Los Angeles Times* vividly portrayed the white suburban victims of the month-long outbreak of "youthful 'wolf packs'" that "cruise the county in hot-rod cars spreading terror," attacking a twenty-two-year-old housewife from Lakewood, a real estate agent in Westwood, and teenagers at the beaches of Santa Monica and Malibu. Politicians and law enforcement officials in the city and county of Los Angeles immediately declared "all-out war against 'wolf packs'" and rounded up dozens of Mexican American youth from the East Los Angeles barrio, a few for specific acts of violence but most on mere allegations of gang affiliation.[1] This racial criminalization of Mexican American teenagers by white authorities and the mass media reprised the infamous state crackdown on "hoodlums" and "gangsters" during the Sleepy Lagoon trial and Zoot Suit Riots of 1942–43, when white mobs assaulted nonwhite youth and police responded with mass arrests targeting the "foreign" immigrant threat. The 1950 mobilization against the "wolf pack" menace demonstrated that Mexican American youth continued to loom largest in the white racial imaginary of crime, drugs, and delinquency in

Los Angeles County. The rapidly growing and deeply segregated region contained an 88 percent white (non-Hispanic) majority along with routinely criminalized Mexican American (5.8 percent) and African American (5 percent) enclaves.[2]

Based on little if any evidence, the chief of the Los Angeles Police Department (LAPD) proposed that marijuana addiction had caused the wave of indiscriminate violence by Mexican American hoodlums, a variant of the "reefer madness" mythology promoted since the late 1930s by Commissioner Harry Anslinger of the Federal Bureau of Narcotics. The Los Angeles County Sheriff's Department (LACSD) circulated a pamphlet warning that marijuana caused ferocious crimes of aggression and sadism, making users "very dangerous to handle—they have no fear. . . . Marijuana becomes the master of soul, mind, and body, and the user becomes a slave to the unknown demands of an enemy to all mankind."[3] In letters to the newspapers, frightened and angry residents from white areas of the city and suburbs alike demanded a "get tough" approach to juvenile crime and condemned liberal "bleeding hearts" and "sob sisters" for "coddling" hoodlums and preventing police from protecting "decent, law-abiding citizens."[4] Civil rights groups countered that the media had fanned public hysteria, and they promoted traditional antidelinquency remedies of more parks, recreation centers, and vocational training for low-income youth in East Los Angeles and other nonwhite areas. The Progressive juvenile delinquency coalition of civic and municipal agencies that had formed after the Zoot Suit Riots denounced all of the major metropolitan newspapers for "increasing racial tensions" by once again sensationalizing a false epidemic of "gang lawlessness of youth in minority groups." After a month of inflammatory headlines, the *Los Angeles Times* implicitly acknowledged this critique by reporting the consensus of the juvenile justice authorities that there was no delinquency epidemic after all and that rates of youth crime in the metropolitan region had actually declined during the previous year when adjusted for population growth. The newspaper informed its white readership that while "wolf gangs" might be dangerous and depraved, it would be wrong to stereotype all Mexican American youth as "an entire delinquent and unassimilable minority."[5]

In cultural and political discourse, the fabricated "wolf pack" epidemic helped cement the connection between racial gangs, juvenile delinquency, predatory addicts, and dope pushers who targeted innocent white teenagers, especially for a suburban audience that primarily encountered these images through the mass media. During 1950–51, the LA newspapers chronicled

Mexican American "peddlers" who smuggled narcotics across the border, "preyed" on high school students in Long Beach (by selling them reefer), and operated a wholesaling ring that allegedly distributed marijuana to white youth from the upscale beachfront enclaves on the Westside to the middle-income neighborhoods of the San Fernando Valley. A narcotics prevention organization with close ties to law enforcement informed parents that juveniles of all races were buying marijuana at bowling alleys, drive-in restaurants, malt shops, and pool halls—but most "large-scale peddlers are in the so-called minority group." In a radio broadcast reprinted in the newspapers, a prominent state judge delivered a jeremiad about the "narcotics invasion sweeping America," threatening "your boy and mine," with dope pushers prowling around high schools hawking reefer cigarettes that can "push the psycho-neurotic type of person from sanity to madness." The judge advocated the death penalty for providing narcotics to minors, justified with an apocryphal tale about a Mexican man, "crazed as a result of marihuana intoxication," who raped and murdered a California infant.[6] In the early 1950s, the LA-based Narcotic Educational Foundation of America issued frequent warnings that the Mexican marijuana "invasion" was causing degenerate crimes of sex and violence, with dope pushers targeting teenage "victims" in all types of neighborhoods—no longer just on the "wrong side of the tracks." The California Bureau of Narcotic Enforcement endorsed these assessments in a 1951 report that addicts were responsible for a "general crime wave" and that marijuana users in particular were "dangerous, hard to handle, and might resort to any act of violence."[7]

The state of California responded by establishing lengthy mandatory-minimum sentences for distributing narcotics to a minor (including marijuana and heroin) in the summer of 1951, three months before the U.S. Congress enacted a similar penalty structure in the Boggs Act. That spring, civic groups in metropolitan Los Angeles and the California Congress of Parents and Teachers began calling for tougher laws, and Governor Earl Warren pledged to crack down on dope pushers who victimized teenagers. The state legislature passed the measure with no evident dissent, setting the minimum sale penalty at five years for the first offense and ten for the second, with parole officials empowered to keep dangerous pushers incarcerated for life. The law also removed the possibility of probation for first offenders, requiring a three-month sentence for all possession convictions and a six-month minimum for sale to adults, with a six-year maximum on both counts. The legislation specified that all noncitizens who broke narcotics laws would be reported to federal immigration authorities for deportation, a reflection of the pervasive racial criminalization of Mexican nationals as the invading pusher-villains in postwar California. The 1951 statute also provided a misdemeanor jail term for being "addicted to the unlawful use of narcotics"—a status criminalization that applied to illegal, but not licit medical, drugs—justified by implausible data such as the claim that dope fiends stole $2 million worth of merchandise annually in downtown LA alone. The legislation further merged punitive crime control and coercive public health policy through a civil commitment procedure that allowed judges to divert addicts to state psychiatric hospitals for an indeterminate period of three months to two years, except for anyone of "bad character apart from his habit." And finally, the 1951 law criminalized business establishments and private residences "where narcotics are illegally obtainable," which permitted law enforcement to initiate asset forfeiture of buildings and vehicles utilized by illegal drug sellers and users, and to arrest everyone present.[8]

The new law intensified rather than quelled an expanding grassroots movement for even harsher punishment for pushers who allegedly targeted innocent youth. The nonpartisan California Federation of Women's Clubs promptly labeled the legislation insufficiently punitive, warning that dope pushers were still infiltrating white suburbs in search of new victims. During 1951–52, Governor Warren received an increasing number of letters and petitions demanding capital punishment or life imprisonment without parole for providing narcotics to a minor, including one from a white suburban mother who blamed pushers for turning her son into an addict after he tried marijuana for kicks. Women's groups based in segregated white suburbs of Los Angeles County led this movement for a tougher crackdown, with calls to action arriving from Glendale, Alhambra, Manhattan Beach, Long Beach, Hermosa Beach, and similar middle-class communities. The California Congress of Parents and Teachers recommended closing the Mexican border to unaccompanied juveniles, a rare admission of how most white suburban youth actually obtained marijuana—not through corruption by evil pushers but by driving to Tijuana and buying it themselves, or by obtaining the drug from other white Americans who had.[9] The state government paired the 1951 get-tough law with a new antinarcotics educational curriculum, designed by law enforcement agencies, that featured a white female from suburban L.A. who experimented with marijuana and became a hopeless heroin addict after a pusher stuck a needle in her arm without her consent. This preposterous scenario formed the basis of the narcotics prevention campaign in high schools and community forums, accompanied by warnings that most girls who tried marijuana would become heroin addict-prostitutes and that boys would inevitable turn into thieves, with both groups destined for jail or psychiatric institutionalization. The educational film praised parents' groups and media outlets for bringing attention to the narcotics crisis and clearly contributed to inflaming the political climate.[10]

The racialized pusher-victim framework and marijuana-to-heroin gateway hype also operated to justify racial segregation as necessary to safeguard innocent white youth from crime, delinquency, and addiction. Civil rights groups launched a major campaign against government-sanctioned housing segregation during the postwar era and advocated construction of public, racially integrated projects spread throughout Los Angeles County. They condemned segregationist federal policies in mortgage financing and redlining, restrictive racial covenants in white subdivisions, suburban municipalities that barred public housing through exclusionary zoning, and other methods to maintain a Jim Crow residential market. Civil rights leaders also argued that integrated housing would ameliorate the delinquency problem among Black and Mexican American youth, which they attributed to racial discrimination and overcrowded slums. They emphasized that the prevailing white belief that racial minorities would "lower the moral tone of the neighborhood" and "teach the children wicked ways" was a pernicious stereotype reinforced by housing segregation itself.[11] Massive white opposition to housing integration proved the point, with frequent charges that scattered public projects would bring the infiltration of crime, delinquency, and narcotics identified with Mexican American and Black slums. White voters defeated three consecutive statewide or LA County ballot referendums to promote racially integrated housing between 1948 and 1952, and the LAPD released a particularly explosive—and statistically invalid—report linking nonwhite public projects to high crime rates during the final campaign.[12] By the mid-1950s, the state of California was officially endorsing housing segregation as the best way to protect "normal" youth from the crime and drug scourge of nonwhite "delinquent neighborhoods."[13] The Federal Bureau of Narcotics also recommended racial segregation as the best defense for white Americans while escalating its nationwide war on nonwhite pushers and urban addicts during the 1950s, the next stage in this story.

1

Pushers and Victims

COMMISSIONER HARRY J. ANSLINGER of the Federal Bureau of Narcotics (FBN) started his 1961 book *The Murderers: The Shocking Story of the Narcotic Gangs* with a gallery of despicable drug pusher villains: Italian Mafia syndicates that imported heroin to the United States, street-corner "hoodlums" who sold the poison to psychologically weak residents of urban slums, marijuana peddlers who handed out reefer cigarettes to high school students to indoctrinate them into a deadly spiral of heroin addiction. Anslinger then channeled his rage and sympathy through the story of a singular white victim: "a flaxen-haired eighteen-year-old girl sprawled nude and unconscious on a Harlem tenement floor after selling herself to a collection of customers throughout the afternoon, in exchange for a shot of heroin in the arm." This racialized and gendered pusher-victim narrative—the evil nonwhite male predators, the lost innocence of the young white female—had shaped the American war on narcotics since its escalation a decade earlier and would continue to justify selectively punitive enforcement for decades to come. The unnamed "white girl" was a lost daughter from Minnesota who descended into heroin addiction and prostitution across the color line in New York City, a desperate and tragic victim who ended up dead. The criminal in the story was "Billy, a Negro, . . . the curbstone pusher in that section of town, and the pimp for a blonde eighteen-year-old addict." Billy allegedly gave the white female constant shots of heroin and cocaine to prostitute her for other "young hoodlums" and then dumped her body in the wealthy suburb of Greenwich, Connecticut. Anslinger highlighted a second story about a white teenager named Peggy, based on a nationally syndicated profile that had circulated as the federal government established harsh mandatory-minimum penalties for sale and possession of both heroin and marijuana in 1951. Peggy came to New York City from Michigan, got involved in the jazz scene, and purportedly became a heroin junkie because her musician boyfriend started her on marijuana. Anslinger advocated coercive medical institutionalization for addict-victims such as Peggy, and ruthless punishment for their pushers.[1]

The racialized pusher-victim binary operated as a consensus framework in postwar America and played a central role in the enactment of every major federal and state law that intensified the war on narcotics during the 1950s. As a cultural and political script of innocence lost, the pusher-victim trope emphasized the dual imperatives of protecting white middle-class youth from the illegal drug markets through the criminal control of their urban nonwhite counterparts. This rationale underlay the federal mandatory-minimum sentencing structure established unanimously by Congress in the Boggs Act of 1951 and stiffened with negligible dissent in the Narcotic Control Act of 1956, as well as similar get-tough state laws passed even earlier in California, New York, and Illinois. In its most shocking and scandalous formulation, conveyed in forums ranging from congressional hearings to mass magazines to the educational curriculum, sinister villains turned pretty white females into addict-victims through a marijuana-to-heroin gateway progression that invariably descended into the "living death" of prostitution in urban slums. This imagery of the innocent and racially violated white middle-class female tapped into the long history of representations of narcotics addiction and the broader captivity narrative in American political culture. Precedents include the nineteenth-century fears of small-town youth seduced by urban vice, the anti-Black apogee of the film *Birth of a Nation* (1915), the anti-immigrant "white slavery" prostitution sensationalism that led to the Mann Act of 1910, the anti-Chinese "opium dens" campaign that informed the Harrison Narcotics Act of 1914, and the white child-victims centered by the "demon alcohol" crusade that culminated in Prohibition during the 1920s.[2] Commissioner Anslinger was by no means the script's foremost purveyor during the 1950s, because he insistently claimed that the FBN had all but eradicated the underground market and that almost all drug addicts were Black "hoodlums" and "colored children," because "normal" white youth who stayed out of slums were not susceptible.[3]

During the 1950s, the drug-war focus on white middle-class youth victims and endangered suburban spaces emerged first and foremost from the racially segregated landscape and bipartisan get-tough political ethos of Southern California, not from the instrumentalist agenda of the Federal Bureau of Narcotics. A close examination of California's early war on narcotics provides a broader ideological dimension, and an alternative model of local-national interplay in policy formation, than the traditional scholarly account of a top-down, Washington-centered expansion of federal power and urban control manipulated by Commissioner Anslinger and racial conservatives in Congress.[4] The sustained grassroots mobilization of white suburban parents and organizations in metropolitan Los Angeles was nonpartisan and bipartisan, not a product of the New Right, grounded in widely shared beliefs that protecting white youth required maintaining neighborhood-level housing segregation and policing racial boundaries on the rapidly expanding automobile-centered landscape.[5] The immediate trigger was the false media and political hype that Mexican American gangs and hoodlums were invading white communities to commit violence and peddle marijuana and heroin to innocent teenagers. This moral crusade rested on a greatly exaggerated "epidemic" of youth addiction and a fundamental misunderstanding of the dynamics of the illegal market, because the relatively small number of white middle-class teenagers who smoked marijuana generally acquired the non-addictive drug by driving across the border to Tijuana or from dealers and acquaintances of the same race, and very few "graduated" to heroin use. In response to white suburban demands for a legal crackdown on Mexican and Mexican American "pushers" and predatory narcotics addicts, the state of California established a series of landmark mandatory-minimum laws and repeatedly escalated racially targeted enforcement while carving out discretionary loopholes to divert "good" youth from "good homes" into rehabilitative treatment or informal juvenile probation.

The racial and spatial logics of California's war on narcotics, and its counterparts in other states and at the federal level, collectively criminalized and dehumanized nonwhite and foreign "pushers" and dangerous "hoodlum addicts," while removing responsibility and agency from white middle-class Americans who likewise violated the drug prohibition laws. Commissioner Anslinger's influential depiction of the criminal narcotics scourge in postwar America—a vision foundational to the consensus politics that shaped drug policy development, including the bureaucratic dominance of law enforcement over medical expertise—was arbitrary, unscientific, legally contrived, and racist at its core. The FBN portrayed the real narcotics threat, which its own policies had constructed and criminalized, as a racially segregated market where nonwhite pushers and nonwhite addicts trafficked and consumed extremely dangerous banned substances, especially heroin and marijuana, that had no legitimate medical use. Anslinger denied that almost any white Americans, except a few helpless victims and foolish hipsters, participated in this illegal "narcotics" market and instead celebrated their "medical" drug consumption as a therapeutic gift from his close allies in the pharmaceutical industry, for which he advocated self-regulation. The FBN commissioner consistently suppressed the clear evidence that prescription barbiturates and amphetamines taken primarily by white middle-class citizens were potentially addictive, even though they constituted a much greater public health hazard than heroin and circulated illicitly in large quantities because of deliberate overproduction by pharmaceutical companies.[6] In reports to Congress and the public, the FBN produced this racial knowledge and segregated market of "drug addiction" with improbable precision based on arrest records alone: 61 percent Negro, 28 percent white, 5 percent Puerto Rican, 4 percent Mexican for 1953–56 combined (fig. 1.1). This fallacious methodology evaded the impact of discriminatory law enforcement and rested on the broader racial contrivance of the legal/illegal divide.[7]

The construction of a bifurcated market separating criminalized substances from corporate-manufactured drugs and alcohol, based on racism and politics rather than evidence-based public health policies, generated almost no mainstream dissent during the 1950s. During this pivotal era in the expansion of the carceral state, the policy discussion in Washington and in the state capitals revolved around the two-track law enforcement approach of arresting illegal drug traffickers and pushers and incarcerating them for a long time, and arresting the addict-victims in order to force them into narcotics hospitals and psychiatric institutions. The liberal Democrats who led the special Senate committees to investigate crime and delinquency, as well as Progressive stalwarts such as Governor Pat Brown of California, strongly advocated this policy of criminalizing heroin and marijuana markets, sending the pusher-villains to prison, and coercively rehabilitating their addict-victims through civil commitment procedures. Although liberal drug warriors believed that institutional rehabilitation was the humane alternative to incarceration, both approaches were punitive and operated in tandem to marginalize the small group of medical experts who advised decriminalization through noncoercive public health policies. White liberal policymakers never addressed or even seemed conscious of the racial discrimination inherent in discretionary law enforcement, and their main disagreement with Anslinger-style conservatives revolved around their view that so-called "addict-peddlers," a group presumed nonwhite, suffered from urban inequalities and psychiatric disorders and should also be diverted into coercive rehabilitation. During the 1950s, even as the FBN continued to promote the nonsensical and widely believed "reefer madness" mythology that marijuana caused crimes of violence and perversion, the law enforcement and political establishment consensus increasingly made the case

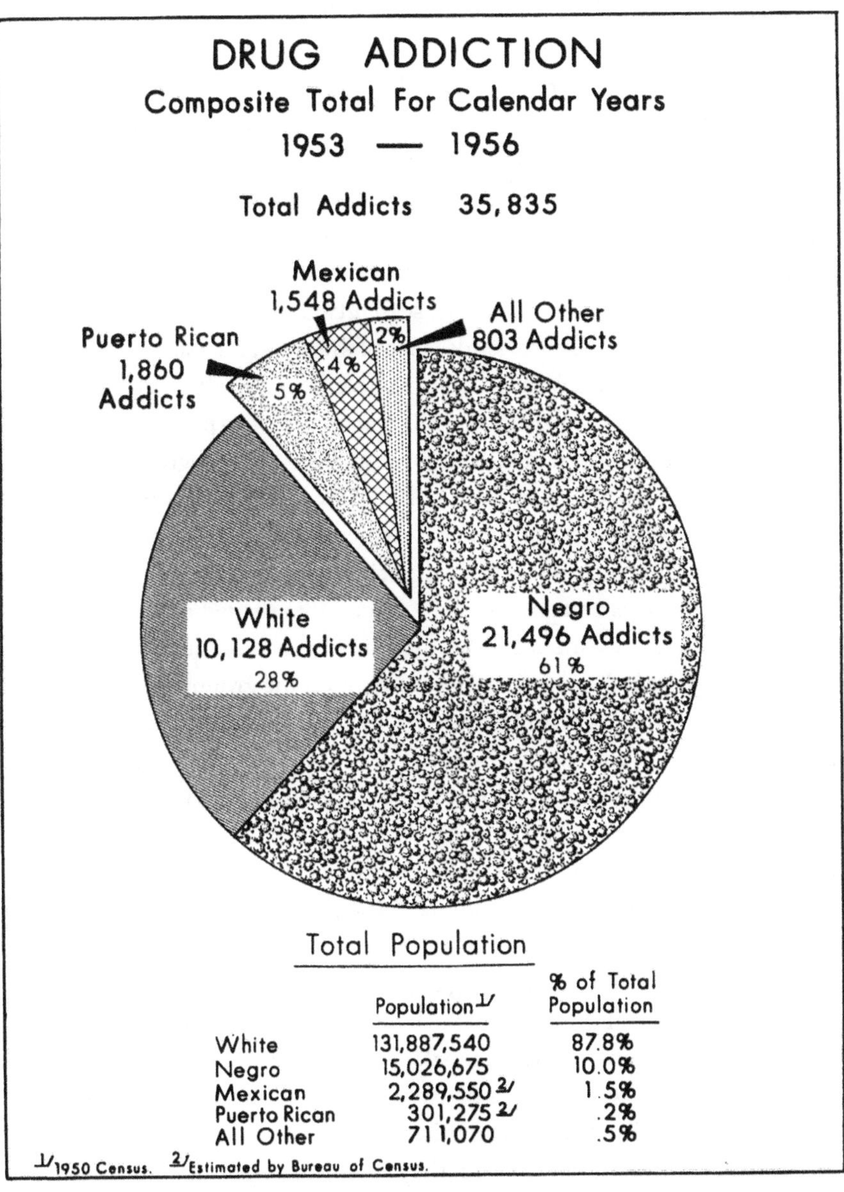

FIGURE 1.1. Racial composite of alleged number of drug addicts in the United States, 1953–56, according to the Federal Bureau of Narcotics. Commissioner Harry J. Anslinger portrayed drug addiction as a primarily Black criminal problem based on invalid statistics drawn from arrest data alone and excluding corporate pharmaceuticals. The FBN circulated this graphic widely in Congress and to the media. (Reproduced from its annual report, *Traffic in Opium and Other Dangerous Drugs, 1956.*)

for prioritizing its threat based on the illogic of the gateway-to-heroin-addiction thesis, which ensured that white youth would remain an unsolvable problem.

The mainstream culture and the policy formation process depoliticized American youth comprehensively during the 1950s, dividing them into racialized categories of villains and victims during an era when mass suburbanization generated concerns about an "epidemic" of juvenile delinquency and drug addiction that was spreading across all racial, socioeconomic, and geographic boundaries. The pusher-victim framework resonated because it fused the categories of race, gender, class, age, sexuality, and space in potent ways—constructing both the physical landscapes of the segregated single-family suburbs and the symbolic terrain of white middle-class society as utopian ideals threatened by dystopian nightmares. The war on narcotics played a critical and underappreciated role in sanctioning racial and economic segregation in metropolitan housing patterns as essential to protect white middle-class youth from the crime, drugs, and delinquency associated with their nonwhite urban counterparts, a preemptive strike as the civil rights movement escalated its challenge to the laws and government policies that shaped racial discrimination across Jim Crow America.[8] This mobilization had pernicious and lasting consequences, including ad hoc development on the ground of a discretionary multi-track (rather than two-track) drug control apparatus that sorted participants in the criminalized market into predatory pushers and addicts deserving of lengthy incarceration, innocent addict-victims who necessitated psychiatric confinement, and a third category of thrill-seeking and misguided white middle-class youth who should be diverted from facing consequences entirely. What is striking is how similarly the teenagers and young adults divided into these categories described their willing participation in the illegal drug markets, almost never blaming the "pushers" and strongly disputing the political consensus of the dangers and evils of marijuana and even heroin, on the rare occasions when congressional investigations or media exposés or scientific researchers gave them a platform at all. A foundational flaw of the American war on drugs was that neither segregated suburbs nor law enforcement could control the white youth they promised to protect.

Producing the White Teenage Narcotics Crisis

In June 1950, Commissioner Harry J. Anslinger of the Federal Bureau of Narcotics informed the Special Senate Committee to Investigate Organized Crime that a "more severe" mandatory-minimum sentencing law combined with additional enforcement resources "would just about dry up the traffic" by dope smugglers and peddlers in the United States. Anslinger, the director of the FBN since its formation two decades earlier, was riding high in early Cold War America, lauded in national magazines as the tenacious general in charge of "our global war on narcotics," the sophisticated architect behind the United Nations international narcotics control regime, the determined leader of a crime-fighting agency "nearly as tough and a whole lot smarter than the worst the underworld can produce."[9] During the 1930s, the FBN commissioner had resurrected the federal government's drug enforcement authority after the disastrous failure of alcohol Prohibition (1920–33), a moral crusade in which Anslinger played a leading role, by mobilizing public opinion and state resources against racially stigmatized heroin and marijuana traffickers and addicts. In 1937, Anslinger capitalized on growing pressure from the Southwest to criminalize marijuana, based on its association with Mexican migrants, by enhancing the FBN's power through federal enactment of the Marihuana Tax Act. This law subjected marijuana violators to the same penalties that heroin offenders received under the Harrison Narcotics Act of 1914, justified by the infamous and fallacious "reefer madness" myth that evil "peddlers of this poison" were targeting innocent school-age children and that smoking the weed caused crimes of maniacal violence and sexual perversity. Commissioner Anslinger rallied support for this mission with propaganda such as "Marijuana: Assassin of Youth," claiming that Mexican reefer cigarettes turned boys into murderers and rapists, girls into sex deviants and prostitutes, and innocent victims into "slaves to the narcotic" (marijuana is not a narcotic, scientifically speaking) and degenerate, crazed, often-dead addicts.[10]

During the 1950s escalation of the war on narcotics, the FBN shifted its definition of the racial-criminal threat by placing Italian crime syndicates and African American pushers and predatory addicts in the crosshairs of its enforcement campaign. In his 1950 testimony to the Special Senate Committee to Investigate Organized Crime, Anslinger blamed Italian American traffickers for the importation of heroin from Asian source nations yet insisted that the illegal narcotics market was largely under control except for "young hoodlums" in urban centers. He boasted that the FBN's efforts had dramatically reduced the problem during the previous two decades, down to an estimated fifty thousand "nonmedical" addicts concentrated in the ghetto areas of the largest industrial cities—mainly New York, Chicago, and Los Angeles. Anslinger did concede that the instability of the World War II years had caused an increase in youth addicts, but the FBN insisted that most of these teenagers were "of the hoodlum type and not school children," already delinquent and criminally inclined. In internal FBN documents, Anslinger made clear his view that youthful addiction primarily involved "colored boys and girls" who hung out at jazz joints, started out smoking marijuana, and soon became "hooked" on heroin—alongside a few wayward white teenage victims who associated with "young hoodlum" types. Notably, Anslinger barely mentioned marijuana imported from Mexico in his 1950 testimony, as he did not yet recognize the utility of conflating reefer with heroin by hyping the gateway-progression thesis in order to achieve the tougher sentencing laws and additional enforcement manpower that the FBN desired. Anslinger urged Congress to provide the FBN with the necessary resources to crush the organized heroin syndicates, a "vicious commercial racket which lives on the slow murder of its customers." The commissioner endorsed the stringent mandatory-minimum penalties in the Boggs bill, introduced in 1950 by a segregationist Democrat from Louisiana, but the proposal failed to gain any political momentum that year.[11]

The national climate shifted toward a more punitive war on narcotics only after the mobilization of Progressive reformers, African American groups, and liberal politicians in the urban centers of Chicago and New York City. In 1949, after alarmist reports of surging narcotics addiction among Chicago high school students, antidelinquency organizations established the Crime Prevention Bureau to coordinate government and private agencies behind a "war against dope—public crime problem No. 1." Lois Higgins, a white middle-class antidelinquency activist and social welfare caseworker in the Chicago Police Department, directed the Crime Prevention Bureau and advocated the traditional Progressive fusion of tough punishment for sinister purveyors of vice markets and coercive rehabilitation of their youthful victims. Under her leadership, the Crime Prevention Bureau helped popularize the myths that marijuana smoking led inevitably to heroin and that narcotic "peddlers inoculate teen-agers free of charge . . . so that they will become addicts." Higgins, who believed that "there should be no conflict between police work and social work," advocated lengthy prison terms for dope peddlers, funding for new local treatment facilities, and a compulsory hospitalization law to cure or at least quarantine addicts.[12] African American organizations and churches on Chicago's South Side launched an affiliated "Dope Must Go" crusade for tougher penalties to save teenagers "victimized" by pushers "from outside of the community," part of the decades-long struggle against the concentration of vice markets in Black communities, generally with the complicity of corrupt police. In a yearlong campaign, the Crime Prevention Bureau and the Dope

Must Go coalition successfully lobbied the state legislature to change the misdemeanor penalty for sale of narcotics to a felony range of one year to life, with an enhanced two-year minimum for dealing to anyone under age twenty-one. Illinois governor Adlai Stevenson, a liberal Democrat and soon-to-be presidential nominee, signed the nation's harshest narcotics control law to date on May 3, 1951.[13]

The racial implications behind Illinois's new mandatory-minimum law soon became clearer in a series of Black pusher/white victim cases that revealed more about the discretionary mechanisms of the criminal justice system than the actual workings of the illegal drug market. The first person arrested under the law, identified by race in the *Chicago Daily Tribune* (along with all other nonwhite narcotic defendants), was George "Greasy" Gilbreath, Negro, fifty years old, for providing two heroin capsules through intermediaries to a white fifteen-year-old teenager named Phillip Petress. A Chicago judge sentenced Gilbreath, who had not known the ultimate destination of the product, to twenty-five years to life. Two other men involved in the transaction process, "Negroes" in their late twenties, received fifteen years to life in exchange for testifying against the supplier.[14] In its "Children in Peril" exposé (June 1951), *Life* magazine included a melodramatic image of white juvenile/victim Phillip Petress, flanked by his parents, pointing an accusing finger at Homer Stigger, the Black man who made the actual sale, in open court. *Life* warned that "'pushers' are selling narcotics to thousands of teen-agers," a threat illustrated with pictures of African American, Italian American, and Hispanic dope dealers from Chicago and Harlem. The magazine explained that while "Negro youth [were] particularly susceptible" to narcotics addiction, given the pathologies of slums and poverty, children from "excellent families" also remained at risk since the "brazen pusher" constantly sought victims through the free-sample method.[15] U.S. Representative Sidney Yates, a liberal white Democrat from the upscale Chicago lakefront, highlighted another case of interracial violation when he introduced a federal bill to stiffen narcotics penalties: David Deitch, a white high school junior who (allegedly) progressed from marijuana to heroin addiction under the corrosive influence of a "colored musician." In the first case tried by Chicago's new specialized Narcotics Court, Deitch received probation, while the jazz musician and three African American accomplices faced long felony sentences.[16]

The leading white reformers in Chicago's antinarcotics movement portrayed the crisis of dope addiction as a universal threat, because evil pushers and peddlers might target any child in any community, a racialized framework that decisively reshaped the national political debate in the early 1950s. Lois Higgins characterized teenage addiction in Chicago as an epidemic of "shocking proportions," a wildfire that "can break out anywhere," which in her view accounted for the bipartisan consensus behind Illinois's tough new law. The Crime Prevention Bureau warned that the dope scourge on the Black South Side and in "foreign" (immigrant) areas was rapidly "spreading" north and west, infiltrating the affluent lakefront neighborhoods and the white suburbs, overwhelming "many young people from socially well-adjusted families." Higgins illustrated these developments through tales of professional peddlers handing out free samples at playgrounds and soda fountains, thrill-seeking teenagers who tried marijuana and became heroin addicts, and a seventeen-year-old white female from a "good family" transformed into a helpless victim-prostitute. In April 1951 testimony to Congress, Higgins criticized Anslinger and the FBN for depicting teenage narcotics addiction as a small-scale problem restricted to inner-city hoodlums, warning that "somewhere right at this minute a little boy like yours, or a little girl like mine, is getting a first taste of the needle, . . . the drug that will soon destroy them."[17] Chicago's antidelinquency network reinforced this message with the educational film *Drug Addiction* (1951), an early and influential component of the postwar narcotics prevention curriculum in public schools. The sordid saga, set on a suburban/small town landscape, featured Italian-American pushers preying on white middle-class teenagers who travel down the path from marijuana experimentation to the "living nightmare" of heroin addiction. The film explained that narcotics addicts come from "all walks of life," not just the "teeming slum areas," and urged Americans to demand tougher national laws to incarcerate the pushers and rehabilitate the addict-victims.[18]

In New York City, the mobilization against the teenage narcotics crisis likewise began with a broad multiracial coalition of Progressive antidelinquency organizations, quickly evolved into a political obsession with racial boundary crossings, and played a key role in structuring the national policy environment. The grassroots initiative began in December 1950, a year after the similar formation in Chicago, when the Welfare Council of New York City organized dozens of civic groups and public agencies in a campaign to address the "alarming, widespread use of narcotics by teen-agers." The Welfare Council's investigative report, "The Menace of Narcotics to the Children of New York," portrayed teenage addicts collectively as the innocent victims of nefarious "pushers"—a repudiation of the FBN's stance that dope appealed mainly to hoodlums and gang members. Without specifying race, the study also emphasized the clustering of teenage addiction in the "economically and socially deprived areas of the city," especially among those traditionally considered most vulnerable to delinquency: juveniles from broken homes with maladjusted personalities and inadequate parental supervision. Although the number of youth (under age twenty-one) arrested for drug violations in New York City remained limited—from 27 in 1946 to 252 in 1950—antidelinquency activists highlighted the exponential growth and "epidemic proportions" of the crisis. The Welfare Council demanded tougher state and federal laws to deter pushers, called for a local treatment center (instead of sending addicts to the federal facility in Kentucky), and organized a comprehensive narcotics prevention campaign through affiliated churches, schools, and civic organizations.[19] The centerpiece of the prevention curriculum, a 1951 comic book titled *Trapped!*, exclusively featured white students ("victims") from a prosperous high school who begin smoking marijuana for thrills, start making bad grades and losing interest in sports, descend into heroin addiction after free samples from a professional trafficker, and are ultimately arrested and then rehabilitated in the federal narcotics hospital.[20]

In June 1951, the Welfare Council and other groups in the New York City coalition helped organize dramatic state hearings that probed the lives of white and Black teenage victims and led directly to a tough mandatory-minimum law to punish illegal drug dealers. The opening session produced the shocking allegation that one in every two hundred public high school students in the city currently used narcotics (meaning heroin or marijuana), a shot-in-the-dark estimate that immediately solidified into media hype and political truth. The hearings disproportionately highlighted, and the local newspapers and national magazines promptly amplified, the anonymous testimony of white youth who recounted drug use and prostitution in racially integrated urban settings. One white fifteen-year-old on probation for marijuana possession attributed his crimes to the influence of "some colored guys" at his Manhattan school and reported that 90 percent of the Black male students and 40 percent of their white counterparts smoked reefer cigarettes. A white female from an upscale family told of buying narcotics in Harlem, serving time in jail for prostitution, and eventually ending up in the federal hospital in Lexington. The *New York Times* reprinted her testimony verbatim, and both *Time* and *Newsweek* reproduced the story of her interracial urban odyssey as the "most startling" discovery of the hearings and the nightmarish underworld. This framework of lost innocence misrepresented the actual story told by the white female "victim," whose addiction began under medical care with the legal prescription painkiller Demerol and who demonstrated sophisticated knowledge of how to track down dealers in Harlem, Coney Island, and Times Square ("if you come up to the peddler, if you talk right, he'll sell you some drugs"). But the pusher-victim trope pervaded the political reception of the state hearings and the bipartisan turn to more punitive narcotics policies. The New York legislature immediately passed a tougher law, signed by Republican governor Thomas Dewey, providing a mandatory five-to-fifteen-year sentence for selling narcotics to a minor, with a two-year minimum for dealing to other adults or for possession with intent to sell.[21]

The mass magazines began hyping tragic stories of white teenage addict-victims in early 1951, nationalizing the message of the antinarcotics movements in Chicago and New York City. Combined with the parallel mobilization in metropolitan Los Angeles (see prologue), this helped transform the campaign for tougher federal laws into a consensus issue in Washington. In major urban centers, Progressive reformers generally deployed color-blind rhetoric and considered teenage drug users of all races to be victims of criminal syndicates and malevolent pushers. This universalistic framework represented a strategy to elicit public sympathy for the policy of rehabilitation by stigmatizing the supply side, where prevailing tropes did identify pushers as nonwhite and foreign, while denying that "susceptibility to drug addiction has anything to do with race," in the careful language of the Chicago Crime Prevention Bureau.[22] But as an almost ironclad rule, national media coverage of the teenage dope crisis individualized only white addict-victims, such as Phillip Petress of Chicago and the anonymous female addict-prostitute from New York, in the feature-length profiles designed to generate public alarm and outrage. In "Don't Let It Happen to You!," published in the popular magazine *True Story* (February 1951), the "hopeless victims" of the New York City narcotics crisis are represented by a pretty white middle-class girl named Bonnie who becomes "crazy on marijuana" and quickly descends into heroin addiction amid the dope fiends and pushers on the hellish streets of Midtown. Bonnie is cured at the federal hospital in Lexington, graduates from high school, and marries a handsome young man—with the moral that "the problem is nationwide," spreading across big cities and small towns, as "dope peddlers find ready victims among reckless young people." A New York City psychologist offered the same message to readers of *National Parent-Teacher Magazine*: "unscrupulous" pushers hanging out near schools and playgrounds offering marijuana and heroin "as bait" to innocent children (all pictured as white), "thousands of innocent victims" in communities across the nation, a crisis that threatened to "destroy our American way of life."[23]

In the spring of 1951, the liberal leaders of the Special Senate Committee to Investigate Organized Crime began to focus in depth on the teenage narcotics situation in response to media coverage of a runaway youth epidemic and the public pressure from Chicago and New York. The select committee, which had primarily targeted gambling and urban political corruption during its first year of operation, expanded its scope in response to direct appeals from African American churches and civil rights organizations, as well as a shifting media narrative that portrayed the Bureau of Narcotics as "powerless" and "ineffectual" in stopping heroin traffickers.[24] In a delicate balancing act, FBN Commissioner Harry Anslinger continued to urge Congress to pass a tougher mandatory sentencing law for dope pushers, which he claimed would make the "narcotic traffic melt away," but did not exactly welcome a comprehensive political investigation into illegal drug markets. After March hearings in New York City, Anslinger informed the Crime Committee that newspaper sensationalism and public "hysteria" had obscured the real, quite manageable problem: marijuana and heroin addiction by "young hoodlums, . . . confined mostly to certain segments and certain neighborhoods in some of the larger cities. . . . The high school student is the exception." Without specifying race, by "certain" the commissioner clearly meant young Negro hoodlums/criminals, as the FBN's internal records illustrate. In a typical analysis, the FBN adopted the dubious methodology of extrapolating national addiction trends from the 120 Black and 38 white teenagers (most from Chicago or New York City) currently institutionalized in the two federal narcotics hospitals in Lexington and Fort Worth, Texas—rather than considering the dynamics of selective enforcement and discretionary punishment in the criminal legal system. In a coercive public health approach, Anslinger endorsed local or state compulsory hospitalization laws for these addict-hoodlums, to be indefinitely "quarantined" until certified as cured by physicians, which mirrored the arrest-and-rehabilitate philosophy of the liberal reform coalitions in Chicago and New York.[25]

During May and June, the Senate Crime Committee held additional hearings that played a pivotal role in popularizing the marijuana-to-heroin gateway thesis, the alleged epidemic of teenage narcotic addiction, and the tragic fates of white middle-class victims of the "despicable drug peddler." In a confidential planning session, the committee staff argued that the FBN's repeated assurances of a situation under control did not represent an "adequate exploration" of the narcotics crisis and that the combination of media attention and public anxiety demanded a full-scale federal response.[26] The Crime Committee next visited two Maryland prisons and the federal narcotics hospital in Lexington, without media coverage, to hand-select ideal witnesses for a high-profile public session in Washington. The Maryland inquiries featured only African American narcotics prisoners, mostly from Baltimore, who almost unanimously rejected the pusher-victim, marijuana-to-heroin gateway scripts that the investigators from the Senate Crime Committee relentlessly sought to impose. Queried about being "hooked" by free samples from peddlers, the convicted drug users responded that they started smoking reefer or shooting heroin with friends and out of curiosity, often strenuously denied that they were addicts, and described an illicit market in which they purposefully sought out dealers. Three witnesses alleged that police had framed them and that corrupt officers in Baltimore protected narcotics peddlers in exchange for payoffs—an angle the elected representatives showed no interest in pursuing. At Lexington, the Senate Crime Committee continued to emphasize the marijuana-gateway and evil-pusher themes, despite contradictory stories told by the institutionalized patients, who spoke of addiction as a contagious "disease" but generally did not blame their suppliers. One white nineteen-year-old college dropout from Brooklyn, when informed that tough penalties would stop the pushers, expressed skepticism that any amount of law enforcement could eradicate such a profitable market and told the stunned and dismayed politicians that the only realistic solution would be to legalize and provide narcotics to all confirmed addicts.[27]

The Lexington hospital investigation also uncovered explosive stories of addiction and prostitution across the urban color line, and the Senate Crime Committee summoned the most resonant witnesses to Washington for theatrical, nationally televised hearings designed to produce a moral-racial panic about the teenage dope crisis. Harvey, an eighteen-year-old Black male and heroin user from Chicago, told the investigators that "white and colored" girls at his integrated high school engaged in prostitution to pay for dope and that peddlers had brought a beautiful white female addict "into a colored neighborhood . . . [to] entice the Negro men." In the second act in Washington, watched by millions nationwide, the senators led Harvey through dramatic revelations that "there is no segregation in the use of dope" and that white girls as young as fifteen were shooting heroin and committing prostitution "with colored men" in Chicago. The Lexington inquiry also revealed the saga of Jeanne, a twenty-year-old white showgirl from Cincinnati, who confessed to buying heroin from "colored" peddlers in multiple cities during her teenage years and "conning" older men for the money required. At the Washington hearing, the senators transformed Jeanne into a victim of dope pushers spreading marijuana into the "small villages" outside the inner cities and triggering the inevitable progression to heroin addiction and prostitution (ignoring Jeanne's account of seeking out dealers in the "colored section" of large cities where she worked and her insistence that marijuana was harmless). The Washington session also included a white mother from an integrated Baltimore neighborhood who accused a "colored fellow" of addicting her son to heroin and said she had always believed "it couldn't happen to my child," but "it happens to anyone's child." As intended, the national media coverage highlighted the "pretty blonde" from Cincinnati and other sympathetic white female addict-victims who descended into prostitution, "sometimes with Negroes," juxtaposed with stories of African American and Puerto Rican males from Chicago and New York City driven to lives of crime for their heroin fixes.[28]

In its final report, the Senate Crime Committee urged ordinary citizens to mobilize against the "insidious evil" of teenage narcotics addiction and concluded that "no penalty is too severe for . . . the peddler who is willing to wreck young lives to satisfy his greed." The bipartisan investigation praised the antinarcotics activism of Lois Higgins in Chicago and the Welfare Council in New York and reiterated their warnings that the dope crisis "cuts across all social and economic lines," invading "every corner of the country," from the largest cities to the "Main Streets throughout America." The report portrayed teenage marijuana and heroin users, of all races, as helpless victims: "the innocent prey of the lowest form of criminal known to society," the "captive of the greedy criminals who have him hopelessly trapped." This framework implicitly rejected Anslinger's insistence that almost all young addicts were nonwhite criminal hoodlums and explicitly silenced the testimony of the teenage witnesses who repeatedly challenged the marijuana-gateway and seductive-pusher narratives. The Senate Crime Committee instead medicalized and psychopathologized the entire demand side of the illicit drug market, arguing that narcotics addiction "should be treated as a contagious disease," spread by bad associates as well as pushers, and that "its sufferers should be treated as patients, not as criminals." Teenage thrill-seekers who became "hooked" were at best "mildly neurotic" and likely addiction prone because of deeper personality disorders: "This is the weak, irresponsible creature on whom the parasitic narcotic trader feeds." The report amplified the FBN's claim that a global network headed by alleged Mafia kingpin Charles "Lucky" Luciano of Italy imported most heroin into the U.S. and concluded that doubling federal enforcement personnel and toughening narcotics laws would "kill the source of supply" completely. Senator Herbert O'Conor of Maryland, a mainstream Democrat who chaired the Crime Committee, introduced a bill mandating twenty years to life for selling heroin or marijuana to anyone under the age of seventeen.[29]

In the House of Representatives, the Boggs subcommittee on narcotics control legislation held parallel hearings during the spring of 1951 that served as an effective vehicle for the FBN's political agenda and simultaneously demonstrated the bipartisan consensus behind tougher mandatory penalties. Rep. Hale Boggs, a conservative Democrat from New Orleans, took advantage of the "alarming growth in juvenile addiction" to reintroduce his mandatory-minimum bill, which was initially motivated by reports of habitual dope peddlers receiving lenient sentences in his home city. The Truman administration endorsed the Boggs bill, and the hearings also featured demands for harsher punishment by Progressive activists, including Lois Higgins, and liberal Democratic politicians from Chicago and New York. The General Federation of Women's Clubs, a nonpartisan coalition dominated by Progressive reform groups, lauded the Boggs proposal because "these rats who peddle drugs are more of a menace than even a potential murderer." In his testimony, Commissioner Anslinger lambasted soft-hearted judges who let dope pushers off the hook and claimed that "where heavy sentences are meted out the traffic just disappears."[30] In late June, the Boggs subcommittee approved mandatory-minimum narcotics control legislation that covered marijuana as well as heroin and punished trafficking, sale, and possession alike. The penalty structure included two to five years for the first offense, five to ten for the second, and ten to fifteen for the third, with no probation or suspended sentence for repeat violators. Boggs argued for the inclusion of possession, the only controversial aspect, as leverage to force addicts to enter the federal narcotics hospitals via the first offender loophole, a coercive vision of public health rehabilitation through criminal law enforcement. Several liberal Democrats objected to this specific provision in the House floor debate, based on concerns that a "sick" teenage addict or a twice-arrested marijuana user should not face a felony sentence, but almost everyone agreed on the urgent need for tougher penalties for the "professional peddler."[31]

The House and Senate approved the mandatory-minimum legislation with minimal dissent, and President Harry Truman signed the amendment to the Narcotic Drugs Import and Export Act in November 1951. The ubiquitous pusher-victim framework set the boundaries of political debate in Washington, leading to a broad consensus in favor of harsher punishment for dope peddlers, with disagreement mainly over the most effective method to coerce young addicts into rehabilitation. No politician of either party publicly questioned the inclusion of marijuana alongside heroin as a dangerous narcotic, the reduction of all teenage drug users to the status of helpless addicts, or the depiction of the underground market as an encounter between villains and victims rather than sellers and consumers with responsibility and agency—even though multiple incarcerated or institutionalized youth in the Senate Crime Committee hearings challenged all of these interpretations. Representative Emanuel Celler of Brooklyn, the liberal Democratic chair of the Judiciary Committee, did argue for maintaining judicial discretion in order to help "the unfortunate victims of narcotic drugs," but he expressed no sympathy whatsoever for pushers. Rep. Edwin Hall, a Republican from upstate New York, articulated the prevailing view: "Do we dare defy these sordid gangsters who are engaged in ruining our youth, . . . degenerated by the sordid criminal who should be exterminated." After the House passed the Boggs bill by voice vote in mid-July, President Truman urged the Senate to act quickly in order to advance the federal war on organized crime. The bipartisan members of the Senate Crime Committee, who claimed primary credit for awakening the "recent nationwide indignation" against narcotics traffickers, sponsored identical legislation that passed by unanimous consent in late October. Truman signed the law, known as the Boggs Act, with enthusiasm for the crackdown on peddlers who targeted youth and an admonition that prison sentences were not appropriate for "unfortunates who are merely addicts and not engaged in the traffic for their own profit."[32]

Congress's deliberate decision to exclude barbiturates from the Boggs Act revealed both the power of the pharmaceutical industry to promote an ultimately political distinction between legal and illegal drugs and another way that the FBN drew racial boundaries between the medical and criminal spheres. During the 1951 hearings, public health advocates urged the Boggs subcommittee to tighten federal regulation of legal barbiturates, given that two-thirds of states had no effective controls at all, and they also portrayed the illicit circulation of depressants (known as "goof balls") as a serious problem. By the late 1940s, more than one thousand Americans per year were fatally overdosing on barbiturates, including accidents and suicides, a far greater public health threat than heroin (or marijuana). Physicians generally prescribed so-called "sleeping pills" to white middle-class women, and pharmaceutical companies claimed that barbiturates were "harmless" and "not habit-forming," despite ample scientific research classifying the drugs as potentially addictive.

Commissioner Anslinger primarily blamed a few rogue doctors and pharmacists for the illicit market in barbiturates, even though the FBN's internal documents conceded that pharmaceutical companies knowingly manufactured far more pills than the "legitimate amount needed for therapeutic purposes" and "over-advertised these products . . . in their zeal for easy profits." In his testimony to the Boggs subcommittee, Anslinger adamantly opposed bringing barbiturates under the narcotics control regime and even asserted that marijuana was much more hazardous—in theory because of the heroin progression syndrome, but in reality, because the FBN commissioner formulated policy in alliance with the pharmaceutical lobby and only believed in criminalizing nonwhite drug use. Congress did pass a separate 1951 law that, for the first time, required prescriptions for barbiturate sales nationwide, with weakened regulation left to the Food and Drug Administration. Anslinger argued that a law enforcement crackdown on the illicit barbiturates trade would be more difficult than Prohibition of alcohol and would make the FBN "very unpopular" with the public—a revealing admission that he had no desire to police a drug market populated by white middle-class consumers.[33]

A number of public health officials and medical researchers criticized the Boggs Act for criminalizing drug addiction and also challenged the racial presumptions of the escalating war on narcotics in several significant if politically marginalized ways. A public affairs pamphlet on the "drug menace," prepared by public health experts in the New York state government and published by the National Association for Mental Health, distinguished between professional pushers who deserved "severe punishment" and narcotics addicts, including low-level "addict-peddlers," who needed medical treatment rather than incarceration even for crimes "arising from that addiction." The pamphlet also stated that both alcohol and sleeping pills represented far greater public health problems than heroin, the real reason that "no economic or social class is immune to addiction." But affluent Americans had medical access to legal painkillers and depressants, especially prescription barbiturates, while underprivileged and nonwhite groups usually self-medicated through the underground market, leading to a political culture that labeled "addiction a disease when applied to the wealthy, and a vice when applied to the poor." The 1951 Senate Crime Committee hearings were notable for portraying all youth "addicts," white and nonwhite, as innocent victims of organized crime, but public health officials in New York went further by declaring that disproportionate heroin addiction in urban slums resulted from racial segregation and "restricted opportunities of Negro children." The pamphlet refuted the "hysterical" claims of a national epidemic of teenage addiction but still embraced the marijuana stepping-stone concept and warned that the heroin menace might thereby "spread like wildfire through all classes of adolescents" without more local treatment centers and a global crackdown on the narcotics supply. Harry Anslinger responded to such critics by mocking the "purely" medical approach that the addict is "misunderstood, frustrated, . . . to be coddled and pitied, . . . nothing more or less than a sick person. . . . His *vicious* and *law breaking* features are ignored."[34]

The solidification of the marijuana-to-heroin gateway mystique proved to be the most consequential outcome of the legislative investigations, law enforcement warnings, and media hype that led to enactment of the Boggs Act of 1951 and its predecessor laws in California, Illinois, and New York. While heroin was a geographically confined problem in a few large cities, marijuana was a much more plausible entry point into illegal drug markets that seemingly typical (i.e., white) American youth might encounter in college, urban leisure pursuits, or thrill-seeking high school activities. Although Commissioner Anslinger claimed that such "normal" youth were not at great risk, he sensationalized the stepping-stone thesis in order to bring both marijuana and heroin under the punitive narcotics control structure. Congress also did so to universalize the crisis as a potential threat to any American community, a narrative with a resilient afterlife in subsequent decades of escalating drug-war enforcement. The FBN then deployed the marijuana-to-heroin gateway warnings in promoting the Uniform Narcotic Drug Act, which a majority of states adopted to align the penalties for both drugs with the federal system. In his 1953 book *The Traffic in Narcotics*, Anslinger included an elaborate section on how marijuana users were in grave "danger of progression" to heroin addiction and how reefer on its own was "one of the most dangerous drugs known," because it transformed its victims into raving lunatics, violent criminals, sexual degenerates, and moral reprobates. Anslinger based these claims not on any scientific research but rather on sordid anecdotes about alleged marijuana fiends sent in by law enforcement sources nationwide, which he assiduously collected in his personal files.[35] The FBN paid no attention to contradictory research from pioneering scholars such as sociologist Howard Becker, whose ethnographic field work revealed that smoking marijuana was a casual, pleasure-seeking "recreational" activity among small subcultural groups and that the drug was not addictive, compulsive, or dangerous.[36]

Commissioner Anslinger promptly capitalized on passage of the Boggs Act by orchestrating a major media counteroffensive that depicted narcotics addiction as an illegal, nonwhite problem in a few big-city slums and essentially advocated racial segregation as the effective antidote. In late 1951, Anslinger crafted a message directly to white middle-class America through a *Reader's Digest* article titled "The Facts about Our Teen-Age Drug Addicts." He began by lamenting the false impression of a national epidemic created by the New York state investigation and the Senate Crime Committee hearings and then assured readers that "rarely in our experience does a boy or girl from a normally balanced family in any income bracket become an addict." The real threat came from "neighborhood gangs of discontented, uncontrolled young people" in the crowded slums, with bad parenting and no moral values. But the media disproportionately hyped the exceptional cases, which Anslinger defined as a small number of "pleasant and intelligent" (i.e., white) youngsters who sought the company of jazz musicians, experimented with marijuana, and could easily be rehabilitated with parental intervention. Although the message was technically color-blind, the meaning was clear: keep white children safe by keeping them away from urban slums, interracial settings, and bad company. A religious publication with close ties to Anslinger summarized his meaning thus: most young narcotics addicts were "colored . . . big city" hoodlums with no work ethic or proper guidance, and so "your son and daughter are not in danger UNLESS THEY COME INTO CONTACT WITH UNDERWORLD CHARACTERS." The FBN commissioner supplied similar material for revisionist articles in *Pageant* and *Parents* (magazines aimed at white middle-class mothers) that criticized the recent media-fueled "hysteria" and promised that well-adjusted children from loving homes had little to fear: "It's seldom the clean-cut high school football captain and the queen of the junior prom who become addicts. The more likely victims are slum kids from bruised or broken homes."[37]

In early 1952, the Federal Bureau of Narcotics launched a coordinated roundup of five hundred dope peddlers in urban centers, and Anslinger promised that the narcotics traffic would soon be eradicated completely if every state enacted the penalty structure of the Boggs Act. The national media coverage lauded the "rugged" FBN commissioner, "armed at last with a tough law," who boasted of giving "shoot first" orders to his men, the "shock troops" in the federal war on narcotics, fighting against dope smugglers and pushers "with a sort of holy hatred." Democratic and Republican politicians alike praised Anslinger's leadership, with liberal Senator Paul Douglas (D-Illinois) providing typical acclaim for the FBN's "devoted and tireless" crusader.[38] In the aftermath of the high-profile raids, Anslinger appeared on numerous national radio and television programs to urge all states to adopt lengthy and inflexible mandatory penalties for pushers and compulsory hospitalization laws for addicts in order to crush the narcotics traffic in the urban slums. As a model, he championed a New Jersey judge who sentenced a "marihuana peddler" to the statutory maximum and railed against the defendant as "worse than a murderer," because smoking reefer "destroys all sense of moral responsibility" and "no girl walking the streets would be safe with a man under the influence of this devilish drug." The FBN commissioner continued to insist that the narcotics trade only threatened "certain segments of the population" through the racialized culture of pathology argument that proper parenting was the "all-important factor, because we do not see these addicts from good homes." Anslinger also collaborated with and then championed a much-discussed story in *Harper's Magazine* (February 1952) that portrayed white middle-class families as "victims of the great national drug scare" and fearful of a menace that "simply doesn't exist." The article reassured Americans that the narcotics traffic centered on slum areas with a "large permanent Negro population" and explained that the only way for a normal high school student to obtain heroin or marijuana would be to venture, unwisely, into a nonwhite ghetto area or urban vice district.[39]

The FBN even fought against the establishment of narcotics education programs in the public schools, a preventive approach that most public health officials and civic reformers advocated in response to the perceived epidemic of teenage addiction in the early 1950s. Anslinger believed that white students from safe communities and "normal" family backgrounds might be tempted rather than deterred by images of thrill-seeking teenagers breaking rules and defying authorities, especially plotlines where the inevitable descent into addiction culminated in a happy ending through rapid rehabilitation. The commissioner argued that "impressionable young minds" should be protected from too much "direct propaganda" about the narcotics trade, including films that demonstrated injection methods and inadvertently provided advice on how to pay for dope through stealing or the "art of prostitution." The Senate Crime Committee disputed the FBN on this point, urging federal public health officials to "lift the veil of secrecy" and develop a narcotics education program to be implemented nationwide.[40] Public school officials in metropolitan areas generally agreed and began adding narcotics education to the alcohol awareness classes already required in most states. The New York legislature mandated a narcotics prevention program in 1952, and many civic clubs, religious groups, and social welfare organizations participated in awareness campaigns as well. Across the nation, the prevention curriculum adopted the lost-innocence and gateway-to-doom tropes of the pioneering efforts in Chicago, New York, and Los Angeles: stories that begin in seemingly safe white middle-class neighborhoods; ordinary teenagers who start out smoking marijuana for kicks and to fit in with the crowd ("drug addiction is contagious"); racialized boundary crossing into dangerous and darkened urban areas where peddlers "prey on" these misguided victims; instant heroin addiction that forces boys into theft and girls into street walking; and finally arrest followed by diversion into a rehabilitation program that probably cannot avert a "lifetime of pain and torment."[41]

Despite Anslinger's keep-calm offensive, media outlets and popular magazines continued to churn out pusher-victim stories of white middle-class youth crossing racial borders and succumbing to the tragic effects of narcotics addiction. In late 1951, the nationally syndicated saga of a former Michigan beauty queen offered a stark warning to parents "who smugly think, 'this couldn't happen to my child.'" The "young, beautiful, talented" Peggy had it all—singer in the church choir, captain of the cheerleading squad, a college-bound future—but she frequented dance clubs and consorted with an interracial group of musicians who supplied her with marijuana and heroin and left her better off dead. "Addicts are not born of poverty, slums, ignorance," Peggy explains. "I and most of the addicts I know came from what society calls fine, upstanding, respectable families." In "My Son Is a Dope Addict," published in the *Saturday Evening Post* (January 1952), a white middle-class mother laments the seduction of her boy by the urban jazz scene and a "heartless" heroin pusher accompanied by a "husky Negro," with a stay in the federal narcotics hospital providing no cure. Later that year, *Woman's Home Companion* published "It Happened to Amy: The Story of a Teen-Age Addict," excerpted from a 1952 book called *H Is for Heroin*. The exposé, one of the first to locate the white middle-class victim in a suburban setting rather than an affluent urban neighborhood, recounted the saga of a pretty seventeen-year-old female whose parents settle in a commuter town south of Los Angeles in order to keep her safe from big-city dangers. But Amy begins hanging out with bad friends at the beach, then starts smoking marijuana and sneaking off to downtown jazz shows, all with a crowd that engages in a "shocking amount of indiscriminate sexual intercourse." Inevitably she progresses to heroin addiction, under the influence of a white addict-peddler who hooks her with free samples. They eventually start buying heroin through a Mexican connection in Tijuana and get busted after forging barbiturate prescriptions. Amy ends up on probation and sent to a narcotics hospital, but she will probably never be cured: "once a hype always a hype."[42]

California's Early War on Narcotics

During the 1950s, neighborhood groups and civic organizations representing more than one million residents of California petitioned the state government for lengthy mandatory-minimum sentences for dope "pushers" who supplied marijuana and heroin to teenagers, with considerable public sentiment for life imprisonment or the death penalty.[43] California's war on narcotics enlisted a broad and ideologically diverse spectrum, led by nonpartisan alliances such as the California Federation of Women's Clubs and the statewide PTA network and advanced by Republican and Democratic policymakers alike. White parents from the racially segregated suburbs of Los Angeles County constituted the most vocal advocates of the grassroots tough-on-drugs movement, especially residents of middle-class communities located in close proximity to the Mexican American barrios in East LA and the San Gabriel Valley. These suburban areas mobilized in response to recurring local media hype about gangs of Mexican American "wolf packs" and "rat packs" invading white communities to peddle drugs and commit violence, a series of racialized "epidemics" both falsely constructed and politically consequential. The ubiquitous discourse of "narcotics pushers" and "dope peddlers" conflated recreational marijuana use with heroin addiction and transformed white teenage lawbreakers into the helpless victims of external villains who lured their prey into an urban dystopia of crime, prostitution, and racial boundary crossings. These tropes distorted the actual workings of the illicit drug market, as most white middle-class teenagers in Southern California acquired marijuana from friends and acquaintances, or by driving across the Mexican border into Tijuana, and rarely progressed to heroin. To protect and rehabilitate white youth who broke the law, the state of California designed a discretionary narcotics control system that repeatedly escalated felony penalties for pushers, criminalized addiction in order to selectively incarcerate or institutionalize illegal drug users, and contained loopholes to divert thrill-seekers from "good families" without a record.

The "narcotics crisis" in Southern California during the early 1950s was the first to unfold primarily on the real and imagined landscape of white middle-class suburbia, which made metropolitan Los Angeles the pacesetter for political and policy developments statewide and nationwide. The antinarcotics mobilization in California began before federal enactment of the Boggs Act and focused obsessively on white teenage "victims" from racially segregated suburbs, the same demographic cohort that Commissioner Anslinger insisted could not succumb to the urban cesspool of heroin and marijuana criminality. But white drug markets operated with significant autonomy in the automobile-centered built environment of California's sprawling suburbs, where middle-class youth enjoyed considerable freedom of mobility and also had easy access to Mexican border towns, long a "vice" destination for Americans in search of illegal drugs, illicit sex, and other criminalized leisure activities.[44] The cultural understanding of the vulnerability of white middle-class suburbia also differed in Southern California, compared to urban heroin centers such as New York City, because nonwhite youth (racialized as "hoodlums" and "gangsters") also had cars and could move more easily across both physical and symbolic boundaries. In fast-growing Los Angeles County, which was 88 percent white (non-Hispanic) in 1950, more than half of the 4.15 million residents lived outside the city limits, as did the large Mexican American population in unincorporated East LA. These suburban trends intensified as the county's population topped 6 million by 1960, and many other white families lived in the city of Los Angeles's outlying suburban-style neighborhoods, including the annexed San Fernando Valley. Housing segregation prevailed across metropolitan Los Angeles, where the vast majority of white neighborhoods employed restrictive racial covenants until their judicial invalidation in 1948, and where comprehensive discrimination in the real estate market and federal mortgage policies restricted 97 percent of new developments to whites only during the 1950s.[45]

The state of California's landmark mandatory-minimum narcotics law, enacted in summer 1951 in response to the political and media crusade against Mexican American "wolf packs" and "hoodlum" pushers, established lengthy penalties for providing either heroin or marijuana to a minor and a discretionary misdemeanor/felony sentencing range for all other sale and possession convictions (see prologue). The legislation permitted judges to utilize a civil commitment procedure to divert "addicts" of otherwise good character to state psychiatric hospitals but, at least on paper, removed the probation option and required a jail term even for possession violators. In reality, police departments and prosecutors operated with total discretion in deciding whether to bring formal charges under the new law, plea down to a public order offense,

TABLE 1.1. Adult Narcotics Prosecutions in Los Angeles County, 1950

Category	Total	Male	Under 21 (18–20 yrs.)	Caucasian	Mexican descent	Negro	Oriental
Marijuana	615	580 (94%)	127 (21%)	209 (34%)	217 (35%)	186 (30%)	3 (0.5%)
Heroin	414	333 (80%)	43 (10%)	109 (27%)	133 (32%)	164 (40%)	8 (2%)

Source: California Bureau of Narcotic Enforcement, "Evaluation of Narcotics Prosecutions Conducted by the District Attorney's Office of Los Angeles County, California, for the Calendar Year 1950," June 12, 1952.

Note: Racial categories in table match the original source. The under-21 category does not include sixty-two teenagers processed in the juvenile justice system. The heroin data includes other opiates and also cocaine.

or dismiss the case entirely. The records from Los Angeles County, which processed two-thirds of narcotics cases statewide, reveal that California officials were mobilizing against a relatively minor law enforcement issue at the time. In 1950, the district attorney prosecuted 1,029 adults, 60 percent for marijuana, an overwhelmingly male class of defendants with a median age of twenty-seven (table 1.1). Almost all narcotics charges in LA County involved working-class or poor defendants, which reflected discretionary policing and prosecution of the "illicit" market based on race and geography. Despite the overwhelming focus on Mexican pushers and addict-hoodlums in popular narcotics discourse, white Anglos, Mexican Americans, and African Americans each represented about one-third of total prosecutions in 1950—although racial minorities faced charges at six times the population share for both groups. Law enforcement also detained 109 juveniles on narcotics charges in 1949 and another 179 in 1950, representing less than 1 percent of total delinquency arrests and in no way constituting an "epidemic" of teenage illegal drug use, much less addiction (table 1.2). The available evidence reveals that in the "ethnically stratified marketplace" of Los Angeles County, heroin remained a working-class drug used almost exclusively by adults and usually acquired from dealers of the same race, while a fairly small number of teenagers smoked marijuana whether in white suburbs or the barrio.[46]

In this early stage of the war on drugs, the political system in California produced a narcotics crisis that at times acknowledged the racial elasticity of the "dope pusher" but reserved the sympathetic status of addict-victim for white middle-class youth and suburban teenagers, the demographic and spatial categories fused together on the symbolic landscape of utopia besieged. In 1951, the Juvenile Court for LA County collaborated in the production of *The Terrible Truth*, an educational film designed to alert students and PTA

TABLE 1.2. Juvenile Narcotics Arrests in Los Angeles County, 1946–50

Year	Total juvenile arrests	Juvenile narcotics arrests	% narcotics arrests/ total juvenile arrests
1946	12,281	120	1%
1947	12,412	154	1.2%
1948	15,961	94	0.6%
1949	21,743	109	0.5%
1950	22,307	179	0.8%

Source: Assembly Interim Committee on Judiciary, California State Legislature, *Preliminary Report of the Subcommittee on Narcotics*, March 24, 1952.

Note: The narcotics category includes marijuana arrests and represents combined totals by the LA Police Department and LA County Sheriff's Department. Racial breakdown for juvenile narcotics arrests is not available.

groups about the epidemic of "hundreds and hundreds of teenage boys and girls becoming hopeless dope addicts," an expensive and incurable habit that inevitably turned males into thieves and females into hookers. The "true story" chronicles the tragic fate of Phyllis, a once pretty high school senior from an outlying LA suburb, who starts smoking pot with her nice-looking but delinquent male classmates, thanks to the cars that let them escape parental scrutiny. But marijuana leads rapidly to heroin addiction, after a shady older white peddler who supplies the high school hooks an unsuspecting Phyllis by jabbing a needle into her arm. The LACSD circulated the same message in *Subject: Narcotics* (1951), a police training video distributed nationwide, featuring a motley assortment of white and ethnic pushers pressuring delinquent white teenagers to graduate from marijuana to heroin. In the climactic scenes, a pretty white girl wearing pearls succumbs to a pusher's needle while sitting on a shooting gallery bed beside a male African American addict and then turns into a haggard prostitute at a sleazy motel. *Subject: Narcotics* warns that peddlers constantly scheme "to convert the youthful marijuana user" to heroin addiction and target "people of all races and professions, the privileged and the underprivileged." The California Department of Education distributed a teachers' manual explaining that peddlers "recruit new customers by giving the first 'shot' of dope for free," illustrated by the scenario of a white high school junior who moved from reefer to heroin after a free sample from a "colored musician." The state government certified more than two thousand police officers to bring these delusory messages to student assemblies and community groups in its narcotics prevention campaign.[47]

The mass circulation of pusher-victim warnings and marijuana-to-heroin gateway tragedies galvanized the white suburban movement for even tougher laws to deter the criminals who targeted innocent youth. In 1951, the California Federation of Women's Clubs warned that suburbs and small towns were not safe from the big-city narcotics plague because dope pushers sought "new converts" everywhere and had recently corrupted an entire high school in an outlying area. The nonpartisan federation demanded a life imprisonment penalty for providing narcotics to a minor. Governor Earl Warren, a moderate Republican, received hundreds of similar letters and petitions from women's clubs in the white suburbs of Los Angeles, interspersed with calls for capital punishment. An internal narcotics review by state law enforcement agencies later labeled this pressure campaign to be "public hysteria" and found that "there can be no doubt that the 'epidemic spread' of teenage drug addiction was exaggerated."[48] Patricia Williams, a white suburban teenager "from a good family" in Pasadena, provided the most shocking account of all in a nationally serialized confession (*American Weekly*, 1953) of how she ended up as a heroin addict consorting with "Mexican pushers" in East Los Angeles (fig. 1.2). As a sixteen-year-old, Patricia began smoking pot for kicks with her older white boyfriend but quickly "graduated" to heroin under the spell of "Chelo, the little Mexican who kept me in supplies." Once arrested, she went undercover to send the East LA pushers to prison before entering a rehabilitation facility in Pasadena, a therapeutic outcome that reinforced her innocence and decriminalization. Hollywood soon dramatized this racial and gendered suburban victim/foreign villain story in *Teen Age Devil Dolls* (1955), featuring a pretty teenager named Cassandra who first smokes reefer with a motorcycle gang of white middle-class delinquents and then crosses the spatial and symbolic boundary into intimate heroin addiction and implied sexual relations with Mexican pushers in East Los Angeles. In the western frontier–style finale, they make a run for the border with the law in hot pursuit, with Cassandra ultimately rescued and sent to the narcotics hospital and the Mexicans headed for prison.[49]

The pusher-victim and heroin-gateway frameworks obscured the material practices that shaped the illicit white middle-class drug market in metropolitan Los Angeles, where autonomous teenagers acquired and circulated marijuana through creative subcultural methods facilitated by the freedom to roam across boundaries on the car-centered landscape. In 1952, the Los Angeles Police Department commissioned a study of "juvenile drug addiction" from its actual case files, focusing on arrested youth who agreed to work with the

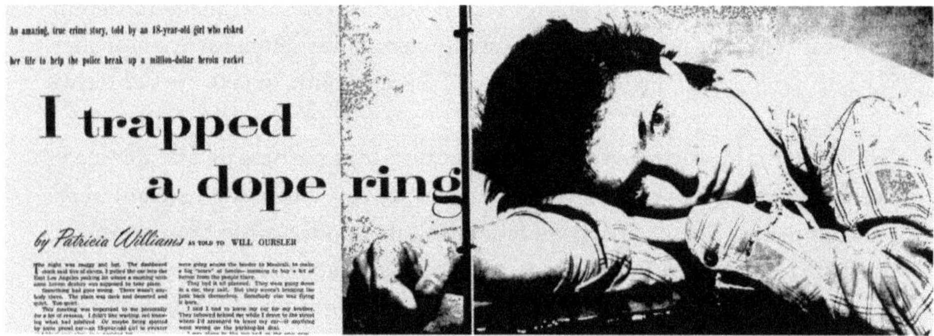
An amazing, true crime story, told by an 18-year-old girl who risked her life to help the police break up a million-dollar heroin racket

I trapped a dope ring

by Patricia Williams as told to WILL OURSLER

FIGURE 1.2. Patricia Williams became a white suburban poster child for California's war on narcotics through this 1953 confessional serialized in *The American Weekly*, a Sunday newspaper supplement. This staged image, allegedly from a Los Angeles County jail, accompanied the tragic chronicle of her descent from a churchgoing girl in Pasadena who experimented with marijuana and turned into a sixteen-year-old heroin addict under the sway of "Mexican pushers" from East Los Angeles.

narcotics squad in exchange for probation or dropped charges. Edward, a fifteen-year-old caught with marijuana at the Venice beach, showed undercover cops how to locate dealers in the waterfront communities south of Santa Monica and introduced them to Mary, also fifteen, who took the police to an adolescent reefer party where they found the alleged main supplier. James and his friends, 16-year-olds from Canoga Park in the San Fernando Valley, bought pot at a pool hall from a neighborhood dealer who made his connection from an eighteen-year-old Venice teenager. LAPD officers also busted a group of resourceful juveniles who grew marijuana in a vacant lot and another network that exchanged reefer cigarettes through predetermined drops at downtown jazz shows. A few of the profiled teenagers had tried heroin, and several of the females took illicit barbiturates, but most of the "narcotics" supply chains involved marijuana originally bought in Tijuana and brought across the border by a small-scale dealer or just a casual user who shared with friends. The teenage market was "not localized in nature," the LAPD concluded, because the "high mobility of both addicts and peddlers" enabled circulation of illegal drugs throughout the metropolitan region. Despite the pusher-peddler language, officers in the LAPD's Juvenile Narcotics Squad acknowledged that marijuana generally spread into white middle-class and wealthy areas because one or two enterprising male teenagers either drove to Mexico or obtained small quantities from an older teenage or young adult supplier and then proceeded to "contaminate . . . other juvenile members of his group." While law enforcement could only speculate about the scope of the illicit teenage market beyond the small number apprehended, the LAPD report concluded with dire warnings of a "frightening menace" and "contagious form of vice."[50]

Law enforcement officials in metropolitan Los Angeles policed the teenage drug market through the absolute statutory discretion central to the broader juvenile delinquency system, an apparatus of social control that provided no formal due process rights for minors but usually enabled middle-class and wealthy white lawbreakers to avoid formal punishment (see chapter 2). During the early 1950s, police most often apprehended teenage males for alcohol, theft, traffic, or curfew violations, and females for status crimes such as sexual delinquency or running away from home. Juvenile probation agencies in LA County only sent about 10 percent of detained minors to Juvenile Court and released the rest to parental custody. The standard "pre-detention" investigation assessed the reformability or criminality of wayward youth based on normative white middle-class standards such as degree of parental involvement, intact versus broken home, regular church attendance, and participation in "character-building" institutions such as the Boy Scouts and the YMCA/YWCA.[51] Minors accounted for 8 percent of total drug arrests in LA County in the early 1950s, with formal adjudication more likely than for most other youth offenses, but still less than half charged in Juvenile Court (fig. 1.3). Internal state documents classified 5 percent of juveniles incarcerated for narcotics as "habitual users," a far cry from the official public line that all were "addicts." In a majority of cases, the police did not arrest teenagers with illegal drugs in their possession but rather discovered the crime during the pre-detention interrogation or rounded them up based on marijuana referrals from schools and recreational clubs. The Juvenile Narcotics Squad also profiled and frisked teenagers at music concerts, trained patrol officers to search suspicious youth during traffic stops, and made occasional mass arrests by busting house parties involving marijuana, barbiturates, and alcohol. According to a suburban probation official, the media focus on Mexican American gangs obscured the considerable marijuana and alcohol use in white middle-class areas with "many youngsters not coming statistically to the attention of the police or juvenile court."[52]

Additional investigations in the early 1950s illuminated a recreational drug market in Southern California where white middle-class teenagers primarily acquired marijuana from contacts in the same racial and age demographic or directly from suppliers in Tijuana, a frequent destination for dealers and adventurous users alike. In 1952, in a special narcotics report distributed to public

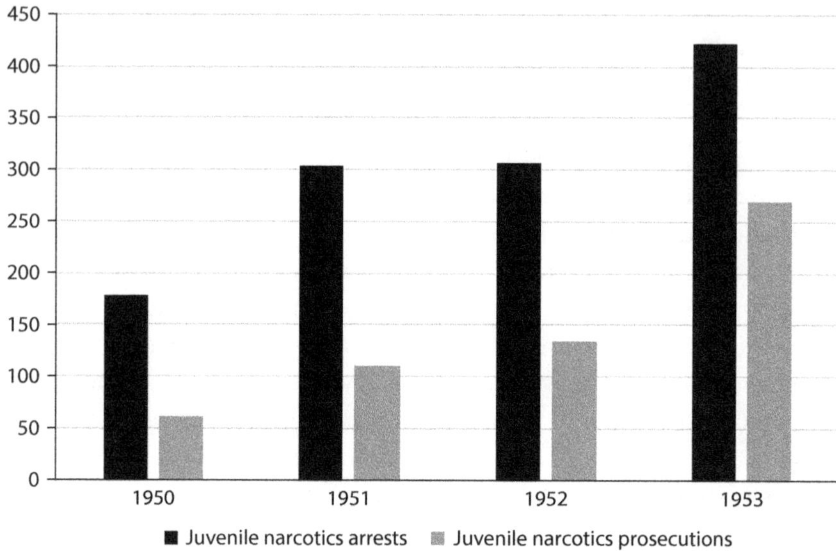

FIGURE 1.3. Juvenile narcotics arrests and prosecutions in city and county of Los Angeles, 1950–53. Juvenile narcotics arrests in LA County more than doubled after passage of California's 1951 get-tough law, and they tripled inside the LA city limits. Juvenile arrests resulted in prosecution (adjudication in Juvenile Court) in 63% of cases by 1953. That year, the LAPD began adding juveniles apprehended for any reason to the narcotics arrest category if they admitted illegal drug use under interrogation, the primary reason for the statistical increase. Most juveniles arrested and prosecuted for narcotics were recreational marijuana users, not heroin addicts. (Los Angeles County Youth Committee, *Monthly Bulletin*, November 1954).

schools statewide, a teacher from the Westside area of Los Angeles chronicled a thriving network of marijuana distribution outside high school buildings and "nearby malt shops and hamburger stands" in upscale white neighborhoods. While many Californians believed the narcotics scourge "is confined to the Mexican-American group and to slum areas," this account emphasized that not only marijuana customers but also the "young peddlers" on the Westside were all "Anglo-Americans from middle-class backgrounds."[53] That same year, the *San Diego Union* published the results of a collaboration with police in Coronado, a beachfront suburb, to uncover the supply lines following the marijuana busts of a group of affluent white teenagers. "I expected to meet a dirty-faced 'pachuco,'" the newspaper series began, but instead police introduced the reporter to a clean-cut seventeen-year-old "weedhead . . . from a respected middle-class family," a shocking discovery that opened up a world of dope "addicts" and heartbroken parents in San Diego's upscale suburbs.

These unsupervised youth got high at beach parties or just driving around in their cars, apparently shared marijuana with one another as a friendship ritual, and occasionally moved on to barbiturates or heroin. Suburban teenage dealers bought their stashes in Tijuana, just a twenty- or thirty-mile drive away, and large numbers of white juveniles also crossed the border nightly to drink beer and smoke reefer. The reporter even witnessed a "jitterbugging mass of humanity" at a Tijuana jam session—Mexican American pachucos, Negro hipsters, Anglo boys with "beautiful blond" girlfriends—with white teenagers driving in from as far as Orange County, Los Angeles, and Santa Monica.[54]

This transnational market in illicit drugs prompted political demands to close the Mexican border to American teenagers and bipartisan momentum to toughen California's penalties for narcotics smugglers and adult peddlers. In early 1953, law enforcement and elected officials in Southern California launched a campaign to pressure the federal government to ban youth under age twenty-one from entering Mexico without a parent or guardian. They also called on the Federal Bureau of Narcotics to intervene more aggressively in order to interdict the supply of narcotics in source nations. FBN Commissioner Harry Anslinger instead praised U.S.-Mexico narcotics cooperation as a "model of international relations" and informed critics that selectively closing the border would be impossible (around 5.5 million automobiles and 18.5 million people traveled between Southern California and Mexico in 1953).[55] California Attorney General Edmund (Pat) Brown, a liberal Democrat, then initiated a summit meeting with Tijuana officials to request (unsuccessfully) that Mexico unilaterally raise the age of legal entry for unaccompanied teenagers from fifteen to eighteen, part of a strategy to show voters that he was "in this battle against narcotics with fists flying and attacking every second of the way."[56] White suburban parents from Los Angeles and San Diego praised Brown's declaration of war on dope pushers and urged him to promote tougher laws to protect "defenseless juveniles versus powerful narcotics syndicates," including the death penalty for peddlers who were "the same as murderers." Newspapers and law enforcement organizations from Southern California also issued calls for an "open war" on marijuana pushers who "prey on our youth [and] do not respect boundaries of cities or counties" or the border with Mexico. In his comprehensive 1953 program to "rid the state of narcotics," Brown endorsed lengthier sentences for all illegal drug sellers and a mandatory life sentence for adults who provided heroin or marijuana to minors.[57]

In the summer of 1953, the California legislature unanimously increased the upper range of penalties for narcotics distribution while restoring the discretionary probation option for possession and casual sale by first offenders. A Republican assemblyman from the Los Angeles suburb of Glendale sponsored the legislation, which reflected the efforts of a coalition of state and local law enforcement officials, including Democratic attorney general Pat Brown. A broad and bipartisan consensus underlay the increased sentences aimed at racially stigmatized "dope pushers," symbolized in the legislative hearings by a twenty-nine-year-old Mexican American man caught with four pounds of marijuana.[58] The simultaneous decision to repeal the mandatory-minimum penalty for possession, first enacted in 1951, represented a pragmatic solution to the unanticipated problem of the increasing number of older teenagers and young adults who encountered the criminal justice system. The probation reform followed complaints by judges in Los Angeles County that mandatory incarceration of first offenders on possession charges resulted in a "great injustice" for misguided youth who did not belong in jail with hardened criminals, even for the three-month misdemeanor minimum, a category that included violators of all races but especially applied to white defendants. One prominent judge criticized mandatory minimums for teenagers "from a good environment" who experimented with marijuana "out of a spirit of bravado," and law enforcement officials warned that juries were increasingly refusing to impose harsh punishment on such first offenders. State records reveal that prosecutors routinely plea-bargained these cases to lesser charges, to require probation and monitor rehabilitation, and the legislative reform essentially sought to standardize and codify this discretionary practice. Political leaders agreed that indeterminate sentencing for first-offense possession cases, ranging from conditional probation to a ten-year felony term, would allow prosecutors and judges to impose punishment or mercy based on the status of the offender rather than the actual offense.[59]

Armed with more flexible penalties, Attorney General Pat Brown announced an enforcement crackdown to "smother the illicit marihuana trade among juveniles," with the goal of arresting and rehabilitating experimenters and teenage peddlers alike before they took the "stepping stone to the heavier addiction to heroin." The initial campaign resulted in only a modest increase in juvenile drug arrests statewide—from 301 in 1952 to 364 in 1953—but the Governor's Advisory Committee on Children and Youth warned that "the problem is much more widespread" because of the challenges in policing the underground market. The state of California mobilized women's clubs, PTA chapters, and civic groups in a parallel drug awareness campaign and frequently praised this network for keeping the "narcotics evil" out of wholesome neighborhoods. Government officials simultaneously sought to reassure middle-class parents that almost all illegal drug use among delinquents took place in urban minority slums, a trend overshadowed by false, media-inspired rumors of rampant marijuana consumption among white teenagers from privileged areas. But the state's zero tolerance rhetoric about doing whatever it would take to prevent innocent children from "being drawn into the narcotics evil" helped to galvanize a grassroots suburban movement that overwhelming blamed outside pushers rather than internal causes or teenage consumers for the youth "epidemic."[60] In late 1953, an organized campaign demanding harsher trafficking penalties emerged in the white Los Angeles suburbs of Redondo Beach, Gardena, Manhattan Beach, and Inglewood—all located near the Mexican American and African American districts to the south and east of downtown (fig. 1.4). Governor Goodwin J. Knight, a Republican from LA, received an outpouring of letters and petitions from frightened parents and women's groups, with many correspondents adopting identical language that advocated life sentences without parole for "those who sell narcotics to children," and a significant number arguing that "dope peddlers deserve the death sentence."[61]

In December 1953, only a few weeks after the start of this grassroots get-tough campaign, another deluge of media hype about Mexican American "rat pack" gangs further fused the political imperative of urban crime control with the white racial imaginary of evil pushers and deranged addicts invading middle-class communities throughout metropolitan Los Angeles. The drama began with the arrest of four Mexican American teenagers for the murder of William Cluff, a white businessman who lived in a Los Angeles suburb and was on the way to meet his wife at a downtown restaurant. Cluff died while attempting to break up a confrontation—the details remain unclear—between the Mexican Americans and a group of young white off-duty Marines from nearby Camp Pendleton, with each faction apparently inebriated.[62] For the rest of the month, the LA newspapers headlined the rampages of a "'mad dog' mob" of "street-roaming hoodlums" and portrayed every arrest of a Mexican American youth as part of the "new outbreak of rat pack outrages," including sensational stories of home invasions and street assaults in the white suburbs.[63] Under intense pressure from fearful and outraged constituents, elected officials warned that Los Angeles was on the verge of becoming a "gang controlled city," and police chief William Parker stated that his department was "losing the war against crime." The *Los Angeles Times* demanded forceful police action and long prison sentences for the "youthful gangs" responsible for the

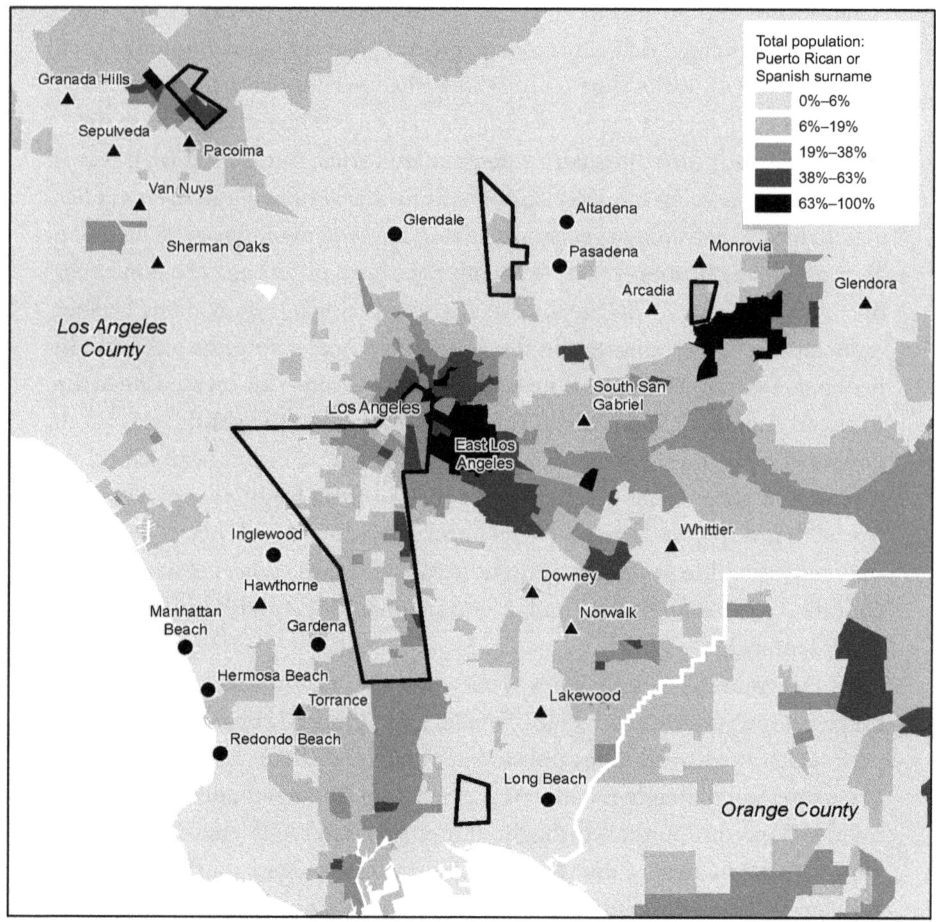

FIGURE 1.4. Location of white suburban antinarcotics activism in Los Angeles County during the 1950s. This map shows the location of Mexican American and African American residential districts in relation to the almost all-white suburban municipalities in LA County that generated the greatest pressure for tougher narcotics laws in letters and petitions to three successive governors. The circles indicate suburban areas at the forefront of the first wave of demands between 1951 and 1955 that "pushers" receive life imprisonment or the death penalty. The triangles denote white suburbs that joined the get-tough movement during a second-wave mobilization between 1958 and 1960 (covered in the final section of this chapter). These white communities were located in close proximity to the predominantly Mexican American district of East Los Angeles, the overlapping Black sections of South Central Los Angeles, and smaller nonwhite enclaves in Long Beach, the San Gabriel Valley, and the San Fernando Valley. The darker shades on the map, including East Los Angeles, are areas of concentrated Spanish surname residents based on the 1960 census. The five polygon-shaped black outlines are approximations of the main distribution of the African American population, which did not figure prominently in public antinarcotics discourse during the 1950s. (Map and 1960 U.S. census data courtesy of Social Explorer.)

"senseless 'rat pack' beatings" that made decent citizens afraid to walk the streets, a sentiment shared in voluminous correspondence that blamed lenient judges and soft-hearted juvenile authorities. "It is time we stop regarding these vicious criminals as juveniles," a Los Angeles woman informed the governor. "I'm afraid to be on the streets after sundown knowing these Rat Packs are allowed to do as they please to decent citizens."[64]

In an incendiary six-part exposé published in mid-December, the *Los Angeles Times* warned readers that waves of juvenile gangsters and youthful hoodlums were "roaming after dark" throughout the city and its suburbs, peddling narcotics and assaulting women, mugging and murdering without conscience. The *Times* claimed that at least five thousand boys and young men, mostly of Mexican descent, belonged to organized gangs in Los Angeles County, and that almost all of them took dope and/or sold narcotics for profit. One particularly notorious unit, the Rose Hill Gang, allegedly distributed marijuana and heroin to white teenagers at dances and parties in Pasadena and other upscale suburbs nearby. Drug-addicted juvenile gangsters often committed terrifying acts of violence, "just for kicks." Their mobility in the car-centered metropolis allowed hoodlums to target suburban "housewives, walking home from movies or stores, [who] are dragged into automobiles and whisked to isolated areas where they are beaten or criminally attacked" (meaning sexually assaulted).[65] Civil rights groups and social welfare agencies accused the *Times* and other local newspapers of "inflammatory, prejudicial, and unfounded generalizations" about Mexican Americans and warned that the media construction of a false juvenile crime wave would undermine public support for progressive programs that attacked the root causes of delinquency in high-poverty areas. The head judge of the juvenile court system emphasized that only one-fourth of the monitored delinquents in Los Angeles County were Mexican American teenagers, while 97 percent of that community were "law abiding, self respecting, and God fearing" people. Six weeks into the saga, the Los Angeles County Youth Committee summoned local media and elected officials to a behind-the-scenes briefing where the LAPD police chief and county sheriff acknowledged the "unnecessary hysteria," admitted that juvenile crime had not spiked, and categorized most of the "so-called gangs" as "street corner societies" rather than narcotics traffickers or violent addicts.[66]

In the white middle-class imagination, the latest "rat pack" epidemic provided a vivid illustration of the frightening consequences of dope trafficking and a racialized explanation for how innocent teenagers from wholesome communities could be lured into a life of delinquency, addiction, and crime.

While some interpretations also portrayed Mexican American addict-gangsters as the victims of narcotics syndicates, the overriding view demanded protection of suburban boundaries and white spaces through a tougher crackdown on invading peddlers and predatory addicts alike. "I am greatly concerned about the way our teenagers are being enticed" into trying marijuana and heroin, a Redondo Beach woman wrote Governor Knight; only the deterrent of life without parole for peddlers might stop the "drug addicts, resulting in rat packs and gangs, committing crimes, even murder! We must do something!" "The peddlers of dope should receive the death penalty," a man from Los Angeles bluntly informed the governor. "I don't think that there is a more horrible type of murder," agreed another capital punishment supporter from Santa Cruz, "than to induce our young people to acquire the dope habit." "Nothing but strong harsh measures will be effective," a business executive insisted, for "rat pack gangs and certainly those who encourage our youth in the use of narcotics." "Some of these peddlers do not hesitate to prowl around high school campuses [and] snare a few victims," a teacher explained, and it was past time for "heavy penalties for such corrupters of our youth." Parents of addicted children in suburban towns such as Pasadena, Inglewood, and Anaheim demanded harsh punishment for the pushers, part of the ubiquitous characterization of drug suppliers as sinister intruders and the corresponding removal of any responsibility from white teenage consumers for their criminal participation in the underground market. "To just think of these sweet young girls and boys," lamented a woman from North Hollywood, with "their whole future blotted out" by dope pushers who deserved to be locked away for life.[67]

California's political system responded in a rapid and bipartisan manner to this moral crusade led by mobilized white parents from the middle-class suburbs. Republican governor Goodwin Knight pledged all-out war on dope pushers, and Democratic attorney general Pat Brown announced a comprehensive assault to "halt the growth of the narcotics habit and eradicate it entirely." Both politicians continued the pattern of merging recreational marijuana smoking and heroin addiction into a single narcotics scourge, and few of the vocal residents of metropolitan Los Angeles appeared to recognize any distinction either in their demands for life imprisonment without possibility of parole for all dope peddlers. In a televised address in March 1954, Knight labeled teenage narcotics addiction "one of the most terrifying social problems of our day" and thanked the women's clubs and other concerned citizens who had alerted the public to the crisis.[68] In a concurrent emergency session, the state legislature again toughened the mandatory-minimum sentencing range by making all penalties for distribution of heroin or marijuana equal to the current punishment for providing narcotics to a minor: five to life for the first offense and ten to life for the second. The final package received only one dissenting vote, after Pat Brown and the state district attorneys association successfully resisted pressure from conservative Republicans and the Federal Bureau of Narcotics to repeal the probation option for first offenders. Prosecutors considered such a policy unworkable and even counterproductive, because of the difficulty of securing jury convictions under an excessively harsh sentencing structure and since probation allowed lengthier supervision and rehabilitative control than a short-term jail sentence.[69] "Dope peddlers are rats," Governor Knight told a series of follow-up conferences on youth and narcotics, in language technically color-blind but thoroughly racialized. "Every day and every hour the peddlers and pushers" stalked the high schools to lure thrill-seeking youngsters into their deadly trap. They "'hook' a young boy, or a young girl, and they will have slaves for the rest of their days. . . . They deserve no mercy whatsoever."[70]

In April 1954, Attorney General Pat Brown proposed a shift in narcotics control policy toward more effective treatment and rehabilitation of addicts and nonprofessional "addict-peddlers," based on a liberal philosophy that fused criminalization and medicalization so that "penalties meted out to these two groups should be on a mental-health approach." The coercive public health blueprint came from the Citizens' Advisory Committee to the Attorney General on Crime Prevention, which Brown established to help mobilize the public behind his declared war on narcotics. The committee recommended a three-tier system involving outpatient clinics for treatable narcotics addicts, indefinite and compulsory hospitalization for "incurables," and long prison sentences for the "professional non-addict peddler" and for any addict-peddlers that a judge found to be dangerous to society. This vision did not contemplate the existence of any illegal drug users in the state of California who were not "addicts," although the report did acknowledge that barbiturates were deadlier than heroin and that alcohol caused more delinquency and violent crime than marijuana. The advisory committee labeled narcotics addiction (defined as heroin and marijuana use, alcoholism, and barbiturate dependency) "primarily a psycho-biological illness, and only secondarily is it a legal or criminal problem." Under the medicalization plan, anyone arrested for possession or distribution could petition the judge for an addict classification, which would trigger a ninety-day institutionalization for cold-turkey withdrawal followed by five years of probation and court-supervised outpatient treatment. The advisory committee also recommended that mandatory-minimum penalties for narcotics peddling only apply to heroin, not marijuana, but Pat Brown refused to promote this reform. Overall, the Brown report captured the postwar liberal psychiatric model of crime control, with racial minorities clearly included in the scope of potential victims deserving of rehabilitation, and discretionary mechanisms designed to sort offenders into compulsory medicalization or prison.[71]

Law enforcement organizations defeated the coercive hospitalization bill as insufficiently punitive in 1954 and in several subsequent legislative showdowns. The Federal Bureau of Narcotics attacked the Brown committee's proposal for "coddling of dangerous criminals," based on the "soft" rehabilitative stance toward "addict-peddlers" and charges that outpatient clinics could not control dangerous dope fiends (Anslinger only supported indefinite civil commitment). Prosecutors from Southern California and the statewide police officers' association also condemned the treatment bill, mischaracterizing it as a backdoor legalization scheme and arguing that the criminal act of breaking narcotics laws required a term of punishment in jail or prison before entry into a rehabilitation program. The racist political framing of marijuana smugglers and dealers as illegal Mexican "wetbacks" further discredited the effort to medicalize the addict-peddler category. Legislators also objected to the financial cost of opening two narcotics hospitals in California, leaving the federal facility in Texas as the closest dedicated institution.[72] Public sentiment toward narcotics addicts hardened alongside continued media sensationalism of interracial crime and violence, most notably the rape and murder of Doris Moulton in 1956. Two Mexican American teenagers out on bail were arrested for assaulting Moulton, a white housewife and twenty-nine-year-old mother of four who lived in the suburb of Whittier, not far from East LA. Before she died, Moulton allegedly told the police that "they beat me apparently for the sheer joy of it," pausing (according to the implausible official report) only "to give themselves hypodermic injections" of narcotics. "Something *must* be done" about lax laws and lenient judges, a desperate woman from Long Beach demanded of the governor, or "can a dope addict go around raping as often as he wants until he kills someone?" William Parker, chief of the LAPD, reinforced these fears by claiming that narcotics addicts committed half of all crime in metropolitan Los Angeles and reiterating the "reefer madness" fiction that marijuana in particular caused "unpredictable" violence and "very serious sex crimes."[73]

The grassroots suburban crusade against dope pushers continued to escalate during the mid-1950s, with groups representing more than one million

Californians ultimately petitioning for even tougher laws to protect the youthful victims of the narcotics scourge. From the Long Beach area of Los Angeles, around one thousand people collectively requested a special law enforcement campaign against pushers and demanded the deterrent of capital punishment or life without parole for providing marijuana or heroin to youth. "The dope pusher is no better than a murderer," a woman from the upper-middle-class suburb of Altadena explained, destroying innocent lives by "enticing our teenagers into the dope habit." The California Federation of Women's Clubs called on the state to double the current penalties for narcotics peddlers, and many other constituents denounced lenient judges and advocated the death penalty for pushers who were "a thousand times worse than any murderer."[74] But Governor Knight and the state legislature resisted pressure for extreme and inflexible measures in the war on narcotics out of recognition that the criminal justice system needed discretionary authority to rehabilitate illegal drug users, especially first offenders, who did not fit the categories of the "professional, non-addict peddler and international wholesaler." The cultural and political stigmatization of "rat packs" and Mexican pushers continued to obscure the actual social practices of the "victims" in the white middle-class suburbs, where the typical "narcotics peddler" was an older white teenage dealer or recreational marijuana user providing small quantities to friends and classmates. This racial and spatial context helps to explain why state legislative committees bottled up legislation to impose capital punishment or life imprisonment for "peddling narcotics to a minor" during the mid-1950s, even as white suburban parents who placed all blame on external villains proved unable to comprehend these market dynamics.[75]

During California's early war on narcotics, the discretionary features of state policy and metropolitan policing institutionalized new double standards that helped to justify racial segregation and increasingly punitive crackdowns on nonwhite youth. The political culture in Los Angeles had long displayed a divided attitude toward "delinquents" from Mexican American and Black areas, with the crime containment approach to gangsters and hoodlums competing with the Progressive rehabilitative philosophy that youth who joined "street corner societies" were victims of poverty, racial discrimination, family breakdown, and the psychopathology of addiction. Attorney General Pat Brown encapsulated the mainstream liberal stance on the spatial and psychological roots of juvenile delinquency and racial inequality, supporting public housing as an antidote for crime in the slums and distinguishing hardened criminals from misguided teenagers who could be rehabilitated from inadequate parenting and bad influences.[76] But in the mid-1950s, liberal delinquency officials in LA County began advocating transfer to adult court for juveniles who were "dangerous to the community" and teenage addicts who were "sophisticated young criminals," in order to salvage rehabilitative programs for the majority of delinquents given the "get tough" political mood.[77] At the height of the narcotics crisis, the state of California also officially began promoting residential segregation as a core antidelinquency strategy, recommending that the best way to prevent teenage drug use and other vices was to live in a neighborhood of single-family homes alongside others of the same "racial, cultural, and economic" identities—a message transparently aimed at white middle-class families. The Governor's Council on Children and Youth simultaneously categorized juvenile delinquency as a product of "delinquent neighborhoods" characterized by minority populations, urban-industrial locations, and dense, multifamily housing—signifying the increasing criminalization of nonwhite spaces and the official embrace of the utopian ideal of suburban whiteness.[78]

Nationalizing the Suburban Narcotics Crisis

The war on narcotics in California played a crucial and largely forgotten role in nationalizing the suburban delinquency crisis in the mid-1950s and shaping the federal campaign to protect white middle-class youth victims from dope pushers and other invading villains. In November 1953, the Senate Subcommittee to Investigate Juvenile Delinquency opened hearings under the leadership of Robert Hendrickson (R-NJ) and Ernest Kefauver (D-TN), a follow-up to the Special Senate Crime Committee that first highlighted the teenage narcotics "epidemic" two years earlier. Although most scholarship on the Juvenile Delinquency Subcommittee has focused on its campaigns against violence and sex in comic books and movies, from the start the federal inquiry prioritized the crisis of teenage drug addiction and resolved to draw public attention to "existing problems, including the use of narcotics, relating to juvenile delinquency and the commission of [criminal] offenses by youths throughout the country." The advance materials gathered by the subcommittee staff prominently included the nationally serialized saga of Patricia Williams, the sixteen-year-old from a white upper-middle-class family in suburban LA who graduated from marijuana smoking to heroin addiction under the sinister influence of "Mexican pushers." The subcommittee also solicited exploratory guidance from law enforcement officials such as Walter Creighton, the director of the California

Bureau of Narcotic Enforcement, who explained that teenage drug violations used to be restricted to the "underprivileged class" and nonwhite juvenile gangs but had recently escalated among college-bound adolescents from "more cultural families, those of higher economic and social standards." Creighton argued that materialistic values and economic prosperity distorted the psychology of affluent white youth, specifically blaming parents who "supply the child with funds and luxuries far in excess of his needs" and the unsupervised freedom provided by automobiles, as "there is no more effective and convenient spot for the use of marijuana than in a car."[79]

The Juvenile Delinquency Subcommittee's initial hearings highlighted the spreading threat of youthful narcotics addiction in the white middle-class neighborhoods of large cities and nearby suburbs. Senator Hendrickson, a resident of suburban New Jersey, pledged in opening remarks to "determine the extent to which unscrupulous adults contribute to juvenile delinquency through the sale of alcohol and drugs to our young people." Karl Holton, the head of the LA County probation department, testified that the recent epidemic of teenage marijuana use was caused by Mexican smugglers and "degenerates" based in the slums who peddled narcotics to youth throughout the metropolitan region. FBN Commissioner Harry Anslinger, however, rejected the "alarmism" of parents and politicians in Southern California and reiterated his mantra that narcotics only tempted criminally inclined teenagers in "areas of social and economic deprivation," whereas better communities with "emotionally normal adjusted youth" (i.e., white youth) were not susceptible. Multiple witnesses directly contradicted Anslinger's portrait of a narcotics situation under control, including a national journalist whose recently syndicated "Dope, Unlimited" exposé warned of "thousands of American children" across the nation who had fallen "prey to vicious dope peddlers." According to the state prosecutor for Cook County, covering Chicago and its suburbs, "This is not a slum problem. This is an American problem." The head of the General Federation of Women's Clubs even insisted that narcotics-related delinquency was primarily a middle-class rather than a ghetto crisis, because youth "who have greater economic security" could afford illegal drugs.[80] In its first report, the Juvenile Delinquency Subcommittee categorized youth narcotics addiction—marijuana, heroin, and illicit abuse of synthetic drugs—as a scourge in the largest metropolitan areas that had spread from the slums to the "higher economic class levels." The subcommittee endorsed tough punishment for "drug pushers" and coercive rehabilitation for their teenage victims.[81]

In September 1954, the Juvenile Delinquency Subcommittee held high-profile hearings in California to focus the nation's attention on the "vicious impact of the narcotics racket on our youth." The subcommittee's advance announcement echoed Anslinger in placing primary blame on organized crime syndicates (and a Communist Chinese conspiracy), but the evidence from Southern California instead elevated the Mexican border explanation in the national narcotics debate. In San Diego, local law enforcement reported that teenagers often crossed into Tijuana where marijuana, alcohol, barbiturates, pornography, and prostitution were readily available—despite a curfew and road blockade by the sheriff's department to send unaccompanied juveniles homeward. Subcommittee investigators visited Tijuana undercover and returned with dramatic stories of hundreds of American teenagers (including Navy sailors) partying at nightclubs where prostitutes allegedly provided "free bundles of heroin" to hook their victims, and "young girls in the company of many older boys" drove back to California after 4:00 a.m. to avoid the sheriff's roadblock. Several federal and local agencies insisted that policing the border effectively was impossible, and they (correctly) attributed the drug trade to small-scale American traffickers and adventurous adolescents with automobiles rather than organized syndicates or Mexican youth gangs. At the Los Angeles hearing, delinquency officials reported that marijuana could be found "in every part of the community," including the "high-class" suburbs, even though affluent white youth more often avoided detection. Law enforcement officers blamed the supply on "pushers and peddlers" who smuggled drugs from Tijuana and advocated closing the border not only to unaccompanied minors but to all youth under twenty-one. The head of the LAPD's narcotics squad provided the key takeaway: in a rapidly suburbanizing metropolis with a highly mobile population, with parents working and children encountering new environments, "every young person . . . is very vulnerable" to drug addiction regardless of geography or class status.[82]

The Juvenile Delinquency Subcommittee interpreted the Los Angeles findings as alarming proof that narcotics traffickers represented a "threat potentially to every American youth" and therefore no community was safe from the teenage drug crisis. The subcommittee's second major report, released in March 1955, proclaimed that "one of the most sinister of all delinquency problems is narcotics addiction among children." To illustrate the national tragedy, the report highlighted the testimony of a distraught white mother from an upper-middle-class suburb near Pasadena whose churchgoing son started smoking marijuana and ended up a heroin addict incarcerated in state prison for robbery. The mother emphasized his wholesome upbringing—"He is not from a broken home"—and demanded tougher federal laws to protect such teenage victims from the "big peddler of narcotics." The 1955 report portrayed marijuana and barbiturate use as the twin gateways to heroin addiction but warned that the scope of the crisis remained unknown because arrest data did not include many middle-class and wealthy youth who generally ended up in private medical facilities. Based on the Southern California hearings and similar discoveries in El Paso, Texas, the subcommittee called for federal action to close the Mexican border to unaccompanied minors. The policy recommendations also included drug education and prevention programs for teenagers, compulsory hospitalization laws to rehabilitate addicts, and stricter controls on the illicit diversion of prescription medication. The report further endorsed a major increase in the enforcement capacity of the Federal Bureau of Narcotics in order to launch a supply-side crackdown against "peddlers and pushers," from the international to the local levels. And finally, the mainstream liberals who dominated the Juvenile Delinquency Subcommittee advocated the punitive step of doubling the mandatory-minimum sentences in the Boggs Act to deter or incapacitate the narcotics traffickers who exploited innocent youth and profited from "human misery and death."[83]

In addition to California, get-tough campaigns in states such as Ohio and New Jersey propelled the antinarcotics crusade back into national politics during the mid-1950s and demanded harsher laws to protect white middle-class communities from evil pushers and dangerous addicts. In Ohio, more than one hundred civic groups and public agencies joined forces in 1953 as the Citizen Narcotics Advisory Committee to launch a war on "dope pushers" who targeted innocent teenagers with marijuana and heroin. The coalition's literature visualized the threat exclusively through images of affluent white high school students "hooked" by shady peddlers who had invaded "all types of communities, large and small, rich and poor alike." Law enforcement allies also hyped the threat of "addicts from the big cities" committing crimes in outlying suburbs to get money for their drugs. In 1955, the legislature responded by passing the nation's most stringent mandatory-minimum penalties to date: thirty to life for providing narcotics to minors, twenty-to-forty years for sale to adults, and two-to-twenty years for possession. Commissioner Anslinger promptly cited the state's punitive law as a national model and repeatedly claimed that all pushers had fled Ohio to avoid inflexible sanctions.[84] In New Jersey, suburban women's clubs and other civic groups launched an initiative, inspired in part by the Ohio campaign, to toughen a 1952 state law that mandated two-to-five years for first offenders convicted of sale or possession of heroin or marijuana. The coalition blamed the escalating narcotics crisis on lenient judges who found loopholes for so-called "addict-peddlers," especially nonwhite street dealers in Newark who allegedly worked for organized syndicates. Encouraged by the FBN, the New Jersey movement advocated a mandatory twenty-to-life sentence for anyone over age twenty-one who provided illicit narcotics (including marijuana) to a minor, and ten-to-twenty years for the first offense for selling to an adult. The law targeted professional traffickers and addict-peddlers alike, to protect victims from their "cold-blooded, premeditated murder."[85]

Racial, class, and geographic assumptions about deserving victims and evil villains pervaded the mid-1950s debate about narcotics policy in New Jersey. Jane Tompkins, the leading figure in the campaign for stricter laws, lived in suburban Maplewood and was married to William Tompkins, a former federal attorney and state legislator who coauthored *The Traffic in Narcotics* (1953) with Harry Anslinger. She served as director of the New Jersey Commission on Narcotic Control, the architect of the harsh legislation and a vehicle for the mobilization of civic groups from upscale suburbs. In a delicate balancing act, Jane Tompkins repeatedly urged women's clubs to "alert the general public" to the narcotics crisis while reassuring them that teenagers in "first class suburban area[s]" remained safe because their parents taught clear moral values and their communities provided "wholesome character-building programs." She informed white suburban audiences that most dope pushers and addicts came from "crowded industrial areas . . . inhabited primarily by economically and socially deprived minority groups [with] mental disorders and emotional instabilities." But Tompkins also warned that "out-of-town" addicts might invade "your fine community" to commit robbery, prostitution, even murder.[86] In spring 1956, the state legislature approved the tough narcotics package, which restricted compulsory hospitalization to addicts who committed no other crimes—the specified, implicitly white, categories included thrill-seeking teens tempted by marijuana and "highly skilled professional people" with a medical dependency. Democratic governor Robert Meyner still vetoed the law as insufficiently flexible and practically unenforceable, arguing that prosecutors and juries would not tolerate lengthy mandatory sentences for many young offenders. As an example of "peddlers" who deserved mercy and discretion, Meyner cited the case of four white college students who had provided marijuana to friends and had been rehabilitated into "useful and valuable citizens" through probation and suspended sentences.[87]

FBN Commissioner Harry Anslinger urged elected officials and grassroots activists across the nation to adopt the Ohio model of lengthy and uncompromising penalties for all narcotics pushers and "addict-peddlers," rather than the New Jersey and California alternatives of probationary loopholes for first offenders. In his coauthored 1953 manifesto, *The Traffic in Narcotics*, Anslinger praised the women's clubs and PTA groups that were leading the battle for tougher state laws to remove discretion from the soft-hearted judges who refused to incapacitate the "murderous drug peddler." As outrageous examples, the commissioner cited a man who served only six months for supplying marijuana to fifteen-year-old girls and another "soul-destroying peddler" given a light sentence who later allegedly raped a ten-year-old girl "while under marihuana intoxication." *The Traffic in Narcotics* provided a how-to manual for an "aroused citizenry" to "strike at the roots of the drug traffic in your community" by demanding laws that included life imprisonment for corrupting minors with narcotics and mandatory hospitalization for addicts.[88] By 1955, more than half of the state legislatures had adopted mandatory-minimum penalties for narcotics violators (including marijuana) equivalent to or harsher than the federal provisions in the Boggs Act. A dozen of these laws authorized a higher maximum sentence for first offenders convicted of sale than the five-year federal threshold—most notably in the coastal and border states with large cities that served as distribution centers. Michigan's exceptionally punitive law, a response to reports of pushers targeting teenagers in Detroit, mandated twenty to life for sellers alongside an indeterminate penalty of up to ten years for a first possession offense. California and Illinois likewise permitted maximum life sentences for any sale of narcotics, as did New York for the second offense. But these and other states also maintained the discretion to rehabilitate drug criminals classified as addicts through involuntary commitment to medical institutions, and the disposition of possession cases generally depended upon prosecutorial and judicial assessment of the offender's character, background, and perceived victim status.[89]

During 1955–56, a bipartisan coalition in Congress collaborated closely with the FBN in a successful campaign to double the federal penalties for sale and possession of heroin and marijuana by capitalizing on the perceived crisis of adolescent drug addiction and manipulating the racial and gender categories of the pusher-victim narrative. The U.S. Senate authorized a special nationwide investigation into the illegal traffic in "narcotic drugs and marihuana" on March 10, 1955, based on that same day's Juvenile Delinquency Subcommittee report advocating tougher mandatory sanctions to safeguard innocent youth.

Another subcommittee of the Senate Judiciary Committee opened the proceedings in June, the very month that the citizens' coalition in Ohio prevailed in its punitive crusade against urban pushers and predatory addicts. Senator Price Daniel, a segregationist Democrat from Texas, chaired the investigation and held almost forty hearings in thirteen of the nation's largest cities between June and December. The Daniel subcommittee consulted with the FBN throughout the process and clearly designed the televised hearings as political theater to mobilize public opinion and rally elected officials behind a more punitive law enforcement war on illegal narcotics traffickers and dangerous addict-peddlers. The Senate investigation adopted the FBN's flawed methodology of directly extrapolating national "nonmedical" addiction data from the arrest and incarceration records in major cities, without ever considering the role of racially targeted policing and differential treatment in the criminal legal system. These assumptions overwhelmingly defined "criminal drug addicts and drug peddlers," in Anslinger's phrase, as a nonwhite and especially African American problem that could only be addressed through lengthy and inflexible prison terms or indeterminate and compulsory hospitalization. The investigation simultaneously portrayed juvenile addicts as more amenable to rehabilitation and constructed this category through conventional tropes of small-town white females victimized by big-city evils.[90]

The Daniel subcommittee hearings targeted traffickers and pushers for retribution, blamed narcotics addicts for a sensationalized urban crime wave, and lumped heroin and marijuana together as national security threats emanating from Mexico, Red China, and Italian Mafia syndicates. At the first hearing in Washington, Harry J. Anslinger boasted of the FBN's success in fighting these foreign smugglers but attributed the persistence of the illegal market to "extremely cunning drug addicts and peddlers" who took advantage of insufficiently tough laws and lenient revolving-door sentences. The commissioner estimated between fifty thousand and sixty thousand addicts in the United States, mostly of heroin, concentrated among the "lower social levels" in the slums of New York, Los Angeles, and Chicago. Anslinger asserted that 70 percent of these addicts worked as street peddlers (a distorted inference from arrest records) and that most paid for their habits through petty theft and often committed "major crimes" under the influence of narcotics. Such addicts therefore deserved the same lengthy prison terms as traffickers, with mandatory hospitalization reserved for true "victims" who broke no other laws. The FBN commissioner unequivocally absolved pharmaceutical corporations of responsibility for the illicit market, claiming that they had not "in any way contributed to this spread of addiction" (he later made the incompatible concession that Americans of "professional" status were most likely to misuse synthetic drugs). Although Anslinger labeled heroin the primary threat, he also portrayed marijuana as an "increasing problem" that led directly from youthful experimentation to narcotics addiction and even had caused "sadistic, terrible crimes" and "sex slayings." This marijuana-heroin connection underpinned the Daniel subcommittee's agenda to generate public outrage against "pushers" and "addict-peddlers" who targeted teenage victims.[91]

The most dramatic revelations of the televised Senate investigation involved the deliberate juxtaposition of nonwhite and immigrant dope pushers with white female addict-prostitutes carefully selected as examples of lost innocence and sympathetic victimhood. The Daniel subcommittee borrowed a top FBN agent as its chief investigator, and before each hearing he consulted with local law enforcement and interviewed incarcerated "addicts" to find witnesses who best fit the racial and gender categories that would resonate in media coverage and public opinion. At the second hearing in Philadelphia, the police reported that most narcotics peddlers and addicts were "of the Negro race," but the subcommittee chose to highlight Barbara Lee Roman (pseudonym), a white nightclub dancer and heroin user arrested multiple times for prostitution, as a tragic saga that must be "told to the American people." The senators also subpoenaed the Italian American man serving a five-year sentence for selling narcotics to Ms. Roman, presented as a small-town girl destroyed by urban depravity, and lambasted him for creating "addicts for life." As intended, *Reader's Digest* featured the "attractive twenty-five-year-old" as the foremost example of how pushers had spread addiction out of the slums and corrupted "youths of every race."[92] Just before the New York City hearings, a local tabloid warned that "teenage hoodlums" in Harlem were committing narcotics-fueled crimes and that pushers were "turning their attention to the children of well-to-do families, particularly in the Long Island and Westchester suburbs." To illustrate the crisis, the Daniel subcommittee subpoenaed Italian American traffickers who refused to cooperate and presented an anonymous white female from Rhode Island who moved to New York City, started smoking marijuana for "excitement," and became a heroin addict on the road to jail instead of college. She begged Congress to "treat addiction as a disease" rather than a crime, and the senators praised her as a "young girl" from a good background, victimized by pushers (which she never claimed), courageously telling her story to prevent other innocent youth from "suffering as you have suffered."[93]

The Daniel subcommittee employed visual props as well as the congressional subpoena power to orchestrate racial showdowns between nefarious pushers and their defenseless victims. The materials prepared for July hearings on the Washington, DC, narcotics trade included a perp-walk photograph of William "Blue" Miller, an African American man appealing a six-to-twenty-year conviction for distribution of heroin. In a spectacle duly featured in the *Washington Post,* the white senators forced Miller and another accused Black heroin peddler to assert the Fifth Amendment right against self-incrimination hundreds of times and berated the two men for claiming poverty while driving expensive cars and wearing fancy clothes. They called the second man to the stand on three separate dates and repeatedly mocked his insistence that the DC police had beaten a false confession out of him.[94] The extensive hearings in Price Daniel's home state of Texas highlighted a dozen arrest photographs of Mexican American peddlers and cross-border smugglers, including a woman named Simona Cavazos whom the chairman demonized as deserving of the death penalty for addicting white youth to heroin. The subcommittee juxtaposed these Mexican American villains with images of fatal overdoses of white men in Houston tourist hotels, a story of a twenty-two-year-old white woman from a respectable background who died because of "dope pushers," testimony from a desperate white mother of an addicted son, and multiple white teenage males who admitted crossing the border for a fix.[95] The planning documents for the Los Angeles hearings listed the racial and ethnic identity of every projected witness, and the proceedings incorporated photographs of "Negro pushers" and extensive interrogations of alleged Mexican American traffickers and "addict peddlers" charged with smuggling heroin from Tijuana. The LAPD's narcotics squad even arrested one Mexican American man specifically to force him to admit cross-border smuggling to the subcommittee's FBN investigator, and the senators discredited his testimony that the police had tortured the confession out of him, as did the *Los Angeles Times* in its prejudicial coverage.[96]

Many of the white teenagers and young adults hauled before the Daniel subcommittee as cautionary addict-victims challenged the prevailing marijuana-gateway and heroin-pusher scripts and instead blamed criminal drug enforcement for their predicaments. Senator Daniel, who was planning a run for governor of Texas, returned often to the shocking tale of an adult peddler in San Antonio who allegedly hooked "40 or 50 boys and girls of high-school age" by giving the first dose of heroin away for free. At the Houston hearing, asked by Daniel, "Who led you to use marijuana?" an eighteen-year-old white male replied that "nobody led me into anything" and that he later tried heroin out of "curiosity" rather than free samples from a pusher. He refused to implicate "Mexicans in Houston" as the cause of his addiction and explained unapologetically that he often crossed the border "for a good time" and might have brought illegal drugs back for friends. A twenty-three-year-old white female named Mary Ann, currently incarcerated after the Houston police timed a mass narcotics round-up for the subcommittee's arrival, also testified that she first tried marijuana and heroin out of "curiosity" as a high school student in suburban Los Angeles. She admitted to smuggling heroin across the Mexican border on numerous occasions and had unsuccessfully sought treatment in the federal narcotics hospital before her recent arrest. Mary Ann also rejected Senator Daniel's invitation to blame pushers and addict-peddlers for her problems and then surprised the subcommittee by questioning the underlying policy of criminalization itself. When Daniel asked what Congress should do to protect other youth from "ruin[ing] their lives like you have," she replied that "it wouldn't be fair to lock all of us up for the rest of our lives just because we got on it when we were young and didn't know any better, because we haven't done anything that serious to break the law." This led to an extraordinary interchange between the crusading senator, the subcommittee counsel, and a young heroin user who advocated legalization and actually understood the market forces of supply and demand.[97]

SENATOR DANIEL: You think whenever you are allowed to get out of jail here, or whatever they do to you, you will go back on it?

MARY ANN: I will try not to, but I couldn't promise, because I don't know. . . . I think the only thing that could be done that would stop the narcotics traffic would be if they open up clinics where addicts could get it. (. . .)

SENATOR DANIEL: That wouldn't break anybody of the habit, cure the habit.

MARY ANN: No, but it would stop drugs from coming from Mexico.

MR. GASQUE [COUNSEL]: Hasn't it ruined your life?

MARY ANN: Well, yes, on account I have gotten in trouble [by being arrested]. (. . .)

MR. GASQUE: Do you think that Houston, one of those cities affected by this, can do nothing to keep it from spreading to the boys and girls of this community?

MARY ANN: I don't know what you can do. It wouldn't be fair to put all the addicts in jail for a long time. That wouldn't be fair. (. . .)

SENATOR DANIEL: If there was a life sentence provided for addicts, . . . if they went back to it for a second or third time, they could be put in some type of colony or some kind of institution; do you think that would help keep you off drugs? (. . .)

MARY ANN: Just anybody using drugs, put us away for life? (. . .)

SENATOR DANIEL: Do you think that kind of a penalty hanging over you might cause you to stay off of drugs after you had been given treatment?

MARY ANN: I don't think so. . . . I don't think that would be fair. . . . Are we going to be sent to a hospital or the penitentiary? (. . .)

SENATOR DANIEL: Under the Texas law it would be possible to send you to the penitentiary, but I understand you will have ample opportunity to be cured.[98]

The fall 1955 hearings in Los Angeles illustrated the subcommittee's tricky balancing act of justifying imprisonment or institutionalization of addicts based on their propensity to commit predatory crimes while simultaneously presenting those who fit sympathetic racial and gender categories as victims of pushers and social companions redefined as "addict-peddlers." Senator Daniel first convinced Chief William Parker of the LAPD to agree that narcotics caused half of all crimes in Los Angeles, a calculation based on zero evidence that justified the policy of preventive incarceration of known addicts. Other law enforcement officials testified—also absent actual evidence—that heroin and marijuana fiends committed not only property crimes and prostitution but also violence, rape, and murder. Then the subcommittee called multiple witnesses drawn from the ranks of recently arrested heroin users and interrogated them about Mexican American and African American suppliers. One young white woman, whose photograph ran in the *Los Angeles Times*, disputed Daniel's characterization that peddlers forced her to try heroin and insisted that she was not an addict, "not guilty of a real crime," and "only harming myself." The subcommittee then summoned a white man who shot heroin with her, all in an effort to trace the supply chain from Mexicans in East Los Angeles to a major trafficker based in Tijuana. Another white female serving a one-year sentence for narcotics addiction admitted that she worked as a prostitute, had crossed the border to buy heroin, and sometimes patronized local Mexican American (and white) dealers. She angrily informed the subcommittee that she belonged in psychiatric counseling rather than jail and then endorsed the medical provision of legal narcotics to addicts to "take the profit out of" the underground market. Despite overwhelming evidence that these white heroin users started in recreational settings and sought out their connections, Daniel concluded by advocating the death penalty for traffickers and peddlers "who are crossing our border with dope and who are selling to juveniles."[99]

The Daniel hearings stigmatized and demonized the nonwhite and foreign suppliers in the illegal narcotics market but also exploited and humiliated the white women repeatedly chosen to illustrate the sympathetic side of the pusher-victim equation. In Chicago, the subcommittee's strategy documents outlined plans to expose the "Italian mob" traffickers and "many well-to-do 'big' colored men" who supplied heroin and, as expected, took the Fifth Amendment. With only a few exceptions, the subcommittee subpoenaed white females to represent the addict-victims, even though about 90 percent of narcotics arrests in Chicago involved African Americans (and disproportionately males), the same racial pattern as in every other destination except the Texas cities and Los Angeles. The Chicago media hyped the appearance of Lila Leeds, the former movie star exiled from Hollywood after her infamous marijuana conviction with co-defendant Robert Mitchum in the late 1940s. FBN Commissioner Harry Anslinger personally supplied the subcommittee with Leeds's narcotics record, which included a jail term for heroin possession and a stay in the federal hospital in Lexington after the state took her two young children away. In front of television cameras and newspaper reporters, Senator Price Daniel led Lila Leeds through the ritual of confessing the marijuana-to-heroin progression of dope addiction starting with bad associates (e.g., addict-peddlers) and later from street pushers, although she did insist that "they never tried to force it upon me." The subcommittee also interrogated two white female addict-prostitutes, both featured prominently in the *Chicago Daily Tribune*, after ascertaining in advance that one would admit to buying narcotics from Black street peddlers on the South Side and the other would concede to marijuana and heroin use with a multiracial clientele.[100] This racial theater continued in the final hearings in Detroit and Cleveland, where the subcommittee highlighted Black heroin pushers and demeaned a white twenty-nine-year-old female addict described in Daniel's notes as "married to Negro pimp and prostitutes with Negroes."[101]

The Senate narcotics investigation elicited thousands of letters from residents of the targeted metropolitan regions who followed the hearings in the media and overwhelmingly demanded tougher punishment for traffickers and pushers who victimized American youth. Many came from the already mobilized white middle-class suburbs of Los Angeles, where outraged correspondents often demanded the death penalty for the "beasts who systematically destroy human souls" and the "wretched misfits who peddle dope to children in their teens." An Arcadia man believed that capital punishment was "too soft" because "smugglers and peddlers of dope are worse than killers," while a professional from Long Beach recommended flogging followed by execution for "the luring of young people into the dreadful addiction." Several leaders of women's clubs and antinarcotics groups in suburban LA blamed the Mexican border and a Red Chinese conspiracy and demanded extreme and inflexible penalties for pushers who were "worse than murderers."[102] Similar letters from the suburbs of New York City and Chicago advocated the death penalty for initiating youth into narcotics addiction and denounced judges for not sentencing pushers to the maximum.[103] White residents of Houston and San Antonio wrote in to attack Mexican peddlers and endorse the ultimate punishment for those who "make prostitutes and criminals out of girls and boys."[104] Senator Daniel responded with a form letter expressing the subcommittee's gratitude for the "support for the death penalty of narcotics smugglers from so many loyal Americans."[105] A number of white parents with addicted children wrote to Daniel pleading for medical rehabilitation, not incarceration, of innocent youth who were "ready prey for the dope peddler," as a Bronx woman reported. An anonymous "American mother" from Los Angeles asked for mercy, and even a legal source of narcotics, to keep her addicted son and other "college students and college graduates" away from the traffickers. She informed the subcommittee of the heartbreak faced by many "good, honest, hard-working" parents whose children had experimented for adventure and now "need help desperately."[106]

The national media reinforced the framework of innocent white youth targeted by evil pushers and effectively functioned as an echo chamber for the Daniel subcommittee and the Federal Bureau of Narcotics. In October 1955, right after the hearings in Philadelphia and New York City, *Coronet* staged the same drama of white female victimization in "The Peddler of Living Death," a photojournalistic essay (with professional actors) designed to horrify its middle-class readership. A foreign trafficker and an ethnic male American pusher represent the "contemptible traffic in human misery" and know that "thrill-seeking teenagers make excellent prospects." The pusher hangs out in an urban entertainment district and "hooks" his victim, a young and pretty white female, with a reefer cigarette from Mexico that makes her need a stronger drug—"virtually all heroin addicts began on marijuana." At the pusher's apartment (the intimate "trap"), he sticks a heroin needle into her arm and soon the "victim" descends into the nightmarish world of addiction and prostitution. She somehow helps the police catch the pusher and then recovers in a psychiatric hospital, but the moral of the story is Commissioner Anslinger's warning that the mandatory-minimum sentences in the Boggs Act are "too lenient." *Pageant*, another general-interest magazine, featured "9 Hours in Hell with a Dope Addict," a true photojournalism account of a twenty-five-year-old white junkie-prostitute going through withdrawal in a Chicago hotel. The article blamed pushers for hooking her with free samples—a charge *none* of the witnesses in the hearings sustained—and recirculated the Senate investigation's manufactured claim that narcotics addicts committed half of all crimes nationwide. *Reader's Digest* also centered the white victims of pushers and underworld traffickers—once pretty female addict-prostitutes and a teenage boy from a "decent family" hooked by free heroin samples—in its report on the Daniel hearings and demanded that the American public rally behind the FBN's call for stricter laws and "get angry enough to force Congress and the judges to crack down."[107]

Despite its deliberate emphasis on white female addicts and nonwhite pushers, the Daniel subcommittee's approach to African American narcotics users also contained elements of pity and sympathy, dependent on the convoluted and often overlapping categories of innocent young victim and dangerous addict-peddler. The Senate investigation conceived and therefore uncovered a hierarchical market in which major traffickers and wholesalers were usually "white" (meaning Italian and Italian American), street peddlers and border smugglers were African American or Mexican, and most illegal drug users also were nonwhite (extrapolated from arrest records). Senator Daniel, a racial conservative, expressed sadness for the slum youth at the bottom of this pyramid and stated that "white people are just so much to be blamed, if not more so, than the Negroes themselves." He often pointed out that "the colored" accounted for almost all addict arrests in the cities of the North and Midwest and wondered if it "may be the fault of the way we have taken care of certain races," meaning the failure to pass tough enough laws to protect "our colored friends" from Italian Mafia pushers.[108] But the broader construction of heroin addicts as dangerous criminals who almost inevitably became peddlers constrained this critique, and the senators rarely humanized nonwhite witnesses as they did for the white females who testified. In one Washington hearing, Daniel offered symbolic victim status to a twenty-eight-year-old Black woman in exchange for turning in her suppliers, but she brusquely refused to play along with the marijuana-gateway, heroin-pusher, and addict-prostitute confession rituals. Another Black female subpoenaed in Chicago similarly disputed the subcommittee's characterization of the market and stated that people took narcotics "because they want to use them. No one entices them." The Daniel subcommittee also ignored pleas from community groups in Harlem to distinguish between "the addicted and non-addicted pusher" and treat the former as a "sick person" who deserved psychiatric help, not incarceration or coercive institutionalization.[109]

During the Senate narcotics investigation, a dissident group of medical and legal experts offered the most direct challenge to the punitive agenda of the Federal Bureau of Narcotics, but the Daniel subcommittee disregarded their arguments by deferring to law enforcement witnesses as the true authorities on drug addiction. In June 1955, as the hearings began, two prominent leaders of the New York Academy of Medicine published a mass-magazine essay titled "Should We Legalize Narcotics?" They argued that providing drugs to confirmed addicts through clinics would reduce crime and put dope pushers out of business, just as ending Prohibition had nearly eradicated the underground alcohol market. In response, Senator Daniel staged a fall hearing in New York City so that Harry Anslinger could denounce and discredit the FBN critics ostensibly given a forum. Hubert Howe, a physician active in the New York initiative, argued that federal interdiction had failed and "no threat of legal punishment" would deter narcotics addicts because they were sick people and not criminals. He endorsed the British model of providing a controlled supply to registered addicts, which would "destroy the black market" and keep nonwhite youth out of prison. Howe also rejected Daniel's assertions that marijuana caused addiction and that heroin led to crimes of violence, but the subcommittee dismissed academic research by citing police testimony to the contrary. Rufus King, the head of a parallel narcotics inquiry by the American Bar Association, then informed the subcommittee that "it is precisely our law enforcement efforts, and nothing else, that keeps the price of drugs . . . so high as to attract an endless procession of criminal entrepreneurs." King labeled the approach of eradicating addiction through harsher penalties "preposterous" and argued that the federal government had no constitutional authority to incarcerate a "diseased person." Commissioner Anslinger, in an orchestrated power play, then denounced the "free clinic" scheme as a radical left-wing conspiracy and insisted that all historical evidence proved that legalizing narcotics would triple the size of the illicit market and lead to a runaway addiction-fueled crime wave.[110]

In January 1956, the Daniel subcommittee released its recommendations for an enhanced war on narcotics to combat "one of the most serious problems facing the nation." The Senate report blamed "Mexican operators" for the flow of marijuana and heroin across the Southwest border and a Communist Chinese plot to demoralize the American people through narcotics addiction. Ignoring expert medical testimony, the investigators accused heroin pushers of "selling murder, robbery, and rape" and attributed half of all crimes in large metropolitan areas to narcotics addicts who spread their "contagious disease . . . with cancerous rapidity" and should be "removed from society." Embracing the FBN's circular logic, the subcommittee argued that current federal laws were too weak to deter traffickers in a $500 million annual market but that tougher penalties enforced without exception would all but eliminate heroin and marijuana smugglers and peddlers. This recommendation included a maximum penalty of death for providing narcotics to children, defined as "murder on the installment plan," a scenario illustrated through the San Antonio pusher who (ostensibly) hooked dozens of high school students. The subcommittee's FBN investigator drafted a second report on "treatment and rehabilitation of narcotics addicts" that attacked the "free clinic" plan as "totally unworkable" and called for the indeterminate confinement of illegal narcotics users and mandatory minimums for addict-peddlers.[111] The Daniel subcommittee hashed out the details of the narcotics law in confidential sessions with the FBN and other federal enforcement agencies. In private, the policymakers conceded that interdicting drugs at the border remained an impossible mission, and they reluctantly decided that barring addicts with U.S. citizenship from entering Mexico would be unconstitutional. The group also expressed hope that extreme penalties would function as a "psychological deterrent" but acknowledged that mandatory minimums would generally sweep up the "small" smugglers and street-level dealers rather than the "big" traffickers.[112]

The political debate over the Narcotic Control Act of 1956 again revealed a broad and bipartisan consensus in Washington in favor of harsh punishment for dope traffickers and street pushers, with disagreement mainly over how to rehabilitate their "victims" and whether to incarcerate or institutionalize "addict-peddlers." In February, a report by the Eisenhower administration's Interdepartmental Committee on Narcotics recommended toughening the Boggs Act and applying severe mandatory minimums to all traffickers and sellers, including first offenders. The FBN-dominated committee racialized and stigmatized "addict drug peddlers" as predisposed to delinquency and criminality, often members of urban juvenile gangs, disordered psychologically and particularly resistant to rehabilitation. The Eisenhower committee reserved true victim status for (implicitly white) addicts who engaged in no other criminal activity and urged state and local governments to provide better treatment through commitment to psychiatric hospitals followed by community-based supervision.[113] In April, Senator Daniel introduced the Narcotic Control Act by highlighting the teenage victims of dope pushers and declaring "open warfare on the illicit drug traffic," focused on heroin and marijuana. The bill doubled existing mandatory-minimum penalties for the importation or sale of both drugs, with no probation or suspended sentences for first offenders, and authorized life imprisonment or the death penalty for a third narcotics conviction or any sale of heroin to a minor. In the House, Representative Hale Boggs introduced similar legislation based on his own public hearings on the illicit narcotics trade and extensive consultation with the FBN. The Boggs report attributed dope peddling to juvenile gangs and "young hoodlums" and declared that the "addict trafficker is just as vicious a person as the nonaddict trafficker," deserving of equally severe punishment. Boggs also backed the possibility of probation for first offenders guilty only of possession, a loophole for "misguided youth" (i.e., deserving victims) that survived in the final package.[114]

The most significant opposition to the Narcotic Control Act of 1956 came from public health organizations and academic researchers who advocated a medical rather than law enforcement approach to drug addiction. The physicians leading the narcotics reform project for the New York Academy of Medicine denounced the criminalization of addiction and blamed the FBN for creating a "flourishing black market" that Daniel's law would inevitably expand. The American Psychiatric Association also emphasized that the heroin addict "is made a criminal by law," condemned the policy of "extreme punishment for peddler addicts," and endorsed provision of narcotics "under medically controlled conditions" to undercut the illicit market. Writing in *The Nation*, sociologist Alfred Lindesmith accused Anslinger of misleading Congress about the viability of the medical clinic approach and attacked the FBN's disastrous and futile multidecade crusade "to control the problem of drug addiction by prohibition and police suppression." Lindesmith also raised concerns about racial and socioeconomic discrimination in police enforcement of narcotics laws, an issue that had received almost no attention in the political discussion or media coverage of the Senate narcotics investigation.[115] Psychologist Isidor Chein's ethnographic research on juvenile narcotics users in nonwhite urban neighborhoods repudiated the "common belief that street gangs are the centers of organized drug selling activity," a prominent feature of news coverage and the rhetoric of drug warriors such as Harry Anslinger and Hale Boggs. Chein also found that, contrary to popular myth, "most [juvenile] addicts were not initiated into the habit by an adult narcotics peddler," but rather through friendship rituals, and that more than half of teenagers who experimented with marijuana and heroin never became habitual users or addicts.[116] None of these scientific findings proved any match for the pusher-victim, marijuana-to-heroin gateway, instantaneous/predatory addict, and other law enforcement tropes that prevailed in Congress with little dissent or even debate.

In July, the U.S. Senate and House of Representatives unanimously approved the Narcotic Control Act of 1956. The law established mandatory-minimum penalties for sale of narcotic drugs and marijuana of five to twenty years for the first offense and ten to forty years for subsequent convictions, with no possibility of probation or parole. An adult (eighteen or older) charged with selling or furnishing heroin to a minor faced a ten-year minimum and a maximum life sentence, with a jury option for the death penalty. Illegal possession of narcotics and marijuana carried a two-to-ten-year sanction for first offenders, with probation and suspended sentence possible, and mandatory five-to-twenty and ten-to-forty-year ranges for second and third convictions. The legislation further authorized deportation of immigrant aliens for any narcotics violation and addressed the Mexican border problem with an unenforceable requirement that illicit narcotics users register at federal customs stations before leaving the U.S.. The final version expanded the FBN's ability to undertake warrantless searches, although civil libertarians managed to remove a wiretapping provision sought by Anslinger. The brief deliberations in Congress seemed anticlimactic, even foreordained, after the six-month political theater orchestrated by Price Daniel's investigatory subcommittee. No member of the Senate opposed harsher punishment for narcotics traffickers, publicly questioned the equation of heroin and marijuana in the control structure, or challenged the framing of teenage drug users as "defenseless victims." Herbert Lehman, a liberal Democrat from New York, did criticize the failure to include federal funding for treatment, but he supported the bill despite skepticism of the exclusively "punitive and repressive approach." A few senators objected to the death penalty provision on religious grounds, but they also voted in favor and denounced dope pushers as "evil characters" and the "lowest form of humanity." President Dwight Eisenhower signed the Narcotic Control Act without fanfare on July 18.[117]

The political consensus behind the Narcotic Control Act of 1956 confirmed the bureaucratic power of the FBN and solidified the racial construction of an American drug market demarcated by evil nonwhite pushers, dangerous nonwhite addict-peddlers, helpless white victims, and the conflated threats of heroin and marijuana. In its year-end 1956 report, the Federal Bureau of Narcotics abandoned previous euphemisms and described the illegal narcotics market explicitly and almost exclusively as a problem "among Negroes" in the urban slums. While foreign traffickers and "Mexican smugglers" imported heroin, domestic distribution and street peddling ensued because of "illicit narcotic rings . . . among the Negroes" in the underworld. The FBN further emphasized the "close correlation between narcotics addiction and major crime" and provided a stark graphic "proving" that "Negro addicts" represented 61 percent of the national total despite being only one-tenth of the population (see fig. 1.1).[118] Although Anslinger remained opposed to classroom narcotics education, the FBN did produce a 1956 pamphlet called *The Living Death: The Truth about Drug Addiction* to warn youth never to experiment because "the smoking of the marihuana cigarette is a dangerous first step on the road which usually leads to enslavement by heroin." *The Living Death* redefined the recreational adolescent drug subculture as a "vicious environment" of contagion and exploitation where "teen-age addicts" provided heroin and marijuana to other youth in order to "snare" them and therefore generate funds for their own continued access to illegal drugs. The FBN categorized these so-called "addict-peddlers" as criminals in the "foulest racket in existence" and also threatened youth who even purchased illegal drugs with lengthy prison terms. For the rest of the decade, Anslinger continued to insist that narcotics crime and addiction remained a problem mainly in the Black slums of the urban North and publicly theorized that "Negroes" were simply "more susceptible" than white people to heroin addiction and related pathologies.[119]

After passage of the 1956 legislation, Commissioner Anslinger quickly returned to his standard portrayal of a narcotics problem under effective federal control, a political vision that depended on the continued maintenance of artificial divisions between white and nonwhite drug use and between medical/licit and criminal/illicit drug markets. During the lead-up to the Narcotic Control Act, the Boggs subcommittee hearings in the House revealed extensive abuse of illicit barbiturates and amphetamines, but the FBN's allies in Congress excluded these drugs from the federal mandatory-minimum structure in deference to fierce opposition from Anslinger and the pharmaceutical lobby. The FBN commissioner repeatedly drew a racialized and unscientific distinction between the dangerous underground market and the licit (and illicit) circulation of pharmaceutical drugs, including barely regulated amphetamines and barbiturates used and misused disproportionately by white middle-class Americans. Throughout his tenure, Anslinger advocated self-regulation for pharmaceutical companies and repeatedly denied the medical evidence that prescription tranquilizers and other legally manufactured barbiturates caused addiction (and far more deaths annually than heroin). Anslinger instead described the mission of the FBN and the pharmaceutical industry as mutually reinforcing: to "keep the narcotics traffic under control" by eliminating illicit competition so that the medical profession could heal people through legal opiates while law enforcement "remove[d] criminal addicts and peddlers from the street."[120] During the late 1950s, Commissioner Anslinger continued to denounce public health proposals to provide narcotics to licensed addicts through clinics and instead maintained that enforcement of the tougher federal and state laws had reduced illegal trafficking "almost to the vanishing point" in most of the United States. The FBN claimed that mandatory minimums had essentially eradicated narcotics addiction in Ohio and Washington, DC, and significantly diminished the problem in New York City, Chicago, and Los Angeles. Anslinger argued that local police could adequately address the lingering heroin problem in the Black ghettos of these cities, although he did concede that the FBN had not made "too much headway" in stopping marijuana from entering Southern California across the Mexican border.[121]

California Drug Enforcement and the Mexican Border

In September 1956, two months after the enactment of the Narcotic Control Act, an attorney in San Diego wrote to Senator Price Daniel asking if Congress had really intended for a five-year mandatory-minimum sentence to apply to his client, a twenty-one-year-old college student caught at the border with ten marijuana cigarettes. The young white man, who lived in the coastal community of Oceanside and had no prior criminal record, had driven to Tijuana with a nineteen-year-old friend and consumed alcohol before they paid $2.50 to a street dealer in a "moment of thoughtlessness." The attorney argued that the inflexible federal penalty for narcotics smuggling should not apply because "youngsters who are not peddlers nor addicts will from time to time experiment with marijuana cigarettes, the same as their fathers experimented with forbidden whiskey twenty-five years ago." Under California law, he noted, state judges retained considerable discretion for first offenders and would most likely have given a sentence of straight probation to his client, an otherwise law-abiding student who was "no different from thousands of other young men." Around the same time, a white father from a middle-income Los Angeles suburb wrote a letter to state officials asking for his brand-new car back, after the San Diego County sheriff's roadblock caught his nineteen-year-old son driving north from Tijuana with seven pounds of marijuana in the trunk. The father accepted the punishment for his adult son under California law, since the county prosecutor exercised the discretionary authority to transfer the older teenager to the juvenile court system, which sent the "irresponsible boy" to a youth facility for rehabilitation. Attorney General Pat Brown's office raised no objection to the relatively light penalty for the felony committed by this white marijuana smuggler but upheld the forfeiture of the car since "narcotics are such a horrible thing."[122]

Between the mid-1950s and the early 1960s, the war on narcotics in Southern California continued to intensify alongside recurring hype about marijuana and heroin spreading to the middle-class suburbs and the persistent inability of government officials to control white teenagers and young adults who crossed the Mexican border. According to the California Youth Authority, "scores of fine appearing boys and girls, many from good homes," traveled to Tijuana to buy marijuana (the "threshold drug") and soon became "hopelessly hooked on heroin." "Even the bobby soxers cross over the border" to buy drugs, a housewife from the upscale Orange County community of Corona del Mar reported in a letter to Governor Goodwin Knight, a rare acknowledgment from a suburban parent of the entrepreneurial network of white dealers and consumers on the middle-class side of the distribution system.[123] In late 1956, the Senate Subcommittee to Investigate Juvenile Delinquency emphasized the unique features of the metropolitan drug market in Southern California in hearings designed to highlight the need for better treatment facilities for teenage addicts, which liberal reformers considered the necessary complement to the tough penalties for pushers in the Narcotic Control Act. The Beverly Hills attorney who headed the Citizens' Advisory Committee on Crime Prevention, which devised policy for Attorney General Brown's war on narcotics, told the subcommittee that "it is simple and easy for young persons . . . [to] buy all the heroin and all the marijuana they want in Mexico." The narcotics problem in California therefore "cuts across all phases of society," had spilled from the big cities into the suburbs, and "has no connection whatever with race or locality"—a definite exception to Commissioner Anslinger's assurances that tough enforcement had contained the crisis to nonwhite urban slums. Brown's suburban advisor recommended closing the Mexican border to juveniles, hospitalizing addict-peddlers before they corrupted their friends, and claimed that "most, if not all, heroin addicts in California start in their teens through marijuana parties."[124]

In April 1957, Attorney General Brown convened a Good Neighbor Conference of American and Mexican officials to promote transnational cooperation between California and Baja California against narcotics traffickers and "uncontrolled juvenile crossings." Brown began by acknowledging the pressure from Southern California PTAs and law enforcement agencies for a complete ban on entry into Mexico by unaccompanied youth, which the State Department had rejected as unworkable and presumptively unconstitutional. Sheriff Bert Strand of San Diego County demanded tougher action from the Mexican government and blamed the "environment in Tijuana" for luring "children seeking thrills and adventure" across the border, where peddlers corrupted "good" teenagers with narcotics and pornography. Strand reported that his curfew enforcement and car blockade policy had accosted and thwarted at least ten thousand juveniles, a majority from Orange and Los Angeles counties, but extralegal action restricted to the evening hours could not solve the problem. The mayor of Tijuana then denounced the "offensive measure" of border restrictions and placed responsibility on American criminals and juvenile delinquents, whose numbers paled in comparison to the legitimate tourist traffic, fourteen million visitors annually. The conference ended without resolution, as Mexican delegates attributed the narcotics trade to American consumer demand (including military enlistees), and California enforcement officials fingered the heroin and marijuana suppliers who took "refuge behind some international boundary" (they did acknowledge that U.S. companies shipped the barbiturates and amphetamines in the illicit California market to Tijuana pharmacies). In subsequent public remarks, Brown praised his Mexican counterparts for increased cooperation but warned that narcotics enforcement in California could not succeed as long as traffickers south of the border operated with impunity. His office emphasized the federal government's ultimate responsibility and advocated a treaty with Mexico to extradite Tijuana kingpins such as "Big Mike" Bautista.[125]

Most suburban parents and civic organizations in Southern California denied any agency to white middle-class participants in the recreational drug market and instead advocated even tougher crackdowns on the villainous

FIGURE 1.5. U.S. customs inspectors at the San Diego, California, border station check automobiles returning from Tijuana, Mexico, November 11, 1958. Federal, state, and local authorities proved incapable of meaningfully impeding the ability of teenagers and young adults from Southern California to drive to Tijuana and bring back marijuana, heroin, and illicit amphetamines and barbiturates. (AP Photo.)

pushers and Mexican smugglers who allegedly victimized their children. In mid-1957, the Los Angeles County Council of Women endorsed the Ohio model of extreme mandatory penalties and urged California to adopt the federal policy of no probation or parole for "pushers" and indefinite confinement for all "addicts." In 1958, a San Fernando Valley affiliate of the California Federation of Women's Clubs recommended twenty years for first offenders and death for a second conviction "for dope peddlers pushing narcotics to minors." A petition drive in five Los Angeles suburbs called on Attorney General Brown to lobby the federal government to cut off all foreign aid to Mexico and other countries that refused to cooperate in controlling the cross-border flow of narcotics.[126] Occasionally, politicians received desperate letters from suburban parents of addicted children who recognized that the get-tough movement against dope pushers was not addressing the root problem. A father from Redondo Beach, for example, begged Governor Knight to support a narcotics hospital in California and asked why his son could not receive methadone legally as a substitute for heroin dependency.[127] But such voices gained little traction in a political culture organized around the systematic conflation of marijuana experimentation with hopeless heroin addiction and the racial construction of nonwhite and foreign pushers victimizing white middle-class youth. The mass media even hyped the exploits of an "attractive thirty-year-old housewife" in Orange County who went undercover to bust twenty dope (marijuana) peddlers working for a "big pusher" in Tijuana who "gladly destroyed the lives of children" out of greed. She volunteered for the dangerous job to rid her suburban community of narcotics and to show "that monster" that there were no limits "to what a mother will do when she feels her home and family are threatened."[128]

Law enforcement officials and their allies in the mainstream media shaped the punitive public ethos through distorted portrayals of the illicit drug market, especially by promoting unreliable arrest data that conflated sellers and users and maximized the alleged Mexican threat. In 1956, the LAPD and LACSD announced the success of an extensive undercover operation, "unparalleled in the history of the nation," after rounding up almost two hundred heroin and marijuana "pushers," targeting the Mexican American area of East Los Angeles. Narcotics squad officers celebrated the arrest of Jose Torres, the alleged mastermind importer of Mexican heroin, and claimed that most of the rest were "peddlers rather than addicts." The *Los Angeles Times* reprinted the LAPD's press release almost verbatim as an objective news article and praised the interagency crackdown and subsequent mass indictments as a major victory in the war on narcotics. A month later, a confidential state investigation revealed that "many of these weren't charges that were substantiated—they made a mass grab, hoping they could make a case on some of them." And despite initial claims, most of the arrests did involve users ("addicts") or small-scale street dealers, as was common in undercover busts; one superior court judge in Los Angeles County estimated that possession cases outnumbered "peddlers" by a twenty-to-one ratio.[129] An internal California Department of Justice assessment of narcotics arrests between 1955 and 1957 also emphasized the inaccuracy of police data, especially regarding teenage party busts, because "frequently officers take a large group into custody for investigation when only one defendant is actually guilty." Members of Attorney General Brown's staff expressed further surprise that, "notwithstanding all of the publicity to the

TABLE 1.3. Adult Felony Arrests, Convictions, and Dispositions for Narcotics Violations, California and Los Angeles County, 1953–58

Location/Category	1953	1954	1955	1956	1957	1958
California—Total arrests	6,612	7,457	7,313	9,140	10,353	10,440
California—Conviction %	31%	31%	25%	22%	22%	22%
California—Total convictions	2,076	2,343	1,834	1,974	2,291	2,342
Disposition—Prison	28%	34%	33%	43%	38%	37%
Disposition—Youth Authority	5%	5%	4%	6%	5%	5%
Disposition—Jail	50%	23%	24%	15%	16%	17%
Disposition—Probation	17%	38%	39%	35%	40%	41%
LA County—Total arrests	4,690	5,220	5,639	6,853	7,731	7,780
LA County—Conviction %	25%	27%	19%	17%	17%	19%
LA County—Total convictions	1,156	1,391	1,054	1,168	1,314	1,451
Disposition—Prison	21%	28%	25%	39%	34%	32%
Disposition—Youth Authority	5%	5%	4%	6%	6%	5%
Disposition—Jail	36%	24%	26%	16%	19%	19%
Disposition—Probation	37%	43%	45%	39%	44%	44%

Source: Bureau of Criminal Statistics, California Department of Justice, Exhibit in "Juvenile Delinquency," Part 5, *Hearings before the Subcommittee to Investigate Juvenile Delinquency, Committee on the Judiciary*, U.S. Senate, November 10, 1959, 728–30.

Note: California law permitted the discretionary transfer of adults ages eighteen to twenty to the juvenile justice system (Youth Authority). Prosecutors and judges generally diverted first offenders to misdemeanor jail or probation sentences under the loophole in the 1951 law, using the threat of felony incarceration as leverage to gain plea bargains.

contrary," arrest totals for both Mexican Americans and juveniles were substantially lower than media coverage would seem to indicate. State officials did recognize that female drug violators were underrepresented in the official data because of the "reluctance to commit women and girls to penal and correctional institutions."[130]

Statistical records from California and from Los Angeles County reveal that most adult drug arrests during the mid-1950s did not lead to felony prosecutions, and that a majority of guilty verdicts resulted in probation or a short jail term rather than a prison sentence (table 1.3). These disposition trends illuminate the extensive use of the first offender loophole by prosecutors and judges, especially the unwillingness to apply mandatory-minimum narcotics penalties to the marijuana market and to the possession violators that police primarily detained. The surprisingly large gap between felony arrests and successful prosecutions reflects not only the diversionary techniques common to the criminal legal system but also dismissals and acquittals resulting from fruitless investigative detentions and rampant police misconduct. The routine tactics of narcotics enforcement included extralegal investigative arrests, undercover entrapment operations, anonymous informants, and searches of persons, cars, and homes based on intuition and suspicion—methods that revolved around profiling based on race and ethnicity, socioeconomic class, age, and geographic location. As one LA County prosecutor observed, California law "authorized a narcotic officer to grab the contraband whenever and wherever he could, go into court, and prove that the defendant had possession of that contraband and that he knew it was a narcotic, and no questions would be asked or be permitted relating to how the officer got that contraband." This legal landscape changed with the 1955 *Cahan* decision, when the California Supreme Court adopted the federal exclusionary rule and limited the introduction of evidence obtained by illegal or unreasonable means of search and seizure. Law enforcement agencies protested this constitutional doctrine vehemently and blamed the subsequent 10 percent decline in conviction rates on excessive judicial scrutiny of their methods. The district attorney in San Francisco even warned a conference of narcotics officers that the state courts were becoming less tolerant of standard police practices such as fabricating the existence of informants and "committing perjury . . . to avoid the implications of the *Cahan* case."[131]

The bipartisan get-tough political consensus in 1950s California rested on a fundamental, and often willful, distortion of how the intersection between drugs markets and law enforcement really operated. Internal documents from multiple state agencies reveal a clear understanding, as leading bureaucrats informed Governor Knight as early as 1953, that "extreme penalties will not accomplish your objective." At decade's end, the California Board of Corrections reported that the rate of narcotics arrests (adjusted for population) had doubled between 1952 and 1957 but the conviction totals had barely risen, meaning that a "tremendous amount of police activity" had accomplished almost nothing even as illegal drug use escalated. During 1958 legislative hearings, a Los Angeles County judge rejected conservative attacks that the judiciary was soft on narcotics for primarily utilizing the probation option, explaining that the police arrested very few "real narcotics peddlers" and that two-thirds of those sent to trial were young, disadvantaged Mexican American and Black males, most busted for marijuana or heroin possession. Every once in a while, one of these stigmatized drug criminals received a platform and spoke the truth that elected officials denied or could not comprehend. The same hearings hauled a young Mexican American man out of state prison for an interrogation about his actions as a marijuana "pusher" in Los Angeles. He began by telling the legislators that everything the government of California said about narcotics was a "fallacy." He mocked the mythology that "proverbial dope pushers" gave away free samples and seduced "some child . . . pouring a few drops of heroin in his arm." Asked if heroin caused rapes and violence, he replied, "No, never," because it was a depressant, whereas both alcohol and amphetamine made some people belligerent. Asked if marijuana did, he patiently explained that the nonaddictive drug made users relaxed and hungry. The witness concluded by stating that their punitive laws had no impact on the market, that bringing drugs across the border was easy, and that youth of all races smoked reefer for kicks.[132]

The hype about the juvenile narcotics crisis in Southern California during the mid-to-late 1950s also belied the small number of drug-related arrests compared to other forms of youth delinquency, all criminalized and regulated through a discretionary and racially discriminatory system of social control dedicated to coercive rehabilitation and lacking basic due process. During 1957, for example, law enforcement agencies arrested 238,376 juveniles in the state of California, with three-fourths of these cases involving traffic violations or the status offenses of "delinquent tendencies" and "dependency" (table 1.4). Formal "law violations" represented one-fourth of juvenile arrests, a 90 percent male cohort primarily detained for theft, burglary, or assault. Narcotics offenses constituted just 2 percent of these crimes—concentrated in LA County and almost always involving marijuana, barbiturates, or amphetamines—although authorities estimated (optimistically) that they only caught 10 percent of juveniles in the illegal drug market. The police handled almost half of detained minors informally and referred the rest to the juvenile justice system, which placed most adjudicated delinquents on probation and sentenced about 6 percent of those arrested for law violations (defined as the "young hoodlums" and "hard core") to Youth Authority detention centers. The state tracked racial data only at the referral and commitment stages, which reveal that Mexican American and African American youth were slightly more likely to be referred for adjudication but then disproportionately incarcerated.[133] Discriminatory treatment was particularly pronounced in Los Angeles County, where narcotics referrals in the late 1950s included 47 percent white youth, 38 percent Mexican American (4 times the population share), and 7.5 percent African American. While the majority received probation, state data revealed that three-fourths of the juveniles categorized as narcotics users and incarcerated for "rehabilitation" in Youth Authority facilities by the late 1950s had primarily "experimented" with marijuana, not been arrested for heroin.[134]

TABLE 1.4. Juvenile Arrests and Dispositions, California and Los Angeles County, 1957

Category	California	LA County
Total juvenile arrests	238,376	N/A
Juvenile arrests—Law violations	58,502 (25%)	23,012
Law violation arrests—Male total and %	52,599 (90%)	20,865 (90%)
Law violations—Handled informally	24,373 (42%)	11,131 (48%)
Law violations—Referred to social agencies	3,278 (6%)	1,534 (7%)
Law violations—Referred to juvenile system	30,851 (53%)	10,347 (45%)
Narcotics arrests—Total and % of law violations	1,224 (2%)	N/A
Narcotics arrests—Referred to juvenile system	624 (51%)	469
Male law violation referrals—White race	74.8%	65.9%
Male law violation referrals—Mexican descent	13.9%	18.5%
Male law violation referrals—Negro race	9.9%	14.8%
Youth Authority commitments—Total	3,345	N/A
Youth Authority commitments—White race	58.8%	N/A
Youth Authority commitments—Mexican descent	20.7%	N/A
Youth Authority commitments—Negro race	18.2%	N/A

Source: Bureau of Criminal Statistics, *Delinquency and Probation in California, 1957.*

Note: The racial breakdown of LA County (1960 census) was roughly 81% white (non-Hispanic), 10% Mexican American, and 7.5% Black (racial designations in table are from original source).

In early 1958, Attorney General Pat Brown launched a new narcotics awareness crusade aimed directly at white middle-class parents and presented through the framework of suburban crisis. The state initiative revolved around public distribution of *The Narcotics Story,* a police training film made in 1957 and originally titled *Goof Balls and Tea.* The dramatization tells the ostensibly true saga of "Joyce," a white middle-class heroin addict, to "deter others from falling victims to this living death." The film opens with an aerial shot of suburban tract housing in metro LA and ominous narration that narcotics is no longer just a "city story" but now a "problem that knows no boundaries." The scenes jump rapidly from narcotics smuggling across the border, to white teenagers dancing in a malt shop, to a blonde female "hophead" being interrogated in a police station. In a series of flashbacks, this main character progresses from an innocent girl in a wholesome neighborhood to an "unsupervised adolescent" drawn to parties where other white youth introduce her to illicit "goof balls" (barbiturates) and a clean-cut male "pusher" distributes free samples to create "marijuana addicts." The film shows beat cops how to profile and apprehend sneaky teenagers who smoke reefer in parked cars and back alleys, by deciphering their jive talk and taking caution with these potentially violent "addicts." The white marijuana dealer operates out of the malt shop, which turns out to be a front acquired by a major narcotics pusher (the only ethnic character, apparently Italian American) to infiltrate the suburban community. Joyce, his "new victim," progresses rapidly from marijuana experimentation in suburban social settings to heroin addiction in the kingpin's network of male addict-peddlers and young female junkie-prostitutes who descend into urban slums. The heroic police officers arrest everyone in this criminal pyramid by working their way upward from street busts of suburban thrill-seekers to the "vicious and ruthless" mastermind pusher. But it is too late to save Joyce, with either death or medical institutionalization her inevitable fate.[135]

The impact of *The Narcotics Story* illuminates the dynamic feedback loop between the state of California's escalation of the war on narcotics and the mobilization of citizen crusaders who demanded harsher penalties for pushers in order to protect suburban youth. As a political strategy, Pat Brown's initiative was simultaneously responding to the persistent grassroots pressure from civic groups and women's clubs in the white suburbs and burnishing his tough-on-narcotics credentials as part of his campaign for governor in 1958. The California Bureau of Narcotic Enforcement consulted on the production of *The Narcotics Story* and previewed the film for select audiences in Los Angeles and nearby suburban cities such as Pasadena and Glendale, eliciting overwhelmingly positive feedback from the invited teachers, students, social workers, religious leaders, and housewives. Brown then endorsed the "truly authentic . . . documentary" as a public wake-up call, declaring that "it's time we got tough" on the narcotics trade, and related that the teenage daughter "of a prominent family" said she never would have tried marijuana and become a heroin addict if she had only seen it first. *The Narcotics Story* opened in commercial theaters in addition to state distribution to public schools and civic organizations, despite the protests of LAPD chief William Parker and Catholic censorship groups that it violated the Motion Picture Production Code by detailing the methods of rolling marijuana cigarettes and injecting heroin.[136] Brown's awareness campaign received grateful feedback from suburban clubs and high school audiences in Southern California, but the attorney general also faced immediate pressure from a petition drive started by civic groups in suburban Los Angeles that secured more than one million signatures demanding a thirty-year mandatory sentence for narcotics pushers. William Knowland, the Republican gubernatorial nominee, further attacked Brown for ineffective narcotics enforcement and failing to prevent a surge in youth addiction, but the liberal Democrat trounced his conservative opponent in the 1958 election.[137]

The grassroots suburban campaign to save white middle-class victims from evil pushers and Mexican traffickers reached a crescendo during 1959–60, with state officials and media outlets actively shaping the public perception of nonwhite and foreign threats. In February 1959, soon after Brown's inauguration as governor, the California Board of Corrections released a major narcotics report that portrayed marijuana use and heroin addiction as "urban phenomena . . . to be found chiefly among underprivileged groups" in "ethnically mixed depressed neighborhoods," especially delinquent Mexican American youth with "neighborhood gang associations" (with African Americans also overrepresented compared to white Anglos). The state constructed this racial knowledge by extrapolating data based on adult prisoners and juvenile wards to the state population as a whole, a fallacious methodology that did not contemplate the discretionary and discriminatory features of the criminal legal system.[138] That same year, Governor Brown received a deluge of letters and petitions from parents and civic groups in the segregated white suburbs of Los Angeles County, especially those located near the Mexican American and African American enclaves south and east of downtown (see fig. 1.4). A number of correspondents attached newspaper articles about Mexican smugglers, or named specific Mexican American street peddlers who had corrupted their children, and demanded tougher penalties to safeguard "law abiding citizens and teenagers." The Lakewood Women's Club organized a form letter campaign demanding a twenty-year mandatory sentence without parole for dope pushers and the closing of the Mexican border to minors. Similar protests came from constituents in Norwalk, Whittier, Redondo Beach, and Pasadena. A Culver City man called for "all-out war on 'pushers'" to protect the daughters of California from becoming addict-prostitutes, and a woman from Torrance blamed the "teenagers of these Mexican families" in nearby San Pedro for bringing narcotics across the border and supplying "our young people."[139]

In June 1959, the *Los Angeles Times* escalated the racial and international politics of the Southern California narcotics crisis with an explosive weeklong series about the white middle-class victims of Mexican smugglers and pushers. The opening article announced an agenda to awaken the public to the illegal drug traffic coming from Mexico and juxtaposed a heroin wholesaler in East Los Angeles with a seventeen-year-old blonde girl, "cute as a button," confessing marijuana use to the sympathetic police. Then author Gene Sherman reported undercover from Tijuana, a "vile, vice-strewn sump hole of civilization," where street peddlers sold marijuana and heroin to American youth and the corrupt Mexican government did nothing about the major traffickers who flooded the California market. The next installment on the tragic casualties of these narcotics pushers profiled white teenagers from good backgrounds who progressed from marijuana to heroin: a lost boy from an "excellent family" who bought drugs in East LA; a "strikingly beautiful" girl first corrupted by older men at a house party; an eighteen-year-old male on probation despite an "exceptionally high IQ"; a "sweet, innocent-appearing" sixteen-year-old addict-prostitute. "Kids start on marijuana," the article proclaimed. "Marijuana comes from Mexico." The series then emphasized that narcotics addicts frequently committed crimes and were disproportionately Mexican American and African American, without deploying any individual stories of lost innocence to humanize these racial groups. The final article provided police a platform to criticize judges who dismissed cases for illegal search and seizure and asked if the law should "give a dope peddler more protection than his prospective victims." This racist and xenophobic *Los Angeles Times* series, which received the Pulitzer Prize for public service journalism, generated immediate demands from Democratic and Republican politicians in California for tougher border enforcement and increased federal pressure on Mexico, whose diplomats retorted with an angry defense of their country's "relentless war" on narcotics.[140]

Governor Pat Brown promptly declared a comprehensive war to shut down the "vicious" and "inhuman" narcotics traffickers and praised the *Los Angeles Times* for alarming the public and highlighting the federal government's responsibility to combat international supply lines. Brown called on judges to hand down "much stiffer sentences for this vicious crime against our youth," a concise summation of the resilient pusher-victim binary that infused the vision of elected officials, media outlets, and the white middle-class public at large. To dramatize the crisis, a state legislative committee presented the shocking testimony of the anonymous "Miss Jones," a narcotics addict who started smoking marijuana at age sixteen with a crowd of white suburban teenagers before securing a heroin connection through a Mexican-born smuggler. She warned lawmakers that all of the "big dope peddlers are moving out" into the residential suburbs of LA and "you used to find it in Mexican and the colored [areas], but now you can find it with everybody."[141] In the months after the *Times* series, Governor Brown received get-tough letters from "apprehensive parents who live near the Mexican border," a woman frightened by the "dope evils . . . coming out of Mexico," and a suburban Glendale group that demanded diplomatic coercion of the Mexican government to halt the narcotics invasion.[142] Many constituents criticized his refusal to support a bill, sponsored by Democratic legislators from suburban Los Angeles, to increase mandatory minimums and eliminate the probation option for first offenders. Brown, along with prosecutors from LA County and other metropolitan centers, argued for the discretionary justice of indeterminate sentencing and maintained that excessively severe penalties would reduce conviction rates by judges and juries. The governor also continued to champion a statewide program for the rehabilitation of addicts, in recognition that drug treatment was "almost nonexistent" in jails and prisons and in effect available only to those affluent enough to afford a small number of expensive private facilities.[143]

Inspired by the *Times* exposé, the Senate Subcommittee to Investigate Juvenile Delinquency came to California in November 1959 for a week of televised hearings on the problem of youth crossing the Mexican border and the "spectacular rise in crime" by teenage gangs. On the opening day in Los Angeles, the senators sounded the alarm by reporting regular marijuana use among "a large group of students from upper middle class families," including an alleged 59 percent of junior high pupils in a white beachfront suburb. The subcommittee's investigator blamed "moral contamination in the sordid atmosphere of Tijuana," where pushers provided marijuana and narcotics to American teenagers, and played an undercover recording of a Mexican American dealer in East LA who smuggled heroin across the border. LAPD officials attributed the drug supply to "big peddlers" from Mexico, claimed that juvenile gangs "composed largely of people of Mexican extraction" committed almost half of major crimes in the city, and blasted the *Cahan* ruling for handcuffing narcotics enforcement. Sheriff Peter Pitchess of Los Angeles County denounced narcotics peddlers as "ruthless predatory animals" and demanded that the legislature enact "drastic mandatory penalties . . . for these loathsome creatures." During the San Diego hearings, the police department boasted of stopping more than 12,500 juveniles from entering Tijuana since its border checkpoint became a 24-hour operation in mid-1958—a policy of dubious legality when enforced beyond curfew, and often circumvented by teenagers who just drove through Mexicali. Although some witnesses admitted that American consumers created the market for Tijuana vice, most state and local officials continued to attack Mexico for causing California's drug crisis and demanded federal action to "stop these kids from going across." Commissioner Anslinger responded by defending Mexico's cooperation in narcotics enforcement and instead attributed the illicit trade to California's weak laws, especially loopholes that let "evil traffickers" and dangerous addicts avoid prison.[144]

In this volatile and punitive climate, the narcotics-related murder of a white high school student in suburban Los Angeles escalated the grassroots and bipartisan crusade for tougher state action by Southern California politicians, civic groups, and ordinary families. In late January 1960, two white teenage heroin users shot and killed seventeen-year-old Leonard Moore during a botched drive-in robbery in the segregated middle-class community of Lakewood. Moore's parents appeared on television to plead for stricter laws to deter narcotics pushers, and several hundred youth from Lakewood-area high schools formed the Student Crusade Against Narcotics and traveled to Sacramento to lobby Governor Brown to call an emergency legislative session.[145] The LA County Board of Supervisors, joined by their counterparts in four other Southern California counties, demanded "an all-out, State-wide war on narcotics" and new legislation to guarantee "stringent, mandatory sentences on narcotics peddlers." Meeting in Los Angeles, three hundred law enforcement and civic leaders, elected officials, and media representatives formed the Southern California Narcotics Council and unanimously endorsed this initiative. Supervisor Kenneth Hahn, a liberal law-and-order Democrat and the coalition's ringleader, labeled the criminal justice system a "revolving door," proposed the indeterminate quarantine of dope addicts, and charged that innocent Californians were "paying for a whole era of softness toward criminals and crime."[146] The *Los Angeles Times* continued its political crusade against Mexican smugglers, inadequate state penalties for narcotics pushers, lenient judges who abused their discretionary authority, and the Brown administration's "pious protestations of rehabilitation." Please protect "innocent children" from the "dope pushers," implored a female high school student from Covina. "We parents are fed up," wrote a Hollywood mother who believed that Brown deserved impeachment. "California is the pushers paradise," declared an enraged Long Beach man who predicted a day of political reckoning for the governor and his allies.[147]

In March 1960, Governor Brown delivered a major statement on the narcotics crisis that strongly defended California's indeterminate sentencing policy "to make the punishment fit the criminal," which enabled the lengthy incarceration of dangerous offenders and the coercive rehabilitation of the "addicts." In an effort to defuse the pressure from Southern California, Brown announced an enhanced "war on the narcotics menace" that included a state task force to target "major profiteers," special addiction treatment funding for metropolitan

Los Angeles, and a narcotics crime commission led by law enforcement officials. The governor did, however, reject as unconstitutional the LA County proposal to override *Cahan* by allowing evidence in narcotics trials regardless of "the manner in which it was obtained." Brown also pledged again to pressure the federal government to address the source problem in Mexico and endorsed a bipartisan congressional resolution for a White House Conference on Narcotics to promote more effective border controls. Notably, the governor heeded staff advice to "not use a discussion of narcotics to belabor your belief in civil rights," meaning that he made the case for rehabilitation in race-neutral language rather than emphasizing that inflexible penalties and abolition of parole would disproportionately affect nonwhite "addict-peddlers" and possession offenders.[148] Indeed, LAPD chief William Parker immediately attacked Brown's stance by highlighting Mexican American narcotics pushers arrested while on parole, although most of his examples involved distorted evidence. In the aftermath, more than fifty women's groups in suburban Los Angeles, mostly from the San Gabriel Valley and the coastal communities south of downtown, sent petitions and resolutions demanding that Brown support lengthier punishment and parole abolition for narcotics felons. "The narcotics peddler is treated far too soft," a San Fernando Valley man informed the governor. "You seem to be more bent on saving a criminal than protecting the innocent." Brown's files contain thousands of similarly enraged constituent letters sent during the early 1960s as part of this grassroots white suburban mobilization.[149]

In early 1961, Governor Brown announced his endorsement of legislation to increase narcotics penalties and restrict parole eligibility as long as state lawmakers preserved the discretionary probation option for first offenders deserving of rehabilitation. Brown further proposed the indefinite civil commitment of addicts and a state registry to track narcotics offenders after their release. His narcotics commission had recommended this more punitive approach, calling for probation only in "exceptional" cases and emphasizing that "an addict-peddler is just as great a menace to society as is a non-addict peddler."[150] Brown's revised position embraced key aspects of the get-tough legislative program devised by the Los Angeles County Board of Supervisors and sponsored by Democratic legislators, including a new narcotics exception to the correctional system's practice of discretionary early release of felons who had served at least one-third of their terms. The Republican party fiercely condemned the governor's insistence on the probation option and refusal to eviscerate the exclusionary rule against illegal search and seizure. During the

TABLE 1.5. Penalty Structure of Regan-Dills Act of 1961

Category	1st offense (parole minimum)	2nd offense (parole minimum)	3rd offense (parole minimum)
Narcotic (except marijuana)			
Possession	2–10 yrs. (2 yrs.)	5–20 yrs. (5 yrs.)	15–life (15 yrs.)
Possession, intent to sell	5–15 yrs. (2.5 yrs.)	10–life (6 yrs.)	15–life (15 yrs.)
Sale, trafficking, import	5–life (3 yrs.)	10–life (10 yrs.)	15–life (15 yrs.)
Provision to minor (21 yrs. +)	10–life (5 yrs.)	10–life (10 yrs.)	15–life (15 yrs.)
Provision to minor (18–20 yrs.)	5–life (no min.)	10–life (no min.)	No parole possible
Marijuana			
Possession	1–10 yrs. (1 yr.)	2–20 yrs. (2 yrs.)	5–life (5 yrs.)
Possession, intent to sell	2–10 yrs. (2 yrs.)	5–15 yrs. (3 yrs.)	10–life (6 yrs.)
Sale, trafficking, import	5–life (3 yrs.)	5–life (5 yrs.)	10–life (10 yrs.)
Provision to minor (21 yrs. +)	10–life (5 yrs.)	10–life (10 yrs.)	15–life (15 yrs.)

Source: Statutes of California, 1960 and 1961, vol. 1, 1301–9.

Note: The mandatory-minimum felony structure in the Regan-Dills Act contained a loophole permitting probation or suspended sentence for any first-offense category except for provision of narcotics to a minor by a person age 21 or older. Possession violators were eligible for diversion through a civil commitment program established in a parallel law. The California penal code allowed the Adult Authority to grant parole after one-third of the minimum felony sentence, so this statute created a more stringent set of parole guidelines for narcotics and marijuana convictions. The law deployed "narcotic" as a catch-all label for all illegal drugs except for marijuana and specifically exempted medical prescriptions.

debate, Brown warned that extreme penalties and anything-goes policing would be racially discriminatory because "most narcotics offenders are members of minority races and are most often from the lower income brackets," a stance that the *Los Angeles Times* denounced as "special treatment" for nonwhite criminals. The governor came under sustained criticism for softness and weakness from the LAPD, LACSD, Republican leaders, Democratic politicians in LA County, and a groundswell of constituents demanding an immediate and ruthless crackdown. In the end, Brown compromised on the first offender provision and signed a package that received overwhelming bipartisan support. The Regan-Dills Act of 1961 toughened narcotics penalties, severely restricted early parole, created the new offense category of possession with intent to sell, and barred probation for all repeat offenders and for adults age twenty-one and over who provided heroin to minors (table 1.5).[151]

The Regan-Dills Act of 1961 marked a culmination of the state of California's decade-long war on narcotics peddlers and predatory addicts, a campaign thoroughly shaped by the racialized pusher-victim framework, the political mobilization of the white middle-class suburbs, the discretionary features of the criminal justice system, and the punitive overlap between the law enforcement and public health spheres. After signing the law, Pat Brown boasted that his administration had enacted "the toughest program to control narcotics of any state in the nation," while resisting the "sheer hysteria" of extremists and irresponsible critics who opposed mercy for first offenders and rejected the rehabilitative ethos. As an example of "humane" public health policy, the liberal Democrat and his allies celebrated a coercive rehabilitation provision that authorized civil commitment of heroin addicts for six months to ten years, enacted alongside a surveillance mandate that narcotics felons register with local police for five years following release from prison.[152] The Regan-Dills Act did draw a new distinction between possession of marijuana versus more dangerous narcotics, but the retention of similar penalties for sale and for provision to minors revealed that the pusher-victim and gateway-to-heroin mythologies remained intact. In 1962, Brown appeared before the U.S. Senate Subcommittee to Investigate Juvenile Delinquency to report on the success of California's crackdown on the "murderous enterprise" of marijuana and heroin trafficking, which he claimed had combined with the civil commitment program to "remove hundreds of peddlers and thousands of addicts from the streets." Back in 1950, the governor recalled, "evil peddlers" could only receive a maximum six-year sentence, but the threat of life in prison and the "heavy new" minimum penalties in the Regan-Dills Act had empowered law enforcement and (allegedly) deterred many narcotics criminals. He did concede that the porous Mexican border remained a major vulnerability, which meant that only strong federal intervention could bring the smuggling of heroin, marijuana, and illicit pharmaceuticals under full control. "In this war," Pat Brown declared, "we can never declare a truce."[153]

In postwar California, the repeated escalation of mandatory-minimum penalties reflected a basic political consensus around the racialized pusher-victim interpretation of the illegal drug marketplace. So did the belief that the criminal justice system required discretionary loopholes to rehabilitate wayward youth—particularly teenagers from "good families" and white suburban neighborhoods—when they violated the laws designed to safeguard their innocence. But what would it mean to grant white middle-class youth the agency of full political subjects and consider the internal causes of their stigmatized social practices, including responsibility for delinquent and criminal/criminalized activities? In the mid-1950s, the state of California took the unusual step of soliciting advice from delegates to a Youth Conference on Narcotics, which resolved that illegal drug use "starts in an unhappy situation in the home and a craving for excitement." This assessment fit within the emerging psychological model of suburban delinquency, which blamed the law-breaking behavior of white middle-class youth on distorted parenting practices that caused maladjusted personalities and on the thrill-seeking immaturity of the teenage subculture. When given a chance to speak, however, illegal drug users from white middle-class communities rarely blamed their parents, never accused pushers, and generally took responsibility for their own recreational choices. Despite the reflexive pusher-victim binary that infused the 1959 *Los Angeles Times* exposé of malevolent Mexicans and Mexican Americans corrupting innocent white youth, each of the profiled white middle-class "addicts" appeared to have purposefully pursued illicit drugs. "I dig pot. It's cool," explained a teenage male with sophisticated knowledge of where to track down dealers in Los Angeles County. "We usually toke up every weekend," another unapologetic marijuana smoker and occasional heroin user acknowledged, with multiple arrests for possession not seeming to have inhibited his lifestyle. As the white middle-class juvenile delinquents of the 1950s turned into the political rebels of the 1960s, this unresolvable suburban crisis moved to the epicenter of America's war on drugs.[154]

2

Suburban Rebels

IN 1966, as civil rights marches and campus demonstrations against the Vietnam War rocked the nation, CBS-TV traveled to the St. Louis suburb of Webster Groves to investigate the youth generation and "the America we are becoming—affluent, suburban, and secure." The upper-middle-class, 96 percent white bedroom community became the subject of *16 in Webster Groves*, a prime-time documentary designed in consultation with academic sociologists to explore "children of abundance, of privilege." What CBS purported to discover—contrary to assumptions of a white middle-class adolescent "world of rebellion, dissatisfaction, and adventure"—was a dominant suburban ethos of conformity, materialism, contentment, and insularity. One after another, white teens tell the cameras that they are "perfectly happy," that they want to get married and have children, make money and achieve status, live in nice houses with two cars just like the ones they are growing up in, in a community just like Webster Groves. Their parents express the exact same values and aspirations. The main complaint of the youth is that the pressure to make good grades and get into top colleges is extremely stressful. Then the reporter asks a group of upscale white parents what would happen if one of their children participated in a civil rights protest. The parents, who clearly had never considered the possibility, say this is "ridiculous" and "what business is it of theirs," joke about spanking them, and agree that no "sixteen-year-old child should be burdened with the problems of the world." In a final scene, a group of teenagers ponders the same question and responds that recent visits to the downtown St. Louis slums had made them "feel guilty" for their privilege and realize "what a sheltered life I really have had." One earnest female explains that the reason youth rebel is because they eventually find out what the world is really like, and "you begin to wonder whether people have been honest with you all your life." Her friend then says, verging on tears, "When I grow up, I wish that there's something, or now, anything, that I could do."[1]

During the mid-to-late 1960s, the prevailing depiction of white middle-class youth shifted rapidly from a silent generation of sheltered conformists to an activist and alienated cohort of suburban rebels. The periodic obsession with the twin crises of "juvenile delinquency" and "narcotics addiction" in white middle-class suburbs, which had ebbed and flowed since the mid-1950s, expanded into a full-scale generational rebellion with the surge of protests on college campuses, the "hippie" migration to urban countercultural enclaves, and mass refusal to obey the drug prohibition laws. Some of these high school students from Webster Groves undoubtedly went on to become college rebels, political activists, marijuana felons, suburban "runaways," hippie dropouts, and perhaps even class traitors as well. There is no question that a large majority of these "children of privilege" were already breaking the juvenile delinquency laws designed to control the adolescent subculture, in particular the status offense of underage consumption of alcohol. In a follow-up documentary, the same sixteen-year-olds inform CBS-TV that there is "a lot more drinking" in Webster Groves than most parents and the authorities admitted. They also insist that the adult and youth generations were living in "two different worlds" on everything from political consciousness about the Vietnam War to awareness of how often the teenagers drove out of their segregated suburb to explore downtown St. Louis. "Your mom doesn't know half the stuff you do," one white female tells her friend—the daughter of two parents who had adamantly defended the need to protect their children in a safe, segregated suburban bubble—as the entire group of teenagers laughs in solidarity. A few years later, a congressional investigation even labeled one Webster Groves high school senior a New Left "subversive," based on secret FBI surveillance files, because he traveled to Chicago with five other St. Louis–area youth activists to participate in the Students for a Democratic Society/Weatherman "Days of Rage" protest against racial injustice and the Vietnam War.[2]

The "generation gap" explanation for the activism, alienation, and escalating rates of illegal drug use by white middle-class youth during the second half of the 1960s placed a broad spectrum of social practices and criminalized activities into the political framework of suburban rebellion. By this time, law enforcement agencies and the broader American political culture were on a mission to defuse the radical threat of white New Left activists, stamp out the explosion of marijuana and LSD use on college campuses and in affluent suburbs, and redefine the counterculture as a "hippie runaway" crisis of lost suburban daughters victimized by heroin addiction, dope pushers, and nonwhite gangs in the urban slums. But the roots of this youth rebellion actually began a decade earlier—with the seemingly sudden emergence of a white middle-class delinquency "epidemic" in the recently built, racially segregated white suburbs during the mid-1950s. Experts and politicians blamed the external threats of violent mass media and evil dope pushers and the internal problem of psychological maladjustment caused by improper and permissive parenting practices. This construction of a new delinquency crisis among "normal" white teenagers reflected real social practices by the postwar youth generation, in particular the freedom and autonomous spaces provided by the automobile-centered suburban landscape. The adolescent car culture facilitated widespread violation of status offense laws against alcohol consumption and illicit sexual relations, along with a small but growing recreational marijuana subculture and experimentation with other illegal drugs. The sustained middle-class delinquency crisis also exposed the bankruptcy of the utopian quest to shield white children from urban crime and disorder through the racist policies that built and defended segregated single-family suburbs. As a 1956 family manual by a California state agency advocated, protecting youth from crime and delinquency required living among "a homogeneous population welded together by similar racial, cultural and economic backgrounds."[3]

Policymakers and law enforcement agencies in metropolitan America designed a racially discriminatory system to regulate and control the adolescent subculture through status offense laws that potentially criminalized almost every feature of everyday life, combined with discretionary procedures to divert detained college-bound youth from "good families" and white middle-class neighborhoods without scarring them with a formal juvenile record. For these impossible criminals, police departments and juvenile justice authorities occasionally required psychiatric counseling, narcotics addiction treatment, or other forms of coercive rehabilitation, but most of the time they just released affluent suburban youth to the custody of their parents with a stern warning that sometime down the line there would be consequences. The juvenile justice system, based on total statutory discretion and the absence of basic due process rights for adjudicated delinquents until the Supreme Court's 1967 *Gault* decision, produced substantially different outcomes for youth who violated the same criminal laws and status prohibitions, depending by explicit design on variables such as race, gender, geography, high school grades, college aspirations, family income, and perceived level of parental involvement. These social control policies for juveniles, as implemented in the fast-growing postwar suburbs, reinforced and intensified metropolitan racial and economic inequalities but also were extraordinarily futile in preventing affluent white youth from engaging in the vast range of criminalized actions and leisure activities that fell under the delinquency umbrella.[4] The inevitable failure of the utopian suburban formula, refracted through media sensationalism and political processes, brought the recurring outbreak of dystopian suburban crisis. A relatively small number of marijuana smokers became a generation in revolt; a few white middle-class heroin addicts augured a racialized urban invasion; the sudden "hippie dropout" phenomenon meant that white children had adopted "ghetto" values and lost all ambition; rising youth political activism must be part of a drug-fueled radical insurgency that threatened the nation's foundations.

The white suburban delinquency crisis of the 1950s and early 1960s structured the emergence of this politicized generation gap and decisively shaped every major drug law and policy shift during a decade when many high school and especially college students were in open rebellion against everything from traditional moral codes to the Vietnam War. Investigations of white middle-class drug use conducted by liberal Democrats on the Senate Subcommittee to Investigate Juvenile Delinquency played a central role in each landmark federal law enacted during the 1960s, usually modeled on narcotics legislation first established in California, where the suburban youth crisis continued to operate as a national bellwether. The federal government criminalized unlicensed distribution of amphetamines and barbiturates in 1965, and added LSD when its use expanded on college campuses in 1966, but did not make illicit possession a crime based on a stated desire not to punish the "victims" in a white drug market. Congress also created a diversionary civil commitment alternative to the mandatory-minimum narcotics laws in 1966, amid media hype about heroin invading the suburbs and lost white daughters becoming urban addict-prostitutes, and then criminalized LSD possession in 1968 (although only as a misdemeanor) during a perceived "suburban runaway" crisis to dangerous hippie slums. President Lyndon Johnson distinguished between urban narcotics traffickers who deserved lengthy incarceration and the "spread" of marijuana and LSD to college campuses and suburbs, where the so-called victims required coercive medical treatment. As the Johnson administration launched a punitive war on urban street crime, targeting young Black males, this racialized binary between locking up menacing narcotics criminals and psychologically rehabilitating their white middle-class victims shaped the policies of the Federal Bureau of Narcotics, J. Edgar Hoover's FBI, and state and local governments at all levels. It also laid the suburban foundation for the Comprehensive Drug Abuse Prevention and Control Act of 1970 (see chapter 4).

American culture and policy generally operate to deny young people a collective political voice, but the scale of the white generational revolt of the mid-to-late 1960s encouraged analysis of their illegal drug use through a political prism—one almost never applied to nonwhite urban "addicts" and "criminals." At the same time, the discretionary and racially discriminatory drug-war enforcement apparatus constructed to deter mass law-breaking by these suburban rebels, without leaving a formal trace on their records, built directly on the discretionary and racially discriminatory juvenile delinquency system designed to control the subculture of white middle-class youth during the previous two decades of mass suburbanization. The vast majority of arrests of juveniles of all races during the 1950s and early-to-mid 1960s were for "delinquent tendencies," especially alcohol-related status offenses, followed by public-order violations such as "disorderly conduct" and then by nonviolent property crimes. The mass media and elected officials repeatedly proclaimed that a newly universalized delinquency crisis had "spread" from the urban slums and infiltrated the suburbs. Academic researchers consistently found that white middle-class youth were already engaging in a significant amount of criminal and delinquent (e.g., criminalized status) behavior, roughly equivalent to nonwhite urban counterparts in most categories. But police departments and juvenile control agencies almost always diverted white middle-class teenagers who violated the criminal and status offense laws, without processing them into a system that disproportionately placed poor and nonwhite male youth in carceral confinement or under formal supervision. The same law enforcement agencies then deployed the same discretionary and diversionary processes to address the rapid expansion of white middle-class youth drug violations during the second half of the 1960s, with predictably similar discriminatory outcomes, albeit intensified by the very real participation of suburban rebels in campus activism and urban countercultures, and the very exaggerated refashioning of traditional myths about white children lost to heroin addiction, urban slums, and the "drug culture."

Constructing the White Middle-Class Delinquency Epidemic

In November 1953, two sisters from a white middle-class neighborhood in San Diego wrote a letter to the U.S. Senate Subcommittee to Investigate Juvenile Delinquency protesting its plans to blame an alleged "wave of youthful crime and violence" on comic books, television, movies, alcohol, and narcotics.

Senator Robert Hendrickson, the chair of the subcommittee, announced the hearings in *Parade* magazine with stories of gang violence in urban slums, beach riots in white coastal suburbs, and desperate parents who attributed the youth "crime spree" to the external villains of mass culture and vice merchants. To generate public shock and alarm, the Juvenile Delinquency Subcommittee resolved to explore the epidemic in affluent commuter suburbs as well as disadvantaged urban centers and pledged to consult delinquency experts and civic leaders in the search for solutions. The offended sisters from San Diego, speaking consciously on behalf of their generation, instead asked why Congress did not solicit ideas from teenagers themselves. They then rejected the external pusher explanation in favor of an internal community diagnosis that accused parental and local authorities of unjust surveillance and overcriminalization of youth. The girls argued that parents bore significant responsibility for their children's values and actions, but most grown-ups did not try to understand problems from the teenage perspective. They complained of excessive supervision in movie theaters and police harassment at teen dances, which "make the teenagers themselves think they are criminals and act accordingly." They asked why they got in trouble just for socializing with friends from different racial and religious groups, questioning if the parents in their community really believed in equality. They pointed out that adult society provided the "booze and dope to the kids." In conclusion, the sisters accused the news media of greatly exaggerating teenage crimes and explained that living through two wars and the atomic bomb had exposed their generation to ample violence, regardless of the content of comics and movies.[5]

The Senate Subcommittee to Investigate Juvenile Delinquency launched its televised hearings in fall 1953 with the explicit mission of highlighting an epidemic of teenage crime and narcotics addiction in white middle-class communities as well as nonwhite urban ghettos. In internal documents, the subcommittee's staff outlined an agenda to expose the juvenile delinquency crisis in white-collar commuter suburbs "where there is an absence of slums, poor housing, and under-privileged children"—specifying Westchester County (NY), Maplewood and South Orange (NJ), and Shaker Heights (Cleveland). The ongoing war on narcotics in metro Los Angeles, and especially the perception of an addiction outbreak among white suburban youth, also significantly shaped the approach of the Senate investigation (see chapter 1).[6] The subcommittee's interest in uncovering youth crime and deviance in white middle-class areas converged with broader midcentury shifts in delinquency theory that challenged the traditional emphasis on causes such as poverty and racial inequality, the social disorganization of immigrant and Black families, and geographic contagion within urban slums. Instead, academic studies and media coverage increasingly attributed juvenile delinquency to the psychological maladjustment of youth, autonomous adolescent subcultures, violent images in mass culture, and harmful parenting practices. All of these remained disproportionately associated with nonwhite and low-income families but potentially could affect any thrill-seeking or unsupervised teenager from any racial and socioeconomic setting. Sheldon and Eleanor Glueck, the Harvard criminologists and influential delinquency theorists, reinforced this interpretation at the subcommittee's inaugural session by arguing that since 95 percent of slum teenagers did not become delinquent, the search for causes should focus on "family life . . . inside the homes of the children to make them what they are"—especially the personality damage resulting from inadequate parental supervision and permissive disciplinary standards. Under this theory, delinquency could happen anywhere.[7]

The subcommittee's first report, released in March 1954, urged the nation to "declare all-out war on juvenile delinquency" and labeled the crisis "both an urban and nonurban problem" that had spread to communities across the racial and class spectrum. With near unanimity, experts who testified in the initial hearings backed the subcommittee's assessment that, while poverty and racial discrimination disadvantaged slum youth, "economically well-to-do communities also produce many juvenile delinquents." The director of the U.S. Children's Bureau pointed out the inherent statistical difficulty in measuring delinquency because only a small fraction of minors apprehended by police faced formal proceedings in the juvenile courts. But many "children from so-called good families and good neighborhoods" also broke the law—because they suffered from improper parenting and unhealthy personalities. A prominent Boston expert likewise favored psychological over socioeconomic causes, explaining that as many delinquents lived in the commuter suburbs of large cities, "surrounded by the luxuries of . . . material wealth and material goods," as resided in the slums. The report recognized that the concentration of official delinquency caseloads in urban centers was misleading because discretionary practices favored families "of means and status" and kept most lawbreaking teens from middle-class areas out of the system. Rather than "punitive" measures, the subcommittee advocated the (coercive) rehabilitation of youth delinquents and drug addicts, supplemented by prevention campaigns in the home, church, and school. Its multicausal explanation for the nationwide epidemic labeled negative parental influence the most important factor but also blamed narcotics pushers, illegal consumption of alcohol in unsupervised leisure spaces, teenage gang activities, and glamorization of crime and violence by comic books, television shows, and movies. This sweeping indictment of internal and external forces located the delinquency crisis in any and every American community where adolescents experienced the "profound influence" of family life and the pervasive presence of mass culture.[8]

The emergence of a nationwide delinquency crisis in the mid-1950s represented the failure of the utopian suburban solution of safeguarding white middle-class youth in postwar America through maternally supervised domesticity in racially and economically segregated neighborhoods. During World War II, the mass media and law enforcement agencies had fueled fears of a youth crime wave unleashed by population migration to congested industrial centers and the breakdown of the nuclear family structure by the social and economic pressures of the military mobilization. "Youth in Crisis" (1943), a segment of the monthly *March of Time* newsreel shown in movie theaters, attributed the delinquency upsurge to "rotten neighborhoods and bad family situations," especially the wartime movement of mothers into the wage labor force and the temptations that unsupervised children faced in "unwholesome" urban areas. The dramatization showed white teenage boys smoking marijuana on a city street corner and buying pornography from an unscrupulous merchant, while adolescent "Victory Girls" engaged in sexual relations (implied as prostitution) with enlisted men. J. Edgar Hoover, the director of the FBI, then blamed this juvenile crime epidemic on working mothers and "'latchkey' youngsters who are left to roam the streets." He advocated structured recreational programs in community centers and urged American parents to "be constantly alert to their children's activities." Hoover characterized white middle-class delinquency as an exception to his generally punitive approach to crime control, proclaiming that "no amount of law enforcement can solve a problem which goes straight to the home."[9] Delinquency prevention agencies in metropolitan Los Angeles, operating within the ideology of Progressive reform, also merged environmental and psychological explanations by ascribing the wartime outbreak to "crowded quarters" in urban neighborhoods, the lack of organized recreational activities in fast-growing suburbs, and the fundamental problem of "delinquent parents, working mothers, broken homes."[10]

The postwar suburban landscape of single-family residential neighborhoods, stay-at-home mothers, and supervised youth activities emerged as the spatial and ideological fix for the mainstream juvenile delinquency crisis. In 1948, the prominent urban planner Charles W. Eliot II encapsulated this utopian, family-centered vision in "Planning Physical Environment for Youth Welfare," the keynote address at a major national conference held in Los Angeles. Eliot argued that the antidote to juvenile delinquency could be found in the "continued development of individual separate homes in the established American tradition, with plenty of yard space for play and air and California sunshine." The "healthy residential neighborhood" would provide safety, privacy, and community through restrictive zoning to eliminate slum-level density, multifamily apartments, and commercialized vice. The strategic location of schools, churches, and parks would ensure a "wholesome environment in which families can do things together." Eliot, whose blueprint for social welfare through the built environment embodied the Progressive and New Deal traditions of an interventionist state, concluded that the "primary purpose of communities is a healthy environment for youth." He portrayed the decentralized landscape of metropolitan Los Angeles, "a group of suburbs looking for the city," as an ideal setting for structured teenage programs guided by "the parents' example and participation" in their children's lives.[11] Municipal planning and social welfare agencies throughout Los Angeles County shared this agenda and specifically identified juvenile delinquency as a rising threat among white middle-class teenagers in rapidly developing, automobile-dependent suburban communities that lacked the facilities for "wholesome and supervised leisure activities." To address this void, suburban municipalities organized "safe, supervised recreation" through schools and youth centers—from afternoon and summer programs, such as athletic teams, Boy Scouts and Girl Scouts, 4-H clubs, and camps to family-focused events, including potluck suppers, square dancing, parent-child sport contests, and chaperoned teen dances.[12]

The suburban solution—premised on the social control of middle-class teenagers through constant parental and community surveillance, and on the coercive protection of innocent youth from external corruption on a landscape of mobility in a mass consumer society—failed both repeatedly and inevitably throughout the 1950s. In the suburban city of Pasadena, the schools and recreation centers defined "preparation for marriage" as the primary purpose of teenage programs and sought to entice and redirect wayward youth who raced hot rods, crashed parties, committed vandalism, and violated alcohol and marijuana laws. Pasadena's new youth centers stationed police officers at all teen dances, banned boys and girls wearing "improper attire," and strictly enforced prohibitions against alcohol and drugs.[13] While chaperoned leisure appealed to some adolescents, municipalities in Los Angeles County struggled to regulate youth dances because the widespread availability of automobiles enabled "gatherings of teenagers without proper safeguards or supervision," including unauthorized multiracial encounters. As youth agencies reported, too many misguided and thrill-seeking teens would not stop drag racing, illegally smoking and drinking, mixing it up across racial and class boundaries, and avidly consuming violent comic books and movies.[14] In the early-to-mid 1950s, PTAs and civic groups in LA County campaigned to ban the sale of violent comic books to youth under age eighteen, for "destroying their moral fiber and inciting them to crime and juvenile delinquency." The youth agencies in metropolitan Los Angeles also called town meetings to address the persistent problem of beach "riots" by mobile teenagers from affluent communities, following mass arrests for drinking, fighting, disturbing the peace, and alleged "juvenile orgies." Automobile freedom and permissive parenting directly caused the alcohol and marijuana violations among affluent suburban youth, according to the head of the California Bureau of Narcotic Enforcement: "too much ready money, too many late-model cars provided by over-indulgent parents."[15]

Law enforcement and social welfare agencies, in postwar California and across the nation, responded to the escalating delinquency crisis through the comprehensive criminalization of teenage subcultures and spaces, enforced through discretionary and coercive strategies of surveillance, punishment, and rehabilitation. In 1953, the California Youth Authority released a major antidelinquency blueprint, modeled on the Progressive philosophy of the U.S. Children's Bureau, that advocated dedicated police patrols of parks and youth leisure establishments, legal bans of "salacious literature" and "danger spots," and special agencies that would evaluate and remand detained adolescents to their families or the juvenile courts as needed. In the CYA's consensus vision of delinquency prevention, parents in every community should impose rules and enforce moral boundaries through "unified action," in recognition that children were "easy prey for harmful influences." Los Angeles County implemented this mandate with juvenile patrol cars that monitored teenage hangouts "such as drive-ins, malt shops, and playgrounds" and a curfew ordinance that authorized law enforcement to arrest minors in the late-night hours and to prosecute parents who failed to control their children.[16] Although nonwhite and lower-income youth disproportionately faced formal adjudication in the mid-1950s, media hype about the delinquency epidemic in metropolitan Los Angeles focused often on white middle-class "bobby soxers, shaggy-haired boys" gone wrong. Juvenile court judges generally ordered family supervision or informal probation for such suburban youth—females detained for sex delinquency or narcotics use, males busted for marijuana smoking or auto theft—while faulting parents whose "kids are turned loose with cars and money" and the distorted psychology of "the over-privileged [who] get into trouble for the thrill of it."[17] The U.S. Children's Bureau reinforced this alarm about a nationwide delinquency escalation and warned that the estimated 350,000 minors processed annually in juvenile courts represented only the tip of the iceberg, since police informally detained more than 1 million youth per year and far more "hidden delinquents" completely escaped the attention of law enforcement and social welfare agencies.[18]

During 1954–55, the Senate Subcommittee to Investigate Juvenile Delinquency intensified the national focus on white middle-class youth through hearings and reports that connected their deviant and criminal behavior to external "pushers" in the comics, television, and film industries. The charges that mass culture corrupted "normal" youth from "good" families helped to make sense of the unexpected delinquency crisis on the utopian suburban landscape and drew directly from the parallel war on narcotics discourse about invading pushers and innocent teenage victims. In targeting violent comic books, the Juvenile Delinquency Subcommittee built on grassroots censorship campaigns in states such as California and New York as well as the far-reaching impact of psychiatrist Frederic Wertham, author of the melodramatic exposé *Seduction of the Innocent* (1954). Wertham labeled comic books the "marijuana of the nursery," an Anslinger-inspired catchphrase that attributed adolescent criminality directly to the psychological damage caused by their addictive, graphic violence and antisocial themes. The psychiatrist began "What Parents Don't Know about Comic Books," a bombshell *Ladies' Home Journal* article published in late 1953, with reproductions of a villain jabbing a heroin needle into a young girl's eye and lurid scenes depicting the sexual assault of a female on a quiet suburban street. Wertham juxtaposed these sadistic images with photographs of clean-cut white preteens avidly reading comic books in leafy neighborhoods (even though he conducted his clinical research on African American children in Harlem) and awful stories of young boys reenacting these dramatizations through real-life beatings and murders. In his testimony to the Juvenile Delinquency Subcommittee, Wertham explained that images of sex and violence in comic books primarily seduced the "average normal child" and meant that "there are no secure homes" anymore, given the power of mass culture to invade and corrupt otherwise wholesome communities by circumventing the supervision of even engaged parents.[19]

FIGURE 2.1. Members of the U.S. Senate Subcommittee to Investigate Juvenile Delinquency inspect a display of horror comic books at a hearing in New York City, April 21, 1954. Senators Estes Kefauver (second from left) and Robert Hendrickson (center) led the Juvenile Delinquency Subcommittee's investigations of narcotics pushers and violent comic books, charging that each had caused teenage crime and delinquency to escalate in white middle-class communities. (Bettmann / Getty Images.)

The Juvenile Delinquency Subcommittee's moral crusade against crime comics generated an avalanche of opposition from American teenagers, an early indication of the political consciousness and generational awakening of the so-called "silent generation" of white middle-class youth. National media coverage of the spring 1954 hearings hyped Wertham's arguments that violent comics caused delinquency among normal adolescents from "good homes" and incited "juvenile gangsterism in well-to-do neighborhoods."[20] Many parents and women's clubs responded by demanding federal action to censor the violent and obscene literature "peddled to our young people," but thousands of teenagers also wrote to the subcommittee with forceful objections to the premise that comic books victimized them by triggering copycat criminality.[21] A group of twenty-one teenage girls from an outer borough of New York City pledged to organize demonstrations against any government ban, because the view that "comic books are bad for children is nonsense." Forty boys from a Long Island suburb, self-described "sane, normal fun-loving kids," reasoned that since everyone in their neighborhood read horror comics, the claim that they inspired delinquency among well-adjusted teenagers violated common sense. The Juvenile Delinquency Subcommittee had undertaken "the most ridiculous move made by the adults of this United States," according to a sixteen-year-old male from a Dallas suburb. "None of us have gone crazy or tried to kill anybody," explained an exasperated female from Seattle. A number of adolescents specifically derided the idea that reading comics would entice them to take dope. Many more letters arrived after popular horror comics ran editorials encouraging teenage readers to protest, such as the fifteen-year-old from Miami Beach who attacked the "stupid, ignorant, old-fashioned, prude-minded people" behind the crusade. The subcommittee staff responded substantively to correspondence from adults but did not even acknowledge this dissent from teenagers, a revealing window into the general depoliticization of youth and the refusal to consider their perspectives in the socially constructed delinquency crisis of the mid-1950s.[22]

The comic book investigation by the Juvenile Delinquency Subcommittee, closely followed by hearings into the pernicious effects of crime and violence in television shows and films, led directly to industry censorship and intensified the national focus on the alleged white middle-class delinquency epidemic. Its comprehensive 1955 report on violent comic books emphasized that their "sadistic degeneracy" endangered both "normal and emotionally disturbed children." The subcommittee demanded industry self-regulation, on behalf of aroused parents and with the implicit threat of government intervention, to protect youth from indecent and immoral influences. The major publishers complied by establishing the Comics Code Authority to guarantee "wholesome" entertainment by banning graphic or glamorized depictions of violence and sex and pledging to cultivate respect among adolescent readers for their parents, police, and law.[23] The subcommittee's follow-up investigation of crime shows on television determined that the new technology subverted traditional methods of social control of children and created the "permissive atmosphere" in which delinquency flourished. In a circular evidence loop, the report justified this finding based largely on thousands of letters from concerned parents and a Gallup survey showing that 70 percent of American adults believed that comics and television contributed to teenage crime and delinquency. The inquiry into Hollywood films likewise cited aroused parental opinion inspired by the Juvenile Delinquency Subcommittee's own hearings as a self-justifying mandate for reform. Its report on movies concluded that themes of violence and illicit sex threatened to corrupt the "impressionable young minds" of normal teenagers and likely triggered delinquency in the "emotionally unstable children" who could be found in every type of American community. The subcommittee pointedly rejected studio arguments that delinquency films—especially the urban working-class drama *Blackboard Jungle* (1955) and its suburban counterpart *Rebel Without a Cause* (1955)—were socially relevant depictions of the nationwide epidemic. The white middle-class teenagers in *Rebel Without a Cause* were not "living in a tranquil world, Utopia, because it really doesn't exist," the head of Warner Brothers explained. Moreover, the plot made clear that "the parents are at fault."[24]

Rebel Without a Cause simultaneously popularized the psychological interpretation of the middle-class delinquency crisis, highlighted the informal and ineffective policing of crime and deviance among privileged white youth, and foreshadowed the political awakening of an alienated generation of suburban rebels. The film, set on the car-centered landscape of suburban Los Angeles, begins at a police station with the detention of the main character Jim Stark (James Dean) for public inebriation, where he meets the wealthy sex delinquent Judy (Natalie Wood) and the confused, gun-wielding, abandoned rich kid Plato (Sal Mineo). The police decline to press charges, even after Jim tries to assault an officer, and instead release him to the custody of his permissive and materialistic parents (Jim's father: "Don't I buy you everything you want?"). The film's psychological framework attributes Jim's malaise and criminality in this suburban utopia/dystopia to the distorted gender roles of his emasculated father and domineering mother. In scenes of affluent white juvenile crime unprecedented in a blockbuster movie, Jim engages in a switchblade knife fight with the leader of a gang of suburban delinquents, followed by a drag race (just for "kicks") that leaves his rival dead and inspires the gang-girl Judy to switch sides and become Jim's girlfriend. Forsaken by their parents and misunderstood by adult society, Jim and Judy play-act the adoption of Plato and seek to create a genuinely loving family structure in a sexually charged sequence in an abandoned house. The film ends in tragedy when a police officer shoots and kills Plato, who is armed (to defend himself from the gang) but ultimately just a lost, emotionally disturbed, and effectively parentless boy. The clear moral is that permissive and/or absentee upper-middle-class parents are at fault for juvenile delinquency and should supervise their children closely and carefully, and that neither the utopian suburban mythology nor racial and class segregation can safeguard affluent white youth from the crime and disorder previously associated with the urban slums.[25]

In mid-1950s America, the sensational impact of *Rebel Without a Cause* revealed the cultural and political resonance of a narrative fundamentally about the moral innocence of suburban whiteness. The movie shifted blame for the delinquency and criminality of middle-class youth from external to internal villains but as always focused on their victimization rather than their responsibility and agency. In a studio mini-documentary about the film's origins, a Warner Brothers executive displays newspaper headlines reading "Slums Breed Crime" and "Gang War" and then explains that the screenwriters "took a look into some privileged homes, far from the slums, nice homes, very respectable, and nice kids, well-clothed, no slum kids here, but beneath the surface, [dramatic pause, aerial view of cookie-cutter suburbia] *trouble, plenty of it*." "What makes nice kids from nice homes do things like this," the voiceover wonders during scenes from the fatal drag race and Jim's confrontation with his parents at the police station; "What drives them, *what has hurt them*?"[26] Even this explicitly stated agenda of *Rebel*'s cultural politics, as a sociological investigation and racial/class exposé of subcultural delinquency among white suburban youth, could not insulate the film from the ubiquitous charges that mass culture's representations of violence and deviance inspired copycat crimes. Like all films of the era, *Rebel Without a Cause* negotiated the censorship standards of the Motion Picture Production Code, which required the studio to revise scenes that teenage audiences might interpret as the glorification of violence and prohibited direct implication of illicit sexual relations between Jim and Judy and of Plato's homoerotic attraction to Jim. The Code authorities also demanded that underage consumption of alcohol by the adolescent characters take place off screen and specifically rejected a shot that might have been interpreted as marijuana smoking in the suburban schoolyard. After the film's release, the Juvenile Delinquency Subcommittee even sponsored federal legislation that banned interstate commerce in switchblade knives, in another quixotic effort to stem the apocryphal juvenile "crime wave sweeping the nation."[27]

Investigations of the suburban gang activities dramatized in *Rebel Without a Cause* reaffirmed that juvenile criminality transcended racial and economic boundaries but continued to prescribe the conventional social controls of wholesome recreation and better parenting. "More and more of the worst cases," *Life* magazine opined, "come from comfortable or wealthy homes." In *Gang Boy* (1954), an educational documentary set in suburban Los Angeles,

Mexican American youth form a gang in self-defense against harassment by a white middle-class counterpart that cruises the San Gabriel Valley in convertibles and terrorizes drive-ins. For both racial groups, the story ends happily with the establishment of police-chaperoned dances, Boys Clubs, and athletic contests (police agencies in LA County also sponsored hot rod clubs to channel adolescent "gangs" into controlled outlets).[28] In a wide-ranging 1955 report, the Juvenile Delinquency Subcommittee endorsed these solutions and warned that the gang scourge had expanded beyond big-city slums into smaller communities and across the socioeconomic spectrum. The subcommittee defined gang-related activity expansively, in ways that broadly criminalized adolescent male subcultures: underage drinking and fighting at drive-ins, conflicts that followed athletic contests between rival schools, party-crashing by groups "out looking for a little excitement," a white youth drag-racing and (alleged) automobile-theft network in the Maryland suburbs, illegal drug use and illicit sex among clusters of teenagers from "middle and upper economic and social level homes." That same year, FBI director J. Edgar Hoover demanded public shock and alarm to address a "crime wave of grave proportions" and insisted that "families in modern and well-to-do circumstances produce delinquents just as those families in lower-income brackets do." Hoover attributed the nationwide delinquency crisis to Hollywood films, materialism, and immoral home influences and urged formal detention of juvenile criminals "unless an investigation shows the parents are decent, law-abiding persons."[29]

The hardest-hitting exposé of suburban criminality in the mid-1950s demonstrated the racial and spatial double standards through which police discretion and parental influence covered up most lawbreaking by white middle-class teenagers. In *The Shook-Up Generation* (1958), journalist Harrison Salisbury chronicled numerous "vicious gang assaults" by white male adolescents in the New York City suburbs, although neither the media nor the police generally utilized the "gang" label that they readily applied to criminal and deviant activity by Black urban youth. In one upscale commuter suburb on Long Island, a group of white male juveniles committed multiple sexual assaults against African American females who worked as domestics, including at least one group rape at knifepoint. The municipal police acknowledged the incidents but declined to make any arrests because, as one explained, "This is a quiet community and we aim to keep it that way. . . . Sometimes the kids get a little wild. But we try to keep things in the family." More typically, the automobile-centered landscape of affluent suburbia enabled crime and delinquency by groups of white males who stole cars, burglarized homes and stores, vandalized schools, fought rivals, and engaged in premarital sex and underage drinking. But almost none of this activity showed up in official law enforcement statistics, since their "families possess the ability to conceal or wipe out the evidence of what their children do." The few academic experts who studied white suburban delinquency agreed that "there is much more upper-class gang activity than is realized," because the police in affluent communities collaborated with parents to cover up criminal and deviant behavior that would result in formal punishment in poor, nonwhite, and urban areas. Salisbury concluded, however, that white suburban delinquents also were victims of a dystopian landscape and culture of pathology: the "psychologically broken home" of absent commuter fathers and distracted socialite mothers produced "children as emotionally starved as those in the deprived areas of the slums."[30]

A closer examination of official delinquency caseloads in Los Angeles County reveals both the discriminatory practices that kept most white middle-class teenagers out of the juvenile justice system and the discretionary policies through which the state over-criminalized and attempted to regulate the social practices of all youth. During 1956 and the first half of 1957, the LA County Probation Department formally processed 9,507 delinquency caseloads, which represented only 10 percent of the minors initially apprehended by law enforcement. The police were expected to "exercise a high degree of discretion" in the disposition process, according to the official policy of the California Youth Authority, and after interrogation they informally handled most youth (often issuing traffic citations or verbal "reprimands"). The probation department then conducted its own risk assessment on the subset referred by police, keeping a majority on informal supervision and sending the remainder for delinquency adjudication by the juvenile court, which placed most on probation and committed a small group (about 1 percent of initial apprehensions) to carceral facilities. The authorities in LA County often emphasized the increasing delinquency problem in fast-growing suburbs that lacked adequate youth services, but the official probation caseload rate was substantially higher in the Mexican American and African American areas of East and South Central Los Angeles. The vast majority of formal caseloads involved poor and working-class male youth, with a racial breakdown of 64 percent white (non-Hispanic), 19 percent Mexican American (2.4 times the population share), and 14 percent Black (1.75 times the population share). Only two-fifths of these adjudicated delinquents had allegedly committed felony-level crimes—primarily the youth-oriented property infractions of burglary and car theft, with narcotics a distant third. More than half came under formal probation or

TABLE 2.1. Juvenile Delinquency Caseloads in Los Angeles County, 1956–57

Category (crimes = 48%)	Caseloads	Category (status = 52%)	Caseloads
Felonies	3,676 (39%)	Home/Parental situation	3,098 (33%)
Homicide	33 (0.3%)	Unfit home/neglect	1,431
Assault	396 (4.2%)	Beyond parental control	464
Burglary	1,259 (13%)	Lack of supervision	1,098
Car theft	1,487 (16%)	No proper guardian	105
Narcotics	434 (4.6%)		
Rape	67 (0.7%)	Sex delinquent	875 (9%)
		Illegitimate sexual relations	648
Loitering	181 (1.9%)	Homosexual acts/ tendencies	85
Vandalism	132 (1.4%)	Other	75
Disturbing the peace	147 (1.5%)		
		Runaway	332 (3.5%)
Motor vehicle	442 (4.6%)	Truant	216 (2.3%)
Drunk driving	61	Transient	207 (2.1%)
Speeding	100	Liquor	141 (1.5%)
Other violations	281	Improper companions	35 (0.4%)
		Victim of sex assault	25 (0.2%)

Total Delinquency Caseloads Categorized = 9,507
Racial Breakdown = 64% White, 19% Mexican descent, 14% Black

Sources: Los Angeles County Probation Department, *Annual Report*, 1956–1957; Bureau of Criminal Statistics, *Delinquency and Probation in California, 1956*.

Note: Data covers 1956 and January–June 1957 and does not include 696 caseloads listed under "no category." A large majority of caseloads involved male juveniles, and sex delinquency was the only category in which the gender breakdown was roughly equal. Racial data is from 1956 caseloads alone. Estimated population of LA County in the mid-1950s: 84% white (non-Hispanic), 8% Mexican American, 7% Black.

institutionalization by the juvenile justice system through age-based status offenses such as unfit home life, lack of parental supervision, transiency and truancy, or sex delinquency that reflected selective policing based on race, socioeconomics, and neighborhood (table 2.1).[31]

During the second half of the 1950s, the political leadership of California launched major antidelinquency campaigns that hyped the relatively small threat of violent juvenile crime and highlighted the dangers facing middle-class communities as well as urban slums. In 1956, Republican governor Goodwin Knight expanded his initiative against teenage narcotics addiction into a "Crusade for Youth" designed to mobilize the public through a statewide series of town meetings. Knight's Advisory Committee on Children and Youth recommended that parents protect their children by supervising recreational activities, monitoring mass culture, attending church together, and avoiding "delinquency neighborhoods" marked by population congestion, multifamily housing, and urban-industrial locations. Effectively endorsing housing segregation, the state initiative urged (white) families to rear children in racially and economically "homogeneous" neighborhoods in the lower-density suburbs and countryside.[32] Democratic attorney general Pat Brown also asked his Citizens' Advisory Committee on Crime Prevention to build on its antinarcotics efforts through an investigation of the epidemic of juvenile violence that allegedly threatened inner cities and upscale suburbs alike. The Brown committee promoted racial egalitarianism in the tradition of color-blind liberalism but also called for a more punitive approach to "hard core incorrigibles" and violent hoodlums, to be sorted out from "those who would reasonably profit from rehabilitative treatment."[33] During the late 1950s and early 1960s, the racial trends among minors arrested and formally processed into California's juvenile justice system remained fairly steady, although in Los Angeles County the percentage of white and Mexican American youth gradually declined as the proportion of adjudicated Black youth increased (fig. 2.2). Based on statewide data from 1955–57, nonwhite male youth formally remanded into the system were almost twice as likely to be incarcerated in a Youth Authority facility as white delinquents, who disproportionately received probationary supervision.[34]

In its 1957 annual report, the California Youth Authority acknowledged that "the definition of a 'delinquent child' is so broad that it seems doubtful whether there is any child who might not have been delinquent at some period of his life." This assessment captured both the virtually unlimited discretionary power that law enforcement agencies held over juveniles who could be arrested and institutionalized for a broad spectrum of status offenses, and the obvious corollary that "there is undoubtedly much delinquent behavior that never comes to the attention of law enforcement agencies." To little avail, the CYA's Bureau of Criminal Statistics repeatedly warned that political and media sensationalism had created a "delinquency hysteria" that conflated total caseloads with serious offenses and narcotics violations, greatly exaggerated the violent crime rate among juveniles, failed to recognize that statistical increases

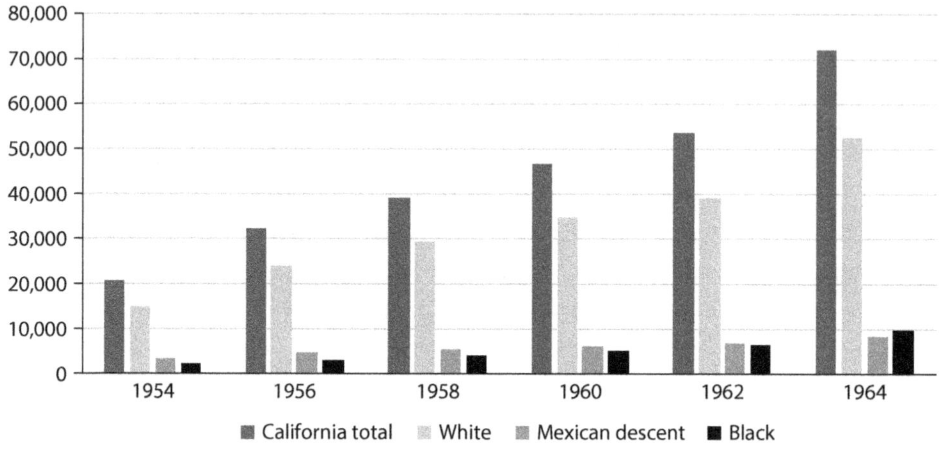

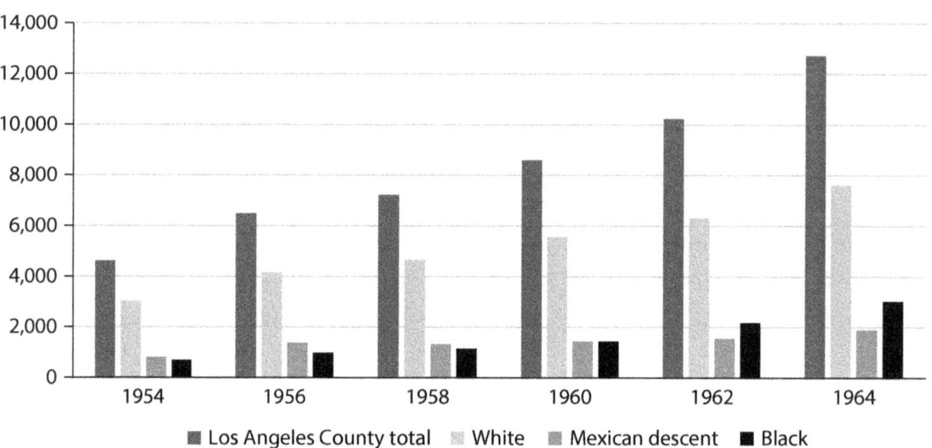

FIGURE 2.2. Racial characteristics and total number of boys referred to the probation department for delinquent acts, California and Los Angeles County, 1954–64. (*Top*) The antidelinquency crusade resulted in a 3.5 times increase in the number of male juveniles processed for delinquency violations in California between 1954 and 1964, significantly outpacing population growth. The proportion of white (non-Hispanic) juveniles under delinquency supervision remained steady during this expansion, averaging 74% of the total, 9 points below the estimated statewide population share of 83% (1960 census). The "Mexican descent" group decreased from 15% to 12% of the total, compared to approximately 9% of the population. Black juveniles increased from 11% to 14% of the total, nearly triple the 5.6% population share (data in "Other" category not listed). (*Bottom*) LA County disproportionately processed nonwhite juveniles in the delinquency control system relative to their population share and to broader statewide trends. Between 1954 and 1964, the proportion of Black juveniles under supervision or confinement increased from 15% to 24%, more than 2.5 times the population share (7.5% in the 1960 census). Mexican American juveniles declined from 18% to 15% of the total, compared to 10% of the population. White (non-Hispanic) juveniles decreased from 66% to 60% of the total, versus 81% of the countywide population (data in "Other" category not listed). (Compiled from annual reports of the Bureau of Criminal Statistics, *Delinquency and Probation in California*, 1954–1964.)

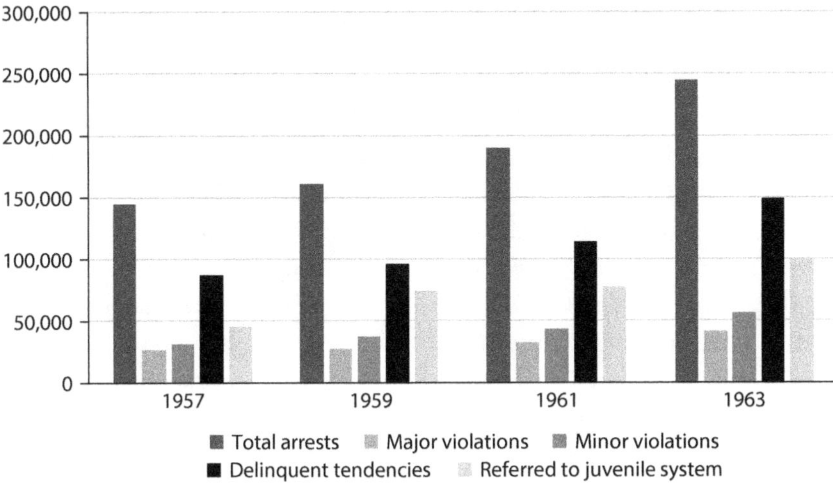

FIGURE 2.3. Juvenile delinquency arrests in California, 1957–63, by category. The political and media portrayal of a delinquency "epidemic" hyped the relatively small problem of violent crime and obscured the reality that most of the increase resulted from intensified enforcement of discretionary status offenses. Only 18% of juvenile arrests in California between 1957 and 1963 involved "major law violations"—a category that included homicide, aggravated assault, robbery, burglary, auto theft, "forcible rape," and narcotics. The vast majority of "major law violations" were for nonviolent property crimes. Minor law violations (23% of the total) covered petty theft, misdemeanor assault, DUI, hit-and-run, arson, weapons possession (usually knives), and sex delinquency status offenses. The largest category of "delinquent tendencies" (60% of the total) involved "incorrigibility," status offenses (alcohol violations, curfew, truancy, running away), discretionary criminalization (loitering, disorderly conduct), and vandalism. The California Youth Authority characterized the significant increase in police department referrals starting in 1959 to expansion of the administrative capacity of juvenile probation departments as a result of increased state and federal funding, not to a shift in actual delinquency patterns. (Compiled from the annual reports of the Bureau of Criminal Statistics, *Delinquency and Probation in California*, 1957–1963.)

usually reflected population growth and intensified enforcement, and routinely portrayed unreliable data as gospel truth.[35] The catch-all category of "delinquent tendencies" accounted for three-fifths of juvenile arrests in California during the late 1950s and early 1960s, based mainly on the status criminalization of alcohol consumption, curfew, and truancy violations; and discretionary enforcement of youth social activities through loitering and disorderly conduct statutes (fig. 2.3). Most other juvenile arrests were for misdemeanors or nonviolent felony property crimes of burglary and auto theft. A large majority were male. Police departments informally "handled" teenagers in 59 percent of these arrests while referring about half of law violators and one-third of "delinquent tendencies" cases to juvenile probation departments. The juvenile system then informally "handled" around two-thirds of this subset through remand to parents or nonadjudicated probationary supervision and sent the remainder to juvenile courts, which primarily placed adjudicated "delinquents" on probation and committed a very small fraction to a California Youth Authority facility. A fusion of race and class pervaded this process by design.[36]

FBI director J. Edgar Hoover, the nation's leading perpetuator of misinformation about juvenile delinquency, habitually conflated the total number of under-eighteen arrests with crimes of violence by "youthful hoodlums," with little acknowledgment that the vast majority were for status offenses, traffic violations, discretionary policing of "loitering" and "disorderly conduct," and nonviolent property offenses. In a 1958 redeclaration of war on delinquency, Hoover announced a "wave" of gang violence and "juvenile lawlessness, . . . mounting in both size and intensity . . . in community after community across the land." The FBI leader urged indulgent parents to discipline their children, his preferred antidote for "psychologically maladjusted" white middle-class youth, while demanding that the juvenile justice system stop "the coddling of young criminals." In public forums, the FBI generally hyped the allegedly exponential increase in delinquency during the 1950s without adjusting for population growth or greater levels of reporting and enforcement by local agencies. The Bureau never admitted the existence of racial and socioeconomic discrimination in the discretionary, status-based enforcement system. Even the "scientific" statistical knowledge produced by the FBI's annual *Uniform Crime Reports* included alarmist graphs and warnings that did not adjust for changes in data collection techniques and obscured the reality that arrests were not the same thing as actual "crimes" and "delinquency," and that a majority did not result in convictions or adjudications. For Hoover, this became an indictment of "coddling" by the juvenile authorities instead of a biased system designed around discretionary criminalization without due process rights for minors. The 1959 *Uniform Crime Reports*, for example, claimed that delinquency had increased 2.5 times faster than population during the previous decade, and that juvenile offenses had skyrocketed at 6 times the rate of adults—invalid statistics enabled by these techniques and by jumbling together violent and property crimes, status offenses, discretionary public order arrests, and minor traffic violations in a society where teenage access to automobiles was experiencing explosive growth (fig. 2.4).[37] Although rarely asked for their perspective, many American teenagers deeply resented the

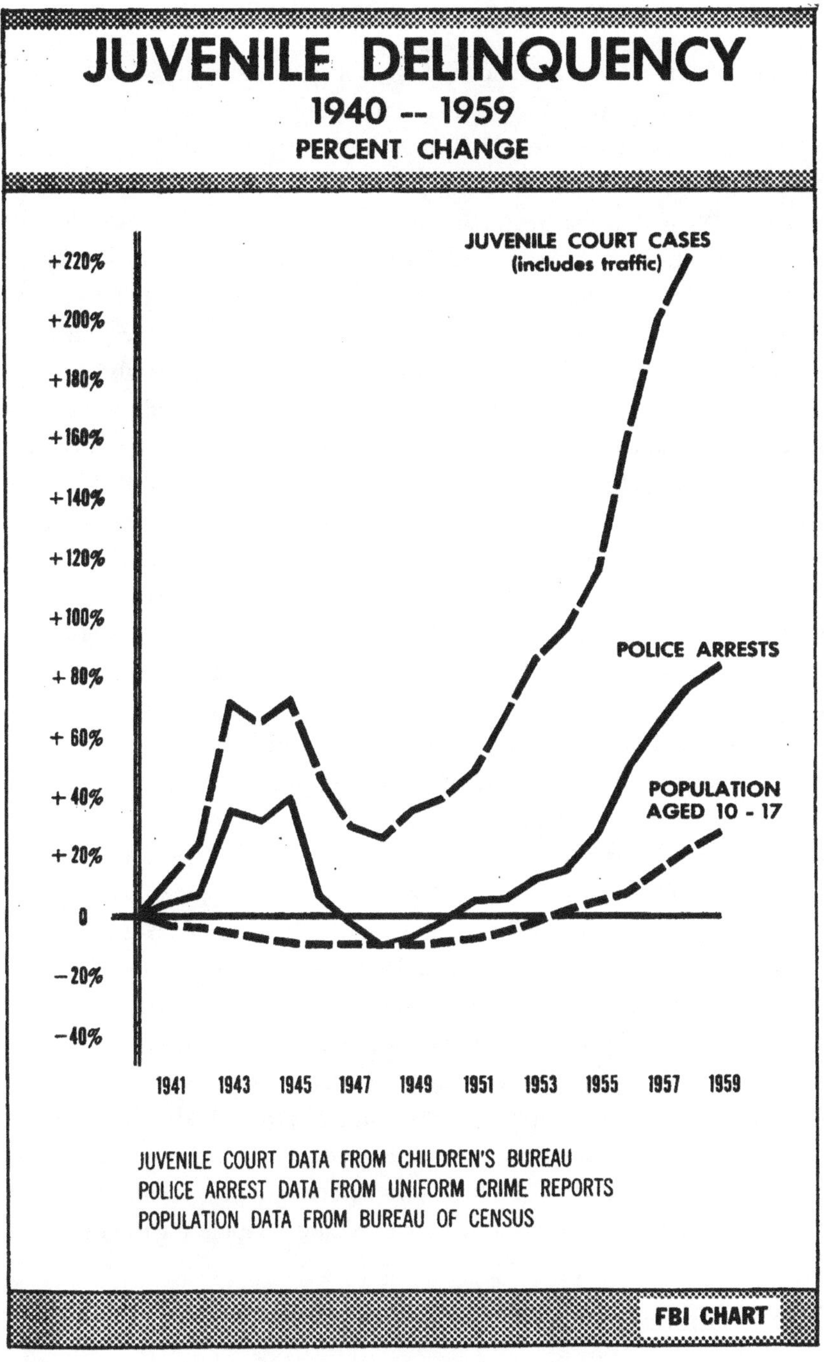

FIGURE 2.4. Purported wave of juvenile delinquency in the United States during the 1950s, circulated by the Federal Bureau of Investigation. Director J. Edgar Hoover hyped a nationwide epidemic of juvenile crime and lawlessness based on manipulation and distortion of statistics, including failure to acknowledge that most juvenile arrests were for nonviolent status offenses or traffic violations. (Reproduced from FBI, *Uniform Crime Reports*, 1959.)

delinquency label and rejected out-of-control epidemic hype, as confirmed by youth opinion surveys and captured in correspondence to national magazines. As a representative teen from Baltimore declared, "I'm tired of hearing my generation berated because of a few."[38]

By the late 1950s, the FBI and the national media increasingly portrayed the juvenile delinquency crisis as two distinct social problems demarcated by race and geography: a contagion of gang violence and narcotics addiction in nonwhite urban centers that demanded a punitive law enforcement response, and a generational subculture of deviant thrill-seeking in permissive white middle-class suburbs where parental engagement remained the desired solution. The Juvenile Delinquency Subcommittee's crusade against violence in mass culture, with its psychological assumptions about the vulnerability of normal youth from wholesome communities, ultimately could not overcome the racialized and specious statistical "truths" produced by the discriminatory and discretionary operations of the juvenile justice system. In a major 1957 investigation of the "catastrophic wave of crime" throughout urban America, *Life* magazine stated as fact that "juvenile delinquency is largely a problem of the depressed areas, the slums, of big cities." According to J. Edgar Hoover and urban police chiefs, "a tremendous proportion of crime is committed by juveniles and Negroes," as well as Puerto Ricans and Mexican Americans in certain cities. Nonwhite juvenile gangs had become "savage and wanton beyond belief," responsible for a "mounting wave" of violence that necessitated police crackdowns in the urban slums.[39] That same year, the *American Weekly* highlighted the growing popularity of the "Conduct Code for Teen-Agers," an internal remedy for white middle-class delinquency pioneered by a "pleasant suburban community" outside Minneapolis. Teenagers who signed the code—illustrated by a clean-cut white couple in a convertible—would discontinue the common practices of underage drinking, party crashing, joy riding (auto theft), drunk driving, and violating curfew. And in line with the utopian suburban solution, parents would pledge surveillance and social control by always knowing "where their sons and daughters are while away from home, what they are doing, and with whom they are spending their time."[40]

Sensationalizing and Medicalizing Suburban Drug Crime

In spring 1961, the Senate Subcommittee to Investigate Juvenile Delinquency announced that "a new 'white-collar' delinquency" of narcotics addiction and teenage crime had infiltrated prosperous suburbs throughout the nation. The warning—in the cyclical pattern of innocence lost through racial contagion—portrayed a sudden epidemic spreading outward from the large urban centers into suburban and small-town areas, "formerly substantially free from the serious juvenile misbehavior associated with the destructive influences of poverty and slums" (making this claim notwithstanding the subcommittee's voluminous reports finding this had already happened in the mid-1950s). Senator Thomas J. Dodd, a liberal Democrat from Connecticut, had recently become subcommittee chair with an agenda to "get the public fully alerted and alarmed" about the intersection of delinquency and narcotics among American teens. He opened the 1961 hearings by highlighting the ostensibly novel problem of the "white-collar delinquent—juveniles who lack the excuse of poverty, a poor home, the confinement and compression of big city slum life." Dodd illustrated the crisis with stories of Mexican marijuana and heroin corrupting the youth of Southern California and an alleged dope ring of 250 white teenagers from "well-to-do families" in the Westchester County suburbs of New York City. In its report, the subcommittee blamed the white middle-class delinquency outbreak on the thrill-seeking teenage psychology, rebellion against parental authority, violence in mass media, and malicious narcotics pushers.[41] During the early-to-mid 1960s, Thomas Dodd frequently charged that "goons and hoodlums" were luring "victims from the well-to-do 'white collar' areas" into lifelong addiction, "turning previously law-abiding and even-tempered youths into wanton criminals." But he strongly opposed the mandatory felony penalties in the Narcotic Control Act of 1956 and instead advocated coercive rehabilitation for most illegal drug users, including "addict-peddlers," based on "individual discretion" assessments. The Connecticut senator also emphasized that illicit circulation of "pep pills" (amphetamines) and "goof balls" (barbiturates) now rivaled marijuana as a threat to middle-class teenagers from good homes, causing males to commit robberies and violence and forcing females into sex delinquency and prostitution.[42]

The perils associated with "dangerous drugs," the common label for illicit amphetamines and barbiturates manufactured by pharmaceutical companies and then diverted from licit medical channels, moved white suburban victims back to the center of national drug politics in the early 1960s. Law enforcement and media reports claimed that barbiturates were replacing marijuana as the gateway to youthful heroin addiction and directly linked teenage abuse of pep pills and goof balls to increased delinquency and crime in white-collar areas. In *The Fantastic Lodge* (1961), the autobiography of a white female junkie in Chicago's bohemian jazz scene, marijuana and bennies (amphetamine) lead to heroin addiction by youth in revolt against their "respectable suburban parents," and the main character ultimately dies of a barbiturate overdose.[43] In August 1962, a few days after Marilyn Monroe's barbiturate-induced death, the Juvenile Delinquency Subcommittee held hearings in Los Angeles to generate momentum for Senator Dodd's legislation to bring habit-forming amphetamines and barbiturates under tighter federal regulation and to impose felony penalties for nonprescription distribution of such "dangerous drugs." The subcommittee's investigation revealed that American corporations were shipping mass quantities of amphetamines and barbiturates to Tijuana brokers who supplied the cross-border smuggling that sustained a thriving underground market in Southern California. But instead of directly attacking the pharmaceutical industry source, Dodd warned that street pushers of "dangerous drugs" were targeting good teenagers with no prior record of delinquency, and California governor Pat Brown blamed "the peddlers [who] seek new ways to prey on the public." Los Angeles County highlighted this "growing menace to society" with a dramatic report, exclusively featuring images of white middle-class youth, of how "the vicious underworld of drugs invades an entire community . . . victim by victim." The pamphlet cautioned that even good parents who lived in safe areas might not be able to prevent thrill-seeking teens from becoming addicted through the pressure of peddlers or by pilfering the family medicine cabinet.[44]

During 1962–63, Governor Brown pledged to expand California's war on narcotics to be "just as tough on those who would create addiction and misery through dangerous drugs as we are now on the evil peddlers of heroin." The Brown administration sought to increase the misdemeanor penalty for illegal sale of "dangerous drugs" to a felony and to make amphetamine and barbiturate "addicts" eligible for commitment to the state's compulsory hospitalization program. The governor also demanded federal intervention to "stem the flood of these drugs which pour in from across our Mexican border," a melodramatic description of an illicit market in which U.S. citizens purchased products that American corporations legally exported to Tijuana entrepreneurs. In the early 1960s, the police border blockade operation in San Diego turned back around ten thousand juveniles per year and reported that illicit amphetamines and barbiturates had supplanted marijuana as the vice of choice for teenage delinquents.[45] During the same period, juvenile and adult arrests for "dangerous drugs" increased significantly in California, especially in Los Angeles County, exceeding the totals for both marijuana and heroin (table 2.2). White violators accounted for almost 60 percent of "dangerous drugs" arrests, and

TABLE 2.2. Adult and Juvenile Arrests for State Drug Law Violations in California and in Los Angeles County as Reported by Law Enforcement Agencies, 1960–62

Area and offense category	1960	1961	1962	% Change
Adults—California				
Marijuana	4,098	3,305	3,291	−19.7%
Heroin + other narcotics	2,244	1,971	1,971	−12.2%
Narcotic addict or user	6,401	5,801	3,532	−44.8%
Dangerous drugs	3,305	4,322	5,578	+68.8%
Adults—Los Angeles County				
Marijuana	2,653	2,316	2,256	−15.0%
Heroin + other narcotics	1,544	1,302	1,187	−23.1%
Narcotic addict or user	4,771	4,193	2,204	−53.8%
Dangerous drugs	2,238	3,013	3,742	+67.2%
Juveniles—California				
Marijuana	677	269	248	−63.4%
Heroin + other narcotics	37	33	24	−35.1%
Narcotic addict or user	120	98	56	−53.3%
Dangerous drugs	503	694	887	+76.3%
Juveniles—Los Angeles County				
Marijuana	499	193	178	−64.3%
Heroin + other narcotics	22	19	16	−27.3%
Narcotic addict or user	71	62	33	−53.5%
Dangerous drugs	385	562	741	+92.5%

Source: Bureau of Criminal Statistics, *Drug Arrests and Dispositions in California, 1962*.

Note: The "dangerous drugs" category includes illicit and nonprescription amphetamines and barbiturates. The decline in "narcotic addict or user" arrests came after the U.S. Supreme Court's 1962 decision in *Robinson v. California* invalidating the state law permitting status incarceration of addicts absent an underlying offense.

not coincidentally the criminal justice system dismissed more than half of these misdemeanor cases. Narcotics enforcement officials proclaimed that illicit use of pharmaceuticals had become the new gateway to heroin addiction and lamented the lack of stigma among teenagers for "socially acceptable" drugs regularly prescribed to their parents.[46] But the pharmaceutical industry consistently downplayed the risks and addictive potential of "dangerous drugs" and successfully blocked Brown's legislation, notwithstanding public health data that barbiturates caused far more fatalities than heroin (840 overdose deaths statewide in 1963). In the aftermath, the governor received hundreds of letters from white parents in the Los Angeles suburbs who demanded protection of their children through stricter controls on illicit pharmaceuticals.[47]

California's war on heroin, marijuana, and "dangerous drugs" played a pivotal role in forcing the issues of white middle-class addiction and suburban delinquency back onto the federal agenda as the Kennedy administration came to power in Washington. Since the late 1950s, California politicians had been demanding a White House Conference on Narcotics to highlight the federal government's responsibility for stopping illegal drugs smuggled across the Mexican border, but opposition from the Federal Bureau of Narcotics and the State Department doomed the initiative until after President Eisenhower left office. During the 1960 campaign, John F. Kennedy pledged to hold a White House Conference as a favor to Democratic officials in California. The Brown administration frequently cited this commitment to refute soft-on-narcotics charges from Republican critics, especially during the governor's reelection triumph over Richard Nixon in 1962. That September, President Kennedy convened the White House Conference on Narcotic and Drug Abuse by endorsing the California agenda of joint U.S.-Mexico border controls, tough punishment for traffickers, better rehabilitation of addict-victims, and stricter regulation of barbiturates and amphetamines.[48] Governor Pat Brown and California law enforcement officials featured prominently at the White House Conference and emphasized that the "dangerous drugs" epidemic was "creating an entirely new class of addicts," the code phrase for white middle-class youth from good homes who were not otherwise criminally inclined. The California contingent demanded enhanced interdiction at the Mexico border and recommended enactment of a federal civil commitment law modeled on Brown's program (which actually had a very limited impact). The Goddard Report, commissioned by the Kennedy administration to guide the White House Conference, likewise warned of growing abuse of synthetic "spree" drugs among teenagers and advocated federal adoption of Brown's compulsory treatment program to target heroin addicts presumably concentrated in low-income slums of the largest cities.[49]

The Kennedy administration promoted the punitive liberal approach in the war on narcotics, which championed lengthy criminal penalties for illegal drug traffickers in tandem with coercive medical treatment through discretionary civil commitment of their addict-victims. Although the liberal rehabilitative position viewed addiction as a medical disease or psychological disorder, its proponents continued to advocate criminalization of nonprescription drug use as the essential foundation of compulsory public health solutions, an ideology aligned with the crime control methods of the Bureau of Narcotics rather than opponents of prohibition. The FBN's policymaking dominance came under increasing attack in the early 1960s, most notably for Anslinger's uncompromising defense of the mandatory-minimum sentencing structure in the Narcotic Control Act of 1956 and his related insistence that heroin and marijuana "addicts" were criminals. In 1961, a joint report by the American Bar Association and the American Medical Association challenged the FBN stance that narcotics was "essentially a problem of criminal law enforcement" and labeled as "hysteria" its pronouncements that addicts often committed crimes of violence and sexual assault. After Anslinger fiercely condemned the report, lead author Rufus King blamed FBN prohibition itself for creating the lucrative illicit market and stated that "if addicts are sick people, it's barbaric to throw them into jail."[50] Then in 1962, the U.S. Supreme Court declared unconstitutional the California law criminalizing the status of narcotics addiction, while sanctioning the public health policy of compulsory confinement for treatment of this "disease." At the White House Conference, Attorney General Robert F. Kennedy endorsed the civil commitment laws recently passed in California and New York as the humane medical alternative to the "punitive" sentences that traffickers deserved, albeit with the leverage of suspended criminal charges to force addicts into rehab centers. As Attorney General Stanley Mosk of California explained, civil commitment "means the involuntary placement of the addict in an institution for treatment aimed at rehabilitation. It is an alternative to punishment."[51]

The liberal rhetoric around coercive rehabilitation concealed the fundamentally punitive nature of compulsory civil commitment programs and operated through the same artificial and racialized distinctions between criminalized nonwhite urban heroin markets and medicalized majority-white drug markets that the Federal Bureau of Narcotics had propagated for the past decade. The ABA-AMA study and the Goddard Report each acknowledged that alcoholism, alcohol-fueled violence, and the abuse of prescription barbiturates (often in combination) represented greater public health threats than heroin addiction, defined as a geographically contained problem that afflicted psychologically disturbed members of "minority groups . . . in the slum areas of large population centers." But the advocates of civil commitment targeted inner-city heroin addicts as a uniquely dangerous racial threat—"spreading terror in our urban centers," as Governor Nelson Rockefeller declared when championing New York's compulsory hospitalization program established by the Metcalf-Volker Act of 1962.[52] In California, nonwhite drug violators represented almost three-fifths of those committed by state courts under the compulsory treatment law through the mid-1960s—48 percent Mexican Americans and 11 percent African Americans. According to sociologist Alfred Lindesmith, a leading critic of the FBN, the California civil commitment program masqueraded as a liberal public health reform but was "actually extraordinarily punitive and was devised by prosecutors and police." Lindesmith contended that "forcible deprivation of liberty is punishment" and also highlighted the racial and economic injustice underlying the Kennedy administration's endorsement of "compulsory cures for lower class addicts and voluntary ones" for the affluent white Americans who generally abused legal prescription drugs and could afford private medical treatment. Isidor Chein, a leading heroin researcher, similarly argued that criminal law should play no role at all in the medical field of narcotics and further charged that politicians and enforcement agencies wildly exaggerated the public health challenge by classifying all illegal drug users as helpless addicts.[53]

In the early 1960s, the Synanon method of voluntary group rehabilitation in therapeutic residential settings emerged as the most prominent middle-class alternative to the policies of coercive institutionalization or incarceration promoted by mainstream liberals and conservatives alike. Synanon House began in 1958 in the beachfront LA suburb of Santa Monica as a private rehabilitation center for narcotics addicts based on self-help methods of "cold turkey" withdrawal and total abstinence inspired by Alcoholics Anonymous. Synanon gained national prominence in 1962 when *Life* magazine published a photojournalistic essay about its "miracles in reclaiming the human wreckage of addiction." Although Synanon House served a multiracial clientele, *Life* chose to highlight white middle-class victims such as a male heroin addict who dropped out of college and a young mother with a heroin habit who overdosed on sleeping pills and lost custody of her son until the rehab program made their reunification possible.[54] Senator Thomas Dodd promptly brought the Juvenile Delinquency Subcommittee back to Southern California for hearings on the purported increase in heroin and barbiturate addiction among the "middle class," featuring eight leaders and patients from the Synanon community to represent these victims. The most resonant testimony came from Jeanne, the white twenty-eight-year-old mother profiled by *Life*, who narrated her downward spiral from an upbringing in a "good middle-class home," to a college student who started smoking marijuana and taking barbiturates, to a dropout and heroin addict until she was saved by Synanon House. Senator Dodd returned to Washington with praise for Synanon's (allegedly) miraculous breakthrough in addressing the psychology of drug addiction, but the framing of this therapeutic alternative only reinforced the racial double standards in public policy and political culture. In its own exploration of Synanon, the *New York Times* contrasted the successful rehabilitation of "'respectable' addicts mixing in polite society" with the heroin scourge in "criminally-oriented, culturally-deprived slums."[55]

The Kennedy administration's racialized interpretation of the juvenile delinquency crisis mirrored its narcotics enforcement agenda through the targeted focus on nonwhite youth in urban slums and the reliance on official crime data that obscured mass illegal activity among their white suburban counterparts. In 1961, President John Kennedy called for the federal government to launch a "total attack" on juvenile delinquency and youth crime, which he attributed to high rates of unemployment, school dropouts, and inner-city family breakdown.[56] Administration officials highlighted the concentration of gang-affiliated crime and narcotics addiction among African American, Mexican American, and Puerto Rican teenagers who lived in urban slums disadvantaged by a fusion of racial discrimination, family disorganization, and community pathologies. Citing FBI statistics, HEW Secretary Abraham Ribicoff informed Congress that the delinquency rate for "Negro boys" was generally five to eight times higher than for white youth in the same metropolitan area, with no acknowledgment of the racial discrimination in the juvenile adjudication system or the vast discretionary policing of youth status offenses (fig. 2.5). According to Attorney General Robert Kennedy, the administration restricted its antidelinquency demonstration projects to nonwhite urban sites because of their "rising tide of law violation" and since "problems of the inner city have an infectious way of spreading outward" to middle-class suburbs.[57] In private strategy sessions, a few of the academic experts who shaped the Kennedy initiative did recognize that "suburban areas have real problems" and that official delinquency rates were higher among nonwhite urban juveniles because of "excessive application of law enforcement." These observations reflected a growing body of academic research on the "considerable unrecorded delinquency among socially advantaged youths," but the Kennedy administration never publicly acknowledged the existence—or even the possibility—of racial and economic bias in the juvenile justice system. The liberal delinquency agenda, as Elizabeth Hinton has argued, merged benevolent antipoverty programs with increasingly punitive law enforcement interventions based on widespread, racist assumptions about Black criminality and "social pathology" in nonwhite urban slums.[58]

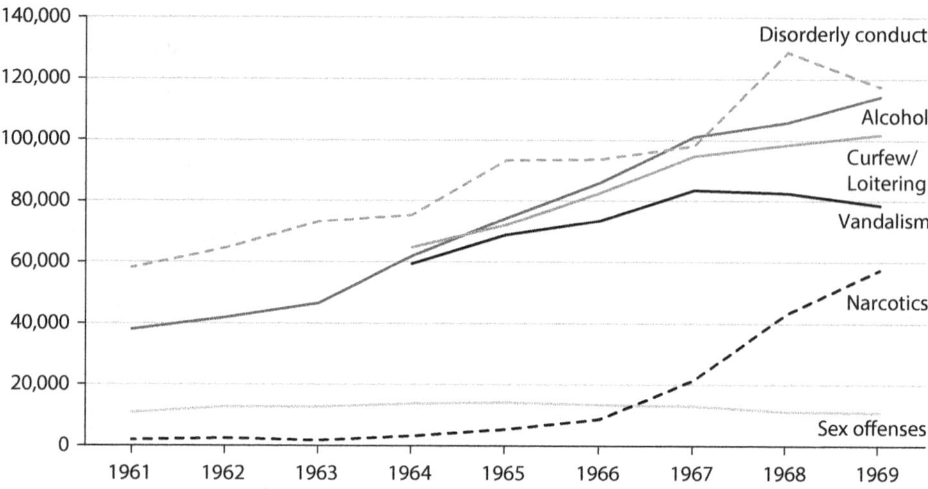

FIGURE 2.5. Arrests of juveniles (under eighteen) in the United States for select status/discretionary offenses and narcotics, as reported to the FBI, 1961–69. The delinquency control system in the United States disproportionately criminalized juveniles based on nonwhite identity, economic class, male gender, and age itself. The "total attack" on juvenile delinquency during the 1960s resulted in a doubling of reported arrests and primarily apprehended teenagers for discretionary and status offenses such as disorderly conduct, loitering, curfew, and underage drinking. The exponential increase in narcotics arrests starting in 1966 mainly involved marijuana. The "sex offenses" category generally involved consensual status offenses, not sexual assault. (Compiled from FBI, *Uniform Crime Reports*, 1961–1969.)
Note: This graphic does not include data on juveniles detained or adjudicated for "delinquent tendencies," the largest arrest category, because the FBI did not report that separately. A majority of these recorded arrests did not result in delinquency adjudications or commitments. Because of demographic growth and changes in local agency reporting rates, these totals represent about 64% of the U.S. population in 1961 and about 72% in 1969.

Academic studies of middle-class juvenile delinquency revealed a different story, finding a widespread if hidden culture of lawbreaking without consequences in the segregated white suburbs during the early-to-mid 1960s. Researchers who conducted ethnographic field work in middle-class suburbia increasingly rejected the fifties-era tendency to blame affluent youth delinquency on parental failure—the psychological interpretation that absentee commuter fathers and domineering and/or permissive mothers created distorted masculine aggression among male adolescents. Instead, the emerging scholarship emphasized the unsupervised freedom for youth on the automobile-centered suburban landscape, the development of an autonomous teenage subculture that mirrored rather than rejected the conformism and materialism of adult middle-class society, and not least the prevailing culture of impunity that all but guaranteed that even "flagrant violations of the law" would have no repercussions. The "dominant role of the car in patterns of middle-class deviance" enabled even typical suburban youth to break alcohol laws, engage in sex delinquency (criminalized premarital sex), commit acts of vandalism, smoke cigarettes pervasively, pop pills illegally, and experiment with marijuana. Sociologists who observed middle-class "gangs"—meaning group deviance in the suburbs that would be labeled gang activity in nonwhite and lower-income areas—highlighted alcohol-fueled activities by college-bound teenagers in autonomous adolescent spaces such as beaches, drive-ins, back roads (for drag racing), music venues, and house parties hosted by the children of absent or permissive parents. Every single study, from suburban Los Angeles to the tristate region of metropolitan New York City, found that official law enforcement records contained almost no traces of the extensive delinquent and criminal activities of affluent white teenagers. Most could only surmise that "the 'white-collar' delinquent engages in as many anti-social activities as do lower class youngsters." Some academics even argued that material affluence and excess leisure time actually resulted in higher (if unrecorded) rates of deviance and criminality among privileged white male youth who avoided manual labor through a culture of protracted adolescence.[59]

The mainstream media then transformed the "normal" delinquency of white middle-class adolescents into a full-blown youth generation crisis that had somehow flipped the utopian promises of safety and happiness in the single-family suburbs upside down. In "The Tense Generation" (1963), *Look* magazine confronted white middle-class suburbia with the question, although not really the answers, of "Why do teen-agers from 'good' homes steal, take dope, and shock their parents with their sexual delinquency?" *Look*'s investigation uncovered a subculture of thrill-seekers, misfits, and alienated youth causing trouble in suburban communities nationwide—"speed, liquor, pills, fights, stealing" by the males; drinking, premarital sex, and often unwanted pregnancies for their female companions. "It isn't a race problem," *Look* emphasized, in an implicit rejection of the Kennedy administration's antidelinquency mantra; "respectable white neighborhoods are as plagued" as anywhere else. The exposé concluded on a note of racial anxiety, warning of the "curious tendency these days for middle-class youth to imitate the slum dweller, to speak his language, to wear his clothes, to act as they imagine he acts." In 1964, the *New York Times Magazine* depicted "The Paradoxical Case of the Affluent Delinquent" as a catastrophic inversion of the suburban promise of the American Dream itself—an epidemic of narcotics addiction among white middle-class

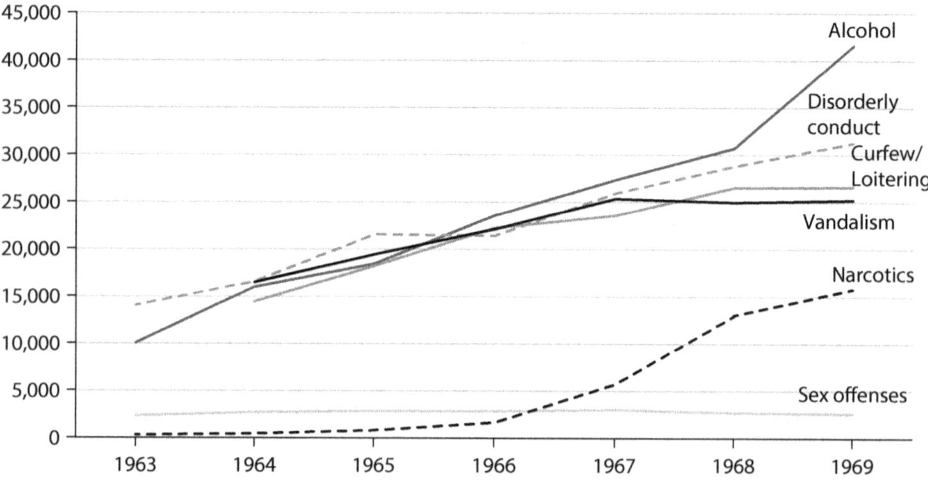

FIGURE 2.6. Arrests of juveniles (under eighteen) in suburban jurisdictions for select status/discretionary offenses and narcotics, as reported to the FBI, 1963–69. Teenagers in locations that the FBI classified as suburban accounted for one-third of all juvenile arrests in the United States by the late 1960s. The number of suburban arrests in most categories of discretionary and status criminalization doubled or tripled during the decade, although some of this growth resulted from an increase in the number of local agencies reporting data. Underage alcohol violations made up the largest category of suburban juvenile arrests, and many offenses in the discretionary categories of disorderly conduct and loitering were also alcohol-related. Narcotics arrests in the suburbs increased exponentially during the second half of the 1960s and primarily involved marijuana busts of white male youth (see chapter 3). (Compiled from FBI, *Uniform Crime Reports*, 1963–1969.)
Note: The FBI first began reporting "suburban" crime and delinquency data separately in 1963.

teenagers in Westchester County, an outbreak of gang fights and group crime sprees in some of the wealthiest towns in the metropolitan region, a spate of drunk-driving deaths following liquor-fueled house parties in the upscale enclaves of Connecticut. The scale of such "hidden delinquency" was unknowable because not only self-interested parents but also local law enforcement officials almost invariably covered it up, given that "suburban towns place a high value on being known as calm islands at the edge of the stormy urban sea."[60]

Underage consumption of alcohol, not illegal narcotics or marijuana use, was the recreational drug most central to the youth subculture of sociability, delinquency, and lawbreaking in the white suburbs during the early-to-mid 1960s (fig. 2.6). Teenage drinking generated some alarm, and was far more likely to be linked to violent crime and fatalities, but remained a normative middle-class activity considered an adolescent rite of passage distinct from the racialized stigmatization of marijuana and heroin as deviant and criminal. Public health studies in white suburbs found that almost all juveniles broke the age-status laws criminalizing underage drinking, that more than three-fourths in affluent coastal suburbs consumed alcohol weekly—but also that 95 percent of high school students drank moderately and responsibly. Even if true, the *Saturday Evening Post* argued in a 1965 report on the youth drinking crisis, that meant at least 350,000 problem drinkers in the teenage cohort nationwide, with particularly high concentrations among affluent males in car-dependent suburbs who paired drunkenness with violent and property crimes.[61] The routine occurrences of white youth "riots" in beachfront communities and vacation getaways also demonstrated the hazards of drunken group behavior in places where police were more willing to confront middle-class lawbreakers. In the white suburbs of Southern California, so-called teenage "beach riots" had erupted annually since the mid-1950s: a mass crowd assault on police officers who arrested a drunken spring breaker in Huntington Beach; an intoxicated melee involving 10,000 teenagers at a 1961 beach party in Malibu; mob violence that twice required riot police in Newport Beach; an "unruly mob" of 400 surfers who fought back during a 1963 police crackdown in Hermosa Beach. During the first half of the 1960s, alcohol-fueled white riots resulted in mass arrests of high school and college students in resort towns from Long Island and Ocean City, Maryland, to the Gulf Coast of Texas and Seaside, Oregon. The National Guard even mobilized to restore order during one Labor Day disturbance by 10,000 teenagers in Hampton Beach, New Hampshire.[62]

In the affluent suburbs of Connecticut, Sen. Thomas Dodd's home state, parallel uproars over teenage drinking and narcotics addiction during the mid-1960s reveal the crisis framework that emerged whenever the "It can't happen here" promise of a safe white nuclear family utopia inevitably shattered. The teen drinking controversy erupted in the upper-income, solidly Republican, 99 percent white town of Darien after seventeen-year-old Nancy Hitchings was killed in a 4:00 a.m. car crash after attending two debutante parties in private homes in summer 1964. The driver, an inebriated eighteen-year-old male, was convicted of vehicular homicide. Two days later, a nineteen-year-old male college student died in a solo drunk-driving crash following another debutante gathering. The Nancy Hitchings incident escalated after a local judge ordered the arrests of thirteen adults, including prominent members of Darien's professional class, for serving liquor to minors at the house parties, which had also involved off-duty police officers providing security. The charges set off a fierce debate within the community over the extent of parental responsibility for teenage lawbreaking and immediately brought the national print media and television networks to Darien. *Time* magazine alone featured the Nancy Hitchings fallout in three separate issues during fall 1964, focusing on both the impossibility of keeping privileged teenagers from drinking alcohol and the shock of affluent white parents who did not realize they could be legally liable for "contributing to the delinquency of a minor." Most of the adults pleaded no contest and received small fines, which did not quell the debate. The police chief and other Darien officials acknowledged that they did not, and perhaps could not, enforce the underage drinking laws either inside private homes or at the beaches and public parks where youth congregated. The subsequent marijuana bust of several Darien teenagers who attended the debutante parties drew a second unwelcome wave of national publicity, including *Time*'s claim that they were "hard-shell hippies" enthralled with New York City's bohemian subculture.[63]

The response to this saga within the Darien community fluctuated between panicked calls for a parental and police crackdown on illegal teen drinking and bitter denunciations that the national media spotlight was damaging the town's image, with almost no attempt to ask youth themselves for their perspective. The local newspaper, the *Darien Review*, declared that "this community stands indicted for a serious breakdown in moral values" and reprinted letters from across the nation praising the judge for holding the debutante parents responsible. Its editorials demanded that permissive parents stop sanctioning underage drinking and sexual delinquency on the beaches and inside private homes, urged families to sign a code of ethical conduct pledging to obey the alcohol and curfew laws, and called on the police department to stop letting wealthy adolescents get away with everything. But then, after the deluge of national publicity, the *Darien Review* condemned the "distasteful barrage of sensationalism" and insisted that all affluent suburban communities had the same problems. Quite a few residents accused the authorities of conducting a "witch hunt" against the parents by "bringing *criminal* charges against honorable people." This faction criticized the age twenty-one legal drinking age in Connecticut, when New York state set its standard at eighteen, and argued that introducing alcohol to teenagers in supervised settings was the safest way to teach responsible behavior.[64] The student newspaper from the all-white Darien High School criticized the hype about "empty and bewildered" suburban youth and instead emphasized the need for a teen center, which opened in fall 1964 after an extensive adolescent-led lobbying campaign. The adult supervision at the alcohol-free teen center certainly did not appeal to all Darien youth, and many continued to violate the age-status law criminalizing underage drinking. Political stirrings were also on the horizon, and the 1966 senior class speech, "Rebels with a Cause?," connected teen drinking and other forms of adolescent "rebellion" to the civil rights protests and anti–Vietnam War activism.[65]

The Darien furor prompted the Connecticut state government to launch a major crusade against the "evils of teen-age drinking" in white middle-class suburbia, part of a broader nationwide mobilization during the early-to-mid 1960s, including linked campaigns in New Jersey and other parts of New England. Governor John Dempsey, a liberal Democrat, blamed unrestricted access to automobiles but argued that parental intervention rather than law enforcement was the solution to the alleged crisis. Dempsey established a Teenage Liquor Law Study Commission whose report rejected calls to lower the legal drinking age to eighteen, even as it acknowledged that the vast majority of adolescents broke the law and that their alcohol consumption was normative behavior modeled on adult society. Instead, the commission recommended an enhanced alcohol education campaign and demanded that New York state raise its drinking age to twenty-one to prevent Connecticut youth from driving there to obtain liquor.[66] Governor Dempsey received an avalanche of correspondence from adult constituents blaming the "blood border" with New York for corrupting Connecticut youth, calling for a get-tough approach toward underage drinkers, and even advocating that teenagers be ineligible for driver's licenses. Letters from dozens of suburban high school and college students conveyed the opposite message, insisting that legal adults age eighteen and older had the right to drink alcohol and labeling the criminalization of this social practice both draconian and unenforceable. Numerous teenage males asked how they could be drafted and sent to Vietnam but denied a legal drink. Other youth asserted the right to "rebel from society" by breaking unjust laws and argued that there was nothing "wrong with this generation" except for the overhyped delinquency panic itself. Suburban towns and state officials in Connecticut ignored these youth voices but also continued to insist that the "primary point of attack must be in the home," explicitly rejecting the law enforcement approach to teenage delinquency that prevailed in nonwhite urban centers.[67]

The political and cultural response to the constructed crisis of teenage narcotics addiction in suburban Connecticut followed a similar pattern of overreaction to a relatively small social problem, conflation of all illegal drug users with hopeless addicts, broad but ineffectual criminalization of the youth subculture, and racialized double standards in law enforcement. In June 1963, a Connecticut television station broadcast a sensational documentary series on the "growing menace" of drug addiction in the state, portrayed as a universal threat in which "a tragic number of victims are teenagers." The centerpiece of both the advertising campaign and the series itself was a twenty-six-year-old white female who had been taking heroin since age fourteen, when pressure from friends lured her into a decade of addiction that ended only after she got clean through the Synanon group therapy method. The documentary profiled a recently established Synanon House in the wealthy suburb of Westport (99% white), just a few miles north of Darien on Connecticut's "Gold Coast," and the first located outside of California. The Westport-based Synanon served heroin and barbiturate addicts from across New England but had no more room for many other teenagers and young adults whose desperate parents wanted access to its miracle cure (Synanon's "success" rate was actually greatly exaggerated). ABC television rebroadcast the documentary for a national prime-time audience, and Senator Dodd of the Juvenile Delinquency Subcommittee celebrated the arrival of Synanon for his constituents as a breakthrough in the war on narcotics addiction. The Connecticut Narcotic Advisory Council also emphasized the inadequate number of treatment centers statewide and proposed a civil commitment law modeled on the California program, combined with a crackdown on the illegal circulation of pharmaceuticals that it labeled the stepping stone for youth addiction to heroin. In affluent suburbs such as Westport and Darien, there was very little evidence of teenage heroin use, but illicit barbiturates were common and marijuana busts were on the rise.[68]

The white middle-class teenage drug crisis exploded back into national political culture in the mid-1960s through dramatic media exposés such as "Dope Invades the Suburbs," a *Saturday Evening Post* investigation of the "carefully hushed up" outbreak of youth narcotics addiction (fig. 2.7). The 1964 article opened with a high school senior from an upper-middle-class enclave in Westchester County, not far from New York City, saying that his parents moved there "because the suburbs are supposed to be good for the kids," but instead marijuana and pills were everywhere. The *Saturday Evening Post* depicted a "tragic and frightening" epidemic of teenage addiction "spreading through the commuter suburbs" and infiltrating "'good' suburban homes" across the nation, as adolescents first moved from drinking alcohol to smoking marijuana and then "graduate[d]" to heroin or barbiturates. Law enforcement officials from suburban communities outside New York City and Los Angeles accused politicians and professional-class parents of covering up the extent of drug crimes by privileged youth. Public health experts emphasized that the illicit use of culturally approved barbiturates and amphetamines was a significantly greater threat than heroin. The article's portrayal of affluent youth as the victims of a suburban invasion existed in tension with the actual social practices that it described, as teenage "addicts" generally drove their cars to Harlem or Tijuana to "buy from pushers," suggesting an entrepreneurial network of white dealers and users on the suburban side of the distribution system. Not surprisingly, after drawing stark racial and spatial distinctions between white suburban addict-victims and their pusher-villains (located in Mexican border towns, inner-city ghettos, and Mafia syndicates), the *Saturday Evening Post* concluded that drug addiction should be treated as a medical illness rather than "a crime to be punished by the law."[69]

The illegal sale and possession of barbiturates and amphetamines was only a misdemeanor under federal law and in all fifty states, because unlike heroin, the licit and illicit market was both profitable to corporations and overwhelmingly white. But the latest suburban "epidemic" of teenage addiction enabled Thomas Dodd and the Juvenile Delinquency Subcommittee to finally advance drug control legislation that the pharmaceutical lobby had successfully blocked during the previous half-decade. Senator Dodd repeatedly charged that half of the ten billion barbiturate and amphetamine pills produced annually by American corporations ended up in the illicit market (as "goof balls" and "pep pills") and primarily victimized "white-collar youths who have never had prior delinquency records." Despite the clear responsibility of the pharmaceutical industry, Dodd placed direct blame on street-level "dangerous drug" pushers who siphoned off the legitimate medical supply and whose contraband allegedly transformed good kids into violent criminals and sex fiends.[70] National media reports such as "Teenagers and the Dope Hazard" (1964), in *Parents Magazine*, reinforced this crusade by portraying pill-based addiction among "white-collar youth" from "good families" as a completely separate problem from heroin crime in "big-city, segregated slums." The article also argued that "normal" youth who took illicit stimulants and depressants, often in dangerous combination with alcohol, were just imitating adult behavior in a society that medicalized fatigue, anxiety, and leisure. In "The Thrill-Pill Menace" (1965), the *Saturday Evening Post* dramatized the plight of white middle-class "pill-heads" who descended into lives of addiction and crime because of a vast underworld that diverted the licit supply. The article

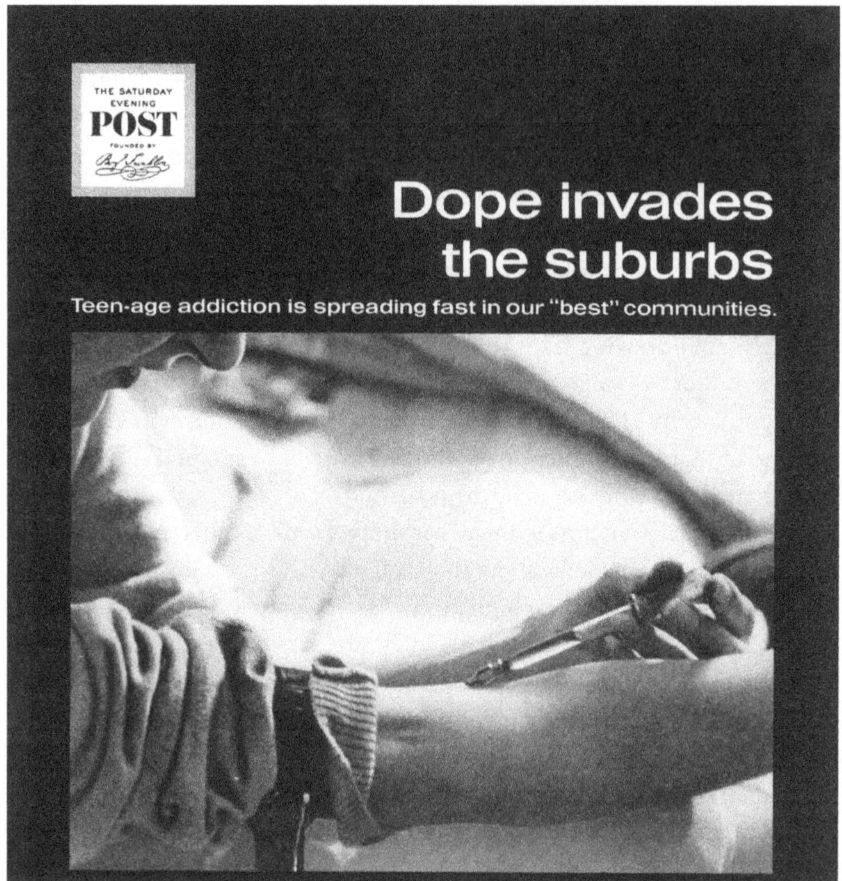

FIGURE 2.7. This cover story in the *Saturday Evening Post* (April 4, 1964) featured two of the most potent and misleading warnings of the era's drug-crisis discourse: the invasion of innocent suburbs by dope "pushers" and the progression of young white victims from marijuana experimentation to an "epidemic" of narcotics addiction. The article advocated medical rehabilitation rather than criminal law enforcement for suburban youth who shot heroin or took illicit barbiturates and amphetamines. (Photo by Archie Lieberman.)

featured a white fourteen-year-old female runaway from a "good family" who became addicted to amphetamine and moved in with a middle-aged heroin dealer, alongside a tragic recitation of white males who committed violent crimes under the influence of pills and alcohol (most dangerous when taken in combination).[71]

Felony penalties for illicit suppliers of amphetamines and barbiturates became the political solution designed to protect these innocent suburban victims of the "dangerous drugs" scourge. This approach reframed both the addiction and the criminality of white middle-class youth as the fault of evil pushers, which absolved the pharmaceutical industry of responsibility, ignored the central role of alcohol in the delinquency patterns being targeted, and justified the continued status criminalization of the youth subculture. In June 1965, Senator Dodd made this agenda explicit in reintroducing the Juvenile Delinquency Subcommittee's bill to increase regulatory controls on the illicit circulation of stimulant "pep pills" and sedative "goof balls." Dodd portrayed a raging epidemic in "wealthy suburban neighborhoods" and on college campuses, especially among pill-popping "'white-collar' youths," which he contrasted with the more limited problem of heroin addiction in crime-ridden urban slums. The legislation elevated the illegal sale and distribution of amphetamines and barbiturates from a misdemeanor to a felony with a maximum sentence of one year for the first offense and three years for the second, with penalties doubled for provision to youth under age twenty-one. The law conspicuously did not criminalize nonauthorized possession of these "dangerous drugs" for personal use, stating that its agenda was to "combat the illegal traffic" but "not to punish individual drug users" or to sanction law enforcement action against them. The U.S. Congress enacted the Drug Abuse Control Amendments Act of 1965 based on these formal provisions of selective market criminalization that insulated both the "legitimate" pharmaceutical suppliers and the imagined white middle-class drug-taking victims. President Lyndon Johnson signed the law and pledged to target "racketeers in this field [who] are making easy victims of many of our finest young people." California, New York, and other states enacted similar penalties for sale but also permitted felony charges for possession to enhance discretionary enforcement.[72]

The selective "dangerous drugs" debate built on the longstanding local policies of ensuring that white middle-class youth lawbreaking remained hidden from official crime records and also epitomized the broader racial double standards that shaped federal delinquency policy during the liberal reform era of the Kennedy and Johnson administrations. During the early-to-mid 1960s, FBI director J. Edgar Hoover continued to define the "all-out war" on youth crime as two distinct fronts: the primary target of "colored gangs" in the inner cities that engaged in crimes of violence fueled by alcohol and narcotics, and the manageable problem of delinquency among "normal" (white, middle-class) teenagers who just needed "the guidance and the discipline which can best be provided by a decent home." In the urban centers, "we have tried the charitable approach toward young hoodlums and it has failed," Hoover declared.

"These are not juvenile delinquents. They are vicious young thugs."[73] In March 1965, President Lyndon Johnson called for a national war on crime, a "malignant enemy in America's midst," but insisted that the law enforcement crackdown on teenage delinquency should be precisely targeted because "the great majority of our young people lead law-abiding, creative lives." Five months later, the Watts riot/rebellion in Los Angeles further racialized the liberal war on crime and delinquency as a crisis "specific to Black urban youth," reinforcing the bipartisan political consensus behind get-tough programs focused primarily on inner-city neighborhoods.[74] The Watts unrest in fact resulted directly from police brutality and other structures of racial segregation and inequality, but the dominant interpretation in the media and the white suburbs highlighted the dangerous criminality of African American juveniles. Newspaper and television coverage claimed that "roving bands" of Black teenagers threatened to "invade the white neighborhoods," and an outpouring of suburban sentiment demanded stronger police action to protect "the vast majority of law-abiding citizens" from urban gangs and "Negro hoodlums."[75]

The Johnson administration's war on Black youth crime, in combination with Watts and other outbreaks of urban disorder during the mid-1960s, contributed to a mainstream political culture that justified housing segregation in metropolitan regions and obscured the everyday reality of parallel teenage lawbreaking in the white middle-class suburbs—an episodic "crisis" periodically hyped and then hidden once again, but always ultimately decriminalized. After Kenneth Hahn, a leading liberal politician in Los Angeles County, blamed Watts on the cultural pathology of African American families and demanded respect for "law and order," a Black woman from the city informed him that the core problem was racist law enforcement and that no white males in suburban Lakewood or wealthy West Los Angeles would ever be arrested for the low-level discretionary violations policed relentlessly in her neighborhood. The McCone Commission's psychopathological interpretation that Watts represented an "insensate rage of destruction" by criminally inclined and culturally "disadvantaged Negro" youth deflected attention from segregationist policies such as the repeal of California's modest fair-housing law by three-fourths of white voters a year earlier.[76] *Ebony* magazine, the leading Black monthly, published a "Crime in the Suburbs" exposé as part of a special 1965 issue on "The White Problem in America" to puncture the mythology that racially segregated communities were "ideal . . . havens for those fleeing cities." The investigative report chronicled frequent "riots" by drunken white youth on beaches and outside entertainment venues, crime and vandalism by "gangs" of white male juveniles, shoplifting and sex delinquency by the females, growing use of marijuana and illicit pills in the exclusive suburbs—and the dominant ethos of making sure that none of this illegality became part of the official record of college-bound adolescents. And in "The Year of the Rebel . . . and the Riots," *Los Angeles* magazine argued that the rebellion was generational and political—not only in Watts but on college campuses and in upscale suburbs, where protest movements and the drug culture had created a volatile, alienated youth scene.[77]

Campus Rebels and the Psychedelic Drug Culture

In 1966, CBS-TV's Webster Groves documentary portraying white middle-class American teenagers as a conformist and apolitical generation cocooned in safe, segregated suburbs captured a prevailing framework that was already on the verge of disintegration, primarily through the activism and dissent of youth themselves. Back in 1960, the White House Conference on Children and Youth declared that "suburbanism" had become the culturally dominant expression of the American way of life, based on "conformity to middle-class values" and almost total racial and economic segregation, which provided youth with an insular and unrealistic understanding of the wider world. In "Suburbia's Coddled Kids" (1960), the *Saturday Evening Post* lamented the "massive overprotecting of the young" in the "near-utopia" of racially segregated single-class communities designed to protect them from the delinquency and dangers of urban life, but which had left them unable to question their society at all. In 1961, the Gallup Poll conducted a scientific survey of high school and college students and found that the "typical American youth" wanted to marry young and have children, live in a suburban ranch house, and in general "likes things the way they are." Gallup concluded that this white middle-class suburban composite "is most unlikely to rebel or involve himself in crusades of any kind," in contrast to the minority of teenage delinquents and the "beatniks" who lived on the margins (meaning white bohemians who congregated in cities). During the early-to-mid 1960s, numerous ethnographic studies of the "shortchanged children of suburbia" criticized the apparent white middle-class parental consensus that kids should be confined to islands of sameness that excluded "undesirables" and insulated teenagers from the multiracial and multicultural world outside their boundaries. This line of analysis viewed affluent white youth in the suburbs as culturally "deprived" of real-world experiences, although the research did reveal that peer group influences shaped adolescent values and behavior more than parents did.[78]

In 1962, Students for a Democratic Society (SDS) opened the *Port Huron Statement* with a striking repudiation of this white middle-class suburban consensus: "We are people of this generation, bred in at least modest comfort, housed now in universities, looking uncomfortably to the world we inherit." "Many of us began maturing in complacency," the New Left's generational manifesto continued, but "our comfort was penetrated by events too troubling to dismiss"—in particular, the civil rights movement against racial segregation and the reckless militarism of Cold War anticommunism. The SDS vision of radical campus-based activism to achieve a genuine "participatory democracy" depended upon the extraordinary idea that affluent white youth actually constituted an oppressed class in postwar America, and therefore that middle-class college students could be the vanguard for societal transformation. The New Left evolved into a mass movement between the 1964 Free Speech Movement at UC–Berkeley, where student leader Mario Savio renounced the American "utopia of sterilized, automated contentment," and the SDS-led protests against the Vietnam War that escalated a year later.[79] In 1966, *Time* magazine named the under-twenty-five youth generation its "Man of the Year" and credited the campus New Left for the "revival of true political dissent," while also classifying most college and high school students as pseudo-rebels and romantics in search of a cause. *Time*'s sweeping assessment identified a widening "generational gap" between adult society and an often-alienated youth cohort in search of authenticity, whether through political activism or more meaningful careers or the "heightened" life experiences provided by marijuana and LSD. The report stated that pot smoking had become a pervasive and "integral part of the generation's life experience" on elite university campuses and estimated that around half of all older high school students in metropolitan Los Angeles had experimented with marijuana as well. The bolder members of the "Now Generation" were also dropping acid for their psychedelic trips.[80]

The simultaneous emergence of protest movements and a mainstream illegal drug culture on college campuses ensured that the use of marijuana and LSD by white middle-class students would be located in a political generation gap framework rather than defined primarily as a criminal problem. In "Drugs on the Campus" (1966), a major investigative report by the *Saturday Evening Post*, interviews at more than fifty colleges and universities revealed an overwhelming student consensus that marijuana was "harmless" and "this generation's illicit pleasure," a relaxing social practice that appealed not only to activists and bohemian "hippies" but also to an increasing number of fraternity and sorority types as well. These recreational pot smokers (every image featured white middle-class students, mainly attractive "coeds") generally made good grades and considered shooting heroin to be completely out of the question, indeed gauche. The article labeled marijuana part of a "general pattern of rebellion against society's values" as well as a "safe way to rebel." The *Saturday Evening Post*'s informants described a casual distribution system where West Coast college students drove to Mexico to purchase marijuana for friends and customers, with similarly informal networks of supply and circulation in the university clusters of Chicago, New York, and Boston. Many students expressed paranoia about law enforcement crackdowns as well as righteous anger over incidents such as Cornell University's enlistment of the local police to round up campus marijuana dealers who allegedly "prey on young people and persuade them to experiment with habit-forming narcotics." In the ensuing backlash, the Ithaca district attorney stated that "these kids are different from slum users. There should be some way to bring across the point that marijuana is wrong and harmful without incarcerating them for five years." The gateway view that marijuana experimentation led to heroin addiction simply did not apply to middle-class students, the *Saturday Evening Post* concluded, and therefore punishing "college rebels" under the narcotics laws was unjustified.[81]

The white drug culture on college campuses was opaque and exotic to the mainstream media, which produced knowledge and shaped popular understanding through broad generalizations and stereotypes of a previously sheltered generation that had suddenly embraced political causes and simultaneously repudiated the constraints of suburban conformity and middle-class morality. Estimates of the extent of illegal drug use on campus varied wildly during the breakout period of 1966–67, but more reliable studies found between 15 and 25 percent of students had smoked marijuana (a felony crime) at the major universities in the Northeast and on the West Coast, with all trends pointing upward. A much smaller subset, approximately 5 percent, had experimented with LSD. Many more college students continued to use other illicit amphetamines or barbiturates, and almost all had broken the underage drinking laws. Heroin use on campus was virtually nonexistent.[82] A 1966 investigation by the *New York Times* claimed that most marijuana and LSD users were either graduate students or undergraduate humanities and social science majors from upper-middle-class backgrounds, "vaguely leftist, disenchanted with American policies in Vietnam, agitated because there are Negro ghettos and bored with conventional politics." These suburban rebels were products of the permissive culture of middle-class childrearing yet filled with "distaste for split-level society," and their collective search for a generational identity was opening up an "immense gap" with the adult world. Other media profiles asserted that "everybody's turning on," not just the politically active campus left and the culturally alienated middle-class hippies, but a broad spectrum of students from the "privileged classes" smoking marijuana and sampling LSD out of "curiosity, kicks, fun, rebellion, boredom, or for the promise of drug-produced insight." "Should I give up a good thing," one college sophomore informed a research team, "just because some freak in the state capitol says it's illegal?"[83]

Most campus participants in the recreational drug scene considered the legal distinction between their own consumption of marijuana and LSD, and the widespread use and abuse of alcohol and prescription drugs by their parents' generation, to be an irrational and unjust spillover of urban narcotics enforcement as well as a symbol of repressive anti-youth policies in line with fundamental American hypocrisies. "Marijuana is this generation's alcohol," proclaimed a sympathetic thirty-year-old *Look* correspondent in a 1967 feature on the ecumenical drug culture at the University of Missouri, illustrated with white middle-class students (faces hidden) passing joints in off-campus apartments and communing with nature while tripping on acid. The article stated conclusively that marijuana was not physically addictive, ridiculed the gateway-to-heroin theory, and labeled the felony laws that classified marijuana as an equivalent narcotic to be unscientific and "absurd." *Look* did warn that taking LSD could trigger psychosis and cause permanent brain damage, but the primary effect on the acid heads that it profiled seemed to be heightened skepticism about materialistic values and the suburban boundaries of the American Dream. "My goals have really been changing," a marijuana smoker who occasionally dropped acid explained. "I really held on to the nice car and the American-Way-of-Life bit. I wanted to make a lot of money and have a comfortable life. Now, more than anything else, I want peace and happiness." *Look*'s correspondent—who actually smoked pot and took LSD with a group of students to become fully immersed in the generational experience—concluded: "We cannot arrest them into submission. These are young, searching, uncommitted, kind, bright, gentle kids. . . . Using drugs is how they wish to live their lives, seek experiences, search for meaning." *Life* magazine depicted surging rates of campus marijuana use as the "greatest mass flouting of the law since Prohibition" and asserted that its very illegality appealed to youth in rebellion against "a middle-class culture they disdain."[84]

Ethnographic studies of the campus drug subculture confirmed the links to political rebellion and a culturally broader antiestablishment ethos while strongly criticizing the continued criminalization of the harmless recreational activities of white youth. *It's Happening* (1966), a sociological investigation of the psychedelic drug scene and the generation gap, found that the sons and daughters of the white upper-middle-class establishment were smoking marijuana and taking LSD as an act of experience and escape, a disaffected yet utopian quest to create a world defined in opposition to the mainstream value system of materialism, violence, imperialism, intolerance, and hypocrisy. "These aren't the pathologically depressed souls of Harlem or Watts . . . using smack to block out the horrors" of racism and poverty, the study concluded. "These are the kids of the Establishment Liberals," the vanguard of a societal revolution for whom illegal drug use was a consequence rather than the cause of their political disenchantment and irreverent "hang-loose ethic." A 1967 survey of one West Coast university revealed that the approximately one-fifth of students who had smoked marijuana and/or taken LSD were three times as likely to have participated in a political demonstration, twelve times more likely to oppose the Vietnam War, and highly "antagonistic" toward establishment values and societal hypocrisies. The analysis concluded that marijuana was a harmless recreational drug whose illegal status was based on moral disapproval of subcultural values, not legitimate crime or public health concerns. Sociologist Erich Goode's pathbreaking research decisively disproved the continued Bureau of Narcotics insistence that marijuana experimentation led to heroin addiction and emphasized its ritualistic role as a subcultural group activity in white middle-class social settings, especially among politically liberal and radical youth. Goode found that marijuana smokers were most likely also to have used LSD or amphetamines and almost always "turned on" with friends in interactions based on sharing rather than dealing for profit.[85]

American culture generally operates to depoliticize youth and deny them any collective platform, but the scale of the white middle-class revolt of the mid-to-late 1960s provided an opening for participants in the campus subculture to articulate their illegal drug use through a political prism—a racial privilege never extended to their nonwhite counterparts. *The College Drug Scene* (1968), an ethnographic investigation of eighty marijuana and LSD adherents at UC–Berkeley, found that these "rebels and nonconformists" expressed extreme hostility to the "square world" of middle-class hypocrisy, suburban tract homes, racial injustice and endless wars. "We realize the things our parents have been telling us over and over and over again are lies," one twenty-one-year-old explained. "We just don't want this society anymore." Another nineteen-year-old student stated that first "you learn that what you have been told is wrong, and that justice doesn't prevail," and then the inevitable next step is to realize that the prohibition and stigma against illegal drug use was unjustified as well. The study distinguished between recreational marijuana users who tended to be active in New Left causes and the politically alienated "heads" who had renounced American society altogether and combined daily pot smoking with frequent LSD trips. Many of the "heads" previously had joined protests against the Vietnam War but had come to believe that nothing would ever change in American politics and society and therefore the best they could hope for was to transform their own lives in small-scale communal arrangements. *The College Drug Scene* emphasized that criminal law was no deterrent for these white Berkeley drug users and also drew a direct contrast between their politically motivated subcultural activities and the deviant combination of heroin addiction and crime in the "lower class Negro slum." Most of the campus rebels interviewed advocated the legalization of marijuana and believed that taking LSD, while not without risk, was an important step in breaking free from the constraints and hang-ups of the square society. [86]

The link between marijuana and LSD in the campus drug scene led to another full-blown crisis about a new gateway dynamic, driven by sensationalistic media reports of the dangers for middle-class youth caught up in the "acid craze." For parents who might be slowly coming to terms with the normalization of marijuana among the college generation, the *Saturday Evening Post* presented worrisome examples such as a female student who cheerfully summarized her coming-of-age experience: "First I came to Berkeley from LA. Then I pierced my ears. Then I went on a few marches. Then I tried pot. Then I lost my virginity. And soon, I'll probably try LSD."[87] In 1966, *Time* published a series of reports on how the frightening "epidemic of acid heads" was leading to psychotic breakdowns of innocent victims, while a *Life* magazine cover story chronicled LSD's spread from "a large underground cult" led by former Harvard professor Timothy Leary into a "dangerous fad on the college campus." The *Life* article included close-up (likely staged) images of a white female teenager who felt the "desire to die" while taking a bad trip at a Sunset Strip party in Hollywood, along with dire warnings that experimenters could suffer "disastrous psychological effects" and might become "permanently deranged through a single terrifying LSD experience." In "The Hidden Evils of LSD" (1967), the *Saturday Evening Post* drew from the cultural script of innocent white females corrupted by nefarious narcotics pushers to highlight tragedies such as a "pretty brunette from a well-to-do middle-class family" who started smoking marijuana and then progressed to acid after allegedly falling for the psychedelic proselytizing of LSD guru Timothy Leary. After two bad trips, the "LSD victim" ended up trapped in a hippie commune and ultimately had to be sedated for several months at the UCLA hospital, whose leading psychiatrist labeled LSD "the most dangerous drug to come down the pike in a long, long time." According to federal law enforcement officials, LSD suddenly represented "a problem worse than the narcotics [heroin] evil."[88]

Psychiatrists and other medical experts argued that LSD held significant therapeutic potential for patients under formal supervision but cautioned of extreme hazards for recreational users, especially those already "hovering on the brink" of mental illness. According to preliminary, unverified research findings relentlessly spread by the mass media, even a single dose of LSD had the potential to trigger paranoid schizophrenia and permanent psychosis. "The Hidden Evils of LSD," the *Saturday Evening Post*'s influential exposé, hyped circumstantial evidence that the hallucinogen caused chromosome damage, leukemia, birth defects, and incurable psychiatric disorders—scientifically unproven speculation based on a very small set of cases that took on the status of truth in the broader political culture. "If you take LSD even once," the article proclaimed, "your children may be born malformed or retarded." These warnings about a novel and mysterious new drug were so specific, pervasive, and medically endorsed that they appear to have slowed the expected rate of LSD growth in the youth population—unlike the completely ineffective marijuana scare tactics. Taking a page from the "reefer madness" era, mainstream news outlets and even some leading psychiatric experts also publicized apocryphal or greatly exaggerated horror stories of otherwise normal LSD users committing suicide by jumping out of windows, leaping off bridges while trying to fly, wandering aimlessly into traffic, and committing assaults and murders during paranoid hallucinations.[89] Later research undermined these claims, distinguishing between the occasional experience of a "bad trip" and the unscientific warnings of instant psychosis or permanent organ damage—with lingering effects most evident in those with prior mental instability rather than randomly induced by the drug itself. The scientists published hunches and tales of terror, one chronicler observed, because they could not accept youth testaments of LSD's "mystic religious experience" when linked to "cultural revolt" by an entire generation.[90]

The white-middle class face of the "acid epidemic" structured the political debate about how to criminalize the supply side while protecting LSD's alleged victims, as did the absence of the racial imaginary of urban and foreign "pushers" that had shaped previous legislative crackdowns on heroin and marijuana. The Johnson administration pledged to increase enforcement against LSD traffickers but explicitly opposed any criminal penalties for use and possession, arguing against "filling up our jails with a bunch of college students." In May 1966, the Food and Drug Administration announced that LSD would come under the regulatory framework of the "dangerous drugs" law passed a year earlier, which had criminalized unauthorized sale, but not illicit possession, of amphetamines and barbiturates. This meant that unlicensed distribution of LSD, a drug portrayed as far more dangerous than marijuana, was still only a misdemeanor, while possession carried no penalty under federal law.[91] Thomas Dodd, the liberal drug warrior from Connecticut, summoned administration officials to justify this situation in a series of hearings during spring 1966, conducted as stories of campus radicals taking acid trips and white youth experiencing LSD-induced insanity proliferated in the mass media. FDA Commissioner James Goddard resisted congressional pressure to make LSD possession for personal use illegal, stating that this would "automatically place into the category of criminals perhaps tens to hundreds of thousands of college students." Dodd's subcommittee then heard from three young white residents of NYC's East Village who extolled the virtues of LSD for a generation seeking a higher spirituality, pledged that criminal sanctions would not deter them in the slightest, and challenged the dismayed senators to drop acid as part of their investigation. The group also disputed Federal Bureau of Narcotics claims that crime syndicates were "pushing" LSD, instead explaining that the supply circulated "through a network of amateurs and friends" on college campuses and in bohemian enclaves. [92] This led to a remarkable exchange:

> PAULA SHERWOOD [COLLEGE SENIOR]: Making criminals of otherwise law-abiding people does not solve any problems. (. . .)
>
> EVE BABITZ [TWENTY-THREE-YEAR-OLD RESIDENT OF THE EAST VILLAGE]: If LSD is made illegal, if possession is made a felony, then I will probably become a criminal. . . . You could make me, and perhaps millions of other Americans, into criminals and we don't feel that we have done anything wrong.
>
> SENATOR EDWARD KENNEDY [D-MA]: Are you aware . . . of the crimes of violence that have been committed by LSD users?
>
> WALTER BOWART [PUBLISHER OF *EAST VILLAGE OTHER*]: Sir, I think we know so little about LSD that no one can make that statement. (. . .)

SENATOR QUENTIN BURDICK [D-ND]: Suppose that the Congress in its wisdom should see fit to make LSD, possession of it illegal?

PAULA SHERWOOD: I am productive and do not do anything illegal otherwise. I feel that prohibition would be pretty unjust. So I would probably go underground. (. . .)

SENATOR BURDICK: Do most of your friends use LSD?

EVE BABITZ: Just about. I would say about 90 percent of them, and I know a lot of people. (. . .)

SENATOR BURDICK: Are there not LSD pushers?

WALTER BOWART: No, it is a social thing, really. (. . .)

SENATOR BURDICK: Where did you get [LSD]?

EVE BABITZ: A friend gave it to me. (. . .)

PAULA SHERWOOD: You will have a very hard time finding out.

EVE BABITZ: Nobody knows.[93]

Pressure to criminalize LSD possession continued to build in response to the massive escalation of political unrest on college campuses, the alarm that greeted the "hippie" dropout phenomenon (covered in the next section), and especially growing fears that taking acid was causing upper-middle-class white youth to lose their so-called "motivation" and abandon productive capitalist pursuits. Sidney Cohen, a UCLA psychiatrist who played an influential role in hyping the LSD menace, warned that the breakdown of middle-class standards—meaning a combination of political nonconformity and the adoption of stereotypically "ghetto" values by white youth—represented an even greater threat than occasional psychosis. LSD adherents "lead a valueless life, without motivation, without any ambition," Cohen informed Congress. "They are 'deculturated,' lost to society, lost to themselves, hung up in fantasy and a dreamlike nonexistence." In May 1966, urged on by Dr. Cohen, California became the first state to outlaw both sale and possession of LSD, with a one-to-five-year felony penalty for distribution and a misdemeanor offense for use. Most states had taken similar actions by the end of 1967.[94] Then in early 1968, under renewed pressure from congressional Democrats, President Lyndon Johnson called for federal criminalization of LSD possession combined with tougher felony penalties for sale, in order to go after the "drug and narcotics peddlers." In the standard racialized formulation, Johnson labeled heroin "largely an urban problem" but warned that LSD and marijuana "had spread to suburban and rural regions, and are taken by far too many American youths." Health officials in the FDA swallowed their opposition to criminal penalties for LSD use after losing a power struggle with the administration's law enforcement agencies, which testified to Congress that the federal government needed the capacity to target the "vicious people" providing acid to vulnerable youth on college campuses and in hippie enclaves.[95]

The get-tough legislation signed by Lyndon Johnson in 1968 included federal criminalization of LSD possession, centralization of drug enforcement in a new agency, and targeted crackdowns on urban Black youth through the Safe Streets Act and the Juvenile Delinquency Prevention Act. The LSD law elevated sale and manufacture to a felony with a maximum five-year sentence and, for the first time, classified possession as a misdemeanor.[96] A separate reorganization plan transferred federal criminal enforcement of all drugs—illicit amphetamines and barbiturates previously regulated by the FDA; heroin, marijuana, and cocaine under FBN purview inside the Treasury Department—to a newly established Bureau of Narcotics and Dangerous Drugs (BNDD) based in the Department of Justice. This was a critical development in America's long drug war, overseen by liberal policymakers in the Johnson administration and Congress, that marginalized the medical approach favored by federal health agencies and concentrated power over policy and science within the DOJ's crime control apparatus. The BNDD operated with greater authority and resources than its predecessor agency, led through five presidencies by FBN Commissioner Harry Anslinger, while carrying on his punitive legacy based on the racialized binary of a permanent criminal heroin problem in the urban slums and the new cultural challenge of marijuana and LSD use among white youth.[97] The alternative drug regulation path not taken during the Johnson administration, advocated by a few dissident medical bureaucrats at the time, would have decriminalized marijuana possession instead of criminalizing LSD use. FDA Commissioner Goddard even publicly stated that marijuana was less dangerous than alcohol and that its prohibition was making "felons of our college students," and he appeared to endorse reducing the federal possession penalty to a misdemeanor before backing down under a fierce political backlash. The new BNDD kept on hyping the old marijuana-to-heroin, and now marijuana-to-LSD, gateway scourge.[98]

Criminal enforcement of the marijuana and LSD laws did increase significantly on college campuses between 1967 and 1969, in response to both the general escalation of radical youth politics and the considerable expansion of psychedelic drug use among white middle-class teenagers and young adults. Marijuana arrests of high school students also rose substantially after police crackdowns in a number of white suburbs, especially in Southern California (see chapter 3). The targeting of pot-smoking and acid-dropping campus rebels under laws designed to protect them from narcotics traffickers provoked enormous outrage from white youth themselves, even though very few of those arrested actually faced felony prosecution. The broader drug-war discourse also continued to draw a racial and geographic boundary between the "otherwise law-abiding" middle-class student market and the criminally oriented urban heroin scene. During the 1968 congressional debate over increasing LSD penalties, the National Institute of Mental Health reported that only 5 percent of enrolled college students had taken acid but at least 20 percent had broken the felony marijuana laws, and that trying to frighten these already "alienated" youth into compliance through scare tactics about heroin addiction was a completely ineffective approach. But many of the medical experts as well as law enforcement officials who testified to Congress justified the criminalization of both drugs based on the constant refrain that judges and prosecutors would utilize their inherent and statutory discretion to send the "hard-core criminal" to prison while diverting the misguided and "innocent" first offender into rehabilitation or psychiatric counseling. Psychiatrist Helen Nowlis, the director of federal drug education outreach to college campuses, disagreed and adamantly denounced the "criminal penalty approach" toward drug use, warning Congress that increased enforcement would make students even more "embittered towards the larger society." She emphasized that the recent surge in marijuana smoking, and the longer history of alcohol status criminalization, disproved the fantasy that legal sanctions could act as a deterrent to American youth."[99]

In January 1968, an armed contingent of two hundred police officers conducted a 5:00 a.m. raid on dormitories of the State University of New York at Stony Brook and arrested thirty-three white youth for narcotics law violations. The campus, located on suburban Long Island, erupted in fury. The operation utilized the testimony of young undercover officers who disguised themselves with long hair and beards to buy marijuana, and some LSD and amphetamine, during a three-month investigation. All of those arrested were between ages seventeen and twenty-one; the *New York Times* published their names and hometowns. The Suffolk County Police Department labeled most of them campus pushers, but students insisted that the majority were just recreational drug users who provided marijuana to acquaintances (the district attorney pleaded the alleged major dealers to misdemeanor possession and probation). The university threatened to expel any students who broke the drug laws and mandated that marijuana users undergo group therapy, while the state legislature opened hearings into Stony Brook's alleged narcotics menace. Enraged students held a series of protests, accused the university and law enforcement of violating their civil liberties and acting as a police state, and demanded the legalization of marijuana. Residents of nearby suburbs attacked SUNY undergraduates as "hideous hippies," and Governor Nelson Rockefeller received a flood of letters praising the police raid and demanding that the state "clean up the mess" at its taxpayer-supported universities. Many correspondents labeled the students arrested on marijuana charges to be "narcotics addicts and pushers," and they described Stony Brook as a "degenerate" place of drug "orgies" and "complete anarchy and moral decay," where permissive administrators and radical faculty encouraged "flagrant disregard and disrespect for our laws." A year later, after a second undercover sting, the Suffolk County narcotics squad again raided SUNY-Stony Brook and arrested eighteen more white youth on marijuana and LSD charges. At least two hundred students rioted in response, stoning and burning police cars and setting fires on campus, and around half of undergraduates went on a multiday protest strike from class.[100]

The Stony Brook raid became an oft-cited symbol of police repression against the youth generation as drug busts on college campuses escalated in the late 1960s, often through politically motivated crackdowns on New Left activists and countercultural radicals. In 1967, the Columbus police arrested a twenty-year-old Ohio State University student after she advocated legalization of marijuana and LSD at a city council meeting. The female, who received a ten-to-twenty-year possession sentence, served one month before agreeing to renounce her views in exchange for early release and rehabilitative treatment under extended probation. At Cornell University, a series of marijuana busts raised accusations of entrapment after undercover narcotics agents befriended regular students, asked them to acquire pot, and then arrested them as "pushers."[101] In 1968, the East Lansing police raided Michigan State University and arrested thirteen youth on narcotics (marijuana) charges based on an undercover operation launched after a majority of students voted for legalization in a campus referendum. Hundreds of MSU students protested under the banner of civil liberties and students' rights, which prompted brutal police suppression of a large demonstration, followed by calls for a "student revolution." That same year, the Madison police targeted the campus "dope traffic" at the University of Wisconsin, a hotbed of New Left radicalism and antiwar protests, and arrested thirty-eight students and other youth for marijuana and LSD crimes.[102] In Berkeley, the police department arrested 3,883 adults and 892 juveniles on drug charges between 1967 and mid-1969, with the majority on or immediately adjacent to the UC campus, predominantly involving white males ages 18 to 23. Plainclothes officers routinely staked out campus and countercultural hangouts and worked closely with federal agents in the Bureau of Narcotics and Dangerous Drugs. Despite this considerable enforcement campaign, most of the detained juveniles received only an informal warning, and almost no busted college students went to jail or prison, either getting off with a threat or at most facing misdemeanor probation and diversion into a rehabilitation program—the latter still a punitive outcome.[103]

The U.S. National Student Association, the main political association that represented the interests of college students, denounced all campus drug enforcement operations and announced a new campaign to legalize marijuana in a December 1968 manifesto. Charles Hollander, the association's director of drug policy, estimated that sixteen thousand college students nationwide had been arrested on drug charges during the most recent semester, compared to two thousand in fall 1967. He further pointed out that almost as many high school students were being busted for marijuana in California alone—ten thousand juveniles during the first six months of 1968. The National Student Association rejected the law enforcement approach as "cruel and inhumane to our own kids in what amounts to a public health or social problem." Its statement emphasized that marijuana was not addictive, not harmful when used recreationally, and a "relatively mild intoxicant" comparable to alcohol. The group also argued that campus crackdowns were politically motivated because marijuana smokers were more likely than other students to be activists working for social change. At a special National Student Association conference to advance the marijuana legalization movement, held at SUNY–Stony Brook because of its infamous undercover raid, speakers ridiculed the federal BNDD and the broader society's "hysterical" fears that smoking marijuana led to heroin addiction and ruined lives. It is important to note that, in condemning the "wave of repression" by law enforcement, the National Student Association declined to take any position on the prohibition of either LSD or heroin, ducking the debate about the hallucinogenic drug that the Johnson administration had recently criminalized and avoiding completely the narcotics issue connected with nonwhite urban populations. The American Civil Liberties Union announced its support for the association's legalization campaign and likewise portrayed white college students arrested for marijuana as the primary victims of the national war on drugs, warning that criminal penalties would harm their careers.[104]

The public vitriol in reaction to the campus drug scene was extensive and part of the broader Middle American backlash against young white radicals in the New Left and counterculture that had been building since the Berkeley Free Speech Movement of 1964–65—opposed by 80 percent of the public—and the emergence of anti–Vietnam War protests soon thereafter. Americans who identified as hard-working, patriotic taxpayers depicted campus rebels as class and race traitors, with little distinction between recreational marijuana use by professionally oriented students, and the political radicals and hippies imagined to be dedicated to overthrowing the social order. The campaign really began with a coordinated assault by political conservatives, including J. Edgar Hoover of the FBI, on the Free Speech Movement as a subversive and communist-infiltrated revolution to corrupt Berkeley students into rejecting "their family, their country, their religion, and their moral standards." Broadsides about the "Berkeley Revolution" created by right-wing organizations in the Los Angeles suburbs connected civil disobedience and antiwar protests to marijuana legalization advocates, dirty "beatniks," and the "almost uncontrollable problem" of pot smoking on campus.[105] By 1966, as antiwar activism escalated, California "taxpayers" who identified as Republicans and Democrats were demanding that Governor Pat Brown crack down on the Berkeley rebellion and the broader campus unrest. A deluge of letters denounced campus activists as degenerates, agitators, hoodlums, traitors, anarchists, malcontents, filthy and long-haired beatniks, "bearded kooks," disgusting scum, cowards, "immature" revolutionaries, anarchists, communists, and more. A number directly compared the protesters and marijuana/LSD criminals at Berkeley to the Watts rioters; the "sons of the Establishment," one man from the San Jose suburbs informed Governor Brown, "are *just* as *violent* as Negroes." Brown, a leading liberal drug warrior, lost reelection in 1966 to Ronald Reagan's conservative crusade linking the "mess at Berkeley" to the violent "jungle" in Watts.[106]

The political mobilization of the "forgotten Americans" and the "silent majority," as Richard Nixon labeled Middle American voters during his 1968 campaign and subsequent presidency, portrayed the white militancy on college campuses and the racial unrest in urban centers as a unified threat to normative middle-class suburban values and therefore the entire American way of life. At decade's end, *Time* named the Middle Americans its "Man and Woman of the Year," three years after giving the designation to the under-twenty-five youth generation, in recognition of a law-and-order backlash that was white, bipartisan, and mobilized against the "defiant young." "Dissent and drugs seemed to wash over them in waves," *Time* proclaimed, "bearing some of their children away."[107] Self-identified members of the silent majority circulated their own political manifestoes to define a collective Middle American identity in opposition to student radicals, the campus drug culture, and urban rioters and criminals. In "Enough Is Enough," a proud member of the middle-class "establishment" angrily asked why he paid taxes for campus riots, "potheads with psychic episodes," and filthy hippies—proposing to "keep America beautiful by flushing the pot-headed protesters down the gutters of their own minds." "You Remember the Real America" waxed nostalgic for the days when "riots were unthinkable, . . . when college kids swallowed goldfish, not acid, . . . when everybody knew the difference between right and wrong, . . . when you knew the law would be enforced, . . . when America was a land filled with brave, proud, confident, hardworking people." In "I Am a Sick American," a suburban father railed against campus anarchists, marijuana legalization, urban riots, pornography, and especially the younger generation's insistence that something was wrong with hardworking, middle-class Americans rather than with themselves. In "My Declaration of War"—mailed to all fifty governors—a suburban New Jersey resident promised that the law-abiding majority would defeat the criminals, rioters, and campus radicals in the end.[108]

The American state criminalized campus activism and political dissent as "internal subversion" and capitalized on illegal drug use as a key pillar of its strategy to harass and undermine the New Left. In 1968, FBI director Hoover labeled Students for a Democratic Society a "band of self-styled revolutionaries . . . [with] a pathological hatred for our way of life" and also observed that most of these class traitors were "reared in affluent homes." The COINTELPRO program, the secret FBI operation to infiltrate and neutralize "subversive" political groups, advised local police to arrest New Left activists on marijuana and LSD charges and also created propaganda portraying SDS leaders as advocates of heroin use and sex orgies in a plot to destroy the "'straight' world."[109] In California, Governor Reagan announced new policies to criminalize campus "dissidents" and "hard core rebels," and law enforcement agencies in Los Angeles released an investigative report accusing New Left subversives of "exhortations to violence" and "incitements to drug abuse," especially by pushing marijuana to undermine the moral and political values of their college student victims.[110] Senator Thomas Dodd, a law-and-order liberal and leading drug warrior, repeatedly attacked the New Left as a communist-infiltrated conspiracy to corrupt "thousands of innocent and idealistic young people" and convened a series of hearings during 1969–70 to expose the internal "subversion" of SDS. One session of this Senate Internal Security Subcommittee highlighted Marjorie King (pseudonym), a nineteen-year-old white female who joined SDS as a high school student and grew up "in the suburbs, . . . a typical middle-class family." King almost certainly was testifying as an FBI informant in exchange for leniency after being arrested at an antiwar protest. She claimed that "a lot of people sell dope within the movement" and confessed to using marijuana, speed, and heroin in the company of Marxist radicals and Black Power revolutionaries while "sleeping around with different guys to prove your freedom."[111]

Students for a Democratic Society certainly did recruit high school students, recognizing them as an already active political force denied basic constitutional rights, rather than as apathetic suburban conformists or psychologically "alienated" rebels without a cause. "High School Reform," a 1967 SDS manifesto written by a Southern California teenager, celebrated the growth of antiwar protests and underground newspapers, the "militant defense of hair and clothing styles," the rejection of the authoritarian drug and sex education curriculum, and the broader student revolt against "administrative totalitarianism."[112] Marjorie King told the Senate Internal Security Subcommittee that she first joined SDS as a fifteen-year-old because of anger at the stifling dress code that banned long hair for males and short skirts for females, regulations that inspired widespread high school protests during the mid-to-late 1960s. The subcommittee's hearings on the "Extent of Subversion in the 'New Left'" chronicled the political activities, including protest-related arrests and drug law violations, of hundreds of individually named college and high school SDS members based on FBI and police surveillance files.[113] The ACLU defended many high schoolers punished for political and nonconformist activities as part of its students' rights campaign to combat the "systematic denials of civil liberties to the young," from bans on protests, to arbitrary dress codes, to punishment of male "longhairs," to undercover police entrapment of recreational marijuana smokers.[114] In the anthology *High School Revolutionaries* (1970), white suburban teenagers denounced the "hypocrisy that lies behind our parents' culture" and the "ideological brainwashing" of a curriculum that evaded racism and inequality. They also defended their rights to engage in civil disobedience to disrupt the Vietnam War and to break unjust marijuana laws in order to seek an "infinitely more real and personal experience" than the "plastic . . . monstrosity" of middle-class suburban society.[115]

Hippies, Runaways, and Heroin

In 1965, reporters from *Life* magazine spent several months in New York City's "Needle Park" searching for charismatic white junkies to become the national face of the latest narcotics crisis, resulting in the much-discussed feature "John and Karen: Two Young Lives Lost to Heroin." The compelling and poignant story begins with an image of an attractive young couple walking across the street, who could be out on a date or on the way to class—"but they are drug addicts, headed for heroin, for a pusher with a fix." Karen fit the dominant cultural script of white female addict-victims from the small-town, middle-class heartland lost in the big-city slums: she had fled her family situation in the Midwest, worked as a prostitute to pay for their dope, and expected to die on the streets. John fit the other longstanding gateway-to-heroin trope: he started smoking marijuana at age thirteen, supported his smack habit with petty theft, and occasionally operated as a "junkie pusher." *Life* presented the white couple as representative of heroin junkies in the "teeming slums," even though the article briefly noted Federal Bureau of Narcotics data that a majority of such addicts were African American. It is clear that the journalistic team intended to humanize urban heroin addiction through a story of white victims that would help create momentum for a medical solution to the crisis. "We are all animals in a world no one knows," Karen laments, alongside dozens of shocking and tragic images of the couple shooting heroin and going through withdrawal, buying dope from street dealers, and cycling in and out of jail and hospital wards with no escape from their "hopeless plight."[116] The second installment of *Life*'s 1965 series on "Drug Addicts" featured two white sisters, ages eighteen and twenty, who left the federal narcotics hospital in Lexington, Kentucky, to return to the "sordid addict world" of heroin and prostitution on the streets of New York City. *Life* concluded that authorities needed to lock up the dope traffickers without mercy but save their victims by enacting "new laws that will force addicts to undergo treatment."[117]

The cultural framing of the heroin crisis through images of runaway white daughters and hopeless suburban junkies bolstered the political case for coercive rehabilitation rather than criminal conviction of narcotics addict-victims. In March 1965, President Lyndon Johnson endorsed the option of psychiatric institutionalization in his declaration of war on crime, calling for greater flexibility in the mandatory-minimum drug laws and urging Congress to enact the California model of civil commitment for "narcotic and marijuana users likely to respond to treatment and achieve rehabilitation . . . for a return to normal life."[118] *Life* magazine combined its recent photojournalistic exposés into a popular book about how drug abuse—heroin, marijuana, LSD, pills—"turns out to be everybody's problem." Reporter James Mills expanded his feature on Karen and John into *The Panic in Needle Park* (1965), a plaintive book later adapted as a Hollywood film starring Al Pacino as the addict-pusher and Kitty Winn as the lost daughter from Indiana. Also in 1965, Columbia Pictures released *Synanon*, a sympathetic film about white middle-class heroin addicts in recovery at the Santa Monica group therapy center, based on the *Life* magazine profile published a few years prior. A *New York Times* investigative report chronicled the "young women from well-to-do families"—in the Midwest and the Westchester County suburbs—who started out with marijuana, became heroin addicts, and ended up as desperate prostitutes working the streets of the Lower East Side. Of the affluent white youth flocking to Greenwich Village, the *Times* claimed that one-third of the pot smokers would become helpless heroin junkies and the rest needed to be forced into psychotherapy to rescue them from a marijuana-fueled "rootless, goalless existence."[119] Congress responded by passing the Narcotic Addict Rehabilitation Act of 1966, providing federal judges with the discretionary authority to divert nonviolent (i.e., deserving) illegal drug users through a civil commitment process to psychiatric hospitals for an indefinite stay of at least six months.[120]

During 1966–67, tens of thousands of white youths began arriving in urban bohemian enclaves adjacent to these heroin markets, part of the so-called "hippie movement" that sent a shock wave through national politics and culture. How could so many middle-class white students from "good homes" drop out of college, renounce materialism and the professional career track, and enlist in the psychedelic drug counterculture? Why were so many high schoolers from "typical American suburbs" escaping to the East Village and the Haight-Ashbury section of San Francisco, denouncing the establishment and the middle-class value system, and bringing radical politics as well as marijuana and LSD back to their hometowns—if they returned at all? What was causing so many young white girls, from the affluent suburbs and the Middle American heartland, to become "juvenile runaways" adrift in urban slums that now contained the new threats of the drug-addled hippie subculture alongside the traditional racial fears of ghetto crime and narcotics addiction? In spring 1967, *Life* magazine introduced many Americans to the "hippie" dropout phenomenon through a profile of the Haight-Ashbury, which housed an estimated six thousand to eight thousand youth refugees from across the nation, with many more predicted to descend during the upcoming "Summer of Love." *Life* portrayed the hippies as the latest stage in the "spreading youth rebellion . . . against established authority and the whole system," consisting of college graduates and dropouts as well as escapees "of high intelligence from well-off homes." The feature praised the hippie ideology of love and peace but labeled the centrality of marijuana and LSD to the psychedelic subculture a "most disruptive sort of escapism" and a "headlong flight from reality." *Life* directly contrasted the hippies of the Haight-Ashbury to the committed political activists across the bay at UC–Berkeley. While both groups deplored the Vietnam War, despised President Johnson and Governor Reagan, and broke the drug laws and other middle-class moral codes, the hippies "are not really doing *anything*."[121]

The extensive mass media coverage of the "hippie revolution" during the summer of 1967 focused national attention on the exotic, dangerous, and increasingly depoliticized illegal drug scene among the young, white middle-class dropouts flocking to urban enclaves. *Time* magazine's cover story categorized the hippies as a novel middle-class subculture, a psychedelic drug cult, a spiritual revival, an internal colony in the urban slums, and a growing migration of "expatriates living on our shores but beyond our society." The article estimated that there were at least three hundred thousand white, middle-class, educated hippies ages seventeen to twenty-five nationwide—"dropouts from a way of life that to them seems wholly oriented toward work, status, and power." Hippies just "feel in the gut that middle-class values are all wrong," one Californian told the magazine. *Time* did credit these alienated youth with a vague, if ambitious, sense of political mission: "Their professed aim is nothing less than the subversion of Western society by 'flower power,'" and most expressed fear of nuclear war and hostility to being drafted and sent to die in Vietnam. But the lengthy cover story mainly obsessed about the psychedelic movement's use of marijuana and LSD in order to take a "magic-carpet escape from reality." The hippies followed a three-step code that justified breaking the laws and sought to recruit other youth into the drug-infused lifestyle: 1. "Do your own thing"; 2. "Drop out"; 3. "Blow the mind of every straight person you can reach. Turn them on." *Look* magazine's similar investigation of the hippie subculture in the Haight-Ashbury portrayed white youth as "utopian-minded idealists" on a quest for religious discovery that rejected the sterility and materialism of mainstream middle-class society. But many spent their days in a drug-fueled stupor—smoking grass and listening to psychedelic rock, tripping on LSD in the public parks, some succumbing to speed and heroin—with "immature minds . . . sometimes permanently derailed almost every day by powerful chemicals."[122]

Ethnographic studies by academic researchers generally located the white middle-class hippie rebellion in a political framework and presented a much less alarmist interpretation of the hallucinogenic drugs at its center. Based on hundreds of interviews in the Haight-Ashbury, one team of psychiatrists concluded that "genuine hippies" self-medicated with marijuana and LSD to subdue their anger about "institutionalized and political violence, war, power struggles, cutthroat competitiveness, aggressive materialism, and the various forms of dehumanization found in modern society." Espousing values of tolerance and liberalism, these college-educated dropouts felt alienated from the hypocritical middle-class world of their parents and viewed LSD sacramentally as the key to transcending "hang-ups engendered by the 'rat races' of life." Marijuana was a harmless social ritual of pacifist values and collective identity, "the cement that holds the movement together." Dropping out was not the end of the line but rather the beginning of a new way of living. The report concluded that *none* of the hippies interviewed should be classified as addicts. A similar ethnography found that ritualistic marijuana use by full-time hippies represented a nonviolent rejection of the Vietnam War and police militarism at home, and that the straight society's extreme overreaction to the psychedelic drug culture was precisely why so many typical teenage rebels wanted to experience it firsthand. One of the most influential investigations of college-educated drug users distinguished between New Left activists ("seekers") who smoked marijuana to push the boundaries of experience and countercultural hippies ("heads") who embraced psychedelic drugs as a full-time lifestyle in alienation from a society that seemed impervious to political transformation. Its author, psychiatrist Kenneth Keniston, argued that the luxuries of affluence enabled these white suburban-reared dropouts to embark on a moratorium from the middle-class career track and that most would reengage with mainstream society on their own terms after one or two years.[123]

The influx of large numbers of high school students and so-called "juvenile runaways" into the Haight-Ashbury during the Summer of Love transformed the meaning of the hippie movement through sensationalistic journalism about lost white children and the hard drugs menace. This framework distinguished between true hippies whose countercultural agenda was political and authentic, versus suburban teenagers who were either "plastic" hippies visiting for a lark, or missing middle-class children in real danger. *The Maze: Haight/Ashbury*, an otherwise sympathetic documentary by the local CBS-TV affiliate, warned that the radical bohemian subculture was recruiting "runaway youngsters swept up in a bizarre world of drugs, sex, and sloth." *Etched in Acid,* the station's follow-up report on these runaways, explained that the hippie mystique had drawn thousands of middle-class teens to San Francisco, where too many ended up hospitalized for psychotic reactions to LSD.[124] In September 1967, the *Saturday Evening Post* published perhaps the most alarmist account of the "missing children" of the Haight-Ashbury, by the up-and-coming writer Joan Didion. Her observations read like a projection of fear and anxiety on the collective behalf of white middle-class parents nationwide. The opening paragraphs describe an America dystopia where "adolescents drifted from city to torn city," of "abandoned homes" and a "social hemorrhaging" centered in San Francisco, where "missing children were gathering and calling themselves 'hippies.'" The first mention of drugs is a sixteen-year-old refugee from the wealthy San Diego suburb of Chula Vista, mainlining crystal meth. Another sixteen-year-old "middle-class chick" gets picked up by a street dealer who "spends all day shooting her full of speed" and then offers her up for prostitution. Runaways offer the thirty-two-year-old journalist grass and acid, and heroin is "now on the scene." Didion concludes that the Haight-Ashbury has become a depoliticized, dangerous, "desperate attempt of a handful of pathetically unequipped children to create a community in a vacuum."[125]

As increasing numbers of increasingly younger white teenagers descended on urban bohemian enclaves, the "Summer of Love" narrative evolved from a hippie revolt against mainstream values into a middle-class family crisis of runaways from the suburbs and small towns of Middle America. *Look* magazine reported that most high schoolers who flocked to the Haight-Ashbury during summer 1967 were experimenting with psychedelic drugs and communal living and then returning home after their temporary hippie vacation. But a hard-core group of runaways—who had "quit parents, homes, schools and careers"—were ending up strung out on speed, hospitalized for LSD-induced psychosis, or addicted to heroin. A second *Look* feature on juvenile runaways in Greenwich Village showed fifteen-year-old females scoring marijuana and LSD from men twice their age while feeling both thrilled and frightened at no longer being "Daddy's plastic kid," in the words of one wannabe hippie rebel. *Time* reported that among the white youth who had "run away to the hippies" of the East Village during summer 1967, a thirteen-year-old girl attempted suicide three times after taking LSD and a fifteen-year-old female was "raped by two young Negroes" in Central Park. *Life*'s story on "Runaway Kids" was particularly shocking, starting with the cover image of a police station bulletin board filled with photographs of missing white teenagers sent in by their desperate parents. "Tens of thousands are now on the loose," the article began, many "fleeing affluent homes in suburbia." These runaways were looking for the loving embrace of the hippie community but ending up as "troubled youngsters adrift in big-city slums." Images of young, pretty blondes standing on urban street corners accompanied stories of a suburban teenager murdered in the East Village and frantic parents wandering the streets in search of lost children. While some tearfully reunited, other runaways such as fourteen-year-old "Janet" refused to leave, explaining that her parents gave her no freedom and "anyone different just isn't accepted" in her Massachusetts hometown.[126]

The East Village slaying of Linda Rae Fitzpatrick, the eighteen-year-old daughter of a wealthy Greenwich businessman, generated extensive national media coverage and considerable racial anxiety in the fall of 1967. A boarding school dropout who wanted to become an artist, Fitzpatrick was found bludgeoned to death alongside her "hippie boyfriend," an older "narcotics pusher" known as Groovy who dealt marijuana and LSD. Initial news reports portrayed Linda as a "happy girl" from the Connecticut suburbs whose parents gave her everything she could have wanted, from equestrian training to top-flight private schools, until she somehow ended up dead in an urban slum. Her acquaintances in the East Village offered a different portrait of an avid user of marijuana and LSD who moved back and forth between the city and her suburban home, crashed with lots of different men, and eventually became "hooked" on speed. After rounding up dozens of hippie suspects for interrogation, the New York City police charged two African American males with committing the murders after luring the couple to an acid party. Young white females slumming in the East Village expressed fear for their safety, citing the escalating tensions between white hippies and the Black and Puerto Rican gangs. "The hippies really bug us," one local Black youth told the *New York Times*, "because we know they can come down here and play their games for a while and then escape. And we can't, man." In the aftermath of the Fitzpatrick murder, law enforcement officials, medical researchers, and even some older hippies all warned that addictive drugs such as amphetamine and heroin had turned into a serious problem among teenage runaways, from the East Village to the Haight-Ashbury. The *New York Times* ran multiple stories about suburban fathers searching the Lower East Side for their lost daughters, while a prominent Long Island psychologist cautioned against blaming the hippies in Greenwich Village because affluent white youth were rebelling against the hollow and hypocritical lives that their parents had created in the suburbs.[127]

FIGURE 2.8. Police station bulletin board near the Haight-Ashbury district of San Francisco featuring photographs of missing children sent in by parents from across the nation, October 12, 1967. *Life* magazine placed the same bulletin board on the cover for its "Runaway Kids" story about the tragic descent of the 1967 Summer of Love into an urban crisis of teenage drug addiction and endangered daughters from white suburbia. (AP Photo / Robert W. Klein.)

For many worried parents as well as a vocal contingent of conservative groups, psychedelic "acid rock" music and the cultish hippie movement had invaded suburban sanctuaries through the auspices of mass culture, luring white middle-class youth into an urban netherworld of marijuana, LSD, sexual promiscuity, and racialized danger. In "She's Leaving Home," released on *Sgt. Pepper's Lonely Hearts Club Band* (1967), The Beatles imagined the desperate and wounded reaction of middle-class parents who "sacrificed most of [their] lives" and "gave her everything money could buy," but still their runaway daughter felt "something inside, that was always denied." A team of psychiatrists reported that many of the well-adjusted "runaway kids" in the Haight-Ashbury believed that this Beatles song captured their "inability to communicate their goals and values to their parents," operating as a mirror rather than a cause of their purposeful decisions to leave home.[128] For right-wing critics, psychedelic rock itself was part of a broad hippie conspiracy to "encourage children to run away from home . . . and enter the drug world," abandoning the middle-class values of hard work, conventional morality, and sexual restraint. Many charged another Beatles song, "Lucy in the Sky with Diamonds," with enticing youth victims to take LSD (the lyrics certainly seem to reference an acid trip). A new version of the dope pusher, the "hippie cult" seduced youth away from parental authority and suburban safety through "the bait of free food, free pads, and free love" in urban communes. One anticommunist organization accused Haight-Ashbury hippies of running an underground operation to indoctrinate and then disguise runaways so that their parents would never be able to find them again. "YOUR CHILD COULD BE NEXT!!" warned a pamphlet produced by another conservative network in the LA suburbs. "That is, *if* he hasn't *already* been enticed and ensnared! Yes, your child could become a hippie—a washout, a dropout from society."[129]

Many adolescents celebrated the freedom and experiences they had achieved by leaving home and rejected the depoliticizing, panic-based depictions of their victimization that circulated broadly in the mainstream media and not just the right-wing press. *The Flower People* (1968), a collection of interviews with young white hippies in the East Village, summarized their collective sentiment as an honest, politically motivated rejection of "a rigidly mechanized society which . . . ignores the individual, glorifies violence, discriminates against minority groups, and persists in clinging to a puritanical sexual ethic which, in practice, it hypocritically ignores." One female who split time between the East Village and a rural commune, and who believed her parents would never understand her values, said that she was happy being part of a love-based community where "anywhere I go, in any part of the country, I can find people who will put me up and feed me and get me high."[130] A careful ethnographic study of "runaway teenagers" in the Haight Ashbury during the Summer of Love disputed the youth-in-crisis narrative and found that these high school rebels primarily smoked marijuana with "self-righteous enthusiasm . . . and scorn for the prohibitions of society and its laws." While many did try LSD, the researchers attributed this willingness to experiment to their harmless experiences with grass, which had convinced teenagers that "all the widely advertised dangers of drugs were establishment lies." A large survey-based investigation of illegal drug use among white middle-class teenagers who stayed in the Haight-Ashbury through fall 1967 revealed that almost 100 percent smoked marijuana, which operated as a "social drug" and an "alcohol substitute," serving essentially the same function that drinking did for their parents' generation and the mainstream youth culture. The study found that the marijuana-infused hippie subculture did encourage experimentation with LSD and speed, but that almost none of these teenagers should be medically classified as either drug abusers or addicts, and that the gateway-to-heroin thesis was completely wrong.[131]

Juveniles who had left home generally disputed the labels of "teenage runaways" and "missing children," which were loaded political and legal labels that allowed parents to file police reports seeking the detention and return of "unsupervised" youth and authorized law enforcement to arrest almost any minor anywhere for this status crime. In the 1967 local television documentary about Haight-Ashbury runaways and the LSD menace, two white high school dropouts (interviewed with faces hidden) object to the "runaway" characterization and insist that they relocated to San Francisco in search of a better life. The male explains that he was learning nothing meaningful in school and that back home, "we have no freedom of mind to think what we want to think." His female companion says that parents in her middle-class community smother their children, won't let them grow up, and tell them to be just like everyone else—but "grass makes you happy" and "the hippies understand." In another scene, two teenage males return home with the film crew just long enough to argue with their mother about why they drop acid—"LSD is fun," plus adults abuse alcohol and pills—and she yells that drugs have turned them into bums without any work ethic and they'll probably still be bums when they turn forty. (LSD had only been illegal in California since December 1966, and possession was not yet criminalized under federal law). In a different San Francisco news broadcast, an older male journalist confronts a fourteen-year-old female in a police precinct station and says that her father reported her as a runaway from home for the third time. "No, I'm not," Sandra retorts. "I don't consider myself a runaway at all." The newsman asks where Sandra spent the previous night. "That's none of anybody's business," she insists, "and I won't tell. I won't tell where I've been for the past two weeks. Ever." Sandra was speaking after being booked in a routine roundup of dozens of white teenagers to be detained until released to the custody of parents who had to travel from across the state and nation to take them home.[132]

During the Summer of Love, the newly established Huckleberry House for Runaways became the leading nonpunitive institutional alternative to the San Francisco Police Department (SFPD) policy of arresting, incarcerating, and forcing "unsupervised" juveniles to return home. Reverend Larry Beggs, a thirty-four-year-old youth minister and trained psychologist in suburban San Mateo, cofounded the Huckleberry House after he attended the "Human Be-In" celebration at the Golden Gate Park in January 1967 and recognized that

FIGURE 2.9. Police in the Haight-Ashbury section of San Francisco arrest a young white female "hippie," presumably as a juvenile runaway, as part of a routine roundup on April 3, 1967. The original caption noted that around two thousand "hipsters from the area" were parading around, and the police also arrested others for unlawful assembly and failure to disperse. (AP Photo / Robert W. Klein.)

the psychedelic hippie movement was on the verge of a teenage explosion. In June, Beggs opened the Huckleberry facility in a Haight-Ashbury row house with financial support from a progressive religious network that included the Methodist Church and the Glide Foundation (which provided social services to marginalized people in the nearby Tenderloin district). Rev. Beggs believed that most teenage runaways were making an autonomous and defensible decision to leave "the suburban world that tries to over-control and over-protect them" through an excessively protracted adolescence, which predictably created youth defiance of rigid and unrealistic rules about curfew, normative sexuality, and alcohol and marijuana use. He advocated decriminalization of running away—the leading category of juvenile arrests across the United States—because the decision was based in family conflict and "often a healthy reaction to an intolerable situation." Huckleberry House provided social services and temporary shelter in what it advertised as a "non-judgmental setting" for youth ages twelve to seventeen who sought its assistance. With their permission, Huckleberry contacted parents to negotiate the terms of a potential return home through family counseling sessions. Beggs based this approach on principles of "maximiz[ing] self-determination for young people" and "honoring the decision-making power of young people" in familial settings and educational and social institutions. "We exert a minimum of pressure to make kids go home," he told the media. "The young person makes the decision—although we might challenge that decision."[133]

The Huckleberry House for Runaways initially experienced significant conflict with the police department and juvenile control system, even though its voluntary services assisted hundreds of teenagers and usually received praise from their grateful parents. During its first year of operation, Huckleberry provided a residential refuge or other support to 664 "runaways," with fifteen the average age, two-thirds from California, and the remainder from thirty-six other states (this was at most 1% of the total in San Francisco during summer/fall 1967). Under state law, juveniles had to call home and receive permission to stay overnight. Around 60 percent of these youth contacted their parents through Huckleberry's auspices, and although not all returned home, those who did were far less likely to leave again than juveniles forcibly sent back by law enforcement. More than one thousand additional families initiated contact with the Huckleberry House in hopes of locating their children. Tensions with the juvenile justice system escalated in fall 1967, after the end of summer break, when large groups of SFPD officers began daily sweeps through the Haight-Ashbury, throwing everyone who looked like a minor into paddy wagons. Undercover narcotics squad operations also increased as part of what the police chief later boasted was a concerted and largely successful two-year crackdown to purge the Haight-Ashbury of lawbreaking hippies as well as runaways.[134] On October 20, the SFPD conducted a late-night raid on the Huckleberry House and jailed nine "runaways" and three adult staffers, allegedly on a tip that youth staying there were smoking marijuana (none was found, and the facility barred illegal drug use on its premises). Rev. Beggs and two other counselors were charged with "contributing to the delinquency of a minor" (dropped two months later). An activist coalition protested the raid as illegal, as did Huckleberry House's religious sponsors and several angry parents who had given their children permission to be there. Larry Beggs accused the juvenile justice authorities of seeking to eliminate a successful youth-centered challenge to their "punitive structure."[135]

Huckleberry House eventually reached an accommodation with law enforcement in San Francisco and became a national model for privately run social welfare centers that opposed the criminalization of the estimated one million annual "juvenile runaways" across the nation. By 1969, Huckleberry was a state-licensed child-care institution that worked with juvenile probation officers who diverted some arrested runaways to its custody, instead of incarceration, until their families arrived. Huckleberry House also became well-known nationwide thanks to glowing media profiles and a popular book authored by Larry Beggs based on testimonials by runaways themselves. Beggs received many heartfelt letters from young teenagers throughout the United States who expressed their desire to come stay at Huckleberry House, related detailed accounts of their family problems and previous runaway escapades, and in some cases confessed psychedelic drug use, railed against conventional American society, and accused their parents of punishing them for radical political beliefs and activities.[136] In the early 1970s, Huckleberry House received federal funding and relocated to a whiter section of San Francisco, after the Haight-Ashbury experienced racial transition and ceased to be the epicenter of the suburban runaway/hippie scene. By then Rev. Beggs had moved north of the city to open a community treatment center for young white heroin addicts in affluent Marin County, where he continued to advocate decriminalization of all juvenile status offenses and to blame suburban society for "overprotecting and controlling the young."[137] This was the prevailing view among the young ministers and doctors who ran similar organizations serving white suburban "runaways" though group homes and free drug treatment/health clinics based on the Haight-Ashbury model, from the Sunset Strip in Los Angeles to Dupont Circle in Washington, DC. They generally criticized the hypocrisy and shallowness of white middle-class suburbia and considered teenage marijuana use to be relatively harmless, but most warned that heroin was a growing threat for runaway youth.[138]

White hippies, especially those categorized as "runaways," also faced substantial criminalization and police harassment in suburban municipalities that sought both to control their own teenagers and to keep out the drugs and disorder associated with the rootless psychedelic generation. In the late 1960s, many beachfront suburbs in Orange County, as well as the city and county governments of Los Angeles, either enacted so-called "antihippie ordinances" or amended existing loitering laws to address the new "middle-class phenomenon." These discretionary measures, which faced frequent constitutional challenges, criminalized standing on the sidewalk and sleeping on the beach, and suburban police also profiled and arrested "hippie runaways" through curfew ordinances and targeting of hitchhikers. Juvenile authorities in Orange County estimated that the runaway total increased 300 percent between 1966 and 1968, with youth from nearby white-collar suburbs and other parts of the nation flooding hippie destinations such as Laguna Beach and Huntington Beach. The *Los Angeles Times* epitomized this crisis with features on a sixteen-year-old female from "comfortable" Garden Grove sentenced to Juvenile Hall after taking LSD and being raped while hitchhiking during her quest for freedom, and a fourteen-year-old runaway male from Costa Mesa ordered incarcerated unless he cut his long hair.[139] Farther north, police in San Luis Obispo jailed two seventeen-year-old suburban males for hitchhiking to camp in Big Sur, with their parents' permission, under a de facto policy to arrest all runaways, long-haired hippie "homosexuals," and otherwise "strange kids." Voters in Laguna Beach elected a new town council on an antihippie backlash platform to restore its status as a "good, clean, respectable community" through aggressive code enforcement and undercover narcotics operations to clear out the pot-smoking, long-haired "transients." In Newport Beach, law enforcement targeted white hippie youth with marijuana raids, street profiling of long-haired males, and rough tactics that inspired an organized anti–police brutality movement.[140]

The criminalization of "running away from home," which resulted in more than two hundred thousand annual arrests nationwide during the late 1960s, produced by far the largest number of formal juvenile records for white suburban youth in this era (fig. 2.10). For most juvenile status offenses and criminal violations, including alcohol and marijuana infractions, law enforcement authorities generally handled white youth from "good homes" informally, in an attempt to deter their behavior without hampering their futures through an official delinquency adjudication. The status offense of running away was different, because processing minors through the formal juvenile system was necessary to hold them overnight until their parents arrived, and also because law enforcement disproportionately detained young white females perceived to be the primary victims of the drugs/sex/urban slums nexus of life on the streets. In fact, most commentators wrongly believed that "running away" was much more common among female than male juveniles, when instead the ratio was almost even. The misperception arose from selective law enforcement combined with the media and political obsession with young white girls in racialized and sexualized urban danger.[141] Running away also was likely the only offense category in the juvenile justice system where white youth were approximately as likely as their nonwhite counterparts to undergo formal adjudication. This racial context played a major role in propelling the movement to decriminalize running away, especially after the Summer of Love turned the relatively common practice into a new nationwide suburban crisis. In addition to the youth advocacy groups that endorsed decriminalization of status offenses on principle, juvenile justice agencies such as the California Youth Authority began arguing that youth detained for running away and other noncriminal status offenses (defined as "one-time contacts") should be diverted without adjudication, in order to protect them from serious offenders incarcerated in juvenile institutions, a reform sentiment with obvious racial overtones.[142]

In 1971, liberal Democrats on the Senate Subcommittee to Investigate Juvenile Delinquency introduced the Runaway Youth Act to promote decriminalization of this status offense and provide federal funding for diversionary private-sector alternatives modeled on Huckleberry House. Senator Birch Bayh (D-IN), the new subcommittee chair, opened the hearings by defining the crisis as white: "Most runaways are young, inexperienced suburban kids who run away to major urban areas" and become "easy victims of street gangs, drug pushers, and hardened criminals." The first witnesses were teenage clients of Runaway House, opened in 1968 to serve suburban refugees in the Dupont Circle countercultural enclave of the nation's capital. Becky recounted fleeing white middle-class Arlington, right across the river, at fourteen years old and experiencing sexual assault, two runaway arrests, and ultimately psychiatric institutionalization after using marijuana, acid, tranquilizers, and speed. William Treanor, the director of Runaway House, testified that most were suburban youth escaping family conflict, not political rebels in search of the Haight-Ashbury or Greenwich Village mystique, and that a significant number abused LSD, speed, and increasingly heroin. He then urged Congress to provide nonpunitive resources for all youth, regardless of race or income level, and contrasted Becky's experience of psychiatric rehabilitation to a Black male runaway who testified that he also used hard drugs but had been sent to juvenile incarceration by the DC police. Such racial distinctions decisively structured the multiyear debate and ultimate passage of the Runaway Youth Act, as Elizabeth Hinton has shown, with white suburban teenagers cast as "youth in trouble" to promote deinstitutionalization of status offenders, and Black urban teenagers targeted as criminals requiring incarceration in other punitive components of the Juvenile Justice and Delinquency Prevention Act of 1974. California passed a similar law decriminalizing runaway status in 1977 while simultaneously "getting tough" on nonwhite urban youth crime.[143]

The suburban runaway crisis reverberated through American culture and politics during the late 1960s and 1970s and profoundly shaped the trajectory of the war on drugs as well as the broader mirror-image policies designed to

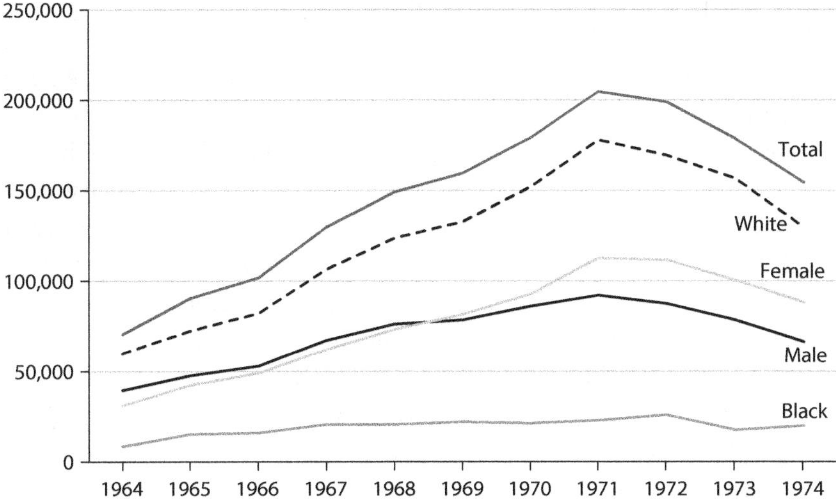

FIGURE 2.10. Arrests/detentions of runaways in the United States, 1964–74, as reported to the FBI. Law enforcement agencies arrested and adjudicated white and female juveniles for the status offense of "running away" at equal to or greater than their share of the population during the late 1960s and early 1970s. The reported increase in female arrests/detentions, from 44% of the total in 1964 to 57% in 1974, primarily resulted from selective enforcement by policing agencies seeking to rescue white middle-class suburban teenagers who chose to relocate to urban centers. (Compiled from FBI, *Uniform Crime Reports*, 1964–1974.)
Note: The data in this graphic is a significant undercount, based only on reported arrests by participating agencies and including only those juveniles taken into formal "protective custody," not those detained and handled informally. The FBI estimated 232,700 runaway arrests nationwide in 1970 and 260,000 in 1971, meaning the reported total was approximately three-fourths of the estimated total. Youth service agencies estimated, conservatively, that one million juveniles "ran away" annually by the late 1960s, meaning that at most one-fourth of the total were apprehended by the police.

protect and control white middle-class youth. The redefinition of the Summer of Love from a hippie rebellion into a lost white daughter epidemic played a pivotal role in the Johnson administration's move to criminalize LSD possession in 1968. President Richard Nixon and congressional Democrats repeatedly hyped the suburban runaway narrative—the white girl from a "good family" who experimented with marijuana and LSD and then became "hooked on heroin"—to enact the comprehensive 1970 drug legislation reform that bifurcated and racialized enforcement policy between coercive rehabilitation for addict-victims and tough punishment for "dope pushers" (see chapter 4).[144] The 1969 murder of Sharon Tate, a young actress who grew up in the wealthy LA suburb of Palos Verdes, led her father to go undercover as a hippie addict to expose the Manson Family cult and helped to redefine the counterculture as a cesspool where evil men controlled young white runaways through LSD and sexual abuse. The bestseller *Go Ask Alice* (1971), allegedly the diary of an anonymous suburban girl who ran away at fifteen, recounted a tragic odyssey from marijuana and LSD experimentation in high school, to heroin addiction and prostitution in urban slums, culminating in death. *Go Ask Alice* (later revealed as a hoax) inspired a made-for-TV adaptation and a wave of similar white runaway-daughter novels and films during the early-to-mid 1970s. *Born Innocent* (1974) advanced the case for decriminalization of runaways in controversial fashion by depicting the prison gang rape of a white fourteen-year-old female sentenced to juvenile detention after leaving home for the sixth time. *Dawn: Portrait of a Teenage Runaway* (1976), at the apotheosis of the lost-innocence genre, featured a fifteen-year-old white middle-class rebel turned victim, lured into prostitution in the sex-and-drugs milieu of Hollywood's vice district.[145]

The sensationalized stories of a runaway suburban daughter epidemic, while certainly capturing the real danger and sexual violence experienced by a relatively small number of white teenage victims in urban spaces, also inflamed racist tough-on-crime politics during an era of punitive escalation and profound double standards in law enforcement. The latest incarnation of these lost-innocence narratives, so deeply embedded in American political culture and the history of drug-war enforcement, further operated to depoliticize white middle-class youth collectively during an era of radical challenges to American politics and society by the New Left and the "hippie" counterculture. But the majority of white middle-class teenagers did not actively participate in either of these radical movements during the mid-to-late 1960s, a time when felony marijuana use accelerated dramatically among high school students in the white suburbs, especially in the affluent communities of coastal states located in proximity to major universities and bohemian urban enclaves. How did these white suburban youth acquire and circulate illegal drugs? What was the political meaning of breaking the marijuana and LSD laws, and participating in other criminalized subcultural activities, as the "generation gap" spread from college campuses and urban countercultural destinations into ordinary white suburbs throughout the nation? How did law enforcement and the juvenile delinquency system, designed to accomplish an impossible mission—controlling the adolescent subculture while diverting white middle-class lawbreakers from "good homes" without scarring them with a formal criminal record—react to the challenge of mass youth defiance of the drug prohibition regime? And how did the response of political authorities and public policymakers to the growing marijuana legalization movement maintain drug criminalization by building on the longstanding racialized dichotomy between "otherwise law-abiding" youth addict-victims in need of coercive rehabilitation and dangerous urban "pushers" and traffickers to be incarcerated without mercy?

3

Generation Gap

"AN EPIDEMIC OF DRUG ABUSE IS SWEEPING THE NATION," *Look* magazine informed its largely middle-class readership in the summer of 1967. "The contagion, centered on college campuses, also infects high-school students and adults in our cities, suburbs and small towns. No one is immune." The exposé warned that, beyond the relatively small number of heroin addicts concentrated in urban ghettos, millions of "white and affluent" Americans also were "hooked" on drugs, from the suburban housewives dependent on amphetamines, to the pervasive abuse of prescription medication and alcohol in middle-income communities, to the spread of marijuana and LSD from the hippie subculture to the general college population. In the typical white middle-class suburb, according to (exaggerated) law enforcement estimates, anywhere between one-sixth and one-half of all high school students had smoked marijuana, and police busts of teenage networks routinely uncovered LSD, speed (amphetamines), and barbiturates as well. Contrary to established myths of adult pushers lurking in the shadows and luring innocent white youth into the living death of narcotics addiction, most of the "major peddlers" in the middle-class suburbs were adolescents who provided marijuana to their friends and classmates. Psychologists believed that the explosion of illegal drug use among white suburban youth reflected a generational rebellion against authority and a search for meaning in modern society, but also not so different from their parents turning to alcohol and pills to escape the pressures and anxieties of "split-level existence" and "middle-class adulthood." *Look* concluded that the crisis of drug abuse should be addressed through public health prevention and treatment programs rather than law enforcement, since it made little sense to arrest otherwise law-abiding Americans for the crime of living in a consumer society that pursued "happiness through chemistry."[1]

During the late 1960s, the national drug debate increasingly focused on marijuana use among white middle-class youth in suburban high schools, which led to probing examinations of the "generation gap" and a racial-political crisis for the carceral state and its two-decades-long war on narcotics. Powerful law enforcement interests, led by the Bureau of Narcotics and Dangerous Drugs, continued to depict marijuana as a menace distributed by "dope pushers" that caused teenage victims to graduate to heroin addiction or LSD abuse.[2] The mass media continued its reflexive hype about the "epidemic" of illegal drug use among white youth and the "spread" of psychedelics from college campuses and hippie enclaves to once placid suburbs. But mainstream journalism also became less deferential to law enforcement and began publicizing medical research that marijuana was not physically addictive (although scientists believed heavy users became psychologically dependent), not a narcotic (despite its legal misclassification), not a gateway to heroin addiction, and probably less harmful than legal corporate-manufactured drugs such as alcohol, barbiturates, and nicotine. In a 1969 cover story on the widening generation gap in affluent suburbia, *Time* compared parents of high school students to Mr. Jones, the "straight middle-class breadwinner" ridiculed in Bob Dylan's "Ballad of a Thin Man," for whom "something is happening here, but you don't know what it is." The magazine explained that white middle-class youth experimented with marijuana based on the social dynamics of their peer networks, but most suburban parents still imagined "the dope pusher standing outside the high school" and believed the discredited myth that pot "inevitably leads to the slow death of heroin addiction." *Time* concluded that recreational use of marijuana had become "a part of growing up" and called for reform of the "inequitable as well as widely unenforceable" criminal sanctions that were turning otherwise law-abiding youth into suburban rebels and exacerbating their political alienation from middle-class values and governmental authority.[3]

A close exploration of policing and adolescent social practices in the white-collar suburbs of major metropolitan regions provides a novel perspective on how illegal drug markets and criminal law enforcement operated during the second half of the 1960s. The media and political hype that marijuana had spread throughout white middle-class American suburbia obscured the ways in which illegal teenage drug use first escalated in affluent inner-ring communities located in close proximity to major urban centers and large universities. Politically conscious youth, other adventure seekers, and suburban drug dealers acquired marijuana and LSD from college campus networks and bohemian "hippie" enclaves such as the Haight-Ashbury area of San Francisco, the

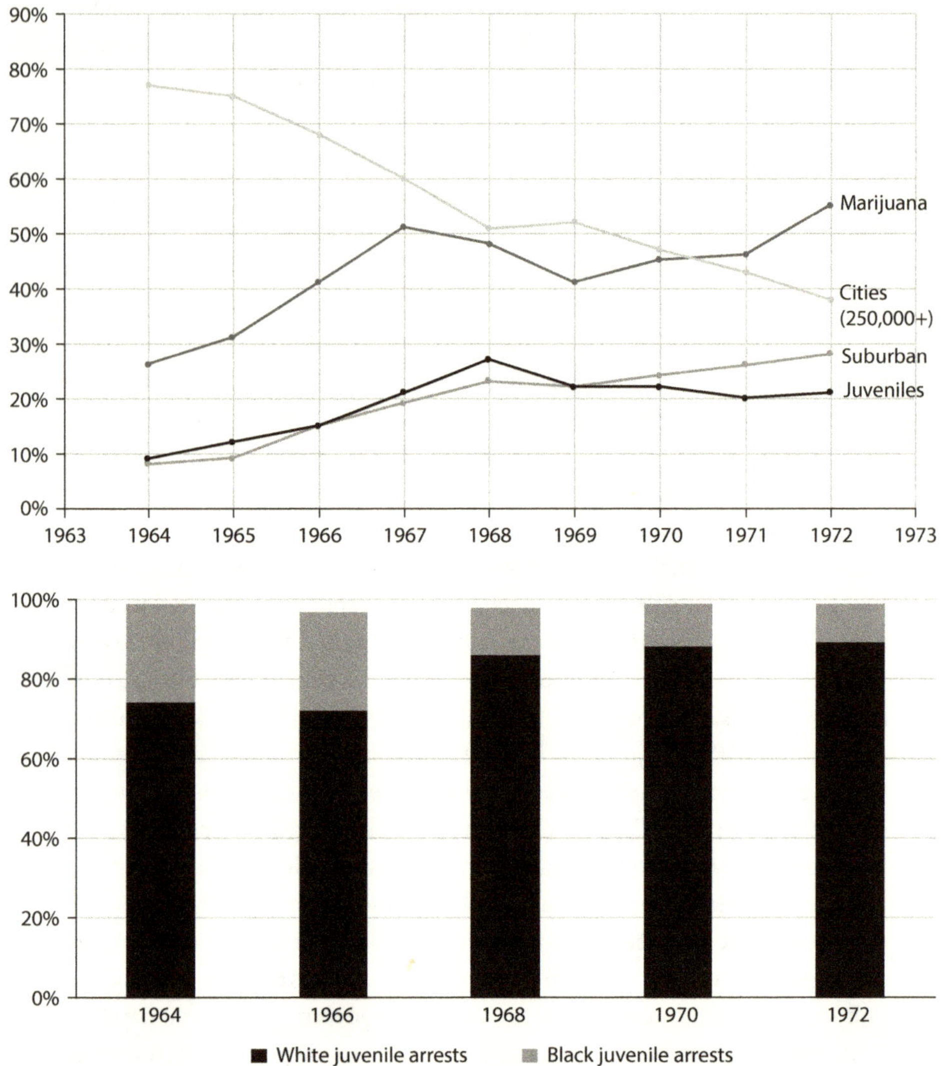

FIGURE 3.1. Select characteristics of the population arrested on drug charges in the United States, 1964–72. (*Top*) The proportion of marijuana arrests relative to total drug arrests more than doubled from 26% in 1964 to 55% by 1972. The percentage of drug arrests in the largest cities declined significantly, while the arrest share in the suburbs increased by 3.5 times during these years. The juvenile arrest share increased from 9% to 21% of the total. The scale of drug arrests also increased by 10.6 times during this period, from 49,700 nationwide in 1964 to 527,400 in 1972. (*Bottom*) The proportion of white juveniles arrested on drug charges jumped from 72% of the juvenile total in 1966 to 89% in 1972, while Black juvenile drug arrests declined from 25% to 10%. Total juvenile drug arrests expanded exponentially during these years, from 4,500 in 1964 to 111,000 in 1972 (figures are rounded). (FBI, *Uniform Crime Reports*, 1964–1972.)

Sunset Strip in Los Angeles, the East Village in New York City, and the Georgetown section of Washington, DC. Ethnographic investigations, academic surveys of high school students, and police crackdowns gradually revealed that psychedelic drugs circulated in affluent suburbs through a decentralized, often nonprofit system of interchange among friends and acquaintances who acted as "suppliers" in a recreational subculture. Local police departments and narcotics squads deployed undercover agents in suburban high schools, profiled and searched teenagers based on age and especially "hippie" appearance, and arrested tens of thousands of white middle-class youths for marijuana possession during the late 1960s and early 1970s. While the consequences of arrest could be substantial, including expulsion from school, supervised probation, and mandatory court-ordered rehabilitation, very few white youths from upscale families ended up in juvenile detention centers or adult prisons. Instead—as revealed in the following case studies of the war on drugs in the affluent suburbs of San Francisco, Los Angeles, New York City, and Washington, DC—the extraordinary increase in felony arrests of white teenagers and young adults resulted in the parallel escalation of discretionary and diversionary procedures by police, delinquency officials, prosecutors, and judges.[4]

As on college campuses, political and cultural discourse most often characterized teenage pot smokers in the middle-class suburbs as "otherwise law-abiding" citizens, a deeply racialized category that captured the simultaneous criminalization and decriminalization of white youth at this pivotal stage of the American war on drugs. During the late 1960s and early 1970s, when both the Johnson and Nixon administrations declared federal wars on urban street crime, local authorities arrested an unprecedented number of young white Americans for drug felonies and misdemeanors. Analyzing the data from the

---

Note: Through 1969, the FBI *Uniform Crime Reports* provided only the actual arrest figures reported by police agencies, but after 1970 the FBI totals included estimates for nonreporting areas. Actual reported data during the pre-1970 period ranged from agencies representing 69% of the population in 1964 to 74% in 1967. For valid comparisons, the top chart standardizes total drug arrests by recalculating the 1964–69 numbers based on the FBI's estimation formula, using the methodology of DrugScience.org. On the FBI's "suburban" category, see note in fig. I.1. The racial breakdown of the U.S. population in the 1970 census was 87.6% white, 11.1% Black, and an estimated 4.5% Hispanic. The FBI did not report data on Hispanics separately during this era, and in a rough estimate, doing so would reduce the white juvenile arrest totals by around 6 to 9 percentage points. In California, which recorded half of all drug arrests in the U.S. in the mid-to-late 1960s, Mexican Americans accounted for around 9% of juveniles arrested.

FBI's *Uniform Crime Reports* requires caution, but the annual surveys clearly reveal that both marijuana and juvenile apprehensions doubled as a percentage of national "narcotics" arrests during this period. Suburban drug arrests tripled as a percentage of the overall total, the proportion of busted white juveniles rose to approximate their population share for the first time in modern history, and arrests of African American juveniles declined steadily from 2.5 times the population share to a 1:1 ratio (fig. 3.1). In a representative sampling of juvenile and adult pot arrestees in 1970, the National Commission on Marihuana found that a substantial majority were under twenty-one with no prior record, one-third were full-time students, and more than three-fourths were white. The criminal legal system dismissed or discharged half of marijuana possession cases for adults and more than two-thirds for juveniles, a law enforcement strategy that the commission labeled "containment." In effect, the carceral state sought to scare white middle-class youth into avoiding illegal drugs through the possibility of arrest but not ruin their lives and destroy their futures when they broke the law. The discursive category of "otherwise law-abiding" youth fused whiteness, socioeconomic status, family background, educational achievement, and geographic residence—the same statistical variables that proved most determinative when police, prosecutors, and judges assessed criminality and exercised discretion following a felony or misdemeanor drug arrest.[5]

What processes enabled law enforcement agencies to arrest so many white middle-class teenagers for felony drug crimes without leaving almost any traces on their permanent records? The archives are full of silences, by explicit design, but the general patterns are discernible through case studies of suburban counties where white marijuana use and police crackdowns escalated in tandem. Key sources include internal law enforcement reports, academic studies, congressional and media investigations—and also the many public forums in which white suburban teenagers openly defended their right to violate unjust drug laws as part of the broader youth political revolt. The political and law enforcement response to the massive escalation of marijuana crimes built directly on the discretionary and racially discriminatory juvenile justice system in place since the 1950s to regulate suburban delinquency and alcohol violations without upsetting affluent parents or saddling their children with the stigma of criminality (see chapter 2). Small police departments in wealthy, racially segregated suburbs generally declined to arrest teenagers for marijuana crimes at all. Prosecutors and judges in larger counties disguised many drug offenses through plea bargains to public intoxication or disorderly conduct, often with informal agreement that parents would send the recreational pot smoker to psychiatric counseling. In metropolitan Los Angeles, where police arrested by far the most white youths nationwide during the mid-to-late 1960s, juvenile officials "counseled and released" the majority of felony drug violators from middle-class suburbs. When this failed to stem the tide, the state legislature reduced marijuana possession to a misdemeanor in a futile attempt to deter teenagers and young adults through formal probation. "Most youngsters do not consider smoking marijuana is wrong," the LA County narcotics commission lamented in 1967. "How can they enforce a law that a whole generation doesn't respect?" a fifteen-year-old white suburbanite hanging out on the Sunset Strip asked a dismayed reporter that same year.[6]

The ubiquitous generation gap interpretation of the illegal drug subculture in upper-middle-class suburbia situated white teenage lawbreakers in a political rather than a criminal framework, which is also how the vast majority of youth defended their own actions. The subcultural practices of smoking pot and dropping acid became highly politicized through association with the antiwar movement on college campuses, the "hippie" counterculture that rejected the capitalist work ethic and the middle-class value system, and the generalized youth critique of the self-absorbed culture of suburban materialism. Psychiatrists overwhelmingly argued that illegal drug use represented a symptom rather than the cause of the generation gap but disagreed over whether the fundamental source of youth alienation resulted from political rebellion or a communications breakdown within the middle-class family. While a vocal subset of suburban teenagers explicitly linked their psychedelic drug use to radical politics, the majority of adolescent pot smokers cited motives of pleasure and leisure and demanded that law enforcement and adult society recognize that marijuana represented a right of personal freedom, a victimless crime, and their generation's version of alcohol consumption. Most parents and politicians, however, viewed teenagers who drank beer and liquor as following in their own normative footsteps, whereas smoking pot in the suburbs seemed to symbolize a rejection of the middle-class values of hard work and upward mobility, a mystifying embrace of the alienation and escapism associated with the Black ghetto and the hippie counterculture, a dangerous and contagious deviation from the path of capitalism and the American Dream. Over time, this interpretation competed with a growing belief that the generation gap crisis signified less a full-blown rejection of American values by suburban rebels, and more that marijuana prohibition itself had alienated too many white middle-class youth by criminalizing a recreational market that functioned as an extension rather than the antithesis of a drug-dependent nation.

San Francisco Bay Area: Drug Markets and High School Politics

The best ethnographic evidence of the emerging generation gap and the underground drug subculture in white middle-class suburbia during the late 1960s came from Pleasant Hill, California, a commuter suburb of thirty thousand residents located thirty miles east of San Francisco in Contra Costa County. In 1966, one year before the problem of illegal drug use in suburban high schools exploded on the national radar, a group of criminologists from UC–Berkeley secured a federal grant from the Department of Health, Education, and Welfare (HEW) to launch an antidelinquency demonstration project in Pleasant Hill and nearby unincorporated areas. The research team selected Pleasant Hill as a "typical" American suburb, middle to upper-middle class and 99.4 percent white, dominated by white-collar fathers and stay-at-home mothers, marked by "conformity and status-seeking," organized around the needs and desires of children. The Berkeley criminologists did not anticipate the emergence of psychedelic drug use among teenagers in Pleasant Hill and initially planned to investigate why middle-class suburban "delinquents" engaged in crimes such as burglary, shoplifting, vandalism, fighting, and alcohol-related mischief. The study theorized that postwar American culture had generated a "distinct adolescent social world" of leisure and deviance that the schools and other suburban institutions had failed to accommodate, except by seeking to control and disfranchise white middle-class teenagers through methods not unlike the subjection of inner-city minorities. As a result, "we find alienation of the average, adjusted, affluent American, and estrangement of the fortunate, the talented, and the privileged." In essence, the Berkeley researchers viewed juvenile crime and delinquency in the suburbs as a symptom of a social system that depoliticized middle-class youth and failed to provide meaningful outlets for their energies and grievances. As a solution, the Pleasant Hill demonstration project facilitated the "formal involvement of youth in decision-making with adults" through a Youth Commission that helped create antidelinquency programs such as a teen center, dances, car clubs, and freewheeling rap sessions with the police.[7]

The most significant finding in the Pleasant Hill study involved the predominant policies of discretion and diversion utilized by law enforcement officials who detained juveniles for criminal and delinquent activities, a process the report labeled "absorption." According to FBI data for 1966, the year after the Johnson administration launched a federal war on urban street crime and nonwhite youth gangs, police departments nationwide "handled and released" 46 percent of arrested juveniles and sent 54 percent into the system for formal delinquency adjudications. Law enforcement in California similarly disposed of 48 percent of juvenile cases informally at the point of arrest. But in affluent and almost all-white Pleasant Hill, police "reprimanded and released" 77 percent of detained minors between 1966 and 1967 without any formal procedure or lasting record at all. Youth from the town's small working-class population were much more likely to face adjudication. The juvenile probation department operated with total statutory discretion and dismissed charges for a majority of arrested teenagers who made it that far, often after parents agreed to place the child in private psychiatric counseling, and the juvenile court often did the same. "There is a gross understatement," the report concluded, "of the amount of deviance in the community as measured by official law enforcement." Other studies of juvenile delinquency in white middle-class suburbs during the mid-1960s confirmed this general pattern, which skewed official youth crime rates and revealed unequal standards of justice based on race, socioeconomic class, and geography. The Berkeley team classified absorption as the "normal method for handling youthful offenders in this middle-class community," an approach widely supported by parents, schools, police, and politicians. The report acknowledged that Pleasant Hill's informal system might appear an "undemocratic" example of racial and class privilege but argued that the methods uncovered in its suburban demonstration project should be extended to disadvantaged urban communities as well.[8]

Large numbers of high school students in Pleasant Hill began smoking marijuana in the summer and fall of 1967, creating a temporary crisis for the discretionary absorption process and a broader exacerbation of the politicized generation gap. The records of the Berkeley project provide an exceptional window into the emergence of an illegal, mainstream drug subculture in white middle-class suburbia since its ethnographers were already embedded in the Pleasant Hill community and actively engaged with a broad cross-section of youth when marijuana use escalated. The researchers estimated that 30 to 40 percent of local high school students began experimenting with marijuana during or soon after the 1967 Summer of Love, and about 10 percent became regular weekly users. These youth constituted a new social category, the "hip type," that identified with the cultural ethos of the Haight-Ashbury, dressed in the mod/hippie fashion, and collectively expressed a pointed critique of suburban values and establishment rules. A smaller but significant subset traveled to Oakland and Berkeley to participate in anti–Vietnam War activism and other political demonstrations as well. The UC–Berkeley project interpreted pot smoking, and the related reverse "flight" of Pleasant Hill teenagers to the Haight-Ashbury section of San Francisco, as "a reaction against those middle-class values which many young people see as having produced seemingly unresolvable conflicts abroad and at home," from Vietnam to urban racial unrest to the shallow culture of suburban materialism and conformity. According to Robert Carter, the director of the investigation, illegal drug use and the trickle-down embrace of mod/hippie lifestyles by Pleasant Hill students represented "*indirect* confrontations" with the adult establishment, part of a broader willingness to challenge the "flaws in the American system." Carter categorized both political activism and countercultural identification by these white suburban youth as "a normal response to a society which abnormally denies a large segment of its population any participation in decision-making."[9]

The seemingly sudden emergence of widespread marijuana use in upper-middle-class suburbs resulted primarily from the power of adolescent peer networks, with behavioral changes triggered by the movement of youth through metropolitan space and the circulation of influences through national culture. According to a follow-up study of Pleasant Hill, teenage delinquency before 1967 revolved around the implicitly sanctioned consumption of alcohol, and the values of most high school students reflected adult suburban society's status obsession, conformity, and political apathy. Then the "hippie" subculture forged in the Haight-Ashbury and popularized by the mass media provided white middle-class youth with the opportunity to become "active members in a movement which they could identify as their own"—a "hang-loose ethic" marked by "do your own thing" values of spontaneity, experience, irreverence, humanism, and tolerance. While some Pleasant Hill teens acquired marijuana by driving to Berkeley or San Francisco, most bought or shared the drug in local parks and other hangouts, or from classmate "suppliers" who operated from home when parents were away. The ensuing parental alarm and police crackdown widened Pleasant Hill's generation gap, as youth who considered their clothing style and marijuana subculture to be harmless markers of individual identity became increasingly confrontational toward authority in general. Drug arrests skyrocketed in 1967–68, and many teens received probation for first offenses that police previously would have handled informally. This influx strained the capacity of the delinquency system, and parents soon began convincing probation officers to dismiss possession cases in exchange for private psychotherapy. The police eventually decided to focus on halting supply lines, but this proved impossible because "dealers were many in number and interspersed within the adolescent social system." Interviews with "hip" teens revealed a widespread conviction that marijuana was safer than alcohol, ubiquitous ridicule of the pusher and heroin-gateway warnings still taught in the schools, and declarations that LSD alarmism was just another "scare tactic" and "plain bullshit."[10]

Politically conscious teenagers in Pleasant Hill mocked the values of middle-class suburbia, condemned the Vietnam War and social injustice, and defended their right to pursue happiness and insight through the use of marijuana and LSD. "We are trying hard," the Youth Commission's newsletter explained, "to break out of an establishment that is turning out kids who do not question or probe anything." A high school columnist for the *Contra Costa Times* described Pleasant Hill as a place of over-programmed childhood where "the world was square and perfectly arranged, . . . when even the pleasures of human existence have been classified, commercialized, and presented in the forms of 'wholesome miniature golf' and 'relaxing drive-in movies.'" Adopting a slogan of the Berkeley Free Speech Movement, he argued that parents as well as conformist youth might as well stamp the warning "do not fold, bend, or mutilate" on the "processed, packaged" children of suburbia. Another Pleasant Hill teenager, presented as an example of the (male) hip suburban typology in the UC–Berkeley drug investigation, explained that he started taking psychedelic drugs during the summer of 1967 "in search of the different," with marijuana providing simple pleasure and LSD spiritual awakening. He labeled the Vietnam War immoral, rejected "the pursuit of riches as the goal of human existence," and renounced his parents' capitalist obsessions with work and respectability. A sixteen-year-old high school student, interviewed in 1967 while on probation for marijuana possession, related that he got stoned because "it's groovy. It makes you feel real good." After first buying pot from Pleasant Hill classmates or student-dealers at a nearby junior college, he began hanging out in Berkeley and started taking LSD as well. "The law is wrong," he informed the nonplussed UC–Berkeley ethnographer. Marijuana "should be legal. . . . I don't think I'm escaping from anything. I just dig getting high. As long as we're not hurting anybody, they should just leave us alone."[11]

The earliest academic investigations of the marijuana "epidemic" in white middle-class American suburbia focused on affluent high schools located near major coastal cities and large universities, where young dealers and bohemians moved easily across spatial boundaries and politically conscious defenses of psychedelic drug use were common. In 1967, a Stanford University research team joined forces with the Santa Clara County Council on Drug

Abuse to uncover the extent of illicit drug violations at upper-middle-class suburban high schools in the Bay Area. The first survey of an affluent town adjacent to Palo Alto found that 72 percent of students had smoked tobacco, 86 percent had broken alcohol status laws (often with parental sanction), while 13 percent admitted marijuana use and fully one-third refused to answer the question. A majority of students expressed resentment of marijuana prohibition, and almost all discounted "pusher" pressure as a factor. Adolescents generally acquired marijuana and LSD from older siblings, friends in college, or by visiting the Haight-Ashbury or the Big Sur surfing mecca. The second survey compared another upper-middle-class community in Santa Clara County to a working-class urban high school and found significantly higher rates of tobacco, alcohol, and marijuana use among the suburban students. Thirty percent of these suburban teens had tried marijuana and 14 percent had taken LSD, nearly triple the proportions of their urban counterparts. A follow-up 1968 survey demonstrated a significant expansion of the illegal recreational drug scene in the Santa Clara suburbs during the previous year, with 55 percent of teenagers at the targeted high school reporting at least one instance of marijuana use and 20 percent having dropped acid. Whether or not they broke the drug laws, most suburban students considered tobacco to be more dangerous than marijuana ("unlike the hypothetical average adult") and resented the prevention curriculum whether delivered by police officers perceived as "ignorant" or "lying," or by teachers who represented the "moralizing" establishment.[12]

In terms of the much-discussed generation gap, white suburban youth who avidly participated in the illegal recreational drug culture in Santa Clara County demonstrated well-developed political sensibilities and displayed a range of antiauthoritarian, libertarian, and countercultural attitudes. "Many of us need an escape hatch from the pressures of this damn Establishment—grades, money, status, college," one student wrote in the 1967 Stanford survey. "You started this and we have to clean up and fix-up everything you messed up in the world. . . . . Freedom now!" "This country is not as free as most people say," another teenager declared. "My parents and most people over twenty-five say work all your life. FUCK." Students who took LSD were particularly fervent about its benefits, defining the hallucinogen as a "religious sacrament," a way to "learn about love and beauty," to discover "what nature is really like," to "be very creative." Many denounced the criminalization of marijuana, often pointing out that "pot is very harmless when compared to alcohol" and wondering how authorities expected to suppress its use given that "nothing happens" when teens violated the alcohol and tobacco laws. "When the Revolution

FIGURE 3.2. Suburban teenagers in the Bay Area often drove into the city of San Francisco to acquire marijuana and participate in subcultural and political activities. This syndicated 1968 image of a young white female casually committing a felony drug violation was originally titled "A hippie woman lights up a marijuana joint in Golden Gate Park." (Ted Streshinsky / Corbis / Getty Images.)

comes," one suburban youth proclaimed, "grass will be legalized." The educational curriculum that portrayed drug dealers as "radicals and 'long-haired kooks'" was nothing but "BULL SHIT," according to another. A number of students expressed anger toward the antidrug organization that administered the survey—a "last-ditch effort by the liberal establishment . . . to patch up a hopelessly perverted society," a "brainwashing campaign to put people down," "this better not be a God Damned bust"—and advised the Stanford academics to "drop acid and see where it's at." The sanguine researchers concluded that the generation gap was foremost a communications breakdown, because these inquisitive, thoughtful, and at times hostile students "have a great deal to say and to ask about drugs," but they did not believe that adults wanted to listen or that authorities would treat them with either honesty or respect.[13]

In adjacent San Mateo County, civic groups did seek answers from suburban teenagers in the crisis atmosphere that accompanied the arrests of several hundred high school students for felony marijuana violations during 1966–67.

Most of the suburban county's approximately five hundred thousand residents (81% white [non-Hispanic], 11% Hispanic, 4.5% Black) lived in a string of peninsula municipalities ranging from white and nonwhite working-class areas just south of San Francisco to affluent, racially segregated white-collar towns along the bay or outside Palo Alto. In spring 1967, the Juvenile Justice Commission of San Mateo County launched an investigation into the causes of the "volcanic eruption" and "flagrant misuse" of illegal drugs by white middle-class youth. Its survey revealed that 25 percent of males and 10 percent of females in the senior class of one upscale high school had smoked marijuana, while about half that number had taken LSD. The report also compared San Mateo youth recently arrested for marijuana possession to "routine delinquents" already in the juvenile system and found that the psychedelic drug users who encountered law enforcement came from higher socioeconomic backgrounds and more stable home situations. The gender breakdown of the data provided the most revealing evidence that marijuana's popularity had created a new criminal class, because three-fourths of female teenagers busted on drug charges were first offenders from middle-class or upper-middle-class families, while three-fourths of female "delinquents" arrested for non-drug-related offenses were repeat violators from poor or working-class backgrounds. Based on extensive student input, the report attributed marijuana and LSD use to the "search for meaning and values in a materialistic, power-oriented culture," where too many youth "feel like cogs in the machinery rather than individuals." The commission concluded that psychedelic drugs were not the cause but rather a symptom of the generation gap, the "persistent problem of inadequate understanding and communication between youth and adults."[14]

The San Mateo County investigation called for political reforms to increase judicial discretion in drug sentencing, reduce the felony penalty for marijuana possession, and toughen the misdemeanor penalty for LSD. These positions reflected the sentiments of a majority of high schoolers consulted in spring 1967, although the findings also revealed that "fear of legal consequences and the attitude of parents have very limited value as deterrence to drug use by juveniles." Instead, the report granted primary influence to the psychedelic hippie subculture centered in the Haight-Ashbury, with its "disrespect for the values of the mainstream" and promises of "excitement, escape, and freedom which is not to be found at home." Teenage informants explained that anyone could obtain marijuana through a nonprofit distribution network where someone's "friend" was always bringing it back from the Haight-Ashbury or a university campus. Many suburban teens featured in the investigation adopted the do-your-own-thing ethos of the counterculture: "Let people decide for themselves if they want to use drugs or not"; "Grass really should be legalized; it's no worse than alcohol"; "Marijuana should be legal—it doesn't lead to other drugs unless you want it to"; "The law is unfair because I believe drugs should be open and free to be used." Whether or not they broke the law, most of the students surveyed believed that casual marijuana experimenters and abstainers had "the same value system," with radical politics associated mainly with regular pot smokers and everyone who dropped acid. San Mateo youth comprehensively rejected warnings from parents and school authorities that marijuana was more dangerous than alcohol, choosing instead to trust their own firsthand experiences and observations, although many worried about the health hazards of LSD. The Juvenile Justice Commission concluded by citing the California Medical Association's position that marijuana produced psychological dependence, "encourages experimentation" with LSD (a "desperately dangerous" drug), and "of course, may lead" to heroin addiction.[15]

The law enforcement response to marijuana smoking by teenagers and young adults in San Mateo County revealed a wide socioeconomic gap between the mainstream drug scene in white middle-class suburbia and the particular violators arrested and processed in the criminal justice system. In 1968, the San Mateo County Board of Education conducted a comprehensive survey of illegal drug use among high school students, with nearly nineteen thousand respondents (table 3.1). In the senior class, 45 percent of males and 32 percent of females had smoked marijuana during the previous year, more than half at least ten times. For ninth graders, 27 percent of boys and 23 percent of girls had tried marijuana, also with half reporting more regular use. One-fifth of senior males and one-tenth of senior females had taken LSD, about double the proportion among their younger counterparts. Overall, 32 percent of high school students in San Mateo County admitted violating the felony prohibition against marijuana, or more than 6,000 teenagers districtwide. During the previous year, a total of 137 individuals faced felony marijuana charges in the southern half of San Mateo County, which included many affluent municipalities along the bay and north of Palo Alto. Judges gave probation or jail time to half of these defendants and, for the rest, either dismissed charges or remanded older teenagers to the delinquency courts. The typical marijuana conviction involved a nineteen-to-twenty-year-old white male from a blue-collar background, classified as a "hippie" in police or probation reports, who had dropped out of high school or junior college and was unemployed. An academic investigation revealed that police profiled and illegally searched San Mateo youth with visible hippie lifestyles, that probation officers were most likely to recommend jail time for defendants who refused to show remorse for

TABLE 3.1. Marijuana Use among High School Students (12th and 9th Grades) in San Mateo County, California, 1968–72

Year	12th male (any use)	12th male (10 or more)	12th male (50 or more)	12th female (any use)	12th female (10 or more)	12th female (50 or more)
1968	45%	26%	N/A	32%	17%	N/A
1969	50%	34%	N/A	33%	22%	N/A
1970	51%	34%	22%	44%	28%	15%
1971	59%	43%	32%	48%	31%	19%
1972	61%	45%	32%	53%	35%	20%
Year	**9th male (any use)**	**9th male (10 or more)**	**9th male (50 or more)**	**9th female (any use)**	**9th female (10 or more)**	**9th female (50 or more)**
1968	27%	14%	N/A	23%	11%	N/A
1969	35%	20%	N/A	32%	18%	N/A
1970	34%	20%	11%	32%	16%	7%
1971	45%	26%	17%	41%	23%	12%
1972	44%	27%	16%	39%	27%	12%

Source: San Mateo County Department of Public Health and Welfare, *Summary Report: Surveys of Student Drug Use, San Mateo County, California*, March 1977.

Note: Survey data denotes the number of times using marijuana during the previous year.

smoking pot, and that students from affluent high schools and colleges were practically exempt from prosecution or juvenile delinquency adjudication. In sum, the legal system had selected working-class nonconformists "arbitrarily for punishment from among vast unpunished numbers of users."[16]

Starting in the late 1960s, public health agencies in San Mateo County secured HEW funding for a decade-long survey of junior and senior high school students that provides the most complete statistical data available regarding the extent of illegal adolescent drug use in a large inner-ring suburban county during this time period (although not broken down by race or income). The findings illuminate many of the general patterns among white middle-class suburban teenagers who lived in coastal metropolitan areas during the late 1960s and 1970s: increasing rates of drug use as students moved from middle school through the senior year; a somewhat greater degree of illegal drug behavior among males than females, with the gap closing over time; a stabilization of LSD and tobacco consumption by the early 1970s, even as marijuana use kept accelerating; an extremely low percentage that ever tried heroin; and the popularity of alcohol above all other drugs (table 3.2). By 1970, 51 percent of males

TABLE 3.2. General Drug Use among High School Students (12th and 9th Grades) in San Mateo County, California, 1968–72

	12th grade alcohol		12th grade tobacco		12th grade amphetamines		12th grade barbiturates		12th grade LSD		12th grade heroin	
Year	Male	Fem.	Male	Fem.	Male	Fem.	Male	Fem.	Male	Fem.	Male	Fem.
1968	77%	71%	58%	55%	21%	16%	N/A	N/A	17%	9%	N/A	N/A
1969	82%	76%	58%	58%	26%	20%	N/A	N/A	23%	11%	N/A	N/A
1970	81%	77%	52%	53%	19%	20%	14%	14%	17%	12%	N/A	N/A
1971	83%	79%	53%	54%	27%	23%	19%	15%	21%	12%	6%	3%
1972	88%	83%	55%	55%	26%	24%	15%	14%	21%	14%	5%	3%
	9th grade alcohol		9th grade tobacco		9th grade amphetamines		9th grade barbiturates		9th grade LSD		9th grade heroin	
Year	Male	Fem.	Male	Fem.	Male	Fem.	Male	Fem.	Male	Fem.	Male	Fem.
1968	61%	52%	57%	52%	12%	13%	N/A	N/A	8%	7%	N/A	N/A
1969	66%	63%	51%	52%	15%	20%	N/A	N/A	11%	11%	N/A	N/A
1970	66%	63%	50%	52%	14%	17%	13%	15%	11%	9%	N/A	N/A
1971	74%	68%	55%	56%	18%	23%	17%	18%	13%	12%	4%	2%
1972	76%	74%	56%	58%	17%	22%	12%	14%	12%	12%	3%	2%

Source: San Mateo County Department of Public Health and Welfare, *Summary Report: Surveys of Student Drug Use, San Mateo County, California*, March 1977.

Note: Data reflects the percentage reporting any use during the previous year.

and 44 percent of females in the senior class had consumed marijuana during the previous year, with more than one-third of this group smoking pot on a weekly basis. In evidence of the continued trickle-down effect, 34 percent of ninth-grade males and 32 percent of their female classmates had experimented with marijuana at least once. Counting all criminalized substances, including alcohol, only 14 percent of males and 16 percent of females in the senior class of 1970 had not broken at least one drug law in San Mateo County. Occasional users outnumbered weekly consumers in every category of drug use, with the exception of tobacco, a finding often lost amid the national political and media hype that conflated the total number of teenagers who had experimented with psychedelics with the chronic "abusers" considered to be psychologically dependent and alienated dropouts as well as heroin-gateway risks. Most of all, the San Mateo surveys revealed that participation in the recreational marijuana market had become a plurality phenomenon by the late 1960s, and a majority practice by the early 1970s, among older white middle-class teenagers in the inner-ring suburbs of the San Francisco Bay Area.[17]

The "generation gap" takeaway from the academic studies of drug use in the suburban high schools of metropolitan San Francisco had a disproportionate influence on the national debate. This interpretation placed the illegal practices of white middle-class teenagers into a political rather than a criminal context and catalyzed discussion of whether changes to marijuana prohibition policies were necessary to resolve the alienation of these "otherwise law-abiding" youth. The investigations connected the attitudes and activities of white middle-class teenagers in the Bay Area directly to the "hippie" scene of the Haight-Ashbury and the political rebellion at UC–Berkeley, in addition to the broader New Left and countercultural critiques of the materialistic values of suburban-corporate America and its undemocratic practices of war, racism, and inequality. Only a subset of white middle-class teenagers articulated their psychedelic drug use at this level of political consciousness, just as only a fraction of suburban youth personally traveled to urban centers and university campuses to secure drugs, drop out, or demonstrate. But the generation gap framework, and the policy of criminal prohibition that served as a key foundation, still turned large numbers of marijuana consumers into suburban rebels by politicizing the recreational drug subculture of white middle-class youth en masse. By the late 1960s, the mandatory-minimum marijuana laws of the state of California had transformed about one-third of all residents between the ages of sixteen and twenty-five into felony criminals, even as the impossibility of enforcement on such a broad scale and the racial and economic discretion within the criminal justice system made the chance of incarceration remote, for affluent white offenders in particular. Even so, as the study of marijuana enforcement in San Mateo County concluded, prohibition and criminalization had resulted in widespread "police misconduct and the alienation of young people," and "even marijuana users who are never apprehended may experience vicariously the deleterious effects of criminal treatment."[18]

The most extensive study of illegal drug use by American high school students during the late 1960s provided even more evidence for the generation gap thesis of political alienation and revealed that older teenagers in the affluent inner-ring suburbs of San Francisco violated the marijuana laws at about double the proportion of their counterparts nationwide. The "Youth in Transition" project, based at the University of Michigan's Institute for Social Research, traced a diverse group of 2,200 male subjects in the class of 1969 from tenth grade through their first year in college or the labor market. The national survey revealed that 21 percent had smoked marijuana during high school, including 6.5 percent on a weekly or daily basis, and about 5 percent had ever tried LSD. The report criticized the mass media for overstating an "epidemic" of illegal drug use among American teenagers while noting the still "rather astounding" confirmation that one-fifth of male high school seniors had committed a drug felony. The "Youth in Transition" investigation also found significant differences in marijuana use based on region and degree of urbanicity, with proportions almost twice as high in the West and Northeast than in the South and Midwest, and greatest in the large cities (40%) and the suburbs (25%). Students from suburban areas effectively caught up during their first year in college, when the proportion that had smoked pot increased to 39 percent. In terms of the generation gap at the high school level, the study found marijuana use most frequently among college-bound teenagers in the highest socioeconomic bracket and a very strong correlation with students who expressed political alienation from the government and opposed the war in Vietnam (65%). One-third of the members of this "ideologically alienated subculture" smoked pot regularly and had taken LSD, persuasive evidence of a vibrant countercultural ethos in the high schools. The "Youth in Transition" study concluded that "selective enforcement" of the marijuana laws, especially against political and cultural nonconformists, "is certain to result in greater alienation."[19]

Suburbs of New York City: Race, Class, and De Facto Decriminalization

In fall 1967, New York Governor Nelson Rockefeller informed a gathering of civic groups in Westchester County that "narcotics addiction has demonstrated that it can travel easily from the slum tenement to the split-levels of suburbia." Rockefeller told the forum, sponsored by the Junior Leagues of Scarsdale (95+ percent white) and two other upscale towns, that parents who moved to the suburbs in search of "a better life for their children don't always find it." As a Westchester resident himself, the governor knew that affluent suburbs were "synonymous with the good life," but more and more, "drug addiction, crime and juvenile delinquency cut across that comfortable image." The increasing problem of drug abuse among teenagers resulted not only from "economic poverty" in the ghetto but also "moral poverty . . . amidst the material plenty" that Westchester had to offer. For Rockefeller, alerting white suburbanites that the narcotics menace of New York City also threatened their own children had become standard fare since he declared a full-scale "war on crime and narcotics addiction" in the lead-up to his 1966 reelection campaign. That special message warned that the "evil contagion" of drug addiction "is spreading into the suburbs," endangering all families regardless of socioeconomic status or geographic setting, and pledged to remove "the pushers of narcotics from . . . our cities and suburbs" alike.[20] In preparation for the Westchester meeting, the governor's staff asked the state police to dig up a story of the perfect suburban victim: "e.g. Johnny M., middle-class respectable family, tried pot at party, eventually hooked on heroin." But the best they could find was a seventeen-year-old model addicted to amphetamines prescribed by her doctor, and another unapologetic teen whose socialite parents didn't care that she smoked pot. Law enforcement officials in Westchester explained that most narcotics addicts held in the county prison were poor African Americans from areas such as Yonkers, while few white middle-class youth had records because the criminal justice system generally handled and dismissed their cases without trial.[21]

As in the San Francisco Bay Area, alarm about illegal drug use in the affluent suburbs of New York City intensified during the summer of 1967, when growing numbers of white teenagers began embracing the psychedelic culture and political ethos of Greenwich Village and especially the East Village (fig. 3.3). These urban bohemian enclaves, the East Coast counterparts to the Haight-Ashbury, generated national media hype about the "runaway

FIGURE 3.3. Hippies gather to "do their own thing" at St. Mark's Place, the cultural hub of New York City's East Village, a frequent destination for white suburban teenagers who embraced radical politics and participated in marijuana and LSD markets, September 6, 1968. (AP Photo / Bob Wands.)

hippie" crisis while providing nearby suburban youth with access to drug markets and political alternatives. Contrary to Rockefeller's warnings of the "pernicious advance" of narcotics pushers and drug addiction, spreading from the inner city into Westchester County, white suburban youth actively sought this physical and philosophical reverse migration. "Somebody finally told me the truth," exclaimed a high school senior who spent a month in the East Village, "staying turned-on" to grass and realizing that "it's what I feel that really matters." She promised to return the next summer, before heading to an elite college in the fall. In a letter to the *East Village Other*, another seventeen-year-old attributed his political enlightenment to the combination of marijuana and the messages of that underground publication. While a high-achieving student with a college scholarship, he now considered himself to be a typical "mass-produced, disillusioned . . . product of our isolated, democratic, and affluent society." Smoking pot helped him to see the light about the "illegal and immoral" war in Vietnam, to recognize that the government had "lied to and cheated" his generation, to realize how much he had been "alienated by a corrupt

Establishment." "The Hippie and Drug Revolution" had reached middle-class suburbia, another high school student excitedly informed the *East Village Other* during the summer of 1967. Marijuana and LSD were readily available, thanks to "two main kids who score drugs from the city," and sometimes directly from Mexico. The "enlightened" teenagers in his suburban enclave often got high and dropped acid at house parties hosted by a few classmates whose parents either also turned on or gave their children permission to do so.[22]

Although smoking pot appeared to trigger political awareness in such generation gap testimonials, a more plausible interpretation is that marijuana played a symbolic role in the process of youth radicalization during the late 1960s, based largely on its illicit status and its ubiquity in the social settings that attracted and produced suburban rebels. "Most hippies are really rather intelligent, sensitive, middle-class kids," an East Village head shop owner observed. "It's marijuana that has kept these hippie kids from dying emotionally in the suburbs. It's jarred them loose." Taking psychedelic drugs, a suburban expatriate in the East Village claimed in the summer of 1967, is when "you change from a straight person to a hippie."[23] While many worried parents also agreed with this conversion narrative, psychiatrists who worked directly with suburban youth were far more likely to view marijuana as a symptom rather than the catalyst for "alienation" and the "generalized rejection of prevalent American values." According to a psychologist based on Long Island, upper-middle-class youth were "rebelling against the nothingness breeding in the suburbs." He argued that the "evil is in Greenwich and Great Neck, not Greenwich Village," and blamed parents for "leading hollow, empty, shallow lives." In the Westchester County suburb of Larchmont, a minister who worked closely with teenagers considered their illegal drug use to be a response to "the hypocrisy of the adult world"—the materialistic values of an affluent society, the narrow boundaries of status and success in middle-class culture, the "moral contradiction" of the Vietnam War. This pastor urged Larchmont parents not to overreact to the seemingly sudden visibility of marijuana, because "it's really a symptom of other things" that were unsettling youth who remained "idealistic about life." While some Westchester officials blamed adolescent drug use on media glamorization of the hippie scene in the East Village, the prevailing interpretation in the upscale suburbs emphasized problems and solutions closer to home, in particular upper-middle-class family culture.[24]

In many affluent inner-ring suburbs of New York City, the official response to increased rates of marijuana use in the high schools operated within the informal "absorption" system of police discretion, de facto decriminalization, and family-centered solutions already in place to handle problems of delinquency and underage drinking. In Scarsdale, a wealthy suburban village in Westchester County, local politicians established a Committee on Drug Abuse in 1967 after reports that one-third of high school students were smoking pot and an unknown number were moving on to LSD and amphetamines. Several arrests of young men from prominent families increased the alarm, including a lawyer's son busted in an LSD raid in Greenwich Village and a twenty-three-year-old marijuana dealer who lived with his clueless parents. The Scarsdale committee involved lawyers, physicians, clergy, and delegates from local government, the school system, PTAs, and the police department. During 1968, this coalition held ten educational forums and attributed the surge in illegal drug use to two main causes: the easy money and automobile mobility enjoyed by affluent suburban youth and the generation gap communications breakdown between parents and children. The police chief then reassured Scarsdale parents that "we are not concerned officially with the kid who is experimenting" but rather focused on "those who are selling to make a profit." According to local police, the recreational subculture involved "four or five loosely organized groups of teenagers" who acquired marijuana from outside the community and supplied friends and acquaintances "as an accommodation." This analysis avoided the racialized, urban categories of "gangs" and "pushers" and left little room for criminal enforcement at all, with only six drug-related arrests in Scarsdale during 1968. Instead, the Committee on Drug Abuse organized parleys between teens and parents to bridge the generation gap, a strategy that had little apparent effect on the marijuana subculture. "They think drugs are wrong," one Scarsdale teenager told the *New York Times*, "and we think they're not."[25]

Parents, law enforcement, and public officials in the affluent suburbs of New York City remained both uncertain and divided over how to respond to the seemingly pervasive presence of marijuana in the adolescent social scene. At a 1967 workshop on "Drug Abuse by Teenagers" sponsored by Westchester County, multiple police officers berated a long-haired teenager who insisted that he would never "squeal" on classmates who used marijuana and LSD, expressing astonishment that the youth would self-identify so unapologetically with a criminal subculture. At another drug conference later that year, a representative from the Westchester district attorney's office explained that "we no longer have the stereotyped problem of pushers selling marijuana to the teenagers. Youths in fine neighborhoods are getting big supplies somewhere and selling it to their friends. . . . No longer is any stigma attached to it."

The county executive warned the audience that pot smokers would "invariably turn to LSD and heroin" and denounced a group of Scarsdale youth who advocated changing the law to treat marijuana the same as alcohol. The police chief of Rye, one of the wealthiest towns in Westchester County, reported that parents were worried about marijuana use but even more opposed to any law enforcement focus on their own children. In a *New York Times* investigation of Port Washington, an affluent white suburb across the Long Island Sound, anonymous teenagers recounted a de facto drug education initiative they had devised for their own parents—being more up front about their marijuana use to defuse adult fears, and explaining that dealers were just ordinary kids trying to make a little cash. While a vocal group of Port Washington parents demanded abstinence-only campaigns and police crackdowns on teenage suppliers, others were coming to agree with local psychiatrists and educators that marijuana was "a social thing" and a "soft" drug like alcohol, and so the emphasis should be on preventing escalation to the "hard" drugs LSD and heroin.[26]

White youth in suburban high schools generally defended the right to smoke marijuana by drawing a direct analogy to their parents' consumption of alcohol, an argument that portrayed criminal enforcement as age-based discrimination and disassociated their activities from the racial stigma of urban heroin markets. In Port Washington, after a wave of police busts of marijuana users and dealers, two high school students conducted an anonymous survey of their classmates in order to combat parental misunderstanding and demonstrate that criminal prohibition provided "no deterrent." The study revealed that 33 percent of high school students in Port Washington had smoked marijuana more than twice, while 12 percent had taken LSD and almost none had encountered heroin. The student-researchers concluded that the drug education curriculum was "worthless" and that adolescent use of marijuana correlated most strongly with permissive parents who drank alcohol to excess. In 1968, after another major undercover operation on Long Island, a high school senior in Great Neck condemned the "persecution" of students who sold and smoked marijuana, a "relatively innocuous" drug, while law enforcement did nothing about the "hard-core addicts and junkies who rob our stores, steal our cars and assault our citizens in their continuous effort to produce or acquire the much-needed money for the purchase of heroin." Rather than crackdowns in the suburbs, this teenager demanded that police start "patrolling the streets of New York, seizing these lawbreakers and arresting those neighborhood junkies." The frequent comparisons of marijuana to alcohol, a legal psychoactive drug, challenged the generation gap framework by positioning white middle-class pot smoking as a mainstream youth practice in a mood-altering society rather than a deviant, criminal, or politicized subculture. But the racial and spatial distinctions between the pleasure-oriented suburban marijuana market and the dangerous urban heroin environment also rested on the failure to acknowledge the equally constructed divide between the illegal menace of narcotics and the legal pharmaceuticals consumed daily by tens of millions of middle-class Americans.[27]

Advocates of a tougher war on drugs in the New York City suburbs conflated the marijuana and heroin threats, as did the felony narcotics category in state law, and advocated harsh punishment for sellers of all illegal drugs. In 1968, the official training manual for the narcotics police in Suffolk County, a 95 percent white jurisdiction on Long Island with more than one million residents, called for the "pusher" of marijuana, LSD, and heroin to be "eliminated from society, . . . no matter who he is or how large or small a supplier he is." According to a neighborhood petition circulated in the county, "our schools are not safe, our streets are not safe, and our communities are not safe while pushers of dangerous drugs are allowed to remain at large." This group praised the police for conducting marijuana and LSD raids in suburban areas and demanded that the Rockefeller administration enact stricter mandatory-minimum laws to stop the "hideous attack on our youth." Another Suffolk petition movement in 1968 condemned "lenient" judges and informed the governor that without more inflexible penalties, "the pushers are getting off too easy." A man from North Merrick, a suburban town in Suffolk County, complained of the light treatment for the drug-dealing sons of "prominent citizens" and insisted that if his "son sold drugs to children I would not object to a thirty-year sentence."[28] In early 1970, a Long Island mother of six wrote Governor Rockefeller to convey her shock at the failure of law enforcement to stop the "great pot party" at the Woodstock music festival, which enabled the hippies to set a terrible example for the teenagers in her middle-class community, where illegal drug use was rapidly increasing. From nearby Westchester County, a mother of three called for the "most severe punishment" for suppliers of all illegal drugs, including marijuana, before they robbed her children of their dreams. "In the suburbs, appearances are deceptive," a Scarsdale mother lamented. "The good-looking, clean-cut boy up the block can be a narcotics pusher. He blends with the scenery. . . . He's not a stranger or a street-corner hoodlum."[29]

In contrast, the parents of suburban teenagers arrested on drug charges in New York typically joined their children in condemning the application of narcotics laws and undercover police tactics to the recreational marijuana market. In late 1969, an upper-middle-class mother wrote Governor Rockefeller to protest the "harassment of youth" by the police, especially the unjustified pursuit of teenage pot smokers. Her high school daughter, an excellent student with no prior record, faced trial for selling marijuana after being arrested in what the mother described as entrapment by a state trooper. At a party, the undercover agent asked the daughter to sell him some pot, and so she "shared what she had" as a favor. At his insistence, she accepted a few dollars in exchange and now faced felony narcotics charges and the possibility of jail or reform school. The mother also accused police of repeatedly pulling over her college-age son and his friends because they had long hair, even though they did not use drugs. She denounced New York state policy for placing nonaddictive "soft drugs" in the same class as heroin and argued that the "law is being used in a vindictive way to punish young people for daring to rebel against the status symbols of today's society." In early 1970, a Long Island woman urged Rockefeller to impose a moratorium on marijuana possession arrests so that teenagers who experimented would "not be scarred for life with criminal records." A judge in suburban Nassau County reported that public opinion did not favor incarceration for marijuana use by young first offenders, but the narcotics law did not permit probation without conviction. He also informed Rockefeller that the state's compulsory medical confinement program was a "futile . . . waste of time and money" because the law required an expert psychiatric assessment of marijuana as well as heroin defendants, even though forcing pot smokers into addiction treatment centers made no sense. In his jurisdiction, therefore, the courts had been reducing low-level marijuana possession charges to public intoxication, a simple violation that did not leave a criminal record.[30]

Marijuana enforcement became a political touchstone for many New York youth who demanded legalization and denounced Rockefeller's frequently declared wars on "drug abuse" with righteous anger. A Suffolk County teenager busted for dealing marijuana wrote the governor that there was no reasonable explanation for its classification as a dangerous narcotic and asked, "Why is alcohol legal and not hash or grass?" "Every day," he lamented, "one of my peers is being arrested," most for possession. At one of Rockefeller's many community antidrug forums, a female who grew up in an all-white town stated that she first smoked pot in Greenwich Village, a place that also introduced her to racial diversity, folk music, antiwar activism, and the realization that "America wasn't the land I was brought up to believe it was." So she chose to ignore the laws and warnings about marijuana, because "if they've been lying to me about so many other things, why couldn't they be lying to me about this." She informed Rockefeller that if the government wanted to close the generation gap, stop lumping recreational marijuana users in with narcotics pushers, churning youth out as component parts of a "machine society," and trying to be "the cops of the world." Multiple other youth speakers at the same forum denounced law enforcement harassment, because "the police are out to get the hippies," and asked how the governor could justify messing up the lives and futures of teenagers arrested in a drug war based on lies. As one male explained, the broader society had alienated a generation with the Vietnam War, criminalized youth for having long hair, and repressed them for smoking grass. Teenagers "would just as soon turn on to drugs because they're more where it's at." Many decried the alcohol double standard and asked of the legal threat to incarcerate recreational marijuana users as felons: "What kind of justice is this?" A particularly discerning teenager told the governor that the problem was not actually a full-blown generation gap but more specific: "Those who are conforming to a certain social pattern and those who don't."[31]

In Nassau County, the probation department compiled the most comprehensive data available anywhere in the nation on how drug-war enforcement and the criminal legal system operated in a large suburban region during the late 1960s and early 1970s. Located on Long Island, directly east of New York City, Nassau County contained a 95 percent white population of 1.43 million, with racial minorities segregated in Hempstead and Freeport. As in many inner-ring suburban counties, drug arrests increased significantly during the second half of the 1960s, from 127 people in 1965 to 3,849 by 1970 (the county spent $10 million on narcotics enforcement that year). The narcotics squad had traditionally focused on white working-class and Black heroin users in the Hempstead area, and the drug arrest proportion for nonwhite residents tripled their share of the county population in the late 1960s. But as the psychedelic drug culture expanded in the New York suburbs, the majority of non-heroin arrests in Nassau County involved white middle-class and upper-middle-class teenagers busted for marijuana possession or on multiple charges that included LSD or pills (table 3.3). In 1969, full-time students accounted for 37 percent of drug arrests in Nassau County, with almost three-fifths still in high school, disproportionately from white-collar families and overwhelmingly male. Based on illegal drug use trends, white females were very underrepresented in the arrest cohort, a reflection of law enforcement profiling and priorities. The data also does not include the significant but unknowable

TABLE 3.3. Drug Arrests in Nassau County, New York, 1969, Comparing Students, Nonstudents, Whites, Nonwhites

Category of arrestee (N = 1,751)	Student	Nonstudent	White	Nonwhite
Total drug arrests	37%	63%	84%	16%
In high school	58% (of students)	—	40% in high school/ college	25% in high school/ college
In college	42% (of students)	—		
Median age	18.3	21.4	19.1	21.5
Race—white	89%	80%	—	—
Gender—male	89%	90%	88%	93%
Median family income	$14,219	$10,350	$12,770	$7,950
Father white collar	66%	48%	62%	18%
Arrest charge—possession	79%	82%	83%	76%
Arrest charge—sale	21%	18%	17%	24%
Arrest—marijuana only	53%	42%	N/A	N/A
Arrest—heroin	7%	25%	10%	61%
Marijuana-only users	51%	28%	41%	17%
Prior record	12%	42%	26%	45%
Disposition—commitment	4%	19%	10%	32%

Source: Nassau County Probation Department, *Drug Abuse in Suburbia: Third Interim Report*, August 1971.

Note: In the arrest cohort, nonstudents were 4.75 times as likely as students to be committed, and nonwhites 3.2 times as likely as white offenders. The discrepancy reveals socioeconomic as well as racial disproportionality, because white nonstudents arrested on drug charges were also much more likely to be committed than white students. "Commitment" in this data includes offenders sentenced to jail, prison, juvenile detention, and hospitalization. The median family income in Nassau County in 1969 was $13,011.

number of youth, especially juveniles from wealthy communities, released to parental custody without charges through the discretion of police or probation officers. The Nassau report broke down arrest statistics by race and student status—revealing that nonstudents and especially nonwhites were far more likely to be arrested for heroin, to come from working-class families, and to have prior criminal or juvenile records. After arrest, nonwhites were eight times more likely than white students to be prosecuted and incarcerated.[32]

The Nassau County analysis, titled *Drug Abuse in Suburbia*, revealed that the unprecedented increase in arrests of white middle-class youth had intensified the discretionary practices of diversion by prosecutors and judges in drug

TABLE 3.4. Demographic and Disposition Data for Drug Arrests in Nassau County, New York, 1969

Category	All drug arrests (N = 1,751)	Marijuana only user group (N = 358)	Multiple drug users (no heroin) (N = 197)	Heroin user group (N = 325)
Age—16/17	20%	31%	34%	9%
Age—18/19	29%	36%	28%	21%
Age—20 to 24	39%	28%	34%	50%
Age—25 and above	12%	5%	4%	20%
Race—white	84%	92%	95%	64%
Race—nonwhite	16%	8%	5%	36%
Gender—male	89%	90%	92%	92%
Gender—female	11%	10%	8%	8%
Disposition—dismissed	17%	9%	8%	17%
Disposition—discharged	30%	34%	19%	9%
Disposition—fined	6%	5%	7%	1%
Disposition—probation	17%	35%	43%	16%
Disposition—pending	12%	10%	8%	9%
Disposition—committed	17%	5%	12%	47%

Source: Nassau County Probation Department, *Drug Abuse in Suburbia: Third Interim Report*, August 1971.

Note: The noncriminal "discharge" of one-third of those classified as "marijuana-only users"—a group overwhelmingly white, male, and young—meant that only one-third received probation and very few faced commitment. "Multiple drug users," also mostly white, were more likely to be sentenced to probation and more than twice as likely to be committed, a process linked to criminalization of their perceived political radicalism. The "heroin user group," disproportionately nonwhite and nonaffluent, was by far the most likely to experience commitment. "Commitment" in this data includes offenders sentenced to jail, prison, juvenile detention, and hospitalization. The three user groups for whom detailed information is available include only those arrestees who admitted drug use for this classification by the probation department, about half of total drug arrests.

case dispositions (table 3.4). For arrests during 1969, the courts dismissed 17 percent of formal charges and "discharged" another 30 percent, especially cases of marijuana possession (a felony at more than one-quarter of an ounce). The discharge category represented a quasi-formal system developed by prosecutors and judges to allow young marijuana offenders without prior records to plea bargain to noncriminal violations, usually public intoxication or disorderly conduct, traditionally utilized in punishment of alcohol-related delinquency status crimes. The data also showed that white students were more likely than nonstudents and almost as likely as nonwhites to be arrested for selling drugs, generally marijuana but sometimes LSD or amphetamines. White student defendants charged with selling pot often plea-bargained down to misdemeanor possession and received probation, a relatively light punishment for a potential felony charge, although more than half insisted that they had only provided marijuana to friends and acquaintances rather than dealt for profit. To assist with court dispositions and assess rehabilitation potential, the probation department separated the arrest cohort into three typologies, based not on observed criminal behavior but on the types of drug use admitted under interrogation. The "marijuana-only user" group, deemed to have high potential for reform, placed most white middle-class offenders into noncriminalized psychological categories such as "situational" drug user (24%), "subcultural identifier" (22%), and "conformist" (21%). The "multiple drug user" group shared similar white middle-class demographics, combined marijuana use with LSD or amphetamines (but never heroin), and more often sold drugs for profit. Probation officials categorized most as "asocial/antisocial" (42%) or "subcultural identifier" (27%)—a political designation for hippies and radicals—and judges sentenced a plurality to formal probation (43%) and sent a couple dozen to jail (12%).[33]

The evidence from Nassau County demonstrates how the criminal justice system in a large suburban jurisdiction modified the impact of drug sentencing laws and devised new discretionary policies to regulate the white middle-class recreational marijuana market (fig. 3.4). The *Drug Abuse in Suburbia* report endorsed the prosecutorial and judicial use of the discharge option as a lenient approach of "wisdom and restraint," even a necessary response to the overburdening of the criminal justice system through police crackdowns on marijuana users, "which many believe has resulted in the growing criminalization of an entire generation." The psychological assessment and demographic classification of individual offenders also shaped the administration of discretion and mercy. Probation officials evaluated defendants and made recommendations based on categories that included educational or employment status, academic achievement and IQ score, religious involvement, personality subtype, family structure and parenting style, and socioeconomic background. Race and economic status fundamentally shaped the nominally color-blind process, with nonwhite defendants disproportionately placed in the category of "social pathology or family disorganization," and white marijuana-only users overwhelmingly categorized as "more intelligent" individuals from "more stable" families and "more solid" middle-class and upper-middle-class communities, "more representative of the general population of Nassau County."

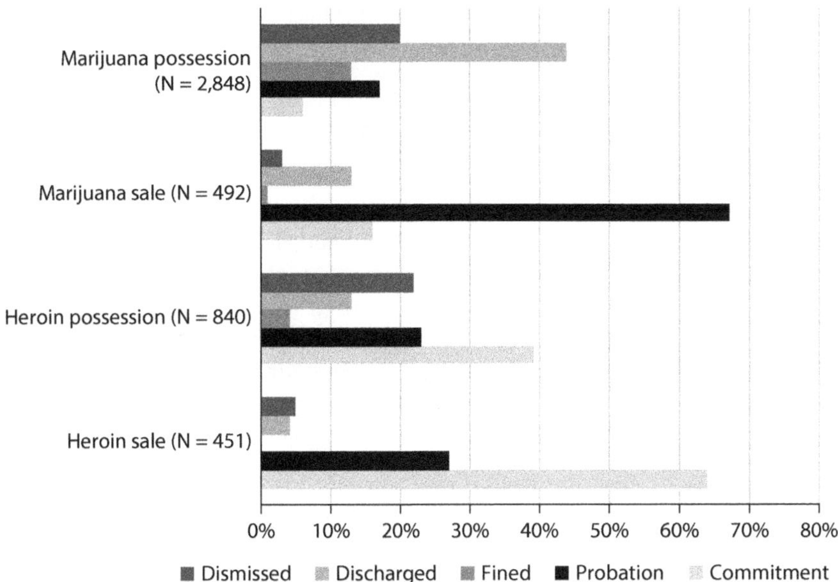

FIGURE 3.4. Disposition of marijuana and heroin offenders in Nassau County, New York, 1967–71. The criminal justice system in suburban Nassau County dismissed or "discharged" 66% of those arrested for felony marijuana possession, a group disproportionately made up of white middle-class youth, while placing 17% on probation and committing only 6%. Individuals arrested for marijuana sale, also a mostly white group, were 4.2 times as likely to receive probation and 2.7 times as likely to be committed. Heroin offenders, a group at least one-third nonwhite and overwhelmingly lower income, were the most likely to be committed for possession (39%) and sale (64%). (Nassau County Probation Department, *Drug Abuse in Suburbia: Final Report*, August 1978.)

Note: Commitment in this data includes offenders sentenced to jail, prison, juvenile detention, and hospitalization.

Through its user-based typology, the probation department drew a spatial and racial distinction between the marijuana and heroin markets, with the former embodied by white middle-class students from upwardly mobile families who were just experimenting, and the latter made up of African American and white working-class "underachievers" from distressed homes who required formal control by the criminal justice system. In sum, the more that Nassau police arrested white middle-class youth for smoking pot, the more the judicial system effectively decriminalized marijuana possession for the majority of offenders who fit the racial and class profile of "otherwise law-abiding citizens."[34]

The de facto decriminalization of marijuana possession for white middle-class students increased over time, although a closer analysis of the Nassau

TABLE 3.5. Communities with Highest and Lowest Drug Arrest Rates in Nassau County, New York, 1967–71, with Median Income and Racial Demographics

All drug arrests	Income rank	Race % white	Marijuana possession	Income rank	Race % white
1. Roosevelt	79	32%	1. Oyster Bay	68	95%
2. Westbury	19	94%	2. Seaford	46	99.5%
3. New Cassel	75	37%	3. Glen Head	49	99%
4. Long Beach	76	92%	4. Great Neck	19	94%
5. Hempstead	78	65%	5. East Norwich	24	97%
6. Freeport	72	81%	6. Massapequa	37	99.5%
7. Island Park	80	97%	7. Freeport	71	81%
8. Elmont	74	96%	8. Long Beach	76	92%
9. Inwood	81	76%	9. Elmont	74	96%
10. Sea Cliff	39	98%	10. Cedarhurst	31	99%
72. Brookville	5	97%	72. Lawrence	7	94%
73. East Hills/Greenvale	6	98%	73. Great Neck Plaza	33	95%
74. Searingtown	11	98%	74. E. Rockaway/ Bay Park	43	99%
75. North Valley Stream	40	99%	75. North Valley Stream	40	99%
76. North Hills	3	93%	76. East Hills/ Greenvale	6	98%
77. Flower Hill	4	99%	77. South Hempstead	36	98%
78. South Hempstead	36	98%	78. Thomaston	10	95%
79. Hewlett Harbor	16	95%	79. Flower Hill	4	99%
80. Great Neck Estates	2	95%	80. Searingtown	11	98%
81. Thomaston	10	95%	81. Great Neck Estates	2	95%

Sources: Nassau County Probation Department, *Drug Abuse in Suburbia: Final Report*, August 1978; Social Explorer, 1970 Census Data.

County arrest records reveals significant disparities in policing practices based not only on race but also economic class and geographic location (table 3.5). Between 1967 and 1971, the Nassau courts dismissed or discharged 64 percent of marijuana possession cases, placed 67 percent of marijuana sellers on probation, and jailed about four hundred defendants for marijuana crimes. The probation department classified the vast majority of these offenders as "low risks . . . with no significant relationship to other types of criminal behavior," whereas lower-income and/or African American defendants with prior records were the most likely to be incarcerated for breaking marijuana laws. During the same period, Nassau County incarcerated or institutionalized 39 percent of heroin possession defendants and 64 percent of sellers, around 615 people in all, disproportionately working class and/or nonwhite. The *Drug Abuse in Suburbia* report concluded that differential arrest rates directly reflected drug usage patterns in the general population, but ranking communities in Nassau County by income as well as race indicates a more complex story (fig. 3.5). About two-thirds of all drug arrests countywide between 1967 and 1971 occurred in the Hempstead area, the location of multiple minority enclaves as well as several colleges, with the highest rates in Nassau's lowest-income and nonwhite sections. For marijuana possession, the highest rates of arrest came in overwhelmingly white suburbs ranked toward the middle or bottom in the income hierarchy, clustered in the southern half of the county. The wealthy white villages along the North Shore had the lowest arrest rates for marijuana possession and for all drugs, indicating that local law enforcement rarely targeted or detained teenage pot smokers or dealers in those areas at all.[35]

In the nearby commuter suburbs of southern Connecticut, modest criminal enforcement of the drug laws quickly led to powerful counterarguments that the solutions rested in public health prevention strategies and better communication within the family. In a 1967 report, the state's Narcotic Advisory Council highlighted the "complete reversal" of the racial makeup of the illegal drug-using population, with whites now constituting a majority of the "victims." While heroin use remained urban centered, the commission emphasized the "alarming" increase in marijuana smoking and LSD experimentation by white middle-class students in high school and college and called for a "total attack on the drug problem" through an educational campaign. According to the (exaggerated) report of a judge in Fairfield County, 75 percent of high schoolers in an expensive suburb had sampled marijuana and 35 percent smoked pot routinely. Fairfield youth faced "absolutely no problem" in securing marijuana, amphetamines, and even heroin from Harlem or Hartford, and federal narcotics agents had busted at least one clandestine LSD lab run by local teenagers. "Our area is literally infested with young drug users and addicts," a Southport woman informed Senator Thomas Dodd in the fall of 1969. Fairfield County (92% white and highly segregated by race and income) used to be a "decent place in which to raise children," but now teenage boys were dealing drugs down the street in her "fashionable" neighborhood and the police seemed powerless to stop such suppliers.[36] Local and state police did launch a series of undercover investigations in Fairfield suburbs during the late 1960s, rounding up dozens of teenage dealers and users, including several from

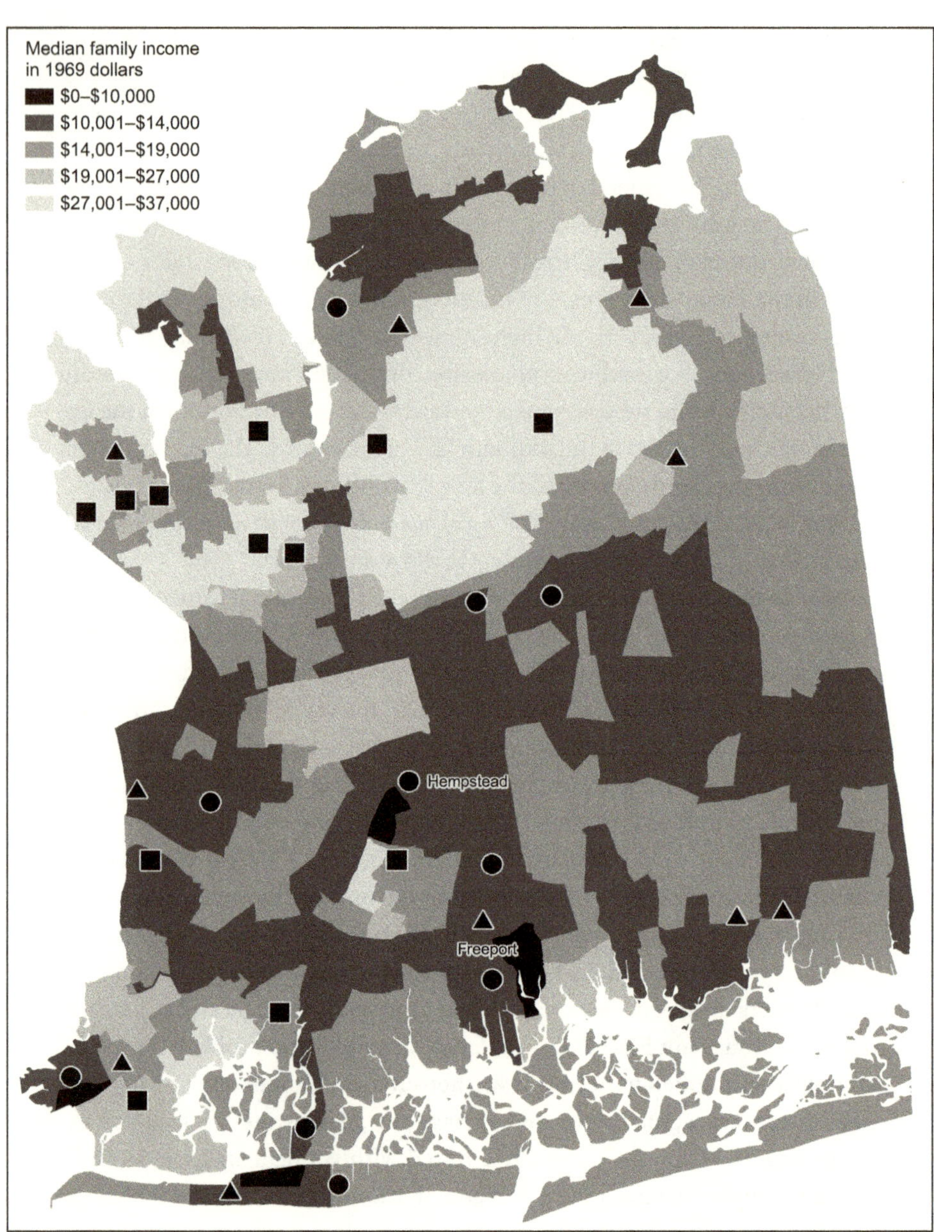

FIGURE 3.5. Drug arrest patterns by income in Nassau County, New York, 1967–71. This map visualizes data from the communities listed in Table 3.5 to demonstrate that the wealthiest and almost all-white suburban towns in Nassau County had the lowest arrest rates (adjusted for population) for all drugs and for marijuana possession, despite considerable evidence that affluent white youth smoked marijuana at higher rates than nonwhite and lower-income counterparts. The squares represent all communities ranked in the bottom ten (out of eighty-one) for marijuana arrest rate and/or total drug arrest rate. They are

"prominent families." Teenage pot smokers denounced such "persecution" by the "repressive hypocrites of the Establishment" and roundly rejected law enforcement's warnings about the marijuana-to-heroin gateway. Public health experts also criticized such "scare tactics" and instead launched prevention programs based on parent-teenager discussion forums to educate suburban communities "which seem to know so little about why [their] children behave as they do."[37]

In 1969, Connecticut became one of the first states to reduce the penalty for marijuana possession from a felony to a misdemeanor, a move designed to address the generation gap and divert white middle-class pot smokers from any possibility of a prison term. Peter L. Costas, the attorney who drafted the reform bill and chaired the state's Committee to Study Marijuana Laws, labeled felony punishment "a joke to our youth, and we have created nothing but disrespect for our law rather than fear of it." Costas's committee reported that marijuana arrests were overcrowding the local courts and that judges were dismissing cases outright or placing violators on probation out of the belief that the mandatory penalties were too harsh. Contrasting marijuana experimentation with the heroin scourge, the committee attributed illicit pot smoking to teenagers and young adults "who partake as part of the peer pressure or desire to experiment in the society to which they belong."[38] Governor John Dempsey, a liberal Democrat, pledged that vigorous enforcement against narcotics traffickers and heroin users would remain a state priority but that community-based drug education and prevention approaches "represent the only means of honestly conveying" the message to the "distinct new group of drug abusers [that] now exists in our society." The Connecticut Drug Advisory Council, so renamed to accompany the legislative reclassification of marijuana as a nonnarcotic, also emphasized family dialogue and compared youth experimentation with marijuana to parental consumption of alcohol. In a

---

clustered in the areas from the highest median family income quadrants (the lighter shades of gray) in the 1970 census, especially in the Great Neck region (top left) and elsewhere in the northern part of the county. All were at least 93% white. The circles indicate the ten communities with the highest arrest rate for all drugs; most are near the bottom of the income ranking, including the heavily Black sections around Hempstead and Freeport. The triangles denote the ten communities with the highest marijuana arrest rates. Most of these are overwhelmingly white areas on the bottom half of the income scale. (Map and 1970 census data courtesy of Social Explorer; arrest data compiled from Nassau County Probation Department, *Drug Abuse in Suburbia: Final Report*, August 1978.)

reluctant acknowledgement of the political as well as social aspects of the recreational marijuana subculture, the Drug Advisory Council highlighted the "desires of youth to experiment and to challenge existing standards and possibly to escape from the problems which our generation allegedly has passed on to them."[39]

A scientific survey of 1,700 students at an elite suburban high school in Fairfield County reinforced the consensus that the ultimate solution to the white teenage drug problem depended upon internal family values. Conducted in 1969, the sociological study examined an almost all-white commuter suburb where 95 percent of fathers worked in the white-collar sector and two-thirds were corporate executives or business owners. The anonymous survey revealed that one-third of students in grades nine through twelve had smoked pot at least once, consistent with findings in other affluent inner-ring coastal suburbs, with little variation among male and female respondents or among Protestant, Catholic, and Jewish youth. But, in its most significant insight, the report distinguished between occasional or one-time experimenters and the "regular" pot smokers who constituted the "drug subculture," defined as only those students who used marijuana on a weekly-to-daily basis. This category encompassed 12 percent of high school students, ranging from 6 percent of ninth graders to 18 percent of the senior class. Two-thirds of these regular marijuana users had taken both LSD and speed (amphetamine), and one-tenth had tried heroin, whereas a large majority of casual marijuana experimenters had never sampled any other illicit drug except alcohol. The findings refuted the alarmist gateway theory that smoking pot would inevitably lead to harder drugs in favor of the more complex analysis (in line with other sociological research) that criminal prohibition itself propelled regular marijuana users into an underground "drug subculture" conducive to "greater acceptance and more favorable attitudes toward various illegal drugs." The Fairfield study did find evidence of a generation gap, although in attitudes more than social practices: almost all parents opposed any marijuana use, while most abstaining teenagers "tolerate and accept it as part of their culture." This reflected the social construction of legality and deviance more than a politicized youth environment, given modern society's message that "every discomfort has a chemical solution" and the fact that alcohol remained by far the most popular mood-altering drug for teenagers and adults alike.[40]

The Fairfield investigation extended the normative assessments of several decades of juvenile delinquency research by concluding that a "rewarding family" environment played the most important role in "curtailing the extent of regular marijuana use." This finding downplayed the generation gap and peer pressure concepts, which were superseding the outside pusher trope as the most popular explanations for the suburban marijuana scene in popular media and political discourse. Instead, the study argued that "integration into the marijuana subculture is a relatively free decision" made for individualistic reasons by a distinct minority of nonconformist teenagers whose motives were "to feel free" and "to feel happy." These regular pot smokers were less likely than both casual experimenters and abstainers to prioritize corporate career aspirations, to view getting ahead in life as the purpose of school, and to fear punishment (as opposed to mere disapproval) from their parents. Regular users of marijuana also were more likely to express resentment of parental pressure to succeed in school, report dissatisfaction with family life (such as feeling misunderstood or ignored), and have fathers or mothers who consumed alcohol or prescription pills to excess. By focusing on avid participants in the illegal drug subculture, the study challenged the broader hype and anxiety about the pervasiveness and centrality of marijuana in the adolescent suburban setting, because "the majority of drug experimenting youths differ little from non-users" in their social practices and cultural values. Instead of causing deviance or widening the generation gap, the smaller-than-recognized marijuana subculture appealed to a subset of privileged white youth who rejected the capitalistic values of the white-collar career track and the "conventional" aspirations of upper-middle-class suburbia. To the extent that this even constituted a crisis at all, the answers should come from within the family rather than through antidrug crusades or criminal law enforcement.[41]

Metropolitan Washington, DC: Diverting the "Normal" Youth Revolt

In the affluent suburbs of Fairfax County, located in Northern Virginia adjacent to the District of Columbia, the marijuana surge of the late 1960s led to futile law enforcement attempts to eradicate the drug supply and new understandings of how the underground white middle-class market actually operated. In fall 1967, Fairfax prosecutor Robert Horan dramatically announced that 20,000 illegal drug users, mostly teenage pot smokers, lived in the prosperous county of 450,000 people, home to many federal government workers and white-collar corporations. Horan pledged a comprehensive assault on "pushers of marijuana" and warned that many of their victims would graduate to LSD or heroin and live unproductive lives. While Horan later charged that "marijuana came out of the ghetto," with heroin close behind, in reality entrepreneurial white teenagers and young adults distributed the drug through contacts in other states and the gentrifying DC enclave of Georgetown.[42] In September 1967, the largest drug bust in Fairfax County's history began with a "local boy" who flew to California with $1,000 and returned with twenty-two pounds of marijuana in a suitcase. Two weeks later, an undercover narcotics cop arrested a twenty-eight-year-old Georgetown bartender for marijuana sale. Fairfax police and federal agents found fifteen pounds from the shipment at the bartender's Alexandria apartment and traced most of the rest to a twenty-year-old female's home in the planned suburb of Reston (94% white) and a nineteen-year-old musician who performed in Georgetown nightclubs and lived with his parents in McLean (98% white). The prosecutor allowed the female, a daughter of Reston's developer, to plea-bargain to misdemeanor possession and a suspended sentence rather than face felony charges. The Fairfax courts also diverted the teenage dealer from McLean to psychiatric counseling but sentenced a twenty-year old member of his network to four years in prison. Worried parents in McLean, located a few miles from CIA headquarters, immediately launched the Parents' Council on Dope Addiction to stop their "children being offered marijuana" at the high school.[43]

In 1968, the *Washington Post* launched an investigation to figure out how and why so many white suburban teenagers in Fairfax County were breaking the felony law by smoking marijuana. Instead of malevolent traffickers "sneaking into town to corrupt children," the *Post* series headlined the discovery that "the modern dope pusher doesn't look the part." The steady marijuana supply in Fairfax came from "young, well-educated, clean-cut suburban types" who lived in the area and imported illegal drugs on their own initiative. "Joan," a female college student who grew up in a local suburb, first drove to New York City to buy ten ounces of higher-grade marijuana on the street and then began selling pot and LSD to her friends and acquaintances. According to "Bob," a seventeen-year-old casual marijuana dealer from an upscale subdivision, "Nobody bothers us, because everybody who sells is just the kind of person you'd never suspect." Bob and a few friends typically would pitch in to buy a $150 stash from a "local pusher" in the Georgetown section of DC (where many adventurous Fairfax teenagers congregated on weekends), keep what they needed, and sell the rest around the neighborhood for a $500 profit. The *Washington Post* attributed Fairfax County's teenage marijuana crisis to a laundry list of suburban disorders and clichés: the shallow sense of community on a rootless white-collar landscape, reflexive habits of denial by status-obsessed parents and school officials, absentee or permissive parenting by commuting fathers and unfulfilled housewife-mothers, high school students seeking relief from the intense pressure to get into elite colleges, teenagers rebelling against the moral hypocrisies of the Vietnam War and antimarijuana propaganda from "The Establishment." But, as in the suburbs of New York City, the *Post*'s psychological indictment placed primary responsibility for illegal drug use on the white middle-class "family environment" and especially the communication breakdown between teenagers and parents, who too often failed to realize "how deeply their actions affect the lives of their youngsters."[44]

The family-centered, psychological analysis of illegal drug use in the Washington suburbs deemphasized law enforcement in favor of the public health approaches of education, prevention, and rehabilitation. Rather than a widespread moral panic, the response to the teenage marijuana market more often involved politicians, law enforcement, and media outlets lamenting and indicting the "apathy on the part of the adult community." Prosecutor Robert Horan blamed "permissive" upper-middle-class parents, whose nonchalance toward underage drinking had encouraged adolescents to disregard the law, and his office organized adult education seminars on drug abuse. The mayor of Falls Church, a wealthy and almost all-white Fairfax town, attributed the marijuana subculture to teenagers "left at home by themselves" by "social climber" parents focused on their prestigious careers. A survey of Falls Church residents revealed that 70 percent of adults definitely would not report illegal drug use by teens in their neighborhoods, while only 22 percent wanted the police to get tougher on such lawbreakers.[45] Although only a vocal minority, alarmed parents and PTA leaders did start a number of drug awareness organizations in the Fairfax suburbs, and some families even took the drastic and authoritarian step of placing their children in residential treatment centers to cure "psychological addiction" to marijuana. The prevention curriculum in the public schools utilized police officers to convey the antidrug message, but law enforcement's reliance on the marijuana-to-heroin gateway threat and other unfounded scare tactics compromised their credibility. After two years, the sergeant in charge admitted that the program had not proved effective because marijuana operated as a "status symbol" and most students seemed to "feel that the policeman and the establishment are synonymous." "How can kids respect adults' opinions when they push this phony crap?" asked one Falls Church student. "We know that it just isn't like that."[46]

As usual, the emergence of new forms of deviance and criminality in the white middle-class suburbs led to searching questions about why children of privilege would turn their backs on the American Dream. This racialized discourse reflected anxiety about white youth adopting behaviors and disorders associated with the pathologized inner city and genuine confusion about why they would seek a psychological escape from landscapes of affluence and opportunity. How, asked the local newspaper in Vienna (99% white), did the drug scourge of the "poverty-stricken ghettos" become so prevalent in the "average, normal, middle-class, middle-income" Fairfax suburbs? Why, the *Fairfax Sentinel* wondered, were so many "well-off kids taking the narcotics-escape route of the ghetto"? Teenagers in Fairfax County generally disagreed with media and authority figures about the meaning of the suburban marijuana scene. Most adolescents did not hold their parents responsible, view themselves as embracing ghetto habits, or seem to believe that their leisure practices represented a crisis for the suburban way of life. In 1969, another community newspaper decided to profile five anonymous youth, ages fifteen to eighteen, as a cross-section of "the white, suburban, middle-class culture" in Fairfax County. Asked if they smoked pot as part of a generational revolt, the teenagers "seemed genuinely startled by the question and looked at each other with expressions of amused tolerance," responding that they genuinely liked their parents. Instead, the group portrayed marijuana as one aspect of a larger desire to create their own authentic experiences, discover their own identities, and even make their own mistakes. The report concluded that these children of suburbia, although not too different from previous youth generations, were in pursuit of individually meaningful lives by "rebelling against the over-organized society, one in which they have been thrown into 'peer groups' from nursery school through Girl and Boy Scouts to high school service clubs."[47]

The informality, decentralization, and—most of all—the whiteness and affluence of the illegal drug market in the Washington suburbs enhanced and justified diversionary enforcement practices throughout the criminal legal system. By 1969, a year and a half after declaring war on drugs, Fairfax prosecutor Robert Horan was making a clear distinction between for-profit "pushers" of heroin and the "very non-professional-type distribution" of marijuana. Horan explained that law enforcement considered the "likely social effect of its decision on the offender," including a "tendency toward leniency in the case of a casual sale or exchange by a juvenile within his circle of acquaintances." The main diversion strategy involved deferred prosecution, designed to "rehabilitate" a misguided or foolish teenager through remand to the juvenile probation department with the "requirement that he seek psychiatric aid." Horan, like many suburban law enforcement officials across the nation, believed that this coercive public health solution was particularly effective for middle-class teens caught experimenting with marijuana who needed a wake-up call but not a criminal record. But only a miniscule number of lawbreakers even faced arrest in Fairfax County, where an undercover narcotics squad of eight officers investigated a population of nearly half a million, albeit with some assistance from local police departments. The head of the narcotics unit explained that "we don't want to lock a child up" for simple possession, so often they just gave the offender a "talking to" and referred the problem to the parents, a longstanding delinquency technique that left no official record. Arrests for narcotics offenses (mostly marijuana) were trending upward but remained quite limited in Fairfax County: thirty-four total, including six juveniles, in 1967; sixty-six total, including twenty-two juveniles, in 1968; seventy total, including thirty-four juveniles, in the first four months of 1969 alone. Similar diversionary practices prevailed in the adjacent Maryland suburbs of Montgomery County (95% white, 523,000 residents), where prosecutors declined to charge half of the 154 minors arrested for drug crimes in 1968. Juvenile courts used "informal adjustment" or "probation without verdict" for most of the rest, with just one youth drug offender countywide sentenced to detention that year.[48]

Starting in 1969, increased hype about the marijuana-to-heroin gateway by media outlets and law enforcement officials reinforced the racial anxiety about the drug problem in wealthy DC suburbs located in Fairfax and Montgomery counties. In February, the *Washington Post* published an exposé headlined: "Heroin Invades Middle Class: White Youth Try the Opiate of the Slums." The story began with six heroin users in Reston, a model suburban community "where poor people do not live." A psychiatrist in Silver Spring, an affluent inner-ring Maryland suburb, estimated (without data) that heroin addicts in Montgomery County had doubled in the past year. The *Post* wondered how a dangerous narcotic used by "the impoverished, the excluded, and the radically disturbed" had infiltrated the "safe, white" world of suburban DC. Upper-middle-class "marijuana users who said they would never use heroin are using it now," the head of the Fairfax County narcotics squad claimed, based on nothing more than anecdotal evidence. "It scares the hell out of me." Teenagers with more sophisticated knowledge of the drug scene explained that heroin appealed mainly to a small number of suburban hippies, runaways, and iconoclasts who hung out in the Georgetown and Dupont Circle areas of the District. Rather than a suburban "invasion," white youth who acquired heroin in these urban enclaves sometimes ended up in psychiatric treatment back home, usually following an arrest or parental intervention. In both Virginia and Maryland, suburban juvenile courts generally sentenced white teenagers arrested for heroin possession to indefinite probation and mandatory rehabilitation or psychiatric counseling, not the available option of incarceration until age twenty-one. This discretionary approach operated within the existing model of diversion and medicalization of suburban youth who broke the drug laws, including the presumption that families could afford private psychiatric treatment in counties that lacked almost any public rehabilitation centers.[49]

White middle-class drug use in the Washington suburbs had a disproportionate impact on national politics because of their proximity to the U.S. capital and immediacy for members of Congress who often lived in the same neighborhoods. In March 1969, the Senate Committee on the District of Columbia held hearings on the drug crisis in metropolitan Washington, part of a broader inquiry into the problem of "crime in the national capital." Chairman Joseph Tydings, a liberal Democrat from Maryland, announced that suburban teenagers who used illegal drugs were "not spurred by criminal motives" and instead blamed "pushers" for turning "law-abiding citizens" into victims by introducing marijuana and narcotics into the high schools. "Most of the drugs sold to suburban students," Tydings declared, "comes from the District." Director John Ingersoll of the federal Bureau of Narcotics and Dangerous Drugs testified that heroin addiction, which used to be contained to low-income DC neighborhoods, was now "spreading to the affluent suburbs." He also lamented the "startling" increase in marijuana and LSD use and blamed "permissivists" who had convinced teenagers that smoking pot was not harmful. Fairfax County prosecutor Robert Horan informed the committee that "all of a sudden," in recent months, suburban high school students who had been smoking marijuana for kicks had started mainlining heroin. While he could understand why Fairfax youth refused to cooperate with the police to arrest pot dealers, because they believed "the marijuana laws are morally wrong," Horan said that teenagers needed to realize that "a heroin seller is a killer." More accurately, narcotics officers from Montgomery County reported that affluent teenagers with generous allowances and their own automobiles just drove to Georgetown or Dupont Circle to purchase marijuana, whereas suburban youth who became involved with heroin tended to relocate to the District entirely. They questioned whether narcotics trafficking was a problem at all in the Maryland suburbs, where the drug market mainly involved teenage suppliers of marijuana who were "not in it for a profit; they perform a service, they think, to their friends."[50]

At the Senate hearings, several witnesses inverted the logic of heroin-gateway advocates by portraying the youth drug subculture as a product of the misdirected law enforcement war on marijuana as well as a generation gap rejection of the suburban-corporate value system. Thomas Murphy, a minister who operated Runaway House in Dupont Circle, explained that the "antiestablishment" teenagers he worked among were revolting against the "deadly sameness" of white middle-class suburbia and the dishonesty of parents who celebrated a "way of life" that "is only great because they stay on tranquilizers or drink." Suburban parents overreacted to illegal drug use because it was "particularly scary to people who have fled the city where they thought that kind of activity was confined." Reverend Murphy agreed that heroin had become a serious problem among some suburban runaways, but he blamed the "absurdity" of a law enforcement approach that "creates felons out of adolescents" by forcing teenagers who wanted to acquire marijuana into the underground drug economy. Dr. Stephen Brown, the director of the Washington Free Clinic in Dupont Circle, characterized white users of marijuana and LSD as "more creative, more intelligent" youth who did not find meaning in the "corporate success" model of their parents. The suburban hippies and runaways who clustered in Dupont Circle felt "alienated" from the promises of the mass consumer society amid national hypocrisy over the war in Vietnam and the racial crisis in the cities. Brown believed that smoking pot was a safe way for white middle-class youth to express these disenchantments. He condemned "police harassment of the hippie marijuana market" for "driving many middle-class kids to the separate market of the ghetto," where they encountered heroin and its serious consequences. A white teenage pot dealer who had served thirty days in jail after an undercover bust in Georgetown agreed that suburban youth turned to marijuana and LSD in rejection of the middle-class culture of "business drudgery" and "money comes before everything" values, which he compared to the motives of heroin users seeking to escape the "oppressive environments" of the slums.[51]

Congressional investigations of the drug crisis in the Washington suburbs provided a rare opportunity for suburban youth to participate in the national debate as full political actors. At the 1969 Senate hearing, two students from Bethesda–Chevy Chase High School in Montgomery County discounted the hype about heroin invading white suburbia and explained that teenagers took marijuana "to increase your awareness," rather than drop out of society or escape responsibilities. One of the youths explained that most pot smokers in his school "are very well adjusted people; people planning on being productive people in society. They just want to take drugs for the experience." In early 1970, the House Select Committee on Crime selected Fairfax County as a "typical suburban community" to illuminate the national problems of white middle-class delinquency and drug abuse. In their appearance at the hearing, four high school seniors from Alexandria disparaged the criminalization of marijuana and rejected any linkage between the recreational suburban market and the dangerous threat of heroin. A seventeen-year-old female endorsed the harshest possible penalties for heroin "pushers" but insisted that marijuana was less harmful than liquor and argued that legalization would be the best way to prevent pot smokers from going underground and trying harder drugs. A male classmate defined marijuana use as a "moral issue which should be left to the individual," since teenage pot smokers were no different from adult drinkers and pill poppers in America's "drug-oriented society." A third Alexandria student explained that marijuana and LSD were part of a youth "cultural movement" in pursuit of meaningful forms of "self-awareness, self-discovery" that the educational system and adult society failed to provide. The "scare tactics" deployed by politicians were only widening the "credibility gap," because many teenagers "know just from personal experience" that taking non-addictive psychedelic drugs would not destroy their lives.[52]

Robert Shephard, another high school senior from Alexandria, turned the 1970 hearing by the House Select Committee on Crime into a political platform for an extraordinary generational manifesto, a suburban teenage fusion of the Port Huron Statement and the countercultural ethos. Shephard categorized youthful consumption of marijuana and LSD as part of a "moral revolution in this country" and a "wonderful tool for demonstrating rebellion" against the hypocrisies and complacency of "adult society." He declared that a majority of Americans under age thirty were "dissatisfied and disillusioned with the way their country is being run . . . and with the sort of meaningless future that our society holds in store for them." Because the system seemed incapable of transformation, "rebellion against middle-class, middle-aged values and norms appears to many young people to be the only valid course open to them." Shephard portrayed marijuana and LSD as more of a cultural than a political insurgency, since both drugs provided users with "euphoric" experiences and "religious, mystical, and metaphysical insights." He argued that most youth believed marijuana should, and soon would, be legalized and therefore criminal enforcement was as futile and misdirected as the earlier Prohibition of alcohol. While Shephard did endorse a "real crackdown" on urban heroin markets, he mocked gateway warnings in the drug education curriculum as preposterous in "upper middle class suburbia," where high school students knew "infinitely" more about marijuana than their parents or instructors. Since young Americans believed they had the right to pursue lifestyles of happiness and meaning, even "massive repression" by law enforcement would have little effect on the suburban drug market, so politicians should stop playing to public fears and distorting the debate with their "abysmal ignorance." Shephard concluded by recommending that Congress face "reality about a subject that the adult world has been harboring delusions about for far too long." It was long past time to legalize "soft, non-addictive" drugs such as marijuana and LSD.[53]

Rather than legalization, the political response to the resilient illegal drug scene in Fairfax County formalized the processes of diversion, coercive rehabilitation, and discretionary penalties designed for the white middle-class market. In 1970, the *Wall Street Journal* selected Langley High School in McLean to represent the drug crisis in "affluent, well-educated, comfortable" suburbia, where a "soaring number" of teenagers were smoking pot, "bored and disillusioned" with the "sterility of life" in uniform, sprawling communities. Almost all high schoolers equated marijuana with alcohol and avoided heroin as a ghetto drug, making prevention and rehab the most effective approach.[54] In May, the Fairfax County Board of Supervisors launched a "frontal attack on drug addiction" by approving construction of Crossroads Community, a publicly funded treatment center "to rehabilitate those individuals who are confirmed users of so-called soft and hard drugs." As an alternative to incarceration and a criminal record, the juvenile courts would work with police, prosecutors, and probation officers to mandate participation in the residential treatment program for teens arrested on marijuana, LSD, amphetamine, or heroin charges. In summer 1970, the Virginia legislature reduced the sentencing range for marijuana possession from a three-to-five-year felony to a minimum of one day and a maximum of twelve months, misdemeanor sanctions designed as leverage for the criminal legal system to divert white middle-class youth to rehab and treatment through formal or informal probation. Two years later, the legislature revised the penalties for sale of illegal drugs through an intent-based formula that combined harsher sentences for the commercial "profiteer" with lighter punishment (including a probation option) for the "accommodator" who merely "share[s] with friends." This policy of formal discretion standardized in law the differential racial and spatial policing of white middle-class youth that the criminal justice system had developed through informal practices since the discovery of the recreational suburban market in Fairfax County back in 1967.[55]

Metropolitan Los Angeles: Mass Arrests in White Suburbia

"What are you doing here?" a shaken mother asked her fourteen-year-old daughter at 3:00 a.m., inside the Hollywood police station during the summer of 1967. "And what are you doing in those hippie clothes?" On July 28, the Hollywood division of the Los Angeles Police Department raided a nightclub on Sunset Boulevard and arrested 190 juveniles for loitering and violating curfew. Their parents were "surprised, shocked, angry, and hurt," an officer told the media. "They were nearly all middle-class people who never expected to see the inside of a police station." The Hollywood police released the white teenagers to the custody of their parents, but not before showing each adult a stash of marijuana, amphetamines, and heroin paraphernalia discovered in the parking lot where most of the youth were hanging out. In mandatory follow-up consultations, officers from the juvenile delinquency unit informed parents that adolescents on the Sunset Strip after dark were "prime targets for narcotics pushers and homosexuals." A conference with a fifteen-year-old daughter in a miniskirt and her clueless "housewife mother" encapsulated the law enforcement agenda of regulating the teenage subculture and deterring illegal drug use by seeking to panic white middle-class parents out of their complacency and permissiveness. While the daughter protested that she "wasn't doing anything wrong" and denounced the curfew law as anti-youth harassment, her mother admitted, "Usually Susan doesn't tell me where she's going and I don't ask." The police sergeant then informed the stunned parent that at the recent Griffith Park "love-in," which Susan attended, hippies danced in the nude and "narcotics" (marijuana) flowed freely. Unless she wanted her daughter to have a criminal record, it was time to keep Susan away from "bad company" through discipline and wholesome family activities. The famous Sunset Strip "hippie riots" during 1966–67, in reality a series of white teenage political protests against curfew laws and police harassment, indicated that neither parents nor cops were capable of controlling this generation (fig. 3.6).[56]

Law enforcement in the city and suburbs of Los Angeles policed the white middle-class recreational drug market more aggressively than any other large metropolitan region in the nation. During the mid-to-late 1960s, LA County accounted for more than half of all drug arrests in California and around one-fourth of the entire United States (fig. 3.7). The traditional militarization of the narcotics war in Southern California intersected with the political geography of the sprawling region, where the LAPD and the county sheriff's department

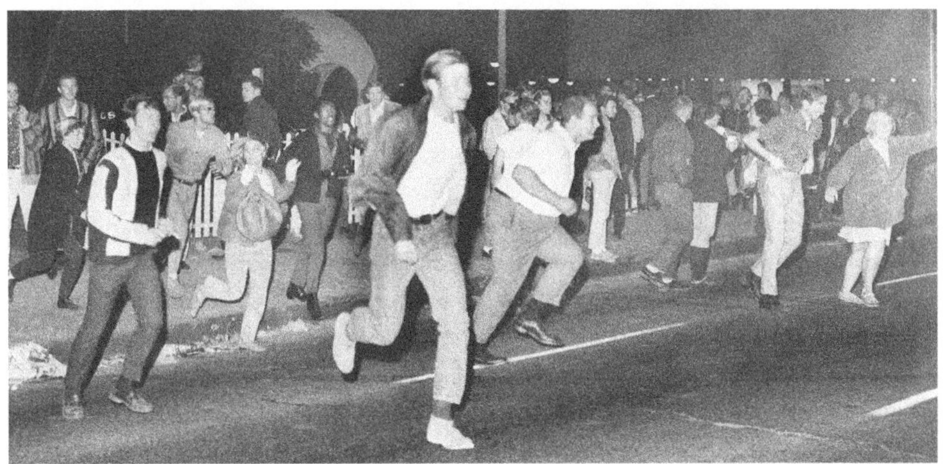

FIGURE 3.6. Juveniles flee a police crackdown at a popular hangout on the Sunset Strip in the West Hollywood section of Los Angeles, November 14, 1966. Law enforcement arrested hundreds of teenagers for unlawful assembly and curfew violations in a series of confrontations during 1966–67. A large youth contingent fought back in protest against police repression in the so-called "hippie riots." (AP Photo.)

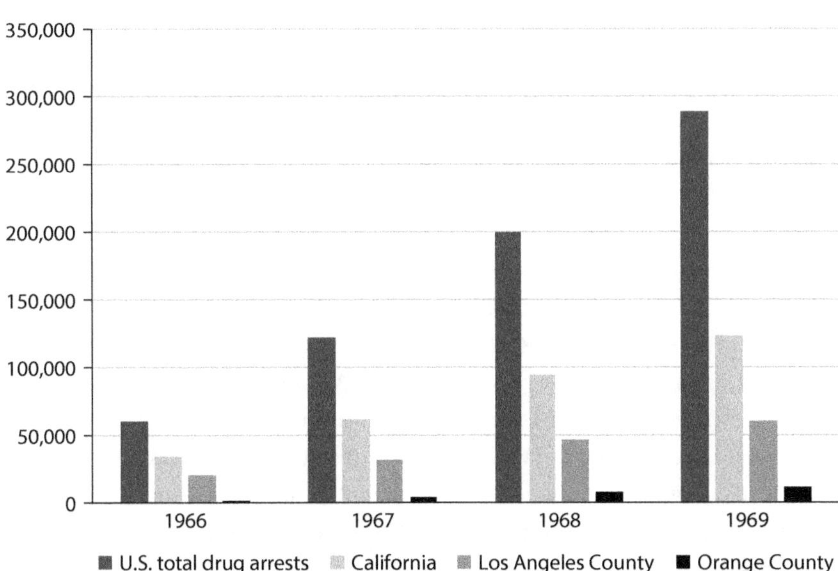

FIGURE 3.7. Drug arrests in Los Angeles County and Orange County as a proportion of estimated drug arrests in California and in the United States, 1966–69. The state of California, with around 10% of the U.S. population, accounted for 47% of reported drug arrests nationwide during the second half of the 1960s. Law enforcement agencies in LA County made more than half of drug arrests statewide, and one-fourth of those arrested were juveniles. The escalation of drug enforcement between 1966 and 1969 brought a fivefold increase in arrests across the United States, a threefold increase in LA County, and a 6.8 times increase in the adjacent and mostly white suburbs of Orange County. (Bureau of Criminal Statistics, *Crime and Delinquency in California, 1972: Drug Arrests and Dispositions*; FBI, *Uniform Crime Reports*, 1966–1969.) *Note*: Data represents combined juvenile and adult drug arrests.

each patrolled much more racially and economically diverse populations than the typical urban or suburban jurisdiction, especially the small wealthy municipalities outside New York City where police rarely chose to make drug arrests. The LA city boundaries encompassed many white suburban-style neighborhoods, including the affluent Westside and middle-income San Fernando Valley, while the county included more than seventy-five suburban towns and the unincorporated and predominantly Mexican American East LA. Unlike in Northern Virginia or suburban Connecticut, policing agencies responsible for white middle-class areas of metro Los Angeles already had much experience cracking down on illegal drug markets when marijuana use skyrocketed among white teenagers in the mid-to-late 1960s. Even as the demographics of the illegal drug-using population expanded, politicians and law enforcement agencies continued to prioritize crime control as the main deterrence strategy, although the diversionary practices that had long advantaged white middle-class delinquents mitigated the impact. Police departments and juvenile authorities operated with total statutory discretion and selected among release to parents, informal probation, or detention "depending upon the juvenile's background, his attitude and the nature of the particular offense." "There is no real rule for it. You just play it by ear," a suburban narcotics officer explained. "Frequently you can best help an individual juvenile right in the police station without involving the juvenile courts and the probation department."[57]

In metropolitan Los Angeles, liberal law-and-order politicians and conservative law enforcement officials alike portrayed marijuana as a catastrophic threat that had flooded white middle-class communities and required escalation of the war on narcotics, rhetoric that anticipated the platform of the Nixon administration a few years later. The LA County Board of Supervisors, which governed a sprawling region of 6.5 million residents, declared in 1966 that marijuana resulted in "violent and unpredictable criminal tendencies" and "leads inevitably to the use of hard narcotics such as heroin." Supervisor Kenneth Hahn, a tough-on-crime liberal and the most powerful Democrat in LA County, called for "all-out war" and "total victory over narcotics" following reports that marijuana and other illegal drugs were infiltrating the affluent suburbs and upper-middle-class neighborhoods.[58] In 1966, when smoking pot still seemed mainly a trend among radicalized college students in much of the country, the LAPD arrested more than 1,200 juveniles for marijuana possession (a felony), and authorities in LA County detained another 1,400 minors—a combined total nearly double the rest of the state. In the city, where racial minorities made up a higher percentage of those arrested, the LAPD's Juvenile Narcotics Unit followed the longstanding discretionary practice of assessing the individual offender's background and circumstances at the point of arrest. Narcotics officers "counseled" and then released about 15 percent of pot smokers to their parents, remanded another 15 percent directly to the probation department, and sent the rest to Juvenile Court for verdicts that ranged from informal probationary supervision to incarceration by the California Youth Authority. "Most kids are experimenting," the head of the Juvenile Narcotics Unit believed, but he emphasized that too many became psychologically addicted to marijuana, losing touch with reality and stunting their development, at risk of graduating to heroin addiction. He blamed permissive parents as well as "pushers, [who] are vicious businessmen out to make money."[59]

The disposition of marijuana cases in Los Angeles County depended on the combined factors of race, gender, socioeconomic status, family background, academic achievement, and residential geography. According to a law school analysis of marijuana arrests in 1966, selective enforcement through formalized policies of discretion shaped every stage of the criminal justice process. At the street level, drug enforcement targeted the Black section of Watts, Mexican American East LA, and white bohemian enclaves in Hollywood and Venice Beach. Most possession arrests occurred during traffic pullovers or "stop and frisk" searches when police profiled male teens and young adults based on probable cause justifications of dubious legality, generally "furtive motions" or "present under suspicious circumstances in a high crime area." Juvenile arrests often resulted from "discriminatory enforcement of curfew violations," with police targeting minorities and white teens "with long hair and 'mod' attire" (multiple cops interviewed for the study expressed contempt for hippies and insisted that profiling them was simply efficient police work). The LAPD and suburban counterparts also busted and turned pot smokers into informants to set up buys, skirting the boundaries of entrapment, and deployed undercover agents "dressed in hippie garb" on the Sunset Strip or posing "in homosexual attire" in Hollywood. In 1966, most of the 8,564 adults arrested for marijuana in LA County were males under age twenty-five, with a racial breakdown of 53.6 percent white, 31 percent Black (almost three times the population share), and 14.6 percent Mexican American (versus 18 percent of the population). The racial and gender proportions for the 2,636 minors officially busted for marijuana that year were nearly identical, but the data undercounted the number of white middle-class youth and especially females apprehended because juvenile agencies had "statutory discretion to counsel and release" teens based on their prior record, attitude, educational situation, family status, and rehabilitation potential. According to the analysis, affluent youth caught with drugs ended up in private psychotherapy and poor kids went to reformatories.[60]

The workings of drug enforcement in LA County raised hard questions about whether the criminal justice system had the capability to deter or punish white middle-class youth who broke the felony marijuana law, especially after rates of use and arrests spiked in suburban areas starting in 1967. In two mostly white precincts in the San Fernando Valley, for example, juvenile marijuana arrests increased from 60 in 1965 to 708 two years later. In Covina, a 99 percent white suburban city in the San Gabriel Valley, police busted seven times as many minors in 1967 as the year before. Overall marijuana arrests of teenagers doubled in LA County between 1966 and 1967, but discretionary and discriminatory practices based on race and class continued to shape the outcomes of juveniles and young adults who encountered the law. A research study at UCLA revealed that despite California's mandatory-minimum statute, prosecutors and judges still exercised leeway to charge or convict an adult marijuana defendant with a felony or misdemeanor, either through plea-bargaining or by dismissing cases when the violator seemed sympathetic and remorseful. While much tougher on dealers, judges in adult and juvenile courts "invariably grant[ed] probation" in possession cases if the accused was employed or in school, a policy that favored white middle-class defendants when their cases even made it that far. One juvenile judge explained that he dismissed almost all possession charges because a teenager with no prior record "had already been punished sufficiently by being arrested, placed in jail." In a representative sample from the 1966 data, which did not include teenagers released to parents or cases dismissed, the juvenile courts acquitted or gave probation to two-thirds of white youth, half of Mexican Americans, and one-third of African Americans—with the most leniency for first offenders with "a repentant attitude, two concerned parents," and good grades. Judicial diversion and even jury nullification, the UCLA study concluded, had expanded in direct proportion to the "tremendous increase" in arrests of white middle-class youth who, "except for their marijuana activity, appear to be law-abiding citizens."[61]

During the late 1960s, police crackdowns in Los Angeles County and in adjacent Orange County yielded thousands more marijuana arrests without slowing down the drug trade or the steady increase in recreational use among white teenagers and young adults. In the San Gabriel Valley, an undercover investigation caught ninety-two members of an alleged narcotics network around Pasadena, accused by police of "preying on teenagers." One-fourth of those busted were juveniles from upscale families who were either dealing marijuana in their schools or just regulars at a "hippie" coffeehouse (California law made it illegal to be present in a place where marijuana was used). In 1967, in the Orange County suburb of Westminster, police arrested nine high schoolers who provided marijuana or amphetamine to a twenty-one-year-old female officer posing as a fellow student. In Laguna Beach, a sheriff's deputy shot and killed a fleeing twenty-year-old white male and alleged marijuana dealer during an undercover raid coordinated with federal agents.[62] The LAPD designed elaborate operations against "dope peddlers" in the semi-suburban areas of Hollywood and the San Fernando Valley, where young-looking undercover agents dressed in miniskirts and mod/hippie outfits impersonated high school classmates to infiltrate popular teen hangouts. Hollywood promptly glamorized this practice with *The Mod Squad*, an ABC-TV drama that premiered in 1968 and featured three former malcontents (a rich white delinquent, a Black Watts rioter, a female hippie runaway) working undercover for the LAPD to protect youth from dope pushers and other dangers.[63] Parents of teenagers arrested for marijuana possession often had a very different perspective, such as the Pasadena father who condemned the presence of undercover cops in the schools after his daughter's expulsion for a "single act of experimentation." The Pasadena school district expelled nineteen students for drug busts in 1968, which generated teenage protests against police entrapment and the adult establishment. The district soon reduced punishment for marijuana possession to a suspension.[64]

Media reports routinely claimed that at least 50 percent of suburban youth in metropolitan Los Angeles were taking illegal drugs, which an academic study labeled a product of "hysterical guesses" by police, politicians, and civic organizations. A scientific survey of drug use among teenagers in Fullerton (98% white), located in the northern part of Orange County and selected as a prototypical white middle-class suburb, revealed that 29 percent of seniors and 22 percent of ninth graders had tried marijuana at least once by the spring of 1968. A majority reported smoking pot for pleasure or out of boredom, not for political reasons or as a countercultural search for heightened self-awareness. Only 5.5 percent of Fullerton's high school students had tried LSD, while 16 percent had taken amphetamines. By 1970, 34 percent of the district's high school students had sampled marijuana at some point, including 41 percent of males and 28 percent of females, and 10 percent had dropped acid. Traditional drug education campaigns made little impression on this population, which was "not affected by the fear of legal or parental authority" because smoking marijuana had become a peer group social ritual. Nor did the threat of arrest provide much deterrent, even after undercover police busted dozens of Fullerton students for "selling narcotics" (marijuana). Recreational drug users viewed pot smoking as a harmless "right" of personal freedom, alongside the rights to have long hair or dress as they wished. The study strongly criticized the overreaction of local police and civic groups, which had unwittingly glamorized marijuana and transformed "drug-escapist behavior" into a politicized expression of antiestablishment values. Just before the report appeared, a Fullerton police sting arrested thirty-eight more high school students on marijuana charges.[65]

In the late 1960s, law enforcement officials in Orange County and other suburban jurisdictions adopted de facto policies of age-based profiling and extralegal search and seizure, techniques that criminalized white youth and exponentially increased the number of teenagers who encountered the criminal legal system. Narcotics squads in Orange County conducted undercover operations in public schools and urged patrol officers to search for illegal drugs whenever they pulled teenagers over for traffic violations, a suburban variation of the stop-and-frisk profiling ubiquitous in nonwhite urban centers. Such practices, and the steady expansion of the recreational suburban market in marijuana and illicit pills, multiplied juvenile drug arrests in Orange County from 67 in 1965 to 2,790 in 1968—almost 4 percent of the estimated population of 65,000 adolescent pot smokers.[66] While policies of discretion and diversion meant that few white middle-class youth actually served time in juvenile facilities, the consequences of a drug-related arrest could still be substantial and disruptive. When a high school in one Orange County suburb expelled two brothers arrested but not yet convicted on marijuana charges, their mother denounced the "unconstitutional" action and the "humiliating and degrading" classification of her sons as dangerous "criminals." The brothers ended up in an alternative school for at-risk youth and complained that local police had marked them as targets and repeatedly stopped and frisked them without cause. Most suburban teenagers who smoked pot were rebelling against legal and parental authority alike, according to a *Los Angeles Times* investigation of Orange County youth arrested for drug crimes. The series profiled the sixteen-year-old son of a corporate executive who got stoned daily to escape his "sterile suburban environment"; a teenager who labeled antimarijuana messaging to be "the biggest lie of all the big lies they've always told us";

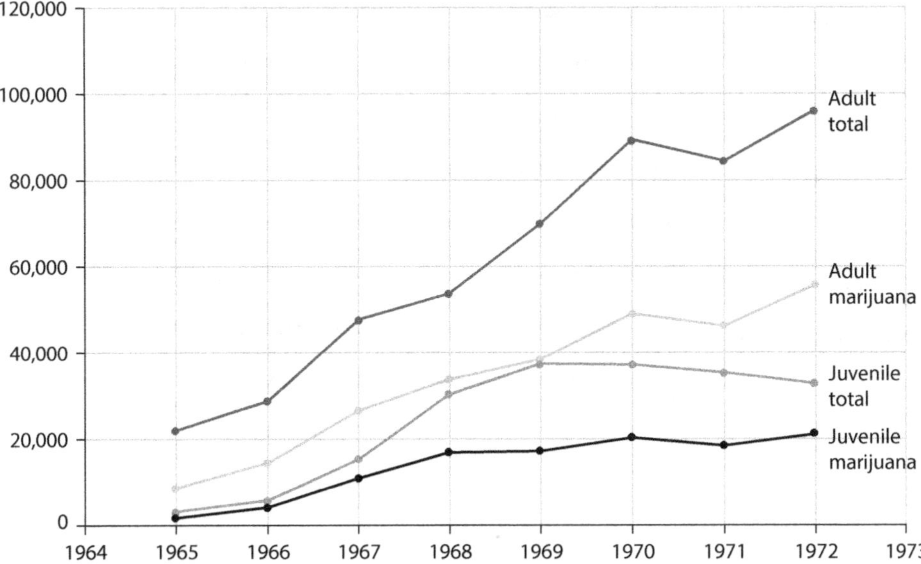

FIGURE 3.8. Adult and juvenile marijuana arrests (estimated) in the state of California as a share of total drug arrests, 1965–72. Total drug arrests increased fivefold in California between 1965 and 1972, and the number of juvenile drug arrests skyrocketed by a factor of twelve. Adult marijuana arrests rose from 39% of the adult total in 1965 to 63% in 1968, primarily involving younger white males. Juvenile marijuana arrests peaked at 74% of the juvenile total in 1967 and accounted for 65% in 1972, also predominantly white male offenders. The decrease in the percentage of juvenile marijuana arrests after 1967 overwhelmingly resulted from the increase in "dangerous drugs" arrests (a two-thirds white offender group). "Dangerous drugs," illicit amphetamines and barbiturates, accounted for two-thirds of nonmarijuana drug arrests, with the remainder primarily involving heroin (a majority-nonwhite offender group). (Bureau of Criminal Statistics, *Crime and Delinquency in California: 1972: Drug Arrests and Dispositions*; "Marijuana Decriminalization," *Hearing before the Subcommittee to Investigate Juvenile Delinquency, Committee on the Judiciary*, U.S. Senate, May 14, 1975.)

and a third upper-middle-class white youth who observed that "I go to school and study during the week, and blow my mind on grass on the weekend. Why should that bug you?"[67]

The racial and economic profile of the population arrested on drug charges changed dramatically in metropolitan Los Angeles and in the rest of California over the course of the 1960s. At the beginning of the decade, 70 percent of drug prosecutions in the state originated in LA County, and half involved heroin. The typical adult defendant was Mexican American, older than twenty-five, a user rather than a seller, and a repeat offender. Juvenile "narcotics" cases that reached the adjudication stage generally involved marijuana or the illegal use

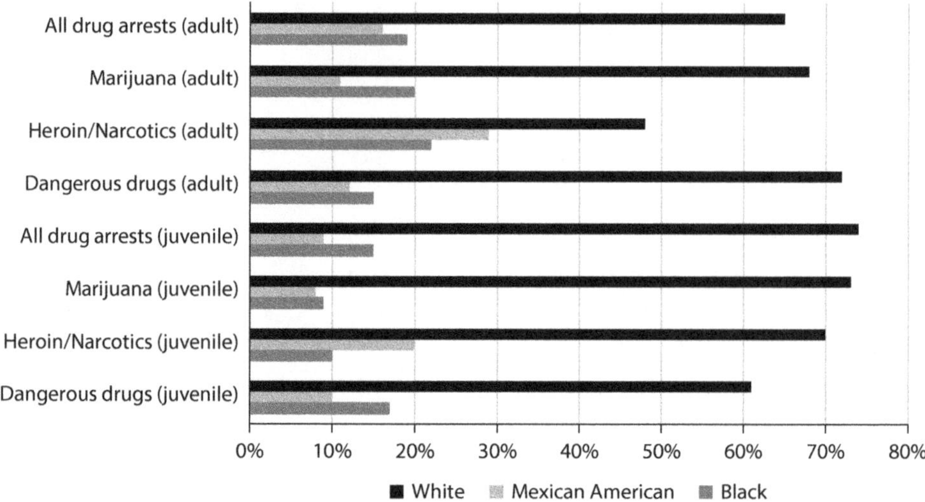

FIGURE 3.9. Adult and juvenile drug arrests in California by race and category of drug, 1967. Law enforcement arrested white juveniles in California for marijuana (73%) and total drug violations (74%) at approximately their population share in 1967. Relative to racial demographics, white adults were somewhat less likely than white juveniles to be arrested on drug charges (65%), with the highest proportions for "dangerous drugs" (72%) followed by marijuana (68%). African American adults and juveniles faced arrest on drug charges at more than twice their population share. Mexican American adults and juveniles were disproportionately arrested only for heroin. (Bureau of Criminal Statistics, *Drug Arrests and Dispositions in California: 1967*.)
Note: In the 1970 census, the racial breakdown of the California population was 76% white (non-Hispanic), 13% Mexican American, and 7% Black. "Other" and "Unknown" categories not included in this drug arrest data.

of amphetamines and barbiturates. The racial breakdown for these minors was 39 percent Mexican American, 37 percent white, and 22 percent African American. The felony marijuana law, revised in 1961, provided a mandatory sentencing range of one to ten years for first offender possession cases. Selling marijuana brought five to life for the first offense (although many defendants pled down to possession). In 1966, marijuana first accounted for more than half of drug arrests in California (fig. 3.8), as did white (non-Hispanic) perpetrators. By 1967, white Anglos made up 68 percent of adult marijuana arrests and 73 percent of juvenile arrests statewide (fig. 3.9). The total number of marijuana apprehensions nearly doubled between 1966 and 1967 alone, and a large majority of the 37,514 arrests that year involved first offenders busted for possession, with the median drug criminal a nineteen-year-old white male student from a middle-class background. Concentrated enforcement in the suburbs and on college campuses created a criminal class that judges and juries proved increasingly unwilling to convict on felony charges that carried mandatory prison time. In 1960, 93 percent of drug defendants lost at trial in California, but by 1967, only 48 percent of marijuana prosecutions were successful. Given these realities, and to discourage rampant diversion of arrested students by prosecutors, the state legislature revised the marijuana penalty in 1968, permitting either a felony or misdemeanor sentence for first offenders, with the latter involving a maximum one-year jail term and more often probation.[68]

The reaction to the marijuana crisis in the wealthy white suburbs of the Palos Verdes Peninsula revealed both the futility and the increasing unpopularity of the law enforcement approach to eradicating the adolescent drug culture. In the summer of 1967, alarmed parents and civic leaders formed the Peninsula Council for Youth after the school board suspended a group of marijuana violators and local police announced that half of area high school students had experimented with illegal drugs. The Peninsula's top narcotics officer explained that it was "virtually impossible" to stop the suburban drug trade, and instead his office adopted a de facto policy of "arresting young users to frighten them but not filing charges." The police did crack down on "pushers" after reports of marijuana parties among sixth graders, but law enforcement officials and educators remained very reluctant to upset rich parents by sending their children to the delinquency courts. In fall 1968, a community newspaper ran a weeklong exposé of the psychedelic subculture on the Palos Verdes Peninsula, starting with a teenage entrepreneur "from a good home" in Hermosa Beach (99% white) who acquired marijuana and pills by crossing the Mexican border or from contacts at the local pier. Until the youth's arrest, his distribution network of twelve "clean-cut" dealers sold the product at high school campuses, house parties, and especially the popular beaches that parents never supervised. Recreational pot smokers told the newspaper that they were not narcotics addicts but rather just bored and stressed suburban kids who were "rebelling against the idea of being sheltered" and having to "follow a narrow path to success like their parents." Many believed, in the words of one unapologetic stoner, that "I'm not hurting myself as much as my parents are hurting themselves with alcohol." Despite hundreds of arrests on the Peninsula, almost none of the teenage dealers or their customers seemed worried about ending up in a detention center, with probation and psychiatric counseling the maximum punishment almost any of these advantaged white youth ever faced.[69]

The Peninsula Council for Youth collaborated with educators, police, and medical professionals to develop a drug prevention program that deemphasized law enforcement in favor of parental mobilization and mandatory rehabilitation. In the late 1960s, the organization held drug abuse seminars attended by thousands of parents and also worked with local churches to set up a hotline for teens in need of assistance. Mel Knight, a Presbyterian minister and council leader, believed that teenage drug abuse was a symptom of growing up "in our chemical-ingesting culture" and criticized parents who responded punitively rather than acknowledging their own culpability. He recognized that marijuana was a "mild psychedelic" that adolescents experimented with out of curiosity, peer pressure, a search for identity, to cope with depression, or often just to relax given the "constant stress" of life in affluent suburbia. Knight therefore urged parents to intervene with equanimity, seeking psychiatric help when necessary but not overreacting to simple experimentation, while making it clear that breaking the law could "ruin your present and jeopardize your future." More alarmist locals continued to warn of the heroin-gateway threat and cautioned that excessive marijuana use would cause the privileged youth of the Palos Verdes Peninsula to "lose their drive and ambition," turning them into "hippie-types or bums." But in 1968, the Peninsula school system replaced this ineffective fear-based curriculum with a program designed by psychiatrists that encouraged teens to "tune in and turn on" through creative alternatives to drug escapism, including mandatory group sessions for teenagers caught by the police and placed on probation. This strategy remained controversial, criticized by hardliners as overly lenient and not well appreciated by adolescent pot smokers who did not believe they should be coerced into therapy any more than incarcerated. A 1969 survey of seniors at Palos Verdes High School revealed that half had smoked pot, and of this group 25 percent had been caught by police, 45 percent reported that their parents abused alcohol, 96 percent planned to attend college, and 78 percent advocated legalization of marijuana.[70]

In November 1968, immediately following the Palos Verdes exposé, political leaders in Los Angeles County issued a redeclaration of war at this shocking evidence that marijuana once again had infiltrated the "upper middle class and high income areas." Supervisor Kenneth Hahn issued the ritual lament that "narcotics use was limited to the ghetto areas five years ago. It has moved to every neighborhood, including the so-called affluent society and college and high school campuses." Hahn called on city police and the county sheriff to step up undercover operations against high school "pushers," and the LAPD's narcotics squad arrested ninety-eight alleged campus dealers in the San Fernando Valley during spring 1969. The county district attorney's office also

TABLE 3.6. Adult Drug Arrests in Los Angeles County, by Race, 1967 and 1969

Category	White		Mexican American		Black	
Year	1967	1969	1967	1969	1967	1969
All drug arrests	55%	66%	18%	12%	25%	21%
Marijuana	58%	71%	12%	6%	29%	22%
Heroin/Narcotics	35%	48%	39%	26%	25%	25%
Dangerous drugs	65%	67%	15%	13%	18%	19%

Sources: Bureau of Criminal Statistics, *Drug Arrests and Dispositions in California, 1967;* Bureau of Criminal Statistics, *Drug Arrests and Dispositions in California, 1969.*

Note: Data includes combined arrests by the Los Angeles Police Department and Los Angeles County Sheriff's Department. Racial breakdown for juvenile arrests at the county level is not available. The proportion of white drug arrests increased significantly between 1967 and 1969 and approximated the white population share for all drugs except heroin. In the 1970 census, the population of LA County was 68% white (non-Hispanic), 18% Mexican American, and 11% Black.

devised a drug prevention curriculum that hyped the marijuana-to-heroin gateway threat and recycled the 1950s-era plotline that pushers seduced "new victim[s] . . . for the favor of some free narcotics." The program advocated "immediate psychiatric assistance" for any teenager who experimented with marijuana and warned that taking LSD would lead to violence, rape, murder, and/or suicide.[71] Los Angeles mayor Sam Yorty, another tough-on-crime Democrat, advocated increased law enforcement as the primary approach, insisted that marijuana "leads inexorably to a preference for hard drugs," and criticized the "permissive" courts for giving misdemeanor probation to most youths prosecuted for smoking pot. In 1969, law enforcement in LA County arrested 7,564 juveniles and 18,038 adults for marijuana crimes alone, more than one-tenth of total drug arrests nationwide. Young white perpetrators made up almost three-fourths of marijuana arrests, although African Americans remained overrepresented in all drug categories (table 3.6). Police and public schools worked together in this crackdown, since most junior and senior highs had a policy of calling the narcotics squad after catching students with illegal drugs, and a new state law required law enforcement to notify education officials about off-campus juvenile arrests as well.[72]

Many Los Angeles area students and some public health experts denounced the law enforcement mobilization against marijuana smoking and the scare-tactics educational curriculum as equally ineffective. In summer 1969, a U.S. House of Representatives subcommittee held a hearing in Los Angeles to consider alternatives to existing drug prevention programs in public education. Larry Diamond, president of the student body of University High School, located in wealthy and semi-suburban West Los Angeles, informed the politicians that it was "inconceivable that any amount of drug abuse education could deter marijuana usage." Diamond stated that smoking pot was so widespread among white upper-middle-class high school students that "the law has become an almost total farce. The law is no longer credible because hundreds of thousands of teenagers are using marijuana much in the same way as their parents use alcohol—and with no harmful effects." Lewis Yablonsky, a sociologist based in the San Fernando Valley and author of *The Hippie Trip*, explained that the "new" category of psychedelic drug users in America—white, upper-middle-class seekers—"are aware that the drugs they are using are illegal but do not believe that they are really committing an illegal act." Unlike narcotics addicts in the ghettos, who (supposedly) understood their actions as "criminal," affluent white youth who smoked pot and dropped acid had "a self-concept of moral righteousness," based on their right to get high for pleasure and freedom or in rejection of the "oppressive, machinelike world they believe the established society and their parents are foisting on them." Dr. Paul Rosenberg, who worked among hippies and suburban runaways as director of the Los Angeles Free Clinic, stated bluntly that smoking marijuana was "innocuous" and "there is no way that society can force adolescents to stop using drugs." The "schools are not teaching," he concluded. "They are propagandizing about drugs. . . . The things that the students learn from experience, from reality, the schools are committed to deny, and to lie about."[73]

Sandy, a high-achieving seventeen-year-old student at another affluent Westside school, informed the congressional subcommittee that she and many classmates would get stoned and laugh through the drug prevention classes because "everybody knew that it was, you know, a bunch of nothing," just worthless falsehoods about how marijuana was dangerous and would lead to heroin addiction. Sandy started smoking pot at age fifteen to escape from her problems but "found that it didn't get me anywhere. I didn't get any insights into myself or anything else." At school, the teachers and police instructors preached that drugs were bad, "but they don't offer you an alternative. . . . What does that leave me? You know, what can you offer me that will be fulfilling, . . . that will make me feel good about myself?" Instead Sandy found the answers she was looking for in an innovative program called DAWN (Developing Adolescents Without Narcotics), launched in 1967 by teachers and guidance counselors at elite Westside high schools in collaboration with a UCLA psychologist. DAWN targeted the "alienated adolescent" (in the white upper-middle-class stratum) and promoted alternatives to the illegal drug scene through "groovy" group rap sessions that encouraged teenagers to "examine societal values" and allowed them to "be accepted for what you really are and really feel." In DAWN's generation gap analysis, frustrated and inquisitive youth turned to psychedelic drug use because the school system and the broader establishment refused to take them seriously as political actors, to let them debate the war in Vietnam, to grapple with the "social revolution"—and then compounded the schism by telling them lies about marijuana and arresting them for experimentation. "You are censored from such an early age; the educational system stifles your creativity and stifles everything," Sandy proclaimed. "The schools should develop experimental programs," Dr. Rosenberg agreed, "where they reopen the question of what the kids need from the society to grow up."[74]

By the end of 1969, the drug policy debate in metropolitan Los Angeles focused primarily on whether crime control or public health measures would best curtail marijuana use among white teenagers in the suburbs. The Narcotics and Dangerous Drugs Commission, an official citizens agency for LA County, produced a report that strongly criticized law enforcement for focusing most of its recent energy on stopping marijuana rather than heroin and blamed the war on drugs itself for driving the recreational adolescent market underground. The commission calculated that more than 90 percent of white middle-class youth who smoked marijuana were casual users rather than drug "abusers" and warned that the "eventual long-term cost to society of criminalizing a major segment of this age group is potentially catastrophic." The police should focus on heroin addicts and the illegal market in pharmaceutical pills, while public health professionals should take the lead in addressing the challenges of recreational pot smoking. The Los Angeles County Board of Supervisors responded by creating a new narcotics task force charged with devising a comprehensive prevention program for youth and pledging to focus enforcement on "the pusher and crime syndicate." Combining the tough-on-drugs platform with coercive rehabilitation, Kenneth Hahn explained that "hardened dope peddlers should get maximum prison sentences" while teenage drug users should undergo "compulsory medical treatment." Teenage arrests for marijuana declined only slightly in LA County between 1969 and 1971, but juvenile authorities diverted a higher percentage of all violators (including working-class and minority youth) to community treatment programs, a coercive medicalization (depicted as benevolent) of recreational drug users. In a follow-up report, the Narcotics and Dangerous Drugs Committee criticized the county's continued prioritization of the law enforcement approach, declared the police to be unqualified to run drug education programs in the schools, and called for the reduction of marijuana possession to a misdemeanor violation.[75]

Drug Prevention and the "Credibility Gap"

In the area of drug prevention, public health experts in the suburbs played a critical role in developing a novel approach that addressed teenagers as rational actors who deserved to be told the truth. "Don't lie to youths about drugs," an addiction specialist implored a community gathering in the San Fernando Valley, because traditional scare tactics had made recreational marijuana users skeptical of everything associated with parental authority and establishment rules. Almost all high school students wanted "more factual information—minus moralizing—coupled with an opportunity to engage in honest discussion about the pros and cons of marijuana," concluded a study of suburban Santa Clara County, California. "A bad program," explained the director of a private treatment center in Fairfax County, Virginia, "is worse than worthless insofar as it creates a 'credibility gap.'" He argued that the willingness of suburban teenagers to experiment with marijuana, LSD, and even heroin "is in some ways a direct result of the scare publicity. . . . Many of the youngsters see friends and acquaintances taking them without the threatened horrible results and come to disbelieve all the dire warnings . . . about the dangers of drugs." Like most medical professionals who worked directly with suburban adolescents, the Fairfax physician considered illegal drug use to be a symptom rather than the cause of the apparent generation gap and broader political-psychological dissatisfactions, an activity that filled the "vacuum" of meaning and authenticity for those "distressed by the contrast between the values they have been taught and the quality of life they experience" in affluent but sheltered communities. Since most white middle-class youth consumed marijuana and LSD either because of peer group norms, or in a "search for greater self-understanding" and an "effort to escape the alienation" of modern society, a successful prevention program needed to "establish an alternative pathway to the insights being reached though use of the drugs."[76]

The Ford Foundation reinforced these findings in a major study highly disparaging of the drug education curriculum that prevailed in American high schools through the late 1960s. The report opened with the frank acknowledgment that "at present, we know almost nothing about how best to reach students on the drug issue," given the inability of both law enforcement crackdowns and school-based prevention campaigns to slow, much less reverse, illegal drug use. Public health experts and academic researchers had reached consensus on what *definitely did not work*: the zero-tolerance, heroin-gateway technique of seeking to prohibit any experimentation with any illegal substance "by emphasizing the horrors of addiction and lumping all drugs together as leading to the same ultimate doom." The Ford report recommended a more realistic approach—an early version of the philosophy subsequently labeled "responsible use" or "harm reduction"—of presenting students with accurate information upon which to base their individual choices, "so that they will at least keep their risk-taking behavior within bounds." An extensive 1970 survey of high school students in California, for example, revealed that 84 percent of illegal drug users and 76 percent of nonusers believed the "decision to use drugs is a personal decision," regardless of criminal law or any moral sanctions associated with adult authority. The Ford study therefore endorsed the group rap session methods pioneered in upper-middle-class white enclaves such as West Los Angeles, where young adult facilitators encouraged teenagers to debate political issues and seek their own answers rather than simply lecturing them that all drugs were bad. "There must be open and free dialogue," the report declared, "in an atmosphere of tolerance for all points of view, free of moralizing and shock reactions." In line with DAWN and similar programs, the Ford Foundation concluded that "emphasis should be placed on the motivational aspects of drug use—why people use drugs, what they hope to accomplish and what they hope to escape, and how they can fulfill those needs in other ways."[77]

Drug treatment professionals were especially critical of instructional films such as *Narcotics: Pit of Despair*, produced by the California Narcotics Advisory Commission in 1967. The main difference between *Narcotics: Pit of Despair* and the fear-mongering marijuana-to-heroin gateway curriculum developed in the early 1950s was the updated representation of the invading dope pusher as a white middle-class "beatnik." The opening scene shows white students outside a stereotypical suburban high school, oblivious to the "peddlers of misery who prey on the unwary, the uninformed, the curious, the thrill-seekers." A bearded pusher named Pete lurks in the bushes watching a clean-cut guy named John, who has a pretty blonde girlfriend and drives a Jaguar, and is a "fish ready to be hooked." Pete lures John to a pot party where hippie kids are making out and dancing to psychedelic rock music. John receives free marijuana and sexual attention from an attractive woman, who is actually a heroin addict-prostitute working for the pusher. They pressure John by assuring him that marijuana is not physically addictive and that being "square" is uncool, and so he "lays his future on the chopping block." Soon John needs a bigger kick, and Pete gives him free samples of heroin until he becomes a junkie, a "victim [who] will never get away." John robs his parents, gets busted by the cops, does a stint in the federal narcotics hospital, and relapses to Pete and his "life-destroying poison" in the end. Denounced by public health specialists as counterproductive propaganda, *Narcotics: Pit of Despair* featured prominently in California's drug education and prevention curriculum in the late 1960s. "A person who could get grass from a dozen good friends sees a film of a bearded pusher jumping out from behind the hedge," recounted one high school student. "Drug education programs in their present form are ludicrous." "It was so phony I about blew my mind," another suburban pot smoker recalled. "In fact, the whole class freaked out."[78]

Leading experts in the drug treatment and prevention field formulated an alternative strategy that acknowledged the legitimacy of the generation gap and portrayed adolescent drug use as a symptom of a broader family and societal crisis. This breakthrough originated with researchers such as J. Thomas Ungerleider, a young UCLA psychiatrist who founded Project DARE (Drug Abuse Research and Education) in response to rising concern over the teenage psychedelic subculture. Ungerleider considered LSD in particular to be a very hazardous drug that had produced an even more dangerous overreaction, leading to "the breakdown of communication between young people and their parents."[79] In 1967, Ungerleider worked with a group of seventy-five high school students to produce *Beyond LSD*, an educational film designed for adults as much as the classroom. Set in middle-class suburbia, *Beyond LSD* begins with white parents watching a traditional instructional documentary filled with frightening images of hippies, psychedelic drugs, and dead teenagers. "Times of rapid change produce anxiety," the *Beyond LSD* narrator observes, but "we cannot help our children if we meet the dangers with hysteria and lies." Cut to scenes of parents alienating their children by wrongly equating hippie clothing, long hair, and psychedelic rock music with drug addiction. Then Ungerleider explains that if adults would be willing to listen when teenagers criticize the shallow materialism of suburbia and the deeper injustices of American society, then youth would be less likely to seek escapism through drugs. He also criticizes the "fundamental hypocrisy" of parents who label LSD and marijuana to be evil and dangerous, while acting like alcohol and tranquilizers were harmless for adults. A sophisticated prevention campaign should emphasize that drug use inhibits rather than expands the adolescent search for identity and new horizons. The film ends with the Project DARE teen rock band singing its theme song, "What Are Parents for, If Not for Listening," and a mother and daughter having a calm and honest conversation about drugs.[80]

Project DARE's widely distributed literature challenged youth to "look for other solutions to growing up than the easy illusion" of drugs, and the program likewise asked their parents to "take a good hard look at yourselves." Did adults also self-medicate when life became stressful, only with alcohol and pills instead of marijuana? Were they not at least equally responsible for the communications gulf with their children? Did they unfairly associate illegal drug use with any young person who adopted generational styles of long hair, short skirts, or listening to psychedelic rock? For its teenage audience, Project DARE warned of LSD's unknown dangers and adopted a just-the-facts approach to marijuana that characterized the apostles of legalization as just as misguided as the proponents of the heroin-gateway mystique, while ultimately respecting the individual responsibility to choose whether or not to take drugs. To improve the curriculum, DARE's high school volunteers ranked dozens of classroom instructional films based on their effectiveness from the modern teenage perspective. The group's rock band, with the motto "get high on life," also performed at a series of "happenings" designed to spread the antidrug message through positive peer pressure and countercultural methods.[81] During the late 1960s and early 1970s, tens of thousands of teenagers in the suburbs of Southern California attended such antidrug "happenings," which drew praise from Governor Ronald Reagan but generated local fears that audiences would riot. Despite their drug-free commitment, youth in Project DARE complained of being harassed by the police and typecast as narcotics users by suspicious adults, just because many of the boys had long hair and most of the girls dressed in the hippie fashion. Young people "have shown an astonishing ability to spot the hypocrisies in our society," Ungerleider declared, although he believed teens could also be extremely naïve about drugs. A resolution of the generation gap depended upon a commitment to genuine dialogue by parents and an honest approach to drug policy by politicians.[82]

Many of the new instructional films attempted to tap into the ethos of the youth revolt by presenting drug dependency as the antithesis of political consciousness. In 1969, the California bureaucrats responsible for the much-maligned *Narcotics: Pit of Despair* released a classroom film that finally abandoned the pusher conspiracy plotline. In stilted language that betrayed its

A TEEN D.A.R.E.
Life Can Be Exciting Without Drug Dreams
D.A.R.E.
HAS SOMETHING TO SAY
*
Youth is the time of life when taking a dare
comes naturally. We dare you to look for other,
perhaps more difficult, solutions to growing up than
the easy illusion of a drugged solution. Take the
time--make the effort to study what scientific research has to say about today's drugs of abuse.
*
FIND OUT FOR YOURSELF
!!!!!

FIGURE 3.10. Project DARE originated in Los Angeles in 1967 as a pathbreaking drug education curriculum, developed in consultation with high school students, that rejected traditional scare tactics and embraced the right of youth to participate in political activism and countercultural styles. White teenagers conveyed Project DARE's "get high on life" message, which emphasized the risks of LSD but maintained credibility by not hyping the threat of marijuana and respecting the authority of students to make their own choices. (Courtesy of Oregon State Archives, Records of Governor Tom McCall's Administration, Administrative Correspondence, folder: Drugs, box 9.)

establishment origins, *Drug Abuse: The Chemical Tomb* warns that even casual marijuana use threatens the potential of youth "to confront, to change a society that somehow hasn't fulfilled all its promise." The film shows young white teenagers in tree-lined LA suburbs who are psychologically addicted to marijuana, arrested by the police, and at risk of ending up as "total dropouts from a world that desperately needs what they can offer."[83] Los Angeles also served as the setting of the educational film *Marijuana* (1968), which opens with the bust of a psychedelic pot party in the suburbs. As police lead a group of teens out in handcuffs, they start yelling: "Grass isn't habit-forming like alcohol," "You'll never go to hard drugs," "What's so bad about feeling good," and "Make marijuana legal." Celebrity narrator Sonny Bono acknowledges that "many average and decent teenagers smoke pot," but if legalized then "too many unstable people" would end up on LSD or heroin. The film then presents two groups of mostly white youth debating the marijuana controversy. To justify pot smoking, the alienated faction blames their parents' generation for sending youth to die in Vietnam, practicing hypocrisy, embracing materialism, and ignoring legitimate youth grievances. "Why shouldn't I smoke grass?" asks a teenager sitting by his backyard pool. "If I don't get killed in the war, or by the big bomb, all I can look forward to is making money like my father, and I know he isn't happy." Instead of letting "the establishment" respond, Sonny Bono turns to the drug-free teens. "What we rebel about," a white female insists, "isn't changed one bit by getting high on marijuana." Young Americans have a responsibility to make the world better, other teenagers declare, "not to cop out on life through grass" and exchange "idealism for a stick of weed."[84]

The generation gap framework also structured network television programming such as *The People Next Door* (1970), an Emmy-winning CBS Playhouse production subsequently distributed as a classroom educational film. Shot on location in Scarsdale, New York, the dramatization follows the entrenched Hollywood formula of upper-middle-class psychological repression and white suburban dystopia. In the opening scene, the mother finds a marijuana joint and blames her hippie college-age son Artie, but it actually belongs to his innocent-seeming teenage sister Maxie. The father yells at Artie for having "girly" hair and preferring folk music to football; Artie responds, "I don't respect you anymore." Then Maxie starts screaming because she is taking a bad LSD trip, and the father kicks the "no good punk" son out of the house for corrupting his sister. The status-obsessed parents are very worried about what the neighbors will think and cannot understand how this could happen in a "normal American family, good Christian values, . . . nice neighborhood, nice home." Both parents (and the neighbors) drink a lot of alcohol, and one of the mothers pops tranquilizers—a plot twist meant to indicate adult hypocrisy. When Maxie recovers, she blames her drug abuse on her parents' "uptight" values, suggests that her unhappy mother drop acid to "see the world better," and runs away to the East Village. Maxie's father and brother reconcile for long enough to discover her in bed with a hippie junkie in a shabby urban tenement. Maxie's brain is fried, and her parents commit her to a psychiatric hospital, apparently for life. It turns out that she bought her drugs from the clean-cut boy next door, who deals marijuana, LSD, and speed. The father assaults this suburban "pusher" and goes to jail, the mother has a nervous breakdown, and the television melodrama ends with the family disintegrated. In its obtuse classroom guide, CBS recommended that students debate the causes of the generation gap and the youth "rebellion against hypocrisy," while pondering the question of "Why aren't all social problems limited to the ghetto?"[85]

Increasingly, the drug prevention curriculum replaced the specter of the nefarious pusher with an emphasis on adolescent peer culture, while letting youth rather than authority figures communicate a modified version of the gateway warning. In New York, the Narcotic Addiction Control Commission produced a series of instructional films that dispensed with the omniscient adult narrator altogether to let teenagers figure it out among themselves, *cinéma vérité* style. In *The Seekers* (1968), high school students talk about how much pressure they face to smoke marijuana in order to be cool and feel accepted by friends and classmates. Two white drug counselors in their early twenties lead the discussion, both of them former heroin addict-dealers who started with marijuana. Without being too heavy-handed, the documentary reinforces gateway tropes of pot smokers becoming heroin junkies and LSD burnouts. But the primary message focuses on the ways that even recreational marijuana use prevents youth from "dealing honestly with your problems" and doing "something much more constructive with your dissent." After one student defends hippies because "maybe the world is simply just not worth adapting to," the counselors respond that "the whole pot scene is one big game" and youth could either "take the easy way out" or engage in political activism. *Grooving* (1970), the second film in the series, starts with a teenager declaring that a convincing antidrug message should not feature adult "experts" or strung-out youth writhing around on the floor. Instead, teenagers themselves debate the pleasures and risks of drugs, with the scare tactics subtle. An innocent-looking white female talks about smoking pot at age thirteen before moving on to LSD, speed, and heroin—which she defends as part of "being happy, being able to love." Other teenagers counter with stories about the gateway dangers of marijuana and advocate turning on through natural highs instead of escapism. The film ends with the original girl saying that she had ignored her mother's antidrug preaching, but hearing the message from youth her own age really made an impression.[86]

Government enforcement agencies seemed incapable of producing a prevention curriculum that did not continue to revolve around the gateway threat that marijuana experimentation would lead to heroin addiction or LSD breakdown. These narratives of lost white daughters and hippie junkie burnouts resonated for elected officials and many parents, especially during an era of crisis coverage about suburban runaways ending up addicted and dead in urban slums, and they played a key role in federal enactment of the Comprehensive Drug Abuse Prevention and Control Act of 1970 (see chapter 4). But the gateway melodrama about marijuana's many dangers fatally undermined the prevention campaign's effectiveness for the target audience of white middle-class youth, in particular the millions of high school students who had actually smoked pot and knew its effects firsthand. Films such as *The Seekers* and *Grooving* were somewhat more sophisticated than the absurd tropes of evil pushers handing out free samples, but simply replacing the law enforcement messenger with a young ex-addict or a hip white teen was never going to be enough. Governor Nelson Rockefeller was proud of his administration's public health policies and therefore quite shocked when not only high school students but also local prevention specialists berated him at community forums for "turning off young people" with a "worthless" program that kept lumping marijuana and LSD users together with heroin addicts as "sick" people in need of arrest and rehabilitation. The federal Bureau of Narcotics and Dangerous Drugs remained even more tone-deaf, as in its 1970 manual for police officers, "Public Speaking on Drug Abuse Prevention." The guidebook did advise officers to stop claiming that "marijuana causes insanity" and instead to emphasize that it creates psychological dependence and benefits the "pusher . . . who profits from 'turning on' youth." They should anticipate student insistence that psychedelic drugs were harmless and respond that anyone who "abuses" them "is taking a 50–50 chance" of dire consequences, potentially death.[87]

In 1969, the U.S. Department of Health, Education, and Welfare published a major drug curriculum guidebook that began with a blunt observation that "traditional methods of deterrence, involving reliance on scare techniques or moral persuasion, have not proved effective." In the opening section, two academic psychiatrists attacked the BNDD for radically misrepresenting marijuana's dangers to maintain the unjust drug laws, which had provided "an ideal target for rebellious youth to point to as an example of adult hypocrisy." The researchers argued that drug prohibition sought to "legislate morality" under the guise of crime prevention because the "passive withdrawal to life of drug-induced fantasy" fundamentally threatened the Protestant work ethic and the capitalist value system. Dr. Stanley Yolles, head of the National Institute of Mental Health (NIMH), wrote that "scare techniques are not only ineffectual but detrimental" because millions of American students knew firsthand that smoking pot did not cause "psychoses or other grave consequences." He warned that many of "our brightest and most competent youth" had become "embittered toward the larger society," and so resolution of the drug crisis required a comprehensive effort to "bridge the intergenerational gap" and "solve the root causes of alienation." The guidebook included an analysis that qualified this assessment by distinguishing between the political alienation felt by hippies and New Left activists, and the "quite normal" preoccupations of most high school students who participated in the suburban middle-class recreational drug subculture. In this view, the generation gap thesis obscured the overlapping reasons—pleasure, boredom, self-medication, self-actualization, self-awareness—that caused teenagers and their parents to consume different types of drugs in America's mood-altering culture. To the extent that suburban youth were alienated, the fault rested with parental and societal overreaction to marijuana, which many teens considered a "normal kind of social activity which is not dangerous to their health or their morals."[88]

The generation gap analysis of widespread marijuana use and felony lawbreaking in white middle-class suburbia laid the groundwork for a major policy shift in the war on drugs. In 1970, *Time* published a curriculum guide that recommended letting high schoolers debate marijuana legalization and instructed teachers to clarify that "neither side has the final answer." The materials blamed the double standard between alcohol and marijuana for creating "widespread disrespect for all law among young people" and contrasted violent crimes associated with drunkenness to the peaceful pot-smoking audience at the recent Woodstock festival. And in a remarkable line given the classroom audience, *Time* observed that the "all but universal acceptance of marijuana by the young raises the question of how long the nation's present laws against its use can remain in force without seeming as absurd and hypocritical as Prohibition." That same year, HEW released a major survey of marijuana attitudes among high school students, part of a series by student journalists to explore the damaging consequences of the generation gap. The vast majority of teenagers drew sharp distinctions between harmful drugs, especially heroin, and the harmless recreational subculture of pot smoking. The student authors labeled conflation of marijuana and heroin to be "utterly ridiculous," an approach that "makes it impossible for anyone with even a modicum of intelligence to respect anything the government says in relation to drugs." Four-fifths of respondents, whether or not they used marijuana, did not consider criminal prohibition to have any effect on the attitudes and social practices of their classmates. Politicians and law enforcement officials, the HEW survey concluded, "must reckon with the fact" that a growing number of American youth "are openly in favor of legalizing marijuana or reducing penalties for its use."[89] Instead of legalization, Congress and state legislatures responded with misdemeanor possession reform that sought, and predictably failed, to deter marijuana use by these "otherwise law-abiding" impossible criminals.

4

Public Enemy Number One

IN THE SPRING OF 1970, Senator Thomas J. Dodd of Connecticut, the Democratic leader of the Subcommittee to Investigate Juvenile Delinquency, warned that "today, drug use is common on the college campus, in the suburban neighborhood, in the high school parking lot, and, most alarming of all, it is beginning to turn up in elementary schools." Dodd claimed that a decade earlier, teenage addiction "was mostly confined to hard-core delinquents from the inner city," but in recent years thousands of otherwise law-abiding white middle-class youth had been arrested for felony drug violations, primarily involving marijuana. He then condemned the nation's "antiquated" drug enforcement policies, especially inflexible laws that sought to "punish the pusher *and* the addict." The federal narcotics laws, enacted in the 1950s during the bipartisan crusade to save youth victims from racialized "pushers" and to punish nonwhite "hoodlum addicts," provided tough mandatory-minimum sentences for distribution and possession of heroin and marijuana (see chapter 1). Most states adopted the federal penalty model and likewise classified marijuana and heroin as equally dangerous narcotics, a law enforcement approach rendered all but untenable by the massive increase in pot smoking by white suburban and college youth in the mid-to-late 1960s. In his campaign for federal drug reform, Senator Dodd continued to endorse the pusher-gateway theory that marijuana experimenters were "just a step away from falling prey to the dope peddler," at risk of lifelong heroin addiction through "murder on the installment plan" (the phrase popularized by FBN commissioner Harry Anslinger). But he also recognized that felony marijuana penalties had widened the generation gap and produced "ideological warfare" between the government and too many white middle-class high school and college students. In negotiation with the Nixon administration, Dodd spearheaded the 1970 legislative reforms that repealed federal mandatory-minimums for individual drug use, reduced marijuana possession and casual sale to misdemeanors for first offenders, and simultaneously increased sentences for major traffickers.[1]

As a racial state-building project, the Comprehensive Drug Abuse Prevention and Control Act of 1970 reflected the bipartisan consensus that white middle-class youth represented the primary victims of both the illegal drug markets and the criminal drug laws. Close attention to the extended debate over federal drug control policy during the late 1960s and early 1970s reveals how the Nixon administration and Democratic leaders in Congress collaborated to produce the racial-political category of the "otherwise law-abiding" victim, especially the white marijuana experimenter from the suburbs and college campuses—unjustly imprisoned by felony laws, politically alienated and/or emotionally disturbed, targeted by pushers and the "drug culture," at risk of "psychological dependence" and the dropout syndrome, in danger of progression to LSD, speed, or heroin. On the ground, neither the criminal legal system nor the recreational drug market actually operated along these lines, given the comprehensive prosecutorial and judicial diversion of white middle-class lawbreakers and the fundamental mischaracterization of the youth marijuana scene by the pusher and gateway tropes. But for a broad spectrum of interests, the production of the white middle-class victim justified both the escalation of interdiction and policing on the supply side and increased public health investments of prevention and treatment on the demand front. Thomas Dodd, a public health liberal who advocated tough punishment for drug traffickers and coercive rehabilitation for their victims, categorized all illegal drug users as "sick" people, whether they injected heroin or smoked marijuana, who therefore should be institutionalized and not incarcerated. During the two-year legislative process, the political and media frame of white youth arrested for marijuana and progressing to narcotics addiction proved so dominant that public health liberals in Congress even convinced the resistant Nixon administration to accept indeterminate sentencing for all categories of possession and sale, even heroin, except for a subset of "professional" traffickers.[2]

During the Nixon era, the criminalization of marijuana became more central than ever to the federal war on drugs and in fundamental ways eclipsed heroin as both a public health and law enforcement priority. The scholarly literature on the drug war during the late 1960s and 1970s has focused too narrowly on the atypical experiences of New York City, the heroin capital of the United States, and not nearly enough on other regions of the country and broader national trends as revealed in social practices, political debates,

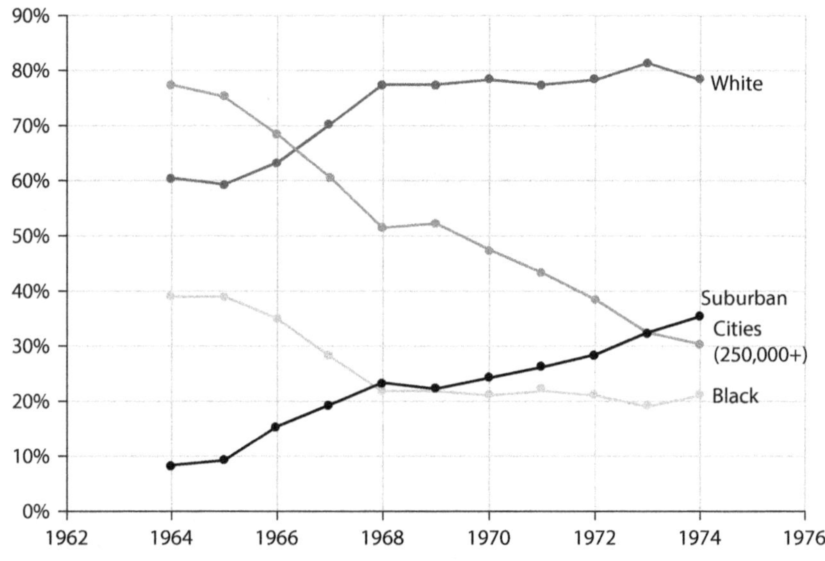

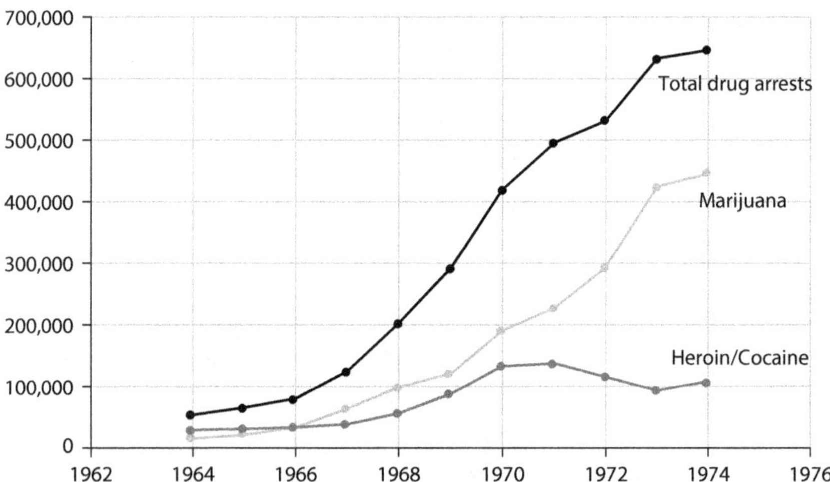

FIGURE 4.1. Select characteristics of the population arrested on drug charges in the United States, 1964–74. (*Top*) The proportion of white to total drug arrests increased from 60% in 1964 to 81% in 1973, an all-time high. The share of suburban drug arrests grew even more rapidly, reaching 35% by 1974. Drug arrests in the largest cities declined to 30% of the total, and Black arrests dropped from 39% in 1964 to the modern low of 19% in 1973. (*Bottom*) The escalation of the war on drugs across the nation produced 12.9 times more arrests in 1974 than a decade earlier. Marijuana arrests increased from 26% to 69% of total drug arrests during this period. The combined heroin/cocaine share fell from 49% to 16% of total drug arrests, directly related to the

and most of all the arrest data. The sprawling and multiracial urban/suburban landscape of Los Angeles County, not New York City and the Rockefeller Drug Laws, provided the template for the escalation of the national war on drugs. This makes sense in a state formation analysis, given that California accounted for half of all U.S. drug arrests in the years preceding the 1970 federal reforms, and white marijuana smokers represented about two-thirds of its detained lawbreakers in the late 1960s. As a proportion of drug-war arrests nationwide, dramatic declines occurred between 1969 and 1974 in the overlapping categories of heroin violators (49 to 16 percent), African Americans (39 to 21 percent), and residents of the largest cities (77 to 30 percent). Arrest shares for the overlapping categories of marijuana criminals (26 to 69 percent), white Americans (60 to 78 percent), and FBI-designated suburban areas (8 to 35 percent) increased to their modern peaks by the mid-1970s (fig. 4.1). White juveniles were even more likely to be arrested than white adults and accounted for between 86 and 89 percent of total juvenile drug arrests between 1968 and 1972. Although the FBI included most Hispanics in the white category during this time period, the vast majority of white drug arrests were non-Hispanic adults under age twenty-five. This massive scaling upward and outward of the carceral state did not ameliorate the inequitable policing of minority communities, but as the Nixon White House appreciated, there were not nearly enough nonwhite heroin addicts in urban America to mobilize public support for a nationwide war on drugs.[3]

As an expanding component of the carceral state, federal policy in the war on drugs merged criminal justice and public health into a comprehensive, discretionary system for the arrest, diversion, and compulsory rehabilitation of recreational drug users and addicts alike. Although scholarly literature and conventional wisdom often portray law enforcement and public health as alternative if not antithetical approaches—punitive versus preventative/rehabilitative—federal lawmakers envisioned their operation in concert as coercive mechanisms for the social control of youth.[4] In 1968, the ACLU began

---

significant decline in the proportion of arrests of African Americans and of residents of the largest cities. (FBI, *Uniform Crime Reports*, 1964–1974.)

Note: For valid comparisons, drug arrest data for 1964–69 recalculated to reflect changes in FBI reporting and estimation techniques that began in 1970. On the FBI's "suburban" category and inclusion of most Hispanic arrests in the "white" category, see note in fig. I.1. The racial breakdown of the U.S. population in the 1970 census was 87.6% white, 11.1% Black, and an estimated 4.5% Hispanic (with overlap between the white and Hispanic categories).

a campaign for legalization of marijuana possession, and four years later the National Commission on Marihuana endorsed decriminalization for personal use and casual sale. A dissident faction of medical experts denounced criminalization as well as the public health establishment's imposition of the disease model on pot smokers. But the Nixon administration and most members of Congress believed that criminal sanctions remained essential to deter white youth from trying marijuana, to arrest and channel them into psychiatric treatment when they did not comply, and to rehabilitate them before they descended into the "drug culture." A broad political consensus also defended marijuana prohibition as essential to waging war on traffickers, thwarting the gateway-to-heroin progression, and saving white middle-class youth from lifestyles of apathy and downward mobility associated with hippies, ghettos, and capitalist nonproductivity. Except for the marginalized civil liberties stance, the national debate almost never presented white pot smokers (indeed almost any illegal drug users) as politically autonomous citizens or willing consumers, rather than as youth to be controlled and victims to be protected. The war on drugs also targeted marijuana and heroin for their symbolic interrelationship and political meanings more than their pharmacological hazards—given that alcohol, tobacco, and the oversupply and abuse of legal prescription medication each presented far greater per-capita health challenges nationwide than all banned substances combined.[5]

The escalation of the federal war on drugs during Richard Nixon's first term depended on a basic bipartisan consensus in favor of harsh punishment for major traffickers and coercive public health solutions for their so-called victims. Only six Democrats in Congress voted against the Comprehensive Drug Abuse Prevention and Control Act of 1970, typical of the longer twentieth-century pattern of omnibus federal drug control legislation passing by overwhelming or unanimous margins. The analytical model of consensus does not mean that politicians from across the spectrum agreed on everything but rather that the shared racialized vision of a national drug "crisis" and the negotiations inherent in the policymaking process overshadowed or defused the differences that did exist. Public health liberals supported more funding for community-based treatment centers, generally opposed incarceration of drug users, and often criticized the Nixon administration for prioritizing law enforcement more than education, prevention, and rehabilitation programs. But they also demanded tougher enforcement against traffickers and street "pushers," focused on the menace of narcotics-fueled urban crime as much as any law-and-order Republican, imposed the disease model on recreational drug users, and hyped the white teenage marijuana epidemic and the spread of heroin addiction to the suburbs. In 1971, when President Nixon officially declared war on "drug abuse," labeled "public enemy number one," he echoed much of the liberal agenda in calling for law enforcement to attack the supply lines and public health programs to rehabilitate the victims. Senate liberals then engineered unanimous passage of the Drug Abuse Office and Treatment Act of 1972, which greatly increased federal funding for prevention and rehabilitation. During this second phase of the Nixon-era war on drugs, the problems of nonwhite heroin addiction and urban street crime moved to center stage, but the Republican administration continued to justify federal mobilization through the marijuana-gateway pusher mythology and to define the crisis as suburban and universal.[6]

At this pivotal stage of carceral state building, the pervasive construction of the war on drugs through the framework of suburban crisis positioned white middle-class youth as impossible criminals, misguided rebels, and innocent victims to be shielded from the organized traffickers and the penal system. The cultural and political image of the white middle-class drug victim proved as foundational to the bipartisan war on drugs as the equally racialized categories of the foreign trafficker, urban pusher, and predatory ghetto addict. Many scholars have examined Nixon's drug war as a racial project of social control of urban minority populations, an extension of the federal war on Black street crime, and the foundation for the "new Jim Crow" of mass incarceration on the horizon.[7] The consensus framework deployed here, and the comparative analysis of urban/Black and suburban/white drug politics, challenges interpretations that this era represented a conservative turn in criminal justice policy, a partisan Republican project of racial backlash, or a consequence of the "rise of the Right." More recent scholarship has emphasized the bipartisan origins of punitive drug policy and the central role of liberalism in promoting urban crime control and building the carceral state, although without sufficiently exploring the real and imagined suburban side of the equation or explaining why federal policymakers shifted from mandatory-minimum sentences to judicial discretion for most drug criminals at this moment of national crisis.[8] The Nixon administration and Congress responded to the same suburban imperatives, and ultimately codified the same discretionary procedures, that local criminal legal systems had already implemented ad hoc to handle the unprecedented influx of "otherwise law-abiding" white pot smokers. Instead of a rightward turn from the liberal ideal of rehabilitation to punitive law-and-order conservatism, almost all federal lawmakers endorsed tough sanctions for traffickers, coercive medicalization for illegal drug users, and the paramount mission of safeguarding and controlling white middle-class youth.

Cruel and Unusual Punishment?

The political and cultural emphasis on young white middle-class pot smokers on the college campuses and in the suburbs set the stage for drug policy reform, triggering an unprecedented national debate over marijuana penalties and raising the prospect of legalization. In December 1968, the American Civil Liberties Union and the National Student Association, the political lobby for college students, jointly launched a campaign to repeal all federal and state laws criminalizing marijuana possession. Citing the harm principle, the ACLU labeled marijuana use a victimless crime and a matter of individual freedom that deserved protection under the constitutional right to privacy recently recognized by the U.S. Supreme Court. The ACLU's position statement criticized law enforcement for harassing citizens through illegal searches, due process violations, and "cruel and unusual punishment" that cumulatively represented "excessive and unconstitutional interventions into personal and private rights." In internal deliberations, ACLU leaders highlighted the problem of police misconduct against white middle-class victims ("students and hippies") and justified legalization because "the user, especially the student, is likely to have his career plans ruined if convicted under the marijuana laws." Initially, the ACLU board planned to recommend that possession be reduced to a misdemeanor but ultimately recognized that anything short of legalization would still allow the jailing of young people and would badly damage its credibility on college campuses. Notably, the ACLU statement declined to take a position on either the "appropriate regulatory measures" regarding marijuana use by minors or the "appropriate restrictions" on sale and distribution of the drug, instead promising to address these crucial questions in the future. Even the nation's leading civil liberties organization remained hesitant to oppose criminalization of the supply side of the recreational marijuana market, a stance that constrained the boundaries of political debate during the Nixon era and anticipated the decriminalization compromise of the 1970s.[9]

During the late 1960s, the ACLU's endorsement of partial legalization created tensions with its campus allies and some state affiliates as well as inside the national headquarters. The National Student Association, which called for full legalization and regulation of marijuana according to the alcohol model, informed the ACLU that its policy was unrealistic because law enforcement charged many college participants in the casual recreational market with sale and not just possession. In early 1968, before the national organization acted, the ACLU chapter in Washington state announced its support for legalization of both marijuana possession and sale through a regulatory system similar to tobacco and alcohol. The Washington chapter warned that marijuana enforcement "threaten[ed] to further alienate an entire generation" and attributed criminal prohibition to moral disapproval of bohemian "hippie" subcultures and misplaced fears that smoking pot caused apathy, escapism, and retreat from the middle-class career trajectory. "The alleged disruption of living patterns and flagging ambition," the Washington state ACLU explained, "is more likely a product of social conditions represented by marijuana laws than it is a product of the hallucinogen itself."[10] The national ACLU internally debated its position on marijuana sale throughout 1969 and 1970, with opponents of full legalization arguing that public sentiment would not accept alcohol-style distribution, that the long-term health effects of smoking pot remained uncertain, and that criminalizing the supply lines would send a message of discouragement to youth who wanted to "escape from reality." Supporters, led by the younger members of the ACLU's policy committee, countered that legalizing possession but criminalizing sale was an "illogical" stance that forced pot smokers to "deal with underworld elements" to exercise their constitutional rights and would allow law enforcement too much discretion to arrest and prosecute marijuana users on distribution charges. The ACLU did not publicly endorse full legalization and regulation of marijuana until late 1971, which makes it less surprising that no elected official in Washington took such a position before then either.[11]

In January 1969, the Massachusetts Supreme Court delivered a major setback to the marijuana legalization movement, indicating that fundamental reform would most likely come through legislative action rather than judicial challenges. The litigation began two years earlier, when a criminal defense firm in Boston launched a test case designed to undermine marijuana laws nationwide as a violation of federal due process and equal protection rights. The defendants, who were all but incidental to the legal debate, were two white men in their mid-twenties caught with five pounds of marijuana at the Logan airport and charged with possession with intent to sell, which carried a five-to-ten-year sentence. The trial court agreed to consider the constitutionality of marijuana's criminalization as a narcotic, leading to lengthy hearings where prosecution and defense experts disputed its hazards relative to alcohol and other "mind-altering" substances. Joseph Oteri, the defense attorney, warned that "there isn't a parent or potential parent in this country who can't be affected by this present law. . . . If marijuana is the innocuous substance scientists say it is, it is a crime to put kids in jail for possessing it, using it, even selling it." The district court judge instead agreed with prosecution witnesses that "marijuana is a harmful and dangerous drug," upholding the narcotics laws and setting up the planned appeal. The Massachusetts Supreme Court likewise ruled that "there is no right to smoke marijuana" to be found in either the federal or state constitution. The unanimous judgment rejected the defense argument that criminalization was "arbitrary and irrational," emphasizing the deference due to the legislature's power to determine criminal law and citing the testimony of the state's experts that marijuana triggered psychosis in some users and led to a "frequent sequence" of escalation to heroin or LSD. The decision also dismissed the "cruel and unusual punishment" challenge with the striking observation that judicial discretion in sentencing should continue to "distinguish between the youth who was experimenting with marihuana or even a constant user of the drug and the 'pusher' or person trafficking in marihuana for financial gain."[12]

Several ACLU affiliates in other states initiated test cases in 1969, based on the same arguments that criminal penalties for marijuana possession violated the Eighth Amendment prohibition against "cruel and unusual punishment" and the constitutional doctrine of an individual right to privacy. The New Jersey chapter filed a federal lawsuit on behalf of two college students busted for smoking pot in the suburbs outside New York City, arguing that each had the positive right to "participate in the future enjoyable use of marijuana whenever the situation arises." The litigation also sought class-action status to challenge the state's narcotics offender registration law, which (selectively) applied to individuals convicted of marijuana possession. According to the complaint, the police had illegally profiled the plaintiffs for having long hair and looking like hippies, part of a broader pattern of discriminatory enforcement against "certain disfavored groups." The federal courts dismissed the allegations as meritless and also declined to certify a follow-up ACLU class-action lawsuit charging the New Jersey State Police with systematic discrimination against long-haired "hippie-like" motorists detained on traffic pretexts and then illegally searched for drugs. In the state of Washington, the ACLU chapter planned a legal test of "cruel and unusual" felony marijuana penalties with a case involving a "socially 'constructive'" (e.g., white middle-class student) plaintiff, but then the legislature reclassified cannabis as a nonnarcotic in 1969 and made simple possession a misdemeanor with a maximum six-month sentence. In response, the ACLU filed an Eighth Amendment claim on behalf of an African American man given a forty-year jury sentence for selling a single joint to a white sixteen-year-old who approached him at a restaurant in Seattle. The Supreme Court of Washington reversed the conviction on the technical grounds that the legislature had subsequently removed marijuana from the narcotics sentencing scheme, which proved welcome news for the defendant but mooted the constitutional challenge.[13]

The ACLU's legal strategy and media connections helped to transform the image of white "hippies" who smoked marijuana from criminalized radicals to misguided youthful victims of an overzealous police state. In 1969, the Virginia affiliate filed an entrapment lawsuit on behalf of James Harold Johnson, a high school senior in a small town outside Richmond who received a twenty-year sentence, with half suspended, for facilitating a marijuana sale to an undercover informant. After some parents in Prince George County complained about drug use in the high school, the sheriff's department enlisted a classmate to solicit a large transaction from Johnson, who agreed to act as an intermediary because he always dealt in much smaller amounts. The prosecutor labeled marijuana an "insidious infiltration" and justified the harsh sentence as necessary to protect local teenagers from "the youth movement in this country and the tendency toward destruction of everything we think is fundamental." Johnson's parents angrily disputed a court psychiatrist's report that their son had a "sociopathic personality" and despaired that ten years in the state penitentiary was "not punishment, that's revenge." The sympathetic coverage in the *Washington Post* characterized Johnson as a "full-time rebel" and "long-haired defier of public and parental authority," scapegoated by the community after some of the "nicest people's children" started smoking pot. In a scathing editorial, the *Post* asked: "Sending an 18-year-old to prison for 10 years because he is doing what thousands of his contemporaries are doing—is that justice?" The Supreme Court of Virginia rejected the entrapment charge because the police had "merely afforded an opportunity for the commission" of a crime, not planted the idea in the "mind of an otherwise innocent person." The decision did remand the case for resentencing based on the inconsistent classification of marijuana as a narcotic in state law, a consolation for Johnson after two years in prison. For the ACLU, the saga also pinpointed the incongruity of supporting the legalization of marijuana possession but relying only on indirect challenges to the lengthy sentences given for the crime of selling the same drug.[14]

In 1969, as the U.S. Congress and most state legislatures began to reconsider the felony marijuana penalties, a white college student in Virginia emerged as the most prominent national symbol of the excesses of the war on drugs. In February, police in the town of Danville arrested Frank LaVarre, a nineteen-year-old at the University of Virginia (UVA), with several pounds of marijuana on a bus headed from Charlottesville to Atlanta. A local judge sentenced LaVarre to twenty years in prison, the mandatory-minimum for that amount, even though the drug courier cooperated under duress by naming his Atlanta contact and UVA supplier. Soon after, *Life* magazine introduced LaVarre to the American public in an exposé about the "disproportionate severity" of felony possession laws for marijuana. A two-page spread chronicled LaVarre's progression from a clean-cut track athlete at his prep school in Tennessee to a longhaired college sophomore who smoked pot to "deepen his already keen sensitivity to music and arts." *Life* labeled the punishment a "travesty" and interviewed a UVA friend who said "the older generation had better get used to pot . . . If they're going to lock up people like Frank LaVarre, they're going to have a violent revolution on their hands." In Congress, Senator Edward Kennedy cited LaVarre's case as the "most shocking" example of the need for a "long overdue reexamination" of the marijuana penalties. *Time* attributed LaVarre's unjust incarceration to a vengeful, elderly judge "who loathes pot smokers and longhairs." After the extensive national publicity and desperate appeals from LaVarre's parents, Virginia governor Mills Godwin commuted his sentence to five years of probation, because the college student had not trafficked for profit and could still "become a useful member of society." The *Washington Post* expressed relief that the conservative law-and-order governor had intervened to "prevent LaVarre's life from being ruined" but denounced the inclusion of marijuana in the mandatory-minimum narcotics penalties and demanded a "more realistic" approach to a drug no more dangerous than alcohol or tobacco.[15]

The attention to the plight of white middle-class students serving long prison terms obscured two of the most important functions of the mandatory-minimum marijuana penalties: leverage for prosecutors to secure plea bargains on lesser charges, often by turning recreational users into informants; and discriminatory enforcement against cultural nonconformists, political radicals, and racial minorities. Law enforcement arrested almost 215,000 Americans for marijuana violations during 1968 and 1969 combined, two-thirds under age twenty-one, out of an estimated 12 million pot smokers nationwide (fig. 4.2). Because of prosecutorial and judicial discretion, less than 1 percent of possession arrests culminated in significant jail or prison time.[16] The ACLU pointed out that the chance of arrest was unlikely and essentially arbitrary for the vast

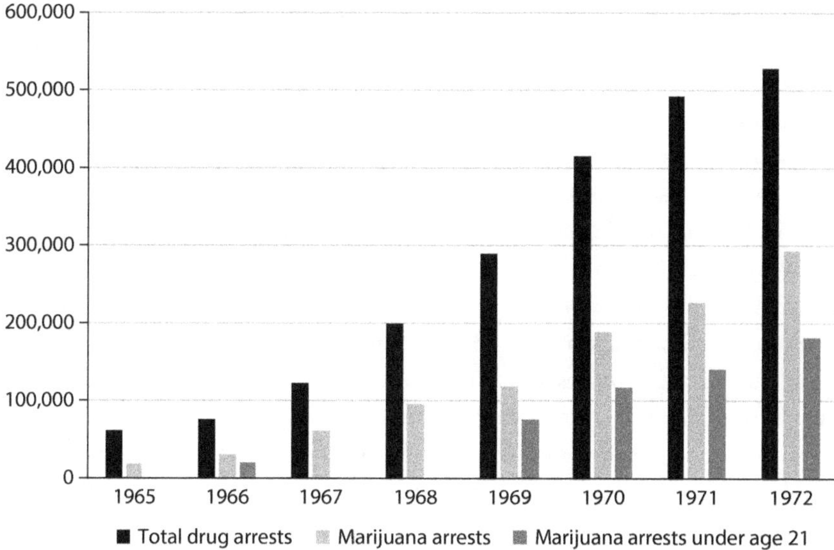

FIGURE 4.2. Marijuana arrests in the United States, 1965–72, compared to all drug arrests and youth (under twenty-one) marijuana arrests. Marijuana arrests increased from 31% to 51% of total drug arrests nationwide between 1965 and 1967, inspiring legalization campaigns and bipartisan pressure to reduce the felony possession penalties, and then dipped slightly as a proportion before rising to 55% of total drug arrests by 1972. The number of marijuana arrests jumped dramatically during this period, from 18,800 in 1965 to 292,200 in 1972, as part of the 8.7 times increase in all drug arrests. Almost two-thirds of marijuana arrests involved youth under age twenty-one (data is not available for 1965, 1967–68), and their proportion of total drug arrests rose from 26% in 1969 to 34% by 1972. (FBI, *Uniform Crime Reports*, 1965–1972.)
Note: FBI data did not break down marijuana arrests by race (racial data on total drug arrests in fig. 4.1). For valid comparisons, drug arrests for 1964–69 recalculated to reflect changes in FBI reporting and estimation techniques that began in 1970.

majority of high school and college-age pot smokers, whereas prosecution and harsh sentences were highly selective for the hippies, political dissidents, and ghetto residents targeted by police—often through entrapment or illegal profiling. The criminal legal system reserved extreme penalties for cases that generated "outraged morality and vindictiveness" based on what marijuana "*represents*—a life style, a political stance, the seemingly alien values of a different generation." LeMar, a loose coalition of marijuana legalization advocates, publicized the most "cruel and unusual" sentences: thirty years for a Black civil rights activist in Texas, busted under suspicious circumstances in 1968; twenty years for a countercultural poet in Michigan, entrapped by two undercover cops; ten years for white radical John Sinclair, convicted by a

Detroit jury in 1969 after giving two joints to an undercover agent. Joel Fort, a San Francisco psychiatrist and frequent expert witness in legalization test cases, observed that "people who publicly oppose the marijuana laws and marijuana mythology of our narcotics police have an unusually high arrest record." Selective marijuana enforcement—invasions of privacy, police misconduct, and discriminatory prosecutions—illustrated the "drift toward a police state."[17]

The national media instead consistently portrayed ordinary white middle-class youth as the main victims of criminal drug enforcement, the "laws broken so often by so many normally law-abiding people." In 1969, Mike Wallace began a CBS-TV special report on marijuana and the generation gap by asking an attractive white professional in her mid-twenties why she disregards the law. "It's very simple," she replies with a smile. "I smoke it because I enjoy it, because it gives me pleasure." The "career girl" clarifies that she is not a political rebel or a malcontent, and for her marijuana is not "such a big deal. The only thing that makes it a big deal is that it's illegal." Like drinking alcohol in moderation, the occasional joint takes the edge off the burdens of modern life. "Pot in itself is innocuous." Wallace then informs the audience: "Marijuana is not the menace we once believed." After scenes that portray the drug's historical progression from Mexican immigrants to Black ghettos to the college campuses and white suburbs, Wallace asks whether prison is an appropriate punishment for otherwise law-abiding youth. Marijuana used to be "a drug used only by society's outsiders" (cut to Black men on an urban street corner), but smoking pot "has now become an escape for the middle class." A judge from Seattle next informs CBS that he just could not give a twenty-year mandatory sentence to a college student who sold a small amount of marijuana to a friend, and young people in America know that the law is "not realistic and uniformly applied." A white high school student tells the show that "the law's stopping nothing, . . . the law sends it underground, . . . the kids don't see any problem." The most evocative segment features a charming young bohemian, joined by his sad wife and newborn child, who faces five to twenty years for a possession conviction. The time has come to change the law, Wallace concludes, given that even conservative politicians were starting to acknowledge that marijuana penalties were unfair and counterproductive.[18]

The white middle-class orientation of the drug debate made marijuana legalization a more legitimate political stance but also exacerbated racial fears that a criminal deterrent remained necessary to prevent suburban teenagers and college students from dropping out and embracing "ghetto" values and lifestyles. The cover of *Life*'s 1969 feature on Frank LaVarre showed a close-up shot of a white male smoking a joint headlined: "Marijuana: At least 12 million Americans have now tried it. Are penalties too severe? Should it be legalized?" The inside story juxtaposed federal narcotics agents policing the Mexican border with images of young white professionals smoking marijuana at social functions in New York City and suburban Boston. Now that marijuana had spread from the "rebellious young" to the respectable middle class, *Life* contended, "the whole question of legalization will have to be faced." In a companion piece, former FDA commissioner James Goddard labeled the prohibition of marijuana as a narcotic "a mixture of bad science and poor understanding of the role of law as a deterrent force." Goddard conceded that alcohol and tobacco were more dangerous but recommended only that marijuana possession be reduced to a misdemeanor, while retaining "serious penalties" for major traffickers. He justified continued criminalization based on alleged evidence that teenagers who smoked pot regularly risked psychological dependence and the dropout syndrome. In its own 1969 cover story about marijuana and white middle-class America, *Time* asked if legalization would be the best response given "youthful defiance of the law unprecedented since Prohibition." The magazine classified marijuana as a "softer" drug, no more harmful than alcohol, and endorsed a public health approach over law enforcement. But, adding explicit racial and anticommunist anxiety to Goddard's warning, *Time* emphasized the hazards of psychological dependence by youthful pot smokers who might adopt the "passive, fatalistic outlook" of Asian nations and the "depression and discouragement of slum life."[19]

The American Medical Association provided significant authority to the emerging middle-ground position of reforming the felony marijuana possession laws but opposing legalization as a dangerous risk for public health and economic productivity in the United States. In 1968, the AMA's flagship journal published an influential editorial labeling marijuana a "harmful drug" and arguing that "legalization would lead to even more serious medical and social consequences than now result from its use." The editorial acknowledged the generation gap caused by the drug's popularity among middle-to-upper-class youth who believed that smoking pot was a harmless social activity. But the AMA countered that "too many"—perhaps 10 percent—would become "chronic users" who suffered from psychological dependence and career "nonproductivity," which harmed both these individuals and society at large. The AMA further warned that the marijuana subculture produced a "substantial number of people who are drug-oriented," open to experimentation with amphetamines and LSD (but rarely heroin, a distinction that highlighted the

AMA's emphasis on white middle-class youth). Directly addressing the most common generation gap accusation, the AMA stated that the "failure of Prohibition made alcohol no less dangerous." The AMA editorial accompanied a position statement by its Council on Mental Health, in collaboration with the National Research Council, that "legalization of marijuana would create a serious abuse problem in the United States" and therefore criminal sanctions remained necessary as a deterrent against psychological dependence and reduced "social productivity." The joint statement did criticize the excessively harsh penalties for marijuana possession, which "needlessly damaged . . . the lives of many young people." The medical commission instead recommended a layered approach of judicial leniency for youthful experimenters, psychiatric treatment for the marijuana dependent, and application of tough law enforcement measures only for the profit-oriented dealers and traffickers.[20]

Federal modification of the marijuana possession laws was always probable during 1969–70, because of the growing political attention to the plight of "otherwise law-abiding" white middle-class youth, but an unexpected Supreme Court decision made congressional action imperative. In May 1969, in an appeal brought by countercultural LSD icon Timothy Leary, a unanimous Supreme Court found the primary enforcement mechanisms in the Marihuana Tax Act of 1937 to be unconstitutional. Three years earlier, a federal judge in Texas sentenced Leary to the thirty-year maximum and a $30,000 fine for bringing half an ounce of marijuana, originally purchased in New York, back across the border after a family vacation to Mexico. Leary contended that he had a "moral and political right" to smoke marijuana and made a religious freedom argument that the psychedelic drug expanded consciousness and enhanced spirituality. After the appeals courts rejected the First Amendment defense, as a smokescreen that would endanger American youth by effectively nullifying criminal prohibition, Leary challenged the Marihuana Tax Act based on the Fifth Amendment safeguard against self-incrimination. The ACLU and the National Student Association filed supporting briefs, with the latter charging that federal marijuana enforcement reflected "popular hysteria" and caused "the alienation of young people in general." The Supreme Court overturned Leary's conviction because the Marihuana Tax Act required importers and sellers to incriminate themselves by registering and paying a federal transaction fee and violated the due process rights of users by basing criminalization on the presumptions that the contraband had been imported and that they knew its origin. Although *Leary v. United States* technically undermined the federal prohibition against marijuana, state laws remained valid and the decision's final line clarified that "nothing in what we hold today implies any constitutional disability in Congress to deal with the marihuana traffic by other means." Timothy Leary predicted "freedom for thousands of young people who are in jail now" and announced his candidacy for governor of California, while President Nixon promised to send Congress a tough, modern program to control illegal drugs.[21]

Bipartisan Consensus for Federal Drug Reform

The suburban politics of marijuana, much more than urban heroin, shaped the trajectory of the federal war on drugs during the first two years of the Nixon administration. During the 1968 presidential campaign, Richard Nixon traveled to Orange County, California, to warn that illegal drugs were "decimating a generation of Americans." The Republican candidate, speaking to a white-collar suburban audience at the Anaheim convention center, pledged to stop marijuana and heroin importers at the border, arrest the drug traffickers, and rehabilitate their youthful victims. Nixon told the audience that a teenage girl inspired his plan by sending him a letter about her struggles with drugs after hearing his convention speech, which promised to crack down on the "narcotics peddlers who are corrupting the lives of the children of this country." The Republican platform likewise called for a "vigorous nationwide drive" against traffickers, with particular emphasis on stopping marijuana and LSD, "the first steps toward addiction."[22] Soon after taking office, Nixon created a special interagency task force to devise a "concerted frontal attack" on the importation, sale, and use of illegal drugs in the United States. Its report, *Narcotics, Marijuana, and Dangerous Drugs,* focused almost exclusively on surging rates of marijuana use and barely mentioned heroin at all, except to claim that chronic pot smokers were likely to progress to harder drugs. The task force defined the nation's primary drug problem as marijuana experimentation by middle-to-upper-class youth and placed the blame on "free-lance smugglers and organized traffickers" who imported the drug from Mexico. The policy blueprint recommended treatment and rehabilitation for regular pot smokers who became psychologically dependent and suffered from "loss of motivation" and a "non-goal oriented lifestyle." On the supply side, the task force endorsed increased interdiction to stop the flow of marijuana and other drugs across the Mexican border combined with revision of mandatory-minimum penalties to provide more flexibility in dealing with major traffickers versus "small-scale" offenders.[23]

The Nixon administration's location of white middle-class marijuana use at the center of the American drug crisis rested squarely within the political and cultural mainstream in the late 1960s. On June 27, the president ordered the Department of Justice to implement the task force recommendations through a "frontal attack on the narcotic, marihuana and dangerous drug traffic" coming from Mexico. Nixon provided only one specific reason for this urgent, high-priority federal initiative: "the alarming increase during the past three years in the consumption of marihuana in particular by our Nation's youth." By seeking to protect innocent teenagers from the illegal drug markets and shield them from the felony drug laws, Nixon's emerging program occupied the same racialized terrain as the national media coverage of the suburban epidemic, the bipartisan congressional investigations of middle-class drug victims, the prosecutors and judges who diverted white lawbreakers in affluent locales, the American Medical Association's belief that nonproductivity by a small subset of stoners justified criminal prohibition, even the ACLU's mission to keep college students and hippies from the stigma of a criminal record. Although participants in the drug policy debate represented a broad political spectrum, almost all still operated within a consensus framework that advocated criminalization and interdiction to disrupt the supply lines while prioritizing public health approaches for young middle-class consumers on the demand side—although the recreational marijuana market did not divide cleanly into these two categories in social practice. In response to the small but vocal legalization movement, the Nixon task force also embraced the new mainstream position that marijuana was in fact more harmful than alcohol and therefore criminal prohibition remained essential, not because smoking pot led directly to heroin addiction or violent crime but because "regular and continuous use" created psychological dysfunction and caused white youth to deviate from the middle-class career track and the capitalist value system.[24]

Liberal Democrats in Congress had been moving toward revision of the federal mandatory-minimum drug laws since 1967, when Lyndon Johnson's crime commission called for greater judicial discretion in sentencing and multiple committees began holding hearings to investigate the marijuana epidemic among white middle-class youth. In April 1969, Senator Thomas Dodd, the Connecticut Democrat in charge of the Juvenile Delinquency Subcommittee, introduced omnibus legislation to eliminate all mandatory-minimum penalties for drug offenses. Like the Nixon administration, Dodd portrayed the several million American high school and college students who had experimented with marijuana as the primary victims of international traffickers and the urgent reason for revising the harsh possession laws. A leading public health liberal, Dodd promised more enforcement funding for the Bureau of Narcotics and Dangerous Drugs and called for a joint United States–Mexico initiative to stop the flow of marijuana across the Southwest border. The bill also funded a major federal study to determine the hazards of marijuana and proposed its reclassification through a three-tiered regulatory structure: Class 1 (banned narcotics); Class 2 (dangerous drugs, including marijuana and LSD, with high abuse potential or no accepted medical use); and Class 3 (therapeutic drugs with low abuse potential). Finally, as a coercive medical alternative to prison, Dodd's legislation expanded eligibility for arrested heroin users under the Narcotic Rehabilitation Act of 1966 and added a provision giving judges the discretion to divert "young marijuana users and addicts" to psychiatric care. In a floor speech, Dodd cited the dramatic increase in juvenile marijuana arrests in Los Angeles County to criticize the punitive approach to illegal drug markets "where the victim and the offender are often the same," and he observed that the generation gap had intensified in middle-class areas "traditionally isolated from routine police surveillance." Dodd concluded that "excessive penalties cannot solve the problem" and that the marijuana laws were "self-defeating" in their practical unenforceability and simultaneously had alienated too many American youth.[25]

Senator Dodd's drug reform agenda played a pivotal role in merging an updated version of the pusher-victim discourse with the prevailing generation gap analysis of the widespread defiance of marijuana laws on college campuses and in affluent suburbs. At the opening session of hearings on his bill, Dodd demanded a tough crackdown on traffickers who victimized American communities but urged leniency for drug users who were not "hardened criminals," a group he defined as "college students and young people of middle and upper economic status." He also distinguished this "alienated," implicitly white, category of youth from the "hardened drug addicts that used to be the main problem in the slums and ghettos of our large cities." Now federal lawmakers faced an extraordinary dilemma: a dropout generation of affluent youth who had listened to the hippies, abandoned the professional career track, rejected "our way of life and our laws," sought to "recruit more youths into the drug culture," and then become even more disaffected when the government cracked down through felony arrests. Rehabilitation and not incarceration, Dodd told a Connecticut audience, was the proper solution for the "new generation of criminals" that joined antiwar protests and engaged in "massive marijuana use." The potent figure of the "drug pusher" helped to resituate these middle-class pot smokers from the criminalized territory of political radicalism to the more sympathetic diagnosis of psychopathology. In hearings, Dodd divided the market into the "professional criminal who viciously pursues the drug trade for profit" and the "victims of this criminal," who succumbed out of "some personal inadequacy or weakness or disenchantment." This latter group of "sick people" needed psychiatric treatment, not criminal convictions. It is important to recognize that the Connecticut senator included inner-city narcotics addicts and nonwhite drug victims within the coercive public health framework, but even this message competed with his hyped warning that "heroin use is growing in the suburbs where it was unknown several years ago."[26]

The Nixon administration initially opposed Dodd's bill out of concern that abandonment of mandatory-minimum penalties would make the president appear soft on drugs, especially regarding "dope peddlers." In July 1969, Nixon sought to burnish his law-and-order agenda with a special message to Congress that labeled drug abuse a "serious national threat" and promised tough action against traffickers, for whom "society has few judgments too severe, few penalties too harsh." The administration's ten-point program revolved around law enforcement priorities of international interdiction, border fortification, and suppression of the domestic market. On the demand side, Nixon's message jumbled together the threat posed by pot smokers and heroin addicts, pledging more resources for treatment and rehabilitation because "psychologically dependent regular users and the physically addicted are genuinely sick people." The crime warriors in the Justice Department assembled the administration's legislative package, the Controlled Dangerous Substances Act, introduced by Republican congressional leaders a few days later. The bill classified marijuana, LSD, and heroin in the same Schedule 1 category of narcotics and dangerous drugs with "no approved medical use." The major change to the prevailing penalty structure was punitive: increasing the punishment for selling LSD from the current five-year maximum to the same sentencing range that governed marijuana and heroin distribution: a mandatory minimum of five to twenty years for the first offense and ten to forty years for the second (double for selling to a minor). The package also created the discretionary category of "possession with intent to sell," which carried the same sentences as distribution. The bill maintained the existing felony penalties for heroin and marijuana possession (two to ten years for the first offense) and moved LSD into this category as well. The administration's proposal did grant judges the leeway to sentence first offenders charged with simple possession to probation, the only concession to the marijuana reform movement.[27]

The federal government's top public health officials, who had lost an internal struggle with the Justice Department over the emphasis on law enforcement over treatment and education, privately and at times publicly disparaged the Nixon legislation. The administration bill consolidated final regulatory authority over both the criminal and medical aspects of federal drug policy with the attorney general, including the scheduling and potential reclassification of all controlled substances. This provision completed a centralization of drug enforcement power that began under the Johnson administration in 1968, when a reorganization plan moved the Bureau of Narcotics from the Treasury Department to the DOJ and transferred the FDA's agency for illicit pharmaceutical control from the Department of Health, Education, and Welfare into a new Bureau of Narcotics and Dangerous Drugs under the attorney general's purview. The psychiatrists and physicians who directed HEW's public health bureaucracies did not believe that the Justice Department had the scientific expertise or political detachment necessary to assess the health hazards of legal or illegal drugs, and they objected with apparent unanimity to mandatory-minimum sentences for use and possession. In the *New York Times*, anonymous administration officials disclosed an internal debate over whether HEW should publicly denounce the Justice Department's proposal, which they labeled a "detrimental" and "regressive" extension of the White House's law-and-order agenda. Dr. Stanley Yolles, the head of the National Institute of Mental Health, ultimately broke ranks by testifying to Congress that the Schedule 1 classification of marijuana as the equivalent of heroin amounted to an "indefensible, established position . . . with total disregard for medical and scientific evidence." Regarding felony possession penalties, Yolles stated: "I know of no clearer instance in which the punishment for an infraction of the law is more harmful than the crime itself." The White House forced Yolles to resign a year later, which the former NIMH director attributed to his refusal to keep quiet about marijuana.[28]

The Nixon administration's legislation generated substantial criticism from liberals in Congress and from public health organizations, although most opponents still operated within the broader consensus framework that law enforcement should target suppliers and that arresting drug users, including marijuana smokers, was the best way to force them into rehabilitation. In Washington, no elected officials or federal bureaucrats questioned the get-tough approach to supply-side interdiction, so the main disagreements revolved around what combination of criminal sanctions, coercive medicalization, and prevention strategies would best deter youth from consuming illegal drugs. In summer 1969, liberal Democrats rallied around a bill sponsored by Ralph Yarborough of Texas, chair of the Senate Committee on Labor and Public Welfare, which maintained marijuana's illegal status but relocated regulatory authority to the FDA. The Yarborough package approached drug abuse primarily as a public health issue, gave HEW scheduling power over controlled substances, and shifted funding to community-based treatment centers and school prevention campaigns. Cosponsor Harold Hughes, a Democrat from Iowa, condemned the administration's support for harsh mandatory-minimum sentences for users and expressed disbelief that "college kids" smoking pot would be in the "same felonious category as the heroin addict." But Hughes, like almost all other congressional Democrats, never specifically addressed racial disproportionality in drug-war enforcement and agreed with Nixon that "pushers" should face "severe penalties." The American Public Health Association endorsed the Yarborough bill and denounced the Nixon administration's "plainly regressive" penalty structure and broader emphasis on law enforcement over sound science. The American Medical Association argued that "drug dependent persons should be treated as patients rather than criminals" and called for HEW to make the ultimate determination about the dangers of controlled substances, in order to "have the penalty in proportion to the public health hazard."[29]

The mainstream media adopted the same basic position of deploring the Nixon administration decision to maintain mandatory-minimum felony sentences for marijuana possession while applauding the crackdown on traffickers and distinguishing white middle-class youth from the inner-city heroin threat. In July, after the DOJ submitted its drug legislation to Congress, the liberal editorial page of the *New York Times* criticized the administration for lumping users of "soft drugs" such as marijuana with urban narcotics addicts who committed street crimes. The *Times* then praised Nixon's supply-side enforcement strategy because "the penalties for those who prey on the innocent by peddling drugs can hardly be too severe." *Life* published a special editorial decrying the administration's unenlightened decision to place "soft" drugs such as marijuana and LSD, favored by "middle-class children," in the same "hard" category as heroin. *Life* imagined, as the prototypical victims of Nixon's policies, the suburban "youngster" serving two to ten years for marijuana experimentation and the college student sent away on a five-year distribution charge for gifting a joint to a roommate—outcomes that almost never happened in the actual, discretionary realm of white middle-class criminal justice. The editorial rejected legalization because of the potential dangers of habitual pot smoking and instead called on Congress to reduce marijuana possession to a misdemeanor. *Ebony* magazine, puncturing the nominally color-blind discourse that shaped the national drug debate, highlighted the racial double standard behind the movement to reduce marijuana penalties because of its sudden popularity among "millions of young whites . . . in the suburbs." "The pot that white folks are smoking today," *Ebony* observed, "is the same old pot black folk and a few white musicians have been smoking for years and that Mexicans have been using for centuries." *Ebony* also endorsed a misdemeanor possession charge so that offenders would not be treated as "hardened criminals," as African American youth caught with marijuana had been for decades.[30]

Advocates of marijuana legalization struggled to break through the bipartisan Washington consensus that criminalization represented the only way to curtail the supply lines and send a message of disapproval to illegal drug users, whether through arrest and incarceration or diversion into psychiatric treatment. Richard Blum, a psychology professor at Stanford University and lead investigator on a major NIMH-funded study of college drug patterns, cautioned public health liberals in Congress that "the social use of marijuana cannot be taken as proof of the illness of the user." In testimony to the Senate Subcommittee on Alcoholism and Narcotics, Blum insisted that "the medical [i.e., disease] model does not fit" the phenomenon of pot smoking by middle-class students because most used the drug safely and moderately, as with alcohol. He also refuted the prevailing "myth that we can be tough on drug dealers without being tough on drug users as well." Blum concluded with a philosophical defense of individual autonomy in a democratic society, in contrast to the overlapping views of law enforcement and public health agencies that "citizens cannot act responsibly, but can only be coerced." Bard Grosse, the drug policy director at the National Student Association, told federal lawmakers that the government had no business arresting Americans who "use drugs very sensibly and sanely," in particular the college students who preferred pot to alcohol as a "relatively mild intoxicant." Grosse advocated marijuana legalization under a regulated system but, in an acknowledgment of political reality, suggested civil fines (as with traffic violations) as an interim step. Aaron Grossman, a young attorney and legalization advocate from Berkeley, denounced Dodd's Juvenile Delinquency Subcommittee for worsening the generation gap by refusing to permit witnesses from outside the public health and law enforcement "Establishment." To impose punitive laws on marijuana users without inviting their participation in the process "is not a participatory democracy, but rather an illusory democracy," Grossman concluded.[31]

The challenge for elected officials, in Congress and in the White House, involved balancing the clear desire to keep white middle-class user-victims out of legal jeopardy with the political imperative of staying tough in the all-out war on crime and drugs. The White House's strategy became clearer in September, when the Subcommittee to Investigate Juvenile Delinquency convened hearings to consider the Dodd bill and the administration's alternative. Internal documents reveal that the Justice Department had decided to accept reduced penalties for marijuana possession, not only because of political pressure but also on the law-and-order grounds that a more realistic approach would result in more prosecutions and convictions. But White House officials wanted Democrats in Congress to appear responsible for taking this "soft" step. In his Senate testimony, Attorney General John Mitchell called for the toughest possible punishment for traffickers but signaled flexibility by conceding that "prison is not the only logical alternative" for experimenting marijuana smokers or mentally ill heroin addicts. Mitchell, who blew smoke from a tobacco pipe throughout his appearance, suggested that Congress might amend the administration bill to provide judges with more discretion to rehabilitate such drug users. John Ingersoll, the director of the Bureau of Narcotics and Dangerous Drugs, labeled drug abuse a staggering epidemic that had "permeated all segments of our society and can now rightfully be considered an American dilemma." He then addressed the controversy over mandatory minimums by distinguishing among three types of criminals: the professional trafficker who deserved the maximum sentence, the dangerous narcotics addict who required compulsory institutionalization, and the young marijuana or LSD experimenter who would likely respond to rehabilitation via arrest and probation. Ingersoll also informed Congress that its revision of the administration's proposal would shape non-federal law enforcement as well by serving as the basis for a new model state law that most legislatures would adopt.[32]

In the fall 1969 hearings, much of the criticism of the Justice Department's bill revolved around its exclusive focus on law enforcement and total neglect to provide funding for the public health constellation of drug treatment, rehabilitation, and education programs. Thomas Dodd told Mitchell and Ingersoll that "the solution will never be found in pure law enforcement" and expressed his opposition to "using punishment for solving mental problems and curing emotional disturbances." When the administration's psychiatrists appeared, NIMH director Stanley Yolles passionately advocated a medical approach to drug abuse that repealed mandatory-minimum penalties as antithetical to the goals of rehabilitation, evaluated marijuana and heroin as "separate and distinct parts of the total problem," and authorized his agency and not the DOJ to determine the legal classifications of controlled substances. Yolles also advanced the generation gap interpretation that smoking pot was "linked with student contempt for the Establishment" and that criminal enforcement had validated the youth critique of "society's hypocrisies." Sidney Cohen, the NIMH's leading addiction specialist, recommended that possession of marijuana and LSD should be misdemeanor offenses, while law enforcement should focus solely on the supply of illegal drugs and leave the rest to the medical profession.[33] Medical associations and pharmaceutical companies also played a major role in negotiations over the Dodd and Nixon bills, defending their interests and profits in the regulatory system by resisting efforts to place prescription drugs with high potential for abuse in the same schedule as any illegal drug. The BNDD estimated that half of amphetamines manufactured by American corporations circulated illicitly, and Thomas Dodd frequently blamed the pharmaceutical industry for marketing products as magical cures, obstructing federal controls that would prevent illegal market diversion, and contributing to the victimization of high school and college students (as well as suburban housewives) who abused "pep bills" and barbiturates.[34]

The seemingly deep divide within the Nixon administration coexisted with a basic consensus that law enforcement should concentrate on stopping the illegal manufacturers and suppliers responsible for the "overwhelming drug menace that confronts our youth," as Dodd summarized the challenge. A few days into the Senate hearings, the White House launched Operation Intercept, a program to search all vehicles entering the United States from Mexico, in order to make marijuana so scarce and expensive that it would be "beyond the reach of our young people." The short-lived border interdiction scheme created massive traffic backups, angered Mexican officials who recognized it was a public relations stunt, and seemed deliberately timed to provide a law-and-order cover for the planned backtrack on mandatory minimums.[35] In mid-October, after extensive negotiations with Senator Dodd's office, the administration formally amended its bill to make first-time possession of the Schedule 1 drugs (including marijuana, LSD, and heroin) a misdemeanor with a maximum penalty of one year in jail. The second possession offense remained a felony, punishable by no more than two years. BNDD director Ingersoll explained that through prosecutorial and judicial discretion, most first-time marijuana offenders would receive probation with the possibility of

TABLE 4.1. Comparison of Select Features of Present Law and Proposed Revisions in S. 3246 (Controlled Dangerous Substances Act of 1969)

Violation	Present law	S. 3246 (Dodd-Nixon bill)
Narcotics Manufacture/ Importation/Distribution	1st offense: 5 to 20 yrs.; 2nd offense: 10 to 40 yrs.	1st offense: up to 12 yrs.; 2nd offense: up to 24 yrs.
Marijuana Manufacture/ Importation/Distribution	Same (classified as narcotic)	1st offense: up to 5 yrs.; 2nd offense: up to 10 yrs.
Manufacture/Distribution by "professional criminal"	No provision	1st offense: 5 to life; 2nd offense: 10 to life
Possession with intent to distribute	No separate offense	Penalties equivalent to distribution/trafficking
Distribution of marijuana on nonprofit basis	No provision	1st offense: up to 1 yr.; 2nd offense: up to 10 yrs.
Distribution to minor	10 to 40 years (no age gap)	Double penalty (3 yr. age gap)
Narcotics and marijuana possession	1st offense: 2 to 10 yrs.; 2nd offense: 5 to 20 yrs.	1st offense: up to 1 yr.; 2nd offense: up to 2 yrs.

Source: *Congressional Record—Senate* (January 28, 1970), 1654.

Note: The provisions in S. 3246, the Dodd-Nixon compromise legislation, are as approved by the Committee on the Judiciary, U.S. Senate, December 16, 1969. This bill, retitled the Controlled Substances Act, ultimately became Title II of the Comprehensive Drug Abuse Prevention and Control Act of 1970. The only major change in the final version doubled the mandatory-minimum sentences for "professional" traffickers, defined as those engaged in a "continuing criminal enterprise" and applicable to narcotics, marijuana, and other Schedule 1 controlled drugs.

an expunged record, including high school and college students who provided small amounts to friends on a nonprofit basis. Thomas Dodd applauded the retreat from rigid minimum penalties for marijuana possession, because "this is what really has got the country upset," although he continued to register disagreement with the BNDD's insistence that "professional" traffickers face mandatory sentences. An anonymous Justice Department official told the *New York Times* that the administration changed course because "the middle-class parent is waking up" and telling the government, "for God's sake, . . . throw the book at the trafficker, but don't lock up my kid."[36]

The merger of the Nixon and Dodd bills established the blueprint for federal and state drug reform in the 1970s: retention of lengthy mandatory-minimum distribution penalties, repeal of felony possession sentences, and continued criminalization of marijuana as the foundation of the national war on drugs (table 4.1). The compromise package offset the possession revisions with "much stiffer penalties for the pusher": five to life for the first offense, ten to life for the second, without possibility of parole and ostensibly applicable only to "professional criminals." Senator Dodd's office considered this a major victory for the public health approach since marijuana "is the major problem in drug abuse" and the flexible, misdemeanor penalty structure for possession would allow courts to rehabilitate such offenders. At Dodd's insistence, the bill also provided discretionary penalties for nonprofessional drug sellers: up to twelve years for heroin "addict-peddlers," up to five years for small-scale marijuana and nonnarcotic dealers, and one year maximum for nonprofit distribution of marijuana (the student/friend scenario). In December 1969, the Judiciary Committee approved the revised bill for consideration by the full Senate. The preamble, composed by Dodd's office, explained that reducing marijuana possession and casual sale to a misdemeanor would help resolve the "serious clash between segments of the youth generation and the government" and the "broader problem of alienation of youth from the general society."[37] This consensus agenda, although rhetorically color-blind, represented above all else a racially motivated policy reform designed to keep white middle-class pot smokers in suburbs and on college campuses out of jail or prison, while maintaining the criminal prohibition of marijuana to protect them from suppliers and, ultimately, from their own choices. And, though rarely acknowledged openly, the Dodd-Nixon compromise effectively codified the discretionary practices of diversion, probation, and coercive rehabilitation that local criminal legal systems had already worked out on the ground for these same white victim-criminals.

Saving the White Suburban Victim-Criminal

As Congress and the Nixon administration debated drug policy reform, public opinion surveys revealed overwhelming sentiment against marijuana legalization and strong support for tough mandatory-minimum sentences for all illegal drug "pushers" and heroin users, with a softening of attitudes only for marijuana possession. In a 1969 poll of California adults, 75 percent said that marijuana laws should either be strictly enforced or made even harsher, and 83 percent endorsed the gateway theory that smoking pot led to harder drugs. That same year, the Gallup organization reported that 84 percent of Americans opposed legalization, with strongest resistance in the South and Midwest, the over-fifty age group, and among women (table 4.2). The only significant support for marijuana legalization came from one-fourth of college students and young adults in their twenties. Gallup estimated that 10 million Americans had at least sampled marijuana, not quite 5 percent of the

TABLE 4.2. Gallup National Survey Questions on Marijuana Legalization (October 1969) and Heroin and Marijuana Penalties (March 1970)

Q. "Do you think the use of marijuana should be made legal, or not?" (October 1969)

Category	Should be legal (%)	Should not (%)
National	12	84
Men	14	81
Women	10	86
21–29 years	26	69
30–49 years	12	83
50 and over	6	91
East	17	78
West	17	80
Midwest	9	87
South	7	89
College	23	72
High school	10	86

Q. "What jail terms, if any, should be given persons 18 years of age and older who are convicted of the following offenses?" (March 1970)

Category (%)	Heroin pushers	Heroin users	Marijuana pushers	Marijuana users
No penalty	—	6	3	15
1 year or less	—	6	6	23
2–5 years	10	27	17	24
6–9 years	3	2	3	1
10+years	43	23	47	14
Life in prison	24	3	16	1
Death penalty	4	—	2	—
Medical help	1	12	Not asked	Not asked
Other	8	2	4	—
Don't know	7	12	2	11

Sources: *The Gallup Poll: Public Opinion, 1935–1971*; Roper Center for Public Opinion Research, Cornell University.

Note: Respondents with "no opinion" (4%) not included in the October 1969 results. Gallup's 1970 survey used the phrase "for a person who sells or 'pushes'" heroin/marijuana and reported the findings as "pushers."

population, including 5 million teenagers and 22 percent of college students, with rates highest among those from upper-income families and participants in campus protests. Respondents who had smoked pot generally disputed claims that it "leads to harder drugs" and caused psychological dependency or medical harm, the effects cited most often by those personally unfamiliar with marijuana. Almost three-fourths of college students and their adult counterparts believed in the existence of the "generation gap," and Gallup noted that "many in the public are offended by the appearance and dress of students, demonstrations, their drug habits and attitudes toward sex." In a follow-up March 1970 poll, Gallup found widespread support nationwide for severe mandatory-minimum sentences for the "pushers" of marijuana and heroin alike. For marijuana possession, 15 percent (the legalization advocates) opposed any punishment, 23 percent called for less than a year in jail, 24 percent advocated a two-to-five-year sentence, and 14 percent endorsed a ten-year minimum. Not surprisingly, younger respondents disproportionately favored legalization or leniency.[38]

The widely publicized suicide of Diane Linkletter, the twenty-year-old daughter of popular entertainer Art Linkletter, reinforced the political positioning of white middle-class youth as the innocent victims of drug pushers and felony laws. In October 1969, Diane jumped out of a sixth-story window of her apartment building in West Hollywood. One of her friends informed the police that she suffered from depression and was distraught about "her identity, her career." Her father told the *Los Angeles Times* that Diane "was murdered by the people who manufacture and sell LSD." He insisted that his daughter, a "loving, happy girl," had jumped while hallucinating on acid. The autopsy revealed no presence of drugs, but Art Linkletter attributed Diane's death to lingering psychosis from a bad LSD trip six months earlier. Within weeks, he announced a crusade "to shock the nation into the realization that this is not happening to other people's children in some poor part of town. It can happen to a well-educated, intelligent girl from a . . . Christian family." The grieving father specifically endorsed the reduction of marijuana possession to a misdemeanor, based on the argument that felony penalties exacerbated the generation gap and discouraged parents from placing their children in drug treatment. In late October, the White House arranged for Linkletter to deliver this message at a bipartisan congressional briefing where he criticized law enforcement policies that were ruining the lives of good kids. "Having marijuana be a felony," Linkletter argued, "is as bad as marijuana being legal." The entertainer urged congressional leaders to fund a drug prevention campaign that would counteract the glamorization of marijuana and LSD by Hollywood and the music industry, a mass culture variation on the pusher-seduction trope. Linkletter, who received more than twenty-five thousand letters and telegrams in the two weeks after launching his mission, also informed American parents that "Diane was not a hippie" and that pressure to take dangerous drugs "not only can happen to their child, but it probably will happen to their child."[39]

This late-1969 forum between Nixon, Linkletter, and the House and Senate leadership, part strategy session and part political theater, illuminated the shared bipartisan agenda as the combined Dodd-administration legislation moved through Congress. President Nixon opened the meeting, which national media outlets covered, by assuring all present that the crisis of drug abuse was "completely above partisan consideration." BNDD director John Ingersoll reported that Operation Intercept had proved a major success in curbing the supply of marijuana and heroin from Mexico (ignoring critics who argued that the temporary shortage had encouraged pot smokers to try harder drugs and would only stimulate domestic cannabis cultivation). He outlined Operation Cooperation, the administration's subsequent plan to work with Mexico to eradicate marijuana crops and fortify the border, and denied that the administration's support for discretionary possession penalties meant going "soft" on marijuana smokers or heroin addicts. Nixon then warned that the drug problem was "moving to the upper middle class" in the affluent suburbs (example: Northern Virginia) and exclaimed that "this educational and rehabilitation thing could be even more important than this whole law enforcement side." Democratic Senator Harold Hughes, a leading public health liberal, agreed that a federal drug education campaign was urgent because "every parent in America is scared to death." Ralph Yarborough of Texas, another outspoken public health advocate, concurred with Linkletter that teenagers unaware of "how dangerous marijuana is" were moving up to LSD and heroin addiction. Nixon promised to go after the traffickers and referenced the recent Gallup poll that the American public strongly opposed marijuana legalization. The Democratic leaders then pledged swift passage of the Dodd-Nixon bill, which the president portrayed as a nonpartisan mission "as important as the defense of the country abroad." The event was "*very* successful," chief of staff H. R. Haldeman recorded in his diary. "Democratic leaders outdid themselves in jumping on the bandwagon."[40]

The pusher-victim and marijuana-gateway themes became central to the Nixon administration's political campaign for drug reform, despite overwhelming evidence from public health research and ethnographic studies that the recreational market simply did not operate along these tracks. In December 1969, at the suggestion of the Democratic congressional leadership, the White House organized a major drug conference for the nation's governors and their wives and children. The agenda, according to the domestic policy staff, involved alerting the public that the drug crisis was "infecting suburban areas" but drawing a clear distinction between the "foolish student" and "casual user," who did not deserve criminal records, and the "pusher" guilty of "using our youth as their prey."[41] In opening remarks, Nixon emphasized again that drugs had spread to the upper-middle-class suburbs and threatened to destroy the spirit of American civilization, an urgent crisis given the ongoing Vietnam War and the broader Cold War struggle against communism. The president then told a story about a churchgoing girl from a "good family" in San Diego who started smoking marijuana in junior high, next tried LSD, and was "now hooked on heroin." He used to believe that "the answer was more penalties," Nixon concluded, but how could the nation put millions of teenagers and college students in prison? Vice President Spiro Agnew—whose own adolescent daughter had recently been arrested for marijuana possession and released in a hushed-up incident—told the gathering that they must resolve the generation gap by "reach[ing] out without caving in." Art Linkletter, the keynote speaker, portrayed his daughter Diane as the "unwitting innocent victim of people who push all kinds of drugs" but then clarified that the real challenge involved combating peer pressure, because marijuana and LSD circulated primarily among people "who are not criminal characters, they are your children and they are my children." They needed help from parents, schools, and therapists, but "no narcotics bureau enforcement and no law can stop them."[42]

The White House's Governors Conference sought to nationalize and standardize drug enforcement policy, especially through the unveiling of the Justice Department's uniform state law, modeled on the Dodd-administration compromise working its way through Congress. Most federal-level drug prosecutions at the time involved border smuggling and domestic trafficking of significant amounts, so while the emphasis on marijuana possession reform in the Washington debate mattered enormously in terms of the political symbolism of white middle-class victimhood, the primary law enforcement impact would come through the adoption of the template by the states. In his remarks, Attorney General John Mitchell asked the governors to ensure their partnership with the federal government through the immediate enactment of the Uniform State Controlled Dangerous Substances Act. Mitchell also assured them that politics played no role in drug enforcement, because congressional leaders of both parties supported the federal law, with its misdemeanor possession penalties and tough mandatory-minimum sentences for traffickers. BNDD director Ingersoll reiterated the need for a "unified federal-state attack" to protect American youth who had been "victimized by the purveyors of narcotics and dangerous drugs and marijuana." He also addressed the governors and their spouses in their role as "concerned parents," stating that the ultimate solution began at home, a demand-side resurrection of family values and communication across the generation gap. Ingersoll concluded with an announcement that the BNDD and National Institute of Mental Health would soon jointly launch a sophisticated prevention campaign to expose the "squareness of hippieness" without resorting to scare tactics. For a sneak preview, the audience watched a film about the secret pro-drug messages coded in psychedelic rock lyrics and another about young people freaking out on acid trips. Unimpressed, the fifteen-year-old daughter of a New England governor told news reporters that she did not think "there is anything wrong with smoking pot."[43]

In January 1970, the full U.S. Senate deliberations on the merged Dodd-Nixon legislation confirmed this Washington consensus that white middle-class youth represented the primary victims of both the organized drug trade and the outdated narcotics enforcement laws. Thomas Dodd introduced S. 3246, the Controlled Dangerous Substances Act, with a plea for urgent action because "every day some of the cream of American youth have their futures and careers ruined because of an arrest for marijuana." While Dodd never explicitly referenced race, nor did any other senator during five days of debate, the Connecticut Democrat defined marijuana smokers as suburban teenagers and college students, "not hardened young criminals," members of "previously drug-free" cultural and economic groups, "victims" of the "criminal drug peddler," and "sick person[s]." Mike Mansfield, the Senate Majority Leader, opened discussion by citing the "shocking" twenty-year sentence for marijuana possession recently imposed on University of Virginia student Frank LaVarre. Thomas Dodd lamented that police arrested a drug user under age twenty-one every five minutes somewhere in America and portrayed his legislation as a "nonpartisan" undertaking for "the parents of our young people." Whether liberal or conservative, Republican or Democrat, every senator who spoke during the extended floor debate supported the repeal of mandatory-minimum sentences for drug possession and nonprofit distribution, with marijuana arrests of high school and college students consistently identified as the main rationale for these reforms. No member of the U.S. Senate raised any objection to severe mandatory-minimum penalties for professional traffickers, and almost all participants advocated the toughest possible punishment for the "pushers" and "peddlers" who victimized American youth: "those who engage in that heinous trade" (Edward Kennedy, D-MA); "those abominable bloodsuckers" (Stephen Young, D-OH); "despicable . . . drug merchants" (Joseph Tydings, D-Maryland); "those who prey upon our young people" (Robert Dole, R-KS).[44]

The bipartisan support for discretionary possession penalties and harsh mandatory sentences for trafficking overshadowed significant disagreement regarding the proper balance between law enforcement, civil liberties, and public health in federal drug policy. Several attempts to amend the omnibus legislation on the Senate floor proved particularly controversial, if ultimately unsuccessful. Senator Sam Ervin (D-NC), an outspoken civil libertarian, led the charge against the Nixon administration's insistence on a "no-knock" provision that authorized federal drug agents with search warrants to break into private homes without warning. Forty senators, including two-thirds of Democrats, opposed this measure, which Ervin labeled a "giant step in the conversion of our free society into a police state." Harold Hughes of Iowa, representing a large faction of public health liberals, offered several amendments designed to shift regulatory authority out of the DOJ. Hughes criticized the bill for empowering the attorney general to make "essentially scientific decisions" and argued that addressing drug addiction and abuse primarily through law enforcement represented the de facto criminalization of disease. Thirty-nine senators backed his attempt to give HEW the ultimate power to determine legal classification of controlled substances in the multitiered scheduling system, a considerable degree of support for a fundamental shift in federal drug authority from the crime warriors to the medical bureaucrats. Thomas Dodd, whose political outlook fused the coercive public health and punitive law-and-order strains of modern liberalism, refused to compromise with these critics from his own party. Instead, he promised to join them in pushing for a subsequent bill to fund rehabilitation, prevention, and educational programs as soon as Congress passed this urgent crime control measure, "so that we can reach the peddlers who are molesting our people, making addicts of them." Hughes reassured his colleague that he would still support the final legislation, because "I abhor the actions of those who are pushing and selling these illegal drugs."[45]

On January 28, the Senate approved the Controlled Dangerous Substances Act by unanimous vote. The final hurdle before passage involved another amendment by Harold Hughes to reduce the maximum first offense penalty for marijuana possession from one year to six months, and for marijuana dealing from five to two years (the Senate bill placed marijuana in the same Schedule 1 category as heroin, with "high potential for abuse"). Hughes considered this proposal the best compromise possible and personally advocated penalties no stricter than those prohibiting possession and sale of alcohol for minors. The Iowa senator argued that marijuana was a "mild drug," safer and less addictive than alcohol, and therefore any extensive jail time even on a misdemeanor conviction risked "destroying the lives of many young people who are experimenting." Thomas Dodd, waving a package of pot in his hand, responded that "marijuana is a personality changer. It is a mind destroyer." Dodd recounted the many parents from Connecticut who had contacted him in desperation, seeking to keep their children out of prison but imploring Congress to stop "this awful problem of marijuana." He agreed that "these youngsters who are smoking this drug are not criminals" but insisted that only a legal deterrent would prevent even greater marijuana use, and "we have to hold the line." In the end, after Dodd's assurance that judges would exercise discretion and not send casual experimenters to jail, Hughes's final amendment failed by a 24–58 vote. Given the punitive drug-war escalation on the near horizon, it is remarkable that no senator during the weeklong debate questioned the first-offense reduction of heroin possession to a misdemeanor or dwelled on the situation of urban narcotics addicts at all, and only a few conservative lawmakers mentioned the problem of street crime even in passing. Senator Joseph Montoya, Democrat of New Mexico, summed up the consensus agenda: "We must sort out the peddlers of hard drugs and crack down on them mercilessly. Yet simultaneously we must segregate them from youngsters who experiment on a one-time basis with marijuana. The latter must be saved. The former must be eliminated."[46]

After the Senate vote, Majority Leader Mike Mansfield emphasized the close cooperation between the Democratic congressional leadership and the Nixon administration in the war on crime, and Thomas Dodd urged the House of Representatives to pass the omnibus drug legislation in equally swift and bipartisan manner. Instead, a barrage of criticism from scientists and medical organizations resurfaced at the initial House hearings, conducted by the Subcommittee on Public Health and Welfare of the Interstate Commerce Committee. In mid-February, more than fifty prominent physicians, psychiatrists, and academic researchers formed the Committee for Effective Drug Abuse Legislation to lobby against the Senate bill for giving the Department of Justice "sweeping power to regulate medical research and practice." While Dodd's Senate subcommittee had refused requests to testify from the main organizers of this coalition, the public health liberals in charge of the House hearings shared and amplified their concerns. Delegates from the Committee for Effective Drug Abuse Legislation denounced the Dodd-Nixon bill for granting the attorney general the final authority to classify controlled substances and accused their colleagues in HEW of caving in to White House pressure by endorsing this approach, however reluctantly. They also strongly disapproved of the absence of funding for treatment and prevention and opposed provisions that gave the Justice Department new authority over legal pharmaceuticals to prevent illicit diversion. The coalition specifically rejected as unscientific the blanket prohibition of marijuana in Schedule 1, alongside heroin and LSD as a dangerous substance with no known medical benefits, while very hazardous drugs such as amphetamines and barbiturates remained in the low-abuse Schedule 3 category. Dr. Daniel Freedman, a psychiatrist and leader of the group, accused the administration-supported bill of exploiting parental panic about marijuana to politicize public health and overemphasize law enforcement in the propagandistic legacy of former FBN commissioner Harry Anslinger.[47]

As in the Senate debate, the initial House hearings in February 1970 disproportionately focused on the two-sided predicament of American youth who allegedly endangered their health by smoking marijuana and then faced unfair punishment when caught breaking the law. The Subcommittee on Public Health and Welfare hearings also extensively addressed the illegal diversion of amphetamines and barbiturates, because a jurisdictional dispute had assigned primary responsibility for the marijuana and narcotics sections of the Senate bill to the House Ways and Means Committee. Representative Charles Wilson, a Democrat from suburban Los Angeles, endorsed the public health approach of misdemeanor rehabilitation and observed that "the kids at the suburban high school . . . may have more serious drug habits than the individual in the inner city slum school." Rep. Lionel Van Deerlin, a Democrat from the San Diego suburbs, expressed his dismay at "watching good kids" in his district suspended from school because the federal government seemed unable to stop the traffickers, including the illicit diversion of millions of amphetamines and barbiturates produced by American pharmaceutical companies. Rep. Richard Hanna, another suburban LA Democrat, rejected the Nixon administration's prioritization of law enforcement and argued that youth consumption of marijuana for mood-altering purposes was really no different from their parents' fondness for alcohol and tranquilizers. BNDD director John Ingersoll, who faced sharp questioning about overcriminalization, portrayed young pot smokers as "the victim of the trafficker" and rejected an analogy to alcohol Prohibition by arguing that only by maintaining marijuana's illegal status could the government deter and rehabilitate the "abuser." The ACLU, which had not received an invitation to testify before the Senate, stated its opposition to the criminalization of marijuana use and possession, while evading the question of sale, and argued that overzealous law enforcement had ruined the lives and careers of students and hippies in particular.[48]

In April 1970, the House's Select Committee on Crime produced a major marijuana report that endorsed misdemeanor possession penalties through the law-and-order rationale that a less punitive and more realistic approach would actually increase conviction rates. The study, based on hearings in six cities, opened with the declaration that marijuana stood at the center of the national drug crisis and "plays a major role in leading increasing numbers of young Americans into tragic drug dependence and into lives of crime and degradation." The Select Committee on Crime denounced legalization advocates for recklessly encouraging youth experimentation and highlighted gateway stories of pot smokers who moved on to LSD, speed, and heroin because of their immersion in the psychedelic subculture. In its most original contribution to the debate, the Select Committee on Crime labeled as "fable and fiction" the widespread belief that thousands of American youth were serving time for marijuana possession. Instead, the report accurately described the prevalent use of probation, suspended sentences, and other diversionary tactics by courts faced with white middle-class defendants (see chapter 3). "When the drug problem was a Negro problem, everyone went to jail," explained a BNDD agent in Boston, but "we have seen a different standard of justice being applied" since marijuana arrived on the college campuses and in the upscale suburbs. A Boston judge confirmed that his circuit never incarcerated high school or college students for possession violations and added that revising the law to reflect reality would undermine the proponents of marijuana legalization. The Select Committee on Crime recommended misdemeanor possession reform as the most effective way to discourage more young people from smoking pot, because judges would be less likely to evade the law and more likely to sentence and rehabilitate offenders through probation. "Uneven enforcement of justice is unfair justice," the report concluded. "Savagely repressive and punitive laws cannot be defended as a solution to the marijuana problem."[49]

The middle-class marijuana phenomenon continued to dominate the second round of hearings in the House, with sustained criticism of the law enforcement approach to public health and a robust debate over whether the government had provided a compelling rationale for the continued criminalization of pot smoking by young Americans. In July, Chairman Wilbur Mills (D-AR) convened the House Ways and Means Committee to consider the Dodd-Nixon bill passed by the Senate. Attorney General John Mitchell warned that "the pusher" threatened the suburbs and ghettos alike, defined the American drug epidemic as pot smoking and pill popping by millions of youth, and said nothing at all about heroin addiction. The administration's public health officials then engaged in a meandering discussion with committee members who asked why pot smokers should be arrested at all, if marijuana was not clearly more harmful than alcohol or cigarettes and did not trigger a progression to heroin. Dr. Roger Egeberg, assistant secretary of HEW, ultimately offered the rationale that liquor and tobacco were culturally accepted drugs, whereas marijuana caused a "tragedy to all of society" by enabling youth to evade reality and digress from the career path. The academic researchers who formed the Committee for Effective Drug Abuse Legislation continued their assault on the "regressive" shift of public health authority to the Justice Department, and the group also recommended a decriminalization approach that would regulate marijuana alongside alcohol and make the maximum possession penalty a small civil fine. The ACLU, in a prescient analysis, cautioned that federal law enforcement officials might exploit the "no-knock" and "professional criminal" provisions to crack down on "ordinary marijuana offenses" and small-scale street dealers, not just major traffickers. The National Congress of Parents and Teachers also denounced the legislation for criminalizing mental health and called for judicial discretion for all drug users and sellers, not just first offenders.[50]

The House of Representatives made several significant revisions to the administration-supported Senate legislation in response to the concerns of public health liberals and medical organizations, although the bipartisan consensus around the penalty structure remained intact. In September, the House opened debate on the Comprehensive Drug Abuse Prevention and Control Act, the retitled and expanded bill (supported by the leadership of both parties) that emerged from negotiations between the two committees that held jurisdiction. H.R. 18583 included a new section that provided funding for education, treatment, and rehabilitation programs administered by HEW, state and local governments, and community health centers. The House bill also gave the HEW secretary an effective veto if the Justice Department sought to shift the scheduling of a controlled substance without a compelling scientific basis—addressing a major concern of both the public health community and the pharmaceutical lobby. The House additionally established a presidentially appointed Commission on Marihuana to examine the medical research and evaluate whether Congress should further revise criminal sanctions for the drug. To confirm its law-and-order credentials, the House doubled the Senate's mandatory-minimum penalties for professional traffickers involved in a "continuing criminal enterprise" (ten to life for a first conviction, twenty to life subsequently). During floor debate, a group of liberal Democrats unsuccessfully sought to amend this provision by eliminating the minimum sentencing requirement and excluding marijuana and LSD from its reach, and they likewise failed to remove "no-knock" authority for federal drug agents. Despite these disagreements, Republicans and Democrats joined together in calling for tough punishment for "the pushers" and medical treatment for their youthful targets, with Diane Linkletter cited as the representative victim of the traffickers and Frank LaVarre as the archetypal victim of the misguided marijuana laws. The House overwhelmingly approved the omnibus legislation, with only six Democrats opposed.[51]

On October 14, the House and Senate each passed the final version of the Comprehensive Drug Abuse Prevention and Control Act of 1970, which removed the federal mandatory-minimum penalties for drug possession established almost two decades earlier. Title II, the Controlled Substances Act, kept marijuana in the most dangerous Schedule 1 category and maintained the DOJ's primary authority over the five-part scheduling system. Rather than a situation where liberals advocated rehabilitation and conservatives demanded law and order, almost all members of Congress supported harsher punishments for traffickers and the overriding priority of protecting young pot smokers from both prison and the recreational market. Public health liberals did factionalize over the validity of coercive rehabilitation through criminal sanctions, but the arrest-and-divert philosophy remained ascendant. During the reconciliation process, a bipartisan Senate coalition attempted a major expansion of the education, prevention, and treatment funding added by the House. The group, led by Harold Hughes (D-IA) and Jacob Javits (R-NY), sought to ensure that "criminal laws be used sparingly," mainly for large traffickers, because "drug dependence is properly regarded as an illness or disease." The DOJ opposed this amendment as potentially jeopardizing all possession prosecutions, and Thomas Dodd promised that Congress would soon revisit

FIGURE 4.3. President Richard Nixon at the October 27 signing of the Comprehensive Drug Abuse Prevention and Control Act of 1970. Attorney General John Mitchell, holding the bill at right, championed its toughening of mandatory-minimum penalties for traffickers. Other Nixon advisors and appointees look on; the congressional Democrats who largely crafted the bipartisan legislation and succeeded in reducing the possession penalty to a misdemeanor are absent. (AP Photo.)

public health funding, but "the country wants us to move first against the peddlers and the pushers." Dodd also lamented the House's refusal in conference to move amphetamines and tranquilizers into a more restrictive control schedule, and he angrily denounced pharmaceutical companies as "white collar drug peddlers."[52] On October 27, Richard Nixon signed the law in a ceremony held at the Bureau of Narcotics and Dangerous Drugs, with 13 pounds of heroin and 250 pounds of marijuana on display (fig. 4.3). The president characterized the legislation as an urgent component of the war on crime and a national mission to "save the lives of hundreds of thousands of young people who otherwise would become hooked on drugs and be physically, mentally, and morally destroyed."[53]

During the two-year debate over federal drug reform, the American political system produced a particular white middle-class victim—suburban teenagers and college students—as the foundation of a racial state-building project that intensified supply-side interdiction alongside an arrest-and-rehabilitate approach to users/abusers/addicts, a constantly conflated category. Government officials and political leaders in both parties consistently portrayed white middle-class youth who smoked marijuana as the primary victims of traffickers, the sympathetic victims of excessive criminal sanctions, and the "sick" and disturbed victims of drug dependency and psychiatric illness. Only rarely did political discourse in Washington depict suburban and campus pot smokers as they saw themselves: as normal adolescents and young adults in an era of generational conflict, as citizens responsible for their own choices, and as consumers in a criminalized market that otherwise did not differ much from the legal products of alcohol and prescription medication. During 1969–70, no government official or member of Congress publicly endorsed marijuana legalization—the position supported by the ACLU (partially), a few dissident drug experts, at least 12 percent of the American public, and around one-fourth of college students. The Nixon administration and a broad bipartisan majority in Congress advocated a law enforcement model that criminalized drug possession and codified discretion for prosecutors and judges to coerce deserving defendants into rehabilitation. "The penalties must have enough teeth in them," Attorney General Mitchell told Congress, "to have a meaningful deterrent effect." Public health liberals did prioritize community-based treatment programs, speak empathetically about heroin users, and lament the criminalization of addiction. A sizable faction failed to achieve a major regulatory shift from the DOJ to federal medical agencies. But they also incorporated marijuana "dependence" and "abuse" into the disease model, welcomed harsh penalties for illegal drug suppliers, and almost all voted for the law in the end.[54]

Marijuana, Heroin, and the War on Drugs

In March 1970, the Nixon administration kicked off a national prevention campaign to alert white middle-class Americans that illegal drug abuse (never "use") among youth was not "only a ghetto problem." The demand-side initiative responded to pressure from Democrats in Congress for more public health programs and revolved around drug abuse education in public schools and the mass media. Although the campaign mainly targeted the recreational marijuana subculture in the suburbs, the president announced the initiative by reciting the tragic stories of two twelve-year-old heroin addicts in New York City.[55] In fact, NIMH scientists did argue that heroin should be the main focus of treatment and rehabilitation, but the White House policy staff contended that the marijuana epidemic "plaguing the homes of middle America . . . should not be ignored, on political or ethical grounds." Nixon's cautionary tale of preadolescent narcotics addiction in the ghetto served two political purposes at once: reassuring public health advocates that the administration did care about nonwhite drug victims and treatment, and seeking to inflame the worst-case-scenario fears of white suburban parents that experimenting with marijuana opened the gateway to heroin overdose. For the launch, the White House worked with the Advertising Council on a national public service campaign, "Why Do You Think They Call It Dope?" that included don't-take-drugs messages from professional athletes and warnings that heroin had spread (yet again) to the suburbs. The administration also summoned network executives to Washington and requested television programming to generate alarm among middle-class parents who still thought that drug abuse mainly happened in the ghettos and hippie enclaves, resulting in specials such as ABC's "Crisis in Suburbia: The Hooked Generation." In a critical assessment, the Ford Foundation questioned the initiative's strategy of grouping marijuana and heroin into a single threat and the "untested assumption that television can 'unsell' drugs," concluding that the real audience was not teenagers but parents and civic groups.[56]

The second major component of the administration's antidrug abuse program combined the resources of NIMH and the Office of Education in an effort to modernize the nation's school-based prevention curriculum. These materials were much less sensationalistic, since public health experts rather than Hollywood and the White House political staff designed them. The target audience also consisted of students with a well-documented skepticism about scare-tactic messaging, rather than parents and voters to be mobilized as foot soldiers in a national crusade. The initiative provided block grant funding for states to train teachers, guidance counselors, and community leaders in the latest prevention techniques. The NIMH also circulated two new drug awareness films for the classroom: *Here's Help* (featuring rehab programs) and *A Day in the Death of Donny B.* (a heroin saga for "inner-city audiences"). The centerpiece of the educational campaign was a new federal resource book that summarized the latest scientific and medical research on various drugs, interspersed—at the DOJ's insistence—with periodic calls for youth to help authorities arrest the suppliers and be alert for the "pusher" who pressured pot smokers to sample more dangerous substances. The introduction attributed the crisis of drug abuse to affluence, easy access, psychological disorders, pro-drug "proselytizers," and "dissatisfied or disillusioned" youth "who have lost faith in the prevailing social system." The publication explained that gateway fears were overblown, and only "a few" youth in the suburbs took heroin, but marijuana was not harmless because "chronic users become psychologically dependent" and unmotivated toward work and life. If faced with demands by children and students that marijuana be legalized, parents and teachers should respond that alcohol was also dangerous and it would be inadvisable to add another "mind-altering chemical to our existing problem." They also should emphasize that a small fraction of "potheads" (regular stoners) risked progression to LSD, speed, and occasionally heroin through immersion in the "drug culture."[57]

The Bureau of Narcotics and Dangerous Drugs responded by commissioning an educational comic book, *Teen-Age Booby Trap* (1970), to counter the "misleading material" entering the drug prevention curriculum through the efforts of public health officials, including NIMH psychiatrists. The law enforcement agency promised a sophisticated resource that the "hip generation . . . will dig," because young Americans deserved "honest and intelligent answers" about illegal drugs. Instead, the BNDD's contribution recycled histrionic, gendered tropes of innocent white victims falling prey to the sinister forces of narcotics addiction, starting with the cover image of two blonde teenagers smoking pot and reaching for the needle (fig. 4.4). The inside panels include a strung-out hippie chick in Central Park, symbolizing the suburban "runaway" crisis; another female hippie smoking marijuana with shady older men; a demonic phantom hovering over a young woman on a bad acid trip; and a heroin octopus ensnaring yet another hooked blonde female. While the comic book did acknowledge that a majority of marijuana users first "turned on" among friends, the most arresting sequence shows a skeleton "dope pusher" jabbing a hypodermic needle into a young pot smoker, with the warning "'Pot' Opens the Door!" The BNDD's production company also created *What If They Call Me "Chicken"?* for the middle-school curriculum. In this cautionary tale about "what might happen anywhere," a white middle-class boy named Timmy faces ridicule from a group of thirteen-year-olds when he declines to smoke marijuana after a game of pickup basketball. After Timmy tells his family, the father explains that "marijuana is a drug to stay away from!" because teenagers who experiment just to be popular often "get hooked," and some end up hospitalized or dead after trying LSD. Then Timmy's older brother, a handsome college baseball player, recalls how the pot-smoking "creeps" who mocked him as a "chicken" back in high school were now hooked on hard drugs and either unemployed burnouts or incarcerated for addiction-fueled street crime.[58]

Although it does not create a physical addiction, marijuana can bring about psychological dependence. In large doses, it offers the same dangers associated with the other hallucinogens. Marijuana serves no useful purpose and has no known medical value.
"POT OPENS THE DOOR!"
The use of one drug all too often leads to experimentation with another and it is rare indeed to find a user of hard narcotics who did not start out on marijuana. Dope pushers have been known to supply hard narcotics free to their victims until they were hooked, but the large majority of narcotics users are first "turned on" by so-called "friends" who are part of "the wrong crowd." It is the mistaken belief that addiction won't happen to them that so many young people move on from marijuana to heroin or other hard narcotics.

FIGURE 4.4. The Bureau of Narcotics and Dangerous Drugs released *Teen-Age Booby Trap* in 1970 to reinforce the Nixon White House's national prevention campaign message that white suburban youth who smoked marijuana were at serious risk of progressing to heroin addiction. The comic book, designed for the drug awareness curriculum, depicted evil older male pushers and demonic narcotics monsters destroying the lives of young white females. This image includes the cover and an inside page of a demon waiting to jab a marijuana smoker with a heroin needle.

The politics of heroin, which played a relatively minor role in the enforcement-oriented debate over the Comprehensive Drug Abuse Prevention and Control Act of 1970, moved back to the center of national discourse in direct relationship to the perception that narcotics addiction was spreading from the ghetto to the suburbs once again. Two weeks before President Nixon signed the omnibus legislation, public health liberals on the Senate Committee on Labor and Public Welfare advanced a more comprehensive federal blueprint to centralize research, education, treatment, and rehabilitation programs in a proposed National Institute for the Prevention and Control of Drug Abuse and Drug Dependence. The report accompanying the bill estimated that 15 million Americans had now smoked marijuana, including almost half of college students, while between 150,000 and 250,000 heroin addicts also lived in the United States. "Whereas formally it [heroin] was only a ghetto drug," the committee warned, "it has been increasingly used in suburban areas and in our colleges and universities."[59] Media outlets in major metropolitan regions also highlighted the "spread" of heroin addiction to the affluent white suburbs, from Los Angeles to metropolitan New York City, where "sons and daughters of the rich and the middle class . . . take their fixes in expensive apartments and suburban homes instead of slum doorways." In a late 1969 exposé, the *Boston Globe* reported that "middle class America's smug assumption that the drug problem is confined to the inner city has been smashed." The series depicted heroin's invasion of upscale suburbs and alleged, implausibly, that "professional pushers have been distributing marijuana that has been laced with opiates—thus getting their customers 'hooked.'" During 1970–71, the *Globe* kept sensationalizing this new narcotics crisis with stories such as "Use of Heroin Is Spreading into Middle Class Suburbia," which repeated dubious BNDD claims that "psychological dependency" on marijuana led thousands of white high school and college students to experiment with and then become addicted to heroin.[60]

The resurrection of the marijuana-to-heroin gateway scourge built on the long history of racial anxiety about ghetto narcotics invading the suburbs as well as specific alarm about the "runaway" white daughter epidemic intensified by the 1967 Summer of Love (see chapter 2). Statistical patterns mattered far less than anecdotal cautionary tales in this political and cultural discourse as, in a very real sense, it only took a few white suburban heroin users to create a full-blown "epidemic" that demanded an urgent response. One oft-cited study of the Haight-Ashbury district of San Francisco found that only 8 of 413 white hippies who smoked marijuana and took LSD also became "heroin abusers" in the late 1960s—but refracted through the media-political hype of smack once again spreading to white America, eight was more than enough. "The kids we're picking up for heroin this year are the ones we were busting last year for marijuana and LSD," a California narcotics agent claimed in the *Los Angeles Times*. "They are the white middle-class kids." Anti-drug networks circulated horror stories such as Percy Pilon, a white all-American high school sports star who allegedly killed himself at age eighteen because "pushers" hooked him on marijuana, LSD, and heroin.[61] Careful studies later revealed that the modest number of white suburban heroin users in the late 1960s and early 1970s clustered in affluent inner-ring areas adjacent to bohemian enclaves and purposefully sought out their connections, often through immersion in multidrug environments. A majority were occasional (or former) heroin consumers, not "junkie" addicts, even though political discourse almost never made any distinction. "The term addict should be reserved for the compulsive drug user," one public health report emphasized. For most heavy heroin users, the so-called gateway generally involved illicit pharmaceuticals, especially speed (amphetamine), and sometimes prescription barbiturates for females. A few suburban youth obtained heroin directly from urban suppliers, but most acquired it through small networks closer to home. None blamed "the pushers" for their situation.[62]

The American political system proved incapable or unwilling to grapple with the considerable evidence that synthetic drugs produced by pharmaceutical corporations, circulating both licitly and illicitly, facilitated white middle-class progression to heroin far more than the group-oriented leisure activity of smoking marijuana. During the late 1960s and early 1970s, multiple House and Senate committees held hearings about the suburban drug crisis featuring white narcotics "addicts" with criminal records (law enforcement agencies brought them to congressional attention). They did not testify to the marijuana-gateway or evil-pusher scenarios as anticipated. "The medical profession . . . are the only legal pushers in America," the anonymous David X informed the House Committee on Crime. The government's "whole drug program is a joke"—as unwinnable as Vietnam. Pressed about the heroin gateway, he responded that "all marijuana laws are ridiculous" and that methamphetamine most often paved the way by making white youth accustomed to hypodermic needles. David X recommended legalization of heroin and insisted that "physical addiction is very overemphasized" (a later federal study found that only one-fifth of heroin users were "addicts"). At the same hearing, Jane K insisted that marijuana had nothing to do with "hard narcotics" and said that taking Demerol (a prescription painkiller) and diet supplements (stimulants widely prescribed to white females) had prepared her "when somebody turned me on to heroin." In another investigation of heroin in suburbia, "Lucy" also named diet pill stimulants as the start of her downfall from debutante parties to cold-turkey withdrawal in jail. She described encountering many different illegal substances in the hippie underground community of Georgetown and Dupont Circle. When asked about pushers, she replied that "I never had to go to the ghetto myself to get drugs," because dealers "sit by your telephone and wait for the people to come to you." Lucy flatly rejected the committee's theory that marijuana led to heroin and said that she took the latter as a painkiller to treat depression.[63]

As rates of heroin use increased among white suburban youth, the pleas of their parents received disproportionate attention from politicians and the media, and this grassroots pressure further reinforced the bipartisan commitment in Washington for a public health approach toward narcotics addiction.

In the late 1960s and early 1970s, the most visibly sympathetic heroin addicts in America (except, for a brief period, Vietnam veterans) lived in the suburbs and towns surrounding New York City. In Fairfield County, Connecticut, organized groups of white parents demanded government funding for narcotics treatment centers in their communities and angrily condemned the incarceration of their addicted children. One mother from the Bridgeport area begged for mercy after a judge sentenced both her sons to jail for heroin possession, asking, "Is that any way to treat an addict?" "The guilty ones are the pushers," another mother declared, whereas her son was sick and needed to be in a hospital rather than prison.[64] In New York, Governor Rockefeller chose Scarsdale for a major 1970 speech demanding more federal action against heroin pushers, in order to emphasize that the crisis affected the affluent suburbs as well as the inner city. The political focus on white suburban addicts angered urban Black groups such as Mothers Against Drugs, since elected officials had largely ignored their demands to fund more treatment facilities in Harlem and arrest the street dealers (not least because of extensive NYPD drug corruption). "You know the best way to deal with the dope problem?" one Harlem activist lamented: "Get as many white kids on it as possible!" Mothers Against Drugs, to draw attention to its 1970 protest march on Washington, even formed a tentative alliance of sorts with the upper-middle-class parents of heroin addicts from Bergen County, New Jersey. The white Bergen mothers, who implored state and federal officials to build a rehabilitation center in their wealthy county, told Congress that "we have it just as badly" as New York City and categorized heroin addiction as "a mental health problem. It is not a criminal problem."[65]

In the national debate, almost every political claim about heroin depended on invalid statistics and hyperbolic discourse, including the extent of the suburban problem, the degree of crime blamed on junkies, the deaths attributed to overdose, and the presumption that all users were hopeless addicts. In March 1970, a suburban New York coalition called March on Drugs launched a prevention campaign with dramatic warnings about the marijuana-to-heroin gateway at an event featuring the preteen, nonwhite Harlem addicts highlighted in Nixon's recent speech. March on Drugs also organized a demonstration in Central Park to raise awareness that "this is a regional problem" and "drugs are rampant in the suburbs." After Governor Rockefeller addressed the mostly white crowd, Black activists interrupted proceedings and denounced the March on Drugs coalition for ignoring the crisis in Harlem until the problem "moved into the white suburbs."[66] The Nixon administration and Congress habitually generalized about national trends based on the heroin politics of New York, where Rockefeller's staff believed that equating the "epidemic" in the city and the suburbs made for "first class public relations." This belied the official data on heroin overdoses, which identified 3,435 "direct deaths due to drug abuse" in New York City and 367 in the rest of the state between 1969 and 1972. But subsequent studies dismantled this "'heroin overdose' myth," which involved rampant misclassification by coroners and failure to acknowledge that most fatalities involved a combination reaction with alcohol or barbiturates.[67] The Rockefeller administration also deliberately hyped and/or ineptly confused the data on narcotics addiction and crime rates, by assuming that all heroin users were inevitably everyday addicts (a large majority were not) who stole everything they spent on the drug and committed runaway street crimes (rather than nonviolent property crimes primarily restricted to poor urban areas). Time after time, from law-and-order conservatives to public health liberals, the consensus political conversation in Washington reproduced these same distortions.[68]

In January 1971, the House Select Committee on Crime released a major report on heroin, a follow-up to its law-and-order endorsement of marijuana possession reform the previous April. Claude Pepper, a liberal Democrat from Florida, chaired the special committee and previewed the findings by alerting Congress that the "menace is no longer confined to the ghetto areas and has spread by geometric progression into the suburbs of every metropolitan area in our country." The House report did locate heroin addiction as primarily an inner-city crisis, "epidemic in our urban slums among economically deprived young people," but also afflicting Americans "at every level of our society." Half of the estimated two hundred thousand heroin addicts in the United States lived in New York, with the highest concentration among poor, young, unemployed African American or Latino males. In line with the liberal public health approach to crime control, the Pepper committee identified racial inequality, psychological alienation, and the lack of jobs as the root causes of urban narcotics addiction and the property crime necessary to support the habit. As the prototypical victim of the heroin crisis, the report offered an unmarried Black mother from the South Bronx who lived in fear, "trapped by poverty and lack of opportunity in an area infested with drug addicts." The Select Committee on Crime called for increased interdiction in supplier nations, at the border, and against street-level pushers but also stated definitively that law enforcement alone could not solve the problem. The report argued that incarceration of addicts was self-defeating, endorsed methadone maintenance programs and compulsory hospitalization as alternative anti-crime strategies, and demanded a vast increase in federal funding for community-based treatment centers. The Pepper committee strongly criticized the Nixon administration for its excessive reliance on law enforcement and specifically rebuked NIMH for making marijuana research and prevention (the white middle-class drug problem) a higher priority than the plight of heroin addicts and inner-city victims.[69]

For the Nixon administration, the entanglement of marijuana and heroin as the two greatest threats in the American drug crisis enlisted a broad range of political interests into the same policy campaign and merged law enforcement and public health into a single mission. In early 1971, the White House asked the domestic policy staff to prepare a memo on drug-related crime and identify the most effective law-and-order posture for the administration to adopt. The response endorsed funding for methadone and rehabilitation centers as an urban crime control strategy and observed that in "Middle America" as well, "treatment and counseling, not punishment, is what most parents want for their children." These recommendations aligned closely with the views of liberal Democrats in Congress, including the recent heroin report by the House Select Committee on Crime and the relentless calls for a "massive federal approach" to control both drug abuse and addiction-fueled street crime by Harold Hughes and his allies on the Senate Committee on Labor and Public Welfare.[70] In March, at a White House drug conference for religious leaders, Nixon conveyed his "anger with the pushers, but not with the addicts," and stated that the drug crisis had "spread to the people in the upper middle class. You don't have to go to Harlem to find it. You find it in Beverly Hills and you find it in Evanston, . . . in the so-called best families." Later that spring, Democrats in the just-formed Congressional Black Caucus asked Nixon to declare drug abuse a "major national crisis," increase funding for urban treatment centers and methadone programs, and crack down on suppliers. The White House endorsed each request, pointed out that current federal spending on public health exceeded law enforcement, and pledged a "complete attack on all fronts against criminal drug trafficking." The federal drug-war budget had more than tripled between 1969 and 1971, but the share dedicated to public health had dropped from two-thirds to just over half since Nixon took office, a trend that the bipartisan commitment to crime control through coercive rehabilitation would soon reverse.[71]

In summer 1971, the Nixon administration formally declared war on "drug abuse" in a political campaign that deliberately conflated the dangers of marijuana and heroin, hyped the pusher and gateway mythologies, and baselessly claimed that narcotics-fueled crime equally threatened low-income ghettos and middle-class suburbs. While public health and law enforcement officials considered heroin the most hazardous drug, the market was localized in nonwhite areas of a few large cities, whereas more than one hundred times as many Americans smoked pot. Heroin arrests also had declined to only one-fourth of total drug arrests by 1971, compared to 46 percent for marijuana.[72] For the administration, this meant that mobilizing public support for a national crusade against drugs depended on the extent to which suburban residents feared urban crime, white middle-class parents linked heroin addiction to recreational marijuana use, and everyone could be convinced that public health solutions for deserving victims would accompany the crackdown on suppliers. Inside the White House, the steering group planning the rollout of Nixon's drug war envisioned a prominent interdiction role for the military and strategized how best to play up the "enforcement pressure . . . against pushers, peddlers." They also schemed to depict heroin addiction as a nationwide "pandemic," based on the invalid assertion that "it directly afflicts the educated, middle-class, churchgoing stereotype of the average American just as it afflicts the black, poverty-stricken ghetto-dweller." (Abuse of legal pharmaceuticals actually did affect white Americans far more than the "ghetto-dweller," but the administration was not interested in fighting that drug war). Nixon personally attended one of the final strategy sessions and laid out his political imperatives: hit the pushers hard, highlight the pot-to-heroin gateway, and recognize that "the line has to be drawn somewhere, and he is drawing it at marijuana." At a June 1 press conference, the president answered a heroin question by denouncing marijuana legalization, which would "simply encourage more and more of our young people to start down the long dismal road that leads to hard drugs."[73]

Richard Nixon declared a "new, all-out offensive" against "public enemy number one," the national crisis of drug abuse, on June 17, 1971. The announcement followed a meeting with congressional leaders, and the president repeatedly emphasized the bipartisan consensus behind this latest escalation of the federal war on drugs. He asked Congress to nearly double the current federal drug budget, with a majority for new public health programs as liberals and community-based advocates had long demanded. To coordinate prevention and treatment policy, Nixon created a Special Action Office for Drug Abuse Prevention in the White House, under the supervision of Dr. Jerome Jaffe, a psychiatrist and pioneering methadone researcher. In a special message to Congress on the "national emergency," the president began by citing the deaths of more than one thousand heroin addicts in New York City during the previous year, but he defined the problem as "universal." Nixon promised that the federal government would address the demand side through prevention and rehabilitation programs, while intensifying law enforcement to "further tighten the noose around the necks of drug peddlers, and thereby loosen the noose around the necks of drug users." Narcotics addicts committed crimes to support their habits, and in their desperation for money they also initiated "other people—young people—on drugs." Nixon then connected marijuana to the heroin crisis by lamenting the misconceptions of "turned on" youth who believed that addiction is "something that happens to other people" and did not realize that they are "too often [on] a one-way street beginning with 'innocent' experimentation and ending in death." The president asked for "compassion" for these "victims of narcotics and dangerous drugs," this threat that "comes quietly into homes and destroys children," overwhelming young people full of "confusion and disillusion and despair." This campaign constituted the domestic equivalent of the Vietnam War, the president concluded, a struggle that could be won if the American people united behind the cause.[74]

Congress unanimously approved the legislation set in motion by Nixon's declaration of war, the Drug Abuse Office and Treatment Act of 1972. After the White House requested statutory authority for its new Office for Drug Abuse Prevention, liberals in the Senate seized the opportunity to incorporate public health measures that Democratic critic Harold Hughes had originally sought to insert in the 1970 law enforcement package. The additions included formation of the National Institute on Drug Abuse (NIDA), funding for community-based prevention and treatment programs, and a requirement that the president formulate an annual "comprehensive, coordinated long-term federal strategy" to combat drug trafficking and abuse. The hearings by the Senate Committee on Labor and Public Welfare focused primarily on heroin and identified three distinct categories of addicts to be rehabilitated: inner-city victims who allegedly committed $8 billion in crime each year (a wild exaggeration), suburban and college youth swept up in the narcotics crisis, and soldiers shooting up in Vietnam. Cracks occasionally appeared in the rhetoric of bipartisan cooperation, such as criticism by Senator Abraham Ribicoff (D-CT) that Nixon had nothing to say about the root causes of heroin addiction and that the administration's war on drugs "has been disorganized, fragmented, and weak." While Senator Hughes expressed gratitude that the administration finally recognized the full value of public health, he stated pointedly that "in the enlightened view, drug abuse or dependence is a sickness, not a crime." But like the administration, public health liberals who championed medicalization of the drug crisis greatly inflated the extent of addiction-fueled crime, compromising their critique of the arrest-first approach. They also ignored dissenting experts such as psychiatrist Norman Zinberg, who rejected the law enforcement and disease models in favor of more measured policies and less militaristic rhetoric, arguing that addicts represented a fairly small portion of illegal drug users, even of heroin, and that social consumers predominated.[75]

In March 1972, President Nixon signed the Drug Abuse Office and Treatment Act and once again celebrated the bipartisan commitment to "mount a frontal assault on our number one public enemy." His remarks portrayed law enforcement and public health as intertwined components of a comprehensive and balanced approach "to wipe out drug abuse in America." Nixon called for tough punishment against "pushers" but rehabilitation for "the pusher's victims," including heroin addicts who "often victimize others" by committing crimes to support their habits. At least in the area of drug policy, the Republican president sounded little different from a frequent Democratic antagonist, Senator Edward Kennedy of Massachusetts. Heroin addiction troubled "parents in the comfortable affluence of Beverly Hills," Kennedy proclaimed, "as much as the mothers whose children are forced to play in the squalor of South Chicago. . . . People are filled with terror at home and in our streets because the victims of heroin stalk the urban byways for money and goods to satisfy their craving. Each of us is in danger of becoming a casualty of the frenzy of the addict." Federal policy should rehabilitate rather than incarcerate these addict-predators, Kennedy concluded, and "pursue drug traffickers relentlessly." For public health liberals, conflating the heroin threat facing urban and suburban youth represented an appeal to their white middle-class constituents but also a tactic to generate broader public sympathy for nonwhite drug addicts. In the words of Abraham Ribicoff, a key architect of the 1972 legislation, "what formerly existed in the inner city ghetto and was . . . long not a matter of serious public attention, has now become such a problem in American suburbs . . . that the nation has finally aroused itself from its former lethargy." Jerome Jaffe, director of Nixon's Special Action Office for Drug Abuse Prevention, later remarked that the public health commitment of a law-and-order GOP administration was unprecedented: "We have never had that proportion of federal resources devoted to intervention on the demand side. We'd never had it before, and we've never had it since" (fig. 4.5).[76]

The war on drug pushers and heroin-related street crime enabled the White House to justify public health as essentially a second front in the federal law enforcement offensive. In early 1972, to launch a "concentrated assault on the

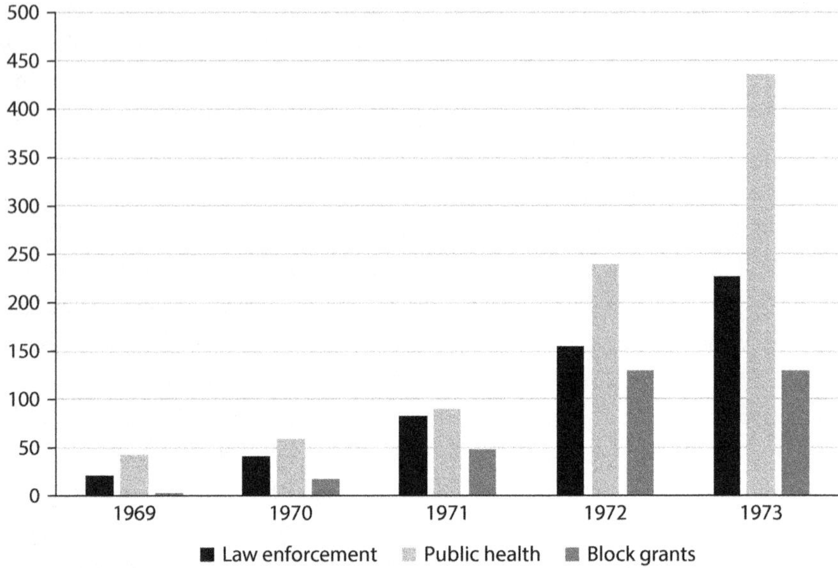

FIGURE 4.5. Federal expenditures on drug abuse and enforcement programs, 1969–73 (in millions of dollars). Federal drug funding increased exponentially after passage of the bipartisan legislative packages in 1970 and 1972. Total expenditures rose from $66.4 million in 1969 to $791.3 million by 1973. Public health programs received a majority of direct federal drug funding, in stark contrast to the pattern during the 1980s (see fig. 7.10). The breakdown in the public health category was 64% for treatment/rehabilitation, 25% for research, and 10% for education/prevention (1973 data). (Congressional Research Service, *Federal Programs Relating to the Control of Drug Abuse*, Report 72–272 ED, December 7, 1972.)
Note: The 60:40 ratio between public health and law enforcement expenditures that most scholarship cites for the Nixon-era war on drugs probably underestimates the percentage of spending on enforcement overall, because of how state and local governments used funds distributed through block grant programs (which peaked at 25% of the total in 1972). In the "war on drug abuse" field, discretionary block grants included programs in each category of law enforcement, treatment, research, and education. The Justice Department provided more than half of all discretionary federal grants through the Law Enforcement Assistance Administration (LEAA), established by the Omnibus Crime Control and Safe Streets Act of 1968, which primarily funded street-level drug enforcement operations.

street-level heroin pusher," President Nixon created a new Justice Department agency, the Office of Drug Abuse Law Enforcement (ODALE), directed to "stop at nothing" in pursuit of this "worst of all criminals." In terms of how the heroin market actually operated, the boundary between "professional" traffickers and street-level dealers remained as fuzzy as the considerable ideological overlap between crime control and public health in the war on drugs, an example of the impossibility of drawing a bright line between supply-side and demand-side policies. The administration understood that street-level enforcement would sweep up so-called "addict-peddlers" rather than major traffickers but believed that ODALE would address public fears of predatory crime while acting as a deterrent to "push people into treatment programs." According to domestic advisor John Ehrlichman, ODALE appealed to the White House because "narcotics suppression is a very sexy political issue. It usually has high media visibility. Parents who are voters worry about narcotics."[77] Designed to demonstrate the national state's power to suppress the heroin supply, ODALE represented a federalization of local law enforcement functions unprecedented since the Bureau of Prohibition in the 1920s. Undercover agents deployed "search and destroy" tactics and their new no-knock authority to arrest more than six thousand people, which ODALE's director labeled a "remarkable success." Critics charged that ODALE swept up addict-peddlers rather than large suppliers and targeted "marijuana dealers with the same zeal they apply to the heroin traffic." According to historian Elizabeth Hinton, ODALE launched a campaign of terror and brutality, mostly in urban Black areas. One of Nixon's main drug advisors later conceded that ODALE "got too close to breaching the wall of what is not acceptable under the Fourth Amendment."[78]

After a year and a half, the White House discontinued ODALE under fierce congressional pressure, following a mistaken raid in which undercover narcotics agents disguised as hippies traumatized two white families in Illinois. Late one night in April 1973, acting on uncorroborated tips and without a search warrant, more than a dozen ODALE agents burst into the Giglotto and Askew homes in the working-class suburb of Collinsville and held the confused and terrified residents at gunpoint while they searched for nonexistent drugs. The home invasion raid generated massive news coverage and turned the Giglottos and Askews into the perfect white victims of federal overreach in the war on drugs, the equivalent of Frank LaVarre for lengthy prison sentences and Diane Linkletter as the innocent target of pushers. An outraged Senator Charles Percy (R-IL), usually one of Nixon's firmest allies, publicized the victims' stories and denounced ODALE for "unconscionable terrorizing of innocent families," "gun-toting terrorism," and "storm trooper tactics." Myles Ambrose, the ODALE director, apologized for the agents' violation of policy in not obtaining a warrant but explained that "drug people are the very vermin of humanity. . . . Occasionally we must adopt their dress and tactics." Harold Washington, an African American political leader in Chicago, pointed out that poor nonwhite communities had suffered systematically from "repressive criminal measures" during Nixon's war on drugs, but white Americans did not care about either "hard dope" pushers or police brutality until it happened in their neighborhoods.[79] The U.S. Congress soon repealed the no-knock authority for Justice Department agents in direct response to the Collinsville abuses. In 1973, Congress also approved the administration's request to create a new Drug Enforcement Administration (DEA) to lead the "all-out, global war on the drug menace." The reorganization plan closed the controversial ODALE agency and absorbed the Bureau of Narcotics and Dangerous Drugs into the DEA's comprehensive domestic and international mission.[80]

"All-Out War, On All Fronts"

During 1972, an election year, the political calculus of the war on drugs led the White House to double down on the marijuana-to-heroin gateway myth and jettison bipartisan rhetoric for a law-and-order platform that blamed liberal permissiveness and lenient judges for the federal government's inability to halt either supply or demand. A national survey conducted in early 1972 revealed that more than three-quarters of adults over age thirty-five believed that experimenting with marijuana "makes people want to try stronger things like heroin," and almost two-thirds still subscribed to the "reefer madness" fiction that "many crimes are committed by people who are under the influence of marijuana." The same proportion of older Americans supported "stiffer penalties" to suppress the marijuana market, although an overwhelming 84 percent opposed the incarceration of teenagers who smoked pot.[81] President Nixon shared most of these views since, as he confided to antidrug crusader Art Linkletter, marijuana caused youth to "lose motivation" and move on to speed, LSD, or heroin. In private, Nixon and his political advisors expressed contempt for the administration's own public health emphasis and pledged to keep control of drug policy away from the "muddle-headed psychiatrists," in the president's phrase, who let "their hearts run their brains."[82] On March 21, the same day that Nixon signed the prevention and rehabilitation law, he told chief of staff H. R. Haldeman that he "god damned near puked" when he saw the cover of the White House's latest drug education publication, which quoted the president himself that the crisis should be "dealt with in a variety of ways." The message should be tough and unambiguous, Nixon demanded: "all-out war, on all fronts." The "gobbledygook about drug addiction" from the psychiatrists "may be the truth," Nixon said. "But it sure as hell isn't the thing to say." The Oval Office conversation continued, based on their racial imaginary of white "kids" smoking pot in the suburbs versus unsympathetic heroin "addicts" in the ghetto, and their shared intuition of how a typical white middle-class mother felt about the war on drugs:

RICHARD NIXON: Just kick the hell out of it. We enforce the law. . . . Who cares about . . . the treating of the addicts.

H. R. HALDEMAN: The mothers don't, because their kids aren't addicts. . . . You just don't worry about that, what you worry about is the son of a bitch that's going to come up—

NIXON: That's right.

HALDEMAN:—and try to slip a packet of marijuana to your kid.

NIXON: Or heroin.

HALDEMAN: Or heroin.

NIXON: Give them a fix. Or LSD, or something.

HALDEMAN: Or LSD, or slip something in his Coca-Cola.

NIXON: Yeah. Right.

HALDEMAN: That's what you worry about, you're not worried about addicts. Nobody knows an addict, but everybody knows a kid who's been smoking marijuana. . . . There aren't enough addicts, addicted kids to matter. (. . .)

HALDEMAN: Stopping the supply is important because people know if there isn't any, then nobody can buy it. . . . And the other thing is getting the god damned pushers, . . . and they'd frankly like to hang them. And then education, educating the kids, they talk about that, but that, that's a tough one to peddle, you know. You can educate the hell out of them but it just—

NIXON: Educate them, shit.

HALDEMAN:—doesn't get anywhere.

NIXON: That's right. Enforce the law, you've got to scare them.[83]

One of the most pivotal moments in the history of the war on drugs came in March 1972, when Nixon rejected the decriminalization recommendation of the National Commission on Marihuana and Drug Abuse, chartered by the omnibus 1970 law. The disassociation of marijuana from heroin in law enforcement would have had profound consequences for national drug policy, separating two markets that criminal sanctions and political rhetoric had jumbled together and removing the main focus of interdiction and arrests in most parts of the country. The White House had not anticipated trouble from the commission, which the president thought he had stacked with "old and conservative" members who would "toe the party line," in the words of its chairman Raymond Shafer, a moderate Republican and former Pennsylvania governor. But the group did include medical experts who favored a public health focus, such as J. Thomas Ungerleider of Los Angeles, as well as public health liberals who opposed criminal sanctions against drug users, especially Senators Harold Hughes and Jacob Javits.[84] In spring 1971, as the Shafer hearings opened, Nixon publicly stated that "even if the commission does recommend that it [marijuana] be legalized, I will not follow the recommendation." The president privately explained his reasoning to domestic policy advisor John Ehrlichman: "I know all the arguments about, well, marijuana is no worse than whisky. . . . But the point is, once you cross that line, from the straight society to the drug society—marijuana, then speed, then LSD, then it's heroin, etc., then you're done." Nixon's prejudgment of the commission's work angered its members, requiring a damage control session with Shafer in the Oval Office. The chairman warned that they would endorse a prevention strategy based on "nonlegal forms of control" that did not "over-penalize use." Nixon agreed that young pot smokers should not be "in jail with a bunch of hardened criminals; . . . that's absurd." But he warned Shafer not to produce a "soft on marijuana report" and ordered: "Keep your commission in line."[85]

The much-anticipated report by the National Commission on Marihuana advocated full decriminalization for personal use and casual sale of the drug, while maintaining criminal sanctions for trafficking. The title, *Marihuana: A Signal of Misunderstanding,* captured the commission's central argument that the recent controversy arose less from the drug's pharmacological hazards or even its illegality than from its status as a "symbol of wider social conflicts." Reinforcing the conventional wisdom, the report located the origins of the crisis in the widespread, visible use of marijuana among middle-class college students and white teenagers in the affluent suburbs. Marijuana, in the Shafer Commission's analysis, had come to symbolize the generational "cultural divide" over the Vietnam War, the counterculture, and youth "disaffection with traditional society." For many youth, breaking the marijuana laws functioned as a "convenient instrument of mini-protest" and an "agent of group solidarity." A large majority of the older generation erroneously believed that marijuana led to crime and heroin addiction, but the anger and anxiety generated by the unapologetic pot-smoking subculture also reflected deep symbolic associations. Many adults linked marijuana use to the "rejection of cherished values" by white middle-class youth and their behavioral patterns of "idleness, lack of motivation, hedonism, and sexual promiscuity." Although the report did not directly connect the dots, this specter of middle-class dysfunction and white pathology closely echoed the racial "culture of poverty" framework imposed on urban ghettos and poor nonwhite families. The copious data compiled by the commission repudiated this alarmism and revealed that adolescent and college-age recreational pot smokers resembled their abstaining peers in social functioning, scholastic achievement, and career goals. The Shafer report hoped to "demythologize the controversy" by disassociating marijuana consumption from its political context altogether, deflating both the unfounded fears and the underground allure.[86]

The Shafer Commission's pragmatic solution revolved around a "social control policy seeking to discourage marijuana use," presented as a middle path between the failure of total prohibition and an alcohol-style regulatory system that would signal implicit government approval. The report strongly criticized the current criminal justice approach of the federal government and all fifty states as arbitrary, selective, a waste of resources, and self-defeating. Around 95 percent of state and local arrests for marijuana involved possession or casual sale, but the vast majority of parents, prosecutors, judges, and the general public did not support any punishment greater than fines or probation for these violators. The commission rejected even those sanctions and adopted the ACLU's right to privacy stance that, absent the now discredited myths about marijuana's dangers, government had not met its constitutional obligation to "show a compelling reason to justify invasion of the home" to penalize users. While the conservative appointees were initially reluctant to take this step, they changed their minds after the commission held secret meetings with doctors, lawyers, and other high-achieving professionals who explained that their personal use of marijuana did not "mark them as radical ideologues or essentially irresponsible individuals." Ultimately, the report portrayed decriminalization as a way to defuse youth anger over facing punishment for an activity that they considered a "pleasurable and socially rewarding experience." But the National Commission on Marihuana declined to endorse legalization, for three main reasons: the depth of public opposition; to retain the justification for outlawing trafficking; and, most of all, out of concern that chronic pot smoking could trigger a so-called "amotivational syndrome" of laziness, disinterest in work, and stunted psychological development in a small percentage of youth. The Shafer report concluded that marijuana use represented "more of a consequence than a contributor" to the social conflicts of the era and should not be viewed "as a major issue or a threat to the social order."[87]

White House officials viewed the decriminalization report as a major political liability and went to great lengths to minimize its impact. Nixon refused to meet with the commission—responding to this suggestion with a "*Violent No!!!*"—and instead accepted the report from Shafer in a brief meeting with no advance media notice. At a news conference a few days later, the president said the report "did not change my mind. I oppose the legalization of marijuana and that includes its sale, its possession, and its use. I do not believe that you can have effective criminal justice based on the philosophy that something is half legal and half illegal."[88] Although Nixon mischaracterized the commission's careful distinction between decriminalization and legalization, his political instincts were on target in rejecting the idea that the policies were fundamentally dissimilar. According to an internal memo, the Shafer report's staff authors had calculated that decriminalizing possession but outlawing distribution "was untenable and would ultimately lead to outright legalization." Removing all criminal sanctions against marijuana possession would have meant a major shift in the war on drugs, but it is important to emphasize the essentially mainstream agenda of the *Signal of Misunderstanding* report, which officially endorsed the already widespread consensus that white middle-class youth were impossible criminals. Major traffickers should be punished to limit the supply to young users; otherwise law-abiding white Americans should not be jailed for recreational drug choices; excessive marijuana smoking was bad for capitalism and middle-class upward mobility; and a more relaxed approach would help ameliorate the generation gap by disentangling pot from both an authoritarian establishment and the radical counterculture. "When the politics have died down" after the next election, the commission's executive director wrote Nixon's main drug policy advisor, perhaps "this Administration can take a far-reaching view of the total problem" and stop using criminalization and law enforcement as the primary weapon in the war on drugs.[89]

On March 20, 1972, the day before Nixon buried the marijuana decriminalization report and signed the Drug Abuse Office and Treatment Act, he traveled to the heroin capital of New York City to redeclare "total war" on narcotics traffickers and street-level "pushers." For such villains, who "destroy the lives of our young people," Nixon called for "no sympathy whatsoever and no limit" in terms of criminal penalties. As part of his reelection strategy, the president asked his political advisors to develop lines of attack that went after the dope pushers and the permissive liberal policies that let them roam the streets. The resulting rhetoric could have come straight out of a 1950s educational film or the political theater of Harry J. Anslinger's many

FIGURE 4.6. President Richard Nixon listens as Myles Ambrose, director of the Office of Drug Abuse Law Enforcement, reports that federal narcotics arrests doubled between 1969 and 1972. This photo opportunity, held on July 24 during Nixon's reelection campaign, was part of the political theater of the White House's racially targeted pledge of "total war" to protect all Americans from heroin traffickers and urban street pushers. (Bettmann / Getty Images.)

congressional appearances. Heroin peddlers were "deliberately enslaving other human beings, . . . young people who are innocent, first-time victims, to a life of degradation, crime and misery." Narcotics pushers were "selling heroin on the streets of our communities, near the schools of our neighborhoods, and at centers where inexperienced young people gather." Lest any suburbanite mistake these dire scenarios for an urban crisis alone, "location, income, race, sex, education, career, family background are irrelevant. No such factor provides a safeguard. Heroin today is *everyone's enemy*."[90] During the fall campaign, Nixon frequently deployed these tropes as he contrasted his "all-out attack on drug pushers" with the permissiveness of soft-hearted judges and his Democratic predecessors, who had allowed violent crime and drug abuse to spiral out of control. Senator George McGovern, his Democratic opponent, tried to outflank Nixon by accusing the administration of failing to halt the spread of heroin to the suburbs and promising his own war on "murderous, unprincipled" dope pushers. The Nixon campaign responded by attacking McGovern as soft on drugs because of his support for legalizing marijuana—an inaccurate depiction since the Democratic candidate actually endorsed misdemeanor possession penalties, although he had reacted favorably to the Shafer Commission recommendations.[91]

The political posturing over the war on drugs during the 1972 election overshadowed the considerable areas of consensus that had shaped bipartisan policymaking in Washington during Nixon's first term, although disagreements remained over the proper balance between law enforcement and public health. Nixon's attacks on permissive judges who gave "light or suspended sentences for drug pushers" repudiated the discretionary penalty structure (for all but "professional" traffickers) in the 1970 reform law, which public health liberals had championed as necessary to hospitalize heroin addict-peddlers and protect white pot dealers from excessive punishment. The president also began combining the "war on crime and drugs" into a single mission and—as in the 1968 election—denouncing liberalism for its "naïve theory that society is to blame for an individual's wrongdoing" and pledging to defend the "first civil right—the right to be free from domestic violence." The 1972 GOP platform portrayed marijuana legalization and heroin-related crime as dual legacies of the permissive sixties and pledged "the most intensive law enforcement war ever waged" against the "pushers" of all illegal drugs. The Democratic platform charged Nixon with failure to keep his promises to reduce violent crime or the scourge of illegal narcotics and declared that the "greatest victims . . . are the people of the ghetto, black and brown. Fear now stalks their streets far more than it does the suburbs." The Democrats championed the disease model for individual drug (ab)users, to be "diverted into treatment before prosecution," a coercive public health approach that depended on arrests and rejected the civil liberties position that the state should leave such citizens alone. The McGovern platform also pledged a "massive law enforcement effort" against the suppliers of heroin "and other dangerous drugs," promised to crack down on the "pusher . . . whether in the ghetto or the suburban high school," and did not explicitly mention marijuana at all. Heroin accounted for one-fifth of drug arrests that year, and marijuana more than half, both mainly for possession.[92]

After winning the 1972 election, President Nixon continued to defend the criminalization of marijuana as a key pillar of the federal war on drugs and the Republican counteroffensive against liberal permissiveness in a crime-ridden society. In March 1973, the administration introduced a heroin trafficking bill to reimpose mandatory-minimum sentences for small-scale dealing (less than four ounces): five to fifteen years for the first offense and ten to life without probation or parole for larger amounts. The president framed the announcement through a series of pusher/gateway tales about a five-year-old boy hospitalized after someone slipped him LSD, a ten-year-old heroin addict who started with marijuana, and a California teenager who committed suicide to escape the drug culture. Nixon then directly connected the war on heroin pushers to his rejection of marijuana legalization, asking, "If we accept the use of this drug, how can we draw the line against other illegal drugs?" For GOP supporters in Congress, the White House circulated talking points such as "It makes my blood boil to think they [heroin pushers] are set free after they have been caught," and "Marijuana has become the most pervasive symbol of the permissive society."[93] The ACLU denounced Nixon for his refusal to abandon the marijuana-gateway mythology, while Gallup reported that two-thirds of the public supported the death penalty for major traffickers. The Nixon administration subsequently amended the heroin bill to double the maximum penalty for cultivating, importing, or selling marijuana to ten years for the first offense and up to fifteen years for the second, while maintaining the judicial discretion established in the 1970 law and designed to protect white suburban teenagers and college students from long sentences. But the U.S. Congress never acted on Nixon's trafficking bill, in part because of the distractions of the Watergate scandal that ended his presidency, but also because heroin politics in most of the country lacked the fear and intensity of New York, which enacted the harsh mandatory-minimum Rockefeller Drug Laws in May 1973 (see chapter 5).[94]

The intertwined and convoluted relationship between marijuana and heroin, and between law enforcement and public health, fundamentally shaped the bipartisan war on drugs during the Nixon era. Dedicated federal drug spending increased tenfold between 1969 and 1973, with the dual targets of marijuana and heroin at the center of this massive state-building project. Public policy toward marijuana remained controversially linked to heroin through the gateway mystique that underpinned the entire war on drugs, while fluctuating between public health techniques designed to overcome the generation gap and the impossible law enforcement agenda of criminalizing the social practices of millions of white middle-class Americans. In national politics, the Nixon administration and the Democratic leadership in Congress remained hostile toward marijuana decriminalization, reflected in the chilly reaction to the Shafer Commission's second and final report in 1973. The National

Commission on Marihuana, which felt badly mistreated by the White House, labeled alcohol abuse the nation's primary drug challenge and reiterated its plea for a rational approach to the youth pot-smoking phenomenon. The report included a scathing critique of America's new "drug abuse industrial complex," which had a "vested interest in the perpetuation of the problem." Policymakers should acknowledge that the United States was a drug-dependent society, rather than reinforce the public's "emotion and fear" by targeting symbolic outcast groups such as the "heroin addict mugger" and "longhaired psychedelic hippie drop-outs." Most striking of all, the national arrest totals for marijuana more than doubled from 188,682 in 1970, the year Congress passed the misdemeanor possession reform, to 420,700 in 1973, representing two-thirds of all drug apprehensions.[95] At the state and local levels, this heightened enforcement led to comprehensive racial and spatial discrimination in criminal justice policies and galvanized the political movement for marijuana legalization or decriminalization, with the white middle-class suburban victim remaining front and center.

5

Impossible Criminals

IN 1973, the California Court of Appeals rejected a "cruel and unusual" constitutional challenge to an indeterminate five-years-to-life sentence for selling marijuana given the year before to a white twenty-four-year-old from the affluent Bay Area suburb of Los Altos. The decision rested on not only the traditional deference to legislative discretion in establishing criminal penalties but also the National Commission on Marihuana's finding that smoking pot remained dangerous because regular use could trigger the "amotivational syndrome" of apathy, diminished ambition, and disinterest in school and career. The trial court sentenced the defendant to the statutory mandatory minimum, which very few marijuana felons in California actually received, after the local police chief labeled him a "major supplier" to teenagers in the suburban community (97% white). The evidentiary record reveals that the young man, by then nineteen months into a sentence at Soledad State Prison, had pled guilty and expected probation because he really just provided pot to friends at cost, out of a misguided "sense of altruism" (according to the court-appointed psychiatrist). Two years later, a desperate father from a suburb outside Cleveland wrote the Senate Subcommittee to Investigate Juvenile Delinquency to register his "righteous anger with a system" that gave his twenty-year-old son a one-to-five-year prison sentence for dealing marijuana. The local narcotics squad had enlisted a young informant (probably in a deal after a possession bust) to seek his son's assistance in obtaining an ounce of marijuana, thereby triggering the felony trafficking threshold. "I am completely helpless!" the father lamented, faced with the "heavy hand of society's police power." Because his son was "in no way" a criminal, by what right did the state of Ohio administer punishment so "wholly irrational and disproportionate to the imprudent, foolish, and victimless act of a twenty-year-old boy."[1]

State and local authorities arrested almost three million Americans on marijuana charges between 1970 and 1977, nearly two-thirds of all apprehensions in the national war on drugs. This group consisted primarily of young white male pot smokers in their late teens and early twenties. Although racial, socioeconomic, gender, age-based, and geographic discretion and discrimination shaped every stage of the criminal legal process, from the point of arrest to the ultimate disposition, this criminalized population contained a greater percentage of white middle-class offenders than ever before or since in America's long war on drugs (fig. 5.1). The Los Altos and Cleveland cases were exceptional in terms of the mandatory-minimum felony sentences imposed on white middle-class defendants, but not in revealing the mechanisms by which law enforcement policed the recreational drug market, and not in illuminating the impossible criminals and suburban victims that animated energetic political movements for marijuana legalization or decriminalization at the state and federal levels. During 1973–74, the proportions of suburban residents and white Americans arrested in the war on drugs reached their all-time peaks, and the percentage of Black offenders hit a modern low (although still almost double the population share). Heroin arrests continued to plummet as a fraction of the total, and Oregon became the first of eleven states to decriminalize simple possession of marijuana. The huge increase in marijuana arrests surprised many observers, but the Nixon administration and a bipartisan majority in Congress had supported the misdemeanor possession reduction for the law-and-order rationale that more realistic penalties would make prosecutors and judges more likely to place first offenders on probation, thereby providing both a deterrent to experimentation and leverage for rehabilitation. While the deterrence theory failed categorically, local authorities did monitor a much higher percentage of white middle-class youth on probation in the early-to-mid 1970s, often with compulsory medical rehabilitation of these recreational pot smokers.[2]

The political movement for marijuana legalization or decriminalization expanded into a powerful grassroots and institutional force for drug-war reform during the 1970s, organized around the evocative racial imagery of the imprisoned white middle-class pot smoker and the demand that law enforcement stop victimizing these "otherwise law-abiding" youth. The American Civil Liberties Union and the new interest group NORML (National Organization for the Reform of Marijuana Laws) coordinated the legislative campaign for alcohol-style legalization in Washington and the state capitals. They adopted the deliberate middle-class strategy of saving "our children" from

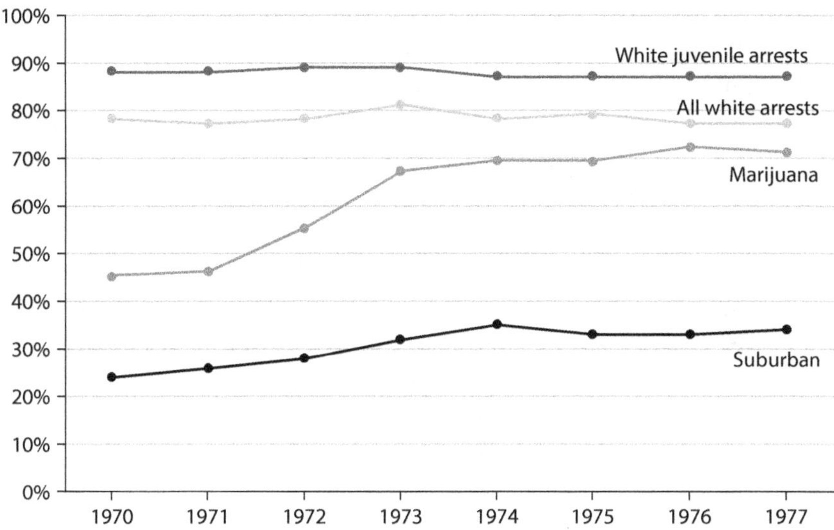

FIGURE 5.1. Select characteristics of the population arrested on drug charges in the United States, 1970–77. The racial distribution of drug arrests stabilized in the 1970s while the total number continued to expand. Marijuana arrests increased to 72% of all drug arrests in 1976, the all-time peak, and cumulatively totaled 2.89 million between 1970 and 1977. The proportion of white drug arrests (adult and juvenile combined) averaged 78% of the total during this period and peaked at 81% in 1973. The proportion of white juvenile arrests alone was even higher, averaging 88% of total juvenile arrests during these years, approximately the population share. The proportion of suburban drug arrests continued its upward trajectory, first surpassing the number of drug arrests in the largest cities (population 250,000+) in 1974, and rising from one-fourth to one-third of the national total between 1970 and 1977. (FBI, *Uniform Crime Reports*, 1970–1977.)

Note: The "white juvenile arrests" category is the percentage of all juvenile arrests, while the other three categories are based on total drug arrests. The FBI did not tabulate Hispanic drug arrest totals separately during the 1970s, but evidence from California shows arrests of Hispanic residents at roughly the population share during this period. The racial breakdown of the U.S. population in the 1970 census was 87.6% white, 11.1% Black, and an estimated 4.5% Hispanic (with overlap between the white and Hispanic categories). The racial breakdown of the U.S. population in the 1980 census was 79.6% white, 11.5% Black, and 6.5% Hispanic.

heroin markets, criminal records, career jeopardy, prisons full of dangerous predators, and the trauma and disruption of any encounter with the carceral state. Potent grassroots movements for marijuana legalization also emerged in the early 1970s, especially among countercultural activists and college students on the West Coast, which played a key role in persuading the legislatures of Oregon and California to enact partial decriminalization reform as a political compromise. Throughout the nation, skyrocketing arrest rates politically mobilized many young pot smokers, and even more importantly, their parents, leading to increased pressure on governors and state legislatures and a massive shift in public opinion. More than one-fourth of Americans supported legalization by mid-decade, and a majority endorsed decriminalization by the late 1970s.[3] Back in 1969, legalization activist Michael Aldrich, who played a leading role in the California campaign, had predicted that once the states adopted the Dodd-Nixon federal penalty structure, marijuana arrests would triple nationwide and tens of thousands of white middle-class Americans would receive misdemeanor criminal records, which "should lead to legalization by about 1975 or so." Instead, in a fateful turn in drug-war politics, the Shafer Commission's decriminalization compromise eclipsed the political momentum behind marijuana legalization, therefore maintaining supply-side interdiction and guaranteeing the continuation of discretionary and inequitable enforcement.[4]

The marijuana decriminalization campaign represented a formation of "political whiteness" that almost never addressed the issue of racial or class discrimination in discretionary drug-war enforcement and instead consistently argued that by leaving middle-class pot smokers alone, police would be able to concentrate on heroin markets and the real criminals in urban centers.[5] This deeply racialized, if discursively color-blind, binary set the "victimless crime" of pot smoking by "otherwise law-abiding" Americans (white, suburban, middle class) in direct opposition to the dangerous addict-predators, heroin traffickers, and violent criminals of the inner city (Black and Latino, urban, poor). The legal and medical scholars whose research informed the marijuana legalization movement promoted the complete disassociation of pot smoking from heroin enforcement, an understandable response to the persistence of the gateway mythology and the Nixon administration's calculated conflation of the two markets—except that every "harm reduction" and civil liberties argument of the futility, selectivity, and criminogenic effects of prohibitionist policies logically applied to illicit narcotics as well.[6] The case studies that follow—of the politics of marijuana reform in Texas, Oregon, California, and New York—reveal that legislative enactment of decriminalization or misdemeanor loopholes for "otherwise law-abiding" pot smokers involved an explicit or parallel tradeoff that toughened mandatory-minimum penalties for heroin sellers and users alike, especially in states with large nonwhite urban populations. Close examination of state and local law enforcement also demonstrates that even during the period of mass arrests of white middle-class marijuana offenders, the incarceration rates of African Americans remained disproportionate and processes of racial and socioeconomic discretion continued to reserve the harshest penalties for nonwhite offenders whether busted for marijuana or heroin—especially those with prior juvenile records and lower educational or employment status, where drug usage presumably indicated "real" criminality.

The political movement for marijuana legalization, and the more limited decriminalization compromise, responded to the historically unprecedented scale of the carceral state's intervention in the white middle-class recreational drug market.[7] As the Nixon administration and the U.S. Congress envisioned, the adoption by most states of the discretionary penalty structure and first offender misdemeanor provisions of the Comprehensive Drug Abuse Prevention and Control Act of 1970 expanded the criminal legal system's capacity to regulate the youth marijuana subculture by merging law enforcement and coercive rehabilitative programs. In California, the advancement of public health through criminal law enforcement diverted at least fifty thousand white pot smokers into psychiatric counseling, drug reeducation classes, and even residential treatment centers in the early 1970s, often taking up spaces once reserved for heroin addicts. New York's pioneering diversion program dropped charges altogether after one year of informal probation for marijuana offenders whom prosecutors and judges assessed as amenable to rehabilitation, part of the increasing divide between punitive urban policy and suburban public health solutions in the era of the Rockefeller Drug Laws. The capacious disease model enabled authorities to justify criminalization by classifying all pot smokers as "drug abusers," rather than recreational users or self-governing consumers. The related "amotivational syndrome" theory popularized by the Shafer Commission also replaced the "generation gap" as the exaggerated symbolic framework for marijuana's middle-class hazards. Even in states that enacted partial decriminalization, the retention of tough but discretionary penalties for marijuana sellers reflected the adaptability of the "pusher" narrative and the resilient racial and spatial logics of white middle-class youth victimization in the war on drugs. The emergence of a political consensus that white pot smokers should not be punished by the carceral state remained compatible with the conviction that criminal law should continue to protect them from consumer behaviors that allegedly caused "amotivational syndrome," threatened suburban ideals, and subverted capitalist imperatives.

Marijuana Legalization vs. Decriminalization

The formation of NORML, the National Organization for the Reform of Marijuana Laws, marked the beginning of a national lobbying campaign to promote legalization as a mission to rescue innocent white youth from the misguided war on drugs. In 1970, a twenty-six-year-old attorney named Keith Stroup started NORML with a seed grant from the Playboy Foundation and a shrewd agenda to emphasize an "effective, middle class approach, not pro-grass but anti-jail." NORML's initial public relations operation, titled "Pot Luck," featured a white teenage girl locked in a cell, looking forlornly at the ground, with an untouched tray of prison food on her lap (fig. 5.2). The accompanying text stated that NORML did not "advocate the use of marijuana," but there was "no medical, moral, or legal justification for imprisoning" any of the twenty million Americans who had smoked pot. Another advertisement, "Pot Shot," featured police mug photos of a young white male facing the lifelong burden of a criminal record, one of many "otherwise law-abiding young citizens" victimized by drug policies that "have wreaked havoc on a whole generation." In its position statement, NORML called for alcohol-style regulation of marijuana distribution, including banning access for minors, while repurposing the gateway argument for the cause of pot reform. Criminalizing marijuana, according to NORML, diverted law enforcement resources from the real dangers: traffickers of heroin, cocaine, and LSD. Marijuana laws also forced recreational pot smokers into a treacherous underground economy, where they often had to "enter the hard-drug culture" and come into "contact with [heroin] pushers." This rather obvious suburban strategy reinforced prevailing tropes about vulnerable white middle-class youth, endangered by the unfair drug laws and the dope traffickers, and effectively endorsed escalation of the urban war on heroin. Keith Stroup deliberately avoided topics such as the racially disproportionate effects of drug enforcement, although NORML did highlight the plight of white political prisoners such as countercultural icon John Sinclair.[8]

In 1972, NORML recalibrated its libertarian agenda and devised a state-by-state lobbying effort in response to the National Commission on Marihuana's call for partial decriminalization, not full legalization. NORML praised the Shafer report for debunking many of the myths surrounding the recreational marijuana market but strongly criticized its refusal to support a legal regulatory system as an unscientific concession to political pressure. NORML circulated an additional critique by Harvard psychiatrist Lester Grinspoon, a member of its advisory board, which disputed the commission's rationale that

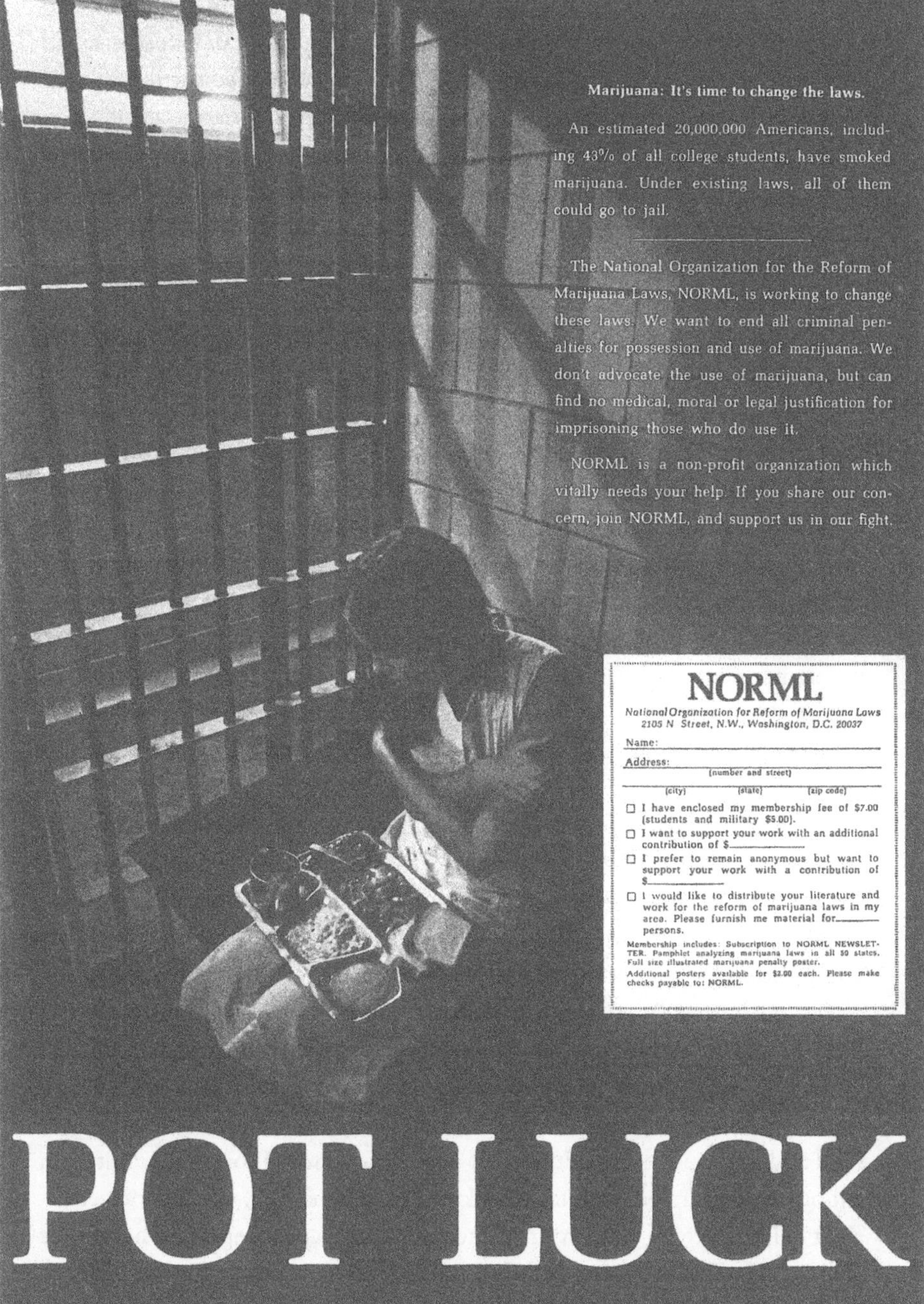

Marijuana: It's time to change the laws.
An estimated 20,000,000 Americans, including 43% of all college students, have smoked marijuana. Under existing laws, all of them could go to jail.
The National Organization for the Reform of Marijuana Laws, NORML, is working to change these laws. We want to end all criminal penalties for possession and use of marijuana. We don't advocate the use of marijuana, but can find no medical, moral or legal justification for imprisoning those who do use it.
NORML is a non-profit organization which vitally needs your help. If you share our concern, join NORML, and support us in our fight.
NORML
National Organization for Reform of Marijuana Laws
2105 N Street, N.W., Washington, D.C. 20037
Name:
Address:
(number and street)
(city) (state) (zip code)
☐ I have enclosed my membership fee of $7.00 (students and military $5.00).
☐ I want to support your work with an additional contribution of $
☐ I prefer to remain anonymous but want to support your work with a contribution of $
☐ I would like to distribute your literature and work for the reform of marijuana laws in my area. Please furnish me material for persons.
Membership includes: Subscription to NORML NEWSLETTER. Pamphlet analyzing marijuana laws in all 50 states. Full size illustrated marijuana penalty poster.
Additional posters available for $2.00 each. Please make checks payable to: NORML.
POT LUCK

FIGURE 5.2. The National Organization for the Reform of Marijuana Laws (NORML) promoted its legalization campaign by highlighting the young white casualties of the war on drugs, especially college students, as in this 1971 "Pot Luck" advertisement. By deploying the racial imagery of white middle-class victimization, NORML responded to the dramatic increase in their marijuana arrests during the early 1970s but also evaded discussion of the disproportionate incarceration of nonwhite Americans in the broader drug war. (Courtesy of National Organization for the Reform of Marijuana Laws.)

the specter of the "amotivational syndrome" among heavy pot smokers justified interdiction of the marijuana supply. Grinspoon labeled the report an illogical political compromise that provided no evidence for the alarm about "strong psychological dependence," casually sanctioned a scenario where lawful users had to venture into the underground market for a product of indeterminate potency and quality, and repeated the mistake of alcohol Prohibition in the fantasy that government could suppress the supply of a popular drug. In subsequent pamphlets, NORML repeatedly challenged the "amotivational syndrome" thesis by publicizing academic research rejecting stereotypes that pot smoking transformed middle-class youth into "non-productive" and apathetic dropouts. Instead NORML sought to depoliticize the issue by portraying cannabis as a middle-class "social lubricant" for students and young adult professionals, rather than a psychedelic escape or an "expression of rebellion against parents and the establishment." To appeal to conservatives, Keith Stroup recruited John Finlator, former deputy director of the Bureau of Narcotics and Dangerous Drugs, to reassure the public that marijuana was a "relatively harmless drug" with no reason to "waste millions of dollars sending young people to jail."[9] NORML also unsuccessfully petitioned the Nixon administration to remove marijuana from Schedule 1 of the controlled substances scheme as an "unlawful" classification based on "emotionalism and misinformation."[10]

NORML's support for an alcohol-style system, and its mainstream positioning as the marijuana lobby for white middle-class professionals, crowded out more radical grassroots legalization movements with roots in the antiwar, racial justice, and countercultural left. In the early 1970s, NORML's primary competition for leadership of national marijuana reform came from Amorphia, a nonprofit "cannabis cooperative" based in the San Francisco Bay Area. Amorphia, the driving force behind the legalization campaign in California, viewed NORML and its Playboy backers as "Establishment interests" seeking to transform the multibillion-dollar marijuana market from the countercultural underground into an immensely profitable sector of corporate capitalism. Amorphia demanded "free, legal backyard marijuana" (fig. 5.3) and viewed the right to homegrown cultivation as the linchpin of a post-repeal, noncommercialized cannabis economy with "minimal interference from government and big business." Unlike NORML, Amorphia immediately embraced the Shafer report, with a twist. Decriminalization, if combined with the added right to private cultivation, appeared capable of excluding liquor and tobacco industries from monopolizing the marijuana market, while avoiding the high taxes

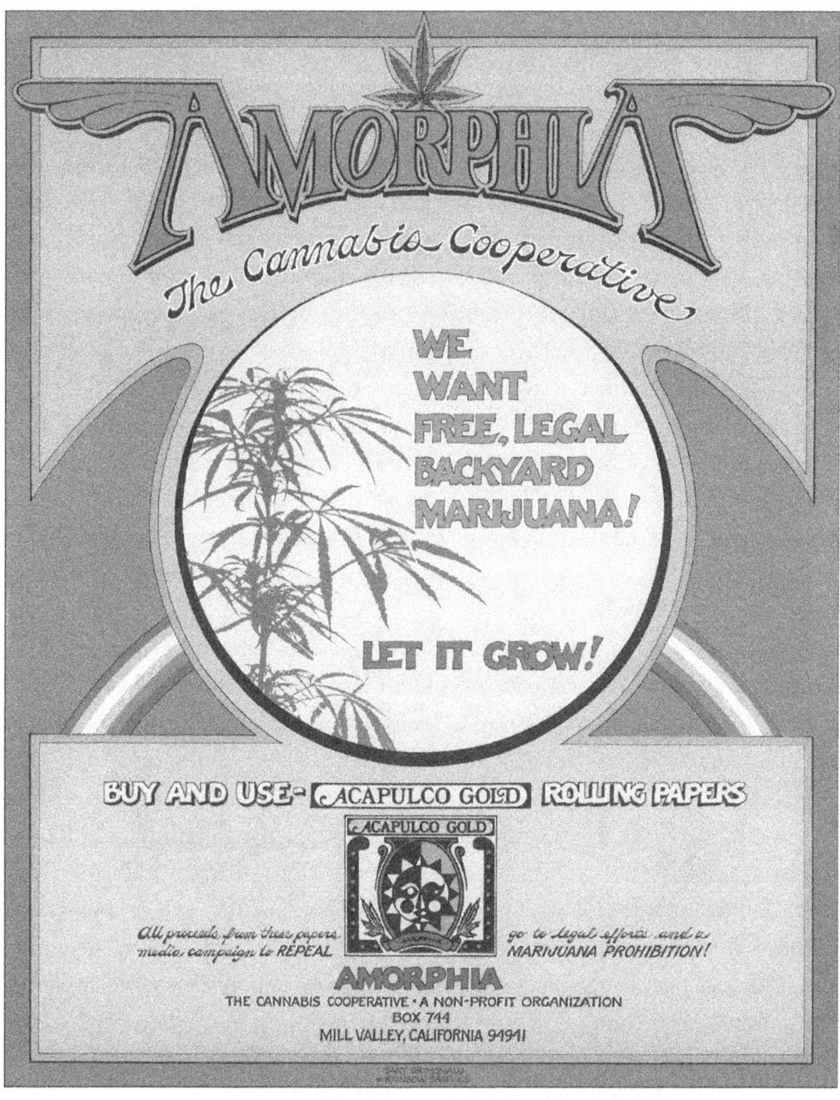

FIGURE 5.3. Amorphia, a radical countercultural organization, led California's legalization movement in the early 1970s with the demand for "free, legal backyard marijuana." This left-libertarian vision rejected the ACLU/NORML proposal for a state-regulated market in favor of an anticorporate system of homegrown cultivation and local exchange. (HS20042, John and Leni Sinclair Papers, Bentley Historical Library, University of Michigan. Poster image © Gary Grimshaw.)

and marketing-abuse nexus of the regulated sectors of alcohol and prescription drugs. Amorphia's alternative model, deeply rooted in California's vibrant environmental and consumer activism movements, proposed a locally based nonprofit distribution system with revenue from "legal weed utilized as an economic foundation for constructive social change." The conflict between Amorphia and NORML boiled over during California's 1972 decriminalization referendum (examined below), which Stroup characterized as a "classic struggle between the middle-class reformers and the people who think they're fighting the revolution." Amorphia's ambitious national plans disintegrated after the failure of that initiative, supplanted by the for-profit regulatory model and middle-class reform agenda championed by NORML and the ACLU.[11]

In 1972, the American Civil Liberties Union joined forces with NORML to launch a nationwide lobbying campaign, targeting Congress and the state legislatures with the slogans "Current marijuana laws criminalize American youth," and "The law is making criminals of our children." After failing to achieve legalization through litigation, particularly in cases charging discrimination against longhaired "hippies," ACLU strategists decided to orchestrate a legislative effort "largely pitched [to] middle-class America." In preparation for the 1972 launch, the national ACLU finally took the much-debated step of extending its legalization position to include the regulated alcohol-model sale of marijuana to adults over age eighteen. Both the ACLU and NORML considered the Shafer Commission report to be inadequate but adopted the pragmatic view that the best possible outcome in many states would be decriminalization of use and possession or, at the most, misdemeanor penalties that did not include jail time. In its legislative manual, the ACLU urged state affiliates to mobilize students, liberal churches, lawyers, women's groups, possibly doctors (with caution because of the AMA's conservatism on the marijuana issue), and to reach out to civil rights groups. On the latter tactic, the manual warned that some Black leaders would resist legalization because of their concerns about heroin trafficking, and many might also resent the fact that a political movement for drug reform only came "after marijuana use spread to white middle-class society." The ACLU campaign materials rejected the "amotivational syndrome" scenario as a confusion of cause and effect, arguing that most pot smokers were "socially perceptive, functioning individuals" with much to contribute to society if they could avoid arrest for a victimless crime. The ACLU also denounced the police apparatus for rampant misconduct in the war against marijuana, condemned the compulsory rehabilitation of drug users as an infringement on freedom, and concluded that criminal prohibition was "perverting our law enforcement system and threatening our civil liberties."[12]

The combined efforts of NORML and the ACLU provided a broader platform for the dissident faction of medical experts and academic researchers who disparaged the bipartisan Washington consensus in the war on drugs. Both organizations drew frequent parallels to Prohibition of alcohol in the 1920s to highlight market realities that almost all elected and appointed federal officials either minimized or denied. Combining law enforcement and coercive medicalization had proved a "complete failure" in the war on drugs, driving up cost rather than eradicating supply, producing the violence and criminality in an underground economy that legal regulation would eliminate, incapable of "curing" either marijuana smokers or heroin addicts through compulsory programs. Both organizations publicized the research of Stanford law professor John Kaplan, author of *Marijuana: The New Prohibition* (1970), which portrayed criminalization as another futile and discriminatory war on youth culture and carefully demonstrated the hypocrisy of arresting pot smokers when alcohol and cigarettes caused far more social harm. Both also promoted the revisionist scholarship of Lester Grinspoon, the Harvard psychiatrist and author of *Marihuana Reconsidered* (1971), which castigated the public health establishment as well as crime control agencies for continuing to operate under the long shadow of Harry Anslinger. Grinspoon rebuked the AMA for its official position that "a person who has a psychological dependence on marijuana is sick," which in the 1970 federal reforms helped to justify both the retention of criminal sanctions and the unwarranted coercion of pot smokers into psychiatric treatment as a condition of probation. *Marihuana Reconsidered* attributed criminalization to anti-youth prejudice, racial anxiety (pot "is *the* non-white drug which is rapidly invading the white community"), and misguided capitalist imperatives (the perception that alcohol "lubricates the wheels of commerce" but potheads renounced the Protestant work ethic). "We must move," Grinspoon concluded, "to make the social use of marijuana legal."[13]

The marijuana legalization movement of the early 1970s, with its explicit agenda to rescue otherwise law-abiding white middle-class victims from drug-war enforcement, generally evaded the question of whether criminal prohibition made sense for any illicit drug. NORML and the ACLU, along with legalization advocates such as Lester Grinspoon, ridiculed the heroin-gateway mythology but popularized two alternative versions: that criminalization of pot smoking drove youth consumers into an underground market pervaded by narcotics pushers, and that misinformation about marijuana in drug abuse education would make skeptical youth more likely to experiment with truly dangerous drugs such as speed, acid, and smack. The ACLU, more than NORML, acknowledged the racially discriminatory enforcement of drug laws but portrayed marijuana legalization as the best way to keep ghetto youth away from "narcotics peddlers," rather than contemplating whether its commitment to civil liberties should extend to ending heroin prohibition as well. Grinspoon considered any analogy between marijuana and heroin to be "ludicrously inapplicable," but several major studies published in 1972 argued in effect for the decriminalization and regulation of all drugs.[14] *Dealing with Drug Abuse,* a Ford Foundation report, labeled interdiction and criminal enforcement a complete failure and called for the repeal of all sanctions for all criminalized drug users. The study recommended a state-provided system of heroin maintenance, as in Britain, to reduce the high cost and addict property crime that the underground market created by prohibition guaranteed. The Consumers Union, in its report on how and why "prohibition does not work," also endorsed state-regulated heroin maintenance and blamed law enforcement for inevitably creating the illicit market that the government futilely promised to eradicate. As for marijuana, "no conceivable law enforcement program can curb its availability," and therefore the only rational government policy would be to legalize and safely regulate the product for American consumers, while freeing all drug-war prisoners.[15]

During 1972–73, the most progressive faction of public health liberals in the Senate tried and failed to generate momentum behind the partial decriminalization recommendation of the National Commission on Marihuana. One month after the Shafer report, commission members Harold Hughes (D-IA) and Jacob Javits (R-NY) introduced a bill to repeal criminal sanctions for personal use and possession of up to three ounces and casual (nonprofit) transfer of small amounts. Both carefully distinguished this reform from outright legalization and emphasized that commercial traffickers "must be prosecuted." Both also lamented the shattered lives of otherwise law-abiding Americans and advanced the generation gap argument that marijuana prohibition represented a hypocritical form of anti-youth discrimination by cocktail-sipping policymakers and middle-aged adults. (President Nixon, discussing the Shafer Commission with Art Linkletter, observed that youth smoked pot "to get a charge, and float," whereas "at least with liquor, I don't lose motivation.") The Democratic-controlled Judiciary Committee buried the Javits-Hughes bill without debate, even though Senator Thomas Dodd and other sponsors of the

Controlled Substances Act of 1970 (Title II of the omnibus legislation) had repeatedly promised to revisit the marijuana penalties after the commission's report.[16] Hughes and Javits reintroduced their decriminalization bill in 1973, arguing that with at least twenty-four million pot smokers in America, the law obviously provided no deterrent and "fair and impartial enforcement and prosecution are impossible." Yet even Javits rejected the Consumers Union's call for a government-regulated marijuana market, part of his broader criticism of the Nixon administration for "wantonly making criminals out of people for casually using marijuana and not successfully prosecuting sellers and pushers." Marijuana decriminalization advocates seemed unable to recognize that a policy criminalizing supply but not personal consumption would actually reproduce the Volstead Act framework of federal alcohol Prohibition in the 1920s.[17]

The Bureau of Narcotics and Dangerous Drugs denounced decriminalization as a smokescreen for legalization and continued to circulate pusher-gateway arguments to justify marijuana prohibition. In 1972, the BNDD responded to the Shafer Commission report by defending the public interest against a "vocal minority" that demanded "approval of 'pleasure drugs' as a basic right." The BNDD insisted on the legal penalty as a deterrent to youthful experimentation and labeled the decriminalization of private use a loophole "to allow traffickers to possess with impunity." Most forcefully, the BNDD attacked the removal of sanctions for casual sale of marijuana as a free license for "proselytizers—those who convert naïve persons to drug abusers." The BNDD promoted multiple versions of this modified pusher-victim interpretation during the early 1970s, including urging censure of the "manifestly pro-drug" messages of psychedelic rock music and the hippie underground press ("initiate them into the drug scene") and condemning pro-legalization academics ("Spockian ultra-permissivists" allied with the "drug cult"). The Drug Enforcement Administration, its successor agency, continued to oppose decriminalization on the gateway-pusher grounds that experimenting youth would soon be smoking highly potent hashish and "become a target of the people who will introduce him into the culture that uses stronger drugs." According to the DEA, "large well-financed, well-organized criminal organizations," not the amateur dealers of the 1960s, had taken over the marijuana market.[18] A 1972 Gallup survey, conducted just before the Shafer report, revealed that most Americans also opposed marijuana legalization, subscribed to the same gateway mystique, attributed physical and psychological damage to smoking pot, and wanted tough enforcement against sellers (fig. 5.4). But almost one-third

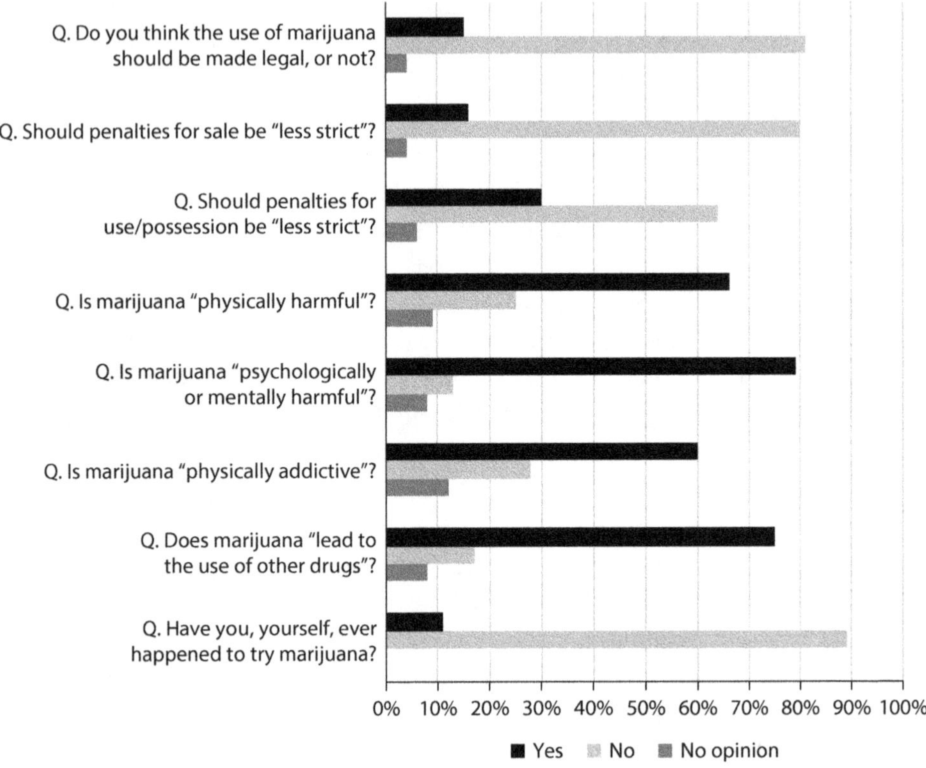

FIGURE 5.4. Gallup national survey responses on marijuana, March 1972. Only 15% of American adults endorsed marijuana legalization in this national survey. Almost one-third advocated "less strict" penalties for possession, revealing a reservoir of support for the partial decriminalization approach. Large majorities continued to believe in the traditional myths that marijuana was addictive and led to heroin or other "hard drugs." (*The Gallup Poll: Public Opinion, 1972–1977.*)
Note: In the eighteen-to-twenty-nine age category, 29% of those surveyed answered yes to marijuana use in 1972. The Gallup totals for all adults reporting marijuana use are also lower than figures revealed in more in-depth federal studies (16% in 1972).

advocated "less strict" penalties for use and possession, evidence of a potential reservoir of support for a decriminalization compromise, and by late 1974 more than one-fourth of Gallup respondents endorsed legalization outright.[19]

The Nixon White House stifled support for the Shafer Commission recommendations by public health officials inside the administration, even as a number of leading establishment organizations endorsed partial decriminalization. In 1971, new NIMH director Bertram Brown questioned the deterrent effect of legal prohibition in his testimony to the commission and then told reporters afterward that the possession penalty should be "minimal or nonexistent, . . . a fine, like for a parking ticket." An enraged Richard Nixon told his political aides to make sure the Justice Department and not the psychiatrists controlled all drug policy decisions and, regarding Brown, "Fire the son of a bitch, and I mean today!" Brown survived but followed orders not to speak out again in favor of decriminalization, although he repeatedly criticized the marijuana-to-heroin gateway mythology, a foundation of Nixon's rhetoric in the war on drugs. In 1973, in a typical exchange, Brown testified to Congress that he did not have White House permission to provide a scientific opinion on whether marijuana should be classified alongside heroin in Schedule 1 of the Controlled Substances Act, even though the law gave HEW the authority to make a new determination.[20] Soon after stepping down, Nixon drug policy advisor Jerome Jaffe informed Congress that public health officials had hoped that, after the 1972 election, the White House would change course and support a civil fine for marijuana possession. While the law-and-order side prevailed, Jaffe believed that "not only should people not go to jail. I do not think they should be threatened with jail." The relatively conservative American Medical Association backed decriminalization of possession and added a call for research into marijuana's potential as a medical therapy. The American Bar Association also adopted a decriminalization resolution while advising law enforcement to "concentrate on detecting and punishing sellers of the drug." In taking this stance, the ABA rejected an internal recommendation and a NORML lobbying campaign to support full legalization through an alcohol-style system regulated by each state.[21]

The most unexpected and volatile development in the national decriminalization debate followed the release of FBI data showing 420,700 marijuana arrests nationwide in 1973, accounting for more than two-thirds of all drug apprehensions that year, and almost 2.5 times the total from 1969 (fig. 5.5). Overall, federal, state, and local authorities made almost 1.7 million arrests for marijuana during Nixon's six years in office, with the proportion rising from 46 percent of drug arrests in 1971, the year the president declared war on drug abuse, to 69 percent in 1974, the year he resigned. More than three-fifths of those arrested were younger than twenty-one, more than four-fifths under age twenty-six, and more than 90 percent involved simple possession.[22] The leading decriminalization advocates in Congress, Harold Hughes and Jacob Javits, convened another hearing in late 1974 to investigate this extraordinary law enforcement effort against a "victimless crime," resulting in "lives disrupted and even ruined, families divided, records besmirched, and the pain of ostracism."

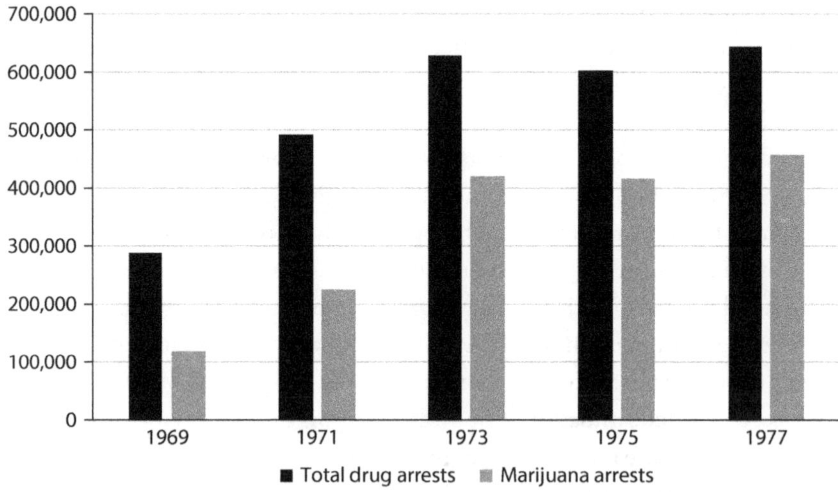

FIGURE 5.5. Marijuana arrests as a proportion of total drug arrests in the United States, 1969–77. Intensified law enforcement and increasing rates of illegal drug use resulted in the doubling of annual drug arrests in the United States between 1969 and 1973. The proportion of marijuana arrests relative to all drug arrests jumped from 41% to 67% during the same period and reached 72% in 1976. This surge was directly linked to the reduction of simple possession from a felony to misdemeanor charge in most states. Most marijuana arrests involved white juveniles and young adults busted for possession. (FBI, *Uniform Crime Reports*, 1969–1977.)

Dr. Robert DuPont, the newly appointed director of the Special Action Office for Drug Abuse Prevention in the Gerald Ford administration, testified that smoking marijuana involved health risks but was "probably safer medically than pills and alcohol." He agreed on the need to curb the "excessive social costs" in the arrest data but explained that the administration would not endorse "decriminalization" per se, because some sort of sanction remained necessary to express federal disapproval of marijuana use. DuPont did encourage Congress to consider making possession subject to a civil fine rather than a criminal penalty, as Oregon had recently done (discussed below), without explicitly endorsing this reform. Keith Stroup, representing NORML, condemned the surge in marijuana arrests as a colossal waste of resources, a violation of civil liberties, and a discriminatory policy of "enforcing moral standards or combatting different lifestyles." And in a tactical shift, Stroup fully endorsed the Shafer Commission's decriminalization proposal, based on the recognition that public opinion and political realities did not yet support a legal, regulated market.[23]

The advocates of marijuana decriminalization rarely if ever questioned whether the enormous increase in arrest totals by the mid-1970s included discriminatory enforcement against racial minorities, lower-income groups, and inner-city residents. On the contrary, both NORML and the small liberal congressional faction that endorsed decriminalization repeatedly urged the government to redirect drug enforcement to the heroin market and escalate the war on violent street crime, categories implicitly coded as Black and urban in the same way that "otherwise law-abiding" pot smokers signified white and suburban.[24] The congressional hearings, NORML publications, and broader discourse almost never discussed the discretionary role of racial, socioeconomic, and geographic discrimination in the disposition of marijuana offenders after arrest: dismissed or reduced charges, user or "possession with intent to sell" status, diversion into rehabilitation or drug abuse programs, probation or a fine, informal supervision or juvenile detention, jail term or prison sentence. The marijuana decriminalization movement, and the national drug-war debate, also did not acknowledge much less address the racial data hiding in plain sight in the annual FBI *Uniform Crime Reports*, a few pages after the inflammatory statistics on police busts of presumably "otherwise law-abiding" pot smokers: the continued drug arrests of Black Americans at 2.5 times their adult population share throughout the 1970s (fig. 5.6 [top]). Although the FBI did not disaggregate marijuana arrests by race, and did not quantify the criminalization of Hispanics at all during this era, the data reveals disproportionate policing of African Americans in all drug categories. The juvenile arrests tell a different story, with Black minors detained at roughly their population share (fig. 5.6 [bottom]). This was a product of both the historically unprecedented crackdown on white teenagers in the recreational marijuana market and the processes of diversion, compulsory rehabilitation, and informal mediation that followed their admittedly traumatic and disruptive encounters with law enforcement.[25]

In 1975, under congressional fire for the extraordinary surge in arrests of pot smokers, the DEA claimed that the war on drugs targeted heroin traffickers and that 85 percent of marijuana possession busts nationwide were "incidental" to other enforcement activities, in particular vehicle stops, loitering and disorderly conduct charges, and "plain sight" searches. Evidence from large metropolitan jurisdictions indicates that targeted marijuana enforcement accounted for a much higher percentage than the DEA's politicized estimate, and the Justice Department also provided massive funding for multiagency task forces and dedicated drug squads even in areas with small or nonexistent heroin markets.[26] But even if true, these discretionary "incidental" categories

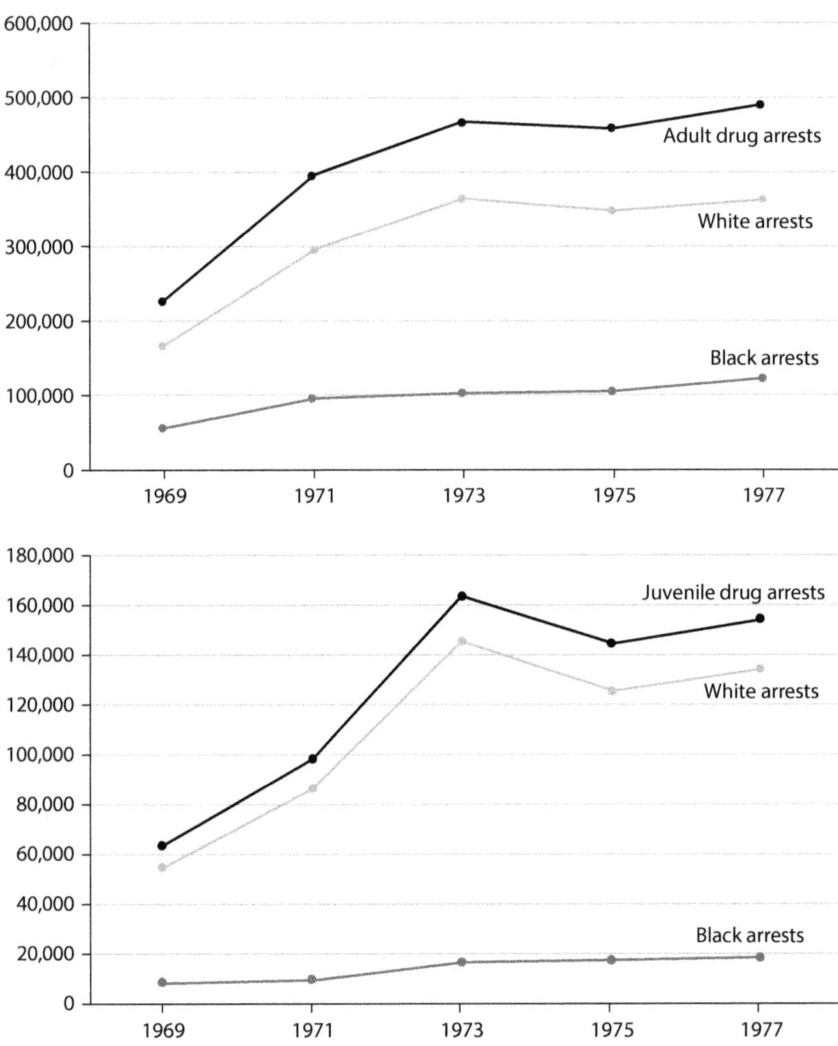

FIGURE 5.6. Racial distribution of adult and juvenile drug arrests in the United States, 1969–77. (*Top*) Around three-fourths of adult drug arrests during the 1970s involved white offenders, a proportion that remained stable even as total arrests more than doubled. The arrest share for Black adults increased only slightly but remained disproportionate at approximately 2.5 times the population share throughout the decade. (*Bottom*) Law enforcement agencies arrested white juveniles on drug charges in close proportion to their population share during the 1970s, a pattern that would shift substantially during the following decade. Black juveniles experienced a historically low proportion of drug arrests during the 1970s, approximating their share of the population. (FBI, *Uniform Crime Reports*, 1969–1977.)

Note. On the FBI's inclusion of most Hispanic arrests in the "white" category, see note in fig. 1.1. The racial breakdown of the U.S. population in the 1980 census was 79.6% white (non-Hispanic), 11.5% Black, and 6.5% Hispanic.

are precisely the mechanisms through which racial profiling in law enforcement has functioned historically and contemporaneously, and through which age- and lifestyle-based profiling of white youth had escalated during the previous decade. By 1976, five years after Nixon declared war on drugs, heroin arrests had plummeted to less than one-tenth the national total, which represented not a victory over narcotics but an enormous expansion of the carceral state—the punitive fusion of law enforcement and public health—into a recreational marijuana market that accounted for 71 percent of all drug busts. This explosion resulted from increased rates of use across the nation, the unprecedented criminalization of white pot smokers, federal subsidies for local drug enforcement, and saturation policing in particular jurisdictions (especially Southern California)—but also the stop-and-frisk tactics, street-level sweeps, quasi-legal or illegal profiling searches, and other forms of racially targeted policing in the urban war on drugs and crime.[27] Since the drug-war debate operated through a formally color-blind discourse, and since detailed national data on marijuana arrests is not available, only case studies of key states and localities can illuminate the convergence of race, class, and geographic space in both the discretionary criminal justice process and the countermovement for drug-war reform.[28]

State-Level Reform: "Concerned Parents" and "The Wrong Kids"

In most states, the marijuana debate in the early 1970s paralleled the federal trajectory of crisis rhetoric about the spread of illegal drugs to the suburbs, followed by the portrayal of white middle-class youth as innocent victims of the pushers, culminating in legal reforms that reduced possession penalties but maintained tough sanctions for distribution. In a special message to the New Jersey legislature in 1970, Republican governor William Cahill labeled drug abuse a "problem that now threatens an entire generation, . . . in the ghetto and affluent suburbs alike." Cahill called for a law enforcement focus on heroin trafficking and "professional drug peddlers" and sympathy for the young "victims of this trade." State lawmakers responded by making marijuana possession the equivalent of disorderly conduct, with a penalty range from a fine to six months in jail. In Illinois, Republican governor Richard Ogilvie introduced his 1971 reforms by acknowledging that the crisis had taken on new urgency since the "children of affluence dropped out and brought the 'drug problem' close to most of us." He warned of the potential decimation of an entire generation and criticized the excessive marijuana laws for driving young pot smokers underground, "toward the dangerous criminals who thrive on the addictive drug culture." The Illinois legislature enacted his proposal to give conditional probation to recreational marijuana users, alongside mandatory minimums for selling drugs to minors. In Florida, the state narcotics task force issued a 1970 report that called heroin an "insignificant" problem and categorized felony penalties for recreational marijuana use as "harsh and unworkable." One year later, the legislature reduced marijuana possession to a misdemeanor while setting the mandatory range for selling pot to a minor at ten years to life. The bill's sponsor, a law-and-order Republican from Sarasota, abandoned his hardline position on marijuana because "my constituents demanded it. . . . Parents just don't want to see their kids imprisoned for something they think may not be as harmful as alcohol or tobacco."[29]

Between 1969 and 1971, every state government altered its marijuana laws, with more than four-fifths reducing punishment for simple possession to a misdemeanor. The Justice Department encouraged states to adopt the penalty structure of the 1970 federal reforms through the Uniform Controlled Substances Act, which also reclassified marijuana as a hallucinogen rather than a narcotic. Thirty states quickly adopted some version of the Uniform Act, generally in alignment with the federal structure setting a misdemeanor penalty range for marijuana possession from probation to one year in jail. More than three-fourths of the states enhanced punishment for selling marijuana to a minor, usually with a three-year age differential in order to exempt college students who supplied other teenagers. Most state laws included the ambiguous "intent to sell" category and preserved felony penalties for possession of more than a specified amount, usually one ounce. More than half of states removed all mandatory-minimum penalties for marijuana sale, with discretionary sentencing usually capped at either five or ten years. Others retained the mandatory-minimum approach, most notably states with large heroin markets in racially diverse metropolitan areas. California's 1970 law made marijuana possession subject to a wide discretionary range, from a misdemeanor to a ten-year felony term, while convicted sellers faced a minimum of five years and a maximum life sentence. Texas modified its drug laws in 1971, providing two to life for felony possession of marijuana and five to life for distribution. In New York, where the politics of heroin and street crime shaped an atypically punitive approach, the 1971 legislature increased the penalty for possession of more than one ounce of marijuana to a mandatory minimum of five to fifteen years, while sale to a minor brought an eight- to-twenty-five-year sentence. In its assessment of state drug laws, the National Commission on Marihuana concluded, "It is unconscionable that penalties should vary so greatly in response to the same behavior."[30]

State laws that adopted the federal model institutionalized the discretionary and diversionary practices that local prosecutors and judges had already fashioned to deal with the influx of white middle-class pot smokers in the late 1960s (see chapter 3), often with formal authorization for conditional discharge and record expungement for first offenders who completed rehabilitation programs. Statutory discretion, of course, simultaneously facilitated various forms of discrimination as prosecutors and judges assessed criminality and decided whether to dismiss or downgrade a charge, remand to probation, or require jail time. Probation provided no panacea for marijuana defendants, especially those compelled to undergo medical therapy or even enter rehabilitation centers as a condition of their plea; in 1974, pot smokers represented 15 percent of patients in federally funded residential programs, and the proportion was undoubtedly higher in locally run suburban facilities.[31] The discretionary leverage of police, prosecutors, and judges increased significantly in cases of marijuana sale, especially in the determination of casual sharing (misdemeanor) versus for-profit distribution (felony), with the potential for five- or ten-year prison sentences even in states that did not retain mandatory minimums. Discriminatory treatment fell most heavily on racial minorities, political radicals, visible "hippies," and random defendants unlucky enough to face a hardline prosecutor or judge. In 1971, in the small town of Woodsfield, Ohio, the sheriff deployed a neighbor to trick a young married couple, ages nineteen and twenty-four, into providing a small amount of marijuana for $5. Ohio's 1970 drug reform made possession a misdemeanor but punished sellers with a mandatory-minimum sentence of twenty to forty years, which both defendants received from a local judge determined to send a message to the community. The ACLU and NORML publicized such cases as outrageous miscarriages of justice, including a Black man in Virginia given forty years for dealing marijuana in a probable entrapment bust, and a longhaired college student in Missouri serving twelve years for selling $5 worth of pot to an undercover agent.[32]

The partial decriminalization compromise that the ACLU and NORML reluctantly supported would not provide any relief for defendants convicted of selling pot, but a pragmatic lobbying campaign aimed at state legislatures seemed the best available option because the federal courts declined to overturn marijuana laws in the face of constitutional challenges. In 1971, the Fifth

Circuit Court of Appeals rejected an Eighth Amendment "cruel and unusual" claim on behalf of a white working-class Dallas man who received a thirty-year sentence for possession of one joint, based on the traditional doctrine of judicial deference to the legislature's statutory authority in the area of criminal law.[33] In spring 1972, however, the Supreme Court of Michigan vacated a twenty-year mandatory-minimum sentence for selling marijuana as a violation of the ban on "cruel and unusual" punishments in the federal and state constitutions. The decision reasoned that "a compulsory prison sentence of 20 years for a nonviolent crime imposed without consideration for defendant's individual personality and history is so excessive that it 'shocks the conscience.'" In a companion case, the Michigan Supreme Court overturned the ten-year sentence for possession of two joints by John Sinclair, the radical marijuana legalization activist, on grounds of police entrapment. Crucially, both decisions came after the Michigan legislature repealed the mandatory-minimum marijuana law and established discretionary penalties of up to ninety days for possession (misdemeanor) and up to five years for sale (felony). Governor William Milliken, a moderate Republican, denounced both marijuana legalization and the "injustices" of inflexible mandatory sentences that turned youth into felons, and he argued that the new discretionary approach would finally distinguish "between drug profiteers and their victims." In 1974, NORML tried to expand the Michigan precedent by challenging all criminal use and possession sanctions as a violation of the constitutional "right to privacy" and the "cruel and unusual" doctrine, but the federal courts dismissed this litigation as "obviously without merit."[34]

The story behind marijuana possession reform in Texas reveals how the racial reframing of the drug war's victims and the political mobilization of white suburban parents could transform the policy debate even in a very conservative political climate. In 1969, as part of the ACLU's campaign for marijuana legalization, the Texas Civil Liberties Union (TCLU) filed a "cruel and unusual" lawsuit on behalf of Jessie Trevino, a Hispanic man serving a ninety-year sentence for possession of eight grams of marijuana. The Texas Board of Pardons and Paroles neutralized the litigation by commuting Trevino's sentence to ten years. A legal study revealed that almost 90 percent of the harshest marijuana sentences (exceeding thirty years) went to African American or Latino defendants, and almost all originated in Dallas or Houston. By the late 1960s, college-educated and middle-class whites smoked marijuana at the highest rates in the state, but 37.5 percent of those incarcerated for felony pot

TABLE 5.1. Prisoners Convicted and Incarcerated for Marijuana Felonies in the State of Texas, 1971

Category	White	Black	Hispanic
Percentage (Race) of all marijuana prisoners	43.5%	37.5%	19%
Percentage (Race) serving 31–40 years	10%	90% (Black/Hispanic combined)	
Percentage (Race) serving 50 years–life	25%	75% (Black/Hispanic combined)	
Percentage (All) without high school degree	95% (all races combined)		
Percentage (All) male	96% (all races combined)		
Percentage of total state drug prisoners	42% (800 marijuana convicts out of 1,892 total)		
Percentage of first offenders	56% (of total marijuana prisoners)		
Percentage of possession convictions	47% (375 out of 800 marijuana prisoners)		
Percentage ages 17–21	31% (245 out of 800 marijuana prisoners)		
Percentage from Dallas County	30% (Dallas County = 12% state population)		

Source: *Marijuana in Texas: A Report to the Senate Interim Drug Study Committee*, March 1972.

Note: The racial breakdown of Texas's population (1970 census) was an estimated 70% white (non-Hispanic), 17% Hispanic, and 12.5% Black.

violations were African American (triple the population share), 19 percent were Hispanic (compared to 17 percent of the population), and 95 percent lacked high school diplomas (table 5.1). About half of marijuana prisoners were first offenders convicted of possession. The Texas pattern reveals the comprehensive racial, socioeconomic, gender, and geographic bias in the discretionary authority wielded at all levels of the criminal legal system, from police and prosecutors to judges and juries. The legislature's 1971 reforms—two to life for marijuana possession, five to life for distribution—maintained the broad discretionary system that invited discriminatory punishment, although without the official misdemeanor loophole for simple possession and casual sale provided by federal law and the model Uniform Controlled Substances Act. Texas therefore retained the technical classification of recreational pot smokers as "an enormous class of felons far too large for law enforcement to apprehend, and far too large to be incarcerated." Although they provided no effective deterrent, the legal investigation concluded, "Texas marijuana laws are the harshest in the world."[35]

In the late 1960s, police agencies in metropolitan Dallas began detaining an increasing number of white teenagers from upper-middle-class neighborhoods for marijuana possession. Before then, media coverage of the youth drug crisis had emphasized the dangers of dope pushers targeting suburban runaways in downtown bohemian enclaves, and police raids to catch LSD and marijuana users at the "hippie pads" near the universities. In 1968, the Greater Dallas Crime Commission, a citizens group dominated by conservative businessmen, leveled explosive charges that an organized criminal enterprise was recruiting teenage girls from affluent areas into prostitution through the lure of "marijuana and ultimately hard dope." Two years later, the Dallas district attorney announced that the wealthiest high schools in the city and inner-ring suburbs were suddenly producing more drug cases than the South Dallas ghetto. A local judge exacerbated civic alarm when he reported that the courts were processing an "amazing" number of teenage marijuana and LSD users from affluent white areas. After complaints from white parents, law enforcement officials sought to clarify that they were "mainly concerned with tracking down hard-core criminals—not teenagers who have been smoking pot."[36] As in other metropolitan regions, the criminal justice system dealt with the influx of white middle-class teenagers and college students by greatly expanding discretionary methods of counsel-and-release, extralegal diversion, downgraded charges, and probation for psychiatric treatment. In 1970, one Dallas County judge sentenced two visiting Black college students from California to three years in prison for possession of marijuana, shortly after his son received probation for the same offense. Most affluent white youth arrested for marijuana possession in the Dallas-Fort Worth area either ended up on probation or found their charges dropped in exchange for a "mild rebuke," in the words of one local politician. But their families often felt extreme distress at "the terrible possibility of being sent to the penitentiary," given the mandatory-minimum law.[37]

In Texas, as in other parts of the nation, political discourse fluctuated between portraying white middle-class youth as the victims of illegal drug traffickers and viewing them as the impossible targets of over-zealous drug enforcement. In 1969, Attorney General Crawford Martin proclaimed that Texas was "losing the war against crime," as narcotics (marijuana) and LSD pushers invaded the senior and junior high schools. "They are the lowest type of criminal," he charged. "Potential murderers of our children." In the capital city of Austin, the district attorney wept in the courtroom while asking a jury to render a life sentence for marijuana possession (of 187 pounds, meaning for a commercial trafficker), sobbing that "my little girl is five years old and this is my country and I want this stuff off the streets."[38] A team of academic researchers delivered a very different message to the Texas Narcotic Officers Association at a 1970 training session. The three most dangerous drugs in Texas, they pointed out, were regulated consumer products marketed by large corporations: alcohol, tobacco, and prescription medication (especially amphetamines). They asked the law enforcement audience if it would even be possible to enforce criminal penalties against the estimated 570,000 Texas youth currently between ages fourteen and twenty-one who had smoked marijuana. In effect, the researchers argued, the state already operated a system of "de facto legalization of marijuana," with participants in the recreational subculture fully aware of what politicians and police were afraid to admit. The main threat to the futures of pot-smoking white youth came from the random, unlikely chance that they might be arrested and branded as felons. The report advocated misdemeanor reduction for marijuana possession and criticized both discrimination in sentencing and the punitive rehabilitation of diverting recreational users into psychiatric treatment. Cracking down on "pushers" provided no practical solution either, because marijuana (unlike heroin) was easily homegrown, and so law enforcement had little chance of cutting off the supply.[39]

By 1972, Texas remained one of only two states (along with Rhode Island) that still classified simple possession of marijuana as a mandatory felony. That spring, a special drug committee established by the state senate reported that rates of marijuana use were highest among younger white-collar professionals and white high school and college students from affluent urban and suburban neighborhoods (nearly one half at UT–Austin and almost one-third of high school seniors in metropolitan centers). Almost all of these technical criminals "secure the drug not from adult 'pushers,' as seems so commonly thought, but from their peers." George Beto, director of the Texas Board of Corrections, told the committee that he did not want these recreational pot smokers in his prisons because they should not be punished and could not be rehabilitated. The marijuana prohibition laws targeted "victimless crimes" and "confuse sins with felonies," he contended. With "these younger middle class marijuana users, . . . we're not necessarily dealing with people who want to be helped. . . . There is not a clear cut conviction in their minds that they've done anything wrong." The senate committee's final report, released in January 1973, echoed the Shafer Commission in calling for the decriminalization of possession combined with much lower felony penalties for sale, with a three-year maximum. The current policy of prohibition through law enforcement was "simply foolish," the committee observed, adding that abstinence-only drug education programs were also unrealistic and ineffective. Like alcohol, "for better or worse, marijuana is here to stay." The report advocated a non-coercive public health approach that focused on the relatively small percentage of drug "abusers," particularly of heroin, and did not force recreational pot smokers into medical treatment any more than jail. Even heroin possession should not be criminalized, the senate committee advised, because addiction was a symptom of underlying problems for people from "seriously troubled backgrounds," not anything that legal sanctions could eradicate.[40]

NORML intervened in the Texas debate through its standard tropes of white middle-class victimization, based on the clear-eyed understanding that even in a conservative state, most suburban parents "don't really want to make criminals of their own children." In early 1973, the organization established Concerned Parents for Marijuana Reform, a quasi-grassroots lobby based in the white-collar suburbs north of Dallas and made up of mothers and fathers of imprisoned youth. At the time, Texas incarcerated seven hundred people on felony convictions for simple possession of marijuana, half first offenders, with an average sentence of 9.5 years. NORML director Keith Stroup toured a Texas prison to highlight the fates of white "dope martyrs" such as a twenty-one-year-old father of two who received five years for possession of two joints, a Dallas hipster and underground journalist serving ten years after a police frame job, and a University of Texas freshman facing a twenty-five-year sentence for dealing marijuana. Frank Demolli, the UT student, had pleaded guilty in his 1971 trial, expecting probation, but the jury had no sympathy after the prosecutor labeled him a hippie pusher who corrupted innocent children. NORML's newsletter instead portrayed these young white men as political prisoners of a culture that "mistakenly identifies marijuana only with long hair and radical politics." NORML also teamed up with Richard Cowan, a young and prominent Fort Worth conservative who had recently endorsed marijuana legalization in the *National Review*. Cowan criticized the Texas state government for applying draconian drug laws to middle-class youth in the marijuana scene, including campus dealers such as Demolli, instead of heroin pushers who deserved to be locked away. NORML's strategy emphasized this implicitly racial and spatial distinction between the unjustified criminalization of marijuana and the legitimate crusade against hard drugs; few reformers highlighted heroin prisoners such as the Mexican American man given a 1,500-year sentence in Dallas, or the Latino defendant who received 1,800 years from a jury in Odessa.[41]

As NORML anticipated, pressure from the affluent white parents of pot-smoking teenagers and college students played a critical role in reforming the Texas drug laws. In early 1973, a conservative Republican state senator named Betty Andujar introduced a bill to reduce possession of two ounces or less of marijuana to a misdemeanor violation with a maximum six-month sentence. Andujar, who represented metropolitan Fort Worth, justified her proposal as a response to the "anguished cries" of upper-middle-class professionals whose children faced jail time, an effort "to get the heat off the very fine families who are enmeshed in this tragic situation." She argued that law enforcement should focus on the "pushers of hard drugs" and compared the social role of marijuana in the youth subculture to the centrality of alcohol for adults at the country club.[42] Andujar received many letters from self-identified "concerned parents" who lived in the Dallas-Fort Worth suburbs and pleaded for new laws that would keep "our" (white, middle-class) children out of prison. A mother from Garland (99% white), a suburb north of Dallas, lamented the family "heart-ache" caused by marijuana laws and asked the legislature to "return hundreds of our youth to their homes." Another mother from an upscale north Dallas suburb wondered how "our boys and girls whose only crime was a marijuana cigarette" could be punished more severely than rapists and murderers and reiterated: "*We don't want our children in Prison!*" A father and "very concerned parent" whose son had been arrested called marijuana a harmless drug and demanded of the legislature, "Are you willing to let our children rot in jail? . . . One day it just could be your child too!" Another mother who lived outside Dallas lamented the "gross injustice" visited upon her son, who could not head to college or "plan for a future" while awaiting his marijuana trial. The superintendent in a Fort Worth suburb informed Andujar that the penalties had to change because half of the high school students were smoking pot—but Texas should keep cracking down on the pushers.[43]

The opposition to marijuana reform in the Texas suburbs revolved around the pusher and gateway tropes, while most younger pot smokers and convicted felons advocated total legalization. A number of Andujar's constituents felt betrayed by her stance and told her, in the blunt assessment of one Fort Worth woman, "You are *not a good Republican.*" Mothers wrote to remind her that pot dealers "are looking for a gullible youngster to 'hook' on the stuff" and to relate tales about how "the drug peddlers kill people with their poison" by introducing children to heroin through marijuana. A physician from suburban Dallas explained that the marijuana counterculture recruited innocent youth in order to turn America into "a society of dreamers and zombies," while another man demanded that Texas protect the "fine children in my community" by taking down the "big money marijuana sellers." From the other side, an incarcerated male from Fort Worth demanded the release of all marijuana prisoners and criticized the misdemeanor reform proposal for still imposing an unfair stigma on otherwise law-abiding citizens.[44] A local high school student echoed this argument in a letter to Chris Miller, a liberal Democrat who represented Fort Worth in the Texas House and who had campaigned on relaxed penalties for possession and tough enforcement against pushers. "Grass must be legalized large sells and small sells," this teenager insisted, or otherwise young people would continue to "hate cops, mistrust government." A Fort Worth lawyer advocated misdemeanor reform by emphasizing the "perverted sexual treatment young boys get in local jails and prisons from old hardened cons," an especially graphic version of the complaints of many parents that Texas laws did not distinguish between the "enemies of society" and "our sons and daughters." The law had to change, a Presbyterian minister from Houston insisted in a letter to the governor, because criminal enforcement was breaking up good families in a futile effort to prevent the "youth-obsessed fling with rebellion and drugs."[45]

The Texas Controlled Substances Act of 1973 ultimately represented a "tough" reform that made simple possession and casual transfer of marijuana a misdemeanor while retaining stringent penalties for dealers and for all other drugs. Betty Andujar would never be "mistaken for a permissive-minded liberal," the Fort Worth newspaper editorialized, but her misdemeanor bill recognized that recreational users should not "be pitched into prison alongside hard-rock murderers and robbers." Drug reform, Andujar explained, would rescue middle-class families that had "confronted the heartache and heartbreak of suddenly being informed that their child is in jail and facing a felony charge."[46] Governor Dolph Briscoe, a conservative Democrat, acknowledged the grassroots pressure to reduce the marijuana possession penalty but insisted that the legislation send a tough message to traffickers and addicts, in order to "expunge the pusher from society and remove the users of heroin and other dangerous drugs from the streets." Texas's new law set a five-to-ninety-nine-year range for distribution of LSD, cocaine, and heroin and a two-to-twenty mandatory-minimum for their possession. For marijuana, the law provided a two-to-ten-year range for possession of more than four ounces and for the profit-oriented sale of any amount. The discretionary penalties for simple possession of marijuana emphasized probation, with a maximum jail sentence of up to six months for less than two ounces and up to a year for between two

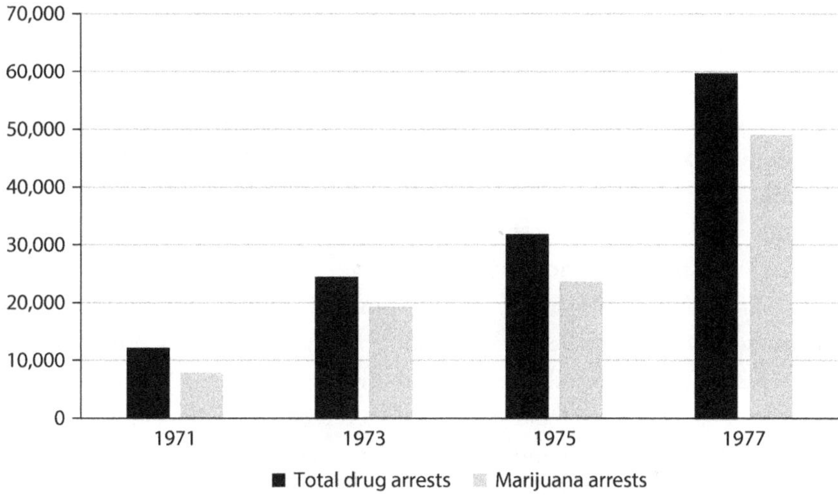

FIGURE 5.7. Marijuana and total drug arrests in Texas, 1971–77. Marijuana arrests surged in Texas after the 1973 reduction of the simple possession penalty from a mandatory-minimum felony to a misdemeanor probation option, a crackdown designed explicitly for the white youth recreational market. The proportion of marijuana arrests increased from 64% of all drug arrests in 1971 to 82% in 1977. Total drug arrests increased 4.9 times between 1971 and 1977, while marijuana arrests increased by 6.9 times. Black and Mexican American residents of Texas disproportionately faced felony incarceration for drug offenses throughout this era. (National Governors' Conference Center for Policy Research and Analysis, *Marijuana: A Study of State Policies and Penalties* [1977], 184; Texas Department of Community Affairs, *Drug Abuse in Texas*, 1980.)

and four ounces. To provide an escape hatch for white middle-class youth, the legislation granted judges the discretion to reduce any felony conviction for marijuana possession or sale to a misdemeanor for sentencing purposes—in theory, the nation's most potentially lenient punishment for dealing pot, offset by very tough mandatory penalties for possession and sale of every other illegal drug. Once "marijuana jumped the tracks from the barrios and black neighborhoods" to the white suburbs, the *Texas Monthly* concluded, the political equation behind reform was straightforward: "Too many of the wrong kids were being arrested."[47]

In Texas, misdemeanor possession reform immediately brought significantly more apprehensions of young pot smokers, following the national pattern, with marijuana accounting for three-fourths of statewide drug arrests by the mid-1970s (fig. 5.7). The arrest surge clearly indicates that before 1973, inflexible mandatory-minimum felony penalties circumscribed marijuana enforcement and effectively compelled police and prosecutors to release or downgrade many violators, despite the state's conservative political culture and law enforcement traditions. California, with double the population of Texas, produced almost ten times as many felony marijuana arrests during the early 1970s, but its penalty structure authorized a discretionary misdemeanor loophole. Texas prosecutors and the large urban police departments supported misdemeanor reform because they considered mandatory-minimum penalties for white violators simply unworkable from a drug control perspective, echoing the Nixon administration's rationale for the federal revision in 1970. Under Texas's new approach, half of marijuana arrests involved youth under twenty years of age, and racial discretion and selective enforcement continued to play a crucial role in the administration of criminal justice.[48] In 1974, the Dallas Police Department analyzed recent drug arrests and determined that heroin addicts and African American marijuana users represented the major crime threats, based on the circular logic that 64 percent of white males busted on pot charges were first offenders, whereas 77 percent of Black males caught with marijuana had prior records. The solution, to focus police enforcement on the "high crime/drug arrest correlation" neighborhoods (including Mexican American ones), reproduced the racial and geographic discretion that created such disproportionally high rates of nonwhite "delinquency" and "criminality" in the first place. By the late 1970s, African Americans represented 12 percent of the population but 21 percent of all drug arrests in Texas, primarily for marijuana, while Mexican Americans at 21 percent of the population accounted for 26 percent of those incarcerated on drug charges.[49]

Marijuana Decriminalization in Oregon

In 1973, Oregon became the first state to decriminalize possession of less than one ounce of marijuana, a response to political pressure from a grassroots legalization movement and the protests of parents of middle-class youth arrested on drug charges. The racial framing of the drug crisis in Oregon differed from get-tough states such as Texas, New York, and California because of its 97 percent white population, which minimized hype about heroin pushers and urban street crime. A 1968 report by Oregon's public health department estimated that as few as 150 residents used heroin, almost all lived in metropolitan Portland, and organized syndicates played no role in the narcotics market. At the same time, marijuana arrests of college and high school students had escalated dramatically since the mid-1960s, leading the state government to replace the mandatory-minimum felony structure with more flexible sanctions. The medical doctor who headed Oregon's drug control agency argued that pot smoking did not lead to hard-drug addiction except in "heroin-risk neighborhoods" (i.e., urban nonwhite). He concluded that the main rationale for keeping marijuana illegal was the moral imperative to discourage "increased indolence, indifference, lack of initiative, and disinterest in acquisitive activity." Governor Tom McCall, a moderate Republican who assumed office in 1967, cited this so-called "amotivational syndrome" in justifying his support for marijuana criminalization, although he did concede that many otherwise law-abiding youth "are labeled as felons who perhaps should not be."[50] In 1969, acting in advance of federal drug reform, the Oregon legislature revised the marijuana law to provide broad judicial discretion for both possession and sale, with available penalties ranging from a misdemeanor fine to a ten-year felony sentence. The Oregon Civil Liberties Union urged McCall to veto any bill that retained criminal sanctions, but he responded frankly that the voters would never forgive such a stance because "people throughout the state are disturbed and upset by the flagrant use of marijuana by many of our young people."[51]

The McCall administration encountered an articulate and passionate movement for marijuana legalization that first emerged in the university towns around 1967. That year, the president of the Young Republicans at the University of Oregon contacted the governor to endorse legalization and condemn the Eugene police crackdowns on pot-smoking students. Marijuana users were "respectable members of society, completely indistinguishable from others," he argued, and "it is indeed a sick society that would deal so harshly with individuals who have done so little to harm it." Writing from jail, an Oregon State University student who faced felony charges for marijuana possession asked McCall for a pardon so that he could join the Peace Corps as planned. "I am *not* a rapist, murderer, larcenist, burglar, or dope addict," the college senior explained, "nor have I ever been, nor will be." According to a legalization petition submitted by a group of University of Oregon law students, the state's "drug laws criminalize young, industrious, and previously usually law abiding citizens." Between 1966 and 1970, the courts in Lane County (which includes Eugene) convicted 375 people on drug charges, with one-third sentenced to jail or prison and two-thirds receiving probation, and the typical defendant a twenty-year-old university student busted for pot.[52] McCall also squared off with Wayne Buhlinger, a twenty-three-year-old Vietnam veteran and University of Oregon honors student, arrested by an undercover cop for selling an ounce of marijuana. Buhlinger predicted campus riots over marijuana stings by the Eugene police and asked what right the state had to label him a "dangerous felon" and ruin his life over a harmless drug. McCall invited Buhlinger to work for political reform within the system but, until then, accept the consequences for breaking the law. Buhlinger wrote back that "marijuana should be legalized immediately" and denounced "a hypocritical society" that was destroying Southeast Asia, polluting the air and water, glorifying corporate values, and winking at the real dangers of alcohol and tobacco.[53]

Oregon residents who self-identified as tax-paying, law-abiding members of the silent majority demanded much tougher punishment for the countercultural rebels of the campus drug culture. A local business owner in Eugene informed the governor that "drug pushers on the rampage" were corrupting children as young as eleven, while hippies swam nude in the public parks in open defiance of the law. A married woman undertook a citizen's sting to prove that hard-drug pushers were using the University of Oregon as their base: she ventured into a coffee shop, "mustered up courage to sit with four long-haired youths, and inquired where I could get a 'fix.'" One of them sold her seven tabs of LSD. Speaking for the "silent majority," the father of a recent University of Oregon graduate charged that pro-marijuana propagandists were trying to dupe the state into ignoring their "distribution of acid and other dangerous narcotics" on campus. He observed that the problem wasn't caused by outside pushers, if this meant "unscrupulous people in the business of selling narcotics," but rather ordinary middle-class Oregon youth who had embraced radical countercultural values. This man demanded automatic expulsion of college students who broke the drug laws, in order to provide a deterrent effect for the younger high school and junior high students who were mindlessly emulating the hippies. The parents of arrested students generally took the opposite position, such as a mother who wrote the governor right after bailing her son, a University of Oregon freshman, out of a Eugene jail. "The majority of our young people are felons," the distressed mother pointed out, but "they just haven't been caught yet." Just like her son, "a fine young man with tremendous potential," many Oregon youths were "serving precious time in jails" for marijuana experimentation, and "what are we gaining by all of this?" She was certain that many other "responsible adults" shared her view that the irrational policy of marijuana prohibition must be repealed.[54]

In metropolitan Portland, parental alarm over increasing marijuana use in the high schools generated pressure for a police crackdown but also revealed significant divisions within white middle-class neighborhoods. In spring 1969, more than one thousand residents of north Portland formed an antidrug organization called Help Kids and demanded that city and state authorities arrest the dealers who were operating in public schools, parks, and consumer spaces. The activists in Help Kids blamed "official permissiveness" for encouraging the marijuana epidemic and lamented that involved parents could not stop the teenage drug culture because too many other families were equally indulgent and "do not share our concern." Indeed, a mother of two teenage daughters who lived nearby asked the governor to "come to grips with the fact that hundreds of thousands of our people use marijuana," and so it was past time to "legalize this harmless practice." This woman clarified that she was "a taxpaying, permanently employed college graduate, a practicing Catholic," who refused to lie to her children about the alleged dangers of pot. Another middle-class Portland mother reported that most of the teenage friends of her three daughters openly admitted smoking marijuana and had convinced her that the drug was far less dangerous than tobacco or alcohol and should probably be legal. Eric Canon, a father who lived in suburban Portland, similarly expressed his refusal to teach his daughter to respect drug laws that drew hypocritical distinctions between marijuana and alcohol. Governor McCall, who personally corresponded with many constituents, retorted that marijuana should remain illegal unless scientific research definitively proved its harmlessness. Canon replied that the pot laws intensified the generation gap by making American youth "really uptight, paranoid of police and their fathers and mothers." He ultimately met with McCall to make his case and, in a follow-up, said the governor must be afraid of a conservative backlash because he could not offer "one single sound reason for not legalizing marijuana at once."[55]

In late 1969, the McCall administration launched a drug education and prevention campaign to address the crisis of "alienated youth" and marijuana use in the middle-class areas of metropolitan Portland. The initiative, Oregon Drug Alert, took its name from a national movement promoted by the Kiwanis International Clubs to upgrade the antidrug curriculum and raise parental awareness about the youth "epidemic." A survey of five high schools in the Portland region, including three in the suburbs, revealed that 28 percent of students had experimented with marijuana at some point, while 8 percent had taken LSD and 1 percent had tried heroin. By a considerable margin, the illegal consumption of alcohol continued to dominate the teenage drug scene, with almost two-thirds of the Portland sample self-reporting this recreational activity. Another study of white middle-class Portland youth argued that smoking marijuana represented a symptom and not the cause of their alienation and frustration with American hypocrisies—and that the drug increasingly appealed to "'all-American,' hard-working" students who were looking for excitement or temporary relief from the pressures of life.[56] Oregon Drug Alert began with a televised conference in Portland, where the audience devised an ambitious agenda of bridging the generation gap on college campuses, formulating a new drug curriculum that offered "straight talk" and not the "hysterical concepts of past decades," and mobilizing families, civic groups, and churches to address the crisis. The ensuing series of statewide meetings often descended into conflict, especially when some younger participants endorsed marijuana legalization, argued for an honest distinction between drug abuse and recreational use, and informed adults who emphasized pusher and gateway themes that they didn't know a "damn thing they were talking about." One thing was certain, the public health officials who planned Oregon Drug Alert concluded in their report: "The youth of today simply will not buy double standards, empty clichés, or hypocritical behavior."[57]

Governor McCall presented Oregon Drug Alert as the beginning of a statewide crusade against the "large, serious, and growing problem of drug abuse" among young Oregonians, whom he labeled "victims." Although the governor often argued that marijuana had become "the unnecessary center of everyone's attention," he sometimes conflated soft and hard drugs in pronouncing that "our twin mission is to reclaim the disengaged and to prevent the detachment of those not yet hooked." McCall, a public health liberal on drug policy, believed that the addict was "not a criminal to be punished, but a sick man to be cured." In 1969, his administration started one of the nation's first methadone programs for heroin addicts, with the controversial treatment available in nine urban and suburban locations. For Tom McCall, this issue was very personal, because his son received methadone through Oregon's pilot project. McCall and his son told the story once on television, but generally the governor declined to discuss the matter publicly, although he commiserated with constituents in similar straits about the "sick despair which clutches at a parent's heart." He received a number of desperate pleas from addicts who begged to be hospitalized rather than incarcerated, such as a Portland teenager "from a very good family" who started smoking marijuana at age fourteen, ran away to Haight-Ashbury, experimented with LSD and speed, and finally ended up on heroin and in prison for burglary.[58] In fact, when McCall testified before the National Commission on Marihuana, he dedicated the bulk of his remarks to the heroin crisis, lamenting that "so many of the young are lost forever." McCall placed the blame on "our generation, our establishment"—for trying to silence rather than listen to "our children," for abandoning Vietnam veterans who came back addicted to heroin, for losing credibility on hard drugs by telling teenagers "scare stories . . . about the evils of marihuana." The governor reiterated his opposition to legalization but pledged that he would maintain an open mind and listen carefully to the young Oregonians who supported this step.[59]

McCall often acknowledged that criminal penalties had "produced alienation between generations" and boasted of the "rap sessions" he held with youth delegations in the state capitol, but the growing public support for marijuana reform also revealed the limitations of the generation gap analysis of drug politics. An academic study of middle-class families in metropolitan Portland found that half of the parents of teenage pot smokers felt that such activity was "not so bad" rather than "harmful," and most attributed their children's drug use to peer culture or the search for "kicks." By contrast, almost all parents of teenagers who had taken LSD considered marijuana to be a "most harmful" gateway drug, as did those who reported that their children had never used illegal drugs at all. The study concluded that the group of parents who had come to terms with teenage marijuana use tended to be more lenient in general and likely had altered their views after personally observing that leisure-oriented pot smoking did not produce detrimental consequences.[60] The most vocal and politically mobilized parents in Oregon continued to be those whose children became entangled with the law. "Our system stinks," an enraged mother from a town near Portland told McCall, after the police busted her daughter for marijuana possession by deploying a heroin addict as an undercover informant. If this outrageous type of entrapment could happen to a "hard working middle class family," then she now understood why "the young people call policemen Pigs." "I am now on a campaign," she warned the governor; "things must be changed." "I'm all for coming down hard on pushers," a mother from suburban Hillsboro wrote, "but dear God, the law seems overly harsh," now that her son faced a felony charge for possession of eleven grams of pot. "Don't you think it is illogical," a Portland woman asked McCall, "to have laws that have no effect in society? Laws that make a large percentage of people in the United States criminals?"[61]

In 1971, in response to this grassroots political pressure, the Oregon legislature revised the marijuana law to make possession of less than one ounce a misdemeanor with a one-year maximum jail term. Judges retained the discretion to sentence up to ten years in prison for felony sale and up to twenty for furnishing to a minor (three years younger). Legalization advocates remained opposed to this "unjustifiable repression" and began a petition drive to place a referendum banning all criminal penalties for marijuana possession on the 1972 ballot. MELO (Marijuana Education for Legalization in Oregon), the Eugene-based group that coordinated the effort, combined a libertarian argument about the individual right to engage in harmless private activity with the fiscal rationale that regulating and taxing marijuana would generate millions of dollars, rather than wasting millions on a futile and highly selective enforcement policy. The campaign labeled marijuana use "a crime for which there is no victim" and portrayed Oregon's pot-smoking demographic as a majority on the college campuses and "a growing minority of middle class adults." MELO also linked its effort to the Shafer Commission report, although the leaders of Oregon's legalization movement privately considered the partial decriminalization recommendation to be an inadequate political compromise. The referendum campaign ultimately failed to qualify for the ballot, despite its adoption of the ACLU and NORML strategy of insisting that supporting legalization did not mean promoting marijuana use.[62] At least a few of its supporters were less circumspect. "I smoke pot regularly," an eighteen-year-old engineering student informed the governor, as did most of his friends on campus, including the conservatives. "It hasn't bothered my studies or changed my values," so why should he be labeled a criminal just because he preferred marijuana to alcohol? Another Oregonian reminded McCall that the hippies had never tried to take any rights away from the alcohol-drinking majority, and so it seemed only fair for the politicians to "help those who wish free backyard grass."[63]

In summer 1973, Governor McCall signed the nation's first law that decriminalized simple possession of marijuana, with less than one ounce classified as a civil violation subject to a maximum $100 fine. Oregon's policy shift—although often celebrated as a repudiation of the "reefer madness" culture and a watershed path not taken in the broader history of the American war on drugs—represented a messy political compromise that remained largely aligned with prevailing national trends. State legislators acted in part to undercut the grassroots legalization movement and preempt a voter referendum that they feared might pass. The Oregon legislature also significantly diluted the original bill's provisions to legalize possession up to eight ounces and to allow cultivation and exchange inside private residences. The 1973 law included a discretionary misdemeanor/felony penalty range of zero to ten years for possession of more than one ounce of marijuana and for the cultivation or commercial sale of any amount. To provide political cover against the inevitable charges of being soft on drugs, the legislature retained the maximum twenty-year felony sentence for distributing to a minor. Governor McCall justified the

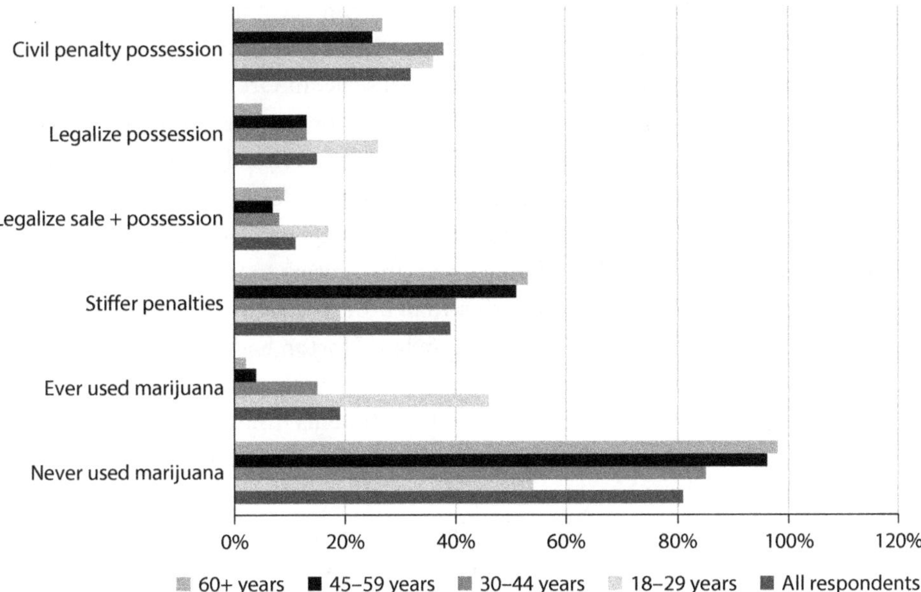

FIGURE 5.8. Drug Abuse Council survey of marijuana attitudes and use in Oregon, October 1974. More than half of Oregon adults surveyed endorsed either the new civil penalty for marijuana possession (32%) or at least partial legalization (26% combined). An average of 37% of adults in the two youngest age categories endorsed the civil penalty decriminalization policy, while 26% in the age eighteen-to-twenty-nine bracket preferred legalization of possession and another 17% advocated full legalization. A majority of adults age forty-five and older, by contrast, desired a return to criminal penalties. Almost half (46%) of the eighteen-to-twenty-nine-year-olds had personal experience with marijuana compared to almost none in the older age categories. (Drug Abuse Council, "Marijuana Survey—State of Oregon," December 15, 1974.) *Note*: The survey asked about penalties for "small amounts," meaning less than one ounce as defined in the 1973 partial decriminalization law. "Undecided" responses not included.

partial decriminalization reform with the standard argument that "the solution is not to toss youthful users into jail," while assuring critics that "stiff penalties for 'pushers' remain in effect and they will be vigorously enforced." He further explained that the legislation "largely reflects existing court practice," meaning the ad hoc diversion tactics by a criminal legal system that only rarely imposed jail sentences or even large fines for possession anymore. In the face of charges that the state now encouraged pot smoking and had become a haven for criminals and countercultural rebels, McCall even denied that the law had decriminalized marijuana possession at all, because of the civil fine. Opponents remained unconvinced, accusing McCall of turning Oregon into a "mecca for hippies," giving pot-smoking teenagers "a pat on the back," unlocking the gateway to LSD and heroin, and opening the door "to invite in all the pushers."[64]

The decriminalization breakthrough in Oregon had a minimal impact on patterns of illicit marijuana use in the state, while significantly narrowing the parameters of drug-war reform on a national scale. In Oregon, as elsewhere, the price of formally removing white middle-class pot smokers from the perils of criminal law enforcement involved a renewed political commitment to supply-side interdiction in the war on drugs and street-level crackdowns in the war on crime. Pat Horton, the district attorney in Eugene, testified to Congress that decriminalization allowed police and prosecutors to focus resources on hard drugs and "serious felons" rather than otherwise law-abiding youth. In 1972, a year before passage of the Oregon law, Horton had implemented essentially the same civil fine policy in his jurisdiction by pleading down cases to avoid criminal records that barred college students from many professions even when they got off with misdemeanor probation. Prosecutors in Portland also welcomed decriminalization since securing possession convictions in front of judges or juries had become almost impossible. Under the civil violation policy, marijuana citations in Oregon increased by 30 percent over the misdemeanor arrest totals, but most went to "teenagers, street people, hippies, the ones who smoke in public places."[65] In 1974, a Drug Abuse Council survey revealed that 58 percent of Oregonians either supported decriminalization or preferred legalization of at least possession, including 79 percent of eighteen-to-twenty-nine-year-olds and 59 percent in the thirty-to-forty-four age bracket (fig. 5.8). A follow-up survey revealed that the proportion of state residents who had smoked marijuana remained stable at 19 percent between 1973 and 1975, reinforcing extensive research findings that criminal law "has had little effect upon [drug] availability and use," either as a deterrent or an incentive. NORML trumpeted this "successful" Oregon model in its national campaign for marijuana decriminalization, which would allow law enforcement to target dangerous crime and spare hundreds of thousands of young people "the debilitating aspects of a lifelong criminal record."[66]

Marijuana Reform and Race in California

In the early 1970s, the marijuana legalization movement came closest to a breakthrough in California, where law enforcement arrested far more recreational pot smokers and white middle-class youth than any other state in the nation. In 1970, Governor Ronald Reagan declared "all-out war on drug abuse," a preview of Nixon's agenda at the federal level and also a continuation of two decades of bipartisan rhetoric in California and particularly in Los Angeles

County. "There can be no compromise with the menace," Reagan proclaimed. "If we surrender, we run the very real risk of losing an entire generation." The conservative Republican governor, who supported tough sentences for suppliers and felony deterrents for illegal drug users, pledged to protect "our youth who are the chief targets of the drug pushers."[67] But instead, as in most states, California's law enforcement agencies publicly advocated the priorities of stopping hard drugs and major traffickers but primarily busted young people for possession or sale of small amounts of marijuana. A National Institute on Drug Abuse assessment of enforcement in Los Angeles concluded that the police "focus on possession and consumption offenses and offenders, rather than on illicit drug traffic or supply. . . . Drug law enforcement is currently controlled by goals that emphasize quantity rather than quality in the arrest of offenders." Between 1970 and 1972, state and local authorities in California detained an average of 70,059 people per year on marijuana charges alone, about 20 percent of all felony arrests in the state, and about 30 percent of all marijuana arrests in the nation, at an annual enforcement cost of more than $100 million. The majority of marijuana arrests in California continued to involve a white male perpetrator younger than twenty-five, initially apprehended on a felony charge involving simple possession. In the 1972 arrest data, white non-Hispanics represented 71 percent of marijuana charges (and 73 percent of the state population), with Mexican Americans underrepresented and African Americans overrepresented, though by significantly less than in the mid-1960s (fig. 5.9 [top]).[68]

Police, prosecutorial, and judicial discretion in the arrest and disposition of drug offenders shaped every stage of the criminal legal system in California, as state policy explicitly envisioned. The so-called "wobbler" law, enacted in 1968, actually increased conviction rates by authorizing prosecutors and judges to choose misdemeanor dispositions for first offenders arrested for felony marijuana possession. Based on the limited racial data that the California Department of Justice released, race-based discrimination after point of arrest did not seem to play a determinative role in sorting the small percentage of adult drug offenders ultimately convicted of felonies in the superior courts (fig. 5.9 [bottom]). In 1972, white Californians accounted for a large majority of both arrests and superior court convictions for sale and possession of both marijuana and "dangerous drugs" (illict amphetamines and barbiturates). Heroin enforcement apprehended and convicted African Americans at more than five times their population share and Mexican Americans at 1.6 times (a massive decline from a decade earlier). Drug offenders with prior records disproportionately received felony convictions and jail or prison time, which

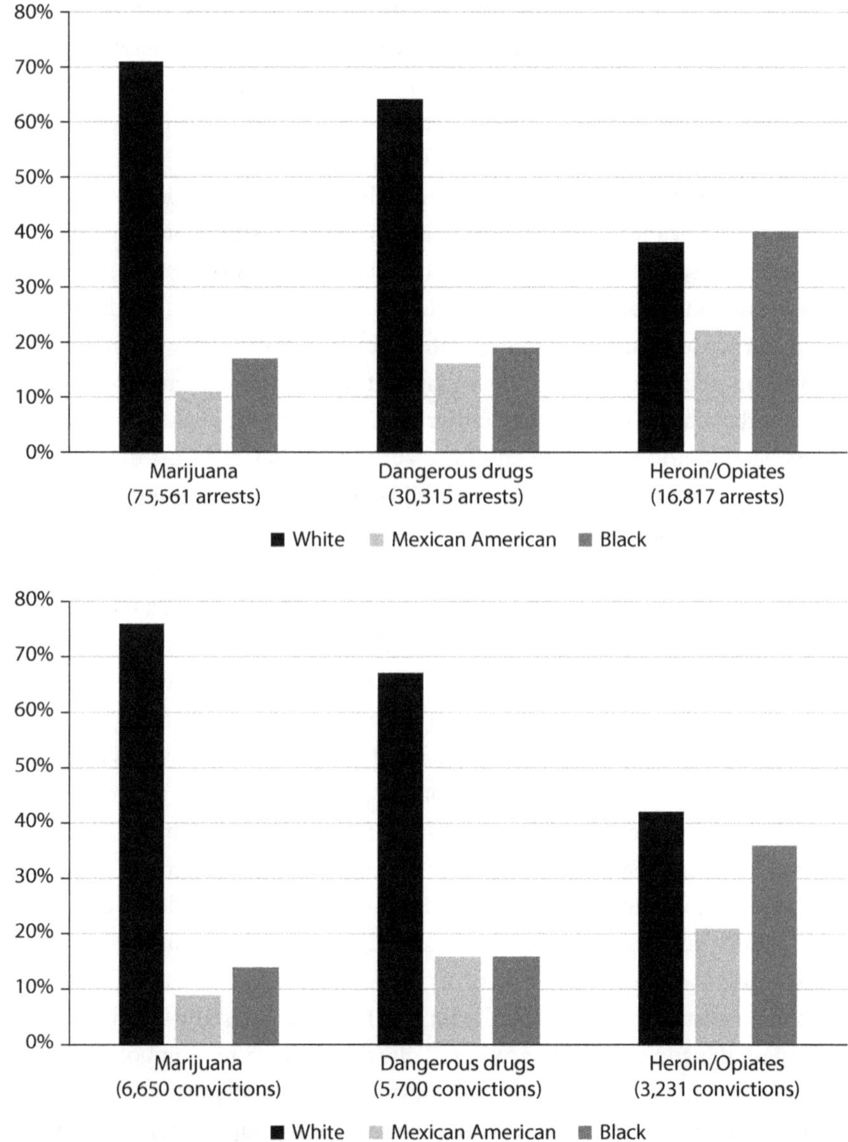

FIGURE 5.9. Total drug arrests and adult felony convictions in California by race and type of offense, 1972. (*Top*) The war on drugs in California prioritized marijuana enforcement in the early 1970s and arrested white offenders at roughly their population share. Mexican Americans, approximately 13% of the state population, were disproportionately arrested for "dangerous drugs" (amphetamines and barbiturates) and heroin. African Americans, about 7% of the population, experienced disproportionate arrests in every drug category, most notably heroin. (*Bottom*) The racial breakdown of felony drug convictions in 1972 closely paralleled the racial distribution of recorded arrests, with whites found guilty on marijuana charges at roughly their

undoubtedly fell most heavily on nonwhite and poor defendants from criminalized communities. The most lopsided discretion involved pretrial prosecutorial diversion and judicial sentencing in the majority-white categories of marijuana and "dangerous drugs," since most arrested adults either received misdemeanor probation or had charges dismissed (table 5.2a). Some marijuana and "dangerous drugs" defendants did serve jail time, especially those convicted of sale, but most misdemeanants ended up with probation, a criminal record, and some sort of rehabilitation mandate (table 5.2b). A large majority of juveniles (80%) arrested for marijuana in 1972 had their cases handled informally or dismissed, with some placed on formal probation and only 8 percent adjudicated as delinquent wards of the state, generally those with prior records and from working-class, poor, and minority families (table 5.2c).[69]

Marijuana legalization advocates portrayed California's war on drugs as an irrational and unjustified commitment of law enforcement firepower and taxpayer resources to incarcerate a very small percentage of offenders and, in the false hope of deterring youth from smoking pot, saddle tens of thousands more with a lifelong criminal record, the trauma of the legal process, the hassle of probation, and often compulsory psychiatric treatment as well. In 1971, the San Francisco Committee on Crime issued a report classifying marijuana use as a victimless crime and recommending a regulated alcohol-style market with sale to minors banned. On civil liberties and right to privacy grounds, the committee compared marijuana prohibition to other futile and selectively enforced laws against gambling, pornography, prostitution, and homosexuality.[70] The Los Angeles Police Department responded with a "Victimless Crimes" study that blurred the line between law enforcement and law-and-order manifesto, part of its longer pattern of overt mobilization in local and state politics. The "research project" ridiculed the ACLU and attacked proponents of marijuana legalization for the rampant "permissiveness in our society" and the "mythical concept of 'victimless crime.'" The LAPD portrayed itself as the thin

---

population share and African Americans disproportionately convicted in all drug categories. Only 19% of felony convictions involved sale, compared to 81% for possession, although the discretionary misdemeanor loophole for marijuana and many other factors meant that only a small fraction of those arrested ultimately received felony sentences. Adults arrested for heroin were about twice as likely as those arrested for marijuana to be convicted of a felony. (Bureau of Criminal Statistics, *Crime and Delinquency in California: 1972: Drug Arrests and Dispositions.*)
Note: Data in the top chart represents combined adult and juvenile drug arrests. The bottom chart includes only adult felony defendants charged in California superior courts.

TABLE 5.2A. Diversion of Adult Felony Arrests for Marijuana in California before Superior Court Trial, 1972

Category	1972
Total felony marijuana arrests—adults	52,027
Felony complaint filed	20,176 (39%)
Misdemeanor complaint filed	21,751 (42%)
Conditional probation (deferred charges)	6,531 (13%)
Charges dropped/unknown	3,569 (7%)
Felony complaint filed (subset breakdown)	20,176
Pretrial diversion (conditional probation)	8,310 (41%)
Charges dismissed (pretrial hearing)	3,875 (19%)
Superior Court trials	7,991 (40%)

Sources: Bureau of Criminal Statistics, *Crime and Delinquency in California, 1972: Drug Arrests and Dispositions*; California Senate Select Committee on Control of Marijuana, *Marijuana: Beyond Misunderstanding* (Sacramento, May 1974), Appendix IV.A.

Note: Prosecutors utilized the "wobbler" statute to downgrade more than half of adults charged (42% of total arrests) to a misdemeanor, which generally resulted in probation. Judges and prosecutors diverted a further 41% of felony charges to misdemeanor probation, indicating use of the threat of felony trial to coerce plea bargains from defendants initially unwilling to take a misdemeanor deal.

TABLE 5.2B. Disposition of Adult Felony Drug Defendants in California Superior Courts, 1972

Disposition	Marijuana	Dangerous drugs	Opiates/Heroin
Superior Court trials	7,991	6,577	4,403
Convicted—total (%)	82%	86%	85%
Dismissed/acquitted (% of total)	18%	14%	15%
Convicted—felony (% of total)	45%	N/A	N/A
Convicted—misdemeanor (% of total)	37%	N/A	N/A
Convicted—possession (% of total)	75%	73%	56%
Convicted—sale (% of total)	25%	27%	44%
Disposition of convicted total	6,540	5,657	3,738
Prison (state)	2%	4%	13%
Jail (county)	37%	45%	40%
California Youth Authority	1%	2%	1%
Civil commitment (medical)	1%	2%	20%
Probation	58%	47%	27%
Fined	2%	1%	0%

Sources: Bureau of Criminal Statistics, *Crime and Delinquency in California, 1972: Drug Arrests and Dispositions*; California Senate Select Committee on Control of Marijuana, *Marijuana: Beyond Misunderstanding* (Sacramento, May 1974), Appendix IV.A.

Note: Media reports and some academic studies cited this data to demonstrate that California incarcerated about two-fifths of marijuana defendants and placed about three-fifths on probation. But as Table 5.2a reveals, the group ultimately convicted in superior courts represented only 12.5% of total adult felony arrests for marijuana. Of the initial arrests, about one-fifth had charges dropped or dismissed, making misdemeanor probation by far the most likely outcome. Only 2% of adult marijuana convictions in 1972 resulted in felony prison sentences (about 150 people out of 52,027 felony arrests).

TABLE 5.2C. Disposition of Juveniles Arrested for Drug Offenses in California, 1972

Disposition	Marijuana	Dangerous drugs	Opiates/Heroin
Total arrests	21,034	6,663	1,180
Handled informally/diverted	9,000 (43%)	3,108 (47%)	786 (67%)
Referred to probation department	12,034 (57%)	3,555 (53%)	394 (33%)
Disposition by probation department	12,034	3,108	786
Investigated and closed	5,332 (44%)	1,209 (34%)	96 (24%)
Informal supervision	2,471 (21%)	658 (19%)	68 (17%)
Petition to juvenile court	4,231 (35%)	1,688 (48%)	230 (58%)
Disposition by juvenile court	3,770	1,675	193
Dismissed	1,365 (36%)	490 (29%)	61 (32%)
Probation as non-wards	577 (15%)	232 (14%)	10 (5%)
Supervision as wards	1,737 (46%)	913 (55%)	103 (53%)
Committed to CA Youth Authority	7 (2%)	3 (0.1%)	7 (4%)
Remanded to adult court	84 (0.2%)	37 (2%)	12 (6%)
Total adjudicated (% of initial arrests)	1,744 (8%)	916 (14%)	110 (9%)

Source: Bureau of Criminal Statistics, *Crime and Delinquency in California, 1972: Drug Arrests and Dispositions.*

Note: The disproportionately high percentage of juveniles arrested for heroin and diverted in the "handled informally" category reflects transfers into addiction treatment programs. The "disposition by juvenile court" total excludes those transferred to a juvenile court in another county.

blue line protecting ordinary citizens and families from crimes that caused great social harm: prostitution, homosexuality, pornography, gambling, narcotics, "dangerous drugs," and not least marijuana. The report blamed the narcotics and marijuana trade on organized syndicates run by the Mafia, Puerto Ricans, and Negroes (not mentioning Mexicans) and recycled arguments that smoking pot caused crime, psychosis, psychological addiction, progression to heroin, and "amotivational syndrome." The LAPD also denounced the National Commission on Marihuana's recommendation to decriminalize possession, and the Los Angeles district attorney added that without a criminal deterrent, young pot smokers would fall "even deeper into contact with the counterculture forces." Los Angeles County arrested more than sixty thousand people on drug charges that year, about 12 percent of the total in a nation that was catching up to the law enforcement mobilization of Southern California.[71]

In 1972, a grassroots legalization movement based in the San Francisco Bay Area qualified a ballot referendum to repeal criminal penalties for possession of any amount of marijuana and to allow unlimited private cultivation (currently punished with a mandatory one-to-ten-year felony sentence). The energy and resources for the petition drive came largely from Amorphia, a nonprofit "cannabis cooperative" that financed marijuana reform by selling rolling papers for joints from its undisclosed Marin County location. Amorphia's cofounders, Michael Aldrich and Blair Newman, met in the late 1960s at a conference of the pro-legalization National Student Association and recruited other activists from the antiwar, environmental, and consumer movements. Amorphia's leaders condemned criminal enforcement against pot smokers but departed sharply from NORML and the ACLU in their radical vision of a noncapitalist, homegrown marijuana economy that would forestall corporate takeover, channel proceeds to progressive social causes, and "fund the entire counterculture revolutionary movement." Unlike NORML, Amorphia also highlighted racial discrimination in drug-war enforcement and argued that police ignored middle-class professionals who smoked pot and selectively targeted "nonwhites, young people, hippies, and political activists." Amorphia popularized the slogan "free, legal backyard marijuana" and simultaneously promised a political campaign "aimed at Middle America," which Newman acknowledged would be tricky because "our supporters and basic constituents are the freaks."[72] To appeal to "straight people," Amorphia hired Gordon Brownell, a libertarian who previously worked in the Reagan and Nixon administrations, as California's first registered marijuana lobbyist. Aldrich and Newman initially collaborated with NORML and the ACLU in planning a legalization initiative but objected to the proposed alcohol-style model and instead settled on language that decriminalized use and possession, with the right to private cultivation replacing state regulation and "corporate industrial control."[73]

The California Marijuana Initiative (CMI), an uneasy coalition, ultimately adopted the mainstream middle-class reform strategy of criticizing marijuana enforcement for sending "our sons and daughters" to jail and "destroying them in the name of saving them." The campaign called on voters to "return to traditional American values and stop making criminals of normal people for personal behavior, . . . destroying careers, disrupting education, breaking up families." This universalistic rhetoric downplayed the racial inequalities in the war on drugs, part of the longer pattern of progressive coalitions making colorblind appeals to the imagined middle-class majority in California ballot referendums, what Daniel HoSang has labeled "political whiteness." CMI literature portrayed the $100 million annual cost of marijuana enforcement in California as a wasteful, discriminatory assault on "youth"—accompanied by an image of police arresting a clean-cut white male wearing a coat and tie—that exacerbated the generation gap and distracted attention from truly dangerous drugs and serious criminals (fig. 5.10).[74] Twenty thousand mostly young supporters

ONE OUT OF FIVE DOLLARS
OF THE ENTIRE CALIFORNIA
LAW ENFORCEMENT BUDGET
IS CONSUMED BY
MARIJUANA POSSESSION
MORE THAN 120 MILLION DOLLARS YEARLY ' GO TO POT '
40% OF THE COURT CASES IN L.A. COUNTY ALONE
THE CURRENT CALIFORNIA LAWS MAKE CRIMINALS OUT OF THE 39% OF OUR 18 TO 25 YEAR OLDS WHO HAVE USED MARIJUANA
THE PRESIDENT'S COMMISSION ON THE CAUSES AND PREVENTION OF VIOLENCE CITED THE MARIJUANA LAWS AS HAVING "CAUSED LARGE NUMBERS OF OUR YOUTH TO LOSE RESPECT FOR OUR LAWS GENERALLY".
A significant decrease in the efficiency of prosecution of felony crimes results from the enforcement of marijuana laws. More police time and effort is expended on marijuana offenses than on all crimes involving personal violence. 21.3% of all felony arrests in 1970 were for marijuana, only 10.6% of these for sale, possession for sale, harvesting, and sale to a minor.
Given the real dangers of other drugs and their traffic, and the need of taxpayers to be secure in their persons and property, WHY IS ONE FIFTH OF OUR LAW ENFORCEMENT RESOURCES WASTED IN THIS WAY?

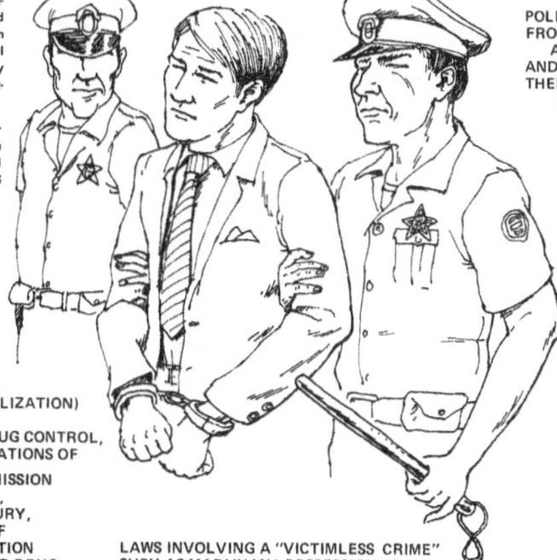

POLICE SHOULD BE FREED FROM THE ENFORCEMENT OF AN UNPOPULAR LAW AND ALLOWED TO DEVOTE THEIR ENERGIES TO SERIOUS CRIMES.
THE DECRIMINALIZATION (NOT LEGALIZATION) OF MARIJUANA, AS A RATIONAL APPROACH TO DRUG CONTROL, FOLLOWS THE RECOMMENDATIONS OF
PRESIDENT NIXON'S NATIONAL COMMISSION ON MARIJUANA AND DRUG ABUSE,
THE LOS ANGELES COUNTY GRAND JURY,
THE COUNCIL ON MENTAL HEALTH OF THE AMERICAN MEDICAL ASSOCIATION
THE COMMITTEE ON ALCOHOLISM AND DRUG DEPENDANCE OF THE AMERICAN MEDICAL ASSOCIATION
LAWS INVOLVING A "VICTIMLESS CRIME" SUCH AS MARIJUANA POSSESSION ARE "PHILOSOPHICALLY UNSOUND AND CONSTITUTIONALLY SUSPECT..." Natl. Comm. on Marijuana and Drug Abuse.
IT'S TIME TO CHANGE THE LAW
VOTE
yes19
"POSSESSION OF MARIJUANA FOR PERSONAL USE SHOULD NOT BE CRIMINAL..." Board of Trustees, American Medical Association (1972)

FIGURE 5.10. The California Marijuana Initiative centered the white middle-class victim of unjust law enforcement in promotional materials for the 1972 referendum campaign to decriminalize possession and private cultivation. This strategy labeled marijuana possession a "victimless crime" and urged voters to direct the police to leave young pot smokers alone and instead "devote their energies to serious crimes." (HS20041, John and Leni Sinclair Papers, Bentley Historical Library, University of Michigan.)

circulated initiative petitions, championed by Amorphia as a "people's movement" led and financed by one of America's largest oppressed groups, pot smokers themselves (by purchasing its Acapulco Gold rolling papers). Because of Amorphia's hostility to a state-regulated corporate market, the CMI welcomed the arrival of the Shafer report as a mainstream endorsement of its decriminalization measure, which "would neither legalize sale nor permit the commercialization of marijuana." But bitter infighting weakened the CMI forces, especially after Amorphia created the spin-off groups Mothers for Marijuana and Jocks for Joynts and then alienated NORML by publicly accusing the Playboy empire of seeking to control the underground marijuana market. Keith Stroup blamed "freaks who wanted to turn on the world" for sabotaging the CMI campaign, while Amorphia denounced him as a "charlatan" and a "genuine menace to the legitimate marijuana reform movement."[75]

Voters defeated Proposition 19, the California Marijuana Initiative, by a 66 to 34 percent margin in November 1972, when the state electorate also reinstated the death penalty, approved a ban on court-ordered busing, and helped reelect Richard Nixon. The marijuana reform coalition had not expected to win and viewed the decriminalization initiative as an educational campaign to accelerate the shift in public opinion, preparing the way for legislative action or a second referendum in 1974. One month before the vote, a group called Citizens Opposing the Marijuana Initiative formed to denounce Proposition 19 as a legalization smokescreen that would increase teenage drug addiction, lead up to one-third of pot smokers to heroin, and corner the marijuana market for the countercultural radicals of Amorphia. NORML's Keith Stroup later attributed defeat to Amorphia's pro-grass evangelism and insisted that "marijuana reform must be made palatable to the middle class," a debate about whether recreational smokers should be in jail rather than whether Middle America approved of getting high.[76] During 1973–74, continued power struggles doomed the CMI's efforts to lay the groundwork for a second referendum campaign, especially the disagreement over whether to support legalization through an alcohol-style system or promote decriminalization via Amorphia's libertarian countercultural vision of a nonprofit homegrown cannabis economy. The CMI petition drive ultimately failed to qualify enough signatures, leaving the future of decriminalization to the reform proposals circulating in the state legislature, none of which included the right to private cultivation. As for Amorphia, the Bay Area radicals attempted to carry out a bold plan to displace NORML as the national leader of the marijuana reform movement and establish affiliates in states from Oregon to New York. This dream soon collapsed, and NORML eventually absorbed the remnants of Amorphia, after most of the original countercultural activists had burned out or left the organization, allowing its libertarian Republican lobbyist to assume control.[77]

In 1972, Governor Reagan opposed the California Marijuana Initiative but sought to undercut public support for decriminalization by endorsing a law granting judges discretion to divert drug offenders—marijuana and heroin users alike—into addiction/abuse treatment programs. The state legislature waited until after the referendum to pass this diversion bill and a Democratic measure to reduce marijuana possession to a misdemeanor. When Reagan vetoed the misdemeanor bill, the CMI denounced him for killing such a "modest reform" and displaying "inexcusable indifference to the suffering caused by the present harsh felony penalties." Marijuana reform became a highly partisan issue in California, unlike in Oregon and many other states, with Democrats demanding an end to felony enforcement and Republican legislators almost unanimously lining up behind Reagan's defense of the status quo. In summer 1974, Democrats sidelined an Oregon-style decriminalization bill in favor of a less controversial misdemeanor penalty revision, and they sought to deflect "soft on drugs" charges by arguing that marijuana enforcement should be redirected to the war on violent crime. Governor Reagan again vetoed the misdemeanor reform, arguing that it would "condone" marijuana use and allow "pushers" to escape felony charges by selling pot in small amounts.[78] Under Reagan's diversion law, local authorities transferred 50,293 adult offenders into rehabilitation programs during 1973 and 1974 combined, representing one-fifth of total arrests in California's war on drugs (juvenile courts already had statutory authority to divert minors into treatment). Racial discretion decisively shaped the process, which primarily sent young white marijuana offenders ("sick people rather than criminals") to drug education classes or outpatient programs (table 5.3). The initiative simultaneously reinforced white privilege and represented a punitive form of coercive medicalization and age-based discrimination against recreational pot smokers, especially given the decriminalization truce enjoyed by their counterparts just north of the border in Oregon.[79]

In 1974, a special state senate committee led by George Moscone, a liberal Democrat from San Francisco, advocated partial decriminalization in the report *Marijuana: Beyond Misunderstanding*. The study drew on research provided by the former leaders of Amorphia and condemned marijuana prohibition in California as an expensive failure—400,000 arrests between 1960 and 1972 at a total cost of $577 million, with no reduction of supply or demand—which had alienated a generation of youth and diverted resources

TABLE 5.3. Characteristics of Adult Drug Offenders Diverted under the 1972 Drug Offender Diversion Law in California, 1973–74

Category	Number
Total adult drug arrests in California, 1973–74	247,516
Total and % adults diverted to drug treatment	50,293 (20.3%)
% Diverted arrested for marijuana	77.5%
% Diverted arrested for opiates/heroin	6%
% Diverted arrested for "dangerous drugs"	5%
White offenders as % of total diverted	83.1%
Black offenders as % of total diverted	7.8%
Mexican American offenders as % of total diverted	7.6%
First offenders as % of total diverted	69%
Under age 25 as % of total diverted	81%
Average length of treatment program	6.8 months
Success rate of treatment program (charges dropped)	86.6%

Source: Bureau of Criminal Statistics, *Drug Diversion 1000 P.C. in California: 1974.*

Note: More than three-fourths of California adults arrested and diverted into drug addiction/abuse treatment programs during 1973–74 were marijuana offenders, an overwhelmingly white and youthful cohort. This coercive public health policy allocated to recreational marijuana users a considerable number of spaces in treatment programs designed and traditionally reserved for narcotics "addicts," during an era when nonwhite urban groups frequently protested the discriminatory lack of rehabilitation facilities in their neighborhoods. The figures for marijuana, heroin, and "dangerous drugs" diversions do not add up to 100% because the reporting agency did not include arrests in the paraphernalia and "visiting premises" categories. LA County did not report individual data, so its total is included in the "% of total diverted" rows but not in the other specific categories.

from the war against serious crime. Marijuana prohibition operated as a "weapon and whipping device to penalize and repress people who have different lifestyles," through selective enforcement against "the Chicano, the Black, and the white long-haired." Although this formulation acknowledged that California's war on drugs targeted a multiracial spectrum, the Moscone committee primarily emphasized the "wrecked careers and ruined lives" of young white middle-class pot smokers transformed into victim-felons by misguided state policy. The report highlighted a judge's lament that he could not "send a long-haired marijuana offender" to jail, knowing that such a "poor young kid . . . [is] going to be the victim of the most brutal type of homosexual, unnatural perverted assaults and attacks that you can imagine." The director of a UCLA marijuana study warned that high-achieving college students had become disaffected and outraged by the criminalization of a social practice they considered harmless, leading them to despise the police and become more receptive to "the whole radical new left philosophy." The Moscone committee concluded that since "marijuana use has become permanent," the state must stop criminalizing the private practices of productive and otherwise law-abiding citizens. The report endorsed decriminalization of marijuana possession for private use but not for homegrown cultivation, in line with the Shafer formula and the Oregon model, and advocated the redirection of criminal enforcement against the "big pusher or trafficker" and those who provided pot to minors.[80]

Law enforcement in California apprehended more than 200,000 adults and juveniles on marijuana charges during 1973 and 1974 combined, about 1 percent of the total population, one-fourth of all felony arrests in the state, and almost one-fourth of all recorded marijuana arrests in the nation (see fig. 5.12). The most controversial events occurred in Los Angeles, where the juvenile police division launched a massive undercover operation in the high schools, with officers posing as regular students, *Mod Squad*–style. In December 1974, the LAPD rounded up 211 "student pushers" between the ages of fifteen and nineteen, a large majority from white middle-class and wealthy areas, mostly for selling marijuana but in a few cases for LSD, amphetamines, or cocaine. The LAPD expressed regret that none of its agents looked young enough to infiltrate the middle schools, followed by outrage when the juvenile pushers were back "swaggering around the campus like heroes" the next day (after release as required by law; the eighteen- and nineteen-year-old adults stayed in jail). The county board of supervisors and the state attorney general demanded a new law permitting pretrial detention of minors arrested for dealing drugs. The head of the LAPD's juvenile division called for reclassification of sixteen- and seventeen-year-old delinquents as adult criminals, and future police chief Daryl Gates warned parents that school hallways were "open marketplaces for narcotics" (i.e., marijuana and LSD; the busts uncovered no heroin). Supporters of the stings labeled the arrested students "drug pushers who engage in the business of peddling death" and complained of "kid glove" treatment by the juvenile system. The ACLU filed multiple lawsuits against the LAPD and board of education and denounced the entire operation as a violation of student rights and a Vietnam-style "destroy the schools to save them" mission. In May 1975, the LAPD trumpeted a second round of undercover arrests of alleged "narcotics peddlers" (again, mainly marijuana), leading liberal critics to charge that the police had designed both investigations to sabotage decriminalization reform in state politics.[81]

The LAPD's campus crackdowns played into the mid-1970s movement to "get tough" with juvenile offenders but backfired in terms of marijuana politics by targeting white middle-class youth so visibly that it generated significant backlash. In the middle of the controversy, the *Los Angeles Times* ran an inflammatory series about the teenage gangs and "hardcore delinquents" in Watts and other Black neighborhoods, highlighting the primary racial villains of the law-and-order campaign to treat juveniles as adult criminals. In the mostly white subdivisions of the San Fernando Valley, where many of the drug busts occurred, high school students organized protests against the LAPD and denounced the violations of their civil liberties. Voters in Los Angeles soon elected a new liberal majority to the board of education, which promptly demanded an end to undercover operations in the schools. Many of the affected families accused the police of entrapment, and trials of the so-called "student pushers" revealed that few of them were even small-time dealers. In most cases, undercover cops had befriended vulnerable teenagers and then arrested them after soliciting joints in the casual manner of the recreational subculture (at times seeking to flip the student as a drug buy informant to find the main source). In court testimony, one juvenile from Venice explained that he had never dealt drugs, but he bought a little pot for his new friend "as a status thing" and "to impress him." Another defendant helped an undercover cop get speed from an acquaintance, "so he would stop bugging me." One local judge told the *Times* that the "whole thing smacks" of entrapment, while another refused to place good kids who had made an error in judgment into juvenile detention with "a bunch of gangsters." In the end, most of the student defendants received probation or had the charges dismissed, although about half served long suspensions handed down by the school system, often without due process. "I seriously doubt," yet another juvenile judge concluded, "if any real drug dealers have been apprehended in this thing."[82]

For advocates of marijuana reform, the LAPD's undercover stings represented almost everything that had gone wrong with California's war on drugs: law enforcement squandering taxpayer money on entrapment operations, rounding up recreational users from white middle-class families, alienating youth and worsening distrust of government, clogging the courts with defendants who were not "real criminals," and hyping the pusher-gateway myth to alarm the public and advance a conservative law-and-order agenda. The LAPD bust in December 1974 also represented a rearguard action against marijuana decriminalization, which seemed likely as soon as Reagan left office. Jerry Brown, the incoming Democratic governor, endorsed the Oregon model during his 1974 campaign, and after the election George Moscone introduced a decriminalization bill to make simple possession a civil infraction subject to a small fine.[83] Shortly before stepping down, Reagan blamed the "permissiveness of the 1960s" for the runaway drug crisis and predicted that marijuana "legalization" would have tragic effects, including "permanent brain damage" for young pot smokers. George Deukmejian, the GOP leader in the state senate, argued that decriminalization would create "another drug-type dropout generation in California." Ed Davis, chief of the LAPD, forecast an epidemic of heroin addiction and attacked Democratic sponsors as "pot peddlers" and "irresponsible, no-good sons of bitches." The LAPD circulated spurious data that marijuana use in Oregon had skyrocketed after decriminalization, but reputable studies of California's northern neighbor ultimately strengthened the case for reform by revealing that ending criminal sanctions barely changed social practices.[84] In March 1975, a Drug Abuse Council survey revealed Californians were evenly divided on the Moscone bill, while 35 percent of the public supported some form of legalization. Most adults under thirty opposed any criminal penalties, not least because one-fourth of them currently smoked marijuana and more than half had committed such a felony at some point in their lives.[85]

NORML worked closely with George Moscone during the 1975 campaign for a state decriminalization law, while young marijuana smokers mobilized for full legalization and lobbied the new Democratic governor directly. Jerry Brown received many letters and petitions from teenagers and young adults who lived in suburban Los Angeles, who were statistically the white middle-class citizens most likely to face felony marijuana arrest anywhere in the nation. Two female high school seniors from Orange County sent Brown a petition signed by 120 classmates, arguing that if they were old enough to vote then they had the right to smoke pot without going to jail. "If a person feels like getting high nobody should interfere with his feelings," a nineteen-year-old daily stoner from Long Beach informed the governor, so why did the law classify him as either a criminal or a sick person? A twenty-five-year-old woman from the San Fernando Valley related the "personal grief and hardship" she experienced when a felony arrest led to mandatory rehabilitation under the diversion law: police invasion of her private home, a lost job as a medical assistant because of the drug charge, and six months of probation while the state of California was "making themselves feel good about 'rehabilitating' hardened criminals like myself" (fig. 5.11). Brown received more angry letters demanding legalization after plainclothes LAPD cops busted 364 juveniles for marijuana possession at a Pink Floyd concert (a "dope festival," according to Chief Davis), along with a seventy-five-stanza poem from one San Fernando Valley concertgoer about her experience in jail.[86] Young constituents from San Diego

Feb. 3, 1975

Governor Brown:

I have never written to an elected official before but I have been involved in something recently that has really disturbed me. Unfortunately, my eyes have been opened to the judicial system in this country and I say unfortunately because I didn't like what I saw. Last June I was arrested on a marijuana charge. I realize it is against the law but is it worth it to the state to handcuff me, take me to jail and book me a felon? I was in my home at the time and I had less than 2 ounces in my possesion. The fact that the charge was later dropped to a misdemeanor is practically irrelevant. I was still arrested and it cost me alot of personal grief and hardship. In all my 25 years I have never been in more serious trouble than a traffic ticket and to be in jail with forgers, burglars and heavy drug addicts was enough of a punishment. By the time the whole thing was over I had lost $750.00, on an attourney I later discovered I didn't need, $500.00 on a bail bondsman because my bail, for a first time offense was set at $2500, a job becuase of the nature of the arrest a medical assistant certainly couldn't be trusted in a doctor's office. I have also spent 6 months being on probation because I chose to go the "diversion route". This is for first time offenders only. You spend 6 months on probation, attend rehabilitation programs and after all this hassle the whole thing is dismissed anyway. Except on my record, I still have an arrest record. Even if no one else knows about it, I do and what bothers me is that I didn't do anything wrong. I was not out on the street and I wasn't bothering anyone else. If marijuana can't be legalized then certainly the law can be humanized. I know the state is doing people a favor by inventing the diversion program so it's over and done with quickly, but I resent being made to feel someone is doing me a big favor when all they are doing is making money and making themselves feel good about "rehabilitating" hardened criminals like myself.

I know you must've heard this request a million times before so let me just add my vote in favor of legalizing marijuana.

Sincerely,

FIGURE 5.11. This 1975 letter to Governor Jerry Brown, from a twenty-five-year-old woman (name redacted) who lived in a white middle-class section of LA's San Fernando Valley, captures the hardships suffered by recreational pot smokers arrested on felony charges and then coerced into rehabilitation through misdemeanor probation. California's 1972 drug diversion law maintained the felony marijuana possession penalty as leverage for prosecutors and judges to send offenders—primarily young and white—into addiction/abuse rehabilitation programs instead of a prison sentence. (Courtesy of University of Southern California, on behalf of the USC Libraries Special Collections.)

to the Bay Area preferred legalization but implored Brown to at least sign the decriminalization bill. They protested the "incarceration of perfectly decent people," denounced police harassment "under an ineffective and prejudiced law," recommended the governor "light one up and turn on the Grateful Dead," and defined themselves as productive taxpayers, intelligent students, ambitious college graduates, successful professionals, and respectable community members.[87]

In summer 1975, the California legislature approved the Moscone bill on a near party-line vote, finally revising what had become the nation's harshest marijuana law. The ultimate version was a weakened Oregon-style compromise that made simple possession or casual nonprofit transfer of up to one ounce an infraction subject to a $100 fine and an expunged record after two years, with possession of larger amounts reduced to a misdemeanor with a maximum six-month jail term. The law created a new category of "low misdemeanor" to encompass the "crime" of simple possession, as demanded by the district attorneys association as a condition of non-opposition. As a "misdemeanor punishable as an infraction," the sanction allowed police to keep conducting "search and seizure" upon discovery of marijuana, as with other arrests, while releasing the individual in the field, as with a traffic violation. The law made possession of hashish (more potent cannabis) a discretionary "wobbler," from a misdemeanor fine to a five-year felony term, and retained the one-to-ten-year felony cultivation sentence. The mandatory-minimum penalties for selling marijuana—five to life for the first offense, ten to life to a minor—remained intact, a concession Moscone labeled "hypocritical" but necessary for passage. Governor Brown said almost nothing publicly throughout the process until, when signing the law, denying that the state had "decriminalized" possession and highlighting retention of "severe" penalties for selling marijuana and the continued ability to commit minors to juvenile detention for any use.[88] In December, just before the law went into effect, the LAPD arrested fifty-nine more alleged "student drug pushers" in another undercover sting, to make a political statement about what decriminalization had wrought. After the ACLU sued, Chief Davis accused the organization of a conspiracy "to destroy America by claiming that kids have a constitutional right to use dope." Overall, the LAPD increased marijuana seizures by 500 percent during late 1975 and early 1976 in a politically motivated enforcement burst to attack the state's new "laissez-faire philosophy."[89]

The arrests of white teenagers and young adults for marijuana offenses, which became both a central mission and the primary accomplishment of

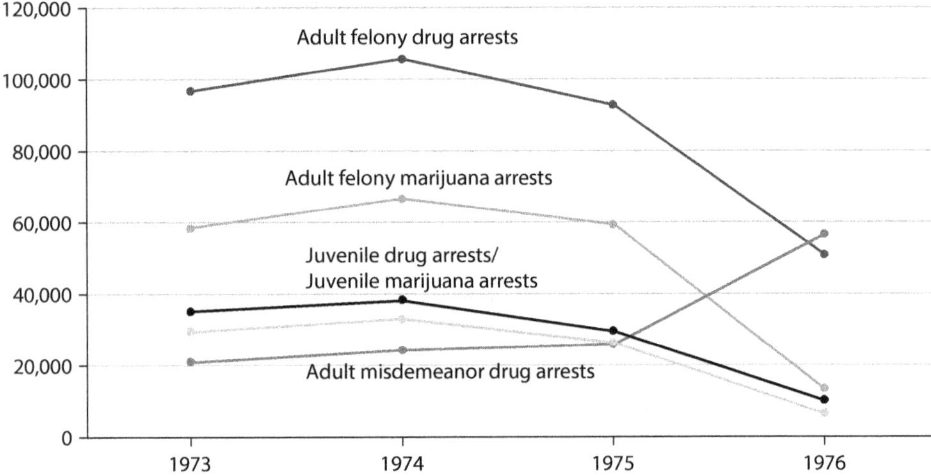

FIGURE 5.12. Marijuana and total drug arrests in California by adult and juvenile categories, 1973–76. Felony marijuana arrests for adults declined dramatically in the immediate aftermath of California's partial decriminalization law, from 64% of total drug arrests in 1975 to 26% in 1976, while the number of adult misdemeanor drug arrests nearly tripled. Juvenile marijuana arrests in 1976 totaled only 24% of the previous year. Between 1976 and 1978, marijuana arrests as a proportion of total felony drug arrests declined much further, from 26% to 5.5% in California. (Bureau of Criminal Statistics, *Crime and Delinquency in California: 1976*; Bureau of Criminal Statistics, *Crime and Delinquency in California: 1978: Part II: Dispositions, Correction, Probation.*)
Note: The California Department of Justice data did not break down misdemeanor arrests by type of drug offense, but the 1975 reclassification of marijuana possession from a felony to a "low misdemeanor" violation is responsible for the doubling of arrests in that category between 1975 and 1976.

California's war on drugs starting in the mid-to-late 1960s, receded rapidly as a law enforcement priority after enactment of the 1975 quasi-decriminalization law (fig. 5.12). Between 1974 and 1976, the reclassification of most marijuana apprehensions as "low misdemeanor" violations cut adult felony drug arrests in half and resulted in at least 30,000 pot smokers emerging from a police encounter with a $100 fine. By 1978, marijuana accounted for only 5.5 percent of adult felony drug arrests (down from two-thirds in the early 1970s), as law enforcement agencies redirected their energies toward the "arrests of heroin addicts," in the assessment of the California Department of Justice. Juvenile marijuana arrests plummeted immediately, from 32,956 in 1974 to 6,281 in 1976, despite no direct impact from the Moscone law. The dramatic decrease in drug arrests of minors reveals how thoroughly marijuana enforcement from the mid-1960s through the mid-1970s had not just been "incidental" to other police activities but rather resulted from targeted investigations of the recreational drug market, such as the LAPD's undercover school operations, rock concert sweeps, bust-and-buy informant stings, and other infiltrations of the youth subculture. The shift away from marijuana enforcement immediately altered the racial breakdown of drug arrests in California for adults and juveniles, as the proportion of whites apprehended declined from 73 percent in 1969 to 57 percent in 1976 and subsequently continued this downward trajectory (fig. 5.13). Since African Americans disproportionately faced drug arrest throughout this period, the mid-1970s resource reallocation affected Mexican Americans the most, as federally funded "multi-agency drug enforcement units" in Los Angeles County and elsewhere did not demobilize but rather policed nonwhite neighborhoods and heroin markets with renewed fervor. State and local police agencies increasingly made marijuana arrests in the context of broader stop-and-frisk tactics and street-level crime enforcement that selectively targeted urban minority communities.[90]

Partial decriminalization reform exempted large numbers of white youth from enforcement crackdowns and criminal sanctions and thus permanently transformed the racial dynamics, geographic targets, and political climate of the war on drugs in California. In September 1975, two months after passage of the marijuana law, Governor Jerry Brown signed mandatory-minimum legislation that removed judicial discretion to divert heroin sellers to probation or rehabilitation, part of his broader political agenda of tough-on-crime liberalism. The measure, sponsored by a Democrat from suburban Los Angeles, passed the legislature with one dissenting vote, amid bipartisan agreement that too many drug "pushers" (generally so-called "addict-dealers") received probation and "our criminal justice system is too often a revolving door." Without the law enabling coercive medicalization of white pot smokers, the number of heroin users arrested and diverted into compulsory drug treatment quadrupled immediately, and the California Department of Justice boasted of the "strong interdependence between the criminal justice system and the drug abuse treatment system."[91] NORML, which had consistently promoted marijuana decriminalization as the way to redirect law enforcement toward heroin markets and street crime, championed California's new approach as a responsible and humane model for the nation. In 1976, a federal survey revealed that 60 percent of California residents either approved of the quasi-decriminalization policy or preferred full legalization, and also that the Moscone reform had no discernible effect on social patterns of marijuana use. Federal and state enforcement in California did continue to prioritize marijuana interdiction in the war on drugs, as the decriminalization compromise presumed, also with no meaningful effect on either supply or demand.[92] And young pot smokers from the white middle-class suburbs continued to lobby

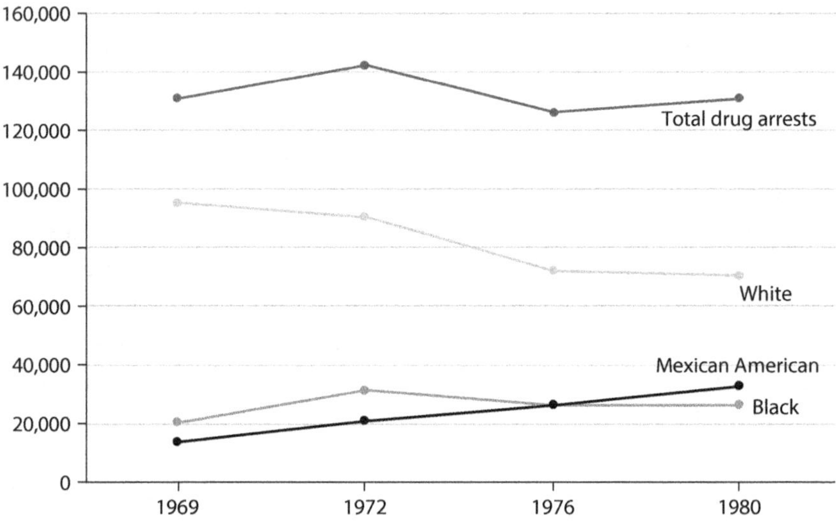

FIGURE 5.13. Combined adult and juvenile drug arrests in California by race, select years. Drug arrests of white offenders in California declined in absolute numbers during the 1970s and also proportionally, from 73% of the total in 1969 (slightly below the white non-Hispanic population share) to 54% by 1980 (12 points below the population share). This trend is largely attributable to partial marijuana decriminalization and the accompanying shift away from law enforcement targeting white youth. While the number of arrests of Black residents increased slightly, and remained the most disproportionate relative to population, the most direct impact fell on Mexican Americans, with a 1980 arrest total 2.4 times higher than in 1969. (Bureau of Criminal Statistics, *Drug Arrests and Dispositions in California: 1969*; Bureau of Criminal Statistics, *Crime and Delinquency in California: 1972, 1976, 1980*.)

Governor Brown to legalize marijuana outright, asking for the ability to cultivate homegrown grass to "put the dope dealers out of business" and the right to "spark up" for a "good, safe high" without fear of police bust.[93]

The Rockefeller Drug Laws and the "Real Criminals"

California's marijuana policies moved into closer alignment with national trends in the mid-1970s, with minimal possession penalties at the center of the decriminalization/misdemeanor compromise of seeking to discourage recreational pot smoking while continuing to wage full-scale war against importation, trafficking, and the supply side of the market in general. Eleven states decriminalized simple possession (less than 1 or 1.5 ounces) of marijuana during the decade, but all of them included misdemeanor jail or felony prison sentences for larger amounts and for selling for profit (table 5.4). In Ohio, a

TABLE 5.4. Marijuana Penalties for First Offenders in States That Decriminalized Simple Possession, 1973–76

State	Year	Possession (simple)	Possession (amount +)	Sale	Cultivation	Sale to minor
Oregon	1973	$100 fine (< 1 oz.)	0–10 yrs. (> 1 oz.)	0–10 yrs.	0–10 yrs.	0–20 yrs.
California	1975	$100 fine (< 1 oz.)	0–6 mos. (> 1 oz.)	5–life	1–10 yrs.	10–life
Alaska	1975	$100 fine (< 1 oz.)	$1,000 fine (> 1 oz.)	0–25 yrs.	No offense	0–life
Colorado	1975	$100 fine (< 1 oz.)	0–1 yr. (> 1 oz.)	1–14 yrs.	1–14 yrs.	3–14 yrs.
Ohio	1975	$100 fine (< 100 gm.)	1–10 yrs. (> 600 gm.)	$100–15 yrs.	6 mos.–5 yrs.	6 mos.–5 yrs.
Maine	1976	$200 fine (< 1.5 oz.)	0–1 yr. (> 1.5 oz.)	0–1 yr.	No offense	0–5 yrs.
Minnesota	1976	$100 fine (< 1.5 oz.)	0–3 yrs. (> 1.5 oz.)	0–5 yrs.	0–5 yrs.	0–10 yrs.

Sources: National Governors' Conference Center for Policy Research and Analysis, *Marijuana: A Study of State Policies and Penalties* (1977), 98–104; Patrick Anderson, *High in America*, 201–3.

Note: Possession and sale of hashish carried higher penalties in Oregon, California, Maine, and Minnesota (usually misdemeanor jail time for possession). Alaska imposed higher fines for "public display" of marijuana, and Colorado up to fifteen days in jail. Ohio's complex weight-based law decriminalized possession of less than 100 grams and sale of less than 20 grams and retained felony sanctions for possession or sale of more than 600 grams. Four other states decriminalized simple possession of less than one ounce of marijuana in the 1970s: New York (1977); North Carolina (1977); Mississippi (1977); and Nebraska (1978).

decriminalization outlier, the legislature passed a parsimonious measure in 1975, after the federal appeals court invalidated its extreme mandatory-minimum sentences (ten to twenty years for possession with intent to sell, twenty to forty years for sale) as "cruel and unusual" punishment out of step with national norms. Every other state adopted the federal model of no mandatory-minimum penalties for simple possession, with misdemeanor probation as the imagined outcome for white middle-class defendants. At the same time, most states maintained severe maximum penalties for the crime of selling pot, typically a discretionary range from misdemeanor diversion to a five- or ten-year felony sentence, designed so that prosecutors and judges could distinguish between misguided first offenders and the "real criminals." Almost one-fourth of states retained mandatory minimums for selling marijuana, and several threatened dealers with a potential life sentence, including California. Four-fifths made private cultivation a prospective or mandatory felony with a maximum sentence of five years or more, which if effective would guarantee the cross-border trafficking and street-level dealing that Amorphia's homegrown solution sought to render superfluous. In general, decriminalization mainly succeeded in mostly white states such as Oregon, with a vibrant youth movement and no racialized heroin "crisis," and in California and New York, where legislatures under pressure from a popular white-led legalization movement carved out a marijuana possession exception to otherwise punitive laws and racially selective enforcement against the urban narcotics market.[94]

The winding history of marijuana decriminalization in New York state provides an opportunity to reassess the meaning of the Rockefeller Drug Laws by demonstrating how racial and spatial discretion operated in both the criminal justice system and in the imagined divide between impossible criminals in the white middle-class suburbs and real criminals in the urban centers. In summer 1970, Governor Nelson Rockefeller relaunched his "all-out war on drug abuse" in New York, four months after the Nixon administration had introduced its national prevention campaign with horror stories of preteen heroin addicts in Harlem and warnings that the epidemic had spread to the white suburbs (see chapter 4). The Rockefeller administration, under fierce pressure from African American groups for failing to address the heroin scourge in their neighborhoods, responded with a statewide series of "drug abuse" community forums held in white middle-class suburbs and college towns (and a semi-suburban location in Queens). The governor, who clearly timed the initiative for maximum benefit in his 1970 reelection campaign, adopted the Nixon strategy of conflating marijuana experimentation with heroin addiction, proclaiming that "every mother and father in America today is gripped by the fear of what drugs can do to their children."[95] In planning the rollout, Rockefeller's political aides consulted with key public health officials in state government, who advised that marijuana and not heroin primarily concerned "middle class parents [who] want most of all to keep their children from becoming enmeshed with law enforcement officials." They recommended that the governor should not use the phrase "drug offender" or portray suburban youth as "any kind of criminal" but instead label them "victims" and attack the "pushers." From the opposite direction, the NAACP strongly criticized Rockefeller for focusing on the so-called "'problems' of suburban experimenters and acid heads" while narcotics pushers targeted Black teenagers and families trapped in the inner city lived in fear of "marauding bands of addicts."[96]

White youth also disparaged Rockefeller's drug-war agenda at the community forums, where the governor championed his pioneering coercive treatment regime for heroin addicts and labeled the "new dimension" of young middle-class drug abuse a "tragic sickness in our society." After the disastrous first event, held in a white suburb of Albany, Rockefeller ordered his speechwriter to change the tone and scribbled notes reading "end hypocrisy," "youth feels society has failed," "can't relate to their parents," "basic problem is they are breaking the law," and an oblique reference to keeping narcotics police off high school and college campuses altogether.[97] At the next forum in Westchester County, his revised speech adopted this generation gap interpretation by redefining drug abuse as "evidence of a fundamental illness in society," rather than a sickness in youth themselves, and pledging that law enforcement would concentrate arrests on the traffickers. Teenagers and college students remained unimpressed, and Rockefeller faced a barrage of demands to legalize marijuana and halt all undercover campus operations. At the Syracuse event, a female high school student informed the governor that his drug abuse program was full of "every single misinformation and misconception, and it's absolutely worthless." Another young woman advised Rockefeller that marijuana and LSD were not dangerous narcotics and that recreational users did not need to be rehabilitated like heroin addicts, but "you are insisting that they label themselves a sick individual, a drug abuser"—a complete misunderstanding "of how drugs are being used in our culture today." In Utica, college and high school students assailed the police for prejudice against longhaired youth and jailing recreational pot smokers as "pushers," alongside broadsides about the generation gap, the war in Vietnam, and the government's lies about marijuana. "Youth make a clear distinction between marijuana and hard drugs," a suburban mother told Rockefeller at another event, and he could not put one-third of the state's teenagers in jail.[98]

After the 1970 forums, the Rockefeller administration continued to declare that "the war against drug abuse is total war," but the moderate Republican governor also moved quickly on marijuana reform and stated that youthful experimenters should not be "ruined for life by the application of harsh and excessive punishment." Rockefeller's advisors warned him of the risks of "coddling young marijuana users," but they also realized that it would be good politics to follow Congress's lead and change the narcotics laws to distinguish the "professional heroin trafficker" from the high school or college student who casually provided pot to a friend. The political staff also worried that a legalization push by the ACLU and a group called the Lawyers Committee for Reform of Marijuana Laws was gaining traction in the legislature.[99] To thread the needle, the administration worked through legislative allies to establish a state commission that would address the fears of parents who wanted "to stamp out the problem" but did not want their children "thrown in jail and branded a criminal for getting caught once smoking pot." Rockefeller personally instructed the chair of the commission, which the administration stacked with "acknowledged hard-liners," to figure out how to reduce the marijuana penalties without giving in to the legalization lobby or surrendering to the "soft" drug culture. In April 1971, the Temporary State Commission to Evaluate the Drug Laws released a report that labeled current marijuana sanctions "grossly disproportionate" and also a hindrance to effective law enforcement because most judges and prosecutors refused to send a teenage pot smoker to prison "with anti-social, disturbed individuals and hardened criminals." Yet the report also emphasized the gateway dangers of marijuana in initiating middle-class youth into a hard-drug subculture and triggering the amotivational syndrome of "lethargy and laziness," marked by disinterest in work and school. The commission specifically warned that marijuana legalization could weaken America through a mass "brain drain" from the colleges and white-collar professions.[100]

The state commission proposed a penalty reduction for possession and the casual "gift" of small amounts of marijuana combined with a coercive public health deterrent that would discharge first offenders who completed one year of rehabilitation under probationary and/or medical supervision. The report advocated the reclassification of simple possession (less than 1/4 ounce) as a violation with a maximum sentence of fifteen days in jail (to provide leverage for the rehab option), available only to those with no criminal record. This recommendation essentially sought to codify the diversionary practices that prosecutors and judges had already worked out on the ground to deal with pot smokers in the white middle-class suburbs. The violation proposal seemed to be a pioneering quasi-decriminalization reform, except that evidence from Long Island reveals that more than half of white marijuana arrestees were already either having their cases dismissed outright or plea-bargaining to public intoxication or disorderly conduct (see chapter 3). Nonwhite offenders in suburban jurisdictions were three times as likely as white counterparts to be institutionalized under the state's civil commitment law, which mandated psychiatric evaluation for all drug arrests, including marijuana. This helps explain why the Rockefeller administration targeted funding for "local treatment programs for soft drugs and youth" in its 1970 campaign.[101] Records from Suffolk County on Long Island reveal how coercive medicalization functioned in the suburbs, as most white commitments involved youth who "habitually use marijuana," allegedly leading to "impaired ability to perform satisfactorily in the area of academic study or employment." One New York mother, distraught after a judge sent her son to a lockdown addiction facility in Westchester County for possession of one gram of marijuana (about three joints), predicted that his "life will be ruined by living with" hard-core junkies and asked how this "communistic" form of injustice could happen in America.[102]

In September 1971, the legislature agreed to a marijuana compromise that sought to defuse the political furor while maintaining the regulation of the recreational suburban market through criminal law and compulsory therapeutic rehabilitation. Almost all of the witnesses before the Temporary State Commission had supported a continued legal sanction to deter pot smoking, except for overwhelming calls for legalization from the students who appeared. Many suburban adults wrote the governor demanding that he stand firm against marijuana legalization, and a number of constituents from all racial and geographic backgrounds called for mandatory life sentences or the death penalty for "dope pushers." Several mothers in wealthy white areas complained of young dealers who "buy their way out" of jail through prominent family connections, while other parents and most young correspondents endorsed legalization and condemned police enforcement against harmless pot smokers. The 1971 law reclassified marijuana as a hallucinogen and made simple possession a misdemeanor with a one-year maximum jail term, rather than the noncriminal violation controversially recommended by the "hard-line" commission. The most innovative feature involved an Adjournment in Contemplation of Dismissal (ACD) procedure, authorizing a judge to suspend charges providing the offender successfully completed twelve months of informal probation, with a discretionary requirement to participate in a treatment or prevention program. The law made it difficult for anyone previously adjudicated a "youthful offender" to receive an ACD, which disproportionately affected nonwhite and poor youth with official juvenile delinquency records. The legislature rejected the casual "gift" reform, instead making sale of any amount of marijuana and possession of more than one ounce a felony with a one-to-fifteen-year mandatory minimum—a clearly unworkable provision that under the current system had guaranteed discriminatory treatment and resulted in the widespread plea-bargaining or downgrading of dealing offenses to misdemeanor charges.[103]

During the early 1970s, the Rockefeller administration faced criticism from all sides as it sought to distinguish the urban heroin crisis from the recreational marijuana market while deploying criminal sanctions and coercive medicalization against all illegal drug "abusers." Nonwhite activists in Harlem, as well as some suburban officials, bitterly complained that the governor had promised money for heroin addiction centers that never arrived, as the politics of public health refocused on the recreational white middle-class crisis.[104] The ACLU and NORML, working with the Lawyers Committee for Reform of Marijuana Laws, demanded alcohol-style legalization and rejected the 1971 reform as a "repressive and totally unrealistic penalty structure" that "victimized" law-abiding youth. The coalition criticized all weight-based and intent-based distinctions as a fundamental misunderstanding of how the recreational pot market operated, because "most users occasionally sell and most sellers are also users." That same year, the state Narcotic Addiction Control Commission released a major study concluding that upper-middle-class drug "abusers" almost exclusively smoked pot, generally at social gatherings where the lines between dealing and receiving were murky at best, and only a small fraction ever used another illegal substance (9% LSD, 12–14% amphetamine). The report labeled heroin a problem mainly in African American (38%) and Puerto Rican (28%) communities, with working-class white adults making up most of the remainder. The NACC study also found that 82 percent of identifiable heroin cases were employed adults or students, contrary to the predominant national and state discourse that all heroin users were desperate addicts who stole every cent they spent on smack and shot up daily. The Rockefeller administration disputed this assessment, arguing that the survey had not uncovered the vast majority of heroin addicts who lived on the street and survived through crime. In the end, hard data would never prove a match for politicized/fabricated numbers and addict-predator hyperbole in the war on drugs.[105]

On January 3, 1973, Nelson Rockefeller delivered his bombshell address to the legislature that the state's heroin rehabilitation programs had failed, that "revolving-door criminal justice" had failed, and that only mandatory life in prison without parole would deter hard-drug pushers and narcotics addicts who committed street crimes. The governor proposed a fifteen-year mandatory-minimum sentence for juvenile pushers (ages sixteen to eighteen), since they also "destroy youth and corrupt society." In addition to heroin, the bill covered LSD, amphetamines, and hashish—even though white dealers and users constituted an overwhelming majority in these three nonnarcotic categories. As usual, Rockefeller defined the crisis as universal, afflicting high school and college students "from every background and economic level." But in a marked break from tradition, he redefined these youth as "victims or pushers or both," and his mandatory-minimum bill did not distinguish among the three typologies that had shaped the discretionary era in national drug policy since 1970: professional traffickers, addict-peddlers, and recreational sharers. Quite remarkably, given the relentless politics of white middle-class victimization in the war on drugs, Rockefeller deliberately capitalized on the story of an affluent suburban addict-peddler to demonstrate that the demand for justice and expiration of mercy knew no boundaries. In late January, an outraged white father published a *New York Times* op-ed, "My Son—Perhaps Yours," about his addicted teenage child who bought heroin in Harlem and resold it to other youth in their Connecticut suburb, with the "profit going back into his arm." The father, who acknowledged that nonwhite heroin addicts would suffer the most under the governor's "inhumane" get-tough plan, then asked if his boy should spend the rest of his life in prison "because he succumbed to a destructive habit." Rockefeller highlighted the case in legislative testimony and answered in the affirmative, labeling the "sharer-pusher" the worst threat of all and asking, "How many have been hooked or died from drugs his son sold?"[106]

The racial politics of the Rockefeller drug debate cut in multiple directions, revolving around whether coercive public health should continue to rehabilitate the predatory addict-peddlers (urban/nonwhite) and the youthful sharer-pushers (suburban/white), or whether a punitive state should incarcerate them all to protect urban Black crime victims and innocent middle-class experimenters. On January 22, three Black preachers and two other Harlem community leaders joined Rockefeller for a press conference/staged political theater that harshly assaulted heroin "pushers" and "addicts" and demanded that the state finally act to protect the decent inner-city residents victimized by both. There is no question that the most intense grassroots pressure for a tough crackdown on heroin pushers and addict-predators came from Harlem, but whether or not this represented a "black silent majority" ultimately mattered less than the ways in which the governor and his allies strategically positioned their demands as the only legitimate voice of the African American community.[107] During his subsequent testimony, Rockefeller championed these Black preachers and then pivoted to the white side of the crisis when an African American legislator condemned his proposal as "dehumanization legislation" and a "ghetto genocide bill." The governor denied that his law was discriminatory because "drug addiction is taking place in the suburbs, on the campuses. . . . It is cutting across all income levels, all racial levels, all social levels." When the inquisitor pointed out that 80 percent of drug criminals sent to prison were Black or Puerto Rican, Rockefeller agreed that suburban judges used their discretion to let white middle-class youth off the hook and pledged that his color-blind mandatory-minimum reform would end this "travesty of justice." Rockefeller also hyped the addict-predator threat with dramatically inflated statistics ("120,000 Addicts Steal $150 per day = $18,000,000 per day or $6.5 Billion per year!") that, if true, would mean that narcotic users in New York annually stole four times the value of all theft reported to the FBI nationwide.[108]

On May 8, 1973, Rockefeller signed what he called the "toughest drug program in the nation" and predicted that the mandatory-minimum deterrent would drive the addict-pushers into treatment at last. The politics of marijuana played a critical, if somewhat submerged, role in the debate, even though the governor repeatedly insisted that it involved an "entirely different problem." In a key turning point, legislative negotiations removed hashish from the bill entirely, to insulate the recreational pot market from the punitive crackdown, a compromise demanded by politicians from both parties and the subject of intense lobbying by NORML and other marijuana legalization advocates.[109] Suburban legislators also insisted on revisions to exempt the "recreational sharer/pusher" from the mandatory-minimum penalties by excluding small amounts of all drugs except heroin, based on concern that an indiscriminate approach would jeopardize two other imagined white categories: the suburban housewife giving diet pills (amphetamine) to a neighbor and the college student sharing LSD with his girlfriend.[110] The slightly less punitive final version established a fifteen-to-life mandatory minimum for selling one ounce or possessing two ounces of heroin, and a six-to-life sentence for sale and possession of smaller amounts of heroin and threshold amounts of LSD and amphetamine. A broad one-to-life range applied to first offenders caught with

see how this new law affects you.

SCHEDULE OF DRUG OFFENSES AND PENALTIES UNDER NEW YORK STATE PENAL LAW (ARTICLE 220)

CLASS	UNLAWFUL SALE OF:	AMOUNT	UNLAWFUL POSSESSION OF:	AMOUNT	PENALTY RANGE	OTHER COMMENTS
A-I Felony	Any narcotic drug	1 oz or more	Any narcotic drug	2 oz or more of a substance containing a narcotic drug.	15 years to life imprisonment	If paroled, life parole; plea bargaining within A-Felony class only.
A-II Felony	Any narcotic drug Methamphetamine Stimulants LSD Hallucinogens Hallucinogenic Substan.	⅛ oz to 1 oz ½ oz or more 5 grams or more 5 milligrams or more 125 milligrams or more 5 grams or more	Any narcotic drug Methamphetamine Stimulants LSD Hallucinogens Hallucinogenic Substan.	1 oz to 2 oz 2 oz or more 10 grams or more 25 milligrams or more 625 milligrams or more 25 grams or more	6 years to life imprisonment	If paroled, life parole; plea bargaining within A-Felony class only.
A-III Felony	First Offender: Any narcotic drug Methamphetamine Stimulants LSD [illegible] Hallucinogenic Substan.	 Any amount to ⅛ oz ⅛ oz to ½ oz 1 g to 5 grams 1 milligram to 5 mgs 25 milligrams to 125 mgs 1 gram to 5 grams	Possession with intent to sell: Narcotic drugs Hallucinogens Hallucinogenic Substances LSD Methamphetamine Stimulants Possession: Stimulants LSD Hallucinogens Hallucinogenic Substances	 Any amount 25 mg 1 g 1 mg ⅛ oz 1 g 5 grams to 10 grams 5 milligrams to 25 mgs 125 milligrams to 625 mgs 5 grams to 25 grams	1 year to life imprisonment	If paroled, life parole; plea bargaining within A-Felony class only.
	Second Offender: Any narcotic drug, methamphetamine, stimulants, LSD, hallucinogens, hallucinogenic substances.	Any amount	Second Offender: Any Hallucinogens, Hallucinogenic Substances, LSD, Methamphetamine, Stimulants with intent to sell.	Any amount		
B Felony	Narcotic preparation to someone under 21. Second Offender of C Felony for dangerous depressant or narcotic preparation.	Any amount	Second Offender of C. Felony except marijuana violations.		1 to 25 years imprisonment	Conspiracy to commit an A Felony is a B Felony, bribery and bribe receiving in a drug case is a B Felony.
C Felony	Any narcotic preparation Dangerous depressants Depressants Marijuana	Any amount 10 oz or more 32 oz or more Any amount	Any narcotic drug Methamphetamine Stimulants LSD Hallucinogens Hallucinogenic Substances Narcotic Preparations Dangerous Depressants Depressants Marijuana Marijuana	⅛ oz to 1 oz ½ oz to 2 oz 1 gram to 5 grams 1 milligram to 5 mgs 25 milligrams to 125 mgs 1 gram to 5 grams 2 oz or more 10 oz or more 2 lbs or more 1 oz or more 100 cigarettes or more	1-15 years imprisonment	Imprisonment is mandatory except for marijuana; probation available for first marijuana violation; rewarding or receiving an award for official misconduct in a drug case is a C Felony.
D Felony	Any controlled substance	Any amount	Possession with intent to sell: Any controlled substance Possession: Narcotic Preparations Marijuana Marijuana	 Any amount ½ oz to 2 oz ¼ oz to 1 oz 25 to 100 cigarettes	1-7 years imprisonment	Probation available for first marijuana violation.
A Misdemeanor			Any controlled substance	Any amount	1 year imprisonment maximum.	Probation available.

DON'T GET CAUGHT HOLDING THE BAG.

The New York State Drug Abuse Program.

FIGURE 5.14. Schedule of drug offenses and penalties under New York State Penal Law (Article 220). The New York State Drug Abuse Program ran newspaper advertisements with the slogan "Don't Get Caught Holding the Bag" to publicize the specifics of the punitive 1973 legislation that came to be called the Rockefeller Drug Laws. The media campaign, part of the Rockefeller administration's get-tough political spectacle, boasted that New York had enacted "the toughest drug law in this country" in order to "make it tough for the addicts, the junkies, the pushers to infect others" and to "make the streets safe for you and your family." (Courtesy of Rockefeller Archive Center.)

possession of any heroin at all and small amounts of acid or speed. In theory and in legislative intent, the hashish exclusion and the insistence on minimum weight requirements for LSD and amphetamine felonies nullified Rockefeller's "sharer-pusher" concept and exempted most white consumers in the illegal recreational drug market. While marijuana reformers expressed relief at dodging the bullet, the New York Civil Liberties Union emphasized the disproportionate effect on African American and Puerto Rican heroin users and denounced the law as "demonstrably inhumane, unworkable, unconstitutional, and essentially irrelevant to the problems to which it is purportedly addressed."[111]

Rockefeller's 1973 program functioned as a "get tough" political spectacle rather than a roadmap for actual drug enforcement in the state of New York. As Julilly Kohler-Hausmann has argued, the Rockefeller Drug Laws marked a shift from "a policy rhetorically committed to reintegrating [nonwhite] drug addicts to a policy of social expulsion." By legislative design, they also furthered the divide between a criminalized narcotics offensive in urban minority areas and a medicalized public health challenge in white middle-class suburbs. Senator Jacob Javits, a liberal Republican and leading advocate of marijuana decriminalization in Washington, endorsed the Rockefeller plan because medical rehabilitation had provided "no viable solution to the tragedy of self-inflicted heroin addiction, therefore society has no alternative but to protect itself."[112] But prosecutors and judges overwhelmingly opposed the mandatory penalties for small-scale dealers and possession, and critics warned that police would take the easy path of arresting users and addict-peddlers rather than the hard work of uncovering trafficking networks (although the NYPD's extensive narcotics corruption made a major crackdown unlikely). One officer remarked that they "could destroy Rocky's program in two months, just by making a lot of arrests, enough to paralyze the courts."[113] The Rockefeller administration hired a marketing firm to publicize the law through radio and television advertisements urging "drug dependent persons" to voluntarily enter treatment or face long-term incarceration. The political staff also planned a ghost-written book about the drug-war triumph, to position Rockefeller for the next presidential election, but a year after the law's enactment they realized that "there is simply not enough positive evidence to present."[114] A comprehensive legal study later found that the Rockefeller law had created massive backlogs in the courts and resulted in tougher mandatory sentences for 1,777 defendants during its first three years, but without any increase in arrest or conviction rates for drug felons and with no impact on use of heroin or any other illegal drug.[115]

In the white suburbs, the response to the Rockefeller Drug Laws ranged from enthusiasm for the assault on dope pushers to wholesale condemnation of his surrender on the public health front, but the dominant sentiment in correspondence to the governor emphasized the need to separate marijuana smokers from the punitive heroin crackdown. "Your death sentence solution is not the answer," a mother of five from a wealthy Long Island community cautioned Rockefeller, given that the "pushers" in her children's schools were just regular students and most teenagers believed they had the right to take drugs no matter what the law said. A SUNY-Binghamton student fiercely criticized Rockefeller for supporting the incarceration of drug users, whether pot smokers or heroin addicts, as a "total avoidance of the underlying social issues involved." But most white middle-class youth and many of their parents focused primarily on the continued unfairness of the marijuana laws, which carried a mandatory one-to-fifteen-year felony penalty for selling any amount and possession of more than one ounce, albeit with a probation loophole for first offenders. From Long Island, a teenager told Rockefeller that his harsh legislation made marijuana legalization imperative, to make sure that recreational pot smokers did not end up in the hard-drug subculture. The mother of an eighteen-year-old denounced the "terrible travesty of justice" that could befall any college student busted for triggering the felony marijuana threshold. University students had "no intention of quitting" their use of marijuana, another correspondent informed the governor, so why didn't he drop the "scare tactics" and focus on arresting the major narcotics traffickers? A young woman asked Rockefeller to reconsider the absurdity of punishing pot smokers at all and asked how drug violations could bring harsher sentences than those reserved for murderers and rapists. Heroin offenders deserved harsh sanctions, another man agreed, but the state of New York should legalize marijuana and hashish instead of turning "millions of good Americans into criminals."[116]

The comprehensive data available on drug arrests and dispositions in Nassau County, the overwhelmingly white middle-class suburban jurisdiction on Long Island, reveal how thoroughly racial discretion and marijuana diversion operated in the administration of criminal justice during the era of the Rockefeller Drug Laws. Through the ACD procedure, established in the 1971 legislative reform, local prosecutors and judges placed the vast majority of possession offenders on informal probation, including almost half of arrests for felony amounts (table 5.5a). In its *Drug Abuse in Suburbia* report, the Nassau County Probation Department characterized the ACD as a wise and necessary method of handling white middle-class teenagers who posed no criminal risk to

TABLE 5.5A. Disposition of Drug Offenders in Nassau County, New York, 1972–75

Disposition	Marijuana possession (N=6,935)	Marijuana sale (N=825)	Heroin possession (N=248)	Heroin sale (N=385)	Barb./Amph. possession (N=419)	Barb./Amph. sale (N=140)
ACD	71%	1%	3%	0%	16%	0%
Dismissed	8%	30%	27%	5%	25%	14%
Discharged	5%	16%	14%	2.7%	16%	19%
Fined	8%	2%	8%	0.3%	19%	0%
Probation	6%	41%	19%	26%	11%	46%
Commitment	3%	10%	29%	66%	13%	21%

Source: Nassau County Probation Department, *Drug Abuse in Suburbia: Final Report*, August 1978.

Note: The ACD (Adjournment in Contemplation of Dismissal) provision involved one year of "informal" probation with the threat of resurrected charges if individuals reoffended or failed to complete drug rehabilitation programs. "Commitment" in this data includes offenders sentenced to jail, prison, juvenile detention, and hospitalization.

TABLE 5.5B. Arrests and Disposition of Marijuana Possession and Heroin Offenders in Nassau County, New York, by Race, 1972–75

Arrests and Dispositions	Marijuana possession (white)	Marijuana possession (nonwhite)	Heroin offender (white)	Heroin offender (nonwhite)
Arrest rate	9.1 per 1,000	20.8 per 1,000	0.4 per 1,000	15.1 per 1,000
% of arrests	91%	9%	37%	63%
ACD	92%	8%	N/A	N/A
Probation	89%	11%	50%	50%
Commitment	67%	33%	29%	71%

Source: Nassau County Probation Department, *Drug Abuse in Suburbia: Final Report*, August 1978.

Note: The "arrest rate" data is for males only (representing 89% of total drug arrests). The disposition data is for all offenders and represents the racial percentage within each category (data for dismissals, discharges, and fines not included). "Commitment" in this data includes offenders sentenced to jail, prison, juvenile detention, and hospitalization.

society, and the agency developed a separate pretrial diversion program to avoid permanent criminal records for almost two-thirds of marijuana sellers as well. Nonwhites made up a small fraction of marijuana arrests but were more than twice as likely to be detained and almost four times as likely to be incarcerated (table 5.5b). The report implausibly concluded that differential arrest rates indicated a lot more marijuana use among nonwhite youth, instead of concentrated stop-and-frisk policing in minority communities categorized as high-crime areas. The stark disposition differential clearly resulted from racial criminalization, but the Nassau authorities instead emphasized that nonwhite pot smokers had prior records, less education, and higher unemployment—factors "associated with criminal behavior in general." In the heroin category, Nassau County incarcerated or institutionalized 29 percent of possessors and 66 percent of sellers, with nonwhites thirty-eight times more likely to be arrested and disproportionately committed (most white heroin offenders were blue-collar workers). *Drug Abuse in Suburbia* praised the Rockefeller Drug Laws as "worthwhile" because heroin addicts harmed society through property crimes, especially the nonwhite group of unemployed high school dropouts that resisted rehabilitation and therefore represented "extremely high risks to the community."[117]

In 1975, new Democratic governor Hugh Carey proposed the decriminalization of possession of up to two ounces of marijuana as part of a tough-on-crime approach to enable law enforcement to focus more effectively on violent predators and offenses "more harmful to society." At the time, New York's fifteen-year maximum sentence for possession of more than one ounce and sale of any amount provided the harshest potential penalty of any marijuana law in the United States, although the ACD provision diverted most offenders. Police statewide also arrested far fewer pot smokers than other tough-on-drugs counterparts (about one-third as many as in California, with roughly equivalent populations). Robert Morgenthau, the Manhattan district attorney, remarked that "we have in a sense decriminalized marijuana here" already in order to prioritize violent crime. While conservative Republican politicians and the *New York Amsterdam News* in Harlem opposed decriminalization with gateway-to-heroin arguments, the state convention of the Parent Teacher Association endorsed the reform because "we don't want our children to have criminal records for getting caught with two or three joints." Keith Stroup of NORML called decriminalization in New York his organization's top priority, and a leading antiheroin activist in Harlem attributed the reform proposal to the simple fact that "the rich and affluent and their children are being caught in the web."[118] After more than two years of political maneuvering, the legislature passed a watered-down partial decriminalization law that made possession of up to 25 grams (7/8 ounce) a civil violation with a $100 fine, more than eight ounces a felony with a maximum four-year prison sentence, and in-between amounts a misdemeanor with jail time possible. Sale of less than 25 grams (including casual "gift") became a misdemeanor, as did any public use or display, and dealing larger amounts brought discretionary felony sentences ranging from zero to fifteen years. Governor Carey signed the marijuana reform with the promise that now law enforcement could focus on the hard drugs and "put the real criminals behind bars."[119]

During the 1970s, the political movement for marijuana decriminalization consistently positioned unjustly oppressed and "otherwise law-abiding" white middle-class pot smokers against the urban heroin markets and "real criminals" that deserved the full attention of law enforcement in the war on drugs and crime. Whether or not individual states enacted partial decriminalization reform, this position came to represent a new national political consensus that formally decoupled marijuana from heroin, and white suburbs from inner cities, both in law and in prosecution of the war on drugs. Marijuana decriminalization sidelined the comprehensive antiprohibition stance of groups such as the Drug Abuse Council, which argued in vain that criminalization rather than heroin addiction caused crime and that get-tough approaches would never succeed in impeding supply or demand.[120] NORML and other advocates of marijuana legalization and/or decriminalization did not instigate the Rockefeller Drug Laws or cause the broader escalation of the war against heroin users and street criminals in urban America, but the racialized binary that they helped to construct played a key role in forging the political culture that made this possible. In New York, as in California and Texas, the legislative reforms that reduced or eliminated criminal penalties for marijuana possession (cast as a white, middle-class, suburban victimless crime) accompanied more punitive laws for heroin sellers and users alike (imagined as Black and Latino, poor, urban predators). Throughout the country, the retention of tough but discretionary penalties for sale of marijuana also guaranteed the continuation of racial, socioeconomic, and spatial discrimination in criminal justice. Provisions such as New York's "public display" misdemeanor further exacerbated racial inequality as police increasingly made pot busts through the stop-and-frisk methods of the war on urban street crime.[121] And in the late 1970s, a grassroots movement of suburban parents remilitarized the selective war on marijuana by repositioning white middle-class youth as the main victims of illegal drug markets once again.

6

Parent Power

AT LEAST TWO OF PAT LOUD'S teenage sons seem obviously stoned when she calls her five children into the living room for a family meeting to discuss some ground rules around the house and request that they stop breaking into her liquor cabinet and taking sexual partners to the loft. "A little late for that, isn't it," one of the longhaired sons smirks as his siblings laugh and his mother gives a stoic half-smile while they gently mock her pretense of discipline and authority. Their father Bill is long gone, after Pat kicked him out and filed for divorce during a previous episode of the nationally televised 1973 cultural phenomenon *An American Family*. The PBS-TV documentary, the first reality show of its kind, chronicled the life and travails of the upper-middle-class Loud family of Santa Barbara, California, for a weekly audience of ten million. By tapping into hot-button issues of family dysfunction, youth sexuality, and permissive parenting, *An American Family* became a cultural benchmark of the subterranean traumas and trickle-down countercultural rebellion of the white suburban landscape. "God, they're lazy," Bill complains of his sons: Lance, the oldest, is a gay college dropout who has decamped to the drug-fueled bohemian subculture of Greenwich Village; Grant, the youngest, refuses to work a summer job in order to play in his garage band and just hang out. "It's your life, I can't control you," Bill concedes during a failed pool-side intervention. An avalanche of commentary transformed the Loud family saga into a "scathing commentary on the American domestic dream," a "symbol of disintegration and purposelessness in American life," a disturbing window into the sexual promiscuity and illegal drug use of unsupervised white teenagers in the "permissive '70s." The series opens with the sons hosting a "weed-smoking bash" in the Loud's garage, and although Pat rejected the media critique and insisted that "my family's fine," the lingering image from the final episode is of a newly single mother in pearls and knee-high boots who has lost whatever control she once had of these fun-loving and unmotivated teenagers—the embodiment of the "permissive" white middle-class culture that was about to set off another suburban crisis.[1]

In the late 1970s, the federal government reescalated the war on marijuana in direct response to the political mobilization of white parents' groups from upper-middle-class suburbs, culminating in their establishment of the National Federation of Parents for Drug Free Youth (NFP) in 1980. Concerted pressure from this self-described "parents' movement" forced the Carter administration to retreat from its initial agenda of marijuana decriminalization, and its prioritization of heroin addiction in the war on drugs, in favor of an interdiction and public health campaign to prevent pot smoking by white suburban teenagers, especially in the middle-school age group. By 1978, nearly 60 percent of high school seniors in the United States had smoked marijuana and 11 percent did so on a daily basis, with the highest rates among white males in large metropolitan centers. The National Institute on Drug Abuse estimated that more than one-fifth of fourteen- and fifteen-year-olds across the country had at least experimented with marijuana, and in some affluent coastal suburbs more than one-fourth of all seventh and eighth graders (twelve-to-thirteen-year-olds) smoked pot.[2] These social trends accompanied an even more dramatic shift in the dominant cultural and political image of the white middle-class drug victim, from the "otherwise law-abiding" college student or early twenties professional unfairly subjected to criminal sanctions, to the increasingly youthful stoner-slacker besieged by adolescent peer pressure and the illegal drug subculture in a hedonistic society filled with permissive or helpless parents. In 1978, a liberal Democrat and mother of three from an affluent Atlanta suburb made this case to President Jimmy Carter in a consequential appeal that linked his administration's pro-decriminalization stance to the widespread use of marijuana by sixth and seventh graders in her neighborhood. Marsha Keith Schuchard charged that the mythology of harmless marijuana sabotaged efforts by "*good* parents" to protect children from illegal drugs and represented a "*short-sighted* and *unnecessary* capitulation to an increasingly aggressive and commercialized 'popular drug culture.'"[3]

Two years later, Schuchard and other local activists founded the National Federation of Parents for Drug-Free Youth, which successfully lobbied for the zero-tolerance approach to adolescent drug use embraced by the Carter and Reagan administrations and provided the direct inspiration for Nancy Reagan's "Just Say No" campaign in the 1980s. The suburban parents' movement emerged as a nonpartisan force in American politics, before Reagan's election and disconnected from the rise of the religious right, a social formation of "moral entrepreneurs" most similar to Mothers Against Drunk Driving and the parallel mobilization of victims' rights groups.[4] The antimarijuana parents constituted "a movement that no one can argue with," Schuchard often observed, because "we can all agree that our children need to get through adolescence free of chemical dependence." This remarkable story reveals how a relatively small number of affluent parent-activists organized a powerful interest group that disproportionately influenced the policymaking process under both parties, placed political constraints on public health messaging, and reinvigorated the recently discredited claim that marijuana represented the most dangerous drug in America. Dr. Robert DuPont, the head of the National Institute on Drug Abuse during the Ford and Carter administrations, renounced NORML and reversed his support for decriminalization after a 1978 meeting with Schuchard and others in her Families in Action organization in metropolitan Atlanta. "The real resolution comes from the community up," DuPont later explained, "when the expert is brought into line by 'watch dog' parents . . . [who] become more expert than the experts." Repudiating a substantial body of NIDA-funded research, DuPont criticized medical specialists who "really believe that drug use is a symptom of some other problem—psychological, social, political." Instead, he praised ordinary parents who recognized the hazards of marijuana, rejected the culture of moral permissiveness, and understood that decriminalization sent a message to youth that smoking pot is "not a big deal."[5]

The parents' crusade against marijuana represented a formation of "political whiteness" and promoted an agenda more deeply rooted in the philosophy of "It-takes-a-village" liberalism and the mainstream perception of a "crisis of the American family" than in the alleged right turn in American political culture.[6] The NFP and its predecessors adopted the slogan "parent power," a rallying cry that emulated radical social movements of the 1960s and 1970s while endorsing positive peer pressure to counteract a deepening sense of malaise regarding suburban family values. Marsha Keith Schuchard characterized the grassroots antidrug movement as a "network of parents who function like an extended family," a necessary response to the acceleration of divorce, mothers working outside the home, and latchkey children during the 1970s and 1980s. She argued that "stronger, intact families" had a responsibility to assist single parents and working mothers by "looking out for their children," because unsupervised teenagers presented a constant "threat to other children in more solid family situations." This analysis reframed the traditional equation of outside pushers and innocent middle-class victims by attributing the adolescent drug "epidemic" of the 1970s to teenage peer pressure, absentee or overly permissive parenting practices, and suburban spaces of youth autonomy. "The first drug won't come from some alien, scary force like a pusher," Schuchard explained, but from a friend or older sibling "who says using drugs is going to be fun." The parents' movement did deploy a variation of the external pusher motif by blaming mass culture, from psychedelic rock music to the drug paraphernalia industry, for infiltrating their homes and neighborhoods and corrupting their children. Although these fears reflected longstanding middle-class patterns of attributing youth crime and delinquency to outside invaders, "parent power" primarily promoted the internal renewal of suburban communities through a help-your-neighbor philosophy of moral policing, authoritarian surveillance, and collective intervention in the lives of teenagers and preteens.[7]

Despite its grandiose self-designation and immediate political impact, the "parents' movement" did not clearly represent the views of even a majority of suburban mothers and fathers during the late 1970s and early 1980s. Rather than interpreting the zero-tolerance parents' crusade as another outbreak of "moral panic" in white middle-class suburbia and therefore in American political culture writ large, it is more useful to trace the ways in which a committed group of grassroots activists collaborated with government officials, and sympathetic journalists and scientists, in a campaign designed to generate moral panic by awakening a complacent, permissive, and demoralized nation to the teenage drug crisis.[8] And rather than a nationwide mobilization, the grassroots antimarijuana lobby emerged from particular spatial contexts during the late 1970s, organized by white mothers who lived in affluent and politically liberal inner-ring suburbs where rates of teenage marijuana use were highest, often located near university campuses and thoroughly embedded in the thriving recreational drug markets of metropolitan centers. Their ideology of "parent power" aimed not only to re-exert control over the youth subculture but also to resolve divisions over child-rearing practices in upper-middle-class suburbia, where families could no longer rely on a consensus about adolescent norms or have confidence that the zone of internal policing and moral sanctuary extended to the basements and backyards down the street. In a sign that marijuana retained its inordinate symbolic power in American culture, the parents' movement argued that recreational pot smoking represented not a symptom but the primary cause of the generation gap and had galvanized a mass "amotivational syndrome" outbreak of apathy, laziness, and alienation in white suburbia. While many American parents and most teenagers did not subscribe to this analysis or endorse zero-tolerance policies, "parent power" succeeded in circumscribing the political debate about the entire war on drugs because no elected official wanted to appear soft on the crisis of pot smoking by twelve-to-fourteen year-olds.[9]

The suburban parents' movement evolved into a powerful national interest group that had lasting consequences for America's permanent drug war, including the deep patterns of racial and socioeconomic inequality produced by the interlinked but spatially distinct policies of public health campaigns in white middle-class neighborhoods and militarized interdiction in nonwhite urban areas. Between 1978 and 1980, the parents' movement extinguished NORML's national drive for marijuana decriminalization and successfully pressured the Carter administration to make the suburban pot-smoking "epidemic" a higher priority than urban heroin addiction. The failure of the federal government to decriminalize marijuana possession, which seemed likely as President Carter took office, represented a momentous path not taken in the long war on drugs. Marijuana continued to account for around 70 percent of drug arrests nationwide, an average of more than 425,000 people per year between 1976 and 1983, with consistently inequitable discretion in criminal dispositions and increasing racially focused enforcement on purportedly "high-crime" populations in urban centers. The parents' movement denounced marijuana decriminalization but operated within its racial and spatial logics of shielding white middle-class youth-victims from the criminal drug laws and the illegal drug markets—not so different from the bipartisan federal reform of 1970, the Shafer Commission's call to maintain the war on traffickers, even NORML's insistence that legalization would allow law enforcement to chase after the real criminals. Parent power groups "didn't want anyone to go to jail" just for smoking pot, as one of the Atlanta-based leaders explained. But the inevitable failure of demand-side prevention campaigns to eradicate the youth recreational drug subculture led policymakers to escalate supply-side militarization, from urban policing to international controls—a renewed war on marijuana to protect suburban family values and address white middle-class anxieties about a lost generation of stoners and slackers ill-equipped to compete in a capitalist society.[10]

Marijuana Decriminalization at the Crossroads

During the early-to-mid 1970s, as rates of pot smoking continued to escalate among high school students and young adults, federally funded marijuana research began to raise new—if questionable—alarms about a broad range of health hazards. In 1972, HEW's annual report to Congress on "Marihuana and

Health" adopted a cautious tone and even disputed the Shafer Commission's concern about "amotivational syndrome," likely a "function of the [preexisting] psychopathological condition rather than of the drug." By 1974, HEW had revised its stance to highlight preliminary academic findings that marijuana damaged lung capacity, chromosomes, memory, brain, immune system, male testosterone levels, and more. Senator James Eastland (D-MS), the conservative chair of the Senate Internal Security Subcommittee, promoted this research in dramatic hearings and a "Marihuana-Hashish Epidemic" report that envisioned a nation "saddled with a large population of semizombies—of young people acutely afflicted by the amotivational syndrome, . . . suffering from irreversible brain damage." Eastland blamed NORML and other "subversive groups" and "pushers" for takeover by a "'marijuana culture'—motivated by a desire to escape from reality and by a consuming lust for self-gratification."[11] NORML's medical experts rebutted the new studies as pseudoscientific misinformation by "researchers who see marijuana as an insidious evil substance that threatens their value system." The Drug Abuse Council, recently established by the Ford Foundation, accused the Nixon White House of censoring and pressuring HEW's medical officials to fall in line with the law enforcement approach and turn science into "a political tool, perverted in order to achieve a desired result." The hyped research had limited political impact at the time, because the decriminalization movement had focused policymakers' attention on the runaway arrests of white pot smokers, but the situation would change a few years later after antidrug parent activists at the grassroots level began mobilizing around the same health concerns.[12]

NORML and its liberal allies in Congress argued that "no drug is totally harmless" and promoted a federal marijuana decriminalization law that would save "otherwise law-abiding youth" from arrest and redirect law enforcement to the war against heroin traffickers and street crime. In 1975, Senator Jacob Javits (R-NY) introduced the Marijuana Control Act to amend the federal penalty for possession or casual sale of less than one ounce to a $100 civil fine, essentially adopting the pioneering partial decriminalization law enacted by Oregon in 1973. Senator Birch Bayh (D-IN), a prominent liberal who had replaced drug warrior Thomas Dodd as head of the Subcommittee to Investigate Juvenile Delinquency, convened hearings and consulted extensively with NORML in promoting the legislation. Bayh argued that instead of the costly and misdirected war on marijuana, government at all levels should target the real criminals—heroin traffickers and the "rising tide of serious crime" in America. Senator Philip Hart (D-MI), a subcommittee member, said that he used to believe in the marijuana-to-heroin gateway but then his teenage son spent twenty days in jail for possession, and "that was all the education I needed to convince me" to support decriminalization. The Drug Enforcement Administration opposed the bill as de facto legalization and warned that most state governments would adopt any federal revision, which for Bayh was precisely the goal. NORML leader Keith Stroup testified that pot smokers were neither "criminal types" nor "the stereotyped long-haired radical" and made the statistically incontrovertible, if politically marginalized, point that "drug use patterns in this country operate almost totally independent of the criminal law." NORML cited growing public support for decriminalization, as revealed in a 1974 Harris poll (fig. 6.1), and endorsed the bill as a temporary "cease-fire" on arrests until the political climate proved ready for legalization. But the Judiciary Committee, controlled by James Eastland, refused to bring the Marijuana Control Act to a vote, and neither party's leadership favored the decriminalization reform.[13]

The Ford administration declined to support decriminalization but called for the de-emphasis of marijuana enforcement in the federal war on drugs, a marked shift from the Nixon White House's strategy of hyping the pusher-gateway mythology as a suburban invasion and a universal threat. In fall 1975, a multiagency task force produced the "White Paper on Drug Abuse," an unprecedented executive branch document in its frank acknowledgment that "total elimination of illicit drug traffic is impossible" and that supply-side interdiction brought "significant adverse side effects," including creation of a profitable underground market and too many "young, casual users . . . stigmatized by arrest." The task force argued for a balanced approach between law enforcement and public health, with federal interdiction targeted at major traffickers not street-level dealers, and rehabilitation focused on narcotics addicts not recreational drug users. The report bluntly rejected the misapplication of the criminal justice system to divert "many non-compulsive marijuana users" into addiction/abuse programs, as envisioned in the 1970 federal law and implemented most comprehensively in California, observing that "these people do not have a serious drug problem and should not be in treatment." The task force also found that while heroin addicts committed most drug-related crimes, illicit abuse of amphetamines and barbiturates represented a greater per capital public health problem. Its internal data estimated that only one-fifth of current heroin users were addicted, while about half of the seven to eight million people who took prescription medication illicitly had serious abuse problems. The report refrained from endorsing marijuana

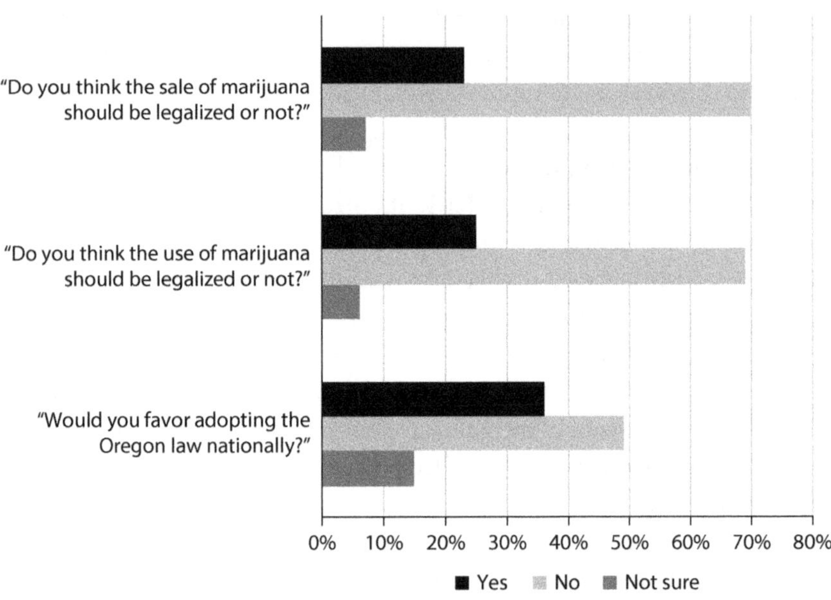

FIGURE 6.1. Harris national survey responses on marijuana policy, February 28, 1974. Only one-fourth of American adults favored marijuana legalization, but more than one-third supported the Oregon decriminalization approach of a small civil fine for possession, and a significant fraction were unsure. In follow-up questions, 48% of eighteen-to-twenty-nine-year-olds endorsed the Oregon law, 35% of thirty-to-forty-nine-year-olds, and 27% of the age fifty+ respondents. Only 29% of total respondents agreed that marijuana was more dangerous than alcohol, a major opinion shift from previous decades. ("Marijuana Decriminalization," Supplement 1, *Hearing before the Subcommittee to Investigate Juvenile Delinquency, Committee on the Judiciary*, U.S. Senate, May 14, 1975.)

decriminalization, which a number of public health officials preferred but the DEA and other crime-fighting agencies adamantly opposed. But the "White Paper on Drug Abuse" did conclude that both supply-side and demand-side policies should prioritize the drugs most dangerous for individuals and for society at large, and of all illegal and controlled substances, "marijuana is the least serious."[14]

In April 1976, when Gerald Ford delivered his only special message to Congress on the war on drugs, he did not mention marijuana at all. The Republican president instead invoked the "disadvantaged minorities" victimized by narcotics-fueled crime and called for mandatory-minimum sentences for heroin sellers, the "merchants of death who profit from the misery and suffering of others." This proposal, which did not pass, revived a get-tough Nixon initiative from three years earlier and would have removed discretionary penalties for street-level dealers established by the omnibus 1970 law. Ford acted under pressure from liberal Democrats, including Rep. Charles Rangel of Harlem and Senator Birch Bayh, to stop the flow of heroin across the Mexican border and address street crime by narcotics addicts.[15] In internal meetings, the White House fixated on heroin interdiction and considered marijuana to be insignificant, except for "legal problems" of those arrested. President Ford did publicly state his opposition to marijuana decriminalization until scientific research had reached a "higher degree of unanimity" on its harmlessness, but the DEA told Congress that the drug was "not our primary or secondary or tertiary priority." When Bayh demanded to know why state and local authorities spent most of their time arresting pot smokers rather than heroin "pushers," White House drug policy director Robert DuPont agreed that marijuana enforcement represented "an unfortunate drain on needed resources" for narcotics traffickers and serious criminals. DuPont, a heroin addiction specialist who recently caused a stir when he seemed to endorse the Oregon approach while speaking at a NORML conference, argued that marijuana was too "politicized" because the public unfortunately did not understand the distinction between decriminalization and legalization. Sensing the political opening, NORML formally revised its policy statement to label marijuana decriminalization a tough-on-crime reform that would enable law enforcement to be "concentrated on commercial traffickers, particularly those who sell truly dangerous drugs."[16]

During the 1976 presidential campaign, Democratic candidate Jimmy Carter endorsed state-level decriminalization for recreational marijuana smokers while promising a federal interdiction strategy that would be "heavy on the pushers." In an interview with the pro-legalization magazine *High Times*, Carter praised the "realistic approach" taken by Oregon and California, a stance that received minimal media coverage and generated little controversy at the time. Carter's three-pronged position stood squarely within the political mainstream by the mid-1970s: "otherwise law-abiding" middle-class pot smokers should not go to jail; marijuana remained harmful for youth, but no more so than alcohol or tobacco; and federal policy should reduce supply by targeting major traffickers. Two months before the election, Rosalynn Carter encapsulated the normalization of marijuana in white middle-class America when she casually told the Associated Press that all three of their adult sons had smoked pot in their younger days. "The only time I worry about my children doing something like smoking marijuana," the future first lady explained, "is if I thought they were slipping around and doing it and not telling me about it." To mitigate this image of permissive parenting, Jimmy Carter quickly clarified his personal disapproval of marijuana use and explained that he and Rosalynn had tried to persuade their sons to stop, but "it's something that most teenagers go through." In contrast to the 1972 presidential election, when the Nixon campaign attacked McGovern as soft on pot, neither Carter's decriminalization stance nor his family situation proved to be political liabilities against Republican incumbent Gerald Ford. In fact, Rosalynn Carter's admission followed similar public comments by first lady Betty Ford, who speculated that all four of her children had "probably tried marijuana" and compared youthful experimentation to "your first beer or your first cigarette." In a sign of the détente in national marijuana politics, President Ford's son Jack and President Carter's son Chip each collaborated with NORML in pursuit of decriminalization.[17]

Peter Bourne, the first director of the Office of Drug Abuse Policy (ODAP) in the Carter White House, energetically advocated the decriminalization of marijuana in order to focus federal efforts on the problem of hard drugs, especially heroin. A medical doctor, Bourne embodied the progressive public health approach to drug policy and had worked in narcotics treatment for both the Nixon White House and Carter's gubernatorial administration in Georgia. In 1975, Bourne delivered a provocative speech criticizing the Nixon legacy for its "unrealistic and unachievable" agenda of "total victory" in the war on drugs. He observed that interdiction programs had simply shifted heroin trafficking to other countries, while the crackdown on street-level dealers in American cities had not affected the supply, except to improve the quality of the product. Bourne then raised the "politically unthinkable notion" that U.S. policymakers might soon have to contemplate the legalization or decriminalization of heroin, in order to curtail the violence that pervaded the drug trade and address addiction as a disease rather than a crime. After taking charge of Carter's drug policy office, however, Bourne oversaw the acceleration of military operations and crop eradication in Mexico and Southeast Asia, a continuation of the ineffective but politically popular focus on reducing the heroin supply in source countries. As for marijuana, Bourne considered the drug to cause "negligible physical or psychological harm," but he opposed outright legalization primarily to prevent corporations from commercializing pot along the lines of alcohol and tobacco. At his Senate confirmation hearing, Bourne stunned the audience when he acknowledged smoking pot "with some friends" a few years earlier and declined to apologize for an activity he deemed much less hazardous than smoking cigarettes. He even spoke at a NORML conference held just before Carter's inauguration and praised Keith Stroup for "remarkable leadership" in the quest for marijuana decriminalization.[18]

During the spring and summer of 1977, the Carter administration struggled to formulate a decriminalization position that maintained a tough approach in the war on drugs while limiting the political fallout of appearing to be "soft" on pot. In March, at Bourne's urging, the White House formally endorsed congressional legislation to make possession of up to one ounce of marijuana a civil infraction under federal law, punishable by a $100 fine. After testifying that criminal sanctions damaged the careers and lives of "otherwise law-abiding young people," Bourne informed Carter of the "minimal adverse reaction" to his position, which he optimistically interpreted to mean that marijuana "no longer raises the passions it did a few years ago."[19] Bourne also assumed responsibility for drafting a comprehensive presidential address on drug policy that linked marijuana decriminalization to the administration's goal of reducing the supply of "those drugs which are truly most dangerous." From a public health perspective, Bourne considered the "unfortunate preoccupation" with marijuana by the media and by American political culture writ large to be a distraction from the urban crisis of heroin addiction and the priorities of interdiction and border enforcement against major traffickers. In the draft section on marijuana, Bourne wrote that federal prohibition policy since the 1930s had "reflected moral disapproval and fear instead of reasoned and dispassionate judgment." He categorized the harm caused by the drug to be "minimal" and labeled the long war on marijuana "an unhappy and misguided chapter in our history." Although forty-five million Americans had smoked pot, "the sky has not fallen." This rhetoric alarmed the Carter White House's political staff, with chief policy advisor Stuart Eizenstat criticizing Bourne's "almost laudatory" tone toward recreational marijuana use for coming close to "a positive recommendation for the drug."[20]

President Carter personally deleted Bourne's most controversial passages from the final statement in order to emphasize that marijuana decriminalization meant that "civil penalties are more appropriate, . . . not that its use should be encouraged." His political advisors then added martial rhetoric and revised or censored the medical consensus that Bourne had summarized. To address Eizenstat's concern that the draft had made "no reference to pushers of marijuana," the administration clarified that major traffickers remained high-priority federal targets. To qualify Bourne's passage about marijuana's limited health hazards, Eizenstat's office added an "amotivational syndrome" warning that chronic use could "deplete productivity, causing people to lose interest in their social environment, their future, and lose other constructive ways of filling their free time."[21] On August 2, the White House released the presidential

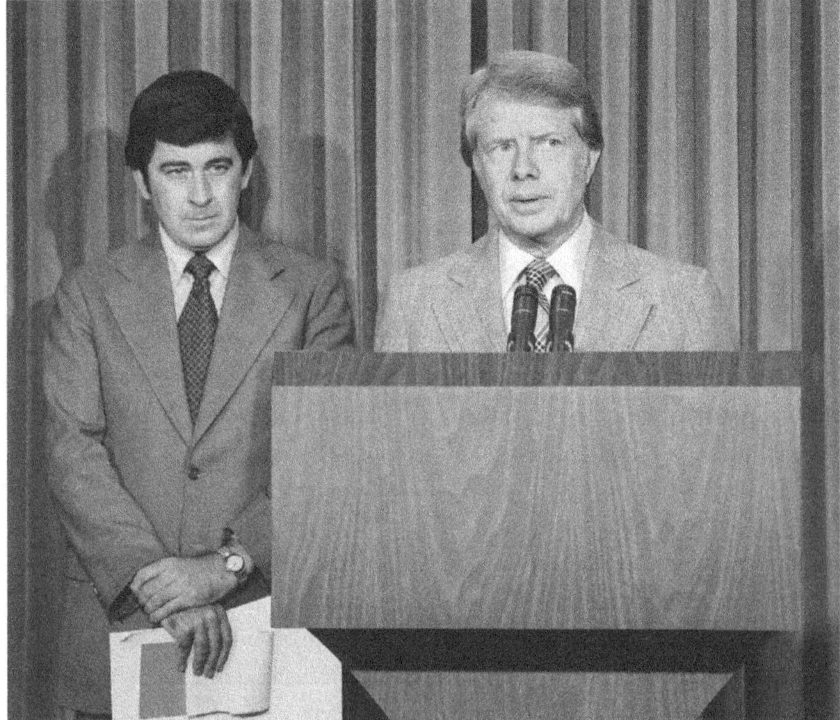

FIGURE 6.2. President Jimmy Carter addressing the media to promote his first drug abuse message to Congress, including endorsement of decriminalization of simple possession of marijuana, on August 2, 1977. Peter Bourne, director of the White House Office of Drug Abuse Policy and the administration's most prominent decriminalization advocate, joins Carter on the stage. (AP Photo / Bob Daugherty.)

message on drug abuse at a press briefing where Carter promised "certain conviction and quick punishment" for drug traffickers (fig. 6.2). The president then insisted that "decriminalization is not legalization" and did not imply approval of marijuana. The formal statement endorsed the recommendations of the Shafer Commission and argued that federal policy should "discourage the use of marijuana . . . without defining the smoker as a criminal." In a reflection of the public health orientation, Carter's message did avoid the gateway and pusher tropes of Nixon's war on drugs in favor of a comprehensive approach that placed "primary emphasis" on the most dangerous substances (heroin and barbiturates) while underscoring that "excessive use" of alcohol and tobacco also constituted a serious social problem. At the same time, the Carter policy intensified the militarization of the war on drugs that flourished under Nixon, especially in the international sphere, although without pledging

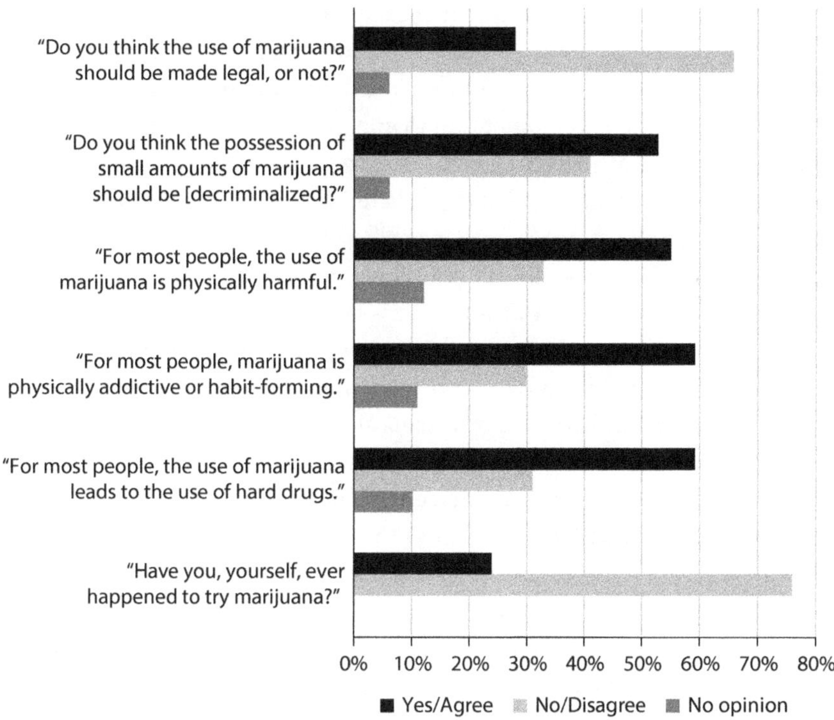

FIGURE 6.3. Gallup national survey responses on marijuana, April 1977. More than half of American adults supported decriminalization of marijuana possession in this survey, in line with the Carter administration's policy stance, and more than one-fourth endorsed full legalization (these categories overlapped). At the same time, around three-fifths of adults continued to believe that marijuana was addictive or habit-forming and a gateway to heroin and other "hard drugs." (For comparison to similar questions in the 1972 Gallup survey, see fig. 5.4). (*The Gallup Poll: Public Opinion, 1972–1977*.)

unconditional victory. "Drugs cannot be forced out of existence," Carter's blueprint acknowledged, but federal policies could reduce the harm caused by their abuse: "broken families, a lost child, or fear to walk the streets at night."[22]

In 1977, public opinion polls and surveys of adolescent behavior sent mixed signals about the competing political imperatives as the Carter administration fine-tuned its marijuana decriminalization stance. In April, a Gallup survey revealed that 53 percent of American adults now advocated the decriminalization of possession, with support highest among the college-educated, the upper-income brackets, and the under-thirty cohort—also the groups most likely to have tried marijuana (fig. 6.3). Slightly more Democrats than Republicans supported decriminalization, as did slightly more nonwhite than white Americans, but age and personal experience remained the major dividing lines. Twenty-eight percent of the public advocated full legalization, similar to survey findings several years earlier, indicating that the decriminalization compromise had stalled momentum to end prohibition entirely. A majority still believed in the gateway progression theory and in marijuana's harmfulness and addictiveness, concerns Gallup predicted would decline but instead soon intensified amid reports than very young adolescents were experimenting with pot. While the Carter administration's call for decriminalization aligned with the views of a majority of voters, the National Institute on Drug Abuse's release of new national data on marijuana use revealed a potential political liability. In summer 1977, NIDA reported that more than half of eighteen-to-twenty-five-year-olds had tried marijuana at some point and one-fourth currently smoked pot, data that did not really exceed expectations. But the survey also found marijuana use by 40 percent of high school juniors and seniors across the nation, and by 21 percent in the fourteen-to-fifteen-year-old age cohort, with half of these students currently involved (fig. 6.4). NIDA presented the marijuana findings cautiously, and emphasized that far more teenagers illegally consumed alcohol and tobacco, but the Carter administration's drug policy officials as well as their quasi-allies at NORML were about to lose control of the narrative.[23]

The Origins of the "Parents' Movement"

The Carter administration's endorsement of marijuana decriminalization, and the new evidence of surging rates of pot smoking among younger teenagers, arrived in the midst of a profound cultural and political crisis over the fate of the "American family" and the intertwined future of the nation. During the late 1960s and early 1970s, the escalation of marijuana use on college campuses and in affluent white suburban high schools appeared to be explicable through the politicized generation gap framework that emphasized the alienation of otherwise normal American youth because of Vietnam, racial injustice, countercultural revolt, and the hypocrisies of suburban materialism and conformity (see chapter 3). By the second half of the 1970s, the political context had shifted substantially: a protracted economic recession meant that fears of downward mobility had replaced worries about complacency in an affluent society; the rising divorce rate meant anxieties about disadvantaged children in "broken homes" were spreading from long-stigmatized poor nonwhite neighborhoods into the middle-class suburbs; the decline of the "family wage"

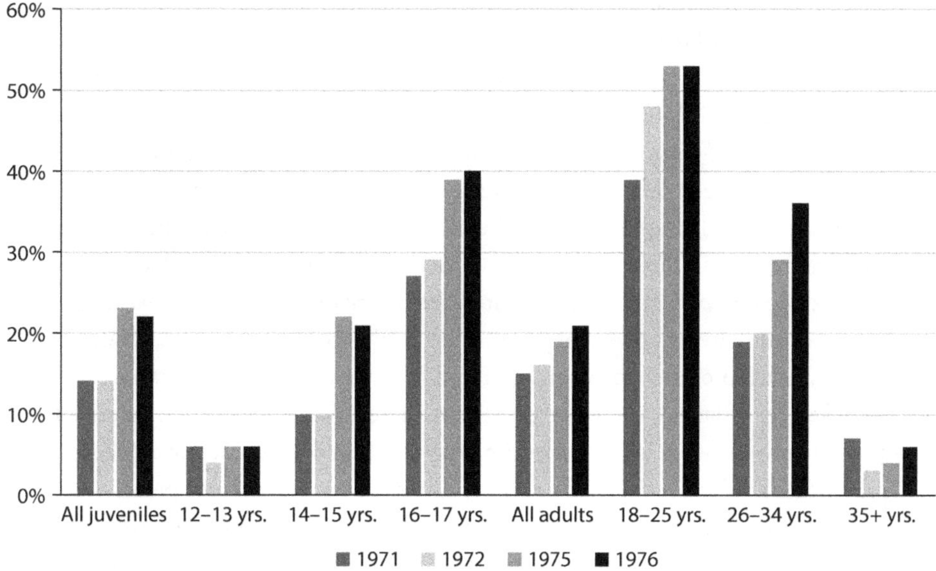

FIGURE 6.4. Trends in marijuana use (% ever used) among juveniles and adults in the United States, between 1971 and 1976. This survey data released by the National Institute on Drug Abuse revealed that marijuana use among fourteen-to-fifteen-year-olds had more than doubled between 1971 and 1976, from 10% to 21%, and that 40% of the sixteen-to-seventeen-year-old group had violated the marijuana laws at some point. Current usage, defined as at least once during the previous month, involved about half of the total that had ever experimented in all juvenile age categories. The survey also found that a majority of young adults had used marijuana at some point in their lives, including one-fourth in the previous month, in an upwardly increasing trajectory. (NIDA, *Marijuana Research Findings: 1976*.)

propelled even more mothers into the paid workforce and generated sustained alarm about the delinquency, crime, and vulnerability of "latchkey children" left behind. The postwar embodiment of the American Dream—a heterosexual nuclear family with a commuter father and stay-at-home mother living in an upwardly mobile (and racially segregated) suburban neighborhood—appeared on the verge of collapse. By the middle of the decade, fewer than half of married two-parent families, and fewer than one-fourth of all American households, conformed to this nuclear family ideal of a breadwinner father and a mother monitoring the home front, charged with the mission of constantly supervising and protecting children from crime, delinquency, and danger. While this suburban utopia was always a mirage, and white middle-class teenagers in an automobile-based society found many ways to break the laws and delinquency status prohibitions even with their mothers at home, the perception of a mainstream American family breakdown decisively structured interpretations of the latest youth drug crisis.[24]

The so-called "crisis of the American family" had been building throughout the 1970s and combined new laments about working mothers and economic strain in middle-class suburbs with the traditional critique that permissive parenting enabled white youth to break drug laws and engage in other types of deviance and delinquency. At the beginning of the decade, the White House Conference on Children warned that "America's families are in trouble—trouble so deep and pervasive as to threaten the future of our nation." *Time* magazine's accompanying cover story linked the implosion of the American Dream to the isolation of the white nuclear family in the suburbs, a predicament intensified by inflation, skyrocketing divorce rates, and mass entry of married women into the wage labor force. The essay attributed the epidemic of teenage rebellion and the psychedelic counterculture to the "benevolent permissiveness" of "many American mothers," a widely shared cultural diagnosis that undercut progressive policy proposals such as government-funded child care and other economic supports for all families of all types. Alarm about disintegration of the white middle-class "American family" amid a "culture of narcissism" represented a mainstream consensus, not just an obsession of conservatives and the emerging religious right. In response to the PBS-TV documentary of the Louds of Santa Barbara, *Newsweek*'s hyperbolic investigation of the "broken family" blamed permissiveness and self-absorbed career women for the "dissolution" of the American Dream, with teenagers lost in a world of sex and drugs without "a father's influence," and ex-wives unable to keep kids in line without "a man to fall back on." In the late 1970s, the Carter administration's White House Conference on Families also sought to "reverse the trend . . . that has destroyed the American family." Despite bitter culture-war showdowns between conservative and feminist groups, a large majority of the 125,000 participants agreed on economic subsidies, controls on sex and violence in the mass media, and drug and alcohol prevention campaigns in the schools.[25]

The mid-1970s revelation that half of all mothers of school-aged children worked outside the home generated a deluge of commentary about the transformation of white middle-class suburbs into dystopian landscapes of "latchkey" kids becoming "dropouts, drug users, and juvenile delinquents." Sociologist Kenneth Keniston, whose influential late 1960s study of psychedelic drug use in the white counterculture and New Left had provided reassurance that most would return voluntarily to the middle-class career track, offered a much more pessimistic prediction about the fate of suburban teenagers who enjoyed material affluence without maternal supervision. "Our middle-class children are awash in skateboards and stereos," Keniston wrote in a *New York Times* series on "Children as Victims" (1976), but "they fall prey to alcohol, drugs, aimlessness and boredom." Keniston and other social scientists contended that because of working mothers and exploding rates of divorce, the traditional role of parental influence on children had been replaced by television and the adolescent peer group (this analysis rarely acknowledged that experts also argued that mass media and peer networks had supplanted parental supervision for suburban youth during the delinquency "epidemic" of the 1950s). In "The Calamitous Decline of the American Family" (1977), published in the *Washington Post*, prominent psychologist Urie Bronfenbrenner portrayed the latchkey child epidemic as a racial crisis that had jumped the tracks from the ghetto to the suburbs. "White families are being fragmented progressively as well as black families," Bronfenbrenner warned, "and middle-class families are now approaching the social disintegration of lower-class families a decade ago." Most academic experts endorsed progressive economic policies such as universal day care to address these trends, but that did not offer a solution for mobile teenagers. So, they constantly reprimanded self-centered parents whether at work or at home for failing to spend quality time with children and for permissiveness that enabled experimentation "with drugs, crime, sex."[26]

The collapse of the utopian suburban ideal, in combination with the very real changes in family structure and the economy during the 1970s, led to a broad range of grassroots parent power crusades to protect America's endangered white middle-class children. Upper-middle-class white mothers generally led these populist movements, operating as "moral entrepreneurs" to arouse a complacent nation and force the political system and the mass media to respond to social developments suddenly transformed into runaway epidemics and existential crises. Many of these campaigns to protect "endangered childhood" were nonpartisan revolts of the center, organized around the defense of white innocence and the ideology of suburban victimization, drawing strong bipartisan support from law-and-order liberals and conservatives alike. The mobilization of the antimarijuana "parents' movement" during the second half of the 1970s paralleled the emergence of the victims' rights movement, which demanded lengthy mandatory-minimum sentences for sexual predators and child molesters and transformed the rare phenomenon of "stranger danger" against young white children into an out-of-control epidemic, even as statistical evidence made clear that only the perception of threat had spiked and that most violence continued to occur within the family and known community. While the religious right's "save our children" crusade scapegoating gay men played a key role, so did the pervasive mainstream alarm about the suburban runaway daughter crisis (see chapter 2) and the emergence of grassroots networks such as SLAM (Society's League Against Molestation), founded in suburban California by white mothers of victimized children. The same white middle-class settings also produced Mothers Against Drunk Driving, the wildly exaggerated child kidnapping "epidemic" of the late 1970s and early 1980s, and related campaigns that historian Philip Jenkins has categorized as part of the populist and bipartisan "child-protection movement," designed to generate moral panic and demand political protection for America's new suburban dystopia.[27]

In this charged context, President Carter's 1977 marijuana decriminalization message alarmed and angered antidrug parent groups at the grassroots, which had not demobilized since their emergence in white middle-class suburbs a decade earlier and had never before had reason to doubt the commitment of Washington politicians to their cause. Making it worse, NORML trumpeted the administration's stance as a reflection of popular sentiment, pronounced 1977 its year of greatest opportunity, and urged the White House to resist pressure from hardliners who wanted to "keep alive the Reefer Madness myth." Drug policy director Peter Bourne applauded decriminalization breakthroughs in three more states (New York, North Carolina, Mississippi) and commended NORML director Keith Stroup in a *People* magazine profile for having "almost single-handedly changed public opinion on this issue."[28] Joyce Nalepka, a suburban mother and antimarijuana crusader from Silver Spring, Maryland, forwarded this article to the White House with a letter claiming that NORML represented only "a very small minority," whereas she spoke for "the *majority of Americans*." Bourne, who definitely underestimated the potential for a grassroots antimarijuana backlash, responded by laying out the difference between legalization and decriminalization, which anti-pot activists considered to be disingenuous and condescending. Nalepka, who later helped establish the National Federation of Parents for Drug-Free Youth, informed Bourne that marijuana remained very hazardous for youth and that both legalization and decriminalization "are entirely wrong [because] either action will create a stronger demand for the drug and where will the supply come from—the very traffickers you think you are going to immobilize." Similar criticism came from a suburban California couple who lectured Bourne that

Dear President and Mrs. Carter,

I am writing to you as the concerned parent of three children and as the worried citizen of a democratic society that seems on the verge of a short-sighted and unnecessary capitulation to an increasingly aggressive and commercialized "popular drug culture." The almost irresistable attraction of this youthful sub-culture for our children was vividly and painfully brought home to my family and community when we learned, much to our dismay and bewilderment, that the majority of our 6th and 7th grade children were using marijuana and alcohol as a regular part of their school and social activities. The most disturbing aspect of their usage--beyond the obvious hazards of intoxication itself for 11 to 13 year-old children--was the consistently matter-of-fact, casual, and "so what?" attitude they revealed when questioned about this premature and immature drug usage. The aspect that should most disturb you and your administration was the constant refrain we heard--"But everybody smokes pot," and then, "Even the President says it's O.K."

As a life-long liberal Democrat, and as a strong supporter of your various campaigns, I certainly recognize that you, as President, do not think it is "O.K." for immature youngsters to use illegal marijuana, much less legal alcohol and tobacco. After two years of research and digging in medical, psychological, and drug-abuse journals, I also now recognize that your policy and that of Dr. Bourne on marijuana decriminalization and related drug problems is based on genuine, humane concerns about the overly-harsh, irrational sentencing procedures of the 1960's. But, I must warn you that I am an historical researcher by profession and that I had to work long and hard to piece together that perception about the administration's drug policy. To the general public—and to your largest and most important constituency--the child-raising parents of the 1970's--the Carter and Bourne message is that "marijuana is harmless" and that official "benign neglect" is the best policy towards increasing marijuana usage.

For parents, teachers, and other adults closely involved with young adolescents, there are growing fears that marijuana usage is producing seriously negative effects on the healthy psychological, intellectual, and physical development of youngsters. These worries are not based on mere ignorance and prejudice about drugs, nor on authoritarian and repressive attitudes toward the young. Concerned adults

FIGURE 6.5. Marsha Keith Schuchard sent this "mad Mom" letter to Jimmy and Rosalynn Carter on Feb. 28, 1978. The suburban Atlanta mother denounced the policy of marijuana decriminalization and the mythology of the drug's harmlessness as an attack on preteens in her white upper-middle-class neighborhood by the "aggressive and commercialized 'popular drug culture.'" Schuchard's campaign helped create the "parents' movement" and directly influenced the Carter administration's marijuana policy shift. This excerpt is from the first page of the seven-page letter. (Reproduced from the White House Central File, Jimmy Carter Presidential Library.)

regular use of marijuana was "tremendously harmful" and caused a "loss of energy and initiative," and a man from coastal Florida who considered the administration's stance on decriminalization "ridiculous" and concluded that "the pushers are happy."[29]

The most influential response came from Marsha Keith Schuchard, the suburban Atlanta mother who sent Jimmy and Rosalynn Carter an impassioned and deeply researched seven-page letter in February 1978 (fig. 6.5). Schuchard held a PhD in English, was married to an Emory University professor, and had founded a local antimarijuana group two years earlier in an effort to stop adolescent drug use in her upper-middle-class white neighborhood adjacent to the college campus. She began by describing herself as a "concerned parent of three children," a "worried citizen of a democratic society," a "life-long liberal Democrat" and a dedicated Carter supporter. Schuchard then described her shock upon discovering that a majority of the eleven-to-thirteen-year-olds in her comfortable neighborhood were smoking marijuana and drinking alcohol "as a regular part of their school and social activities," and even more that these immature children reacted to being caught with a "*matter-of-fact, casual,* and '*so what*?' attitude." Their most common responses were "but *everybody* smokes pot" and "even *the President* says it's O.K." Schuchard acknowledged that decriminalization of marijuana possession by adults represented a defensible response to the law enforcement excesses of the 1960s, but she warned that the administration had completely botched the political messaging for "your largest and most important constituency—the child-raising parents of the 1970s." The Carter-Bourne position had allowed "a new mythology of 'harmless marijuana' to replace the old mythology of 'reefer madness,'" by failing to emphasize the serious dangers of smoking pot for the psychological health and intellectual development of teenagers—in other words, by downplaying the serious drawbacks of the "amotivational syndrome" in a competitive and capitalistic society. Schuchard argued that the administration seemed "so preoccupied with heroin addicts," a very small percentage of the drug-abusing population, that it had abdicated its moral responsibility to "youthful users of non-addictive but still hazardous drugs," especially the so-called "'nice kids from nice families.'"[30]

Schuchard's manifesto occupied a position of real ideological complexity, trafficking in the standard clichés of innocence lost in a suburban dystopia but also making an argument for government regulation of corporate capitalism to protect vulnerable youth from "predatory, profiteering, and proselytizing drug-culture merchandizers." She identified a new and much more sophisticated version of the villainous pusher—a "commercialized multi-drug culture" dedicated to the "no-holds-barred exploitation of the youthful drug consumer." Corner stores sold *High Times* and other pro-marijuana magazines to neighborhood children, while "head shops" provided drug-related paraphernalia to teens who had come to view marijuana as de facto legalized. To drive home this point, Schuchard appended a *High Times* advertisement promising that the marijuana paraphernalia industry "will soon EXPLODE . . .

now that Jimmy has opened the federal doors" with his decriminalization plan. She contrasted the "libertarian Utopia" of legalized marijuana with the right of parents, and responsibility of government, to protect "vulnerable, unstable, and impressionistic" teenagers. Schuchard even expressed "deep shame" that the administration's interdiction policies were wreaking havoc in Latin American countries in order to prevent her seventh-grade daughter from participating in the recreational drug culture, yet simultaneously failing to send a clear zero-tolerance message to American youth. She concluded with a warning regarding the administration's "*extreme political vulnerability*" because of the impression, whether fair or not, that Peter Bourne's office and perhaps Carter himself were "secretly *pro*-marijuana" and "soft on drugs." In a follow-up letter to HEW Secretary Joseph Califano, Schuchard blamed a "lack of strong national leadership" for the "sense of helplessness and bewilderment" felt by many non-permissive parents and requested federal support for a national adult education campaign based on the positive peer pressure model of her suburban Atlanta network, DeKalb Families in Action (named after the county).[31]

The idea that Carter's unenthusiastic endorsement of decriminalization, and the shift to civil possession penalties in a few states, had caused the surge in adolescent marijuana use was somewhere between extremely implausible and completely wrong, yet quite potent as a political threat. Schuchard's one-woman lobbying operation, which she referred to as her "mad Mom" dispatches, first succeeded in forging an alliance with Dr. Robert DuPont, current director of NIDA and former White House "drug czar." After receiving a letter from Schuchard, DuPont visited her suburban Atlanta neighborhood group and came away convinced that marijuana decriminalization might be appropriate for adults but sent the wrong message to adolescents. In 1976, DuPont had appeared alongside Peter Bourne at a NORML conference and declared that the government should not "use the criminal law to try to solve a public health problem." He had endorsed a "a non-criminal policy of discouragement," in line with the Shafer Commission report, but later conceded that the moral symbolism of decriminalization mattered most and "the only thing anybody heard . . . was that the White House drug czar is pro-pot." DuPont soon retracted his support for decriminalization, resigned from the Carter administration, and publicly embraced the parents' movement contention that marijuana was "the worst drug of all the illegal drugs." Before his departure, DuPont connected Schuchard's group with NIDA's Pyramid Project, which provided assistance to state and local drug prevention and treatment programs. Tom Adams, the head of the Pyramid Project, introduced Schuchard to

Dr. Thomas Gleaton, a drug researcher on the faculty of Georgia State University whose own teenage daughter had recently experimented with marijuana. Together they organized a spring 1978 conference in Atlanta to demonstrate that "parent power can win out over peer power and dope power." NIDA also hired Schuchard as a federal consultant and commissioned her to write a handbook for parents, which she previewed in her keynote address at the Atlanta conference.[32]

Schuchard's speech, titled "The Family versus the Drug Culture," combined a detailed analysis of the limited scientific knowledge about marijuana's effects on adolescents with hyperbolic stories of families torn apart by pot in a suburban dystopia. She began by describing her "shocked discovery" that her daughter and other neighborhood youth were under the sway of an "alien drug culture," the "sickening feeling" that all parents—no matter how liberal or conservative—must feel "about their own apparent helplessness and loss of control." Through tropes of white innocence lost, Schuchard lamented the "shattered illusions" of drug and alcohol abuse "by 5th-grade skateboarders, by 7th-grade cheerleaders, by 9th-grade football players," the shocking discovery that teenagers and preteens were smoking pot at school, at the shopping mall, at rock concerts, even at church camps and inside private homes. Schuchard told the middle-aged audience that "kids today are growing up in a vastly different world" from the 1950s era their parents remembered fondly, in a "hedonistic, materialistic youth culture . . . more independent from parental standards and traditional values." In previous decades, parents could feel reassured that the psychedelic drug subculture would attract a small group of youth with "delinquent or hippie tendencies," but now "more and more nice kids from good, stable homes are smoking pot and drinking booze at younger and younger ages." She blamed the "everybody is doing it" peer culture, influenced by pro-drug messages of rock music, films, and other media that portrayed pot smoking as "harmless, acceptable, and inevitable." But instead of sending a clear zero-tolerance message, many drug abuse experts considered pot smoking to be an adolescent rite of passage and "express a scornful, even cavalier attitude" toward concerned parents. The powerful drug subculture and "a wall of official indifference" had intimidated parents into "bewildered permissiveness," Schuchard concluded, but collective organizing at the neighborhood level could reverse the tide and save a generation of lost children through "*parental peer pressure*."[33]

Schuchard's critique of the "newly prevailing mythology of 'harmless marijuana'" reveals how and why the suburban parents' movement resurrected the concept that pot was America's most dangerous drug, the primary cause of teenage dysfunction and family breakdown. She argued that prevention campaigns should also target alcohol and cigarettes but marijuana represented the most urgent threat because "it is usually the first illegal drug used by kids, and it is the drug which most baffles and disturbs parents. . . . It is the popular mythology of marijuana, the rituals and music and glorification of marijuana usage, that set the style of the youthful drug *and* drinking scene." Schuchard specifically warned that smoking pot initiated the stepping-stone process—"many of them also 'progress' to other illegal drugs" such as cocaine, amphetamines, and PCP (a hallucinogen known as "angel dust"). But her analysis mainly portrayed marijuana experimentation as the gateway into an autonomous and frightening youth subculture—a generalized "drug lifestyle" of adolescent freedom, teenage rebellion, and middle-class deviance. "Parents of pot smokers," she explained, "often report that their children seem to become strangers. . . . The parents do not know just *who* they are living with or *who* they are trying to raise anymore." Smoking marijuana during adolescence caused "disturbing personality and behavioral changes," stunted physical and emotional development, induced lethargy and apathy, encouraged sexual promiscuity, and impaired school performance. This interpretation effectively expanded the dubious medical concept of the "amotivational syndrome," usually applied only to long-term daily stoners, into an all-inclusive diagnosis of every youth involved in the recreational marijuana subculture, who were unwittingly "choos[ing] *not* to grow up emotionally and psychologically." The pot-smoking lifestyle sabotaged the middle-class futures of teenage and preteen participants: "The real world out there is tough and it does not make excuses for the supposed young adult who befuddled his adolescence with marijuana."[34]

This message was a depoliticized rearticulation of the late-1960s consensus that smoking pot triggered the generation gap and initiated suburban teenagers into lifestyles of indolence and deviance, refracted through the "amotivational syndrome" framework that marijuana induced personality disorders. Schuchard's diagnosis, based primarily on personal observations of her own children and their friends, also reversed the cause-and-effect analysis found in most recent psychological studies. In 1977, NIDA published a comprehensive summary of marijuana research to accompany its release of explosive data that 40 percent of high school juniors and seniors, and 21 percent of ninth and tenth graders, had smoked pot at least once. According to multiple longitudinal investigations, "rebelliousness was the best predictor of future marijuana use." Teenage pot smokers "placed lower value on achievement, higher value on independence, tended to be more alienated and critical, more tolerant of deviance, less religious, less influenced by parents as compared to friends." The stigmatized attitudes and actions of participants in the recreational subculture "appear more often to precede than to follow" the use of marijuana. Adolescents who had never experimented tended to be "obedient, law-abiding, conscientious, trustworthy, and hardworking," with religiously active and politically conservative youth the most likely to abstain. These findings help to illuminate why liberal white parents, rather than religious conservatives or Republican activists, disproportionately organized the antimarijuana movements that burst onto the political scene in the late 1970s—because their adolescent children were far more likely to be the ones actually smoking pot. NIDA concluded its 1977 report with the observation that like all drugs, "marijuana is not 'safe' in any absolute sense," but only further research could determine its specific hazards. In her "Family versus the Drug Culture" manifesto, Schuchard labeled this "cold comfort to parents who don't want to raise drug-using guinea pigs but more familiar and understandable sons and daughters."[35]

The geographic base of the early leaders of the parents' movement also reflected the spatial dynamics of the white recreational drug market, where rates of middle-school pot smoking were highest in affluent, politically liberal inner-ring suburbs located near urban centers and universities. NIDA's surveys demonstrated that only 6 percent of twelve-to-thirteen-year-olds—the age group generating the most shock and alarm by the nascent parent power movement—had tried marijuana in the mid-1970s. But the limited local-level data that did exist indicated significantly higher rates in the upscale white suburbs of coastal metropolitan centers, such as Joyce Nalepka's home in Silver Spring (91% white) on the DC border, and Schuchard's in Druid Hills (99% white) just outside the Atlanta city limits. Since the late 1960s, NIDA had funded the nation's most comprehensive survey of adolescent drug use in San Mateo County, California, the mostly white suburban jurisdiction in-between San Francisco and Palo Alto. By 1975, one-third of junior high students in the county had smoked pot during the previous year, including 19 percent of seventh graders, 33.5 percent of eighth graders, and 46.8 percent of ninth graders (fig. 6.6 [top]). The trends pointed upward, with a majority of high school students reporting marijuana use throughout the decade, and nearly two-thirds of juniors and seniors by 1977. Almost one-tenth of eighth graders and one-seventh of ninth graders reported smoking pot on a weekly basis, rising to more than one-fourth of the high school students (fig. 6.6 [bottom]).

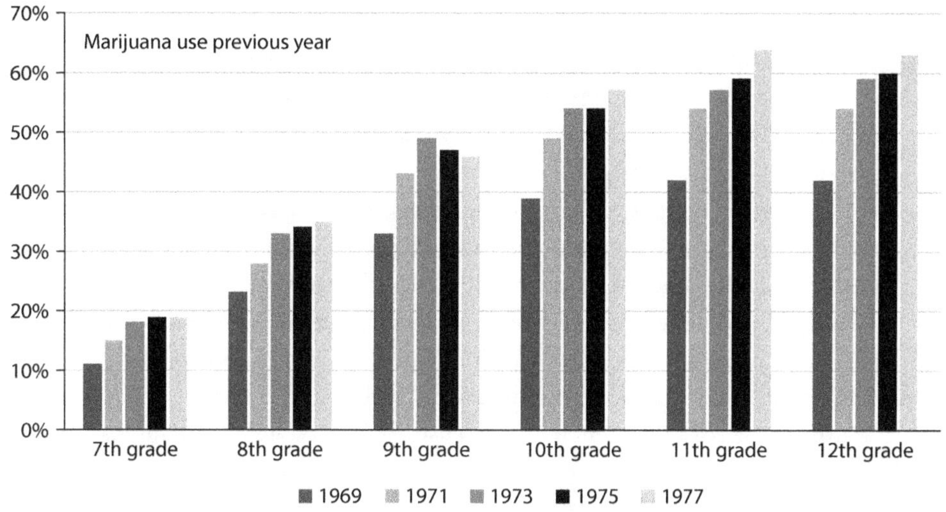

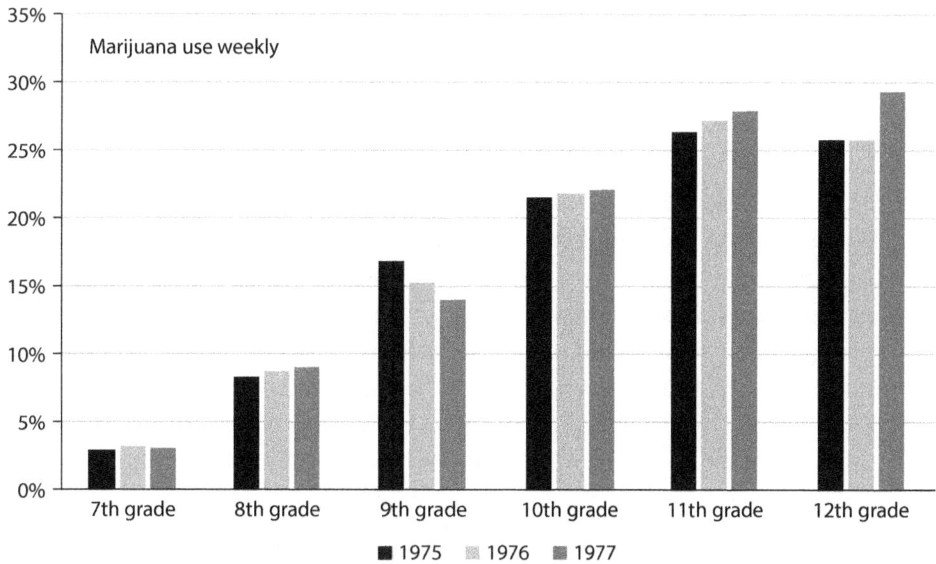

FIGURE 6.6. Student marijuana use in San Mateo County, California, 1969–77. (*Top*) Marijuana usage among junior and senior high school students in suburban San Mateo County increased steadily during the 1970s. By 1977, students self-reporting marijuana use during the previous year included 35% of eighth graders, 57% of tenth graders, and 63% of seniors. (*Bottom*) Regular marijuana smokers (defined as at least fifty times during the previous year) generated substantial alarm about the risks of the "amotivational syndrome" during the mid-to-late 1970s. The survey data from San Mateo County revealed that this category included more than one-fifth of high school sophomores and more than one-fourth of juniors and seniors. The proportion of weekly marijuana users was much lower among seventh and eighth graders, but the 9% weekly figure in the latter category was among the most shocking findings in this widely circulated data. (San Mateo County Department of Public Health and Welfare, *Summary Report: Surveys of Student Drug Use, San Mateo County, California*, March 1977.)
Note: The survey reported male and female usage separately, but calculations in these charts combine them for clarity of presentation, based on an estimate of 50% of each gender in the results. Males generally reported marijuana use around 3–6 percentage points higher than females.

Two-thirds of middle schoolers and most high schoolers also had broken the alcohol laws. NIDA considered San Mateo County to be a suburban harbinger of national trends, and this data circulated widely in federal reports and congressional hearings. In terms of selective law enforcement, it is also illuminating to note that in 1975, the year before decriminalization took effect in California, the rate of juvenile felony arrests for marijuana was five times higher in Los Angeles than in the large, white upper-middle-class suburban city of San Mateo.[36]

In 1978, soon after organizing the Atlanta conference, Marsha Schuchard and Thomas Gleaton launched PRIDE (Parents' Resource Institute for Drug Education) to encourage formation of local antidrug groups and publicize the health dangers of adolescent marijuana use. PRIDE's statement of philosophy proclaimed that the "universal instinct of parents to protect their young is society's best bulwark against the expansion of the commercialized drug culture . . . [and] a walled-in youthful peer culture." Rather than "imposing a sense of guilt and failure" on parents, PRIDE advocated an inclusive approach based in the "rich pluralism of American family life" and explained that "it is not necessarily a parent's fault" if a child succumbed to the cultural pressure to smoke pot and drink booze. To visualize the anti-permissive parent power message, PRIDE's logo replaced the blank space inside the letter "P" with a figure standing with hands on hips, symbolizing the aggressive assertion of adult authority. "Starting a Parent Group," PRIDE's feature publication, repackaged Schuchard's conference manifesto and presented "positive parental peer pressure" as the antidote to the social isolation of individual families and fragmentation of modern communities. Gleaton contributed a section on how parents could tell if a child had started using drugs: suspicious activities included hanging out with a new group of friends, withdrawing from family time, feeling depressed, refusing to do chores, keeping a messy room, listening to rock music, staying out late, changing clothing and hair style, and losing interest in academics and sports. He conceded that many of these symptoms overlapped with "typical adolescent behavior," but other warning signs were more unmistakable: teenagers who demanded the right to drink alcohol, stole liquor and money from parents, left marijuana roaches around the house, vomited in the car, were arrested for burglary or prostitution, and/or attempted suicide. The PRIDE pamphlet concluded with a call for parental surveillance networks to watch out for each other's children and "reestablish a sense of cohesive community values."[37]

DeKalb Families in Action, the model for this national parents' movement, originated in Schuchard's neighborhood antimarijuana campaign and expanded into a suburban Atlanta confederation during the late 1970s. Sue Rusche, the cofounder and main leader of DeKalb Families in Action, lived on the same street as Schuchard and also was a liberal Democrat and spouse of an Emory professor. In her own manifesto, *How to Form a Families in Action Group in Your Community* (1979), Rusche related the shock of discovering an adolescent subculture of recreational drugs—marijuana, alcohol, even cocaine—"going on under our noses without our knowing it." She blamed parental permissiveness and denial, drug abuse professionals who advocated "responsible use" and considered marijuana to be a rite of passage, and the social turmoil that resulted from divorce, working mothers, and middle-class parents who obsessed over their careers instead of spending time with their children. "In our eagerness to raise our kids free of 'hang-ups,'" she asked of the parents in her liberal university community, "had we forgotten they need firm guidance as well?" Rusche advised parents to counteract the pro-drug messages of popular culture by monitoring rock music and chaperoning children at concerts and other venues where pot smoking and underage drinking flourished. DeKalb Families in Action sponsored positive alternatives to the drug subculture, some of which built on traditional antidelinquency strategies and others that targeted the particular challenges of growing up with too much time and money. The chapter in Dunwoody (98% white), which described itself as an "affluent, suburban community" undergoing a "truly awful" marijuana epidemic, started a Neighborhood Jobs Corps for "advantaged" teenagers to fill after-school hours and weekends with productive activities. The Stone Mountain chapter exerted pressure on parents who were allowing their teenagers to throw keg parties with live bands and omnipresent pot, while the Chamblee affiliate opened a Teen Canteen to provide youth a drug-free recreational space.[38]

Despite its ambitious self-designation, the parents' movement faced an uphill battle in its assault on the recreational marijuana subculture in the late 1970s, revealing clear internal divisions in the upscale suburbs that formed its base. Leading activists such as Sue Rusche and Marsha Schuchard often lamented the "solid wall of denial" by affluent, college-educated parents who refused to "worry as much about the so-called soft drugs as the hard drugs." Most mothers and fathers in the upper-middle-class white suburbs either did not agree with this analysis or did not share the sense of urgency. For example, two PTA mothers from Northside High, located in the wealthy Atlanta enclave of Buckhead (98% white, with recently integrated schools through court-ordered busing), started an antimarijuana campaign in 1978 after attending the

PRIDE conference organized by Schuchard and Gleaton. Despite their efforts, only ten couples initially joined the initiative, although many other parents complained when the principal started having students arrested for smoking pot at school. The small group of teenagers whose parents launched the drug-free crusade felt cut off from mainstream peer culture and fiercely resisted the new curfews and zero-tolerance penalties. A larger number of families got on board only through coercion, after the high school and local law enforcement developed a procedure that targeted pot-smoking teenagers for arrest, sentenced them to probation that included mandatory treatment and drug testing, and required their parents to attend a prevention program. The Northside High movement, which eventually claimed success in reversing the adolescent drug culture, revealed that selective police enforcement could play a role in buttressing parent power, conditional on the traditional diversion of affluent white teenagers from criminal penalties. Under PRIDE's auspices, groups at more than five hundred schools in Georgia eventually adopted the Northside High template of "parent-teen cooperation," reinforced when necessary through "creative and effective punishment" by the juvenile courts.[39]

DeKalb Families in Action supplemented its program for internal suburban renewal through parent power with a political and legal campaign against the latest version of the corrosive pusher, the "commercialized drug culture." More than anything else, Sue Rusche attributed the suburban marijuana epidemic to the "outside, alien force" of a drug paraphernalia industry that targeted innocent youth for profit by infiltrating neighborhood stores and local shopping malls. In 1977, Rusche's children were not yet ten, so her involvement represented a preemptive strike against a troubling future, a mission that began after one of her sons picked up a marijuana pipe disguised as a *Star Wars* weapon during a family trip to a record store. Her subsequent investigation revealed pipes and bongs masquerading as children's toys, comic books featuring drug use by teens, "Practice Grass" baggies (allegedly) designed to pre-hook kids too young for the real thing, and *High Times* articles about the constitutional right to get stoned. Rusche accused NORML and *High Times* of a joint conspiracy to recruit youth into the pro-legalization pot culture as part of their profit-driven alliance with a multibillion dollar paraphernalia industry "that glamorizes and promotes illicit drugs to children." Families in Action worked with suburban politicians to close down "head shops" in DeKalb County and successfully pressured the 7-Eleven chain to stop selling rolling paper in its stores nationwide, based on its "responsibility to the public" and not only to shareholders. The group then lobbied the Georgia legislature to pass several laws restricting the sale of drug paraphernalia to minors (head shop owners successfully challenged them as unconstitutionally vague). As part of its supply-side focus, DeKalb Families in Action also urged parents to harass local drug dealers through a neighborhood watch campaign and established a judicial watchdog committee to protest light sentences for traffickers—notable recommendations given that Rusche's how-to manual did not actually mention that pot-smoking teenage victims were breaking the law.[40]

The Carter Administration's "Political Powder Keg"

In the late 1970s, large-scale surveys of adolescent drug trends confirmed the warnings of the parents' movement about surging rates of marijuana use, including hundreds of thousands of daily teenage stoners. The percentage of twelve-to-seventeen year-olds who smoked marijuana doubled between 1972 and 1977, as did the proportion that had tried cocaine. According to NIDA's "Monitoring the Future" project, "there is no question that marijuana use moved in the 1970s from being a deviant, minority behavior among American young people in their late teens and early twenties to become a normative, majority behavior."[41] The annual "Monitoring the Future" survey revealed that 56 percent of high school seniors in the class of 1977 had smoked marijuana, 35 percent within the previous month. One in seven had experimented with hallucinogens such as LSD or PCP, one in ten had tried cocaine, and fewer than one in fifty had used heroin. Almost all seniors had consumed alcohol, 71 percent within the previous month. Three-fourths had smoked cigarettes, and almost one-third did so every day (fig. 6.7). The largest metropolitan areas and the Northeast showed the highest rates of teenage drug and alcohol use, but the gaps among regions had narrowed considerably in the last half-decade (the surveys did not distinguish urban from suburban schools). Non-college-bound students smoked marijuana more frequently than seniors who expected to achieve a college degree, but only by a 51–43 percent ratio; each group drank alcohol at the same rate. In the most politically explosive finding, the survey found that 9 percent of seniors, 270,000 students nationwide, currently smoked pot on a daily or near-daily basis. Males were twice as likely to be daily stoners, and white adolescents twice as likely as Black youth. The upward trends continued in the 1978 survey, which revealed that 59 percent of seniors had tried marijuana and almost 11 percent smoked pot daily. In a sign of the increasingly younger age of initiation, one-fourth of seniors first tried marijuana, and more than half first drank alcohol, before tenth grade.[42]

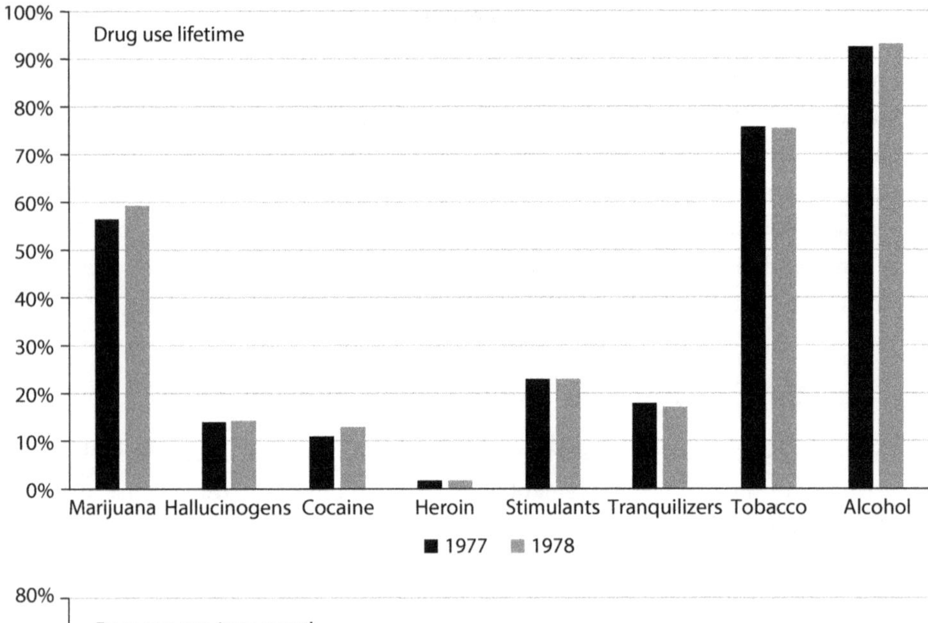

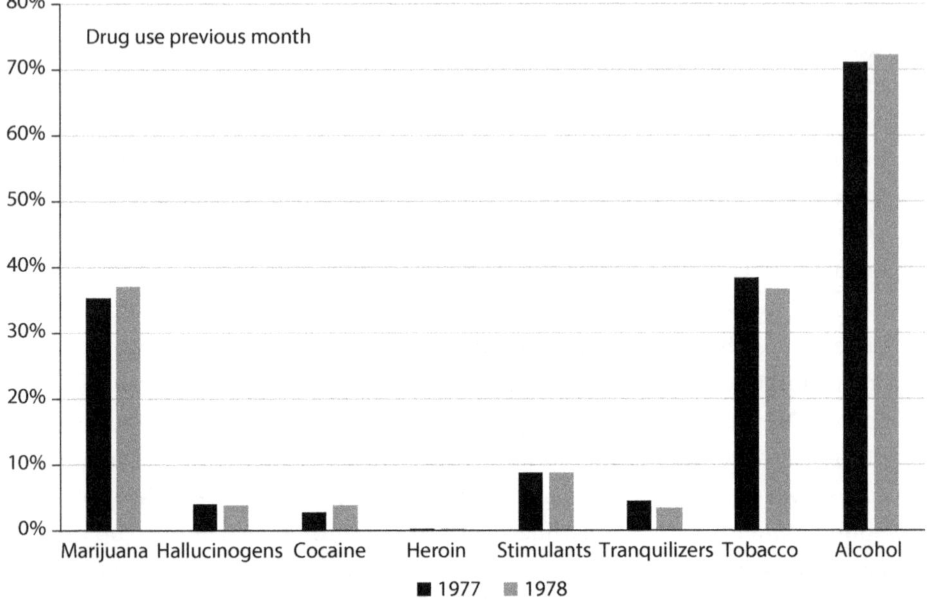

FIGURE 6.7. Drug use patterns among U.S. high school seniors in 1977 and 1978. (*Top*) NIDA's annual drug survey revealed that experimentation with marijuana had become a majority phenomenon among high school seniors by 1977–78. Alcohol and tobacco remained the most popular illicit drugs, as they had been for decades (eighteen-year-olds could purchase both legally in many states). The use of cocaine by more than one-tenth of high school seniors received much less attention than marijuana, which would soon change. Illicit use of legal pharmaceuticals was even more widespread (the data for stimulants [amphetamines] and tranquilizers only include drug use without medical authorization). (*Bottom*) More than one-third of high school seniors smoked marijuana monthly during 1977–78, compared to nearly three-fourths who routinely drank alcohol. Except for tobacco, use of most other illicit and illegal substances by high school seniors was an occasional rather than a regular practice. (NIDA, *Highlights from Drug Use among American High School Students, 1975–1977*; NIDA, *Highlights from Drugs and the Class of '78: Behaviors, Attitudes, and Recent National Trends.*)

The "Monitoring the Future" surveys revealed the persistence of a generation gap in attitudes toward marijuana within the family and undermined the charge that parental permissiveness bore primary responsibility for increased rates of teenage pot smoking. In the class of 1978, a mere 12 percent of seniors believed that occasional marijuana use entailed "great risk," and only 35 percent said the same for getting stoned daily—evidence of the steady downward trend in teenage assessments of the drug's harmfulness. Large majorities believed that routine use of LSD and cocaine was dangerous, although fewer than half said the same for irregular experimentation. One-third of high school students supported legalization of marijuana, and another third endorsed decriminalization. Almost 90 percent agreed that marijuana was "easy" to obtain, and almost all said its legal status had not had, and would not have, any effect on whether they used it. In a significant finding, 91 percent of seniors reported that their parents disapproved of any marijuana use, meaning that the recreational subculture of weekend pot smoking operated outside of familial sanction, unlike underage consumption of alcohol in moderation. On the other hand, antipermissiveness activists could point out that the widespread teenage perception of parental disapproval did not necessarily mean that most mothers and fathers would aggressively intervene to prevent or punish their children's illegal peer-sanctioned drug use. And the zero-tolerance analysis of the parent power movement, which emphasized that a single permissive or unsupervised household could sabotage an entire middle-class neighborhood, could find danger in other aspects of the survey data: 17 percent of seniors believed that their parents would not mind if they tried marijuana once or twice, or if they had five or more drinks over the weekend. Still, as the survey concluded, peer norms and friendship circles overwhelmingly shaped patterns of illicit drug and alcohol use among teenagers, and "there remains a massive generational difference of opinion" about marijuana.[43]

The Carter administration moved quickly during the spring and summer of 1978 to counter the trends revealed by the "Monitoring the Future" survey and to address soft-on-drugs charges from the suburban antimarijuana movement. The parent power network remained numerically small but enjoyed NIDA seed funding and claimed to represent a rising tide of grassroots mobilization. In a missive sent after the formation of PRIDE, Marsha Schuchard and Thomas Gleaton expressed anger about the resignation of NIDA's Robert DuPont and informed the White House that "the great majority of *voting* Americans—the working and child-raising heads of households—are deeply disturbed at widespread marijuana usage by children and adolescents and . . .

confused and resentful at what seems to be the pro-drug bias of Carter's drug advisers." The administration was "sitting on a political powder keg," they warned, since "*masses* of voting parents are observing—with shock and anger—this aggressive drug-merchandising assault on the youth market which is now taking place in their own neighborhoods and shopping centers." Jack Watson, the chief of staff, quickly responded with an assurance that "to the extent that there is any doubt about the President's strong feelings and concerns on this subject, we shall do our best to erase it." Peter Bourne also sought to defuse the anger through a meeting with Sue Rusche, although he later accused the parents' movement of ignoring the urban crisis of heroin addiction because "it's marijuana smoking by suburban white kids—our children—that [they're] worried about." The White House followed up with a personal letter from President Carter praising Rusche and Schuchard for showing the nation how to prevent "drug use among the very young who lack the judgment and maturity to avoid becoming victims." Contradicting his national message of a year earlier, which portrayed illegal drug abuse as a permanent affliction that could be managed but not defeated, Carter adopted the zero-tolerance rhetoric of pledging to wage war until "the drug problem . . . is eradicated."[44]

The White House stance shifted toward wholesale adoption of the parents' movement agenda following the forced resignation of Peter Bourne in July 1978. By then, Bourne's support for both marijuana decriminalization and militarized interdiction had managed to alienate the parent power activists and their enemies in NORML. That spring, pot smokers around the nation became alarmed following reports that the U.S. government had been funding a Mexican program to spray paraquat, a toxic herbicide, on marijuana and opium crops. Peter Bourne defended the strategy as an essential part of the war on heroin and falsely claimed that "the paraquat operation is entirely Mexican." Pot smokers targeted Bourne with a letter-writing campaign imploring the administration to "please stop poisoning me and my friends" and denouncing a "criminally insane policy" worthy of Nixon. NORML accused the administration of having "paid mere lip service to the concept of marijuana decriminalization" and filed a lawsuit in an attempt to halt U.S. aid for the paraquat program, which Congress subsequently terminated.[45] In a fateful turn of events, Keith Stroup felt so betrayed by Bourne's position on the paraquat controversy that he secretly informed a journalist that the White House drug policy chief had snorted cocaine at a NORML party held the previous December. Bourne had just come under investigation for illegally writing a tranquilizer prescription for a member of his staff, and the explosive story sealed his fate. He admitted attending the NORML gathering but denied the cocaine allegation and blamed his downfall on hardline drug warriors in federal law enforcement. After resigning, Bourne told the press that "about half the White House staff" had attended the NORML function and that a "high incidence" of Carter aides smoked marijuana recreationally. The president personally responded with an unprecedented memo warning his staff to obey all drug laws, whether or not they agreed with them, or "seek employment elsewhere."[46]

The leaders of the parents' movement quickly developed a close working relationship with Bourne's successor and former deputy in the White House Office of Drug Abuse Policy, Lee Dogoloff, who embraced the antimarijuana crusade despite his previous stance that heroin addiction should be the administration's top priority. After Bourne resigned, Schuchard and Gleaton warned top Carter advisors that the scandal represented the "tip of the iceberg for almost inevitable further exposure of the multi-drug proselytizing and/or usage" within the administration, and they demanded the firing of staffers and federal bureaucrats who were soft on marijuana. Bourne considered his critics to be "pretty inconsequential gadflies," but Dogoloff promptly wrote an internal memo accepting the charges of the parents' movement that "many people believe that we have pronounced marijuana 'safe' and that we tacitly condone, or will ignore, its use." He agreed that the federal government had "not armed parents and teachers" with sufficient information about the perils of adolescent pot smoking and pledged that the Carter administration would start "taking a stand to support" the zero-tolerance agenda of PRIDE, DeKalb Families in Action, and similar community efforts around the country. The drug policy staff belatedly recognized that Carter's decriminalization message "was misconstrued," according to Bob Angarola, another one of Bourne's assistants. "I'm not particularly upset over a 25 year-old that smokes a joint every once in a while," Angarola explained, "but when you get 12 or 13 year-olds at that age getting spaced out, . . . too many kids are getting screwed up." Dogoloff characterized decriminalization as a politically popular but poorly communicated position that American youth should not be arrested for marijuana possession. He lauded the "resurgence of the parental role of responsibility" as critical to reversing the "public attitude of permissiveness around drug use" and linked the antimarijuana crusade to the administration's broader programs to combat the crisis of the American family in an era of divorce, moral breakdown, and economic malaise.[47]

In September 1978, the new White House drug policy director elaborated the Carter administration's recalibrated position on marijuana in a speech to prevention specialists that could have been written by Schuchard or Gleaton and received their enthusiastic approval. Dogoloff, who resided in suburban Maryland and had a daughter in high school, began with a philosophical lament for the tendency of drugs to "drive a wedge between parents and their children." He listed alcohol, cigarettes, and marijuana as the three most commonly used illegal drugs by American youth but highlighted the dangers of pot in "spearheading the onslaught onto parental authority." Like the parent power movement, this interpretation portrayed marijuana as the primary cause of adolescent misbehavior and family turmoil, an inversion of the popular view during the mid-to-late 1960s that recreational pot smoking constituted an expression of the politicized generation gap, and a departure from the prevailing scientific consensus that drug abuse represented a symptom of deeper psychological problems. In a similar embrace, Dogoloff rejected the "spurious argument" that adolescent use of marijuana was not as dangerous as alcohol or tobacco, which required creative rationalization since the latter two drugs accounted for five hundred thousand deaths per year in the United States. Dogoloff justified the elevation of marijuana as a top priority of the federal war on drugs based on the lack of public awareness and alarm that teenage pot smoking inhibited motivation, undermined study habits, and "can seriously impair physical and emotional maturation and impede the individual's acquisition of intellectual and social skills." He acknowledged that the administration's "badly garbled" decriminalization policy, intended only to keep recreational pot smokers out of the criminal legal system, had left many parents and educators feeling helpless and confused. Dogoloff concluded with a rousing account of the parent power movement in suburban Atlanta and pledged that federal policy would encourage the formation of similar community networks across the nation.[48]

The new White House policy position created a bureaucratic opening for drug warriors in the Department of Justice to secure more resources for marijuana interdiction. Peter Bensinger, the head of the DEA, had never really supported the Carter administration's initial stance on decriminalization, and he refused to abandon the marijuana-to-heroin gateway myth during a 1977 appearance on the ABC television program *Issues and Answers*. When asked whether the federal government should "push the panic button . . . to alert the American people" about the epidemic of teenage drug use throughout the country, Bensinger clarified the DEA's emphasis on heroin traffickers, not the recreational marijuana market, while warning that "we have a situation where drug pushers, drug distributors are getting off without any meaningful punishment." A year later, Bensinger boasted of a "much more significant effort to interdict the flow of marijuana," which he portrayed as far more potent than in the past and much more harmful than most Americans realized. Network television programs trumpeted Bensinger's contention that smoking marijuana caused cancer and birth defects, despite NIDA's assessment that "no convincing evidence" supported such claims. *Time* magazine hyped the DEA's crackdown on marijuana smugglers in the new "Colombian Connection"—which flourished because the paraquat campaign shifted production away from Mexico (American media and policymakers rarely acknowledged the large homegrown domestic supply). NORML denounced the DEA initiative as "paranoid overreaction" and pointed out the impossibility of eradicating a market that, by the federal government's own estimate, grossed more in annual sales than any American corporation except General Motors and Exxon. Blaming the contradictions of decriminalization for the thriving underground market, NORML also changed its platform in December 1978, back to its original demand for full-scale legalization and government regulation of marijuana. Allied publications such as the *Village Voice* also attacked the DEA for resurrecting the era of "reefer madness" and labeled President Carter a "born-again hardliner" on marijuana prohibition.[49]

In the spring of 1979, policymakers in the White House, the DEA, and NIDA held a two-day retreat to debate and clarify the administration's marijuana stance. The decriminalization bill that Carter endorsed two years earlier had stalled in Congress, buried in an unrelated dispute over a get-tough mandatory-minimum crime sentencing package that Senate Democrats supported but influential liberals in the House of Representatives opposed. Before the summit, Charles O'Keeffe, one of Bourne's allies on the drug policy staff, warned in a confidential memo that the DEA had "been filling the leadership void" with a deliberate campaign to exaggerate the hazards of marijuana, which would "reduce our credibility with the ten million Americans who regularly use the drug." The participants at the retreat, however, resolved to shift more resources to the DEA mission of "elimination of drugs at their source" and to craft a unified public relations message about the many health perils of marijuana. DEA head Peter Bensinger argued that interdiction already had succeeded in reducing the heroin supply to the lowest level possible (a dubious claim) and therefore the same strategy could limit the availability of marijuana and cocaine—both depicted as "white" drugs—for American consumers.[50] In Senate testimony, Lee Dogoloff highlighted the administration's Southeast Initiative, which had led to DEA and Coast Guard seizures of two million pounds of marijuana during the second half of 1978 alone, while promising a national prevention campaign to reduce youth demand. Dogoloff soon traveled to Florida for a deeply distressing meeting with Naples Informed Parents, a white middle-class movement that had enlisted the police to crack down on marijuana in the schools. He attributed the crisis to the Gulf Coast community's status as a port of entry for marijuana smuggled from South America, a "truly hopeless" situation that had overmatched local law enforcement and caught innocent teenagers in the crossfire, yet more evidence of the necessity of intensified federal interdiction to support the grassroots efforts of the parents' movement.[51]

The low priority that the Carter administration placed on cocaine interdiction is striking and another indication of how catalytic the white teenage marijuana crisis had become for the federal war on drugs. Cocaine was an expensive "designer drug" associated with Hollywood celebrities, rock musicians, disco clubs, and wealthy white adults in general. Back in 1977, the White House Office of Drug Abuse Policy had considered adding cocaine to its marijuana decriminalization proposal because the stimulant was not physically addictive and "causes relatively few health and social consequences." The internal documents also acknowledged that cocaine prohibition had created "tremendous profits" for traffickers and destabilized source nations in Latin America, even though no interdiction or crop eradication strategy could ever "dramatically reduce the quality of coca being cultivated." In a memo drafted by Peter Bourne, the Carter administration decided against cocaine decriminalization because "unlike marijuana, cocaine possession laws have not resulted in inducting large numbers of otherwise law-abiding young people into the criminal justice system." This extraordinary statement reveals total disinterest in the selective and inequitable enforcement of cocaine laws in nonwhite urban areas and clarifies that marijuana decriminalization was less about public health and more a mission to save white Americans from encountering the punitive police state. President Carter barely mentioned cocaine during his time in office, and the administration publicly touted its Southeast Initiative as an interdiction assault on the new marijuana threat from Colombia. DEA head Peter Bensinger identified Colombia as a "trafficker's paradise" because it had become "the largest supplier of marijuana in the world," even though the nation's $20 billion in annual cocaine exports dominated the American market. The lack of urgency is particularly notable because NIDA surveys showed that 13 percent of high school seniors had used cocaine by 1978, but this too would change once suburban activists targeted the stimulant as a marijuana-gateway threat.[52]

The parents' movement insisted that Washington's nonchalant attitude toward the recreational marijuana subculture obscured the gateway risks of suburban youth moving on to harder drugs, especially cocaine and PCP (phencyclidine, a synthetic tranquilizer). In her 1978 ultimatum to the White House, Schuchard lamented the "frightening PCP overdoses of 'nice kids from nice families'" who started with pot and ended up victims of the "multi-drug advocacy of the drug culture." News reports at the time were sensationalizing a sudden "epidemic" of PCP-induced psychosis in white middle-class suburbs, as the hallucinogen known as "angel dust" and "killer weed" jumped the tracks from inner-city markets. The *Washington Post* claimed that "pushers" targeted affluent youth and PCP was "fast surpassing marijuana" as the most popular hallucinogen in suburban Maryland and Northern Virginia. Similar to the LSD hype a decade earlier, credulous media coverage alleged that "unsuspecting teenagers" were smoking marijuana laced with PCP and circulated stories of psychotic victims wandering into traffic, leaping out of windows, and violently attacking friends and family. In a typical loss-of-innocence narrative, the *Post* revealed how PCP transformed Jimmy, a "happy-go-lucky, affectionate youngster" from a suburban home with bicycles in the driveway, into a "half-crazed" psychotic who stole from his parents and threatened to murder his siblings. Another *Post* exposé contrasted the peaceful ethos of 1960s flower children to the tragic fates of suburban teens who became bored with pot, moved on to PCP, and ended up institutionalized, raped while hitchhiking, or dead of heroin overdoses. The DEA promptly launched a national crackdown on PCP labs, and the U.S. Congress doubled the maximum trafficking penalty. Just a few years after marijuana decriminalization seemed unstoppable, a new version of the pusher-gateway mystique had returned, as had a federal policy environment receptive to Schuchard's demand to halt the "flood" of marijuana, cocaine, and PCP "into ordinary mainstream American neighborhoods."[53]

The Carter administration also faced pressure to join the campaign launched by suburban parent power groups to stamp out head shops and paraphernalia products that had "invaded" Middle American neighborhoods and allegedly "lured" innocent children into the illegal drug culture. Desperate and enraged white mothers, such as Sue Rusche in suburban Atlanta, led the local antiparaphernalia crusades against these outside villains, especially *High Times* and head shop owners. By 1980, more than one hundred municipalities and ten states had enacted antiparaphernalia laws along the lines of the Georgia strategy promoted by DeKalb Families in Action, including Maryland, Florida, Delaware, New Jersey, New York, Connecticut, Colorado, and

California. Grassroots activists denounced the federal government for "frightening complacency" and accused the (allegedly) $5 billion paraphernalia industry of promoting a "drug oriented lifestyle" and "selling the attitudes which make drug use socially acceptable."[54] In 1979, a Senate subcommittee chaired by Joseph Biden, a liberal law-and-order Democrat from Delaware, convened hearings to support the "concern, anxiety, anger, and bewilderment" of ordinary parents under assault by paraphernalia merchants. Biden's investigation focused on the upscale Maryland suburbs and featured parent-activists who condemned head shops as a "blight on our community" and asked how it could be legal to sell pipes and bongs disguised as toys to "encourage and entice" preteens to experiment with marijuana. Former NIDA director Robert DuPont, now in private practice in the DC suburb of Rockville, attacked paraphernalia stores for "commercially exploited flaunting of the drug laws" and even resurrected the heroin-gateway argument to justify his new view that marijuana should be the top priority of the federal war on drugs. The hearings also highlighted pusher-gateway testimony from a female teenager in a wealthy Baltimore suburb who began smoking pot in the seventh grade, moved on to pills and LSD, and frequently bought marijuana and PCP under the counter at the local head shop where the "cool" middle-school kids hung out.[55]

The white suburban mothers at the heart of Maryland's antiparaphernalia crusade claimed to represent a no-longer-silent majority and mobilized around a defense of innocent children designed to resonate across the political spectrum. Pat Burch of Montgomery County blamed the paraphernalia "peddlers" for overriding the efforts of even the "very good parents" and making marijuana a mainstream drug for high school football players and National Merit scholars, not just the "misfits." In a warning to politicians and the paraphernalia industry alike, she proclaimed: "We are angry, we're frightened, and we are beginning to know the real truth about drug abuse. Our message to those who would entice our children to destroy themselves is beware. There will be no tougher adversaries than mothers who are fearful for their children and willing to do whatever is necessary to protect them." Joyce Nalepka, a Silver Spring resident who founded the Coalition for Concern about Marijuana Use in Youth after her son encountered pot at a heavy metal Kiss concert, confronted lawmakers with a similar manifesto of suburban parent power. She began by apologizing for the belated mobilization of the parents' movement, explaining that while NORML and *High Times* were promoting the myth of harmless marijuana, the "good parents" were at "home taking care of their children, . . . participating in scouts, church, school volunteers, baking cookies, and all the rest." Despite their best efforts and wholesome family values, a large number of neighborhood children started smoking pot, and some ultimately took the marijuana-gateway path to cocaine and amphetamines. Nalepka pointed out that she lived on a quiet subdivision street in an affluent suburban community, not in the ghetto, so how could this possibly happen? She blamed the "paraphernalia pushers" for infiltrating her neighborhood, disrupting her family, and targeting her children. And she angrily indicted advocates of marijuana decriminalization, including the Carter administration, for the soft and permissive policies that "keep the drug pushers in business."[56]

Joyce Nalepka pledged that the parents' movement would take down any politician who opposed its antimarijuana platform, because "our children and this country must be protected." Her organization claimed credit for the recent defeat of Newton Steers, a liberal Republican who represented suburban Montgomery County in the U.S. House, because he supported the federal decriminalization bill. The White House drug policy staff took notice of this unexpected development, met with Nalepka on several occasions, and directed the DOJ to develop a model statute for states and localities to prohibit sale of paraphernalia to minors. The paraphernalia industry denied designing products for children and accused "misguided zealots" of scapegoating head shops because they could not stop their own kids from smoking pot. Its lobbyists argued that antimarijuana crusaders circulated "scare stories based on myths and nonsense" and might as well try to ban ashtrays to stop cigarette smoking or outlaw beer mugs to prevent alcoholism. Senator Charles Mathias, a liberal Republican from Maryland, introduced an antiparaphernalia bill in Congress and attacked the industry for targeting children as young as age six.[57] Instead of a constitutionally vulnerable federal ban, however, the Justice Department's solution criminalized paraphernalia designed, sold, or purchased with the deliberate intent to promote illegal drug consumption, which excluded multiuse products such as pipes and rolling papers bought by adults to smoke tobacco. Forty-nine states ultimately adopted the model statute, which survived court challenges that had invalidated the first round of antiparaphernalia laws and forced a significant number of head shops to close. Those that remained in business generally barred minors from entry and posted disclaimers to avoid the intent-based prosecution standard. According to Lee Dogoloff, federal intervention had succeeded in its most important, if primarily symbolic, mission of stigmatizing paraphernalia merchants and standing with parents' groups to "turn around the 'do drug' messages children are receiving."[58]

The Demand-Side Drug War

During 1978–79, the suburban parents' movement supplanted NORML as the interest group that most effectively represented the white middle-class victim in American drug politics. As a result, the twelve-to-fourteen-year-old white pot smoker, suffering from the "amotivational syndrome" and targeted by the "commercialized drug culture," replaced the unjustly imprisoned college student and the wrongly criminalized middle-class professional as the political category that reorganized federal drug policy. This did not happen because "parent power" advocates led a mass social movement of middle-class Americans, or because their antimarijuana campaign represented a "moral panic" sweeping through the white suburbs. Instead, a small number of committed activists who labeled themselves the "parents' movement" gained influence and shaped public policy by adopting political tactics and discursive tropes that paralleled NORML's recent successes, including appealing directly to politicians as ordinary parents themselves, beyond any partisan affiliation or recognizably ideological framework except for the racial and spatial logics of white middle-class victimization. As Lee Dogoloff, head of the White House Office of Drug Abuse Policy and also—crucially—the father of a teenager, later observed, when "you begin to address government officials and others, not in their public roles but as parents, they begin to see the issue with more clarity." Some initial breakthroughs were fortuitous: the suburban Atlanta activists took advantage of administration connections through Carter officials from Georgia, and the suburban Maryland mothers lived right outside DC and among federal policymakers from both parties. But similar antidrug groups existed in the white middle-class suburbs of most metropolitan areas, and the grassroots leaders who first went to Washington would soon collaborate with the Carter administration to organize their counterparts into a national movement, based on their moral authority as mothers and fathers and dedicated to protecting vulnerable adolescents from both marijuana supply and demand.[59]

The Carter administration's 1979 drug strategy elevated marijuana to the center of the federal war on drugs, with interdiction supplemented by the spring launch of a "national adolescent drug abuse prevention campaign." The supply-side marijuana program "should create the greatest amount of legal and economic risk possible at all levels of the trafficking network," alongside priority interdiction of PCP manufacturers and cocaine smugglers, the other two "white" drug problems. In a complete inversion of the Ford administration's "White Paper" and Peter Bourne's vision, the blueprint portrayed heroin as a onetime epidemic that had "subsided" but categorized teenage marijuana use (redefined as "abuse") as a public health emergency. The rationale for this policy shift revolved around the most inflammatory findings of the "Monitoring the Future" surveys: marijuana experimentation by more than half of American high school students and especially daily use by 11 percent of seniors in the class of 1978, which enhanced fears of "serious emotional, developmental, and physical problems" linked to chronic pot smoking. Most alarming of all, 14 percent of fourteen-to-fifteen-year-olds, and 4 percent of twelve-to-thirteen-year-olds, smoked marijuana at least once a month. The Carter report lamented the "growing public tolerance" for the adolescent marijuana subculture and pointed out that much lower rates in the late 1960s had generated national alarm about a youth drug abuse epidemic. In effect, the White House strategy sought to foment a marijuana panic among parents, educators, and civic leaders—but through a positive public health emphasis on the advantages of drug-free living rather than any threat of law enforcement or criminal punishment for these teenagers and preteens. The $386 million demand-side campaign enlisted grassroots parents' groups and corporations, pushed for antidrug programming by TV networks, and worked through the National PTA, Girl Scouts, Boy Scouts, and National Football League. The effort primarily targeted children in the twelve-to-fourteen-year-old age group, and their parents, with new information about the health risks of marijuana and the simple message: "Say *no* to drugs."[60]

The White House's drug prevention campaign moved the zero-tolerance philosophy of the white suburban parents' movement into the political mainstream and established the template that the Reagan administration would follow in its own "Just Say No" version a few years later (see chapter 7). Rather than a Democratic "right turn" that anticipated the conservative backlash on the horizon, the antimarijuana crusade drew from an analysis of the suburban family crisis with deep roots in liberal politics and mainstream postwar developments, especially the casting of blame on a "culture of permissiveness" and the resilient faith in the capacity of government action to strengthen middle-class communities. White House planners envisioned the adolescent prevention campaign as not only a demand-side strategy in the war on drugs but also as a moral intervention to help fulfill President Carter's recent pledge to reinforce the "American family structure," part of the buildup to the 1980 White House Conference on Families. Lee Dogoloff summarized this unusually intimate federal mission: to "discourage youthful drug use through strengthening the family" and building positive relationships between teenagers and adult role models in every local community. In a Gallup survey commissioned by the administration, American parents named the economic recession and the "drug abuse" epidemic as the two greatest threats facing the family in the late 1970s. Dogoloff and other White House policymakers considered these challenges to be interlinked, with overworked and single parents unable to supervise their children adequately, and youth who spent their adolescence stoned and intoxicated unlikely to develop into mature, economically productive adults. The delegates to all three regional meetings of the White House Conference on Families endorsed the adolescent drug and alcohol prevention campaign as a top federal priority, alongside initiatives such as increased government support for childcare and flexible, family-friendly employment policies.[61]

By re-centering the war on drugs around the image of the twelve-to-fourteen-year-old pot smoker in the suburbs, the Carter administration and the parents' movement politicized federal scientific research and narrowed the policy debate to the simplistic question of whether marijuana was harmful or safe for children. The main obstacle to the adolescent prevention campaign came from cautious experts at NIDA who felt that the White House was hyping the dangers of marijuana for political reasons and obscuring the critical public health distinction between drug use and substance abuse. In May 1979, domestic policy chief Stuart Eizenstat informed HEW Secretary Joseph Califano that resistance from NIDA threatened to undermine the adolescent initiative and would leave the administration vulnerable to "justifiable criticism" from the parents' movement. According to Lee Dogoloff, skepticism from public health specialists illustrated the larger "problem . . . that there are not enough parent groups in the government." As a remedy, Dogoloff's office consulted closely with Joyce Nalepka, whose suburban Maryland antimarijuana group successfully demanded the removal of objectionable NIDA publications that advocated decriminalization, downplayed health risks for recreational users, and listed NORML as a resource.[62] The parents' movement specifically attacked federal consultants such as Norman Zinberg, a Harvard psychiatrist and NORML advisor who had once labeled pot smoking "innocuous." Zinberg criticized the antimarijuana crusade for making drugs a "scapegoat" for deeper social problems but agreed, as did NORML, that pot smoking by young teenagers and preteens was a cause for concern. He attributed the increased rates of use among younger adolescents to the lack of the "formal social control" provided by legalization and regulation, which would make marijuana seem less exotic and would concentrate illicit behavior in the sixteen-to-seventeen-year-old category (just under the legal age of eighteen), as with alcohol and tobacco.[63]

The new federal war on adolescent pot smoking empowered a group of antimarijuana crusaders whose alarmist views had been marginalized during the era of decriminalization. A chief beneficiary was Gabriel Nahas, a Columbia University professor whose books *Marijuana—Deceptive Weed* (1973) and *Keep Off the Grass* (1976) blamed the drug for a broad range of physical maladies and psychological disorders, as well as the steady decline of American civilization. Nahas condemned the Shafer Commission report and its compromise solution of decriminalization, which he labeled a smokescreen for legalization. He equated chronic use of marijuana with middle-class downward mobility (implicitly, the white embrace of ghetto values), arguing that potheads "drop out of college, go on public welfare, dress in a slovenly manner, renounce responsibilities." The Shafer Commission's staff director accused Nahas of "blowing up out of all proportion the potential harm of marijuana use." NORML denounced Nahas's "fanatical campaign" to maintain marijuana prohibition by promoting fringe, unreplicated research (such as experiments of massive THC doses on animals) that linked pot smoking to brain damage, cancer, infertility, and birth defects. Reviews in major journals denounced Nahas as a biased scientist who hyped unverified findings, distorted evidence, and even engaged in "psychopharmacologic McCarthyism." But Nahas's extreme views returned to the political mainstream in the late 1970s, when he developed close ties to the parents' movement and found a more receptive federal audience. Soon after the launch of the adolescent prevention campaign, Nahas appeared alongside NIDA director William Pollin at a congressional hearing where both men testified about marijuana's damage to brain, heart, lung, and reproductive functions. Pollin clarified that NIDA scientists were "very concerned about the health hazards of marijuana use," including not only the potential medical risks but also the drug's negative effects on youth study habits and its role in "psychological escapism [that] makes growing up more difficult."[64]

The congressional response to Carter's 1979 drug strategy reveals how thoroughly the policy debate had shifted from the decade-long emphasis on urban heroin addiction and suburban marijuana arrests to an emerging bipartisan consensus around the medical and psychological dangers facing chronic stoners and preteen pot smokers in middle-class America. In 1977, the House Select Committee on Narcotics published a decriminalization report that focused on selective enforcement against youth (with no mention of race) and labeled marijuana's medical effects to be "still undetermined." Two years later, the committee's new Task Force on Marijuana Abuse (not "use") convened hearings to highlight the health hazards for preteens and daily high school stoners, a crisis that "none of us would disagree" about. Dr. Gabriel Nahas led the witness list, and House members assailed NORML and *High Times* for their "vulgar, vicious" conspiracy to create a teenage pot market.[65] When the Narcotics Committee evaluated Carter's broader drug-war blueprint, NIDA director William Pollin all but retracted the previous endorsement of marijuana decriminalization, until "we were effectively able to significantly discourage its use." Jesse Jackson, the Chicago-based civil rights leader, also denounced decriminalization, lumped pot smokers in with other drug abusers as "sick people," and demanded the "severest penalties we can on pushers." Representative Charles Rangel (D-NY) registered his usual criticism that the federal government had not done enough to interdict heroin at the border and arrest street-level "pushers" in Harlem. In general, the congressional debate in the late 1970s no longer focused on the problem of excessive marijuana arrests and continued to ignore the issue of racial inequality in drug-war enforcement more broadly. FBI crime data revealed that marijuana continued to be the main focus of drug interdiction and street-level busts, but a longer-term shift was also underway toward an increased share of arrests in the largest cities and even greater disproportionality in the policing of nonwhite populations (fig. 6.8).[66]

Network television participated in reorienting the drug-war debate toward the dangers facing very young white middle-class pot smokers with exposés such as *Reading, Writing, and Reefer*, a 1979 special report on NBC. The broadcast hyped the "sudden" epidemic of "chronic marijuana smoking . . . by hundreds of thousands of American youngsters." Employing the same fallacy as the parents' movement, the program conflated the statistical increase in daily use by high school seniors with shocking images of preteen suburban stoners. *Reading, Writing, and Reefer* opens with twelve-year-old Brian, a cute blonde-haired boy from coastal Florida who is high on camera and grins while recounting that he started at age eight and now lights up "almost every day," at home or at the bus stop, as do all his friends. "Like most of the children you will meet in this report," the narrator intones, "Brian lives in a pleasant neighborhood. He is not a deprived child. He is not a delinquent." He does have a permissive mother, however, a pleasant lady who admits that she knows about Brian's marijuana use but hadn't realized that he was smoking every day and skipping school often. The ensuing all-white montage includes young blonde girls passing joints outside a rock concert; a fifteen-year-old boy who smokes

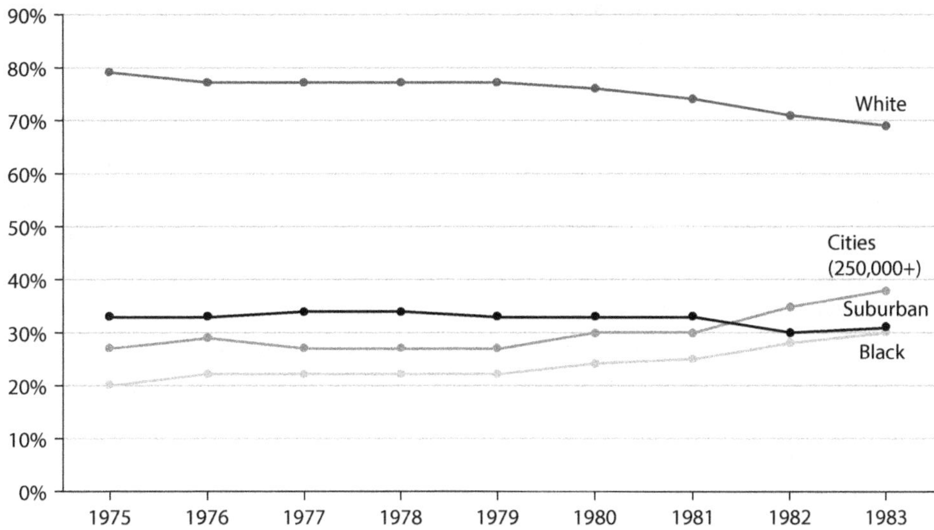

FIGURE 6.8. Racial and select geographic characteristics of the population arrested on drug charges in the United States, 1975–83. The share of white arrests in the war on drugs stabilized at 77% of the total during the first three years of the Carter administration and then began a steady long-term decline in 1980. Black drug arrests simultaneously increased from 20% in 1975 to 30% in 1983. The escalation of drug war enforcement in the largest cities underlay this transformation, and the proportion of drug arrests in these urban centers rose from 27% to 38% during this period, after having fallen dramatically during the orientation toward white marijuana arrests in the late 1960s and early 1970s. The proportion of drug arrests in the suburbs, which were undergoing racial and economic diversification in the aggregate during these years, remained roughly one-third of the total but dropped below the percentage in the largest cities in 1982. (FBI, *Uniform Crime Reports*, 1975–1983.)

Note: Suburban totals approximated for 1978–79, based on historical trends, because of the FBI's temporary decision to report only data from county law enforcement agencies and not the full range of suburban departments. The *Uniform Crime Reports* restored the traditional methodology in 1980, allowing valid comparisons of the geographic areas classified as suburban across time. The FBI data continued to include many, if not most, arrests of Hispanics in the "white" category. In 1980, the FBI also first began reporting arrests by Hispanic "ethnic origin," although the data is not directly comparable to other racial categories because of differences in collection techniques. Hispanic drug arrests (estimated) accounted for 9.2% of the national total in 1980 and 15.1% in 1983. The racial breakdown of the U.S. population in the 1980 census was 79.6% white (non-Hispanic), 11.5% Black, 6.5% Hispanic.

one hundred joints a week, often with friends in his basement; and a suburban Atlanta girl who started getting high in seventh grade to "mellow out" and forget about life's problems. These upper-middle-class stoners, whose "entire lives have come to revolve around pot," matter-of-factly tell the national audience that marijuana is a harmless drug, just a way to relax and escape stress and hang out with friends. A decade earlier, media coverage of the suburban marijuana subculture incorporated similar scenes of older teenagers into a politicized generation gap analysis and acknowledged that adults also sought pleasure and escape through mood-altering drugs. But instead, NBC explains, these very young white children are clueless exemplars of the "amotivational syndrome," the leading edge of a generation of "guinea pigs in an experiment on a national scale."[67]

NBC's special report captured the broader political contradictions of the Carter-era war on marijuana, which renounced the permissive consequences of decriminalization but did not advocate law enforcement against recreational drug users in the white middle-class suburbs. To counter the myth of harmless pot, the second half of the program juxtaposes shots of pathetic teenage burnouts with experts such as former NIDA head Robert DuPont, who warns that chronic use causes psychological immaturity and insists that marijuana is more hazardous than alcohol or tobacco. NORML's Keith Stroup admits that he suffers from bronchitis and agrees that minors should not smoke pot, but he argues that the only way to stop youth participation in the underground market is a regulated system of legal access for adults. *Reading, Writing, and Reefer* depicts the four million pot-smoking juveniles of America as the "receiving end of a vast criminal network" that government interdiction has proved unable to stop, as "many American schoolyards have become retail outlets for the marijuana industry." Using information provided by the Families in Action network from suburban Atlanta, NBC also blames *High Times* for "peddling the paraphernalia of marijuana smoking" and seducing youngsters with pipes and bongs disguised as toys. But despite these tropes of suburban victimization, the teenage stoners given a platform in the exposé cast themselves as autonomous participants in an adolescent subculture where marijuana is very easy to obtain and many users also deal or transfer pot in the casual market. These white suburban youth are breaking the law, the broadcast concedes, but they are not so much criminals as wayward children who do not realize how dangerous marijuana really is, the collateral damage of the political movement for decriminalization of adult pot smoking. NBC, which soon distributed the program for classroom-based drug education, concludes that the need for a national prevention campaign emphasizing marijuana's perils is urgent; the failure to act is the fault of government, schools, parents, "all of us."[68]

ABC-TV answered the federal government's call to highlight the adolescent marijuana crisis through its popular *Afterschool Special* series, which often probed white middle-class family breakdown issues during the mid-to-late 1970s—children of divorce, alcoholic mothers, workaholic fathers, underage drinking, teen sexuality, peer pressure. *Stoned*, which aired in 1980, was the first *Afterschool Special* to focus on illegal drugs, a theme generally proscribed on youth-oriented television under regulatory standards and industry self-censorship. The expert consultant was Sidney Cohen, a psychiatrist with close NIDA connections and a key originator of the "amotivational syndrome" thesis, which he first applied to LSD in the mid-1960s by warning that white youth swept up in the "drug culture" lost all motivation and ambition. *Stoned* dramatizes the fate of Jack, a younger white high school student and shy nerd transformed by marijuana into a cool kid and then a total loser burnout suffering a bad case of "amotivational syndrome," all in less than a week. At first, Jack makes good grades and is bullied by a group of stoners who get high in the schoolyard and boy's bathroom and hide their stash in a compartment under a skateboard. Jack initially resists their aggressive peer pressure to smoke pot, but then the pretty new girl Felicity ignores his advances, his outgoing older brother is too busy with sports and a girlfriend to keep being his only companion, and their mother is gone for good. So Jack shares a joint with the stoner group and immediately starts getting high with them all the time—before school, during school, and in the unsupervised parks and homes of their suburban town. Jack initially gains friends and confidence and impresses Felicity—if a latchkey child had stopped watching halfway through, the message would seem to be that marijuana solves your problems. But then Jack flunks his tests, nearly kills his brother in an accident of stoned stupidity, and Felicity realizes she doesn't like him if he uses grass to hide from his true self. Once Jack gains the courage to say no to the stoners, they end up together in the happy finale.[69]

The extraordinary success of the "Marijuana Alert" series, published by journalist and children's author Peggy Mann in *Reader's Digest* during 1979–80, buttressed the combined efforts of the parents' movement and the White House to overturn the prevailing medical consensus in the war on drugs. The first article drew on resources provided by Schuchard's PRIDE organization, echoed NBC by portraying pot-smoking teenagers as "guinea pigs in a tragic national experiment," and received more than three million reprint requests, the most in the magazine's history. Mann asserted that marijuana was more dangerous than alcohol and highlighted recent studies—with no mention of the skepticism of most drug researchers—that found brain, lung, and reproductive damage in otherwise normal American teenagers who smoked pot on a regular basis. Gabriel Nahas, now recast as a marijuana visionary, warned that users were playing "genetic roulette . . . [with] children and grandchildren yet unborn." In the accompanying essay, "Enemy of Youth," an adolescent psychologist endorsed discredited claims that marijuana was a physically addictive gateway drug and related anecdotes about upper-middle-class stoners who vandalized suburban neighborhoods, failed out of Ivy League colleges, and disappeared into "frightful marijuana-induced lethargy." Peggy Mann's follow-up exposé featured "beautiful" suburban girls suffering pot-induced maladies and labeled the marijuana epidemic the "single most dangerous health hazard facing American youth today." She reiterated these warnings in popular middle-class magazines such as *Saturday Evening Post* and *Ladies' Home Journal*, placing blame on permissive parents who came of age during the 1960s and believed marijuana was harmless, and a paraphernalia industry that deliberately targeted six-to-sixteen-year-old children. One mother's response to Mann's *Reader's Digest* series captures the essence of parent power: "The drug culture is sending our children to cemeteries and institutions. We are sick and tired of apathy in this area and we are going to do something about it."[70]

Peggy Mann also published a marijuana awareness novel, *Twelve Is Too Old* (1980), to highlight the "epidemic" of preteen pot smoking in a generic white middle-class suburb of broken families, latchkey children, and permissive values. The book, coauthored by Mann's eleven-year-old daughter, targeted middle-school students and their parents through the adolescent-narrator-in-suburban-crisis formula popularized by Judy Blume. The main character, a precocious and depressed eleven-year-old named Jody, dreads her next birthday because turning twelve at her middle school means losing your innocence—getting your period, fooling around with boys, smoking your first joint. Half of Jody's seventh-grade classmates already get stoned regularly, teenage dealers openly accost her in the school hallways, and the most popular boy in her class tells the drug education teacher that "everyone *knows* that pot is harmless!" Since the divorce, Jody's mother has been working long hours as a real estate agent, which enables her sixteen-year-old sister Linda to have sex with her boyfriend and gets high in her bedroom every day after school. Their father is too busy with his job and new wife to be involved in their lives, so Jody is left to deal with peer pressure and her identity crisis all alone, with no one to confide in about her problems. She desperately wants a new ten-speed bicycle for her birthday, but instead Linda gives her a pipe, stash box, and joint-rolling lessons in order to "come on real cool with the other kids." But Jody is conflicted, because that very day the drug education teacher demonstrated that smoking marijuana is more hazardous for your health than cigarettes and warned about the "dropout syndrome" of apathy toward school and life that Linda so clearly exhibits. Her older sister assures her that "everything will be great. So don't worry about anything. . . . Most of the best experiences I've ever had have been when I'm stoned."[71]

In its dramatic finale, *Twelve Is Too Old* shifts from a plausible if atypical story of drug pressures and family problems facing a seventh-grade suburban girl to an overblown pusher-gateway morality tale designed to tap into the worst fears of middle-school parents. While Jody is deciding whether to give in to the temptation, Linda smokes the birthday joint, has a paranoid reaction, and attacks her younger sister in a crazed rage. The ambulance paramedic explains that "creeps doctor up low-grade marijuana with PCP" and then denounces "rotten magazines that are helping to ruin a whole generation of our young kids." This indictment is disconnected from the novel's plot but reinforces the parents' movement assault on *High Times* and paraphernalia merchants. In a didactic passage echoing Marsha Schuchard's critique of the "commercialized drug culture," Jody realizes that "the grown-up world—or some of it—was in a conspiracy against kids. Instead of protecting us, they were busy making money off us." Jody resolves to stay away from marijuana and gains the self-confidence to turn twelve and resist the peer pressure. "It makes me mad," she concludes manifesto-style, "to see some of the kids in our school, how they're messing everything up for themselves. They have nice families. They go to a good school. They have plenty of money. They have everything going for them. . . . It makes me sick how they stay stoned all the time and louse things up for themselves and louse up their family life." In the end, the title's double meaning becomes clear: even "twelve is too old" for schools and parents to start educating children about marijuana's dangers, because by then the influences of peer culture and the commercialized drug culture are already too entrenched. In his endorsement, Robert DuPont praised Mann for writing the "first novel to deal realistically with the marijuana scene, which every child in America ultimately confronts." A few years later, the Library of Congress selected *Twelve Is Too Old* in a major compilation of the most important resources available to parents concerned about adolescent drug abuse.[72]

In March 1980, the White House premiered the centerpiece of its adolescent prevention campaign, *For Parents Only: What Kids Think about Marijuana.* NIDA and the DEA jointly produced the documentary, an adult instructional film designed to galvanize and empower parents' groups across the nation. Aiming for the shock value of suburban realism, *For Parents Only* opens with surveillance-style footage of six young, white middle-class teenagers passing a joint while sitting under a tree outside their school (fig. 6.9). "I enjoy getting

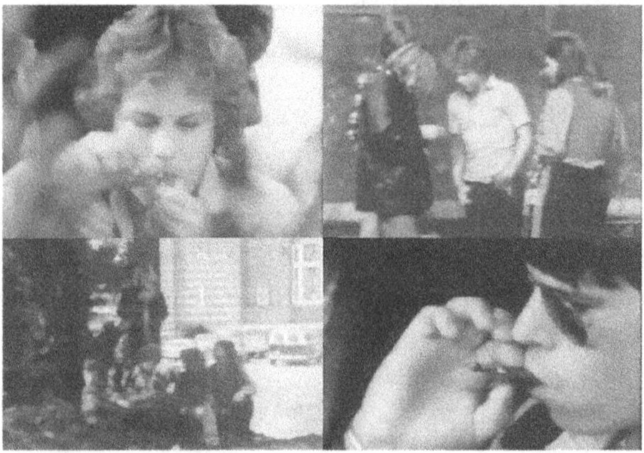

FIGURE 6.9. The Carter administration produced *For Parents Only: What Kids Think about Marijuana* as the centerpiece of its 1980 adolescent drug prevention campaign. This montage of four scenes from the documentary depicts young white teenagers smoking and sharing marijuana outside their suburban middle school with no concerns about law enforcement or interference by "permissive" parents and other adult authorities. The film emphasized the health hazards of marijuana and urged communities to form "tough love" parents' groups. (Reproduced from the Records of the Drug Enforcement Administration, National Archives.)

high," one of the girls giggles in a voiceover; she smokes ten joints a day because "I like the feeling, I'm more cheerful." Toking reefer, a boy explains, is "basically a way just to live it up" with friends, plus his parents don't mind. The most memorable scene is an interview with a cute shaggy-haired boy from the same peer circle, sitting at home on the couch beside his perplexed mother. He says that he smoked his first joint at age eight, became a regular stoner by ten, and meets his friends under the tree before and after school and then again following dinner. His mother asks if maybe she puts too much pressure on him, or perhaps he is trying to escape from family life? Her son just smiles sweetly, tells his mom that he loves her, and says she doesn't need to worry because marijuana isn't dangerous and "I'm leading a pretty good life." Additional footage includes white youth smoking pot while listening to a garage band and hanging out by a backyard swing set, and a drug deal going down inside a station wagon on a tree-lined street. Such images credibly capture the derivative effects of the 1960s counterculture, the many spaces of youth autonomy in the single-family suburbs, and the dominance of adolescent peer culture in middle-class neighborhoods. These vivid scenes indicate that smoking marijuana has become a normal, even culturally acceptable, part of being a middle-class American teenager—although the film distorts social practices by highlighting the rare phenomenon of middle-school stoners rather than the much more common recreational use among older high school and college students.[73]

The federal government warned that youth should not watch *For Parents Only* because it might seem to glamorize the recreational marijuana subculture by presenting the unmediated voices of adolescents, but such realism was necessary to make adults aware of what teenagers really thought, even though their views "are clearly in conflict with current scientific knowledge." Toward the end, psychologists and educators recite all the health risks of marijuana and contradict claims by teenage stoners that getting high helps them perform better in school, be artistically creative, and enjoy a relaxed family life. These authority figures drawn from local communities (not expert talking heads) advise parents to practice "tough love," to be unafraid to assert moral authority and forbid illegal drugs. In conclusion, the obviously permissive mother of the shaggy-haired stoner wonders if the parents in her neighborhood could get together and admit that they have a problem, setting up the resolution promoted by the parents' movement. The film's discussion guide predicted that parents in the audience would likely respond with alarm, anger, despair, permissiveness, or "not my child" denial. The discussion leader should then emphasize that scientists had reached a consensus on marijuana's harmfulness for teenagers, that parents must be willing to discipline children who smoked pot, and that adults should join forces in a community watchdog group. The guide cautioned that "nice" and "good" kids were equally as likely to smoke pot, and so their parents should cut them off from "bad" friends, start chaperoning youth parties, and replace the recreational drug lifestyle with positive activities that "strengthen family ties." NIDA supplemented the film with a *For Parents Only* booklet that attributed marijuana experimentation to peer pressure, not "pushers," and contained additional advice on "how to say 'no.'" The powerful marijuana subculture could entangle "even children of loving parents who have set a good example," according to the federal initiative, and so they had to collaborate through local parent power groups to resolve this national family crisis.[74]

Marsha Keith Schuchard wrote *Parents, Peers, and Pot*, the other key resource in the federal government's adolescent prevention campaign, to turn the experiences of her Atlanta organization into the prototype for a parents' movement nationwide in scope. In the foreword, NIDA director William Pollin praised the handbook as an anti-permissive manifesto aimed at the parents of children in the nine-to-fourteen-year-old age bracket. The agency distributed more than one million copies within a few years. The first chapter, "Learning the Hard Way," recounted the now famous epic of the awakening of suburban Atlanta parents to the marijuana menace through the loosely fictionalized story of Kathy Allen's thirteenth birthday party (based on Schuchard's daughter). Her parents were worried because Kathy, "formerly a model child, cheerful, thoughtful, and responsible," had become bored with school and grown distant from family and friends. Something had gone terribly wrong "in their lovely, tree-lined neighborhood." Strange kids showed up for the birthday celebration, acting rude and stumbling around, and Mr. and Mrs. Allen realized that "this party wasn't going to end up like 'Happy Days.'" They discovered that these "nice and attractive" children of white middle-class suburbia were smoking marijuana and drinking booze right in the backyard. But when Mrs. Allen contacted their parents, many denied the accusations or responded that smoking pot was no big deal. Finally, she found a mother whose son had a severe reaction to a joint laced with PCP, and together they called a neighborhood gathering where the parents of twelve-to-fifteen-year-olds began admitting what they knew or only suspected about "an alien world within their own community." Their investigations uncovered networks of teenage suburban dealers and fake ID manufacturers, with unrestrained pot smoking at school bus stops, pinball arcades, and the nearby university. But school authorities ignored the problem, psychologists told the parents to calm down and recognize that smoking pot was a normal rite of passage, and the police felt powerless to intervene.[75]

Parents, Peers, and Pot portrayed upper-middle-class American suburbia as an internally divided landscape where the (romanticized) 1950s consensus on middle-class family values had collapsed, the drug culture had estranged teenagers from their parents, and a permissive mindset reigned supreme. While one faction of parents at the Allens' neighborhood meeting pushed for punishment and "reeducation," a lenient and "defeatist" group either remained in denial or considered a zero-tolerance crackdown to be excessive or impossible. The truly concerned mothers and fathers adopted the rallying cry of "parent power" and resolved to fight back against the "victimization of our children" by the commercial drug culture. They collectively agreed to ground their children for drug violations, enforce a uniform curfew, and ban them from rock concerts, head shops, the university campus, and nonchaperoned parties. Instead, they resolved to spend more time with their kids through drug-free family activities such as backpacking, sports, yoga, volunteering, and church. The new parents' movement also recognized that "supply creates the demand" for impressionable youth, so they began targeting the neighborhood pot dealers, the permissive adults who allowed teens to smoke and drink in private homes, the shops that sold drug paraphernalia, and the merchants who overlooked fake IDs. According to *Parents, Peers, and Pot,* the children of involved parents came to appreciate the "constant supervision" and firm rules, and they began to realize that stoners and burnouts were not cool. "As the enervating physical and psychological effects of marijuana began to wear off," the story concluded, "the children's energy, cheerfulness, and high spirits returned." The former teen pot smokers jokingly labeled the watchdog group the "Nosy Parents' Association" and warned their younger brothers and sisters to stay off drugs. The shock of innocence lost had given way, if not to the full restoration of a suburban utopia, then to the creation of a "closely knit, friendly neighborhood community" that had once seemed an unattainable relic of the small-town past.[76]

Schuchard pitched *Parents, Peers, and Pot* to a moderate-to-liberal audience of baby boomer parents by contrasting the dire marijuana crisis facing younger teens with the legitimate "generation gap" of the 1960s. After relating the rescue narrative of Kathy Allen and her friends, the booklet endorsed the political analysis that marijuana used to be a "valid part of the opposition to capitalism, racism, militarism" and criticized the overly harsh laws that had inspired the policy shift to decriminalization for adults. But as countercultural values entered the mainstream, the political context disappeared and a sophisticated corporate apparatus emerged to market the illegal drug culture to children. For liberal parents who had smoked pot in their younger days and might feel hypocritical in taking a zero-tolerance stance, these arguments portrayed marijuana as far more harmful for adolescents than for college students and adults and cast the war on drugs as a noble stand to protect exploited children from a ruthless and amoral form of capitalism. Schuchard also contended that drug use inhibited development of youth political consciousness—borrowing a theme from the antimarijuana educational documentaries of the late 1960s—by stifling the "normal adolescent urge to experiment, rebel, reject, and reach out." Most of all, permissive parents who valued their own tolerance and liberalism needed to realize that without establishing boundaries and imposing discipline, they were ceding control of their kids to a powerful adolescent peer culture being manipulated by an even more powerful commercial drug culture. Schuchard did not resurrect the schoolyard "pusher" mythology or remove all responsibility from teenage "victims," stating instead that "dealer" better reflected the "voluntary, two-way, consumer-supplier relationship within the drug culture." But she insisted that teenagers viewed decriminalization as "an open invitation to smoke pot" and warned that the marijuana industry was fast becoming an "entrenched economic interest," following the path of tobacco and alcohol corporations that also profited from marketing hazardous drugs to minors.[77]

Parents, Peers, and Pot concluded with guidelines for a drug prevention campaign through parent power and civic action, representing the most visible expression to date of the federal government's commitment to expanding the scope and influence of the parents' movement. The solution began at home, where parents should communicate often with their children, be unafraid to investigate suspicious behavior, forcefully forbid any use of drugs and alcohol, and mete out punishment when necessary—but "don't become hysterical or exaggerate the dangers of drugs—you will only seem ridiculous and out of touch with reality." This injunction followed a section on the alleged medical hazards of marijuana that highlighted controversial findings from Gabriel Nahas and other researchers on the academic fringe, not to mention Schuchard's framing device of lost innocence in a suburban dystopia and her flawed view that smoking pot represented the cause rather than a consequence of teenage rebellion and family tension. To counter the inevitable youth response that "everybody does it," parents should mobilize at the neighborhood level as "an 'extended family' with uniform rules and expectations," by the time their children entered the fifth grade. Since many adults in highly mobile suburbs did not really know their neighbors, or even many parents of their children's friends, they should forge a genuine sense of community by uniting against the evils of the drug culture. Divorced single mothers and working couples should recognize that their homes provided an unsupervised space for "afternoon pot parties" and ask other adults in the neighborhood to pitch in to monitor their children. Mobilized parents should work through their local PTAs to promote drug prevention programs in the schools and, following the DeKalb Families in Action example, confront merchants who sold paraphernalia and provided alcohol to underage teenagers. "You can make a difference" through collective parent power, Schuchard declared at the end of *Parents, Peers, and Pot*. "And if you don't, who else will?"[78]

National Federation of Parents for Drug-Free Youth

In January 1980, the leaders of seven local parent power groups converged on Washington in a show of force against the latest, and for decades the last, significant attempt to pass a federal marijuana decriminalization law. Public opinion surveys that year revealed that a narrow majority of American adults continued to favor decriminalization of possession while 25 percent endorsed legalization, including 42 percent in California. Senator Charles Mathias (R-MD), who first allied with suburban activists on the antiparaphernalia campaign, called the "Health Consequences of Marijuana Use" hearings after the Judiciary Committee included a modest decriminalization measure in omnibus legislation to revise the entire federal criminal code. Mathias excluded NORML from participation and stated that the debate was not about middle-class adults facing arrest but the "medical and psychological effects of marijuana, particularly on children and adolescents." NIDA director William Pollin emphasized the serious hazards of marijuana being delivered to teenagers by a $12 to $20 billion trafficking industry, and his predecessor Robert DuPont credited the parents' movement for the new consensus that smoking pot caused "amotivational syndrome" among far more youth than most psychiatrists had realized. Prohibition critic Lester Grinspoon, a prominent psychiatrist and NORML ally, argued in vain that marijuana did not "have the capacity to alter personality" and that the "amotivational syndrome" reversed cause and effect for "kids with underlying problems." Sue Rusche, the suburban Atlanta activist, responded that "angry" parents were "organizing to do the job of drug education themselves." Other grassroots leaders blamed decriminalization for transforming teenage marijuana abuse "from epidemic to pandemic" and proclaimed the nation's future to be hanging in the balance. Joyce Nalepka, the Silver Spring crusader, summarized their agenda with a threat: "We see pro-decriminalization as pro-pot; there is no gray area; it is either legal or illegal.... We will defeat pro-pot congressmen, senators, and presidential candidates."[79]

On April 4, 1980, representatives from around one hundred parents' groups and civic organizations from thirty different states gathered for a PRIDE conference in Atlanta and established the National Federation of Parents for Drug-Free Youth (NFP). PRIDE cofounders Thomas Gleaton and Marsha Keith Schuchard laid the groundwork for the new coalition and asked William (Bill) Barton of Florida, the head of Naples Informed Parents and a participant in the Mathias hearings, to be the first president. Barton portrayed the NFP as a "positive cooperative effort between parents and government. The drug epidemic cannot be solved by government or parents alone—it must be a team effort." The initial press release came with an endorsement from Lee Dogoloff, director of Carter's Office of Drug Abuse Policy, praising the "tremendous effectiveness" of parents' groups that were turning the tide of the war on drugs through their zero-tolerance stance on illegal marijuana and alcohol use by adolescents. Tom Adams, the community outreach director of NIDA's Pyramid Project, attended the founding meeting and pledged additional federal support. The NFP platform opposed decriminalization or legalization of marijuana, called for laws against drug paraphernalia, and demanded a ban on government funding for any organization with ties to NORML. The group's officers included Sue Rusche of DeKalb Families in Action, in charge of the antiparaphernalia campaign; Joyce Nalepka of Maryland, responsible for lobbying Congress; and Gabriel Nahas of Columbia University, head of the science committee. In May, at the NFP's first Washington press conference, dozens of politicians from both parties joined officials from the White House, NIDA, and the DEA to endorse the group's agenda—quite a remarkable rollout for a new organization. The NFP emphasized the political diversity within its ranks and pledged to serve as a nonpartisan lobby for the hundreds of parents' groups forming throughout the nation. "We are an idea whose time has come," Barton told his fellow crusaders. "We seem to be the only viable solution."[80]

Bill Barton's family story provided the ideal morality tale for the NFP's message that "parent power" could overcome the adolescent drug crisis and restore the lost innocence of white middle-class American suburbia. Antimarijuana journalist Peggy Mann helped construct the Barton mystique with features in the *Washington Post, Los Angeles Times,* and *Scouting* magazine, including photographs of the attractive couple and their three children, a "typical upper-middle-class family" (living in a 99% white community, which went unmentioned). In 1978, Bill and Pat Barton were attending a Humane Society fundraiser when they found out that their fifteen-year-old daughter Tracy, the "personification of adolescent innocence," was dating a drug dealer. Interrogations revealed that Bret, their sixteen-year-old son, was a daily stoner who began sharing joints when she was only thirteen, and lately Tracy had started using cocaine and pills. The Bartons asked for a police surveillance operation that arrested several students for smoking pot in the parking lot of Naples High School, including Bret (the group received brief suspensions and community service). They subjected Tracy to constant surveillance and then forced her into a drug rehabilitation center after she tried to run away. "Your child will probably hate you," Pat Barton admitted, before it gets better. The Bartons also started Naples Informed Parents, a zero-tolerance community group that initially faced a wall of denial and apathy from other adults but eventually grew into a powerful organization with five hundred members. The Naples activists publicized the medical hazards of marijuana (using information from PRIDE), lobbied for antiparaphernalia laws, and soon expanded into a statewide network, Florida Informed Parents. After her involuntary stay in rehabilitation, Tracy agreed to give up drugs and soon regained her "sunshine child" personality, and Bret also got clean and came to appreciate the necessity of invasive parenting. The Bartons' odyssey "could have happened anywhere in America," Peggy Mann concluded. "It is in fact happening everywhere in America."[81]

Most of the three dozen activists on the NFP's original board were upper-middle-class college-educated mothers who had launched antidrug movements in their affluent, almost all-white suburban neighborhoods within the past two years (fig. 6.10). In a reflection of PRIDE's Southeast-based network and Washington connections, more than one-third of the initial leaders came from metropolitan Atlanta, coastal Florida, or the DC suburbs. Patricia Burch, a veteran of the Maryland antiparaphernalia campaign, lived in the upscale community of Potomac (94% white, 1.7% Black) and ran the Interstate Movement Against Dangerous Drugs before joining forces with the NFP. Geraldine Silverman, from the wealthy New Jersey enclave of Short Hills (97% white, 0.7% Black), organized drug prevention efforts through the local PTA. Other board members represented white-collar commuter suburbs outside Philadelphia, Portsmouth (New Hampshire), Denver, and Los Angeles. Mary Jacobson, who would become the second president of the NFP, had started a door-to-door awareness campaign in her upper-middle-class Nebraska suburb in West Omaha (99% white) in 1978. In an example of the cross-fertilization and chain reaction of the emerging social movement, her group drew inspiration from Schuchard's NIDA publication about the "parent power" movement in suburban Atlanta, circulated Peggy Mann's "Marijuana Alert" exposé from *Reader's Digest,* and screened the Carter administration's *For Parents Only* documentary at conferences. In 1980, Jacobson's coalition secured passage of a Nebraska antiparaphernalia law and opened a Midwestern branch of PRIDE. The Omaha affiliate worked with PTAs to develop a zero-tolerance curriculum for elementary schools, informing preteens that "it's OK *not* to participate in the use of drugs or alcohol." They also asked "parents who care" to sign a public pledge to "promote wholesome social activities for our youth" and refuse to condone any illegal activities.[82]

The NFP leadership included a sizable contingent from California, where liberal white mothers from inner-ring suburbs first organized the parent power movement, mirroring the experiences of DeKalb Families in Action and Naples Informed Parents. Joann Lundgren, a mother of four from Palo Alto, founded Parents Who Care in fall 1979 to combat the "prevailing view" in her progressive high-tech community, where permissive adults often provided

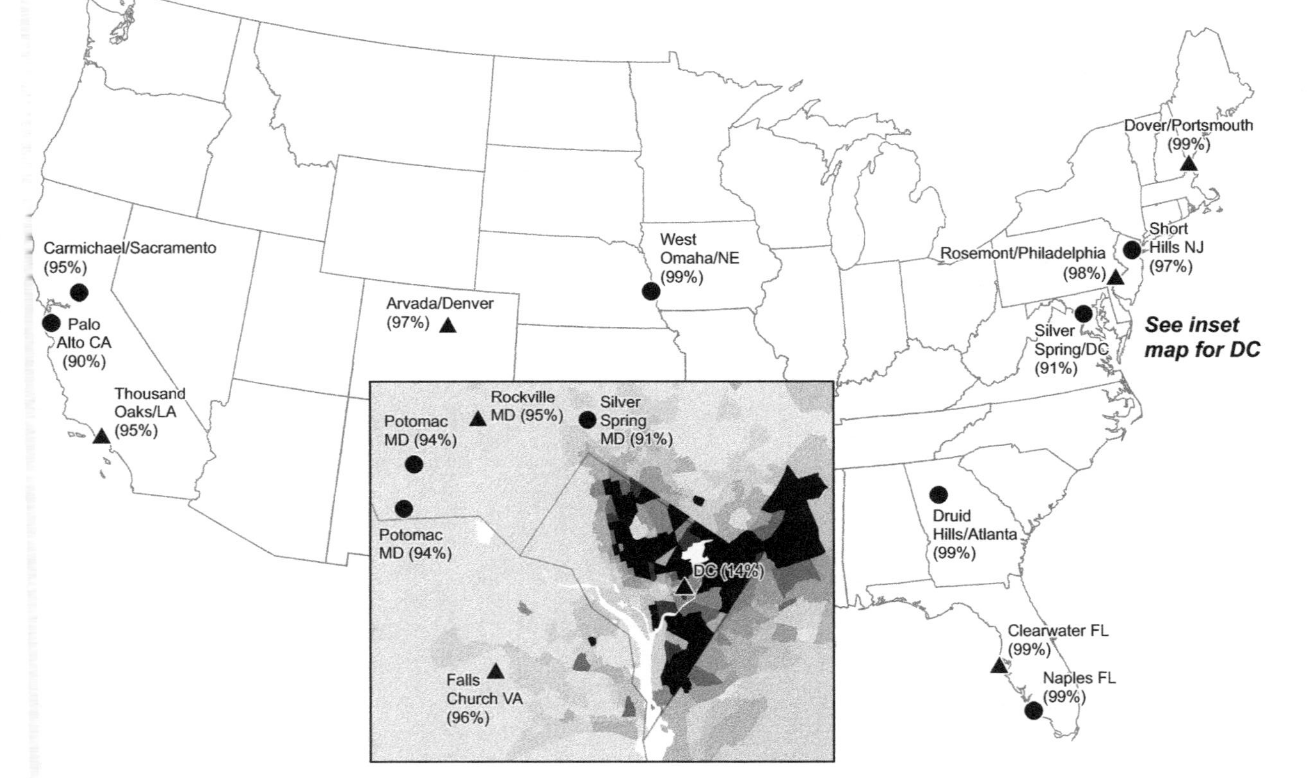

FIGURE 6.10. Geographic base of leaders of the National Federation of Parents for Drug-Free Youth. This map displays the racial demographics (% white) of the home communities of seventeen key activists in the NFP. The circles indicate the almost all-white suburbs where the most influential founders of the NFP first organized local antimarijuana movements between 1976 and 1979. The triangles denote the home bases of leaders who either joined the crusade in 1980, the NFP's first year of operation, or played prominent roles in the early 1980s. The inset map shows the residences of six NFP leaders from the Washington, DC, metropolitan region. The darker shades are areas with the highest concentration of Black residents. The NFP invited Vonneva Pettigrew, who lived in DC itself (in the 14% white census tract), to be its first minority board member in fall 1980 in a conscious attempt to diversify the coalition. (Map and 1980 census data courtesy of Social Explorer.)

alcohol for their children's parties and tolerated teenage marijuana use as a harmless rite of passage. Her children attended a prestigious public high school, located three miles from Stanford University, with "mass acceptance by teenagers that use of drugs and alcohol at their gatherings is the normal and acceptable standard of behavior." After reading *Parents, Peers, and Pot,* Lundgren started her own grassroots movement to forge an alliance of responsible parents and encourage youth to organize social functions without drugs or alcohol. They faced an uphill battle, as a large majority of parents and teenagers declined to participate in the chaperoned parties and antidrug rap sessions, but Lundgren's group still claimed success in shaking up the pro-drug consensus by creating new adolescent norms through positive peer pressure. In barely a year, Parents Who Care expanded to 125 chapters in the San Francisco Bay Area and became a major part of the NFP's statewide affiliate, Californians for Drug-Free Youth. Carla Lowe, the NFP board member who headed the California federation, started an antiparaphernalia campaign in 1978 after her son's suspension for taking a bong to school in the well-to-do Sacramento suburb of Carmichael (95% white). She labeled marijuana "the American parent's nightmare" and lamented the failure to fight back because "parents are under tremendous pressure to let kids do their own thing." Under Lowe, Californians for Drug-Free Youth pushed through a state anti-paraphernalia law and grew into a powerful network with the philosophy that "strong families are the primary line of defense to the 'do drugs' message of society."[83]

The National Federation of Parents, proclaimed Bill Barton in the spring of 1980, "have within our grasp the opportunity to change the course of the nation.... The need is so great that we cannot fail." With photogenic, fired-up white mothers and fathers from affluent suburbs demanding a national war on marijuana, and politicians from both parties scrambling to jump on board, national media coverage often uncritically promoted the NFP's highly questionable claim that America faced "the most massive and pervasive drug epidemic in human history." The NFP received more than seventeen thousand letters and inquiries after a wave of television publicity that included a profile of the Bartons on NBC's *Today Show* and a weeklong series on ABC's *Good Morning, America* about the parents' movement and the adolescent drug abuse crisis.[84] In addition to the widely circulated "Marijuana Alert" trilogy in *Reader's Digest,* Peggy Mann sounded the alarm that "marijuana abuse has reached pandemic proportions among our youth" in multiple women's magazines and other general-interest forums. Mann's articles, accompanied by images of white suburban youth smoking joints and patronizing head shops, advised parents afraid of "losing their children to marijuana" to follow the PRIDE/Families in

Action model of grassroots mobilization and affiliate with the National Federation of Parents. A *New York Times Magazine* feature on the parents' movement reinforced its hype about the "amazing growth" of the middle-school marijuana subculture, illustrated with a photograph of a sixth-grade dealer in suburban Atlanta who hid pot in a compartment under his skateboard. In addition to the Bartons' saga, the article portrayed roller-skating Catholic school girls getting high in Central Park, a head shop proprietor in suburban Connecticut showing fourteen-year-old boys how to hide pot from parents and teachers, school bus drivers who dealt drugs to their passengers, and teenagers turned on by camp counselors and coaches. "Right under our noses," the mother of a twelve-year-old lamented, "our happy, lovely little girl had turned into a sullen, alienated, unreasonable creature."[85]

The NFP grew rapidly in its first year of operation, its grassroots base fortified by such sympathetic/alarmist media coverage and its powerful allies in the Carter White House and on both sides of Capitol Hill, including an affiliated chapter of congressmen's wives. In the organization's inaugural newsletter, Bill Barton laid out the agenda of educating American families about the "dangers of marijuana and other mind-altering drugs" while serving as the national clearinghouse and federal lobby for local parent-activists fighting the war against adolescent drug abuse "in living rooms and kitchens across our country." To coordinate the movement, the NFP distributed a parent group starter kit based on Sue Rusche's DeKalb Families in Action handbook and an antiparaphernalia kit created by the Maryland campaign. After one year of operation, the NFP claimed success in its goal of establishing an affiliated network in all fifty states and boasted of more than one thousand parents' groups in existence across the nation. The NFP leaders also resolved to "encourage development of minority and multicultural parent groups," a response to the somewhat awkward issue that its originally all-white board of directors clearly reflected its political base in prosperous, racially segregated suburbs. In fall 1980, the NFP sought to diversify by inviting Vonneva Pettigrew, an African American mother from Washington, DC, to join the board as its first representative for minority communities. With NIDA's support, Pettigrew had recently started a neighborhood parents' group that spread the antidrug message through Head Start, churches, and PTAs. She offered her organization as proof that inner-city activists could be "as effective" as their counterparts in the white middle-class suburbs because "parent power works—whether you're rich or poor."[86]

The NFP's membership application required parents to sign a pledge that "the best way to achieve drug free youth is through education . . . in a

NON-BLAMING way," a philosophy that captured the complexities and contradictions of the movement's ideological outlook. At its core, this fundamental principle meant that parents who discovered their children using illegal drugs should stop blaming themselves. The NFP adapted the concept from PRIDE's statement of philosophy, which repudiated the "blaming, scapegoating, and denying processes" that divided local communities and undermined parental solidarity. This also meant not blaming divorced couples or working mothers, a common tendency during the 1970s and 1980s. "We do not need to make parents feel guilty," Schuchard explained. "What we need to do is bolster their confidence that they are the most important people to their children in the world." According to Joann Lundgren of the California affiliate, "Parents take total responsibility for their children and blame no one for the present situation." Yet this positive message of moral renewal and collective solidarity within the middle-class family and the suburban neighborhood always coexisted with a lengthy list of internal and external villains—permissive parents who willingly or naively enabled the adolescent culture of "partying" and "getting high," the paraphernalia industry and "commercialized drug culture," Cheech and Chong stoner movies and Eric Clapton's song "Cocaine," mysterious dealers who (inexplicably) laced marijuana joints with PCP, NORML and other advocates of legalization or decriminalization, the hard/soft distinction of prevention experts who favored "responsible use" messaging, even the Carter administration's initial preoccupation with urban heroin addicts instead of young white pot smokers. And despite its "non-blaming" demand-side philosophy, from the outset the NFP demanded aggressive action to curb the supply side of the market, from higher mandatory-minimum penalties for marijuana traffickers to intensified border interdiction and crop eradication abroad.[87]

The Carter administration's immediate, enthusiastic embrace of the NFP cemented the prosecution of the war on teenage drug (ab)use as a public-private partnership between the federal government and the parents' movement. In summer 1980, the White House claimed a considerable degree of credit for the proliferation of parents' groups through its adolescent prevention campaign and for reshaping public attitudes about marijuana's dangers via its media and public health initiatives. In internal memos, Lee Dogoloff and Stuart Eizenstat of the policy staff noted that the NFP "relied on us for leadership and direction" and would provide insulation in the reelection contest against Ronald Reagan, who "will hit hard on this issue" of a runaway marijuana epidemic. The Carter campaign should portray the grassroots parents' movement as "the greatest hope for the future," which they believed to be good politics and also the truth. In his final State of the Union address, President Carter touted his administration's two greatest accomplishments in the area of drug policy: bringing the urban heroin epidemic under control and having "encouraged a national movement of parents and citizens committed to reversing" the crisis of teenage drug abuse.[88] After Reagan won the election, Lee Dogoloff helped establish a NIDA Liaison Committee to formalize NFP oversight to ensure that federal drug publications were "consistent with the basic thrust of the parent movement"—in effect, authority to censor public health materials that did not highlight marijuana's dangers and promote a zero-tolerance stance. As he stepped down, Dogoloff characterized the NFP alliance as one of the Carter administration's greatest accomplishments, because policymakers had realized the power of a "forgotten group," mobilized parents at the grassroots with the federal government "acting as a catalyst." He also predicted, accurately, that the public-private partnership would continue to flourish under the incoming Republican administration because the NFP had become a powerful political force and its drug-free youth mission now represented the firm bipartisan consensus.[89]

The rise of the parents' movement in the late 1970s, and the adolescent prevention campaign launched by its allies in the Carter administration, did play a role in shifting teenage attitudes about the dangers of chronic marijuana consumption but achieved much less success in curbing recreational use. Although the Reagan administration later claimed credit for reversing the culture of public permissiveness that undermined the war on drugs, key downward trends were well underway before the Republican ascension. NIDA's annual "Monitoring the Future" surveys reveal that rates of teenage pot smoking peaked in 1978—the year of Marsha Keith Schuchard's antipermissiveness manifesto, PRIDE's "parent power" launch, and the Carter White House's redeclaration of war on marijuana. Between 1978 and 1981, the proportion of high school seniors who smoked pot daily declined from 11 to 7 percent, and the group that considered regular marijuana use to involve "great risk" increased from 35 to 58 percent (fig. 6.11). Drug researchers attributed this significant shift in behavioral patterns and attitudes to the changing peer norms that accompanied government and media publicity of marijuana's health hazards. The decline among recreational and experimental users was marginal, however, with 46 percent of seniors in the class of 1981 having smoked pot in the previous year and 32 percent in the previous month, versus 50 percent annually and 37 percent monthly in 1978. More than 80 percent of high school

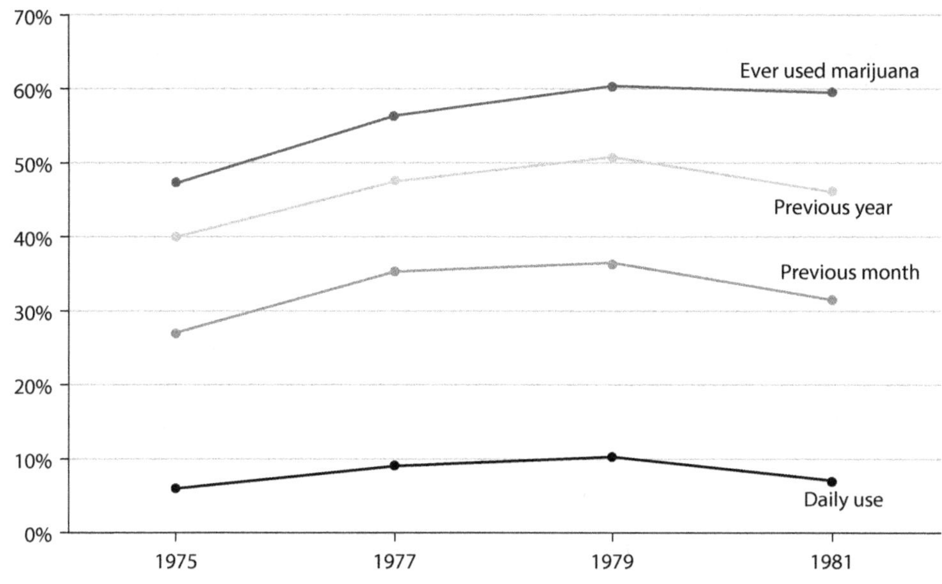

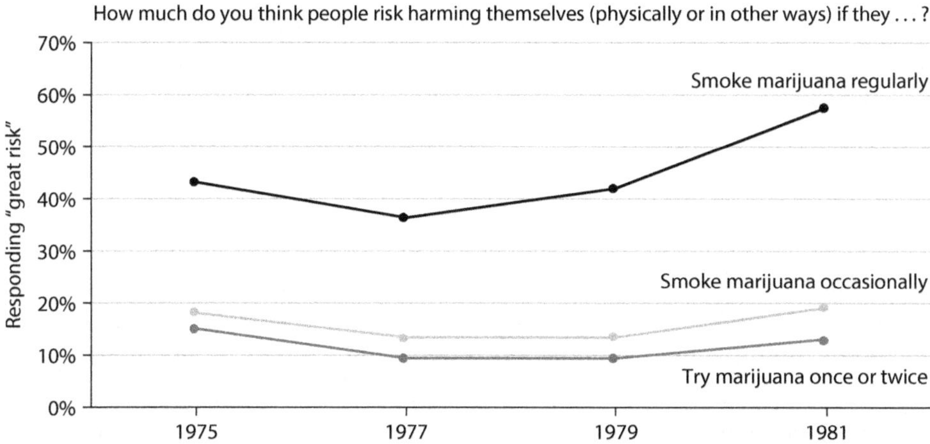

FIGURE 6.11. Trends in marijuana use and attitudes among U.S. high school seniors, 1975–81. (*Top*) Marijuana use among high school seniors peaked in 1978–79 and then began a slow downward trajectory. More than 60% of seniors in the class of 1979 had broken the marijuana laws at some point in their lives, including half within the previous year, more than one-third during the previous month, and more than one-tenth currently smoking pot on a daily basis. (*Bottom*) The vast majority of high school seniors believed that smoking marijuana occasionally or just experimenting did not involve "great risk." Only 36% of those surveyed in 1977 agreed that regular marijuana use involved "great risk," a viewpoint that rose to 58% by 1981 in the context of renewed political and media claims about the physical and psychological health hazards suffered by frequent stoners. (NIDA, *Highlights from Student Drug Use in America, 1975–1981.*)

students in the 1981 survey did not consider "occasional" pot smoking to be a high-risk activity, even though most of their parents disapproved, and almost every teenager said marijuana remained very easy to obtain. In sum, while almost three-fifths of American teenagers now accepted the warnings that chronic stoners jeopardized their health and risked the "amotivational syndrome," an 81 percent supermajority did not find the zero-tolerance messages of the parent power movement to be persuasive, and interdiction policies in the global war on drugs continued to have no impact on either supply or demand in the recreational market.[90]

These social practices and attitudes among American teenagers demonstrate that the "responsible use" approach favored by many public health professionals operated with more effectiveness than the abstinence-only agenda demanded by the National Federation of Parents. The "Monitoring the Future" surveys actually solicited, publicized, and took seriously the views of teenagers themselves—rather than presenting youth as simply the depoliticized and helpless victims of traffickers, NORML, the drug culture, permissiveness, and peer pressure. The survey data reveal that, unlike the parents' movement and the Carter administration (after its mid-1978 course correction), most high school seniors drew considered distinctions between soft and hard drugs, use and abuse, recreational activity and habitual dependency, experimentation and addiction. Three-fourths of seniors in the late 1970s believed that smoking marijuana in private should not be criminalized. Large majorities distinguished recreational use of marijuana and alcohol from the quite distinct practices of getting stoned daily, compulsive drinking, nicotine addiction, and routine use of heroin and cocaine. The public health campaign against adolescent pot smoking had made some inroads, the NIDA report concluded, but American teenagers continued to display "the highest levels of illicit drug use among young people to be found in any industrialized nation in the world." In alliance with the Reagan administration, the NFP's parent-activists escalated their crusade in the early 1980s, expanding the war against teenage "drug abuse" to encompass the rising threat of cocaine and any underage drinking, alongside the primary focus on eradicating the recreational marijuana subculture. This zero-tolerance agenda carried its own risks, as the "Monitoring the Future" researchers warned—and as the disregarded history of the 1950s/1960s scare-tactics approach confirmed—because only prevention strategies based on "credible scientific evidence" would have a lasting impact on the peer norms that fundamentally shaped patterns of adolescent drug use. "An overzealous propaganda campaign," cautioned the NIDA researchers, "however good its intentions, has the danger of backfiring."[91]

7

Zero Tolerance

THE POLICE ARE PATROLLING the parking lot on foot and horseback, and officers with binoculars are up on the roof of the rock music venue, when an extremely stoned longhaired teenager tells the camera that he is also tripping on acid and "they should legalize drugs, that is a fact." He offers the filmmakers a joint, his friend proposes that "burnouts out there" could accomplish this by joining hands across America, and their female companions yell, "Cocaine, baby!" and joke about having sex in the car. Everyone in the mostly white crowd hanging out before the heavy metal concert is drinking alcohol, mainly Budweiser but also a lot of Jack Daniels. Many are drunk, and smart enough to have gotten high before they drove through the gates, because the clear unwritten rule is that police are not going to enforce the underage alcohol laws as long as teenagers keep the illegal drugs out of sight. This scene captured by the underground film *Heavy Metal Parking Lot* is suburban Maryland in the spring of 1986, four years after the Reagan administration declared unconditional war on illegal use of drugs and alcohol by teenagers, four years after the state legislature raised the drinking age to twenty-one, and a few months before the full fury of the federal war on crack cocaine would be unleashed fifteen miles away in Washington, DC. The police had only launched the patrols because a few years earlier, a "parent power" coalition in the upscale DC suburbs began demanding that rock concert venues crack down on the free flow of marijuana and booze inside and outside the shows. This law enforcement campaign seemed both half-hearted and futile, and as one concert-goer in the underground film observes, "Drugs are practically legal in this parking lot." A suburban mother who went undercover to investigate rock shows agreed, angrily reporting their "safe haven" for teenagers breaking marijuana and alcohol laws with abandon. She took her grievance directly to the White House, warning President Reagan that "at the rate we're going, we don't need to worry about a nuclear attack, our enemy can just sit back and watch drugs destroy our people."[1]

The war on drugs during the Reagan administration, and the "Just Say No" crusade championed by First Lady Nancy Reagan, built directly on the momentum of the zero-tolerance parents' movement and the Carter administration's marijuana policy shift in the late 1970s. During the 1980 campaign, Ronald Reagan proclaimed that marijuana was "probably the most dangerous drug in the United States." This declaration, scientifically untenable at the time and widely ridiculed since, nevertheless captured an important political truth, one that his Democratic predecessor had acknowledged as well. Marijuana commanded attention from the American political system, first and foremost, because its "abuse" by young white teenagers and preteens had inspired the grassroots mobilization of "parent power" groups from affluent suburbs. For this powerful social movement, the catastrophe of teenage pot smoking encapsulated the breakdown of the traditional nuclear family in an era of cultural turmoil and explained the apathy and rebelliousness of white middle-class youth at a time of economic crisis and growing fears of downward mobility. The GOP platform in 1980 celebrated the suburban activists in the National Federation of Parents for Drug-Free Youth while charging Jimmy Carter with indifference to the "murderous epidemic of drug abuse [that] has swept our country." This partisan broadside disregarded the Carter administration's actual policies in the war on drugs and in particular its comprehensive alignment with the antimarijuana agenda of the parents' movement. Soon after taking office, Ronald Reagan labeled teenage drug abuse "one of the gravest problems facing us internally in the United States" and lamented that "we're running the risk of losing a great part of a whole generation"—almost the exact wording of his declaration of war on marijuana in 1970 as governor of California. Echoing the Carter administration as well, the new president promised a demand-side campaign of "winning over the users to the point that we take the customers away from the drugs" and praised the NFP as the centerpiece of this national crusade.[2]

The perceived marijuana crisis in the white middle-class suburbs shaped, and in key respects dominated, the federal war on drugs during much of Reagan's presidency. Scholars often have associated the Reagan administration's drug policies with the exploitation of white backlash against urban Black crime and the repressive law-and-order response to the crack cocaine "epidemic." In *The New Jim Crow*, Michelle Alexander argues that Reagan's "drug war from the outset had little to do with public concern about drugs and much to do with public concern about race. By waging a war on drug users and dealers, Reagan made good on his promise to crack down on the racially defined 'others'—the undeserving. . . . The War on Drugs proved popular . . . particularly [among] whites who remained resentful of black progress, civil rights enforcement, and affirmative action."[3] Bipartisan tough-on-crime policies and the Republican administration's "malign neglect" of urban public health unquestionably shaped the repressive crackdown in nonwhite neighborhoods. But this line of analysis simply cannot explain the continuities in federal drug policy between the late Carter and early Reagan years and the responsiveness of politicians from across the spectrum to the marijuana-focused agenda of the suburban parents' movement. Between 1978 and 1986, from the parent power assault on marijuana decriminalization until the discovery of the crack "epidemic," federal interdiction and public health strategies converged to protect the white middle-class victims of the national drug crisis and positioned the twelve-to-fourteen-year-old suburban pot smoker at the moral core of the national crusade. Racial logics certainly did shape implementation of Reagan's war on drugs, but in spatially and socioeconomically distinct ways: a public health campaign created for white middle-class children in the suburbs; an interdiction strategy, designed mainly for their protection, that elevated marijuana above heroin and cocaine as a federal priority; and a targeted law enforcement offensive against crime and addiction in inner-city and nonwhite areas.[4]

As a case study in political mobilization and public policy formation, the NFP's alliance with the Carter and Reagan administrations operated through a series of feedback loops connecting local communities to the federal government, a war on drugs both bottom-up and top-down. The NFP operated simultaneously as a social movement, grassroots lobby, moral exemplar, and most effectively as an interest group with extensive federal contacts, especially because both of Reagan's drug policy chiefs came directly from its ranks. Evaluating the NFP's impact at multiple scales reveals the inadequacy of using public opinion surveys to argue that political elites simply manipulated voters and produced a "moral panic" to advance the punitive war on drugs during the 1980s.[5] The NFP, an initially small network of grassroots activists clustered in wealthy inner-ring white suburbs, pressured and collaborated with Washington policymakers to marginalize bureaucratic and political rivals and magnify the zero-tolerance crusade. This suburban-federal coalition, with eager assistance from the mainstream media, then recruited tens of thousands more parents throughout Middle America to join local organizations affiliated with the

FIGURE 7.1. First Lady Nancy Reagan addresses the inaugural national conference of the National Federation of Parents for Drug-Free Youth, October 11, 1982. The Reagan White House, following the lead of the Carter administration, forged a close political alliance with the white suburban activists in the antimarijuana "parents' movement." (AP Photo / Barry Thumma.)

national campaign. Despite its nonpartisan roots and "non-blaming" philosophy of "It takes a village" suburban renewal, the antimarijuana agenda ultimately overlapped with other parts of the Reagan administration's conservative agenda, in particular abstinence-only sex education and deliberate funding shifts from the public sector to private voluntary initiatives. Although NFP leaders disassociated their unifying, protect-the-children mission from the polarizing politics of the religious right, the organization's rapid expansion in the early 1980s brought in an influx of conservative Republicans and led to an increasingly authoritarian turn at the local level. But the NFP's constituency remained ideologically diverse and its agenda most similar to the simultaneous victims' rights movement, another social formation of "political whiteness" that elected officials in both parties competed to support.[6]

The NFP and the Reagan administration denounced marijuana decriminalization and rejected the entire philosophy of "soft" drugs and "recreational" use, but they advocated private rehabilitation rather than criminal punishment for teenagers who broke the laws, at least for the pot smokers and underage drinkers in the white middle-class suburbs. At the national level, both the NFP and the Reagan White House embraced the Mothers Against Drunk Driving crusade, added alcohol to marijuana as an alleged gateway drug, and endorsed the increase in the national drinking age to twenty-one that federal lawmakers enacted in 1984.[7] This grassroots-driven, bipartisan, and completely ineffective reform criminalized the social practices of millions of legal adults, most of them college students or employed workers—justified as a zero-tolerance measure to curb adolescent drunk driving but fundamentally part of the broader mission to regulate and control the recreational youth subculture. In the white suburbs, zero-tolerance parents' groups promoted a range of authoritarian policies, rationalized as an antipermissive "tough love" approach: lockdown rehabilitation for uncooperative pot smokers and underage drinkers, school suspensions or expulsions for illicit drug users and especially "pushers," cooperative ventures with local police who busted teenagers at rock concerts or school functions and diverted them into treatment programs, random drug testing for high school students, even the arrests of parents who permitted their children's friends to consume alcohol at parties in private homes. The NFP's zero-tolerance program almost certainly did not represent the views of a majority of American parents in most suburban communities, and neither did the Reagan administration's revised gateway argument that experimenting with marijuana or alcohol would lead to cocaine "addiction," but small and organized factions operating through the crisis discourse of a white youth drug epidemic could disproportionately influence policy implementation at the local level as in Washington.

The national arrest patterns in the war on drugs changed dramatically during the 1980s, with the ratio of Black-to-white and cocaine/heroin to marijuana apprehensions returning to their pre-1967 levels, before mass pot smoking by white youth began a fifteen-year interregnum in the racial priorities—though not the actual imprisonment rates—of the carceral state. Even before the arrival of crack cocaine, the racial and spatial demographics had begun to shift because of marijuana decriminalization in states such as California and New York, combined with the stop-and-frisk policing and zero-tolerance "broken windows" philosophy of the militarized war on street crime and urban gangs.[8] The Reagan administration's funding cuts for public health programs, and the expensive private rehabilitation alternatives supported by the NFP and its White House allies, further distanced the white recreational drug market from carceral penalties while criminalizing the urban and nonwhite markets with unprecedented reach. A flurry of mandatory-minimum

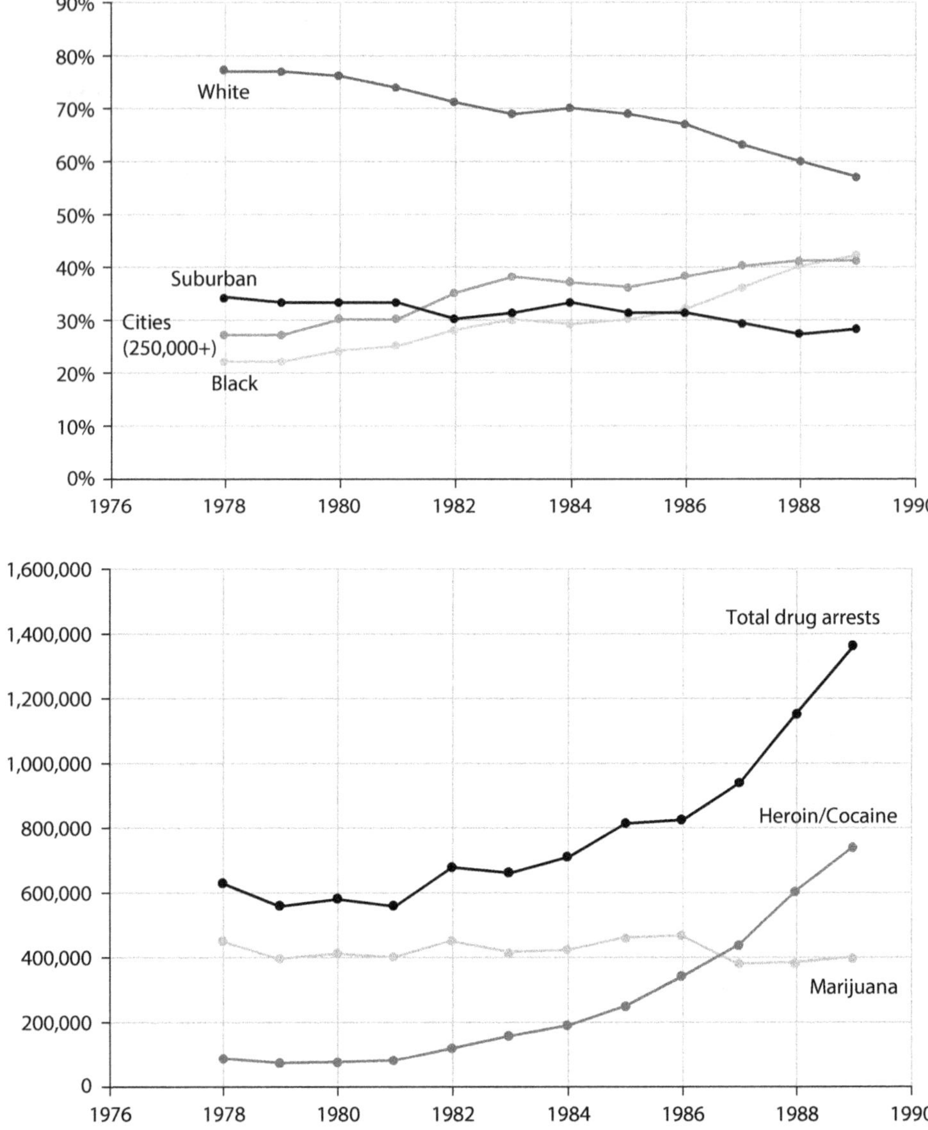

FIGURE 7.2. Select characteristics of the population arrested on drug charges in the United States, 1978–89. (*Top*) The proportion of Black drug arrests nearly doubled during the 1980s, while white drug arrests declined from 77% to 57% of the total. Shifting arrest trends in the largest cities and the FBI-designated suburban areas reflected this racially targeted urban crackdown. (*Bottom*) Arrests in the combined category of heroin/cocaine increased from 12% to 54% of total drug arrests during the 1980s. The white-dominated marijuana market declined from 70% to 29% of the total, although the actual number of annual marijuana arrests remained fairly constant. The number of heroin/cocaine arrests increased tenfold, and the 1.36 million drug arrests nationwide in 1989 was 2.3 times the total at the start of the decade. (FBI, *Uniform Crime Reports*, 1978–1989.)

sentencing laws, state-level policies that permitted prosecutors to charge juveniles as adults, and other bipartisan tough-on-crime measures then intersected with the militarized response to the crack cocaine "epidemic" to accelerate the hypercriminalization of urban and nonwhite neighborhoods, young Black males in particular, and produce the racially disparate outcomes of modern mass incarceration. Between 1978 and 1989, the proportion of marijuana to all drug arrests declined from 70 to 29 percent, white apprehensions dropped from 77 to 58 percent, and the suburban proportion also decreased even as these areas continued to diversify. Total drug arrests more than doubled during this period, combined heroin/cocaine arrests expanded from 13 to 54 percent, the Black arrest share skyrocketed from 22 to 42 percent, and the largest cities increased from 27 to 41 percent (fig. 7.2). In the starkest transformation, the percentage of white juvenile drug busts fell from 87 to 51 percent (this data includes Hispanics), and the Black juvenile arrest share quadrupled from 12 to 49 percent nationwide.[9]

The Reagan-era war on drugs rested on a solid bipartisan consensus, from the immediate embrace of the NFP agenda through enactment of omnibus legislation in 1986 and 1988. With marijuana legalization advocates completely marginalized and civil liberties in retreat, the most vocal criticism came from liberal Democrats who demanded that the GOP administration move even more aggressively on the law enforcement and public health fronts to subdue international traffickers and the urban crime associated with heroin and cocaine markets. Although President Reagan has often received the credit, punitive crime policy was not only a racial project of law-and-order Republicans, and Democratic drug warriors such as Senator Joseph Biden of Delaware and Representative Charles Rangel of Harlem pushed through the legislative

---

Note: Racial data on juvenile drug arrests is available in fig. 7.11. On the FBI's inclusion of most Hispanic arrests in the "white" category, see note in fig. I.1. The FBI began separately reporting Hispanic arrest totals in 1980 and then discontinued this "ethnic origin" tabulation in 1987. The Hispanic data came from fewer local reporting agencies than the other racial categories and therefore is not directly comparable. According to the estimates, Hispanic drug arrests accounted for 9.2% of the national total in 1980, 15.1% in 1983, and 19.9% in 1986. These numbers indicate that the white (non-Hispanic) share of drug arrests plummeted during the 1980s and that combined Black and Hispanic drug arrests likely approached half of the total by the middle of the decade. The racial breakdown of the U.S. population in the 1980 census was 79.6% white (non-Hispanic), 11.5% Black, and 6.5% Hispanic. The 1990 census totals were 75.6% white (non-Hispanic), 11.8% Black, and 9.0% Hispanic.

initiatives that exponentially increased rates of incarceration during the 1980s and beyond. Democrats crafted the Anti-Drug Abuse Act of 1986 that Congress passed with minimal dissent, inverting the funding ratio between public health and law enforcement established during the Nixon era and establishing harsh mandatory-minimum sentences, including the racially inequitable and now infamous (but at the time uncontroversial) 100:1 powder-to-crack cocaine disparity. During this pivotal phase in the expansion of the carceral state, Ronald and Nancy Reagan persisted in lumping recreational pot smoking together with heroin addiction and crack cocaine as the multifaceted epidemic that was "killing our children." They reminded American parents that "no one is safe" and urged teenagers to resist peer pressure by joining "Just Say No" clubs, operating within the universalist discourse and suburban crisis framework that had long shaped the war on drugs as a racial state-building project. The political culture also portrayed white middle-class youth as the most sympathetic victims of cocaine traffickers, as innocent children to be protected and at times forcibly rehabilitated, even as federal, state, and local law enforcement launched a targeted offensive against nonwhite teenage "gangsters" and "pushers" in urban America.[10]

The Reagan Administration and the "Parents' Movement"

The National Federation of Parents for Drug-Free Youth responded to the presidential transition by emphasizing its political centrism and maneuvering to influence the direction of drug policy in the Reagan White House. At a meeting right after the 1980 election, NFP president Bill Barton expressed cautious optimism about the incoming administration but warned his group "to be careful of extremes in either direction." In public statements, Barton portrayed himself as "pure middle America," a concerned parent with a nonpartisan agenda—to save the nation's children from the drug abuse crisis—that had galvanized a unified political response. He explicitly distanced his organization from the culture warriors in the Moral Majority, a vocal element of Reagan's conservative Republican base, explaining that the NFP operated with a "no-blame attitude." They promoted a positive drug-free message of parental involvement in children's lives and were "truly a grassroots movement of people helping themselves." Marsha Keith Schuchard, the NFP's suburban Atlanta cofounder, likewise declared that the "marijuana issue should never have been politicized" because the mission of the parents' movement "can unite us, despite many differences of lifestyle, behavior or political and religious beliefs." The NFP leadership lobbied the Reagan White House either to reappoint Lee Dogoloff, its close Carter administration ally, as head of the Office of Drug Abuse Policy (ODAP) or choose another director with ties to the organization.[11] The incoming administration ultimately selected Carlton Turner, an original member of the NFP board. Turner held a pharmaceutical research position at the University of Mississippi and had energetically promoted controversial new findings regarding the medical hazards of cannabis. He became the first White House drug policy director since Nixon established the position whose background and expertise revolved around marijuana rather than the urban-oriented field of heroin addiction and treatment, a reflection of Turner's political base in the suburban parents' movement against recreational pot smoking.[12]

During Reagan's first year in office, NFP leaders pressed the Republican administration to demonstrate that its commitment to the zero-tolerance crusade for drug-free youth matched the actions of its Democratic predecessor. In Senate testimony, Schuchard (a self-described liberal Democrat) denounced the media presumption that antimarijuana parents were "puritanical reactionaries" and insisted that protection of vulnerable teenagers "should never be an issue of liberals versus conservatives, or Republicans versus Democrats." Her presentation, titled "How the Federal Government Can Better Serve the Parents' Movement for Drug Free Youth," contrasted the vibrant and effective "do-it-yourself" mobilization of grassroots parents' groups with the inaction thus far of the Reagan administration. Schuchard demanded a "massive public educational campaign" to highlight the dangers of the "marijuana epidemic" and asked why "no one at top levels of government seems to be taking the broader public health implications seriously," except for her former NFP associate Carlton Turner. "Many parents wonder why" even President Reagan, despite his "strong anti-drug convictions," rarely addressed the crisis and were starting to question what the administration's priorities really were. Thomas Gleaton, the cofounder along with Schuchard of the Parents' Resource Institute for Drug Education (PRIDE), the NFP's parent organization, criticized administration plans to cut the NIDA budget, which would compromise the Pyramid Project that provided operational grants to "parent power" groups and limit circulation of effective Carter-era prevention materials such as the *For Parents Only* film and Schuchard's *Parents, Peers, and Pot* handbook. Carla Lowe, the head of the NFP's Californians for Drug-Free Youth network, implored Reagan to issue a "loud, clear statement" against marijuana traffickers and "join the parents in declaring war on an industry that has the potential of destroying our country by eating out the heart of our society—our youth."[13]

In fall 1981, the NFP mobilized for a Senate hearing on the health risks of pot smoking to publicize its main message for politicians and the public: "MARIJUANA IS DOING INCREDIBLE DAMAGE TO AMERICA'S CHILDREN." During the build-up, NFP leaders exerted pressure on the scientists at the National Institute on Drug Abuse through their Liaison Committee, which Carter officials had established, including demands for zero-tolerance messaging about adolescent marijuana use and the relabeling of cocaine as a dangerous and additive drug. The Senate proceedings opened with NIDA director William Pollin praising the parents' movement for its efforts to save "our young people [who] have been the tragic victims of a major public health menace." Pollin highlighted the many hazards of marijuana, including the "amotivational syndrome" (which had not been scientifically documented), and emphasized that pot smokers were more likely to abuse cocaine. He concluded with an optimistic assessment of the NIDA prevention campaign launched by the Carter administration, based on declining rates of teenage marijuana use since 1978. Representing the NFP, Marsha Schuchard countered that this hardly constituted a policy success because illegal use of marijuana and alcohol was "still a majority phenomenon" among American teens. Schuchard credited the "populist movement" of amateur activists and PTA mothers for slowly but surely convincing Washington officials to abandon the mid-1970s philosophy that "marijuana was a harmless substance, and that we should allow our seventh graders to smoke it"—an inflammatory description of decriminalization policy and the "responsible use"/"harm reduction" public health approach. She also argued that obsession with "hard drugs" had obscured "the pivotal role of marijuana as the gateway into the drug culture." Schuchard championed the parent power strategy of positive engagement but also called for admittedly "authoritarian" measures, including drug testing of rebellious teenagers and "monitored abstinence" (though not prosecution) for all youth caught breaking the law.[14]

The testimony of Donald Ian MacDonald, a Florida pediatrician and NFP board member who later replaced Turner as Reagan's second ODAP director, further revealed the increasingly authoritarian tactics and feverish rhetoric of the parents' movement. MacDonald, a family practice doctor with no specific expertise in drug or alcohol abuse, served as the medical director of Straight, Inc., a controversial "tough love" rehabilitation center in St. Petersburg. He joined the parent power crusade in 1979 after catching his fifteen-year-old son

Andy with marijuana and eventually institutionalized him for a year in the Straight facility as a multidrug "addict." MacDonald informed the Senate subcommittee that he lived and worked in a suburb of Clearwater (99.3% white), "a beautiful little town with middle-class people who do very well," except for the catastrophic marijuana epidemic among their children. He predicted that one-third of the teenagers in Clearwater, and millions more around the nation, "will either die early or go on to lead unhappy and unproductive lives as chemically dependent adults." MacDonald asserted (with no evidence) that more than half of all teenagers who experimented with marijuana would fall victim to the "amotivational syndrome," and significant numbers would commit suicide or take the gateway progression and add cocaine, PCP, and LSD to their burnout lifestyles. He advocated a parenting strategy based on suspicion and constant surveillance because "chemical use is the norm," including routine searches of children's rooms and drug screening by family physicians, followed by involuntary commitment to a treatment center if necessary. "We need to control our kids," MacDonald insisted, by protecting teenagers from marijuana in the same way that a new parent would not let a toddler run loose on the highway. "There is no such thing as moderate or controlled use of drugs," he concluded.[15]

The NFP's zero-tolerance campaign to eradicate the "marijuana epidemic" increasingly supplemented the message of parent power with previously discredited or marginalized ideas about pot addiction, gateway dangers, pusher evils, and the utilization of law enforcement and medical institutionalization against recreational drug users. In October 1981, the national headquarters publicized the recommendations of Dr. MacDonald and another suburban pediatrician from Ohio who testified that the explosive growth of middle-class "marijuana addicts" meant that every state needed a zero-tolerance treatment facility such as Straight, Inc. The NFP circulated the first-person confessional of MacDonald's son Andy, a boy from a loving upper-middle-class family who started smoking pot in the eighth grade to escape from reality and because he thought it was "harmless." Andy began failing his classes, resisted his parents' efforts to break his marijuana habit, and soon graduated to cocaine, PCP, and LSD before the cold-turkey Straight program cured his addictions. In its fall 1981 newsletter, the NFP issued an alert that shadowy partisans of the drug culture were trying to corrupt children by circulating LSD hits on Mickey Mouse lick-and-stick tattoos, an apocryphal (sub)urban legend that echoed alarm over PCP-laced joints and other pusher tropes of decades past. PRIDE released a "community-school plan" that counseled parents' groups and education officials to involve local police and juvenile justice authorities in a drug prevention approach that would arrest and then divert teenagers into involuntary addiction treatment programs. In this new blueprint for the war on drugs, PRIDE called on government officials to reinforce the demand-side prevention campaign through "strict enforcement" of existing laws rather than the "widespread failure to arrest public marijuana smokers." The NFP's parent organization advocated the coercive treatment and rehabilitation of teenage lawbreakers, not the "non-productive incarceration of naïve users," combined with the demand that "criminal traffickers should receive swift, mandated sentences."[16]

As coordinator of the Reagan administration's drug policy, Carlton Turner energetically advanced the NFP's agenda of keeping marijuana at the center of the national war on drugs and generating public alarm about an epidemic that "affects all citizens from all socioeconomic groups." He frequently proclaimed that "marijuana is a major gateway drug," a rationale not heard from a White House policymaker since the waning days of the Nixon administration. In fall 1981, Turner informed Congress that marijuana interdiction and prevention represented the administration's top priority, because more than eleven million teenagers and young adults currently smoked pot, while only a "statistically insignificant" number of Americans were addicted to heroin (estimated at four hundred thousand). Turner then criticized previous administrations for downplaying the abuse of illegal substances "once considered 'soft' and less dangerous," especially marijuana but also cocaine, the two recreational drugs most closely associated with upper-middle-class white consumers. Although the Reagan administration condemned the permissive policy of decriminalization, there was no talk of actually incarcerating marijuana smokers, even as Turner promised a law enforcement crackdown on the supply side and called for higher mandatory-minimum penalties for traffickers. In this sense, the ethos of decriminalization continued to apply to social practices, physical spaces, and impossible criminals imagined as white, middle-class, and suburban. Like the growing strain within the parents' movement, Turner did advocate the "detoxification" and "rehabilitation" of youth who "abused" marijuana, a significantly more coercive public health approach. But instead of demand-side law enforcement in the suburbs, Turner pledged that the White House would join parents' groups in their "unequivocal and united stand against drug use" by sponsoring a national prevention and education campaign.[17]

The Reagan administration faced considerable pressure from Democrats in Congress to wage a more robust war on drugs on both the law enforcement and public health fronts. In fall 1981, liberals on the House Select Committee on Narcotics Abuse and Control excoriated Carlton Turner at a hearing designed to expose the White House's budget cuts and failure to devise a comprehensive drug strategy. Leo Zeferetti, the Brooklyn committee chair, announced that "apparently this administration does not place a high priority on the serious problem of drug abuse and drug trafficking threatening our nation." He demanded more aggressive interdiction, additional funding for the private-sector drug prevention campaign and parent power groups, and increased efforts to publicize the "harmfulness of marijuana." Charles Rangel, the tough-on-drugs Democrat from Harlem, lamented the explosion of street crime by narcotic addicts and singled out heroin for "destroying a substantial part of the population" in his district. After Turner's presentation, which focused as usual on the white crisis of teenage marijuana use and the parent power solution, Rangel angrily responded that the Republican answer to mass unemployment and heroin addiction among Black youth in the inner city was "to persuade them, either spiritually or through a volunteer effort, that they don't need drugs."[18] That accurately summarized the White House's suburban-oriented drug policy blueprint, which explicitly prioritized the public health campaign against teenage use of marijuana and alcohol because they represented "two of the most common drugs of introduction into the drug culture." The NFP leadership could have drafted Turner's strategy blueprint, which condemned "pro-drug" messages in popular culture and portrayed "the family unit" and "reverse peer pressure" as key pillars of the war on drugs. In announcing the prevention initiative, President Reagan likewise credited the parents' movement for charting the path forward by branding "drugs such as marijuana exactly for what they are—dangerous, and particularly to school-age youth."[19]

The Reagan administration did not formally unveil its comprehensive drug policy until fall 1982, but the president previewed the strategy in a major anticrime speech to a law enforcement convention a year earlier. When talking about crime in the streets, Reagan deployed the racialized specters of the narcotics-addicted "predator" and the implicitly urban "drug pusher" and promised tough punishment for the villains who "prey on the innocent." The most striking feature of this law-and-order rhetoric involved its deep continuities with the decades-long, overlapping liberal and conservative agendas in the war on drugs. The addict-predator-pusher discourse also differed little from that employed by Democratic critics in Congress, with the significant exception of Reagan's distinct inattention to public health funding for urban constituents and heroin abusers. Among other tough-on-drugs measures, the president called for higher mandatory sentences for traffickers, stepped-up interdiction overseas and at the border, and the deployment of the U.S. military in domestic antitrafficking efforts. Then Reagan's tone shifted as he praised the NFP and promised the federal government's full support for its demand-side approach to "the customers," victims to be targeted by prevention programs rather than law enforcement.[20] The House Select Committee on Narcotics remained unimpressed, bluntly declaring in its 1981 report: "Despite the Administration's strong rhetoric concerning drug abuse and drug trafficking, there is little evidence at this time of an equally strong commitment within the Administration to make these issues high national priorities." The House Democrats urged President Reagan to "declare war on drugs" through a formal message to Congress and even contrasted the White House's passive approach with the vigorous work of the National Federation of Parents, yet more evidence that the organization's defense of the young white middle-class victim in the recreational market transcended partisan politics, despite the suburban coalition's transparent lack of concern for either heroin addiction or urban social welfare.[21]

The launch of Nancy Reagan's drug-free youth campaign formalized the Republican administration's alliance with the parent power movement. In April 1981, when the NFP gathered in Atlanta for its first anniversary, Nancy Reagan sent a message praising the organization for showing that "parents who care can make a difference." This communiqué was part of a developing White House plan to associate the first lady with the "burgeoning parents' movement" by making her the public face of the prevention campaign to reverse the "epidemic use of drugs and alcohol among children and adolescents." The project reflected a convergence of various agendas: the traditional expectation that each first lady in the modern era would promote a particular cause, Nancy Reagan's genuine concern about the youth drug crisis, and a public relations strategy to counter her image as an out-of-touch elitist with a designer wardrobe and rich Hollywood friends. The campaign would work with parents' groups, recruit celebrities to deliver the drug-free message, and mobilize a "Children's Crusade" of positive peer pressure. The main goal would be to shift public attitudes, because "most people believe marijuana is harmless, and most parents are grateful if their children 'only' drink." Nancy would emphasize that smoking pot created the "space out" effect of apathy and withdrawal, while the alcohol component would align with the Mothers Against Drunk Driving crusade.[22] Marijuana and alcohol should be the first lady's primary focus because they were "the two major starter drugs," as Carlton Turner articulated the gateway philosophy in internal planning memos, a strategy of "prevention before the young person graduates to heroin." Nancy Reagan's antidrug crusade represented a "golden opportunity to create a climate where young people begin to realize there is no 'soft' drug and you must pay a price for drug use." In one of her initial events, the first lady visited a rehab facility in suburban Maryland and asked narcotics addicts if they had started with pot before criticizing popular culture for spreading the myth of harmless marijuana.[23]

The orchestrated rollout of Nancy Reagan's antidrug campaign began in November 1981 when she held a White House meeting with Bill Barton and other NFP leaders (the official "Just Say No" slogan did not arrive until 1985). "We're in danger," she told the gathering, "of losing our whole next generation"—repeating back a diagnosis taken directly from their own publications, which the White House carefully gathered and archived. The first lady labeled the drug crisis the "most democratic illness there is," a sympathetic reference to the white upper-middle-class backgrounds of the NFP visitors, before reaffirming their motto that "parents are the answer." The accompanying White House press materials portrayed Nancy as the administration's "newest recruit" in its war on drugs and a committed ally for the one thousand parents' groups mobilized around the nation. "As parents, we all know it's great to say yes, but there are times you have to say no," the first lady, also a mother of two children in their twenties, informed American families. "Children need and want discipline and supervision because that means love. . . . It will strengthen the family and, in turn, the country." Her staff recommended that she project the image of a "concerned mother" during public appearances and media interviews—alarmed about the adolescent drug crisis and hopeful about the future, all with the "non-blaming attitude" at the center of the NFP/PRIDE philosophy. At the same time, the first lady should praise the parents' movement for rejecting the permissive ethos of the 1960s and 1970s, the view that "maybe alcohol and marijuana weren't bad for our kids, that we needed to be less of a disciplinarian and more of a friend." Parents constituted "the first line of defense" in the war on drug and alcohol abuse, she emphasized to the daytime ABC-TV audience of *Good Morning, America*. "This battle will really be won at the grassroots level in every community in this country." Nancy Reagan then promised that if worried parents wrote to her at the White House, her staff would connect them with a local NFP affiliate to join the drug-free crusade.[24]

During the first half of 1982, the first lady visited more than a dozen treatment centers and local groups, including the Straight, Inc., program in Florida and the Dallas headquarters of Texas War on Drugs, a parent power movement headed by business executive H. Ross Perot. Nancy Reagan appeared on the *Today* show with Bret Barton, the rehabilitated former pot smoker and son of the NFP president, and commiserated with nonwhite heroin addicts at several inner-city facilities. She admonished all American parents to "be tough" and wake up to the crisis, because drug addiction "cuts across economic and racial lines." She told the national PTA conference an Anslinger-era "reefer madness" story about a teenage boy who tried marijuana and ended up hospitalized after a violent paranoid outburst, and she warned a gathering of governors' wives that "the enemy is drugs and it is taking captive millions of our children, and even killing them." The first lady often informed audiences that mothers would win the war on drugs because "a woman is like a tea bag. You never know her strength until she is in hot water."[25] In April, Nancy Reagan attended the annual PRIDE conference in Atlanta, the epicenter of the parents' movement, accompanied by drug policy advisor Carlton Turner and NIDA director William Pollin. She praised the mostly white audience for their crusade to rescue innocent victims of marijuana and alcohol abuse, the "frightening number of drug orphans lost to themselves and their families." In a subsequent speech to the Advertising Council, she related the PRIDE conference's critique of the "drugs are cool" messages of pop culture—Hollywood movies, TV comedies, rock lyrics that "shout at kids to get high and get stoned," paraphernalia stores that "cater to kids as surely as candy stores once did." Assessing the flurry of events, the staff director of the first lady's campaign acknowledged that "we have talked the concept of parent groups almost to death" and so the time had come for real executive branch action, because thus far "Mrs. Reagan has been at the forefront of the Administration's drug strategy."[26]

In March 1982, the first lady hosted a White House conference on "Drug Use and the Family" that revealed how completely the agenda of PRIDE and the NFP had moved to the center of national policy. The program officially kicked off an adolescent drug and alcohol prevention campaign sponsored by ACTION, the federal government's agency to coordinate private-sector volunteerism, which developed a close relationship with the parents' movement as part of the Reagan administration's war on drugs. National media coverage included a photograph of Nancy Reagan sitting next to Marsha Keith Schuchard and Bill Barton (fig. 7.3), confirmation that the PRIDE/NFP leadership had secured an even greater degree of White House access than its already impressive inroads during the Carter era. Nancy opened proceedings by contrasting the "age of innocence" that marked her own youth to the "age of

FIGURE 7.3. The Reagan White House hosts the leaders of the National Federation of Parents for Drug-Free Youth at a "Drug Use and the Family" conference, March 22, 1982. First Lady Nancy Reagan, whose recently launched initiative sought to capitalize on the group's mission, is joined on the stage by PRIDE cofounder Marsha Keith Schuchard (*left*) and NFP president Bill Barton (*center*). (AP Photo / Charles Tasnadi.)

vicious drugs" in modern America, where marijuana transformed happy and smart children into "listless burnt out remains of their former selves." Barton portrayed the NFP, now claiming nearly three thousand local affiliates, as the nonpartisan political representative of Middle America—"concerned about our kids and concerned about our country." Schuchard lauded parent power as the antidote to the media's glamorization of illegal drugs and the "tremendous crushing peer pressure on our children," while her neighbor Sue Rusche delivered a briefing on the evils of the paraphernalia industry. H. Ross Perot, director of Texas War on Drugs, focused on the enormous profits in the illegal drug market, part of a pitch for donations from the corporate executives in attendance, including pharmaceutical executives sensing a good opportunity to distract attention from the inconvenient truth that their products were far more deadly and addictive than marijuana (the NFP received $50,000 in donations from the event). Carlton Turner promised that the White House was all-in for the zero-tolerance approach that renounced the distinction between hard and soft drugs and permissive rhetoric such as "recreational use of drugs, responsible use of drugs."[27]

To reach the youth audience, ACTION introduced Melissa Gilbert, the teenage star of NBC's traditional family values show *Little House on the Prairie*, as the celebrity spokesperson for the new national prevention campaign. The drug-free lifestyle that once seemed square was becoming cool again, Gilbert announced, because "reverse peer pressure" was rapidly shifting the youth culture in America. "I'm not going to do what I don't want to do. I just say 'no,'" she explained. "I find my friends eventually come around. . . . They respect me for my position." (In her 2009 memoir, Gilbert admitted getting high on marijuana with members of Hollywood's Brat Pack soon after she started traveling the country as "America's antidrug cheerleader"). Gilbert's message particularly resonated with preteen fans such as an eleven-year-old girl from Orange County, California, who wrote Nancy Reagan to thank her for enlisting the *Little House on the Prairie* star. "I'm almost afraid to be a teenager now," the youngster lamented, "because I know that if you're not on drugs other drug-addicted teenagers will try to get me on drugs." Another eleven-year-old girl from Illinois wrote the first lady that "a lot of people do party a lot" in her town, but "I hope that when I get into high school I will not be tempted to use drugs." And from the San Francisco Bay Area, a fifteen-year-old sent a poem to President Reagan to capture her lonely stand against the peer pressure to smoke pot: "My name is Kelley and I am in my teens/At my school drugs are as popular as jeans/Everybody does it or so I am told/ . . . I am not into drugs and never will be/Why is it that nobody else can see/How they are ruining their lives by turning-on to pot." The young correspondent concluded: "I am writing to you for all of those people who do not/All of those who are hooked on pot/If only you could help to stop drug solicitation/Then I think that this would be a much better nation!"[28]

Through ACTION, the Reagan White House helped expand the parents' movement while simultaneously advancing the principles of voluntarism and federally subsidized privatization central to its broader strategy of conservative governance. The administration asserted that the success of grassroots antidrug groups revealed that the private sector was "almost invariably far more efficient than government in running social programs." As a public-private partnership, ACTION channeled significant federal funds to PRIDE, the NFP, DeKalb Families in Action (to distribute Rusche's manual on how to form a parents' group), and other nongovernmental organizations committed to the antimarijuana and zero-tolerance platform. The agency awarded twenty seed grants to help transform local groups into statewide networks, including Californians for Drug-Free Youth, Florida Informed Parents, and NFP affiliates in Ohio, Colorado, and Virginia. According to Carlton Turner, this enabled the administration to circumvent public health professionals and educators at the state and local levels who did not take unequivocal, abstinence-only stands against adolescent drug and alcohol use. As with abstinence-only sex education, this ideological project shifted federal funding away from "harm reduction" and "responsible use" approaches that treated students as rational actors, avoided scare tactics, and had much higher success rates than zero-tolerance programs. ACTION director Thomas Pauken, a conservative Republican from Texas, stated that the nonnegotiable principles of drug prevention included parents' groups as the first line of defense, repudiation of "the lie" that marijuana or any other drug was "soft," and agreement that "there can be *no* 'responsible use' of illegal drugs by youth."[29] Through ACTION's "Good News Report," Pauken highlighted NFP activists such as Otto Moulton, who fought against "purveyors of marijuana" in metropolitan Boston, and circulated gateway stories about white teenagers from upscale suburbs who experimented with pot and ended up addicted to cocaine before being saved by interventionist parents and institutionalization in private drug treatment centers.[30]

By the early 1980s, cocaine addiction had dislodged heroin as the most hyped and feared fate for white middle-class youth who succumbed to the marijuana-gateway process, a symbolic framework based not on scientific data but on the political demands of the parents' movement and its government allies. Cocaine in powder form was a stimulant and an expensive "party drug" used primarily by upscale white Americans, classified as nonaddictive by mainstream medical research, and a low priority for street-level law enforcement because of the racial and class makeup of its consumer demographic. Its chemical properties were completely different from heroin, a "ghetto" drug that few white suburban youth ever encountered or desired, whereas cocaine had a glamorous reputation and was not a big leap for affluent high school students in communities where legal and illicit stimulant drugs circulated widely. By 1982, one-sixth of American high school seniors had taken cocaine, compared to only 1 percent who had tried heroin. The national media portrayed cocaine as the "all-American drug" and a "middle class high . . . unchecked by law enforcement" but also began warning of the risks of psychological dependence for white professionals and students "who would never remotely think of themselves as criminals." The Reagan White House, urged on by the NFP, worked closely with network television to transform cocaine's reputation through programs such as NBC's "Pleasure Drugs—The Great American High," which aired in April 1982. The prime-time exposé claimed that cocaine was far more dangerous than realized by the estimated twenty million Americans ("not slum dwellers") who had snorted the glamour drug, illustrated anecdotally by a nineteen-year-old white female and recreational weekend partier who allegedly took a fatal overdose and a white stockbroker who lost his family after he became psychologically dependent. NBC's follow-up, "Cocaine: One Man's Poison" (1983), was sheer propaganda about how the drug destroyed a white suburban California family by turning the father into a violent raging addict.[31]

The Reagan administration's embrace of the priorities of the suburban antimarijuana movement drew substantial criticism from inner-city activists and public health professionals long focused on the heroin threat. In the lead-up to the 1982 White House conference featuring the National Federation of Parents, the African American director of a DC addiction treatment center lambasted ACTION and Nancy Reagan's office for a segregationist strategy "aimed at the 'white' drug problem only." "Multiracial problems will take multiracial solutions," Mahmoud Baptiste of the Hurricane House declared. "There are now and have been Blacks involved in a continued war against drug abuse and the deterioration of family and community." When Black community groups questioned whether the White House even understood the urban drug crisis, Carlton Turner responded: "We're aware of it. We don't know the solution. I've asked all my black friends for any possible solution they think will work." Later in 1982, an ACTION-sponsored conference to launch the Colorado branch of the NFP drew similar charges that the white-dominated event ignored minority groups. Thomas Pauken denied accusations of racial insensitivity and emphasized the Reagan administration's color-blind commitment to fight drug abuse "as a problem that afflicts young people of all socioeconomic backgrounds, including black, Hispanic, and white youth." ACTION then tried to organize parent power groups in low-income and nonwhite urban neighborhoods—a strategy to reproduce the zero-tolerance suburban movement rather than work through existing, underfunded drug treatment centers and community organizations. Turner conceded the "hard feelings toward the Administration" from addiction treatment professionals who opposed its public health budget cuts and reallocation of federal funds to NFP amateurs. In Congress, Representative Charles Rangel leveled especially vocal criticism against the administration for slashing resources for treatment centers in New York City and completely failing to stem the flood of heroin and cocaine across the border.[32]

In mid-1982, Reagan issued an executive order placing Carlton Turner in charge of interagency oversight for all domestic and international policies in the federal war on drugs. The president pledged to "stop the flow of drugs into this country," lauded the parent power movement, and declared that "we can win." While the Justice and State Departments exercised considerable autonomy on the enforcement and interdiction fronts, Turner's office supervised the public health side and handled political communications. During 1982 and 1983, Turner met frequently with NFP leaders and consulted them on a broad range of issues, from vetting NIDA's prevention literature to interdiction efforts in the Caribbean. To buttress the parents' movement, the administration directed Surgeon General C. Everett Koop to issue a formal report on the severe health hazards of marijuana for teenagers, especially the "amotivational syndrome" of listlessness, falling grades, and generational conflict within the family.[33] The White House ODAP files during this period reveal an overwhelming focus on stopping the overseas marijuana supply, instead of prioritizing heroin or cocaine, even in South Florida. As part of this mission, the DEA expanded marijuana eradication programs from seven to forty states and escalated its efforts to halt domestic cultivation in the interior. Carlton Turner successfully pushed for congressional repeal of the 1978 prohibition on U.S. foreign aid for spraying paraquat on marijuana crops abroad, arguing that the health risks of youth pot smoking justified use of the herbicide.[34] The NFP lobbied Congress for all of the Reagan administration's major interdiction measures, including lifting the paraquat ban, increased penalties for marijuana traffickers, and the controversial Posse Comitatus amendment to allow military participation in domestic drug enforcement. In laying out the White House strategy, Turner envisioned such rapid progress against both the supply and demand of marijuana that, by the fall of 1983, Reagan's war on drugs would constitute "a major accomplishment and a possible campaign theme."[35]

Marijuana and Alcohol: The Gateway Drugs

In late 1982, when President Reagan officially launched his administration's war on drugs, the priorities of the suburban parent power movement and especially the focus on marijuana remained at center stage. In a national radio address on October 2, the president began by asking his wife Nancy to report on her trips to visit parents' groups around the country. The first lady painted a dystopian portrait of family crisis in Middle America, where "lying replaces trust, hate replaces love," parents were clueless or felt powerless to intervene, once smart and extroverted teenagers turned into burnouts and often wound up dead. But there was hope for the future, thanks to the dedication and rapid growth of the parents' movement. Ronald Reagan then took over and pledged "to win the war on drugs" by combining the zero-tolerance prevention and treatment approach with crime control and border interdiction. "We've taken down the surrender flag," Reagan declared, "and run up the battle flag." He claimed that the South Florida initiative had seized large quantities of marijuana and cocaine and targeted the "drug pushers who were terrorizing Florida's citizens." Reagan contrasted this border control strategy with the previous administration's complacency, even though the South Florida program began under Carter. On the supply side, the White House pledged increased interdiction abroad and stepped-up domestic law enforcement, including a crackdown on homegrown marijuana cultivation. On the demand side, the administration said almost nothing about the primarily urban issue of heroin addiction but instead singled out the "bogus glamour" surrounding the marijuana subculture and pledged "to let our nation's kids know the truth" about its dangers. In addition to Nancy's alliance with the parents' movement, the White House championed MADD's grassroots campaign against drinking and driving (covered below), another indication of how directly the suburban crusade against marijuana and alcohol use among teenagers shaped Reagan's initial drug war.[36]

Leading Democrats in Congress continued to attack the Reagan administration for failing to dedicate adequate resources to the national war on drugs. In response to the radio address, Senator Joseph Biden of Delaware charged the administration with a lackluster strategy for fighting street crime by predatory addicts and an "insufficient emphasis on heading off illegal drugs before they reach our shores." Biden, the head of the Senate Democratic Task Force on Crime, told a convention of police chiefs that Reagan's budget policies meant that "young and old, black and white, rich and poor will find themselves increasingly unable to go about their daily lives free from fear." While Reagan officials talked about interdiction policies in the context of stopping elementary school children from trying marijuana and "beautiful people" from snorting cocaine, Biden and other Democrats highlighted heroin overdoses and violent narcotics-related crime in urban centers.[37] In December, Congress overwhelmingly approved a legislative package introduced by Biden that increased mandatory-minimum penalties for heroin traffickers and centralized federal drug policies under a cabinet-level "drug czar." Reagan vetoed the bill because of the drug czar provision, arguing that it would complicate the federal bureaucracy and undermine existing initiatives. During 1983, the House

Select Committee on Narcotics Abuse and Control escalated its criticism of the administration's policies in the war on drugs and demanded a comprehensive crackdown on pushers. Carlton Turner testified about the progress of the prevention campaign thanks to parents' groups, the first lady, and corporate sponsors. Charles Rangel emphasized the flood of heroin into the big cities, the glut of cocaine on the market, no reduction of the domestic marijuana crop, long waitlists for urban treatment programs, and surging crime rates because of underfunded law enforcement. "In short," Rangel concluded, "we appear to be losing the battle against drug abuse on nearly all fronts."[38]

One week after the Reagan administration relaunched the federal war on drugs, the National Federation of Parents held its 1982 national conference in Arlington, Virginia. The group's new president, Mary Jacobson of Omaha, reflected the organization's geographic expansion, with leaders from California and New York particularly well represented on its board of directors. The meeting also premiered the NFP's strikingly dystopian logo, a fraying American flag alongside the theme "Drugs and Youth: An American Crisis." Despite this image of teenage dysfunction and national decline, the NFP celebrated its substantial accomplishments in a few short years, including passage of antiparaphernalia laws in thirty-one states and the broader transformation of national attitudes about adolescent use of drugs and alcohol. Nancy Reagan, recently named the NFP's honorary chair, greeted the delegates with a $40,000 donation from the National Football League and a warning that "the victims are getting younger all the time." The first lady expressed nostalgia for the innocent days of her youth, when girls wore saddle oxfords and hadn't even heard of drugs, until the disruptions of the 1960s brought the scourge "into every segment of society—regardless of economics or race or education." She praised the parents' movement for removing the stigma that mothers and fathers once felt if a child developed a drug problem and for showing the professional experts that all illegal drugs were dangerous—whether hard or soft, including marijuana and alcohol. Carlton Turner reinforced this message by telling the conference that the Reagan administration would target illegal teenage drinking just as vigorously as pot smoking. The NFP leadership proclaimed that the adolescent drug epidemic represented "the single most uniting issue this nation has ever seen. . . . Drug involvement for children is unacceptable to parents across this nation, regardless of ethnic, economic or religious background—there is no division."[39]

Starting in 1982, the Atlanta-based PRIDE network collaborated with the Gannett Corporation to produce a series of "Epidemic" documentaries that urged American parents to take back their families and neighborhoods from the illegal drug and alcohol subculture. The first installment, *Epidemic! Kids, Drugs, and Alcohol* (1982), highlighted the health dangers of marijuana and the scourge of teenage drunk driving and then blamed popular culture for glamorizing illegal drug and alcohol use. The sequel, *Epidemic: America Fights Back* (1983), adopted a much more hopeful perspective, with a framing device that anticipated Reagan's "Morning in America" message of national renewal during the 1984 presidential election. In the opening scene, soothing music accompanies a sunrise and voiceover message that "there is a change coming over our nation, a change sweeping over the landscape of America, . . . but it comes hard, with pain and struggle, a war fought by the mothers and fathers, teachers, kids, community leaders of this country, and some have died, others are injured, for years the war will continue." With a jarring shift to pulsating rock music, images of white teenagers smoking joints and chugging beer flash across the screen. A businessman asserts that addiction to drugs and alcohol costs the U.S. economy $100 billion a year. PRIDE's Thomas Gleaton explains that marijuana use among teenagers had decreased in recent years but remains at epidemic levels, while consumption of alcohol and cocaine continues to escalate. A pretty, innocent-looking white girl explains that "practically everyone is drinking; I mean, I don't really know anyone that's not," followed by a snapshot of a dead teenager in a wrecked car. The reporter-narrator then says that this program is not just another tragic accounting but instead a hopeful story of ordinary parents mobilizing to defeat the enemy: "an epidemic of drug and alcohol abuse, the worst of any nation of the western world, of any time in our history."[40]

A lengthy segment of *Epidemic: America Fights Back* featured Naples Informed Parents, the antimarijuana movement started five years earlier by future NFP president Bill Barton and his wife Pat. From a suburban living room, a group of upper-middle-class white adults relates the lessons learned: collective parent power is essential because "you can be a good parent and it can happen to you"; your teenage children might rebel against strict supervision but will come to appreciate it in the end. The documentary portrays this affluent and all-white slice of Naples as a community resurrected, with images of happy families walking together down the sidewalk and teenagers who believe, in Bret Barton's words, "it's not cool to do drugs; who wants to be a burnout?" After this inspirational feature, the program visits a drug prevention event at an interracial public school in Tampa and a gathering of middle-class Black parents holding a neighborhood meeting with their children. These scenes emphasize that the parents' movement has become a racially diverse phenomenon, an expansion of the standard political and cultural frame of recreational teenage drug use as a white upper-middle-class suburban crisis. The inclusion of these scenes also reflected the well-intentioned, if historically uninformed and somewhat condescending, efforts of the NFP, which boasted in 1983 of having "organized minority communities" to join its drug-free crusade. At the end, the cameras shift to unsupervised youth wandering the streets of West Dallas, a high-poverty area of Black and Hispanic residents, drawing a clear contrast between the absence of parent power in this urban slum and the energized middle-class neighborhoods that are turning the drug crisis around. Thomas Gleaton has the last word, juxtaposed with an over-the-top image of a large group of white middle-class slacker-stoners smoking enormous (Cheech and Chong–sized) joints. "It's going to be a long war," the PRIDE director acknowledges, "and we're going to lose a lot of kids before we get there," but the rise of parent power meant that the fight could be won.[41]

The Reagan administration and its allies in the parents' movement sought to counter the "pro-drug" messages of popular culture by mobilizing corporations and media institutions behind a "massive assault . . . to truly stun America into action," in the words of NFP president Mary Jacobson. In spring 1983, Carlton Turner's office launched the "White House-Private Sector Drug Abuse Awareness Program," an initiative that deliberately sidelined NIDA's public health experts to promote a business-funded drug education curriculum subject to NFP oversight.[42] The NFP leadership returned to the White House for the launch of Pharmacists Against Drug Abuse, sponsored by McNeil Pharmaceutical to discourage experimentation with the "gateway drugs" of alcohol, marijuana, and cocaine. (This corporate strategy to obscure the widespread abuse of prescription medication almost backfired when McNeil's CEO made the inopportune comment that by reducing marijuana use, "we can force kids back into the medicine cabinet.") Celebrity spokesperson Michael Landon, who played Melissa Gilbert's father on *Little House on the Prairie,* emphasized his real-life daughter's narrow escape from addiction during the era before parents realized the harmfulness of so-called recreational drugs. Network television also advanced the White House mission to "encourage the mass media to convey the truth about drug use and 'deglamorize' the drug culture." In March, Nancy Reagan appeared on the popular NBC sitcom *Diff'rent Strokes* in an episode where Arnold (Gary Coleman), a Black kid who had escaped the dangers of Harlem thanks to a millionaire benefactor, goes undercover to expose a white "drug pusher" classmate at his Manhattan elementary school. The principal and parents don't want to admit there is a preteen drug crisis, but the first lady saves the day by coaxing several students to admit that they had experimented. The principal promises to call the police next time, and Arnold's father says, in the takeaway for America, "I think we should all open our eyes a little wider" and make sure "all the parents know what's going on."[43]

The Chemical People, the centerpiece of the White House drug prevention campaign, aired on PBS in November 1983. The National Federation of Parents cosponsored the production and mobilized its supporters to watch the two-part series at "town meetings" held throughout the nation. The program, developed by the WQED affiliate in Pittsburgh, promised an assault on the "wall of denial" and "not in our town" illusions of so many communities, followed by the solution of forming an NFP-affiliated parents' group. The NFP emphasized the ecumenical and nonpartisan nature of the mission, with participation "not limited by race, age, religion, socioeconomic class, or political persuasion." The organization also praised the wonderful turnaround of the mass media, "where drugs are all too often glamorized," now conveying its messages of parent power and the inherent harmfulness of marijuana and alcohol for American youth. Behind the scenes, NFP leaders placed considerable pressure on the PBS team to remove any suggestion that "use is not necessarily abuse," succeeded in forcing many changes to the initial draft, and demanded that the accompanying guidebook label cocaine a highly addictive drug, contrary to scientific research (they compromised on "psychological dependence"). At the White House briefing to announce the *Chemical People* initiative, Carlton Turner explained that marijuana "helps introduce kids to the drug habit" and labeled alcohol the second most important "gateway drug." He also charged the news media and the scientific community with failing to communicate the health dangers of marijuana to the American public, from memory damage and reproductive risk to loss of "motivation to study, to work, and to get along with their families and friends." The rapid growth and national scope of the parents' movement demonstrated that "the mood of the country has changed," Turner proclaimed. "People want action." The Reagan administration's goal "is to create a drug free generation."[44]

The agenda of *The Chemical People*, in line with the broader NFP-White House adolescent drug campaign, aimed to generate a collective moral panic among parents of teenage and preteen children. Nancy Reagan, the program host, introduces teenage drug and alcohol abuse as an "urgent community problem that crosses all boundaries, rich and poor, educated and uneducated, black, white, brown, no one is immune." Speaking as a parent, she empathizes about "how difficult it is to face a painful truth about your children. It's much easier to say, this isn't happening, not in my community, not in my family, not my child." *The Chemical People* then highlights the multiracial character of the drug crisis through a cross-section of teenagers—white, Black, Latinx, Asian American—who speak of the difficulty of resisting peer pressure and the "everybody does it" culture of marijuana experimentation and drinking. A series of skits then shows a racially mixed group of parents/actors joking about their children driving drunk, asking why should they worry about a few beers or an occasional joint because "kids will be kids," and explaining that they don't have the time or inclination to watch over teenagers all day long. *The Chemical People* instructs such parents to abandon the state of denial and culture of permissiveness and, in effect, to panic. They should follow the example set by Nancy, who says she is "scared to death for our children." According to ODAP's Carlton Turner, "One word summarizes our drug and alcohol problem: epidemic." Robert Kramer, a suburban Maryland politician and NFP leader, warns of the serious "psychological damage" for millions of pot-smoking and binge-drinking youth who were "18 going on 15, or 23 going on 16, in terms of their emotional, social, and intellectual development." Television actors Michael Landon of *Little House on the Prairie* and Bruce Weitz of *Hill Street Blues* also make appearances to emphasize the need for community mobilization before more children succumbed to the drug culture, risking not just "amotivational syndrome" but also addiction and death.[45]

The PBS–White House–NFP collaboration resurrected marijuana-gateway and dope-pusher tropes that public health experts had largely purged from the drug education curriculum by the mid-1970s. The target audience of *The Chemical People* appeared to be young parents of elementary and middle-school students who had not yet been tempted by drugs, parents who presumably did not know very much about actual social practices among teenagers and could be mobilized to join a preemptive crusade of antipermissiveness and zero tolerance. Several real-life teenagers featured in the program state that they are addicted to pot, and a young white boy reports, "I wasn't satisfied with just marijuana, you know, and I moved up" to whisky, then LSD, and finally heroin. A cute white girl explains that she first smoked marijuana because of peer pressure and soon ended up a twelve-year-old addict-prostitute on the Chicago streets, under the control of her supplier-pimp. The program even features a skit involving an older teenage pusher named "Magic Bill" who pulls up outside a school and hands out free samples to entice a group of younger kids to buy marijuana, liquor, speed, and cocaine. For more discerning audiences, the "Magic Bill" scene would probably have come across as even more implausible and absurd than the pusher-gateway educational films that American high school students had laughed out of the classroom in the late 1960s and early 1970s. The runaway daughter and heroin-gateway anecdotes did presumably involve actual teenagers and tapped into suburban loss-of-innocence narratives with a long history in American drug-war mobilization, but most prevention specialists believed that such scare tactics backfired because recreational pot smokers had firsthand knowledge that marijuana was highly unlikely to trigger such outcomes. *The Chemical People* also warned that drug use was causing many adolescents to consider or attempt suicide, potentially dangerous misinformation given the much more scientifically credible scenario that depressed and unstable teenagers were self-medicating with alcohol and marijuana.[46]

The Chemical People's dystopian, panic-oriented message that "it could happen to anyone, anywhere" addressed mothers and fathers who presumably did not need to be convinced that heroin addiction, prostitution, and death were common outcomes to become alarmed that the worst might be possible. This emotional appeal accompanied dire warnings about an epidemic of teenage alcoholism and drunk driving and pseudo-scientific claims that smoking marijuana frequently produced psychological dysfunction, emotional dependence that bordered on addiction, and "amotivational syndrome." There was no mention that even the small subset of experts who endorsed these controversial findings acknowledged that they mainly affected a small fraction of chronic pot smokers. The second installment of the PBS program, *The Chemical People: Community Answers*, urged all American adults to join or start a neighborhood parent power group as part of the nationwide crusade. An ideal parent-activist, a white mother with an eight-year-old and a five-year-old, explains that she became involved to help solve the crisis before her children entered junior high. Another, a pregnant woman with a one-year-old, exclaims that "like a lot of you I'm concerned, and I'm scared" about the future. Baseball star Willie Stargell appears to urge grandparents and retirees, who have plenty of time on their hands, to sign up in order to make the world safer for the younger generation. Nancy Reagan returns to endorse abstinence-only drug education starting in elementary school, followed by a scene from a multiracial third-grade classroom where students wearing "Proud to Be Drug Free" buttons are learning about peer pressure and slang terms for marijuana. "Our kids are worth fighting for," an upbeat suburban mom summarizes, and they need help rather than punishment—from parents, teachers, doctors, coaches, and drug-free friends.[47]

The Chemical People: Community Answers advocated mandatory drug treatment for any youth caught with marijuana or alcohol, an authoritarian approach that resurrected the coercive public health initiatives of the late 1960s/early 1970s and went well beyond the initial parent power collaboration with the Carter White House. In keeping with the Reagan administration's formal position that there were no "soft" or "recreational" drugs, the program portrayed numerous teenage "addicts" who credit residential rehabilitation centers for putting their lives back on track. In a restoration of suburban utopia, one white middle-class female and former alcoholic expresses gratitude that now she can "get married and have kids and live a real normal life," while another ex-pot smoker exclaims that she is so excited to go to prom. A white high school student from suburban Minnesota relates that she considered herself a weekend social drinker but, after falling grades and two drunken episodes, her mother forced her into an abstinence-based treatment center for alcoholics that set her straight. The segment concludes with the daughter riding her bicycle down a path in an idyllic suburban setting, followed by praise for the mother for institutionalizing her child before events spiraled out of control—glossing over the crucial question of whether the daughter was actually an alcoholic or just a typical middle-class social drinker and weekend partier. Another white mother says she became worried when her teenage son stopped hanging out with family and stayed in his bedroom a lot—a behavior pattern common among adolescents—but then she realized he was a marijuana addict who needed professional help. To create an effective antidrug movement, according to another local parent-activist, start "fantasizing about what you would like to see if you could have a perfect community." *Community Answers* concludes with the injunction: "Take a long close look at ourselves. Are we the best parents and neighbors we can be? Do we really know just what our kids are doing? And do our kids really know just how we feel about their use of drugs?"[48]

The Chemical People succeeded in focusing significant public attention on the issue of teenage drug and alcohol use, with parents and students gathering to watch and discuss the program at more than ten thousand town meetings throughout the country. In California, an organizing blitz by the NFP's statewide affiliate resulted in more than one thousand community forums, including fifteen thousand people in eighty-six public school auditoriums in Orange County alone. The local PBS station publicized the event with data showing the skyrocketing arrests of adolescent drunk drivers and the (unverified) claim that thirty thousand teenage alcoholics lived in the suburban county. In the upscale suburb of Huntington Beach (95% white, 1% Black), parents acknowledged that "no family is immune" when confronted with evidence that 89 percent of local students drank alcohol, 57 percent had smoked pot, and 23 percent had used cocaine. More than half of older teenagers, according to school figures, had attended a house party where a parent provided the alcohol. "Everyone thinks it's a problem somewhere else, but, oh no, not here," one Huntington Beach resident explained. "It's supposed to be in downtown L.A. or the ghetto, anywhere but here." At a gathering in University City (93% white, 0.5% Black), an upscale residential area in San Diego, mothers of middle schoolers responded that the *Chemical People* message on teenage marijuana and alcohol use was "really startling" and had left them "shocked and scared." High school students in the panel discussion were less surprised and more composed, explaining that "getting stoned, drunk or whatever makes everything you do just a little more fun" and "it is the normal, accepted thing around here for a kid to get high, every day, any way." Parents and teenagers alike did criticize the "Magic Bill" pusher skit as "unconvincing, unrealistic, and rather silly," according to a journalist in attendance. The injunction to take action to counter the peer pressure culture proved more compelling, as more than forty parents' groups promptly formed in San Diego County alone.[49]

In a powerful feedback loop, the federal zero-tolerance campaign initially inspired by a small network of grassroots "parent power" activists mobilized a much larger white suburban constituency behind the national war on drugs. The producers claimed that *The Chemical People* sparked thousands of new parents' groups and civic task forces, and PBS also provided an educational guide for teachers and community organizations. "Young people are wary of scare tactics," the manual advised, without irony; "they resent and are turned off by this approach." The guidebook refuted teenagers' "false belief that they can obtain some kind of higher awareness through a drug induced altered state," recommended scared-straight class field trips to drug rehab centers, and proposed the positive alternative of "getting high on life." Local parents' groups responded to *The Chemical People* by pressing school districts to start drug and alcohol awareness education in elementary school, before it was too late. Many also embraced the contract approach, asking high school athletes to pledge to avoid illegal substances or face suspension, and circulated lists of parents who promised not to allow alcohol at house parties. In the wealthy Los Angeles suburb of Glendale (94% white, 0% Black), the parent power group launched a campaign to pressure liquor stores not to sell to minors. In suburban

Bucks County, north of Philadelphia and 96 percent white, a newly formed coalition began a grassroots drive to raise the federal drinking age to twenty-one years old. In the affluent and almost all-white Connecticut suburbs, Citizens Against Substance Abuse organized alcohol-free dances and parties for teenagers, while the New Canaan Chemical People asked parents to sign a "safe homes" pledge promising to supervise teenage gatherings and ban booze and drugs. "It isn't the children, it's us," admitted one father from suburban Los Angeles, "our whole society, the breakdown of our values and family structure. The program says it all—we live in a chemical society, we surround our children with a life style based on a great deal of acceptance about drinking and pills."[50]

The most influential, and ineffective, zero-tolerance response came from the Los Angeles Police Department, which took advantage of the opportunity provided by the NFP's nationwide campaign to wrest control of the drug education curriculum back from public health experts who had taken charge during the 1970s. The LAPD launched Project DARE (Drug Abuse Resistance Education) in fall 1983 as a partnership with the Los Angeles Unified School District that brought uniformed officers into elementary and middle-school classrooms to deliver the don't-ever-try-drugs message. The initiative was the antithesis of its late 1960s namesake, which had revolutionized the prevention curriculum through peer-to-peer methods of harm reduction that kicked out the cops, renounced scare tactics, respected individual choice, and recognized serious drug abuse as a symptom of underlying issues (see chapter 3). Police Chief Daryl Gates presented the new Project DARE as the complement to the undercover sting operations that had arrested three thousand high school campus dealers since the mid-1970s, albeit without reducing the "plague of drug abuse." This required a second law enforcement front "to inoculate the next generation," starting in fifth grade, by teaching children how to resist the overwhelming peer pressure to smoke pot and drink alcohol. The LAPD claimed that its approach avoided traditional scare tactics, despite the centrality of zero-tolerance warnings that any experimentation with a "gateway drug" could ruin your life. Project DARE targeted marijuana as the primary gateway to drug abuse and addiction, and within three years the LAPD declared that even though stopping the supply was a losing battle, the initiative had proved a great success and was the "ultimate solution to the demand problem." Project DARE spread to all fifty states during the mid-to-late 1980s, facilitated by billions in federal funding for the zero-tolerance prevention campaign, even though a large body of academic research has found its officer-in-the-classroom program to have no long-term impact on rates of illegal drug use among youth.[51]

The National Federation of Parents and the White House also collaborated on the other linchpin of the 1983 federal drug awareness campaign, a *New Teen Titans* educational comic book series for students in the fourth, fifth, and sixth grades. In line with the public-private partnership strategy, DC Comics prepared the materials and the Keebler and IBM corporations provided the funding. The New Teen Titans, seven teenage superheroes fighting evil villains throughout the universe, was the best-selling DC Comics brand at the time. The venture represented a calculated effort to redeploy popular culture, which the parents' movement blamed for glamorizing drugs, in service of positive peer pressure and the zero-tolerance agenda. A survey co-commissioned by the White House and NFP reported that 25 percent of fourth graders, and more than 50 percent of seventh graders, felt peer pressure to drink alcohol or smoke marijuana. Through the New Teen Titans, the Office of Drug Abuse Policy hoped to convince elementary schools to start the drug education curriculum several years earlier than the typical approach of beginning with the sixth or seventh grade. In the teacher's guide, Carlton Turner criticized the "responsible use" prevention curriculum that became widespread during the 1970s for "tending to encourage experimentation" by avoiding the unequivocal zero-tolerance stance now being promoted by the Reagan administration. The White House distributed more than 1 million copies of the first comic book to fourth graders in 1983, and around 5.5 million in the series by the end of Reagan's presidency. Each comic included a wall poster of the Teen Titans saying "We Want You to Be a Hero . . . Stay Drug Free!" and a "certificate of heroism" signed by Nancy Reagan for participating in the President's Drug Awareness Program. The first lady's message implored students to become warriors in "one of the most important battles the nation has ever fought. . . . Declare that you will stay drug-free. At any cost. . . . You'll be a hero—to your mother and father, family and friends, but most of all, to yourself."[52]

The White House's comic book curriculum combined the contemporary solutions of parent power and positive peer pressure with 1950s-era plotlines about innocent young victims succumbing to sinister dope pushers and the gateway consequences of marijuana and alcohol experimentation. *Plague!*, the fourth-grade comic, begins with Debbie, a cute thirteen-year-old white girl with blonde hair who tearfully confesses to being a "druggie"—since age ten, she has been hooked on marijuana, alcohol, hash, PCP, and mushrooms. Debbie started by sneaking liquor from her parents' cabinet and then began smoking pot, which made her hate her mother. Four other kids from her multiracial druggie circle share similar stories of starting with pot and ending up

FIGURE 7.4. The White House Office of Drug Abuse Policy teamed up with DC Comics, multiple corporate sponsors, and the National Federation of Parents for Drug-Free Youth to create the *New Teen Titans* educational curriculum as part of its 1983 national prevention campaign. In this scene from *Battle!*, designed for the sixth-grade classroom, a Black "addict-peddler" and the pink-haired girlfriend of the evil pusher Adam pressure the innocent white boy Teddy to smoke a marijuana joint laced with PCP.

on cocaine, PCP, and LSD. After one of the kids ("helpless victims") dies of an overdose, the Teen Titans swoop in and beat up a syndicate of older men ("drug-pushing creeps") who deliberately laced joints with PCP in order to kill their young customers (which makes no sense as a business model). They also catch some adult pushers who are passing out free cocaine samples to preteen kids (almost as implausible). The Teen Titan superheroes put Debbie into a detox center and inform her friends that if "you start experimenting you don't stop." The druggie kids and their parents reconcile through a neighborhood group and the story ends happily, with readers asked to sign a drug-free pledge. *Problem Child*, the fifth-grade version, conveys a similar message through the saga of Jesse, a blonde-haired surfer boy passing out PCP-laced joints to his friends in the schoolyard. Jesse gets marijuana and cocaine from his older brother, a heroin addict who works for a syndicate of dope pushers and sells drugs to young kids. Their weeping parents are helpless until the Teen Titans arrive to bust up the syndicate, force the brother into a treatment facility, and convince Jesse that all illegal drugs are addictive. Jesse's family joins a parent power group, and he persuades his friends to go straight in the end.[53]

Battle!, the New Teen Titans comic for middle-school students, recycled one of the most common plots of postwar educational films, the corruption of the new kid in a seemingly safe suburban town by a villainous pusher and his seductive girlfriend. A white middle-class boy named Teddy moves to Blue Valley, "a great place to grow up in," to get away from the big city and the drug addiction that almost killed him there. He meets a wholesome and pretty girl named Amy, and everything seems to be going great. But then two classmates, a Black guy and the pusher's pink-haired punk girlfriend, pressure him into smoking PCP-laced joints and snorting cocaine. Teddy abandons Amy and spirals out of control, until she devises a way to get him into a parent-child support group started by one of the Teen Titans, who informs everyone that marijuana and cocaine are "psychologically addictive." All seven Teen Titans attack the traffickers who are infiltrating Blue Valley with marijuana and cocaine, asking, "How many kids have you ruined? How many minds have you destroyed?" They rescue Teddy and his Black addict-peddler friend, who end up together in a treatment center, reconcile with their parents and good girlfriends, and realize that it is cool to be drug-free heroes.[54] The White House received many expressions of gratitude for the New Teen Titans curriculum from local school officials, although a number of districts that already provided drug education courses for younger students rejected the comic books as pedagogically unsound. The harshest criticism came from the superintendent of a suburban Boston school system who denounced the comics for their "blatant sexism, unmitigated racism, stereotypical characters and appalling violence." He asked how the White House could dare to disseminate "this pile of worthlessness" in the same month that the Reagan administration condemned the mediocrity of American public education in its *A Nation at Risk* report. Effective drug prevention required credible information presented in a positive manner, not scare tactics "so demeaning as to be counterproductive."[55]

The Chemical People and New Teen Titans emphasis on evil pushers, gateway horror stories, and coercive rehabilitation for recreational drug "addicts" showed how comprehensively the suburban parents' movement and its White House allies had transformed the federal war on drugs into a moral crusade to save innocent children. In November 1983, at a hearing of the House Select Committee on Narcotics Abuse, Carlton Turner cited both initiatives as proof that the Reagan administration was turning the tide, with thousands of parent power groups leading the way toward the ultimate goal to "eliminate drug and alcohol abuse in future generations of Americans." NIDA director William Pollin echoed the NFP's hype about cocaine addiction and explained that federal prevention efforts targeted marijuana because it was "clearly the gateway drug which determined whether young people particularly will go on to use other drugs or not." He credited the parents' movement for clarifying the health risks of pot smoking and moving American political culture away from the excesses of decriminalization. Thomas Pauken, head of the ACTION volunteer agency, likewise praised parents' groups as "the new counterculture" for their efforts to reverse the "responsible use," allegedly "pro-drug," approach that took hold in the mid-1970s. To illustrate the crisis, he told a suburban gateway story of a seventeen-year-old female from Northern Virginia who started with pot and alcohol at age thirteen, graduated to cocaine and pills, and habitually took drugs at a high school where clueless "teachers considered [her] a good kid." Pauken then touted the Reagan administration's supply-side crackdown but stated that the drug war could only be won with a demand-side focus on youth culture, assisted by Hollywood and Madison Avenue. Narcotics committee chair Charles Rangel responded that "we want to laud you and the administration for *Chemical People* and *Diff'rent Strokes*," but the supply of heroin and cocaine kept increasing, drug treatment centers remained underfunded and overwhelmed, and "we have to lock up the traffickers" as well.[56]

In fall 1984, President Reagan assessed his administration's war on drugs as a noble quest to "save a generation" and proclaimed that the "unique American spirit of voluntarism" had proved more effective than any big-government program could ever be. When Reagan talked about the supply side of the market, he sharply distinguished the "pushers" from the victims and pledged that "retribution must be swift and sure for those who decide to make a career of preying on the innocent." But "real victory will only come," he again declared, "when we take the customers away from the drugs." The president then praised the parent power movement and its corporate sponsors for replacing the "permissive attitudes" of the 1970s with the "say no to drugs" philosophy of zero tolerance.[57] The NFP's new president, Maryland activist Joyce Nalepka, celebrated Reagan's position of "'no responsible use' of drugs by children" as the basis of a nonpartisan crusade in which "everyone in our country will truly lay differences aside and pull together." Nalepka briefly addressed the critique of urban politicians such as Charles Rangel by reciting the gateway stance that had long informed the war on drugs: "marijuana must be taken seriously—or we'll never solve the heroin problem." But she mainly emphasized the quotidian concerns of white suburban parents' groups: rock music, movies, and television that glamorized drugs and alcohol; stores that sold booze to underage customers; schools that did not crack down on flagrant pot smoking; and, of course, youth peer pressure. The NFP's 1984 slogan summed it up: "Come On, America! Stick Your Neck Out for Kids and Help Stop Adolescent Drug and Alcohol Use." Watching with dismay, former Carter advisor Peter Bourne lamented this thorough redefinition of America's drug abuse crisis, especially the neglect of urban heroin addicts because of "hysteria" about marijuana experimentation by white teens, which he labeled a "smoke screen" to cover up the Reagan administration's failure to address either narcotics trafficking or genuine dependency with sufficient resources.[58]

The unsolvable problem for the parent power movement and the Reagan drug warriors remained teenagers themselves, especially the impossible criminals in the white suburbs—not the outside invasion of "pushers" and mass culture, or even the enemy within of adult "permissiveness." The zero-tolerance assault on recreational pot smoking and social drinking as the addictive gateways to ruined lives and the "amotivational syndrome" was an unwinnable war, and not only because it was based on bad science, the symbolic politics of restoring a white suburban utopia that never existed, demand-side scare tactics that had historically backfired, supply-side interdiction that had failed for decades, and the longstanding fallacious distinction between dangerous illegal drugs and therapeutic pharmaceuticals in a mood-altering society. The crusade for "drug-free youth" was unwinnable and indeed counterproductive because it treated American teenagers as depoliticized victims when most of them actually understood how the market operated, knew the difference between "responsible use" and helpless abuse, and did not consider criminal prohibition to be any more of a deterrent than their parents' generation had back in the 1960s. NIDA's annual "Monitoring the Future" surveys revealed that 57.6 percent of high school seniors in 1986 had broken the drug laws in their lifetime, compared to 64.1 percent in 1978 at the pinnacle of the "permissive" era—a slight decline, but still a substantial majority (fig. 7.5). After eight years of zero-tolerance messaging from the Carter and Reagan administrations, more than half of seniors had still smoked pot, 75 percent of them within the previous year. The upward trend in cocaine use by one-sixth of twelfth graders revealed that the gateway warnings had no impact on teenage social practices and also explains why the suburban zero-tolerance crusade had shifted away from heroin to a new demonized drug villain at last. And violation of underage drinking laws by more than 90 percent of those surveyed meant that placing alcohol alongside marijuana as a totally forbidden "gateway drug" could never work.[59]

The "responsible use" and "harm reduction" approaches to illegal teenage drug use, which many American schools (as well as so-called "permissive" parents) continued to follow, had a greater impact on adolescent norms than the zero-tolerance crusade that condemned everything short of abstinence-only

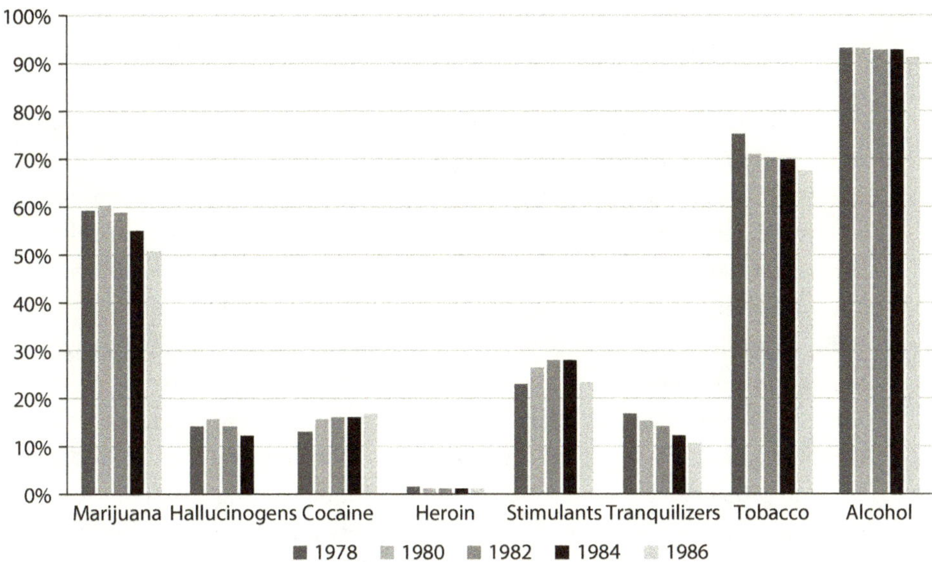

FIGURE 7.5. Drug patterns (% ever used) among U.S. high school seniors, 1978–86. Illegal drug use trended slightly downward during the 1980s, but experience with marijuana remained a majority phenomenon among high school seniors in 1986. The use of cocaine and other stimulants (amphetamines without medical authorization) continued to rise, more than two-thirds of high school seniors had smoked cigarettes, and almost all broke the underage alcohol status laws. (NIDA, *Monitoring the Future: National Survey Results on Drug Use, 1975–2006*, vol. 1.)

mandates. Most public health professionals, including many censored federal experts, recognized that collective risk assessment within the teenage subculture was not responsive to legal deterrents, threats of punishment, and hyperbolic campaigns designed to scare elementary and middle-school children and their parents. The most successful programs sought to meet adolescents on their own terms, through peer-to-peer messaging and an emphasis on how excessive drug and alcohol use could compromise their goals, taking care not to conflate social drinking and any marijuana experimentation with serious substance abuse, dependency, addiction, and destroyed lives. While the Reagan administration and NFP warnings of a mass outbreak of "amotivational syndrome" were clearly overblown, and based on racialized fears rather than medical data, most high school students understood that being stoned during class and getting drunk every afternoon was unproductive behavior. Even during the mid-to-late 1970s, more than two-thirds of seniors had expressed personal disapproval of daily marijuana use; what did change by the mid-1980s was that an equivalent number came to view being constantly high as involving "great risk" of self-harm. The number of current daily stoners also declined from 10.7 percent in 1978 to 4 percent in the class of 1986, although 15 percent of the seniors had smoked pot routinely at some point in their lives (fig. 7.6). These teenagers did not require *Chemical People*/Teen Titans–style disinformation about evil pushers and gateway-to-doom tragedies to alter their risk perception, and zero-tolerance rhetoric also did not stop a majority of students during the early-to-mid 1980s from violating marijuana prohibition laws or a supermajority from continuing to believe that occasional pot smoking was not harmful.[60]

The zero-tolerance parent power campaign against the dystopian "teenage drug culture" during the early-to-mid 1980s was ultimately a movement to restore the lost innocence of a suburban utopia by reestablishing social control over white middle-class youth. This was part of a broader, mainstream racial project to protect and defend "endangered childhood" during an era of widespread anxiety about the fate of the nuclear family unit, the vulnerability of latchkey children with mothers working and fathers gone, and the future of a capitalist society mobilizing to win the Cold War while too many of its best and brightest suburban youth were too stoned and drunk to play their expected roles. The mass diagnosis of marijuana-fueled "amotivational syndrome," which inverted cause and effect and originated in racial anxiety rather than rigorous research, paralleled the Reagan administration's overwrought call to arms in *A Nation at Risk* (1983), which attacked the public school system for a "rising tide of mediocrity that threatens our very future as a Nation"—illustrated on network news with imagery of white suburban slackers who could barely stay awake in class.[61] The NFP's hyperbolic claims about the deadly drug crisis in Middle America intensified in the same context as the early 1980s political crusade to save millions of white kids from kidnappers, sexual predators, and other forms of "stranger danger"—a dramatically sensationalized "missing children epidemic" that heightened the culture of fear and punitive law-and-order climate of this era. While the Reagan administration certainly sought to capitalize on these save-the-children social movements by demonizing racial/sexual minorities and advancing conservative priorities, the antidrug and victims' rights mobilization to protect the white suburban family from external threats and internal breakdown was fundamentally nonpartisan and inevitably bipartisan. "The child protection movement," scholar Philip Jenkins concludes, "was immensely successful in establishing its views as a component of social orthodoxy and winning acceptance from virtually all ideological camps."[62]

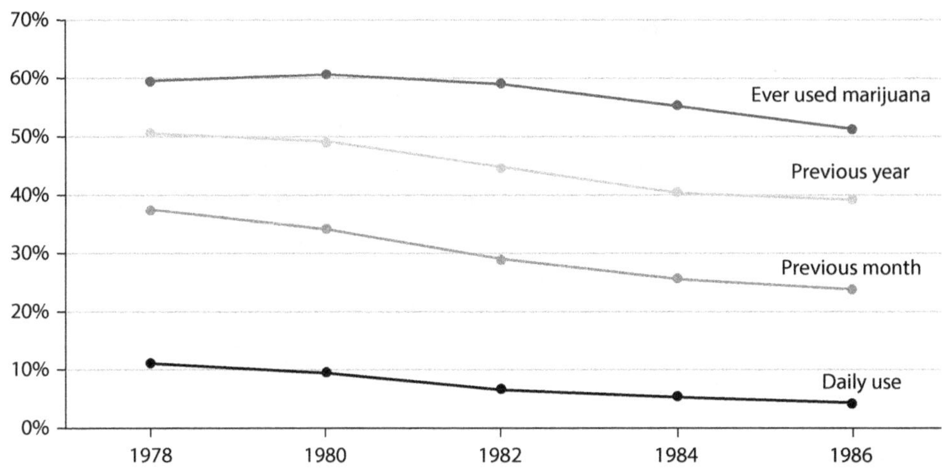

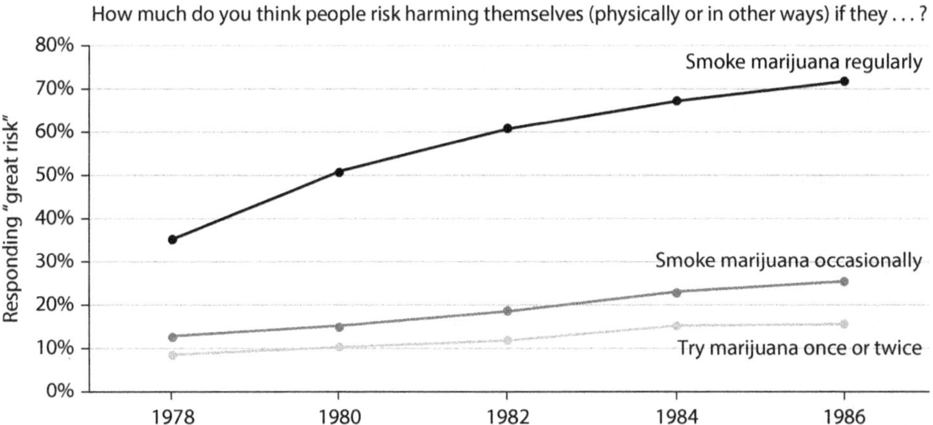

FIGURE 7.6. Trends in marijuana use and attitudes among U.S. high school seniors, 1978–86. (*Top*) While half of the senior class of 1986 admitted breaking the marijuana laws, the percentage that reported smoking pot during the previous year and previous month declined somewhat between the late 1970s and mid-1980s. The category of daily stoners underwent the largest statistical decrease, but in 1986 almost one-fourth of seniors still acknowledged marijuana use during the previous month. (*Bottom*) A large majority of older teenagers in the mid-1980s continued to believe that occasional marijuana use or experimentation did not constitute a "great risk," although the minority view was trending upward. The anti-marijuana crusade was most successful in altering teenage attitudes about the "great risk" of smoking pot regularly, as the proportion of seniors who agreed with this viewpoint doubled from 35% in 1978 to 71% in 1986. (NIDA, *National Trends in Drug Use and Related Factors among American High School Students and Young Adults, 1975–1986*.)

"Tough Love" at the Grassroots

During the early-to-mid 1980s, parent power groups in many local communities turned toward increasingly punitive and authoritarian tactics of "tough love" in the quest to eradicate drug and alcohol use by white middle-class youth and to control the adolescent subculture more broadly. In addition to the NFP's grassroots network, the ToughLove movement generated more than 1,500 neighborhood chapters during this vibrant era of zero-tolerance parental mobilization. Phyllis and David York, married family therapists in suburban Philadelphia, founded ToughLove in 1978 after two of their teenage daughters became "druggies." The Yorks objected to the psychiatric interpretation that family problems and parental mistakes caused teenage drug use, believing that their only failure came from not being tough enough, soon enough. They kicked their oldest daughter out of the house and then, following an arrest, refused to pay bail until she agreed to extended confinement in a rehabilitation center. *ToughLove*, their 1982 manifesto, echoed the NFP/PRIDE mantra that parents should adopt a "non-blaming attitude," by which the Yorks meant that mothers and fathers should blame their children and the broader drug culture rather than themselves. "Most of the young people who are manifesting outrageous behavior today are not 'crazy,'" the Yorks wrote in their assault on psychiatry and permissiveness, "they are 'stoned.'" *ToughLove*, with a sullen-looking white boy on the cover, told dystopian stories of pot-smoking, boozing, hostile, rebellious, and suicidal teenage and preteen children yelling at parents to "leave me the fuck alone." The self-help manual urged parents to start neighborhood solidarity groups, to discipline "uncontrollably rebellious teenagers," to "be willing to risk losing" their children by kicking them out, to use police and courts as leverage to force kids into drug rehabilitation, and to stop protecting them from negative consequences. The Yorks deliberately distanced ToughLove from the religious right and appealed directly to mainstream suburban parents overburdened by grief and guilt over "druggie" kids who just needed firm discipline.[63]

ToughLove chapters proliferated in the early 1980s after extensive media exposure and a glowing feature on its antipermissive philosophy by Ann Landers, the "most widely read columnist" in the nation and the voice of conventional Middle American morality. "You need ToughLove," Landers wrote, "if you feel helpless and unable to cope with your teenagers' behavior or if you feel victimized by them." Stop blaming yourself, because this crisis was universal: "These feelings are experienced by the affluent, the disadvantaged, middle-income families, the uneducated, intellectual, single, divorced, married, permissive, repressive, black and white, [a]nybody." Landers claimed that one-third of American teenagers got high on marijuana *every day* and attributed the drug and alcohol epidemic to permissive psychiatrists, television, economic affluence, and the 1960s protests that first gave middle-class youth permission to act "like bums." America faced a runaway crisis of "keg parties, getting drunk, smoking dope, popping uppers and downers, snorting cocaine, using angel dust and acid and having sex."[64] In Falls Church (93% white), a wealthy Northern Virginia suburb, a grateful mother who founded a ToughLove chapter reported confronting her unrepentant daughter to "do what needs to be done to help you, even if you don't love me anymore." From a "luxurious" suburb of Philadelphia, parents who developed the courage to expel drug-using teenagers praised the movement for helping them realize the "neighbors are facing the same problems with their kids." ToughLove parents often expressed relief after a child's arrest, and sometimes called the cops themselves, as long as the outcome involved medical treatment and not prosecution, especially diversion to private rehabilitation facilities. The *ToughLove* newsletter reduced all teens who used illegal drugs or alcohol to the identity of "druggies," urged parents to enlist juvenile agencies to help catch and confront their children, and—most of all—never, ever blame themselves.[65]

The "tough love" philosophy also encapsulated the controversial methods associated with Straight, Inc., the lockdown rehabilitation center for adolescent drug and alcohol users that started in St. Petersburg, Florida, in 1976. Straight targeted "good families in bad trouble" and portrayed any adolescent use (not just "abuse") of alcohol, marijuana, and other drugs as a "disease" that caused rebellion, family breakdown, and the dissolution of the American Dream into a terrible "nightmare." *Epidemic*, the organization's newsletter, informed parents in denial that what might seem like recreational use of marijuana and alcohol by teenagers was usually debilitating psychological dependency and most likely represented "only the tip of the iceberg." Because middle-class parents retained the "image of the 'drug addict' as the hardcore heroin user seen sprawled on the streets of big city slums," they often failed to recognize that affluent suburban youth also suffered from a psychological "habit," the "'need' to get high." Straight urged parents to have the love and courage to force their children into its residential program, which involved the entire family in a months-long group therapy process that combined methods of cold-turkey heroin rehabilitation with the self-help recovery philosophy of Alcoholics Anonymous.[66] The medical director of Straight, NFP board member Donald MacDonald, acknowledged threatening his son Andy with court-ordered institutionalization before he "voluntarily" entered the program. Andy initially considered Straight "worse than being in jail," but the techniques of total surveillance and confrontational peer pressure ultimately transformed him into an advocate for the drug-free lifestyle. Straight assured parents that if a child takes drugs,"It's not your fault," but it was imperative to practice tough love by "holding children accountable for their behavior." The Straight philosophy blamed teenage "druggies" comprehensively and exclusively: "You screwed up everything in your life. You've blown your family, your school, your ability to walk around free, the privilege of people trusting you."[67]

Straight's involuntary zero-tolerance approach meant that teenagers struggling with serious drug addiction and mental illness experienced confinement alongside more typical adolescents whose parents had overreacted to recreational use of pot and alcohol in the context of adolescent rebellion. In 1982, an in-depth series in the *St. Petersburg Independent* highlighted Straight patients who clearly required some sort of therapeutic support. Jenifer started smoking pot at age twelve and then received probation for dealing drugs in middle school. She ran away with an older man, did cocaine and heroin, and worked as a prostitute until her parents committed her to Straight. Christopher began drinking at age eleven and smoking pot at thirteen, started dealing drugs and served two years in prison after high school, and descended into cocaine and acid as his girlfriend committed suicide. Justin was expelled from middle school, incarcerated for drunk driving, overdosed on alcohol and pills, took everything from cocaine and heroin to LSD and PCP, and entered Straight under court order. Desperate parents of such youth often sought out Straight as a last resort, after traditional psychiatric counseling had failed and law enforcement became involved. But two-thirds of Straight's teenage patients in the early 1980s were just typical recreational pot smokers and adolescent social drinkers whose parents forced them into long-term institutionalization under the zero-tolerance and gateway-drug philosophy. Since many marijuana and alcohol users refused to admit that they were "druggies" and addicts, the process of overcoming denial and breaking down "chemical dependency" often took at least a year. Straight's seven-step program fused the abstinence-only, spiritual approach of Alcoholics Anonymous with private-sector incarceration; teenagers typically spent three to twelve months in the rigidly controlled facility while undergoing aggressive peer counseling and group therapy, eventually earned the right to go home at night (with parents required to lock children in bedrooms), and finally regained the privilege to return to school or work.[68]

Straight's techniques generated increasing scrutiny after Nancy Reagan praised its methods and the for-profit corporation opened branches in the suburbs of Atlanta, Cincinnati, and Washington, DC. By 1982, the expensive program had treated around three thousand youth between ages twelve and twenty-one, almost all from white upper-middle-class backgrounds, and claimed a drug-free success rate of 57 percent for graduates (but only 25 percent counting dropouts and runaways). When Straight opened its center in Fairfax County, Virginia, at the request of more than one hundred local parents who had sent their children to the St. Petersburg facility, the organization promised to turn "adolescent drug users into highly motivated, goal-oriented, drug-free members of society." Many parents credited Straight with saving their children's lives, but outside critics and some former patients accused the organization of brainwashing tactics and physical as well as psychological abuse. The ACLU denounced Straight as a "concentration camp for throwaway kids" and filed a lawsuit that led to greater state oversight of the Cobb County facility in suburban Atlanta. The most damaging publicity came after Fred Collins, a college student from Fairfax County, escaped following more than five months of rehabilitation and then won a false imprisonment lawsuit against Straight in 1983. Collins, a legal adult, was visiting his younger brother in a Straight facility when his parents and the staff conspired to commit him to the program as well (his father testified against him at trial). He had consumed alcohol and smoked pot in the past but considered this to be normal behavior and refused to admit that he was a "chemically dependent person." Straight counselors strip-searched Collins and then held him in solitary confinement except for twelve-hour sessions of "reality therapy" where other teenagers yelled at him to stop denying his drug addiction. Several other former patients/prisoners supported his account by testifying of physical abuse, marathon sessions lasting up to eighty hours, and being kidnapped by Straight staff (with parental authorization) after running away.[69]

The Collins lawsuit led to significant media coverage of Straight, Inc., including a *20/20* feature on ABC and a *60 Minutes* exposé by CBS. The *20/20* program labeled Straight "strict, militaristic, even cultish" but also portrayed its techniques as effective for the exclusively white families portrayed in group therapy confrontations, with adolescents crying and confessing while parents expressed fear and fury over losing them to the drug culture. The much more critical *60 Minutes* profile juxtaposed a tearful suburban Maryland father who believed that drug addiction would have killed his son without Straight's intervention with a group of white teenage girls who told harrowing stories of psychological intimidation and physical restraint. "I wanted to die," one of them sobbed on national television; "I didn't think I was ever going to get out." Straight's new executive director, an Atlanta businessman with no medical credentials whose daughter had completed the program, told *60 Minutes* that teenage drug abusers would never agree to enter rehabilitation unless "someone, somewhere—a parent, a government official, a probation officer—someone is literally forcing that child to make a voluntary decision." Another father informed CBS that since "all druggies are con artists," adolescents inevitably resisted the zero-tolerance approach at first, but Straight's remarkably successful techniques not only saved his addicted child but also made his family whole again. Following the Fred Collins wrongful imprisonment verdict, dozens of Straight parents took out a full-page advertisement in the *St. Petersburg Times* to defend and praise the tough love approach for salvaging their families by halting the downward spiral of teenage drug addiction. In a typical formulation, a Tampa couple credited Straight for transforming an "abusive, combative, suicidal" daughter who smoked pot, drank alcohol, and took pills back into a "straight, beautiful, caring daughter." Many called the program a "miracle" and rejoiced, in the words of a Fairfax County woman, that its rehabilitation of her sons had made her "the happiest mother in the world."[70]

Not My Kid, a tough love parental guidebook turned into a TV melodrama, introduced the zero-tolerance Straight philosophy to an even larger national audience. The book version, published in 1984, was coauthored by Miller Newton, formerly national director of Straight, and Beth Polson, the television journalist who produced the *20/20* episode that portrayed the Florida facility as remarkably successful for white suburban youth in crisis. "Too many of us assume that drugs are exclusive to the ghetto, or to the 'bad' kids in class," the book began. Your children may be popular and good-looking, smart and college-bound, the homecoming queen or the athletic star. "So you think you're safe. You're not." *Not My Kid* identified parental denial as the primary obstacle in America's losing war against teenage drug and alcohol use: "Any parent high on the denial drug is an accomplice to the conspiracy that leads a child to a druggie lifestyle." The manual absolved parents of any blame for their children's initial decision to experiment but demanded immediate intervention and an inflexible zero-tolerance stance at the first sign of trouble—because the "gateway drugs" of marijuana and alcohol almost invariably led to chemical dependency and multidrug addiction, the burnout "amotivational syndrome," and a life of criminality, sexual promiscuity, and ultimately early death. The authors condemned psychiatrists who believed that drug use was a symptom of other problems rather than the underlying "disease," transforming teenage pot smokers and underage drinkers into manipulative and untrustworthy "con artists" who required comprehensive monitoring. *Not My Kid* also criticized adult "enablers"—parents, school officials, police—who protected teens from the consequences of their illegal activities ("You may as well be selling him the drugs"). The book urged parents to "know the enemy" and embrace "authoritarian" solutions—try grounding as punishment, or report children to the police as a scare tactic, but it was probably too late for any cure except commitment to an abstinence-only residential facility such as Straight, Inc.[71]

The tough love movement repudiated the "permissive" view of illegal drug use as a "victimless crime" based on the insistence that its destructive consequences not only harmed teenagers themselves but cast the entire family into a downward spiral of pain and suffering. Tough love advocates also departed from the dominant suburban ethos of shielding children from the criminal justice system at all costs, albeit a hardline stance that advocated coercive medicalization rather than prosecution and counted on the willingness of local law enforcement to divert white middle-class teenagers to private treatment programs such as Straight. The CBS-TV adaptation of *Not My Kid* (1985) reinforced these messages by showing how a Straight-style program saved a fifteen-year-old "druggie" and transformed her initially clueless and permissive parents, a dystopian saga based on the customary plotlines of white innocence lost and runaway daughter in suburban crisis. Susan, a pretty girl with a surgeon father and mother in denial, hangs out with heavy metal burnouts skipping school, smoking pot, guzzling booze, and shooting speed. After a drunk-driving accident sends Susan to the hospital, her parents find the stash in her room and take her to a psychiatrist, who labels her behavior "natural rebellion" and recommends giving her more freedom. But when she runs away to her bad drug-taking friends, her father enlists the police to track her down and then forces her, against the mother's wishes, into a lockdown treatment center. Susan resists admitting she is a "druggie," briefly escapes until her father recaptures her, but ultimately breaks down under the relentless pressure of the peer counselors and admits multidrug addiction (including heroin). Confrontational family therapy sessions also break down the denial and shame of her parents, who realize they are not at fault and are powerless to control a child with the "disease" of chemical dependency. In the triumphant finale, the treatment center allows Susan to return home; in a coda, Nancy Reagan endorses the solutions of antipermissive parenting and tough love rehabilitation.[72]

The evolution of the parents' movement in Fairfax County, a generally affluent and 89% white suburban area in Northern Virginia, reveals how the zero-tolerance agenda at the local level quickly broadened from a disciplinary project targeting individual sons and daughters into a public policy campaign against recreational marijuana and alcohol use by all youth. Fairfax's main parent power group, PANDAA (Parents' Association to Neutralize Drug and Alcohol Abuse), formed in 1980 in the upper-middle-class community of Annandale, located a dozen miles outside DC. Joyce Tobias, a mother of seven, founded PANDAA after discovering that her two oldest sons were smoking pot and getting drunk. As she recounted, both boys made good grades, played sports, and worked jobs, but "it was obvious that they were unhappy people, filled with hate, and dependent on alcohol and marijuana." The parent power method of adult supervision and positive peer pressure failed to stop their behavior, counseling backfired when the psychologist said marijuana was no big deal, and "finally we realized our boys were powerless over their drug use and we, also, were powerless." In 1981, Tobias and her husband committed both sons to the Straight program in Florida, which in her telling worked wonders in only six months. The couple helped lead the fundraising campaign to bring Straight, Inc., to Fairfax County with the motto: "Parent power and professional help together can get kids off drugs." PANDAA's newsletters featured Straight rescue narratives such as an apology from a self-confessed "druggie" to his AP English teacher for constantly being stoned in class, followed by the promise to be back soon because "I am *straight,* and I will never touch another drug or alcohol for *the rest of my life!*" In another lost-innocence confessional titled "I Thought I Had It Made," a wealthy Fairfax mother explained how both her daughters started dealing drugs and hanging around with "disgusting" friends, despite a luxurious family life that provided yacht trips and European vacations, and "would have died" without the rehabilitation program.[73]

PANDAA's energetic political lobbying promoted coercive measures ranging from involuntary private-sector confinement of "marijuana users" to raising the drinking age to twenty-one. In 1982, PANDAA joined dozens of local groups to form the Virginia Federation of Parents, the NFP's statewide affiliate. The alliance demanded vigilant enforcement against drug dealers but also called for policies to discipline and rehabilitate teenagers who used illegal drugs, reflecting the increasingly punitive approach to the demand side. The Virginia Federation of Parents pressed state politicians for a tougher antiparaphernalia law and advocated age-21 legislation to curb binge drinking and drunk driving among teenagers. In its backyard, PANDAA ran a family crisis hotline, encouraged ToughLove groups in the DC suburbs, and promoted drug-free chaperoned parties modeled on the Parents Who Care movement in California. In 1983, the group began a court-monitoring program to pressure county judges to give stiffer sentences for drug violations, especially to "pushers" (mainly marijuana dealers in the recreational market). PANDAA also orchestrated a long campaign to convince police departments and private venues in metro DC to crack down on the "open use" of pot and booze at arena rock concerts. The group demanded police stings against "drug pushers" at these venues and even (unsuccessfully) requested drug-sniffing dogs to catch teenage fans with marijuana and alcohol. After infiltrating a heavy metal concert undercover, one PANDAA mother reported rampant drinking in the parking lot, pot smoking everywhere inside, and an unintended contact high for herself: "The kids were completely out of control. They were in a 'free zone' atmosphere which allows them to abuse drugs and alcohol with no fear of getting caught. . . . Within this mob atmosphere, law enforcement agencies are helpless." In the PANDAA newsletter, amends-making youth who had graduated from Straight confessed to "smoking pot in front of the police," admitted buying LSD and PCP from older strangers, and advised parents to ban their children from all rock shows.[74]

PANDAA's influence demonstrates how a small but dedicated group of zero-tolerance advocates could transform public policy in a large suburban county of nearly six hundred thousand people. The group demanded a "get tough" approach in public schools and accused Fairfax officials of denying the prevalence of drug use on campus. In its newsletter, PANDAA published first-person accounts by teenagers who bought drugs between classes, kept stashes in their lockers, and reported that parent chaperones allowed pot smoking and drinking on overnight field trips. PANDAA applauded Robert DuPont, the antimarijuana crusader and former NIDA director, when he told Fairfax educators that "schools and parents must support each other in creating an environment of suspicion and enforcement." In fall 1983, based on PANDAA's incessant pressure, the Fairfax County school board adopted much tougher disciplinary policies that automatically suspended students caught with illegal drugs or alcohol and pledged expulsion of campus "pushers" (four alleged dealers received this penalty in 1984). At a White House event, Nancy Reagan praised the Fairfax district's zero-tolerance approach as a model for the rest of the nation. PANDAA also condemned parents who supplied alcohol for their children's parties and then "look the other way" when everyone drove home drunk. After PBS broadcasted *The Chemical People,* a number of Fairfax schools asked parents to sign pledges not to serve alcohol to minors at house parties. To reinforce the initiative, the Fairfax parent power movement lobbied for police busts of keg parties in private homes, which led to juvenile citations for many teenagers and multiple arrests of mothers and fathers for "aiding and abetting" underage drinking. The Fairfax police department recommended PANDAA, along with Straight and ToughLove, to parents whose children used drugs, and a county task force endorsed the group's campaign for the age-21 drinking standard. "We have been absolutely astounded," PANDAA leader Joyce Tobias said, "at how much impact we can have."[75]

In the early-to-mid 1980s, zero-tolerance parents' groups in cities and suburbs across the nation endorsed law enforcement crackdowns on the teenage subculture of recreational drug and alcohol use, even if it meant arrest of their own children. In Maryland, the NFP-affiliated Parents' Action Network of Anne Arundel County applauded a police initiative to bust "in-school pushers," acknowledging that "none of us wants our child involved" but drug dealers needed "constructive, firm discipline." A number of California police departments reactivated undercover sting operations after parent power chapters demanded tougher punishment for students caught with drugs. The LAPD arrested 303 "juvenile pushers" on high school campuses in December 1982 and another 218 a year later, concentrating on the San Fernando Valley and upscale Westside (the same mostly white areas where undercover busts elicited parental backlash in the mid-1970s). The Beverly Hills school board enacted a policy making all drug violations subject to arrest and expulsion, rather than the previous stance of warnings and in-school discipline. In metropolitan San Diego, undercover police disguised as students arrested more than two hundred campus "dealers" in 1983–84, focusing on high schools in affluent white areas, at the behest of NFP chapters in Californians for Drug-Free Youth. The Fort Lauderdale chapter of Florida Informed Parents worked with police to regulate illegal activities at the beaches and waterfront bars where thousands of teenagers congregated and cruised each night. The Texas War on Drugs Committee, and affiliates such as Houston Informed Parents, proved especially vigilant in their demands that police target the marijuana market and arrest any youth caught with any amount. These "parent power" and "tough love" organizations did not want white suburban youth to be incarcerated, or even to receive formal criminal records, but rather operated within the arrest-and-divert framework first developed on a mass scale to regulate the middle-class delinquency and drug subcultures of the 1950s and 1960s (see chapters 2 and 3).[76]

The grassroots "tough love" movement claimed to represent a Middle American awakening but embraced coercive methods and collaborated with law enforcement because many suburban parents, as well as most teenagers, did not share its absolutist philosophy and reliance on criminalization to control the white middle-class youth subculture. PBS, which promoted the NFP's nationwide expansion through *The Chemical People*, offered a much more balanced and critical assessment of the zero-tolerance crusade in a 1987 *Frontline* documentary about the stark internal divisions over drug abuse prevention policies in upper-middle-class suburbia. The feature begins with a law enforcement crackdown on high school drinking and marijuana use at the behest of the NFP chapter in East Greenwich, Rhode Island, a 99 percent white suburb of Providence. The police search students' cars in the school parking lot, surveil them at dances, and bust up house parties—an initiative requested by the sixty families in the NFP affiliate, which also sponsors a high school club that enlists 5 percent of teenagers (who concede they are a fringe group). Other parents strongly object to these tactics, arguing that it makes more sense to teach adolescents to practice responsible behavior and to acknowledge that the underage drinking subculture in particular was there to stay. Most East Greenwich students express disdain and hostility, defending their social right to consume alcohol. One female states, "I drink often; I get good grades," and points out that plenty of college-bound classmates smoke marijuana and some even do cocaine. *Frontline* then visited an all-white Boston suburb that utilized the "responsible use" curriculum with more effective results. Students there tell PBS that it is okay to drink alcohol or smoke pot as long as they "know when to stop" and that they understand the difference between socializing with beer and getting drunk all the time. The program ends by contrasting the federal government's abstinence-only policies with the consensus of many drug prevention specialists that "responsible use" worked best.[77]

Failure in the impossible mission to eradicate teenage drug and alcohol use inspired the zero-tolerance movement to champion even more punitive methods of family surveillance, coercive medicalization, and other disciplinary projects to retake control of the youth subculture. Robert DuPont, the former Ford/Carter NIDA director who helped forge the initial federal alliance with the parents' movement, contended that "any continuing use of an illegal drug is drug abuse" and urged parents, educators, and politicians to enforce zero tolerance for all marijuana experimentation and underage drinking. In his polemical guidebook, *Getting Tough on Gateway Drugs* (1984), DuPont blamed the decriminalization-era mythology of marijuana as a "soft" and harmless drug for the disastrous 1980s epidemic of teenage chemical dependency and mass "amotivational syndrome." He elevated the family as the most effective instrument of social control, advised parents to conduct random urine testing at the first hint of suspicion, recommended "using the powers of the law" to control uncooperative children, and endorsed involuntary institutionalization for marijuana and alcohol dependency. Donald Ian MacDonald, the former Straight leader and Reagan's future drug policy director, reinforced this message in his own get-tough manifesto, *Drugs, Drinking, and Adolescents* (1984). The book highlighted an American "disease of epidemic proportions"—widespread marijuana "addiction" among middle-class suburban youth combined with a drinking subculture that allegedly produced three million current teenage alcoholics. MacDonald endorsed regular urinalysis screening of all adolescents, called for schools and police to arrest every teenage violator in order to force them into drug treatment, and depicted Straight's lockdown methods as the most effective recovery program in the nation's history. That same year, despite (or more likely because of) MacDonald's lack of expert qualifications, the Reagan administration appointed the Florida pediatrician and NFP leader as federal director of the Alcohol, Drug Abuse, and Mental Health Administration.[78]

Teen Drinking: Get MADD

During the early-to-mid 1980s, the zero-tolerance agenda of the National Federation of Parents for Drug-Free Youth converged with the victims' rights mission of Mothers Against Drunk Driving (MADD) to forge a political consensus behind legislation to increase the national drinking age to twenty-one. This grassroots-driven and bipartisan reform, although often justified as a public safety measure to curb fatalities caused by teenage drunk driving, also represented the parent power movement's elevation of alcohol alongside marijuana as a major "gateway drug" and its comprehensive assault on the "responsible use" philosophy that took hold during the 1970s. Thirty-five states lowered the minimum drinking age to either eighteen or nineteen between 1970 and 1973, part of the broader shift toward treating college students and other young adults as full political citizens who deserved the right to vote and other responsibilities and privileges. Academic studies consistently showed that, as with marijuana prohibition, the legal drinking age had very little effect on usage rates among American teenagers, with more than 90 percent of high school students consuming alcohol before turning eighteen, and half of sixteen-to-seventeen-year-olds doing so on a regular basis. Under the "responsible use" approach, school-based prevention programs recognized recreational drinking as a normative teenage behavior and concentrated on discouraging drunk driving and frequent intoxication by "problem drinkers," defined as the 15 percent of high schoolers who became inebriated weekly. The federal government's National Institute on Alcohol Abuse and Alcoholism (NIAAA) promoted this prevention curriculum to teach youth to "drink in a responsible manner if they choose to drink," based on the practical assessment that teenagers as well as adults lived in a culture that revolved around the social consumption of alcohol. In a typical pamphlet from the early 1980s, the NIAAA urged parents to "set realistic goals" rather than "hand down ultimatums," because "most teens do drink on some occasions" and therefore the main goal should be to help them "find ways to not *mix* drinking and driving."[79]

In 1982, the Reagan administration took the unprecedented step of including the total prevention of underage drinking as a priority in the national war on drugs, a reflection of the political influence of the parent power movement and a policy in direct tension with the promotion of "responsible use" of alcohol by federal public health agencies. That same year, the NIAAA (a division of Health and Human Services) sponsored a series of regional conferences on teenage drinking that praised the "outstanding" alcohol and drug abuse educational programs developed in locations such as suburban Westchester County in New York. This public school curriculum presented "responsible use" and abstinence as equally viable options, based on overwhelming evidence that an effective approach should not simply "tell youngsters not to drink." The NFP and PRIDE first protested, unsuccessfully, to the secretary of Health and Human Services and then demanded that the Reagan White House bring federal public health programming into alignment with the administration's stated opposition to "responsible use."[80] In November 1982, the NFP adopted a resolution that "resoundingly rejects any educational, prevention, or treatment program which advocates or condones the 'responsible use' of illicit drugs including the use of alcohol by minors and further rejects our tax dollars supporting a 'responsible use' message." PRIDE also released an anti–"responsible use" manifesto that compared the toleration of social drinking by "immature" adolescents to the harm previously caused by permissiveness toward marijuana experimentation and demanded that parents, schools, and the government enforce the criminal ban on alcohol consumption by minors. And, in a simultaneous expansion of the zero-tolerance crusade, the National Federation of Parents mobilized its local affiliates behind the growing movement to restore the legal drinking age to twenty-one in every state, in order to reduce drunk driving crashes and limit the "gateway" progression of teenage experimenters to full-fledged alcoholics and multidrug addicts.[81]

The drive to recriminalize alcohol consumption by eighteen-to-twenty-year-old adults began gathering steam at the local and state levels in the late 1970s, a half-decade before its emergence as a pressing national issue. The first major reversal came in Michigan, where the PTA launched a "Coalition for 21" campaign based on the insistence that rampant drinking in high schools and colleges inhibited the academic achievement and career prospects of students defined by their "emotional and psychological instability." Proponents also cited traffic deaths caused by teenage drunk drivers but focused primarily on behavioral problems at high school football games and dances, suburban house parties, and college keg blowouts—paralleling the social control agenda of antimarijuana activists. In 1978, 57 percent of Michigan voters ratified the Coalition for 21 referendum, against the resistance of college students and bar owners who formed Citizens for a Fair Drinking Age and unsuccessfully litigated the result as unconstitutional age discrimination.[82] In New Jersey, suburban PTA leaders organized a similar campaign and achieved success in 1982. The New Jersey activists highlighted the "trickle-down syndrome," alleging that older teenagers who could legally purchase alcohol supplied underage kids in elementary and middle school, alongside the need to curb vandalism, drunk driving crashes, and the out-of-control party culture in high schools and universities. College students and the liquor industry again provided the main opposition, but the New Jersey coalition recruited law enforcement, allied with the statewide NFP affiliate, and aggressively lobbied legislators with the slogan "No Kid Ever Died Because He Wasn't Allowed to Drink."[83] Maryland also restored its age-21 law in 1982 after a campaign by the PTA and suburban chapters of the NFP and MADD. The Maryland NFP claimed that 3.3 million American teens were alcoholics (conflating this with weekly drinkers) and maintained that "alcohol is a drug" that severely damaged youth, who were inherently not social drinkers like most adults because they sought only to "get 'high,' 'drunk,' 'stoned.'"[84]

By 1982, legislatures in a dozen additional states had increased the drinking age to either nineteen or twenty, a threshold designed to criminalize alcohol consumption by high school but not most college students, and an incomplete victory that caused the age-21 movement to shift its focus to campaign for a uniform national standard. In July, four months after the Reagan administration included underage drinking in its formal war on drugs blueprint, the

National Transportation Safety Board (NTSB) issued a public safety recommendation urging every state to raise the minimum legal drinking age to twenty-one. The NTSB, an independent federal agency, acted after nine teenagers perished in a high-profile crash in a Long Island suburb, when a nineteen-year-old driver with a .09 blood alcohol content ("impaired" but not "inebriated" under state law) struck a moving train. Citing data from Michigan, the NTSB emphasized the "direct correlation" between enactment of age-21 laws and "dramatic reductions in alcohol-related accidents," a debatable finding based on selective academic studies that almost immediately achieved the status of gospel truth in news coverage and political discourse. In media outlets and congressional testimony, antimarijuana crusader Peggy Mann added a related alarm about a youth epidemic of "drugged driving," claiming that one-third of eighteen-to-twenty-four-year-olds smoked pot regularly and most drove while high (e.g., the "typical" attendee at a high school or college keg party drank four to five beers and smoked two to three joints before driving home).[85] In Congress, liberal Democrats allied with MADD and the age-21 movement introduced drunk-driving legislation to establish a "national standard for alcohol-related offenses" or lose federal highway funding, but the Reagan administration opposed the mandate on states' rights grounds. In the Surface Transportation Assistance Act of 1982, Democratic legislators and the administration compromised on a carrot rather than stick approach that provided incentive grants to states that adopted tougher drunk-driving penalties and/or increased the legal drinking age to twenty-one.[86]

In 1983, Mothers Against Drunk Driving placed its considerable political influence behind the campaign to establish a national drinking age of twenty-one. This move epitomized the new focus on adolescents as the primary drunk driver villains and represented a partial abandonment of the "responsible use" philosophy that had shaped the group's public health stance. Candy Lightner, a real estate agent from a white middle-class area outside Sacramento, founded MADD in 1980 after a middle-aged adult male with four prior drunk-driving arrests struck and killed her thirteen-year-old daughter Cari as she walked "down a quiet suburban street." The grieving mother, who had not previously been politically active or even registered to vote, turned into a self-described "crusader with a cause"—demanding justice for "thousands of victims across the United States . . . innocently slaughtered by repeat offender drunk drivers."[87] Lightner began by picketing the California State Capitol in Sacramento, accusing Governor Jerry Brown of "doing nothing" while prosecutors, judges, and juries went easy on drunk drivers and ignored the suffering of their victims. Brown soon acknowledged the unrelenting pressure from "concerned citizens" in MADD and appointed a task force, including Lightner, to overturn the "social acceptance of drinking and driving" by toughening enforcement and sanctions. The committee's 1981 report embraced the rhetoric of the victims' rights movement, criticized prosecutors for the tendency to plea-bargain DUI offenses to reckless driving, and endorsed mandatory penalties ranging from license revocation to jail time. The California legislature quickly passed the task force's get-tough package, which covered "drugged" as well as drunk driving, celebrated by Lightner as a model for the rest of the nation. During its early years, MADD almost exclusively portrayed youth as the victims of adult drunk drivers, rather than as the primary social or criminal problem, and promoted the "responsible use" position. In Lightner's words, "Be realistic, be mature. Call a taxi, call a friend. It isn't realistic to expect people not to drink."[88]

MADD played a pivotal role in transforming the anti-drunk-driving agenda into an urgent federal cause but only belatedly embraced the age-21 movement's zero-tolerance stance on teenage drinking. In fall 1980, Candy Lightner held a press conference in Washington to pressure the Carter administration to name a presidential commission to address the national drunk-driving crisis, because "what happened to my daughter Cari could happen to anyone." Lightner joined forces with Cindi Lamb, a suburban Maryland mother whose infant daughter Laura had been paralyzed in a wreck caused by a repeat-offender drunk driver, as the coleaders of a national MADD campaign that drew extensive media coverage and immediate support from prominent public health Democrats in Congress. The National Highway Traffic Safety Administration (NHTSA) provided seed grants for the expansion of MADD chapters as well as the parallel grassroots movement of Remove Intoxicated Drivers, headquartered in New York. Lightner and Lamb maintained the MADD pressure on the new Reagan administration with additional DC protests and a petition drive that secured two hundred thousand signatures, including a majority of members of Congress, by spring 1982.[89] The Reagan White House at first refused to consider a national commission but changed course for political reasons, as drug policy advisor Carlton Turner acknowledged, "to buttress the President's concern for the family and . . . show this Administration is concerned with all aspects of the drug issue." In April, Reagan announced the formation of a Presidential Commission on Drunk Driving and praised grassroots activists such as Candy Lightner, an appointee, for bringing the nation's attention to the "slaughter of the innocent" on America's roads and highways. In an interim December 1982 report, the commission backed the get-tough criminal sanctions demanded by MADD and Remove Intoxicated Drivers and also endorsed the NTSB's position that all states should adopt age-21 drinking laws in order to reduce fatal crashes caused by teenagers and young adults.[90]

The policy solution of criminalizing the alcohol market for all Americans under the age of twenty-one eclipsed the substantial evidence that "responsible use" messaging was increasing public consciousness about drunk driving among teenagers and young adults, thanks in large part to MADD and especially the new organization Students Against Driving Drunk (SADD). The SADD movement, which promoted alcohol education based on teenage responsibility rather than zero tolerance and social control, began in fall 1981 with a group of high school students in the Boston suburb of Wayland (98% white). They devised a "contract for life," to be signed by teenagers who agreed never to drive while inebriated or ride with someone else who was drunk, and parents who promised to provide safe transportation home for children who called for help—"no questions asked and no argument at that time." The Massachusetts state government quickly embraced SADD and its positive peer pressure campaign, which popularized the slogan "Friends don't let friends drive drunk." SADD's central philosophy—"It is the teenagers themselves who must solve their problem"—resonated because it treated high school students as rational political actors and distinguished between "acceptable and unacceptable" drinking practices. SADD chapters spread quickly—often after a fatal drunk driving crash—in the suburbs of Northern Virginia, Chicago, Southern California, and many other localities. Unlike zero-tolerance methods, SADD's acknowledgment of the reality of underage alcohol consumption increased its appeal among teenagers who considered social drinking and weekend parties to be the norm. "Everyone drinks," a seventeen-year-old female from a wealthy suburb of Boston explained. "It's natural. It's no big deal. But it's crazy and stupid and wrong to drive when you're messed up." Preaching the abstinence-only message "'do not drink' is not to live in the real world," agreed a public school administrator in suburban Maryland who supported SADD. "We're not encouraging kids to drink, just to make responsible decisions when they do."[91]

SADD's vision of teenagers as citizens who could be trusted to make sensible choices involving alcohol consumption created a schism in the anti-drunk-driving movement and drew censure from parent power groups that demanded authoritarian policies of zero tolerance. In the early 1980s, SADD's parent-child contract expanded into programs such as Safe Rides, in which teenage volunteers drove inebriated or stranded counterparts home with no questions asked and no involvement of law enforcement. State and local officials credited such efforts with significant reductions in drunk-driving crashes and fatalities, and the NHTSA promoted Safe Rides alongside the "designated driver" concept as part of its "national drunk and drugged driver awareness" campaign.[92] This federal endorsement of SADD's "responsible use" agenda, including praise from the secretary of Health and Human Services, provoked a backlash by zero-tolerance groups and then a course correction from the White House. From suburban Chicago, the leader of the Deerfield Citizens for Drug Awareness, an NFP affiliate, denounced SADD's "Just don't drink and drive" slogan and demanded that the Reagan administration stand with the parents' movement through an uncompromising "No Drug message for adolescents." The New Jersey PTA, which was coordinating the national organization's campaign for age-21 laws, charged that SADD's methods "unintentionally create underage alcohol abusers" and called for the "immediate elimination of programs that offer contracts or rides to teenagers under the legal drinking age." Carlton Turner responded by eliminating any praise for SADD from President Reagan's speeches and other executive branch policy blueprints, in order to appease grassroots antidrug activists and the age-21 movement. MADD did continue to support SADD and the Safe Rides initiative as "very effective" in reducing teenage alcohol-related crashes, and Candy Lightner unequivocally rejected criticism from antidrug groups that promotion of pragmatic life-saving measures necessarily condoned underage drinking.[93]

In January 1983, the national MADD organization formally endorsed the campaign for a national twenty-one-year-old drinking age to implement the recommendations of the Presidential Commission on Drunk Driving and save "at least 380 innocent young lives" annually. The number of local MADD chapters also doubled during that year alone after NBC-TV aired *Mothers Against Drunk Driving: The Candy Lightner Story*, how "what began as a one-woman crusade for personal justice" forced first California and then Washington politicians to support MADD's victims' rights agenda.[94] Although a late convert, Lightner immediately emerged as the telegenic face of the age-21 movement in media appearances and congressional hearings, where she collaborated closely with public health Democrats who promoted a national mandate to force recalcitrant states into line. Lightner blamed the liquor industry lobby for the refusal of many state legislatures to adopt the uniform standard and repeatedly insisted that federal age-21 legislation would "save the lives of thousands of Americans." She also advanced the trickle-down theory that criminalizing access for eighteen-to-twenty-year-olds was essential to prevent alcohol "from being almost universally available to high school students." Asked why adults old enough to vote should be prohibited from buying alcohol, Lightner responded that "no one is killed, crippled, or maimed from voting," a zero-sum equation that captured the anti-drunk-driving movement's increasing stigmatization and depoliticization of youth. In November, the Presidential Commission on Drunk Driving issued its final report, which attributed the get-tough political mood to the "crescendo of voices" from grassroots victims' rights groups and endorsed the legislative efforts of congressional Democrats to withhold federal highway funds from any state that did not increase the drinking age to twenty-one. After the Reagan administration reiterated its states' rights opposition to a mandatory national drinking age, Lightner told *NBC Nightly News* that MADD would escalate pressure on the White House and expected to win in the end.[95]

College student groups and the alcohol beverage industry provided the main opposition as the political campaign for a federal age-21 standard gathered steam in Congress. The lead sponsors of the National Minimum Drinking Age Act were liberal Democrats from New Jersey and Maryland, two states where the suburban grassroots age-21 movement had recently emerged victorious. At congressional hearings during 1983–84, these politicians joined with MADD and private-sector organizations such as the National Safety Council and the National Council on Alcoholism to portray the connection between a higher drinking age and reduced drunk-driving fatalities as a consensus position supported by irrefutable statistics. A careful state-by-state meta-analysis by Michael Birkley, an alcoholism treatment specialist from Wisconsin, labeled this position "speculative in the extreme and clearly at odds with reality." Birkley found that increasing the drinking age tended to exacerbate public safety problems, because barring youth from "supervised settings" such as bars just shifted their alcohol consumption to cars and illicit "remote settings" that increased drunk driving. Instead, Birkley argued that the legal drinking age should be as close as possible to sixteen, "the normative age for onset of social drinking," because studies overwhelmingly confirmed that underage youth had no trouble obtaining alcohol anywhere. The National Licensed Beverage Association then hired Birkley as an expert witness, which allowed MADD and its allies to dismiss his findings as "very biased," although numerous other studies challenged the oversimplified claim that age-21 laws saved lives.[96] The U.S. Student Association denounced the legislation as age discrimination because legal adults should have the right "to make responsible decisions

FIGURE 7.7. Candy Lightner, founder of Mothers Against Drunk Driving, pins a MADD button on President Ronald Reagan after he signed legislation raising the national drinking age to twenty-one on July 17, 1984. The Reagan administration initially opposed the Democratic-sponsored bill but changed sides in response to MADD's media-savvy pressure campaign. Secretary of Transportation Elizabeth Dole (left) looks on with a group of Republican politicians. (AP Photo.)

concerning their own personal actions and lifestyle." The college student lobby also accused politicians of scapegoating eighteen-to-twenty-year-olds, given that older adults caused the vast majority of drunk-driving fatalities, and criminalizing the "young citizens" whose Safe Rides and designated driver programs actually worked.[97]

Congress approved the National Minimum Drinking Age Act of 1984 soon after MADD and the National PTA held a "Save Our Students" rally at the Capitol and the Reagan White House recognized the political risks of continuing to stall the age-21 crusade. Secretary of Transportation Elizabeth Dole announced the policy shift at the "Save Our Students" protest, as politicians from both parties lauded Candy Lightner as an American hero and observed that the general public favored the age-21 mandate (77 percent in a Gallup survey). Senator Frank Lautenberg (D-NJ), the law's primary author, dismissed the opposition as self-interested liquor lobbyists (silencing the positions of the U.S. Student Association and SADD) and portrayed the higher drinking age as a life-saving measure that would help parents control the teenage "environment of drugs and alcohol abuse." President Reagan confirmed his change of heart in a speech at a suburban New Jersey high school, where he credited MADD's grassroots movement for the breakthrough and warned students to avoid "drinking and drugging" as well as drunk driving, because all "drug use is drug abuse." Reagan justified the mandate from a "big and overwhelming government in Washington"—withholding a portion of federal highway funds from any state that did not enact the age-21 minimum—based on MADD's "blood borders" argument (that, for example, teenagers in New Jersey drove to New York to buy alcohol legally). On July 17, with Candy Lightner at his side, Reagan signed the age-21 law and guarantee that it would "save thousands of young lives"—a dubious proposition in terms of its public health effects on underage drinking and drunk driving, but a comprehensive political victory for the zero-tolerance crusade to criminalize the recreational youth subculture of drugs and alcohol.[98] All but seven states complied with the federal mandate by the 1986 deadline, and the loss of highway funds brought the holdouts into line by the decade's end. The law did not deter alcohol use by around 90 percent of all high school and college students (fig. 7.8).[99]

The parent power movement continued to attack "responsible use" programs after passage of the national drinking age law, including SADD's acceptance of the fact that "a large number of teenagers will drink at least occasionally." Remove Intoxicated Drivers strongly criticized SADD for refusing to endorse the age-21 standard, and NFP cofounder Sue Rusche's syndicated column denounced its student-parent contract for excusing lawbreaking rather than demanding abstinence. In 1985, SADD lost its most important ally in the anti-drunk-driving movement when MADD ousted Candy Lightner, who accused "neoprohibitionist" radicals of taking over her organization and later became a "Don't drink and drive" (i.e., "responsible use") spokesperson for the American Beverage Institute.[100] MADD's new leadership entered into a formal alliance with the National Federation of Parents and promptly repudiated both SADD's "contract for life" and Safe Rides programs. In Operation Prom/Graduation, a joint initiative launched in 1986, the NFP and MADD urged parents and educators to organize wholesome parties, ideally chaperoned by local police, to prohibit illegal behavior and reduce drunk-driving fatalities. The initiative condemned Safe Rides and parents who agreed to other "responsible use" arrangements: "A drug- and alcohol-free party is aimed at keeping adolescents free of drugs and alcohol. It does not condone the use and then merely offer accident protection by having someone transport them home." Micky Sadoff, the MADD president in the late 1980s, championed even

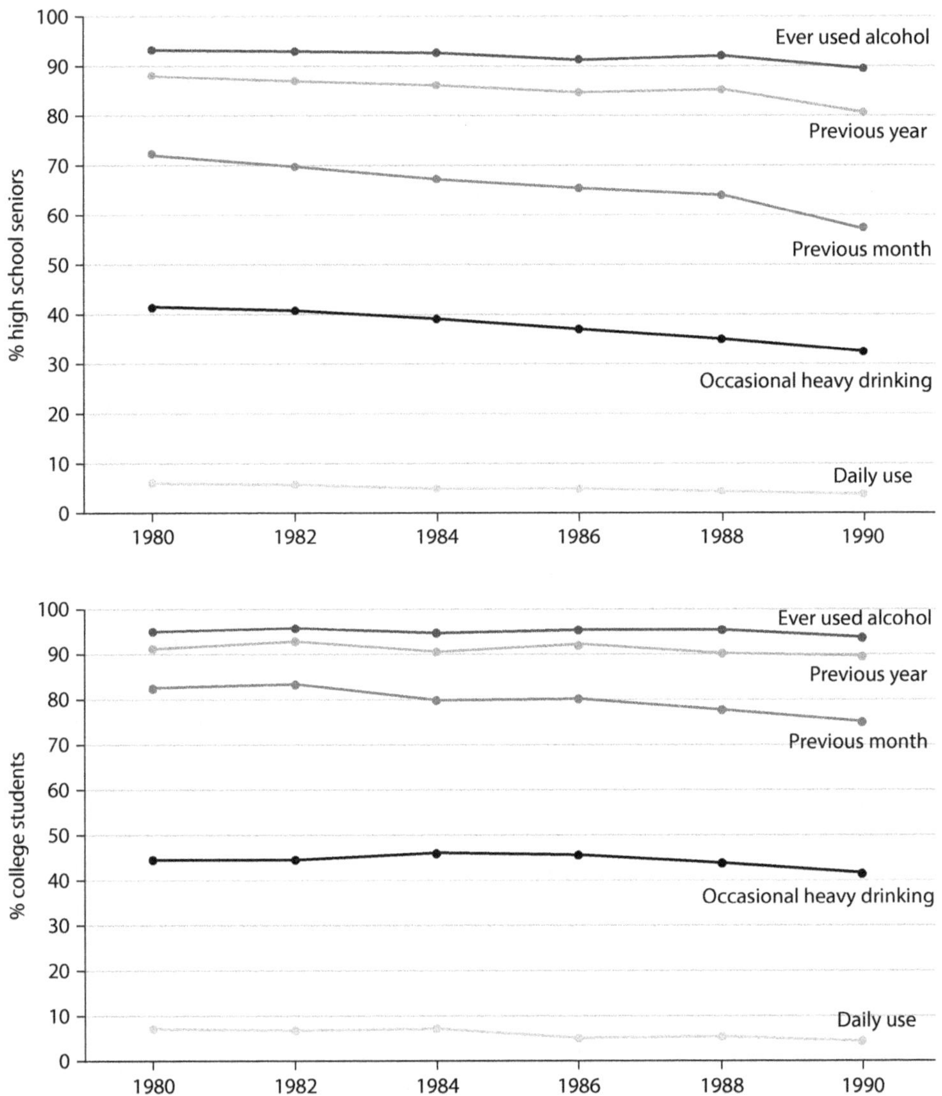

FIGURE 7.8. Trends in alcohol use among U.S. high school seniors and college students, 1980–90. (*Top*: high school seniors) Federal and state age-twenty-one laws had little impact on alcohol usage. Almost all high school seniors in 1990 still broke the alcohol status laws, although self-reported drinking during the previous year and month did decline slightly. "Occasional heavy drinking" (defined as five or more drinks at one time during the previous two weeks) decreased among high school seniors from 41% in 1980 to 32% in 1990. (*Bottom*: college students) Age-twenty-one laws had no effect on alcohol consumption among college students. For legal adults between the ages of eighteen and twenty, the status prohibition campaign represented a sweeping mass criminalization of normative social behavior. (NIDA, *Drug Use Among High School Seniors, College Students, and Young Adults, 1975–1990*, vols. 1 and 2.)

more authoritarian measures in response to persistent illegal drinking by a large majority of high school students, including two-thirds of seniors monthly. Sadoff called for a legal ban on alcohol advertisements purportedly aimed at high school and college students, criminal sanctions and civil liability for parents who provided alcohol to underage youth, heightened police crackdowns on the adolescent party scene, a mandatory one-year driver's license suspension for any alcohol violation, and a 0.0 percent BAC standard for under-twenty-one drivers.[101]

The dogmatic politics of zero tolerance, and the uncompromising assault on SADD's "responsible use" agenda, ultimately led to a major schism within the parent power movement. PRIDE directors Thomas Gleaton and Marsha Schuchard, the pair that largely orchestrated the founding of the National Federation of Parents, resigned from its board in 1983 in a dispute over alcohol policy. PRIDE strongly opposed any toleration of underage drinking but refused to condemn SADD's "Friends don't let friends drive drunk" campaign and also held that "moderate, responsible use of alcohol can be taught to adolescents within their families," a social practice permitted under most state laws.[102] The PRIDE-NFP relationship ruptured publicly over the 1985 television documentary *Deadliest Weapon in America*, the latest installment in the *Epidemic* series produced by Gannett in consultation with Gleaton's organization. The exposé featured horrifying scenes of young children and teenagers from white middle-class suburbs who had been killed or maimed by drunk drivers, followed by a segment on SADD's campaign for designated drivers or Safe Rides home from parents. Following NFP criticism of the initial cut, Gannett added an interview that disparaged the SADD contract as de facto authorization of teenage lawbreaking. NFP leaders nevertheless denounced the final version, while Gleaton and Schuchard criticized their "interest in destroying SADD" and praised the documentary for recognizing that "a majority of teenagers do drink." NFP activists from New Jersey, the epicenter of the national age-21 movement, then launched a vitriolic attack on PRIDE for betraying its longtime opposition to "responsible use," and the national board severed all ties with its parent organization. Gleaton and Schuchard, whose zero-tolerance crusade against marijuana had decisively reshaped national politics and policy, rebuked NFP leaders for allowing the "non-blaming, constructive approach of the original parents' movement to deteriorate into fruitless condemnations of those who do not meet a few people's standards of '100% purity.'"[103]

The criminalization of the normative social practices of millions of college students and employed young adults, after decades of irrefutable evidence that legal prohibition had no deterrent effect on alcohol consumption within the adolescent subculture, represented both the pinnacle of the zero-tolerance assault on teenage drug use and an expression of symbolic politics at its most futile. The save-the-children crusades of the 1980s began with white grassroots activists in "parent power" and "victims' rights" coalitions who mobilized around serious but quite rare social problems—the twelve-year-old daily stoner, the fifteen-year-old alcoholic, nine suburban teenagers killed in a drunk-driving crash, the young white child kidnapped and murdered by a stranger. These "moral entrepreneurs" then portrayed their causes as nationwide epidemics of endangered childhood and suburban family crisis, based on wildly exaggerated statistical claims recirculated by an irresponsible media industry that continued to hype any threat to white middle-class youth as universal, and championed by politicians from across the spectrum who scrambled to jump on the bandwagon. In *Generation at Risk: The Chemical People II*, broadcast by PBS in 1986 in alliance with the White House Office of Drug Abuse Policy, Nancy Reagan returned to reiterate the zero-tolerance movement's mantra that one-fourth of high school students were "problem drinkers" and lament the "terrifying specter of drug and alcohol abuse"—a crisis of "epidemic proportions" that "can happen in any town, in any home in America."[104] These campaigns to "protect" children ultimately sought to control the teenage subculture through strategies of criminalization, coercive medicalization, and depoliticization—vividly demonstrated by the zero-tolerance attack on SADD even though the youth-led movement achieved significant public health success by combining strong disapproval of drunk driving with a family compact that treated teenagers as citizens who could be trusted to make responsible choices. For some, but not all, American teenagers, it was about to get a lot worse.

Crack Cocaine and the Racially Divergent Drug War

In 1986, the White House Office of Drug Abuse Policy was focused on the expansion of Nancy Reagan's campaign to encourage "Just Say No" clubs in elementary and middle schools nationwide when the crack cocaine phenomenon propelled the carceral state and its bipartisan war on drugs toward the most massive and racially inequitable escalation in modern American history. The first "Just Say No" club began in Oakland, California, started by two Black mothers of preteens. The movement spread to other nonwhite urban communities with assistance from NIDA's Pyramid Project, the same agency that had seeded the white suburban National Federation of Parents groups in the late 1970s. Then the eight-year-old white lead of NBC-TV's *Punky Brewster* sitcom and her Black friend resisted peer pressure to do drugs in an October 1985 episode and formed a "Just Say No" club, inspiring their rapid proliferation in diverse communities nationwide. The Reagan White House promptly embraced and branded the "Just Say No" crusade as the first lady's latest contribution to the war on drugs, much to the chagrin of NIDA experts who believed the prevention slogan was good for young kids but a simplistic message for older teenagers and dangerously misguided when preached to actual addicts and substance abusers.[105] The White House transformed "Just Say No" into a media campaign sponsored by Procter & Gamble, alongside Hollywood celebrities delivering the zero-tolerance message in public service announcements. ODAP coordinated television ads through the white suburban crisis formula of a sixteen-year-old male resisting pressure to drink beer and get high and an eleven-year-old girl "from a very loving family" who took the marijuana gateway to cocaine, LSD, and heroin addiction. The Keebler Elves, from the same company that funded the White House's *New Teen Titans* comics curriculum, taught children not to succumb to drugs and alcohol in an "I Believe in Me" film and shopping mall tour. "We are in danger of losing an entire generation," Nancy Reagan reiterated. "The victims are getting younger all the time."[106]

President Reagan made the "Just Say No" campaign a centerpiece of the federal war on drugs in an August 1986 speech designed in large part to refute Democratic charges that his administration was losing the fight as crack cocaine ravaged America's cities and get-tough legislation made its way through Congress. "Illegal drug and alcohol use will no longer be tolerated," Reagan declared. "Starting today, Nancy's crusade to deprive the drug peddlers and suppliers of their customers becomes America's crusade." The president praised the first lady for the formation of ten thousand "Just Say No" clubs across the nation and warned all young Americans that "they must learn to 'just say no,'" which he defined as the foundation of all other antidrug policies. The rest of the Reagan administration's six-point "Campaign Against Drug Abuse" included prevention and policing to maintain "drug-free schools," testing to ensure a "drug-free workplace," addiction treatment programs (badly underfunded), international interdiction, and a law enforcement crackdown of "prompt and severe punishment to drug peddlers, the big guys and the little guys." The president did not mention crack cocaine, but he did call on Hollywood to join the "Just Say No" crusade and praise the Parents Music Resource Center, the organization recently founded by Tipper Gore to shame the rock music industry and restrict youth access to sexually explicit, violent, and drug-oriented song lyrics.[107] The parent power movement had long protested the "pro-drug" messages of rock music and denounced teenage films such as *Fast Times at Ridgemont High* (with a humorous and harmless slacker-stoner character) and *The Breakfast Club* (the 1985 hit where five high school misfits can only bond after they get high). The Reagan administration's "Just Say No" initiative sought to repurpose popular culture by pressuring Hollywood to produce more *Punky Brewster*–style plotlines, such as star Kirk Cameron's don't-try-cocaine bravery in the sitcom *Growing Pains*, as well as drug-free themed events by Major League Baseball and music artists. The "Just Say No" campaign targeted October 1986 for a nationwide surge to enlist eight-to-fourteen-year-olds in its "no drugs/no alcohol" clubs.[108]

Crack cocaine, during the spring and summer of 1986, suddenly "spread" from an inner-city scourge to the latest white suburban crisis even faster than its actual "destructive sprint across America," in the phrase of a breathless *New York Times* headline from a few years later. In reality, the practice of freebasing and smoking (rather than snorting) cocaine for the intense rush first took hold among a subset of the affluent white users who constituted the vast majority of its consumers before the so-called "crack epidemic." By spring 1986, 40 percent of all Americans in their mid-twenties had tried cocaine, as well as 17 percent of high school seniors. That year, as freebase cocaine expanded from upscale white urban and suburban enclaves to mass production in "ghetto" drug markets, the "crack epidemic" erupted and redefined the cultural meaning of smoking the drug as an instantly addictive racial threat that unleashed a wave of crime and violence spilling out of inner cities into Middle America.[109] But the earliest mention of "crack" cocaine in mainstream media came in a *New York Times* article about a new form of drug dependency among white suburban teenagers at a private treatment center in Westchester County. Around the same time, a DEA official labeled cocaine the "marijuana of the '80s" in a *Los Angeles Times* feature on how the Reagan administration's drug war had completely failed to stem the supply and there was "no serious enforcement on the consumer." Then the *New York Times* reported "a new, purified form of cocaine" that emerged on the streets of the Bronx and rapidly spread "throughout the city and its suburbs." The article portrayed urban street-level crack dealers as evil predators and humanized their victims as college-bound teenagers from two of Westchester's wealthiest white suburbs, "addicted almost instantly." By March 1986, when *Newsweek* put a young white teenager on the cover for its "Kids and Cocaine: An Epidemic Strikes Middle America" investigative report (fig. 7.9), the crack crisis was well

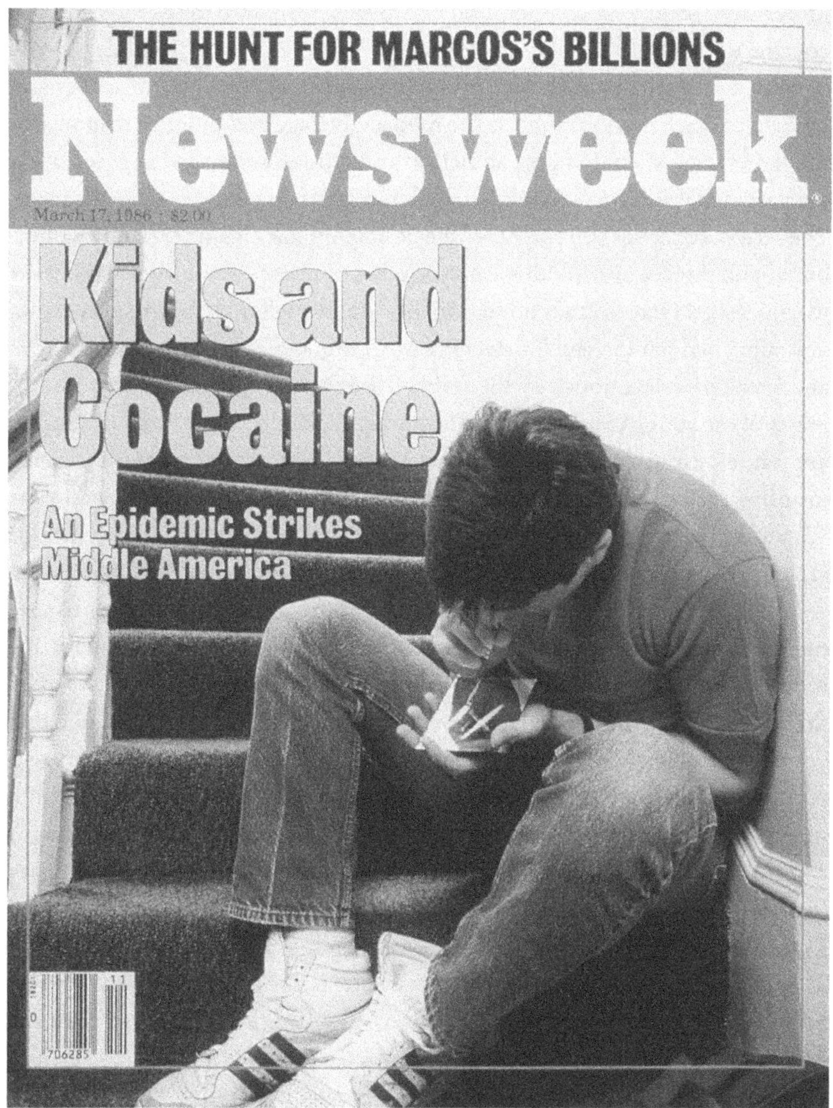

THE HUNT FOR MARCOS'S BILLIONS
Newsweek
Kids and Cocaine
An Epidemic Strikes Middle America

FIGURE 7.9. *Newsweek* highlighted the young white suburban casualties of the "crack epidemic" in this cover story on "Kids and Cocaine" published March 17, 1986. The feature, typical of mainstream media coverage during the bipartisan rush toward tougher crack laws, bifurcated the cocaine market into innocent white addict-victims and the predatory international smugglers and street dealers who targeted "school-age children." (Courtesy of Enveritas Group.)

underway—exposing "a generation of American children to the nightmare of cocaine addiction."[110]

White suburban youth victims of international cocaine traffickers and inner-city crack markets shaped the media coverage and political response to the nation's latest epidemic of addiction and crime, as they had in every other escalation of the carceral state's racially bifurcated war on drugs since the 1950s. The *Newsweek* cover story of how "the contagion has already spread to suburbia" highlighted white middle-class tragedies of innocent teenagers taking the marijuana gateway to crack addiction, inevitably including the greatest fear of any suburban parent, the fourteen-year-old runaway daughter rescued from an inner-city crack house by the police. The feature even included a photograph of the young cheerleader and honors student who underwent this ordeal and ended up in an expensive private suburban treatment center for seven months until she overcame her addiction. Three months later, *Newsweek*'s "Crack and Crime" cover story portrayed the other side of this market: "savage violence" by Black and Hispanic gangs that had transformed urban centers into a "domestic Vietnam," left law enforcement "outmanned" and helpless to stop the flood, and were expanding their networks into the suburbs. *Time* magazine focused primarily on the ghetto "pushers" and violent addicts "deranged by the new drug," claiming that half of the nation's "crackheads are black" and that young "hard-core" criminals in the inner city "are America's newest lost generation." In "I Am a Coke Addict," *Life* magazine profiled the sympathetic and unexpected victims of the scourge with a cover image of a white male smoking crack and a feature on "what happens when nice guys get hooked."[111] To say that the Reagan administration was late to highlight this crack cocaine threat is an understatement. In an internal June memo, ODAP director Carlton Turner labeled crack "basically a media event" based on his view that cocaine addiction was already an "epidemic" in white America, combined with the zero-tolerance, suburban-oriented policy stance that all illegal drug use including marijuana and underage drinking was equally hazardous.[112]

Liberal Democrats in Congress and in the largest cities constantly lambasted the Reagan administration for losing the war on drugs and doing nothing about the crack cocaine epidemic throughout the summer and fall of 1986. Thomas (Tip) O'Neill, the Speaker of the House, announced in July that the Democratic party would assemble comprehensive drug legislation on an emergency timeline, including much more funding for a law enforcement crackdown and for addiction treatment programs. Drug abuse was no longer just an urban crisis, O'Neill warned; "it has spread like wildfire to become not only a tragic national menace but a threat to our domestic peace and security." Senator Joe Biden and Representative Charles Rangel, longtime critics of Reagan's drug-war policies, continued to assail the administration for its failure to control the border, lock up the street dealers for good, and provide adequate funding for urban treatment centers. In June, the shocking death of college basketball star Len Bias from an apparent cocaine overdose generated even more momentum for the war on traffickers and provided one of the only compassionate media portraits of a nonwhite drug victim during the emergence of the crack crisis.[113] As the Democrats escalated the stakes, the Reagan White House remained very reluctant to highlight crack cocaine as a priority threat because the administration did not want to acknowledge that any drug abuse problem had increased on its watch, preferring to boast about the slight statistical decrease in teenage marijuana smoking. The president and his advisors also just did not care very much—in both a racial and a political sense—about addiction and suffering in the inner city and among nonwhite Americans (paralleling their neglect of AIDS victims). Internal White House communications do reveal political calculations about how to outflank the Democrats' hardline program by endorsing harsher laws against criminal traffickers and addicts, while making sure to "hold users accountable" by expanding the "Just Say No" campaign against all illegal drugs and continuing to prioritize "recreational users" over urban treatment funding.[114]

The congressional hearings that produced the Anti-Drug Abuse Act of 1986 depicted the crack crisis as universal and its most innocent victims as white, while demonizing the enemy as nonwhite ghetto dealers and murderers who profited from their misery. A Senate hearing in July portrayed crack as an "egalitarian drug" that had killed many white-collar professionals, and an anonymous witness testified that he operated crack houses in the gentrified parts of DC and in Silver Spring, Maryland, where white suburbanites were the best customers. Soon after, a White House ODAP memo observed that Senator Biden was working with House colleagues on a get-tough law to burnish his presidential bid in 1988 and box Reagan into a corner where he would either have to veto and face the fallout or accede to the big-spending Democratic agenda.[115] The main action took place in the Democratic-controlled House of Representatives, especially in the Select Committee on Narcotics Abuse and Control chaired by drug warrior Charles Rangel. In mid-July, the committee designed its first hearing on "the crack cocaine crisis" to send the Reagan administration a loud and clear message that "we are losing the effort to save our children" and that the first lady's just-say-no rhetoric was not enough. The liberal Democrats excoriated the White House for funding cuts that had devastated treatment programs in nonwhite urban areas, but they also chose to highlight and humanize this tragedy through a twenty-year-old white female and recovering addict from New York City who testified alongside her mother. Lee Ann said that she progressed from marijuana to cocaine dependency and Valium addiction, then started dealing coke and freebasing crack, and only survived because her parents forced her into an expensive private rehab center ($5,000 a week). The takeaway was twofold: Lee Ann said that if it could happen to a middle-class white girl then "it happens to everybody," and her mother urged the federal government to "crack down on drug dealers" (presumably excluding dealer-victims like her daughter) and help out families that could not afford treatment.[116]

The Select Committee on Narcotics Abuse and Control portrayed the crack epidemic as a violent and devastating conflagration as the Democrats devised comprehensive drug legislation and the Reagan White House sought to reclaim the narrative. Rep. Rangel demanded "all-out war on drugs"—heightened interdiction in source countries, tough mandatory-minimum sentences to accompany the law enforcement crackdown, far more funding for treatment and prevention programs—and observed that "we in the black community have suffered out of proportion than the rest of the nation."[117] Reagan kept talking about teenage boys smoking pot, "the young coed popping pills or snorting coke," and the need to "take the customers away from the drug peddlers." On September 8, the House Democrats introduced their omnibus drug legislation, and six days later Ronald and Nancy Reagan addressed the nation in a prime-time televised address while holding hands and sitting on a couch in the residential wing of the White House. "Drugs are menacing our society," President Reagan began. "They're killing our children." He defended his administration's progress, particularly in the areas of marijuana interdiction and Nancy's "Just Say No" campaign against "school-age drug and alcohol abuse," but conceded that cocaine was flooding into the country and the new crack epidemic was "an uncontrolled fire." The first lady took over and reiterated her universalistic and zero-tolerance mantras that "no one is safe" and "there's no moral middle ground," as the young leaders of ten thousand "Just Say No" clubs were teaching the nation. Nancy Reagan then warned that "drug criminals are ingenious" and had created the new temptation of crack—visibly stumbling over this unfamiliar line on the teleprompter—to "steal our children's lives." The president finished by touting his six-pronged Campaign Against Drug Abuse while criticizing the Democratic agenda for wanting to

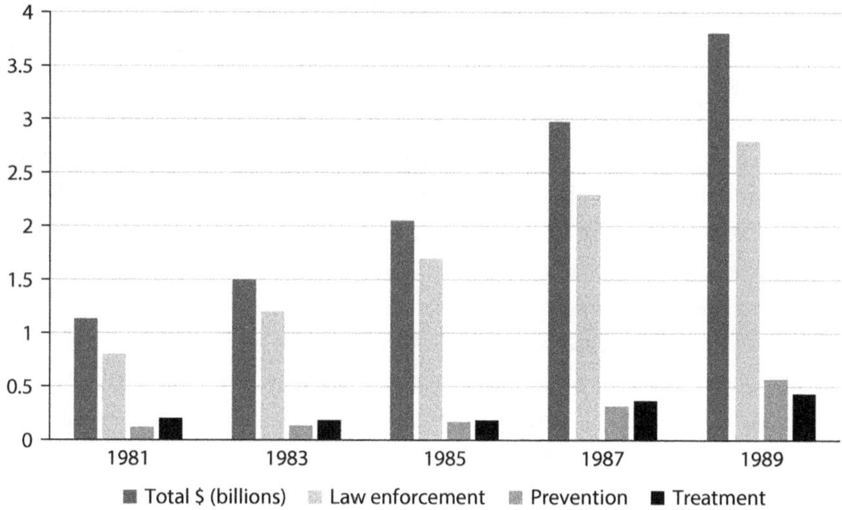

FIGURE 7.10. Federal expenditures for drug enforcement, prevention, and treatment, 1981–89 (in billions of dollars). Federal war on drugs spending dedicated to law enforcement (including border and overseas interdiction) more than tripled during the 1980s and constituted almost three times the combined total for prevention and treatment. The prevention total surpassed treatment after implementation of the Anti-Drug Abuse Act of 1986, meaning that the "Just Say No" curriculum and messaging campaign received expenditures diverted from underfunded rehabilitation centers. By contrast, the law enforcement category represented less than half of federal war on drugs expenditures in the years immediately after passage of omnibus legislation in 1970, and treatment received three to five times as much funding as prevention (see fig. 4.5). (White House Office of Public Affairs, "The Reagan Record on the National Crusade for a Drug-Free America," June 6, 1988.)
Note: Totals are rounded and adjusted for 1989 dollars.

"throw money at the problem." He concluded that the ultimate solution would be for "Americans simply to quit using drugs" and join the national crusade to "just say no."[118]

Congress approved the Anti-Drug Abuse Act of 1986 in a bipartisan and nearly unanimous vote on October 17, and President Reagan signed the omnibus legislation ten days later. The package greatly expanded funding for interdiction and law enforcement, its primary focus, with smaller increases for treatment and especially prevention programs (fig. 7.10). The most consequential provision replaced the flexible penalty structure of the 1970 federal drug law with mandatory-minimum felony sentences of five to forty years for selling or trafficking threshold amounts of all Schedule 1 illegal substances, including 5 grams (0.01 pounds) of crack cocaine, 500 grams of powder cocaine, 100 grams of heroin, and 100 kilograms (220 pounds) of marijuana. The law also doubled penalties for repeat offenders, enhanced sentences for providing to minors, and authorized forty to life if distribution led to death or serious injury. Larger amounts of each drug brought a ten-to-life mandatory-minimum sentence with parallel enhancements.[119] The 100:1 sentencing disparity between powder and crack cocaine, which led to strikingly divergent racial outcomes in the criminal legal system, did not generate any debate at the time. A large body of academic research has demonstrated that the crack/powder differential and the broader political consensus around harsh penalties for traffickers and low-level street dealers alike resulted from the racially targeted hype about violent gangs and predatory addicts in Black and Hispanic neighborhoods, combined with pervasive scientific misinformation spread by network television, the print media, law enforcement, drug treatment professionals, and of course politicians. Scholars have refuted the myths of crack cocaine's alleged "instant" addiction (instead of potential psychological dependency as with many drugs), its propensity to turn users into dangerous predators (most violence in the market results from competition for lucrative profits enabled by prohibitionist policy, not the drug itself), and the unambiguously racist "crack babies" furor (stigmatizing poor Black mothers in underserved communities for developmental problems in infants purportedly born addicted).[120]

The Reagan administration, which had played a reactive role in passage of the Anti-Drug Abuse Act, responded by launching a multifaceted "Crusade for a Drug-Free America." The White House claimed that illegal drug use had declined because teenagers were embracing the "Just Say No" message and federal law enforcement agencies had coordinated an "aggressive attack on drug pushers," securing longer sentences for "those who prey on the innocent." On the user front, zero-tolerance prevention remained a much higher priority than publicly funded addiction treatment, and the executive branch increasingly shifted the budget to "Just Say No" programs in both areas. The Crusade for a Drug-Free America conspicuously targeted all "illegal drug users" for moral condemnation and called for a range of punitive policies toward "even 'casual' use"—involuntary rehabilitation, mandatory testing, asset forfeiture, loss of government benefits including student loans and public housing, revocation of driver's licenses for alcohol violations, and jail time. Internal documents clarify that the strategy was to arrest the "casual user" in order to coerce "rehabilitation rather than incarceration." The point person for the White House crusade was Donald MacDonald, the recently installed director of the Office of Drug Abuse Policy and former NFP leader who advocated mandatory urinalysis screening of all teenagers and lockdown rehabilitation for "marijuana addicts." MacDonald promoted "zero tolerance" as the cornerstone of all sectors of federal drug policy—law enforcement, prevention, and addiction treatment—and championed the administration's pledge to "get tough on the user." He constantly blamed the permissive attitudes and liberal policies of the 1960s and 1970s for an illegal drug culture excused by concepts of "responsible use," "victimless crime," and "do your own thing." In February 1988, Nancy Reagan summed up the mission thus: "The casual user cannot morally escape responsibility for the actions of drug traffickers and dealers. I'm saying that if you're a casual user, you're an accomplice to murder."[121]

The internal White House records, as well as the media orientation of its "Just Say No" campaign, make clear that the "casual user" in this formulation was white, middle class, and suburban, while the "drug traffickers and dealers" remained nonwhite urban youth gangsters—the same racial imagining of the illegal market that had structured the bipartisan drug control legislation of 1970 as well (see chapter 4). "Focus on the User," the Reagan administration's confidential strategy document, resurrected the arrest-and-rehabilitate philosophy of the Nixon era for the "mainstream adults" and "occasional" users who "most often live away from the areas in which they buy their drugs"—both an obvious reference to white suburban consumers who patronized inner-city markets and a fundamental misunderstanding of how white middle-class dealers actually operated. One section of the strategy blueprint called for "arresting the user" in order to force these otherwise law-abiding adults and younger "occasional users" to quit, with the deterrent of jail only as a "last resort." A separate section about "low-income, high-crime areas" called for "special enforcement initiatives aimed at both pushers and users" and aggressive prosecution of juveniles.[122] This racially bifurcated division of the illegal drug market into suburban users who needed moral censure and coercive rehabilitation, and urban criminals who required incapacitation, also underlay and occasionally surfaced explicitly in the "Just Say No" media initiative, a centerpiece of the Crusade for a Drug-Free America. In the opening scene of *21 Jump Street*, a Fox-TV drama that premiered in 1987, two Black teenage drug dealers burst through the glass door of an expensive suburban home, terrorize the white family at gunpoint, sexually threaten the daughter, steal the Jaguar because the son owes them $6,000, and later try to kill him with a speedball (heroin and cocaine). The young undercover cops who are the show's heroes infiltrate the high school to bust the Black criminals and save the white boy, a "user" who is hospitalized and delivers the "Just Say No"/"parent power" lessons in the end.[123]

The bipartisan consensus behind this racialized, two-track war on drugs culminated in the Anti-Drug Abuse Act of 1988, a second round of omnibus legislation co-introduced by the House majority and minority leaders. The urgent atmosphere in Congress responded to the escalating violence in urban centers—exacerbated by the selective militarized crackdown on inner-city cocaine markets—and extreme crisis rhetoric about Black crack pushers and predatory addicts in the media and political culture. The law included mandatory enhancements for violent felonies by juveniles and also applied the five-year minimum sentence for sale of five grams of crack cocaine, established in 1986, to first-time possession offenses as well (while retaining misdemeanor status for illegal use of all other drugs). The Reagan administration did not propose the crack revision, believing that the discretionary "possession with intent to distribute" charge made it superfluous and that the proliferation of harsh mandatory-minimum state laws would cover most simple possession cases. There also was no real debate, as with the singling out of crack suppliers as a uniquely evil threat two years earlier. The White House did take advantage of the second legislative wave to enact priorities that the Democrats had refused to incorporate in 1986, including the death penalty for "kingpins" and punitive "user accountability" measures such as denial of student loans and random drug testing in federally funded workplaces and other pilot locations. The 1988 law mainly pumped a lot more money into street-level enforcement, interdiction, and prison construction. It also budgeted an additional $150 million annually for zero-tolerance prevention programs—shown by all reputable studies to have negligible impact—while flatlining the percentage of funding dedicated to addiction treatment. This legislative free-for-all played out during a presidential election in which each party accused the other of being "soft on drugs" and losing the war to protect America, while Washington politicians collaborated in the passage of an omnibus package that received only eleven dissenting votes.[124]

The intensification of militarized law enforcement in urban centers and poor Black and Hispanic neighborhoods during the late 1980s and early 1990s produced the most racially discriminatory outcomes in the history of the war on drugs (fig. 7.11). The prioritization of a selective war on crack, targeting inner-city dealers and nonwhite youth but not white suburban counterparts, meant that the racially disproportionate arrests of Black Americans reached historically high levels, including half of juvenile apprehensions. As recently as

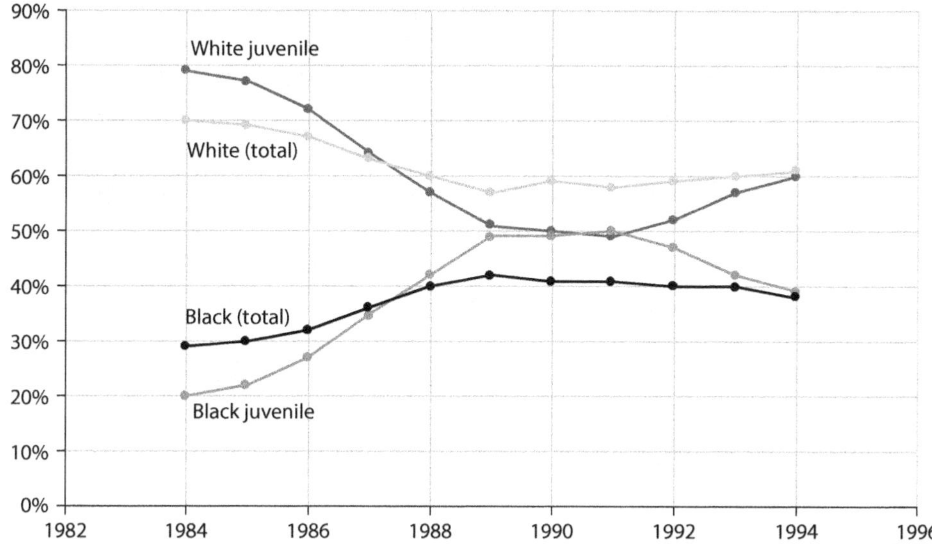

FIGURE 7.11. Racial distribution of juvenile and adult drug arrests in the United States, 1984–94, as a percentage of total drug arrests in each category. The racially targeted war on crack cocaine had the most disproportionate impact on Black juveniles between the mid-1980s and the mid-1990s. Their proportion of the juvenile drug arrest total increased from 20% in 1984 to a peak of 50% in 1991 (about 4.2 times the population share). This was double the proportion of Black juvenile arrests in the mid-1960s (25%), before the enforcement prioritization of the white marijuana market. White juvenile arrests consequently declined from 79% of total juvenile arrests in 1984 to a low of 49% in 1991, even as the proportion of Hispanic juveniles included in this category steadily increased (see note). The overall racial breakdown (adults and juveniles combined) in the annual drug arrest totals paralleled these patterns but without the extreme disproportionality of the juvenile data. Total drug arrests remained above one million per year between 1988 and 1994, and more than half involved cocaine or heroin. (FBI, *Uniform Crime Reports*, 1984–1994.) *Note*: Juvenile drug arrests ranged from 8% to 12% of total drug arrests during these years. Total drug arrests for adults and juveniles combined increased from 708,400 in 1984 to 1,351,400 in 1994. The FBI reported (estimated) arrest data for Hispanic juveniles between 1980 and 1986 and then discontinued the practice through 1994. Hispanic juveniles averaged 18.5% of total juvenile drug arrests during the three-year period from 1984 to 1986, approximately twice the population share, and also double the estimate of 9.1% Hispanic juvenile arrests in 1980. The racial breakdown of the U.S. population in 1990 was 75.6% white (non-Hispanic), 11.8% Black, and 9.0% Hispanic. On the FBI's inclusion of most Hispanic arrests in the "white" category, see note in fig. I.1.

1980, marijuana had accounted for 70 percent of drug arrests nationwide, and white Americans more than three-fourths of the total. After the Anti-Drug Abuse Act of 1986, and the wave of parallel mandatory-minimum state laws, cocaine firmly displaced marijuana and drug arrests of African Americans rose to 3.5 times their population share, and even more skewed for teenagers. Despite the political promises to incarcerate the traffickers, possession busts represented around three-fourths of all drug-war arrests, and most of the remainder involved low-level street dealers and couriers. These stark disparities still tell only part of the story, because systemic racial discrimination in the discretionary processes of prosecution and disposition following arrest meant that African Americans accounted for 63 percent of all recent felony drug violators sentenced to state prisons by 1996, about five times their population share, and around 80 percent of crack defendants. The incarceration of nonwhite juveniles, often through gang enhancements and transfers to the adult system, was the most inequitable feature of the entire drug-war apparatus. This all happened even though white Americans continued to both sell and use illegal drugs at rates greater than their population share and also to constitute a majority of even the crack cocaine market—but for the most part they did not live in the geographic areas prioritized for enforcement. When white students and professionals did happen to face arrest, the criminal legal system generally diverted them into rehabilitative programs or other outcomes that did not leave a criminal record, as the Reagan administration's racialized "user accountability" strategy had explicitly envisioned.[125]

The binary of white suburban addict-victims and nonwhite ghetto predator-criminals structured this political assault on crack cocaine and urban gangs, operating as both the preemptive rationalization and the circular logic of the racially divergent war on drugs. In 1988, *Time* magazine's "Kids Who Sell Crack" cover story introduced the nation to "Frog," a remorseless "cocky prince of the barrio" in East Los Angeles, a thirteen-year-old gangster-dealer in "an ultra-violent street gang, the Crips." *Time* depicted a crack market dominated by Black and Latino teenagers, killing each other and destroying their communities with the "highly addictive" drug, battled by the police in stop-and-search street sweeps that had filled Los Angeles's jails and juvenile detention centers. Then there was Eric, a high school athlete and honors student from the "posh" suburb of Brentwood, and also a "crack addict" scared straight into rehab when a "menacing dealer" invaded his home. That same year, the California Department of Justice distributed a confidential racial profiling manual on "Crips & Bloods Street Gangs" to local police departments, advising the war on crack strategy of searching all "Black males, 13 to 40 years old," especially those wearing the gang fashions of gold chains and brand-name athletic gear. The LAPD's "Operation Hammer" and other street sweeps and racial profiling crackdowns arrested at least fifty thousand Black and Latino youth in the late 1980s, many for low-level offenses or mere allegations of gang affiliation, a comprehensive policy of preemptive criminalization.[126] In New

FIGURE 7.12. This montage of four scenes from the 1989 HBO documentary *Crack U.S.A.: County Under Siege* illustrates the prevailing media tropes that divided the intertwined cocaine market into separate spheres based on race, class, gender, and geography. Set in South Florida, the film juxtaposes the nonchalant criminality of teenage Black male crack dealers with three fifteen-year-old white suburban "addicts" recovering in a private treatment facility. Both the white male "Barry" (top left) and the Black male "Joe" (top right) admit to selling cocaine, but the documentary portrays the former as an addict-victim being saved through rehabilitation and the latter as a menace on streets that "belong to the dealers."

York City, the other epicenter of the urban war on drugs, the "bane of [the] inner city is now gripping suburbs," the *New York Times* proclaimed in a 1989 series about how crack had "leaped across the city lines" to cause rampant addiction among affluent white Americans "living double lives." Everyone featured in this report was in private rehabilitation centers or programs, several through diversion after a felony arrest. A number of these white victims had supplied friends and acquaintances in the suburbs after driving into Harlem to make their buys, a practice known in other contexts as "cocaine trafficking."[127]

The pinnacle of this racially divergent imagination of the intertwined metropolitan drug market came in a 1989 HBO documentary, *Crack U.S.A.*, that juxtaposed the innocent young white addicts of the nation's latest plague with teenage Black street dealers boasting of the "money in the drug game" (fig. 7.12). The film portrays Palm Beach County in South Florida as a once-utopian suburb infiltrated by the "crime and violence of the big cities" and lionizes the police drug squads busting into crack houses and fighting the good war on the streets. *Crack U.S.A.* then takes viewers into a private West Palm Beach treatment center where two fifteen-year-old white girls confess cocaine addiction, staged sitting on a bed with a teddy bear in case anyone missed the theme of innocence lost. The narrator echoes Nancy Reagan's lament that "we're losing a generation to this drug." The most evocative scene is a cute and innocent-seeming white boy named Barry who says he started "working for, like, big-time people," selling cocaine to classmates. An impossible criminal, Barry speaks to the nation from the safety of the rehab facility, joined by his conscientious parents and other white suburban casualties of the crack invasion.[128] The prevailing view that drug and crime control policies shifted from rehabilitative to punitive between the 1950s and the 1980s is based on the fundamental failure to recognize that both approaches have always operated in tandem through a racialized political consensus that reserves the status of innocent victim for the impossible criminals in white middle-class America. And yet, as pernicious as the racial binary between public health solutions for white suburbia and crime crackdowns in nonwhite urban centers has been, the arrest-and-rehabilitate policy designed for middle-class youth is not the opposite of incarceration, because both are coercive and ultimately depend on the carceral state's capacity and authority to criminalize and punish. The opposite of both, and the only truly humane alternative, is the civil liberties agenda of removing criminalization from drug and public health policies altogether.

Epilogue

The most dangerous drug in America is a 12-year-old smoking pot.

—GENERAL BARRY MCCAFFREY, DIRECTOR OF THE OFFICE OF NATIONAL DRUG CONTROL POLICY, 1997

Anyone who gets convicted of a drug crime—not one that is in terms of massive selling, but consumption—they shouldn't go to prison. They should go to mandatory rehabilitation.

—JOSEPH BIDEN, DEMOCRATIC PRESIDENTIAL NOMINEE, 2020

IN THE LATE 1990S at least fourteen white high school and college students died of heroin overdoses in the affluent Dallas suburb of Plano, recently named the safest midsized city in America. The local newspaper proclaimed a "heroin epidemic sweeping Plano and the nation," and media reports invariably described the illegal drug consumers as tragic victims, "clean-cut teenagers" from good families with a "bright future ahead of them." The intensive national coverage highlighted innocent white children in a seemingly idyllic suburb corrupted by sinister outside forces that might strike anywhere, anytime. "Heroin in Suburbia," an *ABC World News* exposé, warned all of white middle-class America that Plano's gated communities faced "a new enemy that has invaded their city and is threatening their children. . . . People thought it couldn't happen here, but it did." *Dateline NBC* lamented that heroin, an inner-city drug, "has jumped the tracks and has been killing kids in some of our most prosperous suburbs." CNN opened a special Plano broadcast with the searching question, "Is your town ripe for picking by drug dealers?" The Plano police blamed illegal [undocumented] immigrants who "peddle Chiva [heroin] to rich suburban kids," and the U.S. district attorney pledged zero tolerance for the Mexican cartels "preying on this community." The federal Drug Enforcement Administration announced a major operation to protect Plano's youth, culminating in the indictment of twenty-nine "drug pushers" for conspiracy to commit murder. Sixteen of these defendants were local white teenagers who sold marijuana and heroin to other students; each took a plea bargain, and most received probation or limited jail time. The Mexican "kingpins"—in reality, low-level operators in the transnational market—received mandatory-minimum sentences of twenty years to life for what prosecutors labeled their "calculated and cold-blooded" decision to "target young people in Plano as a new market." This episode strikingly parallels the 1950s war on narcotics crusade in Southern California to save white teenage victims from Mexican pushers and reveals yet again the structural power of suburban crisis in American political culture and public policy.[1]

The "Crusade for a Drug-Free America," launched in 1988 by the Reagan administration, did not succeed in its stated goal of eradicating the illegal drug market through an even tougher crackdown on the supply side, while eliminating demand with a combination of "Just Say No" moralizing and coercive "user accountability" methods encapsulated in the arrest-and-rehabilitate philosophy. The bipartisan consensus for the racially divergent drug war continued during the George H. W. Bush and Bill Clinton administrations, epitomized by the Violent Crime Control and Law Enforcement Act of 1994. Its punitive provisions included billions for new prison construction, enhanced mandatory-minimum sentencing for gang members and drug dealers, and authorization of adult prosecution for juveniles as young as thirteen. President Clinton embraced the cause of the victims' rights movement, symbolized by the "Three Strikes and You're Out" crusade to avenge the abduction and murder of twelve-year-old Polly Klaas in suburban California, inviting her father to the signing ceremony and declaring that "there must be no doubt about whose side we're on." For the other side of the imagined racial and metropolitan divide, Clinton raged that "gangs and drugs have taken over our streets," tapping into the broader "super-predator" discourse of the mid-1990s that young Black males terrorizing American cities were "hardened, remorseless juveniles" and "wolf packs" trapped in a pathological culture of "moral poverty"—not actual poverty and racial segregation. Senator Joseph Biden, the longtime Democratic drug warrior and a main architect of the 1994 Crime Bill, proclaimed his mission to lock away the "violent thugs" and "predators on our streets" while diverting first-time drug offenders arrested for possession into compulsory rehabilitation programs. The Clinton administration also expanded drug interdiction in the U.S.-Mexico border region and in South America through militarized operations such as Plan Colombia, a bipartisan initiative continued by his successors that spent (squandered) $8 billion on coca eradication between 2000 and 2012.[2]

In the white middle-class suburbs, the "user accountability" front in the war on drugs continued to revolve around "Just Say No" prevention campaigns aimed at teenagers and preteens, with the backup strategy of coercive rehabilitation for the very small fraction of lawbreakers who actually encountered the criminal legal system. The National Federation of Parents for Drug-Free Youth, having accomplished its primary missions of stopping the momentum of marijuana decriminalization and forcing federal policymakers to adopt zero-tolerance messaging for any adolescent use of illegal drugs and alcohol, faded after the mid-1980s as a national coalition although many grassroots activists remained involved in local and statewide campaigns. The Partnership for a Drug-Free America, among its most significant legacies, formed in 1987 as a private-sector collaboration with the former NFP leaders who ran the Reagan administration's Office of Drug Abuse Policy to advance the "Just Say No" crusade through public service advertisements such as "This Is Your Brain on Drugs" (featuring eggs sizzling in a frying pan). William J. Bennett and General Barry McCaffrey, the respective White House drug czars for the George H. W. Bush and Clinton administrations, claimed that the "Just Say No" campaign in general and the widely mocked "This Is Your Brain on Drugs" commercial in particular had achieved significant reductions in teenage drug use and convinced most of its target audience that "kids who are really cool don't use drugs." During the Clinton era, the U.S. Congress also authorized $1 billion for zero-tolerance and "positive peer pressure" advertisements by the new public-sector National Youth Anti-Drug Media Campaign, and McCaffrey's office spread the wealth to major networks in order to review and censor scripts to ensure that television did not glamorize marijuana and underage drinking. Pharmaceutical companies, including Purdue Pharma (maker of OxyContin), provided significant funding for spin-off projects such as Partnership for Drug-Free Kids, in recognition that the obsession with marijuana's dangers distracted attention from the addictive potential of prescription painkillers.[3]

Marijuana remained at the center of the war on drugs during the 1990s, at it had since the Nixon era, because of its symbolic association with jeopardized futures for white middle-class youth and the resilient gateway mystique that any experimentation risked progression to hard-drug addiction. The first Bush administration labeled illegal drugs "the gravest threat facing our nation," championed a harsh law enforcement assault on inner-city crime and gangs, and boasted that Republican "user accountability" programs had succeeded as evidenced by a statistical downturn in frequent pot smoking by high school students. Then in the mid-1990s, NIDA's annual "Monitoring the Future" survey reported that 21 percent of high school seniors had used marijuana during the previous month, compared to 14 percent five years earlier, leading to bitter recriminations about which party was responsible for the biggest jump since the late 1970s (48 percent of seniors in 1995 had taken an illegal drug in their lifetime, and almost all had broken the alcohol laws).[4] The Clinton White House mobilized against this latest suburban crisis, with NIDA convening emergency sessions on the gateway progression of "our children" from marijuana to cocaine addiction and General McCaffrey channeling the NFP to proclaim that the "most dangerous drug in America is a twelve-year-old smoking pot." Public health agencies in the Clinton administration distorted science to warn that "marijuana is addictive," turned adolescents into lazy and unproductive burnouts, and accounted for more than half of teenagers in treatment for "drug abuse"—glossing over the reality that many were recreational users coerced by the criminal legal system or their parents. The next George W. Bush administration reiterated this mantra in a 2002 alert: "The *truth* is that *marijuana is addictive*," "The *truth* is that *marijuana and violence are linked*," "The *truth* is that *marijuana is a gateway drug*." The White House Office of National Drug Control Policy justified this priority mission because more than three-fourths of illegal drug users nationwide smoked pot and "*No drug matches the threat posed by marijuana*."[5]

Marijuana accounted for far more arrests nationwide than cocaine and heroin combined during the two decades after passage of the Violent Crime Control and Law Enforcement Act of 1994. But unlike the interregnum between the mid-1960s and late 1970s, when the vast majority of marijuana apprehensions involved white male teenagers and young adults, this arrest surge occurred disproportionately in the nonwhite urban neighborhoods targeted for saturation policing ever since the bipartisan launch of the militarized war on crack cocaine and gang violence. As the ACLU documented, marijuana busts escalated as part of the "broken windows" and "zero tolerance" law enforcement strategies that deployed racial profiling stop-and-frisk sweeps in selectively policed communities of color, under the philosophy of preemptively incarcerating the "real criminals" through aggressive crackdowns on quality-of-life public order offenses and other minor nonviolent crimes. In New York City, for example, marijuana arrests skyrocketed from 774 in 1991 to 59,000 by 2010, with African Americans detained at ten times the rate of white residents (adjusted for population) despite similar usage patterns. Nationwide, law enforcement agencies arrested more than 8.2 million people for marijuana violations between 2001 and 2010, 88 percent for possession, which the ACLU labeled primarily "a war on people of color." The ACLU's investigation reiterated the case for legalization and observed that the national drug war had cost $1 trillion and arrested more than 40 million people since the early 1970s, "while failing to have any marked effect on the use or availability of drugs." Critics further argued that the state's massive drug-war apparatus reprioritized marijuana enforcement starting in the mid-1990s in order to justify its mission and budgets as the crack cocaine phenomenon waned. Yet it is also essential to recognize that marijuana is "politically the most important illegal drug" because its intertwined but geographically divergent prevention and interdiction fronts aim above all else to protect white middle-class youth from its dangers.[6]

In recent decades, the methamphetamine "invasion" of the Middle American heartland and especially the surge in opioid overdose fatalities in suburban and rural areas has refocused attention on the white face of the latest American drug crises. This has generated extensive commentary about how government policies and media framing have shifted from punitive law enforcement to sympathetic public health approaches because of the racial and class identities of the perceived victims. While the critique of systemic inequalities and double standards in drug control programs and American political culture is compelling, this book has demonstrated that there is little new about these contemporary white suburban drug "epidemics," except the scale of the casualties in the pharmaceutical industry's opioid market. There is nothing at all new about the political consensus that white middle-class victims are not "real criminals" and should be rehabilitated in treatment centers rather than incarcerated.[7] There is also nothing new about the bipartisan rush to blame Mexican cartels for the existence of an illicit and lucrative drug market constructed by the prohibitionist policies of the U.S. government—bringing enormous social damage and human rights abuses in northern Mexico as a direct result—and exacerbated by the profit-seeking criminality of Purdue Pharma and other corporations that denied the addictiveness of prescription painkillers and spread them far and wide, just as Commissioner Harry Anslinger of the Federal Bureau of Narcotics did on their behalf in the 1950s. "Mexican drug cartels have pushed heroin sales beyond major cities into America's suburban and rural byways," the *New York Times* announced in its 2009 series "War Without Borders." The 2010 *National Drug Control Strategy* of the Barack Obama administration elevated prescription drug abuse to a major federal priority while praising the "legitimate benefits" provided by the pharmaceutical industry and pledging to crack down fiercely on Mexican cartels, which Obama labeled "hardened criminals who are bringing drugs like heroin into our country."[8]

The grassroots-driven, state-level marijuana legalization drive is a major departure in the American drug war, achieving majority public support for ending the prohibition policy that resulted in more arrests between the 1960s and the 2010s than any other criminalized substance. But if this campaign remains distinct from the broader movement for racial and social justice, then it risks becoming the latest stage in the segregation of the predominantly white recreational market from the "real criminals," following in the "political whiteness" traditions of earlier marijuana legalization and decriminalization movements traced in this book. By 2008, thirteen states had legalized medical marijuana, often by popular referendum, even though the federal government maintained its unscientific classification under Schedule 1 of the Controlled Substances Act as a drug with "high potential for abuse" and "no accepted medicinal value." The Obama administration's drug czar blamed the marijuana legalization movement for increased rates of adolescent drug use, even though data from the annual "Monitoring the Future" surveys revealed no correlation between state laws and teenage behavioral patterns, reinforcing decades of research that prohibitory policies had negligible impact on the recreational youth market. The breakthrough for legalization of recreational marijuana came in 2012 with successful ballot initiatives in Colorado and Washington state. By 2022, recreational marijuana for adults (age twenty-one and above) was legal in twenty-one states and medical cannabis in sixteen more, a sea change in drug control policy that has not diminished the federal interdiction budget or even changed marijuana's indefensible Schedule 1 classification, although surely that will not last. A surprisingly discordant note came from David Simon, creator of *The Wire* and prominent critic of the "misguided, destructive, dehumanizing" war on drugs. Carving out a marijuana exception primarily for "white middle-class people," Simon warned, would only exacerbate the racial inequalities of drug control policy. The entire system needed "to fall as one complete edifice."[9]

The liberal drug-war strategy of "balanced public health and public safety," in the updated 2010 formulation of the Obama White House, did not substantially depart from the historical boundaries of the bipartisan consensus and its drug control policies of criminalization and punitive law enforcement. The Obama administration promoted "alternatives to incarceration" for nonviolent drug offenders, combined with interdiction against foreign traffickers and domestic crackdowns to "rid our streets of the drug dealers who infect our communities." President Joe Biden's version of this two-track drug control policy is his oft-stated philosophy that the malevolent criminals in the supply side of the market should be incarcerated for a long time while the illegal user-victims, including marijuana offenders, are arrested and diverted to "mandatory rehabilitation." The mainstream liberalism represented by Obama and Biden has belatedly acknowledged the crisis of "mass incarceration" and the problem of systemic racial inequality in law enforcement, and its rehabilitative agenda for "nonviolent" drug users and addicts does extend across racial lines. But liberalism's primary drug-war reforms have focused on reducing racial bias in sentencing disparities, pardons and commutations for a narrow class of nonviolent offenders, and "using the criminal justice system to spur people in need of treatment to get it" by somehow ending discrimination in the discretionary arrest-and-divert rehabilitation process. This seemingly benevolent phrase justifies the continued criminalization of the "disease" of addiction and the illicit recreational market more broadly.[10] The only transformative alternative is the combined legalization and harm reduction agenda endorsed by civil liberties and human rights organizations in recognition that, as the Global Commission on Drug Policy has summarized, "the war on drugs has not, and cannot, be won." The heart of the crisis, so deeply rooted in our racist history of moral crusades and discretionary law enforcement and social control of youth, is criminalization itself.[11]

ACKNOWLEDGMENTS

I STARTED RESEARCHING this book in 2008–9 when I spent a year in California and Oregon, although at the time I didn't realize that I was going to write the whole story about the war on drugs. The origins of the project really go even further back to 2003, when I started teaching an undergraduate lecture course on the "History of American Suburbia," among the first of its kind. As the course evolved, I decided that my "second book" would be a synthetic history of American suburbia, a next-generation variation of Kenneth Jackson's *Crabgrass Frontier* (1985), that would range from the 1950s through the 1990s and trace many different themes in the areas of politics, public policy, and popular culture. I did a fair amount of research for chapters I will never write on housing, schools, electoral politics, the "culture wars" over feminism and gay rights, sex crimes and the victims' rights movement, racial and economic diversification of the suburbs, utopian/dystopian themes in films and novels, and more. Now the idea of cramming all this into a single book seems nuts. That summer of 2008, during a research trip to the California State Archives, I stumbled across an enormous number of letters from suburban LA residents to the governor during the 1950s demanding a harsh crackdown on narcotics pushers to protect their children from marijuana. I had never heard of this movement before and decided to dig in deeper on the suburban side of drug-war politics and policy. This topic began to seem more urgent with the publication of Michelle Alexander's *New Jim Crow* in 2010 and the heightened public and scholarly attention to mass incarceration and racial injustice in the criminal legal system. Eventually, during a 2012 sabbatical, when I started drafting a projected single chapter on the war on drugs and the white middle-class suburbs, it spiraled almost out of control and eventually became the whole project, and so here we are.

Most professors know that scholarship and teaching are thoroughly intertwined, and my first debt of gratitude is to the undergraduate and graduate students whom I have taught at the University of Michigan. I explored most of the big ideas and plenty of the specific parts of *The Suburban Crisis* in dialogue with undergraduates in the "History of American Suburbia" between 2003 and 2013 (although this is not the book I told them I was writing), and in the successor "Crime and Drugs in Modern America" course that I started teaching in 2015 in response to Ferguson and the Black Lives Matter movement. Discussion and debate with graduate students, in my "Urban/Suburban History" and "New Political History" seminars and through working with them on dissertation committees, has been rewarding and invaluable. I cannot list all of them here, but a specific thanks to those whose direct input or overlapping research interests have particularly influenced my thinking about history and methods: Nathan Connolly, Tamar Carroll, Andrew Highsmith, Matthew Ides, Lily Geismer, Clay Howard, Lauren Hirshberg, Drew Meyers, Josh Mound, Anthony Ross, Dale Winling, Katie Rosenblatt, Ronit Stahl, Scott De Orio, Austin McCoy, Nora Krinitsky, Steve Arionus, Cyrus O'Brien, ToniAnn Treviño, Stacey Bishop, Antonio Ramirez, Michael Stauch, Salem Elzway, Allie Goodman, David Helps, Nicole Navarro, Alexander Stephens, Alex Burnett, and Lloyd Simpson.

Friends and colleagues at the University of Michigan and elsewhere have my deep appreciation. I have so many amazing colleagues in Ann Arbor that I will restrict this list to those who provided direct feedback: Howard Brick, Jay Cook, Susan Juster, Kathleen Canning, Anthony Mora, and Stephen Berrey. Dozens of additional people raised great questions at UM talks and workshops, including those sponsored by the Eisenberg Institute for Historical Studies, the Institute for the Humanities, the Urban and Regional Planning Program, the Law School, and the Knight-Wallace Fellows Seminar. Many thanks as well to the organizers and audiences for talks and workshops at Boston University, Princeton University, Oregon State University, University of Oregon, Kalamazoo College, Ohio State University, Northwestern University, UT–San Antonio, Wesleyan University, Purdue University, Claremont-McKenna College, and the University of Virginia. Brian Balogh, Brent Cebul, Daniel HoSang, Elizabeth Hinton, Julian Zelizer, and Nathan Connolly deserve specific mention. And as always, another shout out to Tom Sugrue and Bruce Schulman, whose intellectual camaraderie and professional generosity are models to which I aspire.

The incredible recent historical scholarship on policing and the carceral state, as part of the overdue reckoning with mass incarceration and discriminatory law enforcement, profoundly shaped the trajectory and content of *The Suburban Crisis*. Heather Ann Thompson invited me to join this vibrant community of scholars by contributing essays to the 2015 special issue "Historians and the Carceral State" in the *Journal of American History* and the 2015 special section "Urban America and the Carceral State" in the *Journal of Urban History*. These articles—"Impossible Criminals" and "Pushers, Victims, and the Lost Innocence of White Suburbia"—enabled me to begin to conceptualize the book as a whole and to receive important and constructively critical feedback from Heather as well as Donna Murch, Khalil Muhammad, and Kelly Lytle Hernández. Material first published in the *Journal of American History* or *Journal of Urban History* essays appears, in revised and expanded form, in several chapters of this book. Heather then founded the University of Michigan Carceral State Project in 2016, and soon after I launched the affiliated Policing and Social Justice HistoryLab. Co-leading the *Documenting Criminalization and Confinement* initiative that started with a major grant in 2019, with a research team of more than one hundred students and community members, definitely enhanced my understanding of the carceral state and frankly also delayed this book's publication by about three years. It was definitely worth it, and I'm grateful to the whole team and particularly to the other faculty members who served on the Carceral State Project steering committee: Heather Ann Thompson, Ashley Lucas, Nora Krinitsky, Melissa Burch, Jesse Hoffnung-Garskof, William Lopez, and Ruby Tapia.

Researching and writing a national story with close attention to state and local developments turned out to be even more difficult and time-consuming than I anticipated, and it would not have been possible without the support of many institutions and people. I benefited from a fellowship at the Huntington Library to spend a summer in Pasadena and Los Angeles; a year-long sabbatical at the Center for the Humanities at Oregon State University; a writing fellowship at the UM Institute for the Humanities; and internal grants from the LSA Associate Professor Support Fund, the LSA Michigan Humanities Award, and the Richard Hudson Research Professorship. Archivists and librarians pulled a lot of boxes and provided a lot of assistance along the way, as I conducted research in at least twenty-five archives in thirteen different states and Washington, DC. Many of these archives are spread out across the sprawl of Los Angeles and Southern California, and thanks especially to Doug Smith and Andy Lewis for their hospitality and friendship during my frequent research trips there. Andy also accomplished what I thought was going to be impossible when he figured out how to secure Governor Jerry Brown's permission to allow me to look through his closed, unprocessed papers at the University of Southern California. Three undergraduate research assistants at UM digitized articles from magazines and inventoried other material from media databases: Briana Green, Lucas Schaefer, and Elana Firsht. On the homestretch, Bill Deverell and Abby Gibson helped track down an elusive image from the USC Special Collections, Peter Knoop generously contributed technical support to finalize the maps, and Josh Mound provided crucial assistance with several charts and graphs.

Three colleagues read the entire manuscript before final revisions and provided insightful and abundant comments: David Freund, Julilly Kohler-Hausmann, and Kevin Kruse. I hope they will recognize my heartfelt gratitude in the many improvements made and not go too hard on me for the occasional advice not taken. Lily Geismer read multiple sections of the book and came through at the last minute with her typical speed and brilliance when I asked for help to resolve some conceptual and organizational issues with the introduction. Eric Crahan acquired the book for Princeton University Press, guided me through the first round of revisions, gave me the flexibility that I requested for an atypical hybrid of humanities and social science methods (meaning all the tables and graphs), and pinch-hit again near the end. Bridget Flannery-McCoy joined Princeton University Press midway through this process and has been a great editor, providing perceptive feedback on the introduction and wise advice about much more. Alena Chekanov and Kathleen Cioffi helped me navigate the publication process and answered a volley of questions about images, maps, graphs, and more. Much appreciation also to Dana Henricks for copyediting the manuscript with such care and thoroughness.

Friends and family make it all worthwhile. I won't name everyone who asked, again and again, when I was going to finish the "drugs book"—but thanks especially to Carl Nystrom, Julia Huffman, Graham Griffith, and Rainey Tisdale. Spending summers in Western North Carolina keeps me grounded, and a shout out to the whole crew in Asheville, along with ardent gratitude to Rachel Jones for all of the balance and fun and support. My large immediate family is wonderful in so many ways, and I cannot express my appreciation enough. I very much regret that my mother Sally Lassiter did not live to see this book's publication, and no one else could possibly have expressed as much enthusiasm or asked as many questions about it as she did. I miss her dearly and dedicate this book to her life and memory.

ARCHIVES AND ABBREVIATIONS IN NOTES

Archival Collections

ACLU-Princeton. American Civil Liberties Union Records, Department of Rare Books and Special Collections, Princeton University Library, Princeton, New Jersey

ACLUSC-UCLA. ACLU of Southern California Records, Department of Special Collections, Charles E. Young Research Library, University of California, Los Angeles

AMG-Carter. Annie M. Gutierrez Files, Records of the Domestic Policy Staff, Jimmy Carter Presidential Library, Atlanta, Georgia

APP. The American Presidency Project, Online by Gerhard Peters and John T. Woolley, https://www.presidency.ucsb.edu

AR-CSUN. Alan Robbins Collection, Urban Archives Center, Oviatt Library, California State University, Northridge

BA-UTA. Betty Andujar Papers, AR125, Special Collections, University of Texas at Arlington Library

BATA-SFSU. Bay Area Television Archive, Special Collections and Archives, J. Paul Leonard Library, San Francisco State University, https://diva.sfsu.edu/collections/sfbatv

CET-Reagan. Carlton E. Turner Files, Drug Abuse Policy Office, Ronald Reagan Presidential Library, Simi Valley, California

CM-UTA. Chris Miller Papers, AR381, Special Collections, University of Texas at Arlington Library

CMCC-Carter. Carter-Mondale Campaign Committee Records of the 1976 Campaign to Elect Jimmy Carter, Jimmy Carter Presidential Library, Atlanta, Georgia

CMDA-Nixon. Commission on Marihuana and Drug Abuse, FG 308, Subject Files, White House Central Files, Richard Nixon Presidential Library, Yorba Linda, California

CMM-JHU. Charles McCurdy Matthias Jr. Papers, Special Collections, Milton S. Eisenhower Library, The Johns Hopkins University

CWC-Nixon. Charles W. Colson Papers, White House Special Files, Richard Nixon Presidential Library, Yorba Linda, California

DAPO-Reagan. Drug Abuse Policy Office Files, 1981–1987, Ronald Reagan Presidential Library, Simi Valley, California

DEA-NA. Records of the Drug Enforcement Administration, RG 170, National Archives, College Park, Maryland, https://www.archives.gov/research/guide-fed-records/groups/170.html

DEM-UCSC. Dean E. McHenry Papers, Special Collections and Archives, University of California, Santa Cruz

Dempsey-CSL. Office of the Governor: John Dempsey Records, Connecticut State Library, Hartford, Connecticut

DFM-Kennedy. Dean F. Markham Papers, White House Staff Files, John F. Kennedy Presidential Library, Boston, Massachusetts

DG-Nixon. David Gergen Papers, White House Central Files, Richard Nixon Presidential Library, Yorba Linda, California

DIM-Reagan. Donald Ian MacDonald Files, Drug Abuse Policy Office, Ronald Reagan Presidential Library, Simi Valley, California

EC-Kennedy. Eleanor Charwat Personal Papers, John F. Kennedy Presidential Library, Boston, Massachusetts

EGB-Bancroft. Edmund G. Brown Papers, The Bancroft Library, University of California, Berkeley

EIP-Carter. Exit Interview Project, Oral Interviews, Jimmy Carter Presidential Library, Atlanta, Georgia

EK-Nixon. Egil Krogh Papers, White House Special Files, Richard Nixon Presidential Library, Yorba Linda, California

ERIC-DOE. Educational Resources Information Center, Institute of Education Sciences, U.S. Department of Education, https://eric.ed.gov

ESL-UCB. Ethnic Studies Library, Publications Department, University of California, Berkeley

EW-CSA. Earl Warren Papers, California State Archives, Sacramento, California

GCS-Nixon. Geoffrey C. Shepard Papers, White House Special Files, Richard Nixon Presidential Library, Yorba Linda, California

GJK-CSA. Goodwin J. Knight Papers, California State Archives, Sacramento, California

GJK-Stanford. Goodwin J. Knight Papers, M0244, Department of Special Collections, Stanford University Libraries, Stanford, California

HJA-PSU. Harry J. Anslinger Papers, HCLA 1875, Special Collections Library, Pennsylvania State University

JAF-Huntington. John Anson Ford Papers, The Huntington Library, San Marino, California

JAL-UM. Joseph A. Labadie Collection, Special Collections and Archives, University of Michigan

JB-USC. Edmund G. [Jerry] Brown Jr., Papers, Regional History Collections, Special Collections, USC Libraries, University of Southern California

JD-NA. Records of the Special Senate Subcommittee on Juvenile Delinquency, Record Group 46, Section 13.108, Center for Legislative Archives, National Archives, Washington, DC.

JLS-UM. John and Leni Sinclair Papers, Bentley Historical Library, University of Michigan

JMC-Ford. James M. Cannon Papers, Gerald R. Ford Presidential Library, Ann Arbor, Michigan

JMJO-Carter. Jim Mongan and Joseph Onek's Subject Files, Records of the Domestic Policy Staff, Jimmy Carter Presidential Library, Atlanta, Georgia

KH-Huntington. Kenneth Hahn Collection, The Huntington Library, San Marino, California

LACNDDC-CSA. Los Angeles County Narcotics and Dangerous Drugs Commission Files, Correctional Agencies Records, California State Archives, Sacramento, California

LB-SFPL. Larry Beggs Papers on Huckleberry House, 1967–2009, San Francisco History Center, San Francisco Public Library

LEL-UM. Lee E. Landes Papers, Bentley Historical Library, University of Michigan

LM-Huntington. Loren Miller Papers, The Huntington Library, San Marino, California

LVLM-PHL. Lu Verne La Motte Papers, Pasadena Historical Library, Pasadena, California

MADD-UM. Mothers Against Drunk Driving, Michigan Chapter Records, Bentley Historical Library, University of Michigan

MEB-Reagan. Michael E. Baroody Files, Office of Public Affairs, Ronald Reagan Presidential Library, Simi Valley, California

MK-Huntington. Marie Koenig Conservative Political Collection, The Huntington Library, San Marino, California

MM-CSUN. Max Mont Collection, Urban Archives Center, Oviatt Library, California State University, Northridge

MPF-CSA. Marijuana Project Files, Barry Keene Papers, California State Archives, Sacramento, California

MPPC-AMPAS. Hollywood, Censorship, and the Motion Picture Production Code, 1927–1968 Collection, Margaret Herrick Library of the Academy of Motion Picture Arts and Sciences (digitized in Archives Unbound)

NAR-Rockefeller. Nelson A. Rockefeller Gubernatorial Records, Rockefeller Archive Center, Sleepy Hollow, New York

NCJRS. National Criminal Justice Reference Service, Office of Justice Programs, U.S. Department of Justice, https://www.ojp.gov/ncjrs/new-ojp-resources

NCMDA-NA. Records of the National Commission on Marihuana and Drug Abuse, 1970–1973, National Archives, College Park, Maryland (digitized in ProQuest History Vault)

NDI-WSU. New Detroit Inc. Collection, Walter P. Reuther Library, Archives of Labor and Urban Affairs, Wayne State University

NSA-GWU. National Security Archive, The George Washington University, https://nsarchive.gwu.edu

NSAJC-CSA. Narcotics Subcommittee, Assembly Judiciary Committee Records, California State Archives, Sacramento, California

OMR-Reagan. Office of Media Relations, White House Staff and Office Files, Ronald Reagan Presidential Library, Simi Valley, California

OPD-Reagan. Office of Policy Development, White House Office of Records and Management, Ronald Reagan Presidential Library, Simi Valley, California

PASAJC-CSA. Police Administration Subcommittee, Assembly Judiciary Committee Records, California State Archives, Sacramento, California

PD-NA. Records of the Special Subcommittee on Improvement of the Federal Criminal Code, Committee on the Judiciary, U.S. Senate, Record Group 38, Section 13.123, Center for Legislative Archives, National Archives, Washington, DC [PD = Senator Price Daniel, subcommittee chair]

PGB-Carter. Peter Geoffrey Bourne Files, Jimmy Carter Presidential Library, Atlanta, Georgia

RC-CU. Roper Center for Public Opinion Research, Cornell University, https://ropercenter.cornell.edu

RFK-Kennedy. Papers of Robert F. Kennedy, Attorney General Papers, John F. Kennedy Presidential Library, Boston, Massachusetts

RJR-UCSF. RJ Reynolds Records, Truth Tobacco Industry Documents, University of California San Francisco Library, https://www.industrydocuments.ucsf.edu

RLW-Reagan. Richard L. Williams Files, Drug Abuse Policy Office, Ronald Reagan Presidential Library, Simi Valley, California

RRGP-Reagan. Ronald Reagan Gubernatorial Papers, Ronald Reagan Presidential Library, Simi Valley, California

SCN-CSA. Special Commission on Narcotics, Correctional Agencies Records, California State Archives, Sacramento, California

SEE-Carter. Stuart E. Eizenstat Files, Records of the Domestic Policy Staff, Jimmy Carter Presidential Library, Atlanta, Georgia

SSC-CSA. Special Study Commissions Records, Correctional Agencies Records, California State Archives, Sacramento, California

TAUSC-CSL. Records of the Teenage Alcoholic Use Study Commission, RG 048, Connecticut State Library, Hartford, Connecticut

TCLU-UTA. Texas Civil Liberties Union Records, AR121, Special Collections, University of Texas at Arlington Library

TJD-UConn. Thomas J. Dodd Papers, Archives and Special Collections, Thomas J. Dodd Research Center, University of Connecticut Libraries

TM-OSA. Administrative Correspondence Series, Records of Governor Tom McCall's Administration, Oregon State Archives, Salem, Oregon

WFT-Hoover. William F. Tompkins Papers, Herbert Hoover Presidential Library, West Branch, Iowa

VF-DPL. Vertical Files, Texas/Dallas History and Archives Division, Dallas Public Library, Dallas, Texas

VF-FCPL. Vertical Files, Virginia Room, Fairfax County Public Library, Fairfax, Virginia

WGM-UM. William G. Milliken Papers, Bentley Historical Library, University of Michigan

WHCF-Carter. White House Central File, Jimmy Carter Presidential Library, Atlanta, Georgia

Newspapers, Magazines, and Journals

AJP. *American Journal of Psychiatry*

AJPH. *American Journal of Public Health*

AJS. *American Journal of Sociology*

AW. *American Weekly*

BAA. *Baltimore Afro-American*

BB. *Berkeley Barb*

BG. *Boston Globe*

CD. *Chicago Defender*
CDT. *Chicago Daily Tribune*
CQ. *Congressional Quarterly*
CR. *Congressional Record*
CRS. Congressional Research Service
CSM. *Christian Science Monitor*
CT. *Chicago Tribune*
DMN. *Dallas Morning News*
DR. *Darien Review*
DTH. *Dallas Times Herald*
EVO. *East Village Other*
GPO. U.S. Government Printing Office
HM. *Harper's Magazine*
HT. *High Times*
JAMA. *Journal of the American Medical Association*
LADN. *Los Angeles Daily News*
LAE. *Los Angeles Examiner*
LAFP. *Los Angeles Free Press*
LAHE. *Los Angeles Herald Express*
LAT. *Los Angeles Times*
LHJ. *Ladies' Home Journal*
NVS. *Northern Virginia Sun*
NYAN. *New York Amsterdam News*
NYT. *New York Times*
PM. *Parents Magazine*
PSN. *Pasadena Star-News*
RD. *Reader's Digest*
SDT. *San Diego Tribune*
SEP. *Saturday Evening Post*
SFC. *San Francisco Chronicle*
SFE. *San Francisco Examiner*
TNR. *The New Republic*
USNWR. *U.S. News and World Report*
WHC. *Woman's Home Companion*
WP. *Washington Post*
WSJ. *Wall Street Journal*
VV. *Village Voice*

Note: ProQuest Historical Newspapers and ProQuest Congressional databases utilized for major newspapers and congressional hearings and reports.

NOTES

Introduction

1. "Children in Peril: 'Pushers' Are Selling Narcotics to Thousands of Teen-agers," *Life*, June 11, 1951, 116–25; Testimony of Miss Jeanne———, "Investigation of Organized Crime in Interstate Commerce," *Hearings before the Special Committee to Investigate Organized Crime in Interstate Commerce*, U.S. Senate, Part 14: "Narcotics," June 12, 26, 1951 (Washington: GPO, 1951), 203–210, 294–305; Patricia Williams (as told to Will Oursler), "I Trapped a Dope Ring," *American Weekly*, May 31, June 7, June 14, 1953; "Runaway Kids," Life, November 3, 1967, 18–29; Richard M. Nixon, "Remarks at the Opening Session of the Governors' Conference," December 3, 1969, *Public Papers of the Presidents: 1969* (Washington: GPO, 1971), 986–89; Testimony of Lee Ann Bonanno, "The Crack Cocaine Crisis," *Joint Hearing before the Select Committee on Narcotics Abuse and Control and the Select Committee on Children, Youth, and Families*, House of Representatives, July 15, 1986 (Washington: GPO, 1987), 12–24.

2. Testimony of Mary Ann———, "Illicit Narcotics Traffic," *Hearings before the Subcommittee on Improvements in the Federal Criminal Code, Committee on the Judiciary*, U.S. Senate, Part 7, October 17, 1955 (Washington: GPO, 1956), 2716–34; Gene Sherman, "Boys—and Girl—Tell Drug Addiction Story," *Los Angeles Times*, July 15, 1959; Testimony of Paula Sherwood and Eve Babitz, "LSD and Marijuana Use on College Campuses," *Hearings before a Special Subcommittee of the Committee on the Judiciary*, U.S. Senate, May 23, 1966 (Washington: GPO, 1966), 543–68; Jane Howard, "For the Long-Distance Runner Who Got Caught—a 20-Year Sentence," *Life*, October 31, 1969, 30–31; Testimony of Robert Shephard, "Crime in America—In the Nation's Capital," *Hearings before the Select Committee on Crime*, House of Representatives, February 27, 1970 (Washington: GPO, 1970), 314–18; PBS Frontline, *Stopping Drugs, Part II* (Documentary Consortium, PBS Video, 1987).

3. On the state's relationship to "impossible" political actors in another context, see Mae M. Ngai, *Impossible Subjects: Illegal Aliens and the Making of Modern America* (Princeton: Princeton University Press, 2004). For a sampling of the scholarship on global drug markets and the imperialist project of U.S. drug control beyond its borders, see Alfred W. McCoy, *The Politics of Heroin: CIA Complicity in the Global Drug Trade*, 2nd rev. ed. (Chicago: Lawrence Hill Books, 2003); Paul Gootenberg, *Andean Cocaine: The Making of a Global Drug* (Chapel Hill: University of North Carolina Press, 2008); Suzanna Reiss, *We Sell Drugs: The Alchemy of U.S. Empire* (Berkeley: University of California Press, 2014); Ben Whitaker, *The Global Connection: The Crisis of Drug Addiction* (London: Jonathan Cape, 1987); H. Richard Friman, *NarcoDiplomacy: Exporting the U.S. War on Drugs* (Ithaca: Cornell University Press, 1996); Ted Galen Carpenter,

Bad Neighbor: Washington's Futile War on Drugs in Latin America (New York: Palgrave Macmillan, 2003); Curtis Marez, *Drug Wars: The Political Economy of Narcotics* (Minneapolis: University of Minnesota Press, 2004); Peter Dale Scott, *Drugs, Oil, and War: The United States in Afghanistan, Colombia, and Indochina* (Lanham, MD: Rowman & Littlefield), 2003.

4. The pre-1960s phase of the federal war on drugs has received limited attention from scholars. For top-down approaches, see John C. McWilliams, *The Protectors: Harry J. Anslinger and the Federal Bureau of Narcotics, 1930–1962* (Newark: University of Delaware Press, 1990); David T. Courtwright, *Dark Paradise: A History of Opiate Addiction in America*, rev. ed. (Cambridge: Harvard University Press, 2001); David F. Musto, *The American Disease: Origins of Narcotic Control*, 3rd ed. (New York: Oxford University Press, 1999); Kathleen J. Frydl, *The Drug Wars in America, 1940–1973* (Cambridge: Cambridge University Press, 2013).

5. General histories of drug politics and culture during this era include Michael Massing, *The Fix* (New York: Simon & Schuster, 1998); David F. Musto and Pamela Korsmeyer, *The Quest for Drug Control: Politics and Federal Policy in a Period of Increasing Substance Abuse, 1963–1981* (New Haven: Yale University Press, 2002), 38–139; Jay Stevens, *Storming Heaven: LSD and the American Dream* (New York: Atlantic Monthly Press, 1987); Jill Jonnes, *Hep-Cats, Narcs, and Pipe Dreams: A History of America's Romance with Illegal Drugs* (New York: Scribner, 1996).

6. Most scholarship about the war on drugs during the 1980s focuses on urban crack markets: Craig Reinarman and Harry G. Levine, eds., *Crack in America: Demon Drugs and Social Justice* (Berkeley: University of California Press, 1997); Jimmie L. Reeves and Richard Campbell, *Cracked Coverage: Television News, The Anti-Cocaine Crusade, and the Reagan Legacy* (Durham: Duke University Press, 2004); Doris Marie Provine, *Unequal under Law: Race in the War on Drugs* (Chicago: University of Chicago Press, 2007); Michelle Alexander, *The New Jim Crow: Mass Incarceration in the Age of Colorblindness* (New York: New Press, 2010); David Farber, *Crack: Rock Cocaine, Street Capitalism, and the Decade of Greed* (New York: Cambridge University Press, 2019). Journalistic histories have most often noted the role of suburban antimarijuana groups; see Dan Baum, *Smoke and Mirrors: The War on Drugs and the Politics of Failure* (Boston: Little, Brown and Company, 1996); Massing, *The Fix*.

7. For introductions to these subfields, see Meg Jacobs, William J. Novak, and Julian E. Zelizer, eds., *The Democratic Experiment: New Directions in American Political History* (Princeton: Princeton University Press, 2003); Brent Cebul, Lily Geismer, and Mason B. Williams, *Shaped by the State: Toward a New Political History of the Twentieth Century* (Chicago: University of Chicago Press, 2019); Kevin M. Kruse and Thomas J. Sugrue, eds., *The New Suburban History* (Chicago: University of Chicago Press, 2006); James W. Cook, Lawrence B. Glickman, and Michael O'Malley, eds., *The Cultural Turn in U.S. History: Past, Present, and Future* (Chicago: University of Chicago Press, 2008).

8. On the deeper history of the criminalization and oppression of multiple racially targeted groups in California and Los Angeles, see Kelly Lytle Hernández, *City of Inmates: Conquest, Rebellion, and the Rise of Human Caging in Los Angeles, 1771–1865* (Chapel Hill: University of North Carolina Press, 2017).

9. On diverse suburbs, see Matthew D. Lassiter and Christopher Niedt, "Suburban Diversity in Postwar America," *Journal of Urban History* 39, no. 1 (January 2013): 3–14; Andrew Wiese, *Places of Their Own: African American Suburbanization in the Twentieth Century* (Chicago: University of Chicago Press, 2004); Rosalyn Baxandall and Elizabeth Ewen, *Picture Windows: How*

the Suburbs Happened (New York: Basic Books, 2000); Douglas S. Massey, ed., *New Faces in New Places: The Changing Geography of American Immigration* (New York: Russell Sage Foundation, 2008); John Archer, Paul J. P. Sandul, and Katherine Solomon, eds., *Making Suburbia: New Histories of Everyday America* (Minneapolis: University of Minnesota Press, 2015); Josh Sides, "Straight into Compton: American Dreams, Urban Nightmares, and the Metamorphosis of a Black Suburb," *American Quarterly* 56, no. 3 (September 2004): 583–605. Synthetic accounts of suburban history include Kenneth T. Jackson, *Crabgrass Frontier: The Suburbanization of the United States* (New York: Oxford University Press, 1985); Robert Fishman, *Bourgeois Utopias: The Rise and Fall of Suburbia* (New York: Basic Books, 1987); Dolores Hayden, *Building Suburbia: Green Fields and Urban Growth, 1820–2000* (New York: Pantheon, 2003); Lizabeth Cohen, *A Consumers' Republic: The Politics of Mass Consumption in Postwar America* (New York: Alfred A. Knopf, 2003); Robert A. Beauregard, *When America Became Suburban* (Minneapolis: University of Minnesota Press, 2008).

10. On the punitive structure of liberal rehabilitation policy, see Julilly Kohler-Hausmann, *Getting Tough: Welfare and Imprisonment in 1970s America* (Princeton: Princeton University Press, 2017), esp. 29–78. The carceral state scholarship that most influenced the framework in this book includes Marie Gottschalk, *The Prison and the Gallows: The Politics of Mass Incarceration in America* (Cambridge: Cambridge University Press, 2006); Gottschalk, *Caught: The Prison State and the Lockdown of American Politics* (Princeton: Princeton University Press, 2015); Jonathan Simon, *Governing through Crime: How the War on Crime Transformed American Democracy and Created a Culture of Fear* (New York: Oxford University Press, 2007); Kelly Lytle Hernández, Khalil Gibran Muhammad, and Heather Ann Thompson, eds., "Historians and the Carceral State," special issue, *Journal of American History* 102, no. 1 (June 2015). On coercive and racially inequitable public health, landmark books include Nayan Shah, *Contagious Divides: Epidemics and Race in San Francisco's Chinatown* (Berkeley: University of California Press, 2001); Samuel Kelton Roberts Jr., *Infectious Fear: Politics, Disease, and the Health Effects of Segregation* (Chapel Hill: University of North Carolina Press, 2009).

11. Daniel HoSang, *Racial Propositions: Ballot Initiatives and the Making of Postwar California* (Berkeley: University of California Press, 2010), quotation 86. For a similar critique of the "ideological need to cast race as liberalism's other," see Paul A. Kramer, "Shades of Sovereignty: Racialized Power, the United States and the World," in *Explaining the History of American Foreign Relations*, ed. Frank Costigliola and Michael J. Hogan, 3rd. ed. (Cambridge: Cambridge University Press, 2016), 245–70 (quotation 248).

12. See especially Kohler-Hausmann, *Getting Tough.*

13. Case studies of white grassroots politics include Thomas J. Sugrue, *The Origins of the Urban Crisis: Race and Inequality in Postwar Detroit* (Princeton: Princeton University Press, 1996); Robert O. Self, *American Babylon: Race and the Struggle for Postwar Oakland* (Princeton: Princeton University Press, 2003); Matthew D. Lassiter, *The Silent Majority: Suburban Politics in the Sunbelt South* (Princeton: Princeton University Press, 2006); David M. P. Freund, *Colored Property: State Policy and White Racial Politics in Suburban America* (Chicago: University of Chicago Press, 2007); Lily Geismer, *Don't Blame Us: Suburban Liberals and the Transformation of the Democratic Party* (Princeton: Princeton University Press, 2015). Books on suburban conservatism include Lisa McGirr, *Suburban Warriors: The Origins of the New American Right* (Princeton: Princeton University Press, 2001); Kevin M. Kruse, *White Flight: Atlanta and the*

Making of Modern Conservatism (Princeton: Princeton University Press, 2005); Darren Dochuk, *From Bible Belt to Sunbelt: Plain-Folk Religion, Grassroots Politics, and the Rise of Evangelical Conservatism* (New York: W. W. Norton, 2011); Michelle M. Nickerson, *Mothers of Conservatism: Women and the Postwar Right* (Princeton: Princeton University Press, 2012).

14. On urban policing during the post-1945 period, see Christopher Lowen Agee, *The Streets of San Francisco: Policing and the Creation of a Cosmopolitan Liberal Politics, 1950–1972* (Chicago: University of Chicago Press, 2014); Max Felker-Kantor, *Policing Los Angeles: Race, Resistance, and the Rise of the LAPD* (Chapel Hill: University of North Carolina Press, 2018); Timothy J. Lombardo, *Blue-Collar Conservatism: Frank Rizzo's Philadelphia and Populist Politics* (Philadelphia: University of Pennsylvania Press, 2018); Simon Balto, *Occupied Territory: Policing Black Chicago from Red Summer to Black Power* (Chapel Hill: University of North Carolina Press, 2019); Elizabeth Hinton, *America on Fire: The Untold History of Police Violence and Black Rebellion since the 1960s* (New York: Liveright, 2021). On urban history and carceral studies, see Heather Ann Thompson, "Why Mass Incarceration Matters: Rethinking Crisis, Decline, and Transformation in Postwar American History," *Journal of American History* 97, no. 3 (December 2010): 703–34; Thompson and Donna Murch, eds., "Urban America and the Carceral State," special issue, *Journal of Urban History* 41, no. 5 (September 2015).

15. Alexander, *New Jim Crow*, esp. 40–57; Vesla M. Weaver, "Frontlash: Race and the Development of Punitive Crime Policy," *Studies in American Political Development* 21, no. 2 (Fall 2007): 230–65; Provine, *Unequal under Law*; Katherine Beckett, *Making Crime Pay: Law and Order in Contemporary American Politics* (New York: Oxford University Press, 1999); David Garland, *The Culture of Control: Crime and Social Order in Contemporary Society* (Chicago: University of Chicago Press, 2001); Bruce Western, *Punishment and Inequality in America* (New York: Russell Sage Foundation, 2006); Michael W. Flamm, *Law and Order: Street Crime, Civil Unrest, and the Crisis of Liberalism in the 1960s* (New York: Columbia University Press, 2005). Much of this scholarship advances a top-down interpretation that Republican elites manipulated the public to generate white suburban support for punitive crime and drug control policies, often based on the dubious methodology of analyzing opinion surveys alone. Also see Katherine Beckett, "Setting the Public Agenda: 'Street Crime' and Drug Use in American Politics," *Social Problems* 41, no. 3 (August 1994): 425–47.

16. Elizabeth Hinton, *From the War on Poverty to the War on Crime: The Making of Mass Incarceration in America* (Cambridge: Harvard University Press, 2016); Naomi Murakawa, *The First Civil Right: How Liberals Built Prison America* (New York: Oxford University Press, 2014); Kohler-Hausmann, *Getting Tough*; Gottschalk, *Prison and the Gallows*. For earlier eras, see Khalil Gibran Muhammad, *The Condemnation of Blackness: Race, Crime, and the Making of Modern Urban America* (Cambridge: Harvard University Press, 2010); Michael Willrich, *City of Courts: Socializing Justice in Progressive Era Chicago* (Cambridge: Cambridge University Press, 2003); Jessica R. Pliley, *Policing Sexuality: The Mann Act and the Making of the FBI* (Cambridge: Harvard University Press, 2014); Claire Bond Potter, *War on Crime: Bandits, G-Men, and the Politics of Mass Culture* (New Brunswick, NJ: Rutgers University Press, 1998); Kenneth O'Reilly, "A New Deal for the FBI: The Roosevelt Administration, Crime Control, and National Security," *Journal of American History* 69, no. 3 (December 1982): 638–58.

17. For an elaboration of this argument, see Matthew D. Lassiter, "Political History beyond the Red-Blue Divide," *Journal of American History* 98, no. 3 (December 2011): 760–64; and

Lassiter, "Ten Propositions for the New Political History," in *Shaped by the State*, 363–76. For other explorations of how consensus political culture operates, see Wendy L. Wall, *Inventing the "American Way": The Politics of Consensus from the New Deal to the Civil Rights Movement* (New York: Oxford University Press, 2008); Daniel T. Rodgers, *Age of Fracture* (Cambridge: Harvard University Press, 2011); Bruce J. Schulman, *The Seventies: The Great Shift in American Culture, Society, and Politics* (New York: Free Press, 2001).

18. Dodd quotation in *CR—Senate* (January 24, 1970), 993–997, 1008–1009. On rehabilitative ideology, see Claire D. Clark, *The Recovery Revolution: The Battle over Addiction Treatment in the United States* (New York: Columbia University Press, 2017).

19. On the crack/powder non-debate, see Provine, *Unequal under Law*, 103–19. On the ubiquity of the racialized "culture of pathology," see Daryl Michael Scott, *Contempt and Pity: Social Policy and the Image of the Damaged Black Psyche, 1880–1996* (Chapel Hill: University of North Carolina Press, 1997). On African American support for tough drug and crime control policies, see Michael Javen Fortner, *Black Silent Majority: The Rockefeller Drug Laws and the Politics of Punishment* (Cambridge: Harvard University Press, 2015); James Forman Jr., *Locking Up Our Own: Crime and Punishment in Black America* (New York: Farrar, Straus and Giroux, 2017). For a caution against overemphasizing the political influence of tough-on-drugs politics in urban Black communities, see Donna Murch, "Who's to Blame for Mass Incarceration?" *Boston Review* (October 6, 2015); Murch, "Crack in Los Angeles: Crisis, Militarization, and Black Response to the Late Twentieth-Century War on Drugs," *Journal of American History* 102, no. 1 (June 2015): 162–73. On endemic police corruption, see Eric C. Schneider, *Smack: Heroin and the American City* (Philadelphia: University of Pennsylvania Press, 2008), 106–15.

20. On Anslinger and licit/illicit markets, see chapter 1 and Reiss, *We Sell Drugs*. Scholarship on the separate track of pharmaceutical drugs includes Edward M. Brecher, *Licit and Illicit Drugs: The Consumers Union Report* (New York: Little, Brown, 1972); David T. Courtwright, *Forces of Habit: Drugs and the Making of the Modern World* (Cambridge: Harvard University Press, 2001); Richard DeGrandpre, *The Cult of Pharmacology: How America Became the World's Most Troubled Drug Culture* (Durham: Duke University Press, 2006); David Herzberg, *Happy Pills in America: From Miltown to Prozac* (Baltimore: Johns Hopkins University Press, 2009); Herzberg, *White Market Drugs: Big Pharma and the Hidden History of Addiction in America* (Chicago: University of Chicago Press, 2020); Nicolas Rasmussen, *On Speed: The Many Lives of Amphetamine* (New York: New York University, 2008); Andrea Tone, *The Age of Anxiety: A History of America's Turbulent Affair with Tranquilizers* (New York: Basic Books, 2009); Barry Meier, *Pain Killer: A 'Wonder' Drug's Trail of Addiction and Death* (New York: St. Martin's Press, 2003). On the FHA and metropolitan segregation, see Jackson, *Crabgrass Frontier*, 190–218; Freund, *Colored Property*.

21. Michael Tonry, *Malign Neglect: Race, Crime, and Punishment in America* (New York: Oxford University Press, 1995); Alexander, *New Jim Crow*, esp. 95–136; Marc Mauer, *Race to Incarcerate*, rev. ed. (New York: New Press, 2006); Mauer, *The Changing Racial Dynamics of the War on Drugs* (Washington: The Sentencing Project, 2009). The racial disproportionality of mass incarceration has fallen most heavily on African Americans, imprisoned at almost six times the rate of white Americans by the early 2000s, compared to Hispanics at approximately two times the white (non-Hispanic) rate (state and federal systems combined). Also see Ashley Nellis, *The Color of Justice: Racial and Ethnic Disparity in State Prisons* (Washington: The Sentencing

Project, 2016); Peter Wagner and Daniel Kopf, "The Racial Geography of Mass Incarceration," Prison Policy Initiative, July 2015, https://www.prisonpolicy.org/racialgeography. In 2018, African Americans accounted for 40 percent of state and federal drug prisoners and 13 percent of the U.S. population. Hispanics, at 18 percent of the population, made up 38 percent of drug cases in state and federal institutions. See Drug Policy Alliance, *The Drug War, Mass Incarceration, and Race*, January 2018, https://drugpolicy.org/sites/default/files/drug-war-mass-incarceration-and-race_01_18_0.pdf.

22. On drug control policy from the perspective of Mexico, see Isaac Campos, *Home Grown: Marijuana and the Origins of Mexico's War on Drugs* (Chapel Hill: University of North Carolina Press, 2012). On the "social setting" and internal dynamics of metropolitan narcotics markets, see Schneider, *Smack*.

23. Data compiled from FBI, *Uniform Crime Reports for the United States*, 1964–1989. For census analysis disaggregating the Hispanic and white (non-Hispanic) categories, see Frank Hobbs and Nicole Stoops, *Demographic Trends in the 20th Century: Census 2000 Special Reports* (Washington: U.S. Census Bureau, November 2002). For scholarly critique of the politicized nature of crime statistics, see Weaver, "Frontlash," 245–47; Muhammad, *Condemnation of Blackness*; Hinton, *War on Poverty to the War on Crime*, esp. 18–25. On alcohol Prohibition, see Lisa McGirr, *The War on Alcohol: Prohibition and the Rise of the American State* (New York: W. W. Norton, 2015); Michael A. Lerner, *Dry Manhattan: Prohibition in New York City* (Cambridge: Harvard University Press, 2007). This work emphasizes the disproportionate criminalization and arrests of Catholic immigrants and African Americans and the de facto decriminalization of the alcohol market for the white middle class, which differs from the agenda (if not always the effects) of marijuana-oriented drug war enforcement in the late 1960s and 1970s.

24. Shah, *Contagious Divides*; Ngai, *Impossible Subjects*; Margot Canady, *The Straight State: Sexuality and Citizenship in Twentieth-Century America* (Princeton: Princeton University Press, 2009); Peggy Pascoe, *What Comes Naturally: Miscegenation Law and the Making of Race in America* (New York: Oxford University Press, 2009); Kelly Lytle Hernández, *Migra!: A History of the U.S. Border Patrol* (Berkeley: University of California Press, 2010); Karen M. Tani, *States of Dependency: Welfare, Rights, and American Governance* (Cambridge: Cambridge University Press, 2016); Colin Gordon, "Blighting the Way: Urban Renewal, Economic Development, and the Elusive Definition of Blight," *Fordham Urban Law Journal* 31, no. 2 (2003): 305–36. On the racial formation literature, see Michael Omi and Howard Winant, *Racial Formation in the United States: From the 1960s to the 1980s* (Routledge: New York, 1986); Daniel HoSang, Oneka LaBennett, and Laura Pulido, eds., *Racial Formation in the Twenty-First Century* (Berkeley: University of California Press, 2012).

25. Quotation in Muhammad, *Condemnation of Blackness*, 3. For an introduction to the scholarship on discretionary policing, see Agee, *Streets of San Francisco*; Risa Goluboff, *Vagrant Nation: Police Power, Constitutional Change, and the Making of the 1960s* (New York: Oxford University Press, 2016); Marilynn Johnson, *Street Justice: A History of Police Violence in New York City* (Boston: Beacon Press, 2003); Hinton, *War on Poverty to the War on Crime*; Sarah A. Seo, *Policing the Open Road: How Cars Transformed American Freedom* (Cambridge: Harvard University Press, 2010); Victor M. Rios, *Punished: Policing the Lives of Black and Latino Boys* (New York: New York University Press, 2011). On prosecution, see Angela J. Davis, *Arbitrary Justice: The Power of the American Prosecutor* (New York: Oxford University Press, 2007).

26. Nassau County Probation Department, *Drug Abuse in Suburbia: Final Report*, August 1978, NCJRS, https://www.ncjrs.gov/pdffiles1/Digitization/52204NCJRS.pdf.

27. On NORML, see Patrick Anderson, *High in America: The True Story behind NORML and the Politics of Marijuana* (New York: Viking Press, 1981). On the ACLU's campaign against "victimless crimes" in another policy area, see Leigh Ann Wheeler, *How Sex Became a Civil Liberty* (New York: Oxford University Press, 2012). On the broader role of misdemeanor criminalization, see Alexandra Natapoff, *Punishment without Crime: How our Massive Misdemeanor System Traps the Innocent and Makes America More Unequal* (New York: Basic Books, 2018).

28. Mike A. Males emphasizes the ways in which social control policies designed for nonwhite youth ultimately constrain the freedom of all youth in *Scapegoat Generation: America's War on Adolescents* (Monroe, ME: Common Courage Press, 1996).

29. FBI, *Uniform Crime Reports*, 1964–1989; CRS, *Federal Programs Relating to the Control of Drug Abuse*, Report 72–272 ED, December 7, 1972; White House Office of Public Affairs, "The Reagan Record on the National Crusade for a Drug-Free America," June 6, 1988, folder: CDFA (4), box 2, OA 16758, DIM-Reagan. Julilly Kohler-Hausmann captures the relationship between coercive medicalization and incarceration well in her analysis that for targeted African Americans, the shift of the 1973 Rockefeller Drug Laws "from a policy rhetorically committed to reintegrating drug addicts (even addict-pushers) to a project of social and physical quarantine was significant. However coercive in practice, rehabilitative intent in policy was theoretically democratizing, committed to reabsorbing marginalized citizens into the polity (on elites' terms)." See *Getting Tough*, 119.

30. PM [anonymized] to Governor Goodwin Knight, January 4, 1954, folder 13, box 36, GJK-CSA.

31. *LAHE*, January 28, 1958, clipping in folder 12, box 74, GJK-CSA; Testimony of Paula Sherwood, Eve Babitz, and Walter Bowart, May 23, 1966, "LSD and Marijuana Use on College Campuses," 543–68; Orange County Petition to Governor Edmund G. Brown Jr., November 18, 1974, CC [anonymized] to Brown, February 3, 1975, folder: Bureau of Narcotics Enforcement, box E-26–7, JB-USC.

32. On racial segregation as an antidelinquency strategy, see California Youth Authority, "Crusade for Youth," 1956, folder 4, box 75, Governor's Advisory Committee on Children and Youth, "The Age of Conflict," February 1956, folder 14, box 74, GJK-CSA. On the mass culture angle of the antidelinquency crusade, see James Gilbert, *A Cycle of Outrage: America's Reaction to the Juvenile Delinquent in the 1950s* (New York: Oxford University Press, 1986).

33. Although few historians have examined juvenile delinquency enforcement in the white suburbs, there is a copious literature on racial discretion and inequality in delinquency policing and institutionalization targeting nonwhite and immigrant youth in urban centers, especially during the Progressive Era. See Miroslava Chávez-García, *States of Delinquency: Race and Science in the Making of California's Juvenile Justice System* (Berkeley: University of California Press, 2012); Tera Eva Agyepong, *The Criminalization of Black Children: Race, Gender, and Delinquency in Chicago's Juvenile Justice System, 1899–1945* (Chapel Hill: University of North Carolina Press, 2018); David B. Wolcott, *Cops and Kids: Policing Juvenile Delinquency in Urban America, 1890–1940* (Columbus: Ohio State University Press, 2005); Andrew J. Diamond, *Mean Streets: Chicago Youths and the Everyday Struggle for Empowerment in the Multiracial City, 1908–1969* (Berkeley: University of California Press, 2009); William S. Bush, *Who Gets a Childhood?: Race and Juvenile*

Justice in Twentieth-Century Texas (Athens: University of Georgia Press, 2010). On the broader juvenile control system, see Margaret K. Rosenheim et al., *A Century of Juvenile Justice* (Chicago: University of Chicago Press, 2002); David Spinoza Tanenhaus, *The Constitutional Rights of Children: In Re Gault and Juvenile Justice* (Lawrence: University Press of Kansas, 2011).

34. Some social scientists did document these processes contemporaneously in academic journals; for a synthesis, see Edmund W. Vaz, ed., *Middle-Class Juvenile Delinquency* (New York: Harper & Row, 1967).

35. The Shafer Commission appointed by President Nixon emphasized the symbolic politics of marijuana and popularized the "amotivational syndrome" thesis in *Marihuana: A Signal of Misunderstanding: First Report of the National Commission on Marihuana and Drug Abuse* (Washington: GPO, March 1972). On the mainstream "crisis of the American family" during the 1970s and 1980s, see Natasha Zaretsky, *No Direction Home: The American Family and the Fear of National Decline, 1968–1980* (Chapel Hill: University of North Carolina Press, 2007); Robert O. Self, *All in the Family: The Realignment of American Democracy since the 1960s* (New York: Hill and Wang, 2012); Marisa Chappell, *The War on Welfare: Family, Poverty, and Politics in Modern America* (Philadelphia: University of Pennsylvania Press, 2010), esp. 159–68; Matthew D. Lassiter, "Inventing Family Values," *Rightward Bound: Making America Conservative in the 1970s*, ed. Bruce Schulman and Julian Zelizer (Cambridge: Harvard University Press, 2007), 13–28.

36. *Rebel Without a Cause* (Warner Bros., 1955); *The Graduate* (Embassy Pictures, 1967); *American Beauty* (Dreamworks Pictures, 1999). The utopian/dystopian formulation is indebted to Mike Davis's theoretical analysis of Los Angeles in *City of Quartz: Excavating the Future in Los Angeles* (London: Verso, 1990). Also see Lynn Spigel, *Welcome to the Dreamhouse: Popular Media and Postwar Suburbs* (Durham: Duke University Press, 2001); Catherine Jurca, *White Diaspora: The Suburb and the Twentieth-Century American Novel* (Princeton: Princeton University Press, 2001); Robert Beuka, *SuburbiaNation: Reading Suburban Landscape in Twentieth-Century American Film and Fiction* (New York: Palgrave Macmillan, 2004); Eric Avila, *Popular Culture in the Age of White Flight: Fear and Fantasy in Suburban Los Angeles* (Berkeley: University of California Press, 2004); Kyle Riismandel, *Neighborhood of Fear: The Suburban Crisis in American Culture, 1975–2001* (Baltimore: Johns Hopkins University Press, 2020).

37. Harry J. Anslinger and Will Oursler, *The Murderers: The Shocking Story of the Narcotic Gangs* (New York: Farrar, Straus, and Cudahy, 1961); *Traffic* (Bedford Falls Production, 2000). On Polly Klaas, see Jeffrey Toobin, "The Man Who Kept Going Free," *New Yorker*, March 7, 1994, 38–53; ABC-TV News Transcript, December 6, 1993 (quotation); Bill Clinton, "Remarks on Signing the Violent Crime Control and Law Enforcement Act of 1994," September 13, 1994, *Public Papers of the Presidents of the United States: William J. Clinton, 1994* (Washington: GPO, 1995), 1539–41; Franklin E. Zimring, Gordon Hawkins, and Sam Kamin, *Punishment and Democracy: Three Strikes and You're Out in California* (New York: Oxford University Press, 2001). On gender and female drug victimization, also see Caroline Jean Acker, *Creating the American Junkie: Addiction Research in the Classic Era of Narcotics Control* (Baltimore: Johns Hopkins University Press, 2002); Nancy Campbell, *Using Women: Gender, Drug Policy, and Social Justice* (New York: Routledge, 2000); Karen M. Staller, *Runaways: How the Sixties Counterculture Shaped Today's Practices and Policies* (New York: Columbia University Press, 2006).

38. Robin Bernstein, *Racial Innocence: Performing American Childhood from Slavery to Civil Rights* (New York: New York University Press, 2011); Paul M. Renfro, *Stranger Danger: Family*

Values, Childhood, and the American Carceral State (New York: Oxford University Press, 2020); Philip Jenkins, *Moral Panic: Changing Concepts of the Child Molester in Modern America* (New Haven: Yale University Press, 1978); Philip Jenkins, *Decade of Nightmares: The End of the Sixties and the Making of Eighties America* (New York: Oxford University Press, 2006); Susan Eckelmann Berghel, Sara Fieldston, and Paul M. Renfro, eds., *Growing Up America: Youth and Politics since 1945* (Athens: University of Georgia Press, 2019); Erica R. Meiners, *For the Children? Protecting Innocence in a Carceral State* (Minneapolis: University of Minnesota Press, 2016). On youth politics, also see Joe Austin and Michael Nevin Willard, *Generations of Youth: Youth Cultures and History in Twentieth-Century America* (New York: New York University Press, 1998).

39. On "moral panic," see Stanley Cohen, *Folk Devils and Moral Panics: The Creation of the Mods and the Rockers* (London: Paladin, 1973); Stuart Hall, *Policing the Crisis: Mugging, the State, and Law and Order* (London: Macmillan, 1978); Jenkins, *Moral Panic*; Philip Jenkins, *Synthetic Panics: The Symbolic Politics of Designer Drugs* (New York: New York University Press, 1999); Renfro, *Stranger Danger*; Joel Best, *Threatened Children: Rhetoric and Concern about Child-Victims* (Chicago: University of Chicago Press, 1990).

40. For the original model of "moral entrepreneurs," see Howard S. Becker, *Outsiders: Studies in the Sociology of Deviance* (London: Free Press of Glencoe, 1963).

41. Suburban coalitions such as the National Federation of Parents for Drug-Free Youth and Mothers Against Drunk Driving illustrate "associational" state-building, the ways in which policymakers across the spectrum have worked through interest groups, and vice versa, and the fluidity of the boundaries between public and private actors. See Brian Balogh, *The Associational State: American Governance in the Twentieth Century* (Philadelphia: University of Pennsylvania Press, 2015).

42. For recent expressions of the civil liberties and harm reduction stances, see Global Commission on Drug Policy, *War on Drugs*, June 2011, http://www.globalcommissionondrugs.org/wp-content/themes/gcdp_v1/pdf/Global_Commission_Report_English.pdf; Human Rights Watch, *Nation Behind Bars: A Human Rights Solution*, 2014, https://www.hrw.org/sites/default/files/related_material/2014_US_Nation_Behind_Bars_0.pdf.

Prologue

1. *LADN*, April 22, 24–26, 1950; *LAHE*, April 22, 24–26, 28, 1950; *LAT*, April 24–26, 30, May 22, 1950.

2. On the events of the World War II era, see Eduardo Obregón Pagan, *Murder at the Sleepy Lagoon: Zoot Suits, Race, and Riot in Wartime L.A.* (Chapel Hill: University of North Carolina Press, 2003); Edward J. Escobar, *Race, Police, and the Making of a Political Identity: Mexican Americans and the Los Angeles Police Department, 1900–1945* (Berkeley: University of California Press, 1999); Elizabeth R. Escobedo, "The Pachuca Panic: Sexual and Cultural Battlegrounds in World War II Los Angeles," *Western Historical Quarterly* 38, no. 2 (Summer 2007): 133–56. On the shifting criminalization of Mexican Americans and African Americans, see Hernández, *City of Inmates*, esp. 92–198. On racial patterns, Andrea Gibbons, *City of Segregation: 100 Years of Housing Struggle in Los Angeles* (London: Verso, 2018); Philip J. Ethington, *Segregated Diversity: Race/Ethnicity, Space, and Political Fragmentation in Los Angeles County, 1940–1994* (Los Angeles: John Randolph Haynes and Dora Haynes Foundation, 2000), 12.

3. *LAT*, April 25, 1950; Lt. Ray Huber, Narcotics Detail of Los Angeles County Sheriff's Department, *What Is Marihuana?* (Los Angeles: Narcotic Addiction Research Correlating Organization), n.d. [1950–1951], folder 13, box 98, EGB-Bancroft. Also see H. J. Anslinger, "Marijuana: Assassin of Youth," *American Magazine*, July 1937, 18–19, 150–53; McWilliams, *Protectors*, 63–126.

4. *LAT*, May 15, 22, 25, 1950.

5. Los Angeles Civic and Social Agencies to the Metropolitan Press, May 26, 1950, Los Angeles County Committee on Human Relations, Minutes, June 20, 1950, folder 3, box 9, LM-Huntington; *LAT*, May 5, 15, 19, 1950.

6. *LAHE*, April 17, 1950; *LAT*, May 5, 1950, June 28, 1951; *Narcotics: Questions by Parents* (Los Angeles: Narcotic Addiction Research Correlating Organization), n.d. [1950–1951], folder 13, box 98, EGB-Bancroft; Twain Mickelson, KYA Radio Broadcast, July 22, 1951, folder 10, Mickelson, "Go Out—Get This Killer!" *Hollywood Life*, July 27, 1951, folder 13, box 1, HJA-PSU.

7. Narcotic Educational Foundation of America, *Narcotics: Our Ever Present Social Menace*, n.d. [early 1950s], *Marihuana: The Assassin of Youth*, n.d. [early 1950s], folder 2, box 85, *Youth and Narcotics*, 1951, folder 13, box 98, EGB-Bancroft; Walter R. Creighton [director of CBNE], "Narcotics: Their Legitimate and Illegitimate Use," 1951, Section 213, F3640:2671, EW-CSA.

8. *LAT*, June 26, July 15, 1951; *Preliminary Report of the Subcommittee on Narcotics*, Assembly Interim Committee on Judiciary, California Legislature, March 24, 1952, 33–42, UCLA Law Library; California Board of Corrections, *Narcotics and Hypnotics in California*, January 1953, 17–18, in folder 17, box 36, GJK-CSA; Mrs. Edward T. Walker/California Congress of Parents and Teachers to Earl Warren, March 10, 1952, Section 213, F3640:2671, EW-CSA.

9. *LAT*, July 29, September 27, 1951; CFWC to Members of California Legislature, October 9, 1952, Mrs. Edward T. Walker/California Congress of Parents and Teachers to Warren, March 4, 1952, Section 213, F3640:2671, EW-CSA. Additional letters and petitions in ibid. On the cross-border market, see chapter 1 and San Diego Police Chief J. W. Jordan to Warren, January 27, 1952, ibid.

10. California Division of Narcotic Enforcement, "Narcotics: Their Legitimate and Illegitimate Use," 1951, Warren to California Congress of Parents and Teachers, March 10, 1952, Section 213, F3640:2671, EW-CSA; *The Terrible Truth* (Los Angeles: Sid Davis Productions, 1951), Internet Archive, archive.org/details/Terrible1951.

11. Los Angeles Youth Council, Third Annual Convention Proceedings, May 1–2, 1948, folder BIII-14-a-gg-aaa, box 60, Los Angeles County Committee on Human Relations, Press Release: "Jim Crow Segregation," September 27, 1949, folder BIII-14-d-f, box 65, JAF-Huntington; "Proceedings of the Conference on Housing and Racial Discrimination," February 24, 1945, folder 6, box 25, Loren Miller, Speech to NCADH, March 14, 1955, folder 8, box 44, LM-Huntington.

12. *LAT*, March 25, 1952; California Housing Initiative Committee, "Open to All" flier, 1948, folder BIII-14-d-ff, Committee for Home Protection, "Vote Yes on Proposition 10," 1950, "Arguments against Proposition No. 10," 1950, folder BIII-14-d-cc, box 65, JAF-Huntington; Committee against Socialist Housing, "Vote No L.A. Housing Proposition," 1952, folder 13, box 2, MM-CSUN. Also see Donald Craig Parson, *Making a Better World: Public Housing, the Red Scare, and the Direction of Modern Los Angeles* (Minneapolis: University of Minnesota Press, 2003).

13. Governor's Advisory Committee on Children and Youth, "The Age of Conflict," February 1956, folder 14, box 74, GJK-CSA.

Chapter 1. Pushers and Victims

1. Anslinger and Oursler, *The Murderers*, 3–7, 183–93; Peggy Ellsworth, as told to Norma Lee Browning, "I Was a Dope Addict," *CDT*, October 21, 1951.

2. On this trope in antidrug campaigns, see Acker, *Creating the American Junkie*; Susan C. Boyd, *Hooked: Drug War Films in Britain, Canada, and the United States* (Toronto: University of Toronto Press, 2008); Campbell, *Using Women*; Shah, *Contagious Divides*, 90–97; Susan L. Speaker, "Demons for the Twentieth Century: The Rhetoric of Drug Reform, 1920–1940," in *Altering American Consciousness: The History of Alcohol and Drug Use in the United States, 1800–2000*, ed. Sarah W. Tracy and Caroline Jean Acker (Amherst: University of Massachusetts Press, 2004), 203–24. More broadly, see Rodney Hessinger, *Seduced, Abandoned, and Reborn: Visions of Youth in Middle-Class America, 1780–1950* (Philadelphia: University of Pennsylvania Press, 2005); Pliley, *Policing Sexuality*; Melvyn Stokes, *D. W. Griffith's "The Birth of a Nation": A History of the Most Controversial Motion Picture of All Time* (New York: Oxford University Press, 2008); Richard Slotkin, *Gunfighter Nation: The Myth of the Frontier in Twentieth-Century America* (Norman: University of Oklahoma Press, 1998).

3. Harry J. Anslinger, "The Facts about Our Teen-Age Drug Addicts," *RD*, October 1951, 137–40; Anslinger and Oursler, *The Murderers*, quotation 189; Anslinger and William F. Tompkins, *The Traffic in Narcotics* (New York: Funk and Wagnalls, 1953).

4. For top-down approaches, see McWilliams, *Protectors*; Frydl, *Drug Wars in America*.

5. Almost no scholarship has examined the grassroots pressure during the 1950s for a get-tough war on narcotics. The popular support for mandatory-minimum laws in Southern California represented a much broader suburban and white middle-class base than the grassroots ideological conservatives and Republican activists who have received so much attention from political historians. The local and statewide organizations of California's New Right during the postwar era also did not play central roles in the narcotics debate in state politics. For explorations of grassroots conservatism in the Los Angeles suburbs during this period, see McGirr, *Suburban Warriors*; Dochuk, *Bible Belt to Sunbelt*; Nickerson, *Mothers of Conservatism*.

6. Anslinger, "How to Plug Loopholes That Make Narcotics Addicts," n.d. [1950], folder 15, box 2, Anslinger, "Illicit Traffic in Narcotics Today," *NARD Journal* 77, no. 21 (November 7, 1955), folder 10, Anslinger, "Briefing on the Work of the United Nations Commission on Narcotics," May 29, 1957, Anslinger, "Address by Remington Medalist," December 4, 1962, folder 8, box 1, HJA-PSU. Also see Reiss, *We Sell Drugs*, esp. 192–205; Courtwright, *Dark Paradise*, 145–60; Herzberg, *White Market Drugs*; Tone, *Age of Anxiety*; Rasmussen, *On Speed*; McWilliams, *Protectors*, 86–87.

7. FBN, "Drug Addiction: Composite Total for Calendar Years 1953–1956," *Traffic in Opium and Other Dangerous Drugs, 1956* (Washington: GPO, 1957), 36.

8. The literature on government-sanctioned housing segregation is vast, including Jackson, *Crabgrass Frontier*, 190–230; Freund, *Colored Property*; Richard Rothstein, *The Color of Law: A Forgotten History of How Our Government Segregated America* (New York: Liveright, 2017).

9. Anslinger Testimony, "Investigation of Organized Crime in Interstate Commerce," Part 2, *Hearings before the Special Committee to Investigate Organized Crime in Interstate Commerce*, U.S. Senate, June 28, 1950 (Washington: GPO, 1950), 88–97; On media coverage, see Richard Barr, "Nemesis of the Dope Gangs," *Argosy*, July 1949, 36–37, 106–9, folder 1, Frederic Sondern Jr.,

"Our Global War on Narcotics," *American Mercury*, March 1950, 355–62, folder 8, box 12, HJA-PSU.

10. H. J. Anslinger with Courtney Ryley Cooper, "Marijuana: Assassin of Youth," *American Magazine*, July 1937, 18–19, 150–53; Committee on Finance, U.S. Senate, *Marihuana Taxing Bill*, Report No. 900, July 15, 1937, 75th Congress, 1st Session; McGirr, *War on Alcohol*, 211–19; McWilliams, *Protectors*, 25–106.

11. Anslinger Testimony, "Investigation of Organized Crime in Interstate Commerce," *Hearings*, Part 2, June 28, 1950, 88–97; FBN, *Traffic in Opium and Other Dangerous Drugs, 1950* (Washington: GPO, 1951), quotation 12. On private views, see Anslinger, "How to Plug Loopholes That Make Narcotics Addicts," 1950, Anslinger to John S. Zinner, March 17, 1950, folder 15, box 2, HJA-PSU.

12. "Accomplishments of the Crime Prevention Council and Crime Prevention Bureau from 1949 to 1955," n.d. [1956], folder: Illinois-Chicago, box 921, PD-NA; *CDT*, July 16, 1951 (quotation); Chicago Crime Prevention Bureau, Transcript of Proceedings, October 19, 1949, reproduced in "Control of Narcotics, Marihuana, and Barbiturates," *Hearings before a Subcommittee of the Committee on Ways and Means*, House of Representatives, April 7, 1951 (Washington: GPO, 1951), 82–92; Joan Beck, "Mother of Two Leads Chicago's Battle against Dope Menace," *CDT*, July 16–18, 1951 [three-part series]. On police/reform work, see Lois Higgins, "Women Police Service," *Journal of Criminal Law and Criminology* 41, no. 1 (May–June 1950): 101–6 (quotation).

13. Golden B. Darby Testimony, June 26, 1951, "Investigation of Organized Crime in Interstate Commerce," *Hearings*, Part 14: "Narcotics," 293–94; Southside Community Committee, "The Proposed 'Dope Must Go' Program," ibid., 457–63; Southside Community Committee, "Dope Must Go" materials, folder: General Narcotics, box 60, JD-NA. On the Illinois law, also see *CDT*, February 5, May 4, July 18, 1951. For allegations that narcotics traffickers paid off the Chicago police, see *Chicago Defender*, July 7, 1951. On police corruption and drug markets, also see Schneider, *Smack*, esp. 106–15.

14. *CDT*, June 22–23, 1951.

15. "Children in Peril: 'Pushers' Are Selling Narcotics to Thousands of Teen-agers," *Life*, June 11, 1951, 116–25; Herbert Brean, "A Short—and Horrible—Life," *Life*, June 11, 1951, 126.

16. Sidney R. Yates Testimony, April 7, 1951, "Control of Narcotics, Marihuana, and Barbiturates," *Hearings*, 40–50; *CDT*, April 3, 11, 1951.

17. Higgins series in *CDT*, July 16–17, 1951; Lois Higgins Testimony, April 7, 1951, "Control of Narcotics, Marihuana, and Barbiturates," *Hearings*, 103–9. Bipartisan comment in Lois Higgins Testimony, June 26, 1951, "Investigation of Organized Crime in Interstate Commerce," *Hearings*, Part 14: "Narcotics," 281–86. "Socially well-adjusted families" in Leonidas H. Berry/Chicago Crime Prevention Bureau, "Medical Counseling Clinics for Young Narcotics Addicts," *JAMA* 147, no. 12 (December 4–7, 1951): 1129–32. Also see Lois Lundell Higgins/Crime Prevention Bureau, "Dope-Ology: Articles and Lectures," n.d. [mid-1950s], box 183 (loose materials), JD-NA.

18. *Drug Addiction* (Encyclopedia Britannica Films, 1951), made with the Juvenile Protection Association of Chicago and the Wiebold Foundation, Internet Archive, http://archive.org/details/DrugAddi1951.

19. James R. Dumpson/Committee on Use of Narcotics among Teen Age Youth, *Interim Report: The Menace of Narcotics to the Children of New York: A Plan to Eradicate the Evil*, August 1951, folder 8, box 7, HJA-PSU; Dumpson Testimony, June 26, 1951, "Investigation of

Organized Crime in Interstate Commerce," *Hearings*, Part 14: "Narcotics," 261–71. On arrest data, see Mayor's Committee on Drug Addiction, *Report of Study on Addiction among Teenagers*, July 1951, folder 14, box 8, HJA-PSU.

20. Information Comics Division of Harvey Publications, with the cooperation of the Committee on Narcotics of the Welfare Council of New York City, *Trapped!* (New York: Columbia University Press, 1951).

21. *NYT*, June 13–15, 1951; "Narcotics: Degradation in New York," *Newsweek*, June 25, 1951, 19–20, "Crime: The Junkies," *Time*, June 25, 1951, reproduced in *CR—House* (July 16, 1951), 8198–8199; Mayor's Committee on Drug Addiction, *Report of Study on Addiction among Teenagers*, July 1951.

22. Berry/Chicago Crime Prevention Bureau, "Medical Counseling Clinics for Young Narcotics Addicts," 1129.

23. "Don't Let It Happen to You!" *True Story*, Part 1 (February 1951), 40–43, 124–29, Part 2 (March 1951), 58–59, 111–17, folder 19, box 12, Frank J. O'Brien, "Drug Traffic in Young Lives," *National Parent-Teacher: The P.T.A. Magazine*, September 1951, 4–7, folder 15, box 8, HJA-PSU.

24. Estes Kefauver, "What I Found in the Underworld," *SEP*, April 7, 1951, 19–21, 71–72, 76, 79; *CDT*, January 31, 1951. Quotations in Peter T. White, "Dope, Inc.," *Argosy*, February 1951, 44–45, 84–86, folder 1, box 12, HJA-PSU. Also see Estes Kefauver, *Crime in America* (New York: Doubleday, 1951).

25. Anslinger Testimony, "Investigation of Organized Crime in Interstate Commerce," *Hearings*, Part 12, March 27, 1951, 662–67; FBN, "Addict Patients Under Age 21 at Lexington and Fort Worth Hospitals," June 7, 1951, folder 14, box 8, HJA-PSU. The first round of narcotics hearings took place in New York City and only featured FBN agents and local law enforcement; see "Investigation of Organized Crime in Interstate Commerce," *Hearings*, Part 7: "New York–New Jersey," March 14–15, 1951, esp. 1022–97, 1180–98.

26. Special Committee to Investigate Organized Crime in Interstate Commerce, U.S. Senate, *Organized Crime in Interstate Commerce: Final Report* (Washington: GPO, 1951), quotation 2; "Report of Proceedings, Executive Session—Confidential, Hearing before the Special Committee to Investigate Organized Crime in Interstate Commerce," April 16, 1951, unpublished transcript, 40–53 [in ProQuest Congressional database].

27. "Investigation of Organized Crime in Interstate Commerce," *Hearings*, Part 14: "Narcotics," May 29, June 7, June 12, 1951, 1–229.

28. Testimony of Mr. Harvey———, June 12, 26, 1951, "Investigation of Organized Crime in Interstate Commerce," *Hearings*, Part 14: "Narcotics," 194–202, 271–81; Testimony of Miss Jeanne———, June 12, 26, 1951, ibid., 203–10, 294–305; Testimony of Mrs.———, June 26, 1951, ibid., 323–29; Associated Press story in *LAT*, June 27, 1951 (quotations); *WP*, June 27, 1951.

29. *Organized Crime in Interstate Commerce: Final Report*, quotations 16, 4, 2, 26–29, 35. Also see *NYT*, July 26, 1951; Senator Herbert R. O'Conor, "Watchdogs against Crime," *LAT*, September 30, 1951. *Newsweek* repackaged the narcotics findings of the Senate Crime Committee for civic clubs and the general public in the educational booklet *U.S. Narcotics Problem: Controversial and Unsolved* (Newsweek Club and Educational Bureaus: Weekly Publications, 1952), folder: Narcotics: Educational Pamphlets, box 9, WFT-Hoover.

30. "Control of Narcotics, Marihuana, and Barbiturates," *Hearings*, quotations 1, 111, 203.

31. Committee on Ways and Means, House of Representatives, *Increased Penalties for Narcotic and Marihuana Law Violators*, Report No. 635, June 21, 1951; *CR—House* (July 16, 1951), 8196–8211. The initial bill contained a ten-to-twenty-year sentencing range for third offenders, revised during later negotiations.

32. *CR—House* (July 16, 1951), 8209–8211; *CR—Senate* (October 21, 1951), 13675–13676; Harry S. Truman, "Letter to Chairman, Senate Committee on Finance, in Support of a Narcotics Control Bill," August 24, 1951, APP, https://www.presidency.ucsb.edu/node/230649; Truman, "Statement by the President upon Signing Bill Relating to Narcotics Laws Violations," November 2, 1951, APP, https://www.presidency.ucsb.edu/node/231244.

33. "Control of Narcotics, Marihuana, and Barbiturates," *Hearings*, 3–39, 119–238 (Anslinger quotation 205). For the internal FBN document, see "4,000,000,000 Doses of Sleeping Pills," n.d., folder 1, box 9, HJA-PSU. Anslinger's papers include scientific reports on the addictiveness of barbiturates; see additional documents in folder 1, box 9, HJA-PSU. On the white middle-class female market, also see William Engle, "Sleeping Pills: Doorway to Doom," *Coronet*, February 1951, 25–28. Background and barbiturate overdose data in Herzberg, *White Market Drugs*, 135–293.

34. Albert Deutsch/New York Department of Health, *What We Can Do about the Drug Menace* (National Association for Mental Health, 1952), folder: Narcotics: Educational Pamphlets, box 9, WFT-Hoover; Anslinger, "The Sheriff and Narcotic Enforcement," *International Criminal Police Review* (December 1952), 317–21, folder 11, box 1, HJA-PSU.

35. Anslinger and Tompkins, *Traffic in Narcotics*, 18–26; FBN, *Traffic in Opium and Other Dangerous Drugs, 1953* (Washington: GPO, 1954). Marijuana stories in folder 7, box 9, HJA-PSU. Also see Schneider, *Smack*, 17–74.

36. Howard S. Becker, "Becoming a Marihuana User," *AJS* 59, no. 3 (November 1953): 235–42; Becker, "Marihuana Use and Social Control," *Social Problems* 3, no. 1 (July 1955): 35–44.

37. Anslinger, "The Facts about Our Teen-Age Drug Addicts," *RD*, October 1951, 137–40; "The Teen-Age Narcotic Problem," *The Voice* (Board of Temperance of the Methodist Church), n.d. [late 1951/early 1952], folder 13, box 1, J. D. Radcliff, "A Sane Look at Teen-Age Drug Addiction," *Parents*, November 1951, 76–81, folder 11, box 1, Herbert C. Rosenthal, "How Much of a Menace Is the Drug Menace?" *Pageant*, October 1951, folder 1, box 7, HJA-PSU.

38. FBN, *Traffic in Opium and Other Dangerous Drugs, 1951* (Washington: GPO, 1952); "'The Man' Strikes Hardest Blow Yet against Dope," *Life*, January 14, 1952, 22–23; John M. Conly, "'Shoot First' Is Nation-wide Slogan for Raids on Dope Peddlers," *Pathfinder*, January 23, 1952, 24–25, folder 13, box 1, HJA-PSU; Neil M. Clark, "They're Death on Dope Runners," *SEP*, July 26, 1952, 36–37, 108–11. Endorsements in Anslinger biographical packet, 1952, folder 13, box 2, HJA-PSU. Anslinger's "shoot first" orders emulated the FBI's martial rhetoric in the first federal "war on crime" during the hunt for John Dillinger and other gangsters in the early 1930s; see Potter, *War on Crime*.

39. "Narcotics: A New Social Disease," Georgetown University Radio and Television Forum, February 10, 1952, folders 8–9, box 1, HJA-PSU; John Gerrity, "The Truth about the 'Drug Menace,'" *HM*, February 1952, 27–31. Remarks by Judge Alexander M. MacLeod (Paterson, New Jersey) reproduced in *Traffic in Opium and Other Dangerous Drugs, 1951*, 10–11.

40. James C. G. Coniff, "Do Schools Teach Drug Addiction?" *Catholic Digest*, February 1952, 1–6, folder 3, box 12, "Narcotics: A New Social Disease," folders 8–9, box 1, HJA-PSU; *Organized Crime in Interstate Commerce: Final Report*, 8, 33–34.

41. Science Research Associates, "Facts about Narcotics: Instructors Guide," 1951, folder 18, box 8, HJA-PSU; Attorney General Nathaniel L. Goldstein (New York), "Narcotics 1952: A Further Study of Problems and Plans," January 1953, folder: Narcotics Reports–New York, box 12, WFT-Hoover; Detroit Public Schools, *Instruction Regarding Narcotics* (Detroit: Board of Education, 1952). Film quotations from *Drug Addiction* (Encyclopedia Britannica Films, 1951); also see Information Comics, *Trapped!* (1951); *The Terrible Truth*.

42. Peggy Ellsworth, as told to Norma Lee Browning, "I Was a Dope Addict," *CDT*, October 21, 1951; also see *CDT*, October 28, 1951; "My Son Is a Dope Addict," as told to Cameron Cornell, *SEP*, January 25, 1952, 20–21, 77–84; David Hulburd, "It Happened to Amy: The Story of a Teen-Age Addict," *WHC*, May 1952, 26–27, 103–4, 115, 120–23, 141–45; Hulburd, *H Is for Heroin* (New York: Doubleday, 1952).

43. Figure cited in Kenneth Hahn, Statement to President's Interdepartmental Committee on Narcotics, March 31, 1960, folder 6, box 403, series 6.4.5.19, KH-Huntington.

44. Rachel St. John, *Line in the Sand: A History of the Western U.S.-Mexico Border* (Princeton: Princeton University Press, 2011), 148–73; George T. Díaz, *Border Contraband: A History of Smuggling across the Rio Grande* (Austin: University of Texas Press, 2015).

45. Gibbons, *City of Segregation*, esp. 41–72; Josh Sides, *L.A. City Limits: African American Los Angeles from the Great Depression to the Present* (Berkeley: University of California Press, 2003); Becky Nicolaides, *My Blue Heaven: Life and Politics in the Working-Class Suburbs of Los Angeles, 1920–1965* (Chicago: University of Chicago Press, 2002), 185–214. East Los Angeles was technically "suburban" in census classification, because of its location in an unincorporated part of the county close to the city limits of Los Angeles, but almost never labeled suburban because of the racial demographics of its Mexican American population and the association of suburbia with whiteness. The same is true of multiple other Mexican American enclaves in the San Gabriel Valley and other parts of Los Angeles County. On this generally unmarked suburban diversity, see Jerry González, *In Search of the Mexican Beverly Hills: Latino Suburbanization in Postwar Los Angeles* (New Brunswick: Rutgers University Press, 2018).

46. CBNE, "Evaluation of Narcotics Prosecutions Conducted by the District Attorney's Office of Los Angeles County, California, for the Calendar Year 1950," June 12, 1952, folder 4, box 98, EGB-Bancroft; Statistical Appendix in *Preliminary Report of the Subcommittee on Narcotics*, Assembly Interim Committee on Judiciary, California Legislature, March 24, 1952, UCLA Law Library; LACYC, "Juvenile Narcotics Report," September 7, 1951, F3717:204, SSC-CSA. On the racial/ethnic dynamics of the heroin market in Los Angeles, see Schneider, *Smack*, 75–97 (quotation 75).

47. *The Terrible Truth* (Los Angeles: Sid Davis Productions, 1951), Internet Archive, archive .org/details/Terrible1951 (narrated by Judge William B. McKesson of the Los Angeles Juvenile Court); *Subject: Narcotics* (Narcotic Educational Foundation of America: 1951), in consultation with LACSD Narcotic Detail, Internet Archive, http://archive.org/details/SubjectN1951. On national distribution, see Henry Hall to Price Daniel, March 8, 1956, folder: California (2), box 915, PD-NA. On statewide campaign, see California State Department of Education, "Narcotics: The Study of a Modern Problem," 1952, F3717:195, SCN-CSA; Walter R. Creighton/CBNE, "Narcotics Report to Subcommittee to Investigate Juvenile Delinquency," November 6, 1953, folder 1, box 85, EGB-Bancroft.

48. *LAT*, July 29, September 27, 1951; CFWC to Members of California Legislature, October 9, 1952, and other letters and petitions in Section 213, F3640:2671, EW-CSA; *Report of the*

Governor's Advisory Committee on Children and Youth, Subcommittee on Narcotics, 1953, folder 1, box 75, GJK-CSA.

49. Patricia Williams (as told to Will Oursler), "I Trapped a Dope Ring," serialized in three parts in *The American Weekly*, May 31, June 7, June 14, 1953, in folder: Narcotics, box 181, JD-NA; *Teenage Devil Dolls* (1955, dir. Bamlet Lawrence Price Jr.).

50. LAPD, *Youth and Narcotics: A Study of Juvenile Drug Addiction in Los Angeles*, 1952, folder 15, box 8, HJA-PSU; Juvenile Narcotics Squad in Testimony of Sgt. John McTighe, "Juvenile Delinquency (California)," *Hearings before the Subcommittee to Investigate Juvenile Delinquency, Committee on the Judiciary*, U.S. Senate, September 27, 1954 (Washington: GPO, 1955), 186–93.

51. Testimony of Karl Holton, September 24, 1957, "Juvenile Delinquency (California)," *Hearings*, 133–42; Testimony of Sgt. John A. Hampton, ibid., 170–77; Testimony of S. Ernest Roll, ibid., 215–24.

52. LACYC, *Monthly Bulletin*, November 1954, folder 22, box 84, EGB-Bancroft; California Board of Corrections, *Narcotics and Hypnotics in California*, 33; Testimony of Sgt. John McTighe, September 24, 1957, "Juvenile Delinquency (California)," *Hearings*, 186–93; Testimony of Capt. Kenneth E. Irving, ibid., 177–85; Testimony of John Brewer, ibid., 151–53.

53. Sanford Rothman, "Narcotics Use among High School Boys," *California Journal of Secondary Education* 27, no. 5 (May 1952): 291–92.

54. Gene Fuson, "Narcotics and Youth" series, *San Diego Union*, May 1952 (reprint), folder 22, box 98, EGB-Bancroft; also see Fuson Testimony, September 24, 1957, "Juvenile Delinquency (California)," *Hearings*, 62–71.

55. S. Ernest Roll (Los Angeles County District Attorney) to Edmund G. Brown, January 23, 1953, folder 27, box 95; Attorney General Brown's Office, "California Narcotics Timeline," n.d. [1958], folder 3, H. J. Res. 240, "Joint Resolution to Close the Mexican Border to Unaccompanied Minors," April 16, 1953, folder 8, box 85, EGB-Bancroft; Anslinger, "Remarks at UN Commission on Narcotic Drugs," May 1, 1952, folder 8, box 1, Rep. Samuel M. Yorty to H. J. Anslinger, March 16, 1953, Anslinger to Yorty, March 18, 1953, reproduced in *CR* reprint, March 23, 1953, folder 11, box 8, HJA-PSU. Border crossing data in "Juvenile Delinquency (California)," *Hearings*, 3.

56. Dick Wylie to Brown, Memo on Mexico Narcotics Conference, January 20, 1953, folder 27, box 95, Dick Wylie and Chester Reed, Memo on Narcotics Suppression, February 18, 1953, folder 1, box 85, Walter R. Creighton to Brown, July 3, 1953, folder 29, box 95, EGB-Bancroft.

57. Brown, "Six Point Program to Rid the State of Narcotics," 1953, Southern California Juvenile Officers Association quoted in *South Bay* newspaper, February 27, 1953, William A. Townes, Open Letter, *LADN*, February 2, 1953, *Fullerton News Tribune*, February 12, 1953, folder 1, box 85, Mrs. P. de Shishmareff (La Jolla) to Brown, February 5, 1953, Mrs. Vernon (Huntington Park) to Brown, February 1953, folder 27, Mrs. John M. Woodard to Brown, February 1953, folder 29, box 95, EGB-Bancroft.

58. State of California, Narcotic Act of 1953, folder 14, box 98, EGB-Bancroft; *LAT*, January 30, February 3, 5, March 17, June 8, 1953; *Report of the Governor's Advisory Committee on Children and Youth, Subcommittee on Narcotics*, 1953; Testimony of Karl Holton, "Juvenile Delinquency (National, Federal, and Youth Serving Agencies)," Part 1, *Hearings before the Subcommittee to Investigate Juvenile Delinquency, Committee on the Judiciary*, U.S. Senate (Washington: GPO, 1954), November 20, 1953, 106–17, 124–26.

59. Judge Mildred Lillie quoted in Minutes of the Meeting of the Southern California Advisory Committee on Crime Prevention, June 8, 1953, folder: Los Angeles, box 72, JD-NA; Judge Charles W. Fricke, Address to Narcotic Enforcement Officers, August 25, 1954, folder 29, box 89, Brown to Charles Edward Chapel, February 10, 1953, folder 27, box 95, EGB-Bancroft; California Board of Corrections, *Narcotics and Hypnotics in California*, 17–20; *LAT*, March 17, 1953. Juvenile judges maintained absolute statutory discretion, and California law allowed the criminal courts to certify eighteen-to-twenty-year-olds as "unfit" and try them as adults or remand them to the juvenile system. Some older teenagers, particularly African Americans and Mexican Americans disproportionately classified as "incorrigible" in the juvenile courts, preferred to gamble on a misdemeanor jail sentence in the adult system rather than indefinite confinement of a year or more in a California Youth Authority detention center. See Holton Testimony, November 20, 1953, "Juvenile Delinquency (National, Federal, and Youth-Serving Agencies)," *Hearings*, Part 1, 125–26.

60. Office of Attorney General, Press Release, August 27, 1953, Press Release, March 27, 1954, folder 5, box 85, EGB-Bancroft; *Report of the Governor's Advisory Committee on Children and Youth, Subcommittee on Narcotics*, 1953.

61. Women's Club of Redondo Beach/Mrs. Frank A. Boulger to Goodwin J. Knight, November 17, 1953, Gardena High PTA/Mrs. Floyd E. Pixley to Knight, November 21, 1953, Esther Fish to Knight, November 19, 1953 (sample of form language), Jean Verrill to Knight, November 24, 1953 (death sentence quotation), and similar letters in folders 12–13, box 36, GJK-CSA.

62. *LAT*, December 7–8, 12, 1953. For the less biased version, see LAPD Police Chief William Parker's report in LACYC Minutes, January 20, 1954, folder BIII-7c-cc, box 34, JAF-Huntington.

63. *LADN*, December 7, 1953 (first two quotations); *PSN*, December 7, 14, 16, 18, 21, 1953; *LAT*, December 16, 1953 (third quotation), December 18, 21, 29–30, 1953.

64. *LAT*, December 8–9, 1953; Mary E. Slinkard to Knight, January 19, 1954, folder 13, box 36, GJK-CSA. For letters to the editor, see *LAT*, December 12, 13, 17, 19, 1953, January 1, 6, 1954.

65. "Youth Gangs" series in *LAT*, December 16–21, 1953.

66. William B. McKesson letter to the *Daily Mirror*, December 22, 1953, quoted in LACYC, "Special Meeting Re Juvenile Delinquency," December 22, 1953, LACYC, Minutes, January 20, 1954, folder BIII-7c-cc, box 34, JAF-Huntington; also see Los Angeles County Committee on Human Relations, Memorandum on "Rat Pack" Publicity, December 22, 1953, folder BIV-5-a-cc, box 72, ibid.

67. Gordon R. Eshelby to Knight, December 16, 1953, folder 12, J. A. Woodruff to Knight, December 30, 1953, Cora B. Phillips to Knight, January 22, 1954, Pauline A. Vorachek to Knight, February 1, 1954, W. L. Ford to Knight, March 10, 1954, folder 13, Mrs. Ethel D. Brenner to Knight, March 22, 1954, folder 14, box 36, GJK-CSA. For parents of addicted children [anonymized], see Mr. and Mrs. MCS to Knight, March 11, 1954, Mrs. VO to Knight, March 16, 1954, Mrs. JHB to Knight, March 17, 1954, folder 13, box 36, GJK-CSA.

68. Knight, "The Challenge Ahead: Progress in Combating Narcotics," March 1954, folder 14, box 36, GJK-CSA; Knight, "The Narcotics Challenge: Greater Compassion for the Victims, More Punishment for the Offenders," March 1954, folder: March 1954, box 124, GJK-Stanford; *LAT*, March 10, 14, 1954. Brown in *PSN*, December 7, 1953; Office of Attorney General, Press Release, April 18, 1954, folder 1, box 85, EGB-Bancroft.

69. Brown, "1954 Amendments to the State Narcotic Act," n.d. [March 1954], folder 30, Brown to Charles Edward Chapel, February 10, 1953, folder 27, box 95, EGB-Bancroft; Assembly Subcommittee on Narcotics, "Transcript of Proceedings," October 14, 1954, folder LP164:37, NSAJC-CSA; *LAT*, March 24, 27, 1954; *SFC*, March 22, 1954.

70. Knight, "California's Narcotics Disaster: Can the High School and Junior College Students Help?" September 17, 1954, Knight, Remarks to Governor's Committee on Children and Youth, September 28, 1954, folder: September 1954, box 124, GJK-Stanford; Knight, Speech to Governor's Conference on Youth and Narcotics, December 13, 1954, folder 18, box 36, GJK-CSA.

71. Citizens' Advisory Committee to the Attorney General on Crime Prevention, "Narcotic Addiction," March 26, 1954, folder 6, box 85, EGB-Bancroft. Brown's office released selective summaries of the report in four dispatches; see Office of Attorney General, Press Releases, April 19–22, 1954, folder 1, box 85, EGB-Bancroft.

72. Assemblyman H. Allen Smith, Memorandum, October 1954, folder 15, box 36, GJK-CSA; *LAT*, April 19, October 15, 1954, March 18, 1955; Minutes of the Northern Citizens' Advisory Committee to the Attorney General on Crime Prevention, July 31, 1957, folder 32, box 98, EGB-Bancroft. The advisory committee's report explicitly blamed "wetbacks" as the major source of marijuana smuggling; see Office of Attorney General, Press Release, April 20, 1954, folder 1, box 85, EGB-Bancroft.

73. *LAT*, January 2, 4, 12, 1956; Dolores M. Lawless to Knight, January 18, 1956, folder 15, box 36, GJK-CSA; William Parker, "Statement to the Special Subcommittee on Improvement of the Federal Code," November 1955, folder: Crime and Illicit Narcotics Traffic, box 919, PD-NA.

74. Petition from Long Beach area citizens, June 1955, Mr. and Mrs. Howard L. Rice to Knight, May 25, 1955, Petition to Governor Knight from Petaluma Voters, March 1955, Wesley J. Cole to Knight, November 16, 1955, folder 15, CFWC to Knight, May 14, 1956, Mary Brace to Knight, June 7, 1956, folder 16, box 36, GJK-CSA.

75. Knight to Subcommittee on Narcotics of the House Committee on Ways and Means, November 8, 1955, Assemblyman H. Allen Smith, Memorandum, October 1954, folder 15, box 36, GJK-CSA.

76. Brown, "Slums and Crime Rates," n.d. [early 1950s], folder 3, box 87, Brown, Press Release, March 27, 1954, folder 5, box 85, Brown, "The Problem of Juvenile Violence," 1958, folder 33, box 87, EGB-Bancroft. The rehabilitative view is evident in the reports of the LACYC cited above and others found in box 34, JAF-Huntington. On the resilience of the Progressive Era antidelinquency philosophy in Los Angeles, also see Janis Appier, "'We're Blocking Youth's Path to Crime': The Los Angeles Coordinating Councils during the Great Depression," *Journal of Urban History* 31, no. 2 (January 2005): 190–218.

77. Karl Holton (chief probation officer of Los Angeles County) to John Anson Ford, April 4, 1957, folder BIII-7c-cc, box 34, JAF-Huntington; Testimony of Karl Holton, September 24, 1957, "Juvenile Delinquency (California)," *Hearings*, 139–40.

78. Governor's Advisory Committee on Children and Youth, "The Age of Conflict," February 1956, folder 14, box 74, GJK-CSA.

79. *Juvenile Delinquency: Interim Report of the Committee on the Judiciary*, U.S. Senate, March 15, 1954 (Washington: GPO, 1954), 4; Williams, "I Trapped a Dope Ring"; Walter R. Creighton/CBNE, "Narcotics Report to Subcommittee to Investigate Juvenile Delinquency,"

November 6, 1953, folder 1, box 85, EGB-Bancroft. For the traditional emphasis, see Gilbert, *Cycle of Outrage*.

80. "Juvenile Delinquency (National, Federal, and Youth-Serving Agencies)," *Hearings*, Part 1 (Henriksen quotation 4); Testimony of Karl Holton, November 19, 1953, ibid., 110–13; Testimony of Anslinger, November 23, 1953, ibid., 151–87; Testimony of Edward J. Mowery, November 24, 1953, ibid., 242–56; Testimony of John Gutknecht, November 24, 1953, ibid., 225–42; Testimony of Sally Butler (GFWC), January 22, 1964, Part 3, ibid., 543–47. Also see Mowery, "Dope, Unlimited" series distributed by Scripps-Howard wire service, November 1953, folder: General Narcotics Material, box 60, JD-NA.

81. *Juvenile Delinquency: Interim Report of the Committee on the Judiciary*, March 15, 1954, quotations 21, 23.

82. Subcommittee to Investigate Juvenile Delinquency, Press Release, n.d. [September 1954], Thomas S. Sullivan, Memorandum on Tijuana Investigation, n.d. [1954], folder: Los Angeles, box 72, JD-NA; "Juvenile Delinquency (California)," *Hearings*, quotations 66, 70, 136, 183, 181, 196. Also see Anslinger and Tompkins, *Traffic in Narcotics*. Anslinger routinely blamed "Red China" for a conspiracy to addict Americans to heroin, tapping into the historical legacy of racial stigmatization of Chinese immigrants as narcotics criminals and China's status as a source country for opium and especially as a convenient Cold War enemy. See Douglas Clark Kinder, "Bureaucratic Cold Warrior: Harry J. Anslinger and Illicit Narcotics Traffic," *Pacific Historical Review* 50, no. 2 (May 1981): 169–91.

83. *Juvenile Delinquency: Interim Report of the Committee on the Judiciary*, U.S. Senate, March 10, 1955 (Washington: GPO, 1955), 6, 30–46; Testimony of Mrs. M. C. Shipley, September 24, 1957, "Juvenile Delinquency (California)," *Hearings*, 254–55; first quotation in ibid., 196–97.

84. Citizen Narcotics Advisory Committee, "Crackdown: The Dramatic Story of Ohio's Fight against Narcotics," 1955, folder: Narcotics-Clipping, box 182, JD-NA; Citizen Narcotics Advisory Committee, "Narcotics Facts," n.d. [1954], Attorney General William O'Neill, "Narcotics Recommendations," n.d. [1955], O'Neill, "Synopsis of Senate Bill 214," n.d. [June 1955], folder: Narcotics Reports-Ohio, box 12, WFT-Hoover. Also see Anslinger to William Kurtz, July 18, 1956, folder: Narcotics Legislation, box 9, WFT-Hoover; Anslinger, "Narcotic Addiction as Seen by the Law Enforcement Officer," *Federal Probation* 21, no. 2 (June 1957): 34–41, folder 11, box 1, HJA-PSU.

85. New Jersey Commission on Narcotic Control, *Second Report of Study and Recommendations*, March 1, 1956, folder: Narcotics Control Commission Annual Reports, box 11, *Newark Star-Ledger*, May 11, 1956, *Newark Evening News*, May 25, 1956, Ruth P. Sanborn/New Jersey State Federation of Women's Clubs to William E. Ozzard, June 30, 1956, folder: Narcotics Legislation, box 9, WFT-Hoover.

86. Jane B. Tompkins to Dorothy Siegel, February 29, 1956, folder: Narcotics Correspondence 1956, box 9, Tompkins, Speech to Service League of Maplewood, n.d. [c. 1956], Tompkins, Speech to Republican Women's Group, n.d. [c. 1956], Tompkins, Speech to Women's Club of Irvington, n.d. [c. 1956], folder: Speeches of Jane Tompkins, box 12, WFT-Hoover.

87. New Jersey Commission on Narcotic Control, *Second Report of Study and Recommendations*; Jane B. Tompkins, "Statement at Executive Hearing before Governor Robert B. Meyner," n.d. [June 1956], folder: Narcotics Legislation, box 10, Robert B. Meyner, "Veto Message Assembly Bill No. 488," June 28, 1956, folder: Stiff Penalty Legislation, box 10, WFT-Hoover.

88. FBN, *Traffic in Opium and Other Dangerous Drugs, 1955* (Washington: GPO, 1956), 7; Anslinger to William Kurtz, July 18, 1956, folder: Narcotics Legislation, box 9, WFT-Hoover; Anslinger and Tompkins, *Traffic in Narcotics*, 222, 294–303 (quotations 296); Funk and Wagnalls, Marketing Materials for *Traffic in Narcotics*, 1953, folder 12, box 2, HJA-PSU.

89. Exhibits No. 10 and No. 11, "State Laws Relating to the Treatment of Drug Addiction" and "Minimum Mandatory Sentences," 279–301, in "Illicit Narcotics Traffic," *Hearings before the Subcommittee on Improvements in the Federal Criminal Code, Committee on the Judiciary*, U.S. Senate, June 2–3, 8, 1955 (Washington: GPO, 1955); Anslinger and Tompkins, *Traffic in Narcotics*, 282.

90. Committee on the Judiciary, S. Res. 67, ratified March 10, 1955; Anslinger, "Statement before the Senate Judiciary Subcommittee on Narcotics," June 2, 1955, folder: Anslinger, box 918, PD-NA. Also see McWilliams, *Protectors*, 112–15.

91. Anslinger Statement, June 22, 1955, PD-NA; "Illicit Narcotics Traffic," *Hearings*, June 2, 1955, quotations 13, 9, 11, 35, 18.

92. "Illicit Narcotics Traffic," *Hearings*, Part 2, June 17–18, 1955, quotations 369, 442, 566; Frederic Sondern Jr., "We Must Stop the Crime That Breeds Crime!" *RD*, June 1956, 21–26.

93. "Illicit Narcotics Traffic," *Hearings*, Part 3, June 24–25, 1955, quotations 746, 747; "Synthetic Dope Floods City," *New York Sunday Graphic*, June 13, 1955, folder: Narcotics Clippings 1953–1960, box 9, WFT-Hoover.

94. William Miller Preparatory Materials and Image, July 1955, folder: Hearings of Washington DC (1), box 921, PD-NA; "Illicit Narcotics Traffic," *Hearings*, Part 4, July 12–15, 19, 1955; "Illicit Narcotics Traffic," *Hearings*, Part 6, September 28, 1955; *WP*, July 16, 20, 1955.

95. "Dallas Hearing-Points to Be Emphasized," October 1955, folder: Dallas Hearings, box 922, PD-NA; "Illicit Narcotics Traffic," *Hearings*, Part 7, October 12–14, 17–21, December 14–15, 1955, quotation 3441.

96. "California Hearing-Points to Be Emphasized," folder: Los Angeles Hearing, box 920, PD-NA; "Illicit Narcotics Traffic," *Hearings*, Part 8, November 14–16, 1955; *LAT*, November 15, 1955.

97. "Illicit Narcotics Traffic," *Hearings*, Part 7, October 18, 1955, 2791–2806; Testimony of Mary Ann——, October 17, 1955, ibid., 2716–34.

98. Testimony of Mary Ann——, October 17, 1955, "Illicit Narcotics Traffic," *Hearings*, Part 7, 2716–34.

99. William Parker, "Statement to the Special Subcommittee on Improvement of the Federal Code," November 14, 1955, folder: Crime and Illicit Narcotics Traffic, box 919, PD-NA; "Illicit Narcotics Traffic," *Hearings*, Part 8, November 14–16, 1955, quotations 3655, 3708, 3800; *LAT*, November 15, 1955.

100. "Chicago Hearings: Points to Be Emphasized," folder: Chicago Hearings, box 921, PD-NA; "Illicit Narcotics Traffic," *Hearings*, Part 9, November 21–22, 1955 (Leeds quotation 4271); *CDT*, November 21–25, 1955; *LAT*, November 22, 1955.

101. "Detroit Hearing-Witnesses," folder: Detroit Hearings, box 922, PD-NA; "Illicit Narcotics Traffic," *Hearings*, Part 10, November 23, 25, 1955.

102. George Todt to Price Daniel, January 1, 1956, folder: California (1), Herbert L. Herscher to Daniel, September 28, 1955, Walter W. Strong to Daniel, December 5, 1955, Gwendolyn Bryant to Daniel, October 31, 1955, Joseph Engholm to Daniel, September 21, 1955, Anonymous to

Daniel, December 19, 1955, Ruth H. Millikan to Daniel, December 5, 1955, folder: California (1), box 915, PD-NA.

103. Mrs. Virnal M. E. Truesdale to Daniel, July 16, 1955, folder: Colorado-Connecticut, Harold C. Butt to Daniel, September 24, 1955, folder: New York (1), Mrs. T. P. Cunningham to Daniel, November 11, 1955, folder: Illinois, box 915, PD-NA.

104. Minnie Stein to Daniel, January 9, 1956, folder: Texas (1), William B. Wertham to Daniel, October 19, 1955, folder: Texas (2), box 915, PD-NA.

105. Price Daniel to Etta Davis (form letter), January 30, 1956, folder: Reading File January 1956, box 897, PD-NA.

106. Anne Travers (pseudonym) to Daniel, August 4, 1955, folder: Delaware-Florida-Georgia, "American Mother" to Daniel, September 29, 1955, folder: Anonymous, box 915, PD-NA.

107. "The Peddler of Living Death," *Coronet*, October 1955, 85–100; Archie Lieberman, "9 Hours in Hell with a Dope Addict," *Pageant*, June 1956, 6–21, in folder 10, box 12, HJA-PSU; Sondern, "We Must Stop the Crime That Breeds Crime!"

108. "Illicit Narcotics Traffic," *Hearings*, Part 9, November 21, 1955, quotations 4250–51, "Illicit Narcotics Traffic," *Hearings*, Part 7, October 12, 1955, quotation 2392.

109. "Illicit Narcotics Traffic," *Hearings*, Part 4, July 12, 1955, 997–1017, Part 9, November 21, 1955, 4200–11; Rev. Ransom Hammond to Price Daniel, June 7, July 3, 1956, C. Aubrey Gasque to Hammond, June 21, 1956, folder: New York (2), box 915, PD-NA.

110. Herbert Berger and Andrew A. Eggleston, "Should We Legalize Narcotics?" *Coronet*, June 1955, 30–34; "Illicit Narcotics Traffic," *Hearings*, Part 5, September 19–21, 1955, quotations 1322, 1327, 1379, 1395, 1393.

111. *The Illicit Narcotics Traffic: Report of the Committee on the Judiciary*, U.S. Senate, January 16, 1956 (Washington: GPO, 1956); "Narcotic Addiction and Treatment, Preliminary Report," n.d. [early 1956 draft], folder: Wayland L. Speer, box 896, PD-NA; *Treatment and Rehabilitation of Narcotic Addicts: Report of the Committee on the Judiciary*, U.S. Senate, April 24, 1956 (Washington: GPO, 1956).

112. "Report of Proceedings: Staff Conference, Executive Session," Subcommittee on Improvements in the Federal Criminal Code, February 7, 21, 1956, folder: S. 1043 "Penalties for Narcotics," box 906, PD-NA.

113. *Report of Interdepartmental Committee on Narcotics*, February 1, 1956, folder: Narcotics Legislation, box 9, WFT-Hoover.

114. Subcommittee on Improvements in the Federal Criminal Code, Press Release, April 30, 1956, folder: Press Release, box 924, PD-NA; S. 3760, "A Bill to Provide for More Effective Control of Narcotic Drugs," April 26, 1956; Committee on the Judiciary, *Narcotic Control Act of 1956*, Report No. 1997, May 7, 1956; Subcommittee on Narcotics, House Committee on Ways and Means, *Illicit Traffic in Narcotics, Barbiturates, and Amphetamines in the United States*, May 10, 1956 (Washington: GPO, 1956).

115. Hubert Howe to C. Aubrey Gasque, May 28, 1956, folder: Howe, box 912, American Psychiatric Association, "A Statement Critical of Current Legislative Proposals Dealing with the National Problem of Drug Addiction," June 12, 1956, folder: Narcotics Misc. Reports, box 182, PD-NA; Herbert Berger, "To Dispel the Nightmare of Narcotics," *NYT*, July 8, 1956; Laurence Kolb, "Let's Stop This Narcotics Hysteria!" *SEP*, July 28, 1956, 19, 50, 54–55;

Alfred R. Lindesmith, "Traffic in Dope: Medical Problem," *The Nation*, April 21, 1956, 337–39; Lindesmith, "Dope: Congress Encourages the Traffic," *The Nation*, March 16, 1957, 228–31.

116. Isidor Chein, "Narcotics Use among Juveniles," *Social Work* 1, no. 2 (April 1956): 50–60 (first quotation 54); Isidor Chein and Eva Rosenfeld, "Juvenile Narcotics Use," *Law and Contemporary Problems* 22, no. 1 (Winter 1957): 52–58 (second quotation 58).

117. Narcotic Control Act of 1956, Public Law 728, July 18, 1956; *CR—Senate* (May 25, 1956), 9012–9047, (May 31, 1956), 9300–9316, (July 9, 1956), 12160–12167; McWilliams, *Protectors*, 115–16.

118. FBN, *Traffic in Opium and Other Dangerous Drugs, 1956* (Washington: GPO, 1957), 35–36, 56.

119. FBN, *The Living Death: The Truth about Narcotics Addiction*, 1956, folder 1, box 7, HJA-PSU; Anslinger quoted in "Another Problem for the Big Cities," *USNWR*, April 6, 1959, 74–76; also see FBN, *Traffic in Opium and Other Dangerous Drugs, 1958* (Washington: GPO, 1959), 13.

120. House Subcommittee on Narcotics, *Illicit Traffic in Narcotics, Barbiturates, and Amphetamines in the United States*, 1956. On FBN opposition to regulation of illicit pharmaceuticals, also see Anslinger, "Illicit Traffic in Narcotics Today," *NARD Journal* 77, no. 21 (November 7, 1955), folder 10, Anslinger, "Briefing on the Work of the United Nations Commission on Narcotics," May 29, 1957, folder 8, box 1, HJA-PSU; Herzberg, *White Market Drugs*, 163–69.

121. Anslinger, "Narcotics Addiction Lowered Under New Federal Act and Druggists' Assistance," *NARD Journal* 80 (November 17, 1958), 26–27, folder 12, box 1, FBN, "Graphic Results of Mandatory Penalties against Peddler: Narcotic Control Act of 1956," December 31, 1958, folder 8, box 7, Anslinger, "Narcotic Addiction as Seen by the Law Enforcement Officer," *Federal Probation* 21, no. 2 (June 1957): 34–41, folder 11, box 1, HJA-PSU; "Another Problem for the Big Cities," *USNWR*, April 6, 1959, 74–76.

122. BJB to Price Daniel, September 21, 1956, folder: California (2), box 915, PD-NA; WS to Don Allen, April 21, 1956, Don Allen to Edmund G. Brown, April 24, 1956, Frank J. Mackin, Memo on Shaheen Case, May 1, 1956, Brown to Allen, May 3, 1956, folder 1, box 98, EGB-Bancroft [names anonymized].

123. H. Eugene Breitenbach, "Statement for Narcotics Convention," February 9, 1960, folder 9, box 403, series 6.4.5.19, KH-Huntington; on juvenile border crossings to Tijuana, also see Governor's Advisory Commission on Children and Youth, Minutes, February 28–March 1, 1957, folder 4, box 75, Eleanor Grimstad to Knight, November 11, 1955, folder 15, box 36, GJK-CSA; *LAT*, May 1, 1955, July 13, 1959.

124. Testimony of Robert A. Neeb Jr., "Juvenile Delinquency (Treatment and Rehabilitation of Drug Addicts)," *Hearings before the Subcommittee to Investigate Juvenile Delinquency, Committee on the Judiciary*, U.S. Senate, December 17–18, 1956 (Washington: GPO, 1957), 1–125 (quotations 9, 11, 12).

125. Transcript of Attorney General's Good Neighbor Conference, May 22, 1957, folder 58, box 90, Brown, Press Release of "Excerpt from Address to the Convention of California District Attorneys," June 19, 1957, folder 2, box 85, H. G. Robinson to Brown, Memo on "Good Neighbor Conference," July 31, 1957, folder 31, box 95, Frederick Dutton to Pat Frayne, August 5, 1957, folder 2, box 85, EGB-Bancroft.

126. Los Angeles County Council of Women, "Narcotic Problem Resolution," June 7, 1957, folder 17, box 36, GJK-CSA; Sierra Cahuenga District of CFWC, Narcotics Resolution, 1958,

folder: Narcotics, box 915, PD-NA; Petition to the Attorney General of California from Balboa Island, Fallbrook, Elsinore, Pasadena, and Chula Vista, Spring 1958, folder 27, Brown to Juanita Darwin, May 20, 1958, folder 26, box 95, EGB-Bancroft.

127. [Anonymized] to Knight, September 12, 1956, folder 15, box 36, GJK-CSA.

128. Marshall K. McClelland, "She's Marked for Death," *Pageant*, April 1957, 6–15, folder 10, box 12, HJA-PSU.

129. LAPD, Press Release, March 25, 1956, folder 5, box 85, Norman Nevraumont (CYA) quoted in Minutes of the Southern Citizens' Advisory Committee to the Attorney General on Crime Prevention, April 30, 1956, folder 22, box 84, Judge Stanley Mosk, Testimony to State Senate Committee on Narcotics, September 16, 1957, folder 32, box 95, EGB-Bancroft; *LAT*, March 26–27, 29, 31, 1956.

130. M. M. O'Connor, Memorandum to Brown, October 27, 1958, folder 3, box 85, Memorandum from Pat Frayne and Fred Dutton, June 25, 1957, folder 31, box 95, EGB-Bancroft; California Board of Corrections, *Narcotics in California: Usage Trends and Recommendations for Controls* (Sacramento, February 19, 1959), F3717:205, SSC-CSA.

131. *People v. Cahan*, 44 Cal.2d. 434 (1955); Testimony of Manley J. Bowler, "Juvenile Delinquency," Part 5, *Hearings before the Subcommittee to Investigate Juvenile Delinquency, Committee on the Judiciary*, U.S. Senate, November 9, 1959 (Washington: GPO, 1960), 646; District Attorney Thomas Lynch quoted in Minutes of the Third Conference of the Northern-Central California Narcotic Officers' Association, March 22, 1957, folder 3, box 85, EGB-Bancroft. On entrapment charges, see C. H. Ortel to Brown, December 25, 1958, folder 26, box 322, Tony Geram to Brown, March 5, 1960, folder 24, box 352, EGB-Bancroft.

132. *Report of the Governor's Advisory Committee on Children and Youth, Subcommittee on Narcotics*, 1953, folder 1, box 75, GJK-CSA; California Board of Corrections, *Narcotics in California: Usage Trends and Recommendations for Controls*; Testimony of Judge Louis Burke, May 27, 1958, Testimony of Anonymous Witness, February 18, 1958, "Transcript of Proceedings," Subcommittee on Police Administration and Law Enforcement, LP115:5, PASAJC-CSA.

133. Bureau of Criminal Statistics, *Delinquency and Probation in California, 1957* (State of California, Department of Justice, 1958). Estimate in "Juvenile Delinquency," *Hearings*, Part 5, 928. Quotations in *Medical and Psychological Aspects of Juvenile Violence*, Report of the Northern Subcommittee, Citizens' Advisory Committee to the Attorney General on Crime Prevention, 1957, folder 21, box 84, EGB-Bancroft.

134. Karl Holton, "Narcotics Traffic among Juveniles in Los Angeles County, 1958–1959," reproduced in "Juvenile Delinquency," *Hearings*, Part 5, 884–92; Los Angeles County Probation Department, *Special Report*, June 1956, *Annual Report*, 1956–1957, folder BIII-7-d, box 35, JAF-Huntington; Special Study Commission on Narcotics, "Recommendations," n.d. [c. 1960], folder 3, box 385, EGB-Bancroft.

135. *The Narcotics Story* (Police Science Production, Alpha Video, 1958), Internet Archive, https://archive.org/details/TheNarcoticStory_50; original version: *Goof Balls and Tea* (1957), included in *Classroom Scare Films, Volume 7: Drugs and Beyond* (Something Weird Video, 2000).

136. M. M. O'Connor to Brown, February 20, 1958, O'Connor to Brown, "The Narcotic Story," March 10, 1958, *LAE*, February 26, 1958, Police Science Productions, Synopsis of *Narcotics Story*, n.d. [1958], Audience Preview Comments, February 19, 25, 1958, Clippings of Catholic Newspapers, March 1958, Brown to Louis M. Pesce, May 21, 1958, folder 25, box 95, EGB-Bancroft.

137. Braeme E. Gigas to Brown, June 11, 1958, folder 27, box 95, EGB-Bancroft; on the petition drive and election see *SFE*, August 17, 22, 26, 1958, *LAE*, August 21, 1958, George H. Brereton, Memorandum to Attorney General Brown, August 8, 1958, folder 27, box 95, EGB-Bancroft; *LAT*, February 22, 1959; California Republican Platform, 1958, folder: California Republicans, box 33, MK-Huntington. Also see Totton J. Anderson, "The 1958 Election in California," *Western Political Quarterly* 12, no. 1 (March 1959), 276–300. A Republican group called Citizens for the Right to Know ran advertisements attacking Brown for failing to address the narcotics menace, with an image of a white female student under attack by a heroin needle; see *LAT*, October 25, 1958.

138. California Board of Corrections, *Narcotics in California: Usage Trends and Recommendations for Controls*.

139. Carolyn L— to Brown, n.d. [1958–1959], folder 26, box 95, Mrs. F. L. Mason to Brown, March 10, 1959, folder 28, Lakewood Women's Club form letters in folder 26, Leroy R. Sommers to Brown, February 5, 1959, folder 26, and other letters in folders 26–28, box 322, Mrs. C. E. McNew to Brown, December 6, 1959, folder 28, box 323, EGB-Bancroft; Norwalk Petition to Governor and California Legislature, October 1958, folder 17, box 37, GJK-CSA.

140. Gene Sherman, "Mexican Monkey on Our Back: Dope's Evil Roots" series, *LAT*, July 12–19, 1959. Responses in *LAT*, July 16–17, 21–22, 1959. Also see The Pulitzer Prizes, "1960 Winners," http://www.pulitzer.org/prize-winners-by-year/1960.

141. Brown to *LAT*, July 20, 1959, folder 27, box 32, EGB-Bancroft; *LAT*, July 21, 1959; "Miss Jones," Testimony to Special Narcotics Hearing of the California Assembly, 1959, folder: Drugs (3), box 21, MK-Huntington.

142. L. A. Parkhurst to Brown, November 19, 1959, folder 27, box 323, Mrs. Georgia Kine to Brown, December 14, 1959, folder 26, box 322, Glendale Community Coordinating Council to Brown, January 9, 1960, folder 24, box 35, EGB-Bancroft.

143. Brown, "Progress Report No. 27," August 31, 1959, folder 28, box 323, Charles W. Johnson to Fred Dutton, "Narcotics" Memo, December 3, 1959, Alexander H. Pope to Kristie E. Dixon, November 6, 1959, folder 27, box 323, Laughlin E. Waters to Brown, February 15, 1960, folder 24, box 352, EGB-Bancroft; *LAT*, December 8, 1959. On constituent pressure, see folders 26–28, box 322, folder 27–28, box 323, EGB-Bancroft. On the lack of rehabilitation programs, see *Report of the Subcommittee on Narcotics and Dangerous Drugs, Assembly Interim Committee on Public Health*, March 1959 (Sacramento: Assembly of the State of California, 1959), 7 (quotation), 19–28.

144. "Juvenile Delinquency," *Hearings*, Part 5, quotations 593, 595, 747, 615, 619, 625, 959; "Juvenile Delinquency," *Hearings*, Part 7, quotation 1355. On border enforcement, also see State of California Department of Finance, "San Ysidro-Tijuana Border Juvenile Check Station," January 4, 1962, F3717:187, SCN-CSA.

145. *LAT*, January 28–31, March 13–14, May 25, 1960; Edwin H. Whitman to Brown, February 3, 1960, folder 24, David R. Lyon to Brown, April 23, 1960, folder 25, box 352, EGB-Bancroft.

146. Kenneth Hahn, Press Release, February 16, 1960, folder 3, Press Release, March 3, 1960, March 15, 1960, folder 11, March 23, 1960, folder 12, Hahn, Statement to President's Interdepartmental Committee on Narcotics, March 31, 1960, folder 6, box 403, series 6.4.5.19, KH-Huntington; Hahn to Alexander Pope, February 17, 1960, folder 24, box 352, EGB-Bancroft; *LAT*, February 12, 17, 1960.

147. *LAT*, March 1, 3, 16, 1960; Susan Mallon to Brown, April 25, 1960, folder 26, Mrs. Ralph R. Roberts to Brown, February 1960, Roy H. Coon to Alexander Pope, January 27, 1960, folder 24, box 352, EGB-Bancroft.

148. Brown, "Narcotics Statement," March 15, 1960, Fred Dutton to Brown, Memo "Message on Narcotics," March 11, 1960, folder 24, box 352, EGB-Bancroft. On the evidentiary rule, also see *LAT*, March 3, 1960.

149. Postcard campaign from CFWC chapters, April 1960, L. A. Fuller to Brown, April 4, 1960, folder 26, San Gabriel Valley District CFWC, "Resolution," December 1959, folder 27, Pacoima Junior Women's Club and Pacoima Coordinating Council petitions, folders 26–28, box 352, EGB Bancroft. General narcotics letters to Governor Brown during 1960–1961 in folders 32–33, box 596, folders 29–30, box 604, folders 1–3, box 605, folder 18, box 614, EGB-Bancroft. For LAPD criticism, Charles W. Johnson to Brown, Memo "Narcotics Cases," March 18, 1960, folder 24, box 352, EGB-Bancroft; *LAT*, March 3, 1960.

150. Brown, "Statement on Narcotics," February 28, 1961, Special Study Commission on Narcotics, *Interim Report*, December 9, 1960, folder 15, box 98, EGB-Bancroft; Special Study Commission on Narcotics, *Final Report*, June 1961, F317:169, SCN-CSA.

151. Regan-Dills Act, May 4, 1961, in *Statutes of California, 1960 and 1961*, vol. 1 (Sacramento: State of California), 1301–09; *LAT*, January 10, February 20, March 5, 9–10, April 2, 5, 12, 27–29, 30 (quotation), May 5, 1961; Los Angeles County legislative package in Kenneth Hahn, Press Release, February 16, 1961, folder 1a, box 212a, series 1.24.2.1, KH-Huntington; Republican Legislative Campaign Committee, "California: Dope Peddlers Paradise!" August 24, 1960, F3717:165, SCN-CSA.

152. Brown administration, "Supplemental Budget for Attack on the Narcotic Problem," September 6, 1961, Brown to Joseph P. Kesler, July 14, 1961, folder 5, box 35, EGB-Bancroft; *LAT*, May 7, June 8, 16, 1961; "Registration of Narcotic Offenders" and "Commitment and Corrective Treatment of Narcotic Addicts," June 24, 1961, in *Statutes of California, 1960 and 1961*, vol. 1 (Sacramento: State of California), 2221–30.

153. Brown, "Testimony to U.S. Senate Subcommittee to Investigate Juvenile Delinquency," August 7, 1962, Brown, Press Release, August 6, 1962, folder: Governor Edmund G. Brown, box 70, JD-NA.

154. "Student Recommendations of Youth Conference on Narcotics," December 13, 1954, folder 18, box 36, GJK-CSA; Gene Sherman, "Boys—and Girl—Tell Drug Addiction Story," *LAT*, July 15, 1959.

Chapter 2. Suburban Rebels

1. CBS Reports, *16 in Webster Groves* (New York: Carousel Films, 1966).

2. CBS Reports, *Webster Groves Revisited* (New York: Carousel Films, 1966); "Extent of Subversion in the 'New Left,'" *Hearings before the Subcommittee to Investigate the Administration of the Internal Security Act, Committee on the Judiciary*, U.S. Senate, Part 4, June 10, 1970 (Washington: GPO, 1970), 415.

3. Governor's Advisory Committee on Children and Youth, "The Age of Conflict," February 1956, folder 14, box 74, GJK-CSA.

4. *In re Gault*, 387 U.S. 1 (1967); K. A. Banks, "Juvenile Justice in California: The Probation Officer and the Minor's Right to Due Process," *Criminal Justice Journal* 4, no. 1 (Fall 1980): 181–98. Also see Vaz, ed., *Middle-Class Juvenile Delinquency*; David Loth, *Crime in the Suburbs* (New York: William Morrow, 1967); Chavez-Garcia, *States of Delinquency*; Bush, *Who Gets a Childhood?*; Rosenheim et al., *Century of Juvenile Justice*.

5. Pat and Beverly Hall to Parade Magazine, November 13, 1953, Senator Robert C. Hendrickson, "Are U.S. Kids on a Crime Spree?" *Parade*, November 8, 1953, box 122, loose materials [no folder], JD-NA.

6. Herbert J. Hannock to Charles C. Deubel, October 27, 1953, folder: Subcommittee I Hearings, box 81, JD-NA; Walter R. Creighton/CBNE, "Narcotics Report to Subcommittee to Investigate Juvenile Delinquency," November 6, 1953, folder 1, box 85, EGB-Bancroft.

7. Testimony of Sheldon Glueck and Eleanor T. Glueck, November 29, 1953, "Juvenile Delinquency (National, Federal, and Youth-Serving Agencies)," *Hearings*, Part 1, 73–105; Gilbert, *Cycle of Outrage*, 127–42; also see Ralph W. England Jr., "A Theory of Middle Class Juvenile Delinquency," *Journal of Criminal Law and Criminology* 50, no. 6 (March–April 1960): 535–540. For an example of the traditional emphasis, see National Commission on Law Observance and Enforcement, *Social Factors in Juvenile Delinquency* (Washington: GPO, 1931).

8. *Juvenile Delinquency: Interim Report of the Committee on the Judiciary*, March 15, 1954, quotations 14, 7, 19, 8, 9; Testimony of Martha M. Eliot, November 19, 1953, "Juvenile Delinquency (National, Federal, and Youth-Serving Agencies)," *Hearings*, Part 1, 7–32; Testimony of George Gardner, ibid., 49–58.

9. "Youth in Crisis," *March of Time*, episode 3, vol. 10 (New York: Time-Life, 1943); J. Edgar Hoover, "A 'Third Front'—Against Juvenile Crime," *NYT Magazine*, February 27, 1944, 8, 32. Also see Gilbert, *Cycle of Outrage*, 24–41.

10. "Report of the Juvenile Crime Prevention Committee to Board of Trustees, Los Angeles Bar Association," n.d. [c. 1944], CYA, "An Outline of a Community Program for the Prevention of Juvenile Delinquency," 1943, loose materials, box 33, Community Chests and Council Inc., "A Community Plan for Recreation and Youth Services for Los Angeles," January 1, 1946, folder BIII-14-a-gg-aaa, box 60, JAF-Huntington.

11. Charles W. Eliot II, "Planning Physical Environment for Youth Welfare," 1948, folder BIII-14-a-ff, box 60, JAF-Huntington. On this normative suburban vision, also see Clayton Howard, *The Closet and the Cul-de-Sac: The Politics of Sexual Privacy in Northern California* (Philadelphia: University of Pennsylvania Press, 2019), esp. 85–147.

12. LACYC Report, June 18, 1948, West Los Angeles Coordinating Council, "Report to California's Youth Committee," 1950, folder BIII-14-a-ff, box 60, Los Angeles County Department of Parks and Rec and County School Districts, "Cooperative Playground Program," 1950, folder BIII-10-a, box 41, JAF-Huntington.

13. Pasadena Department of Recreation, "Youth Clubs," November 1950, folder: Pasadena Schools, box 6, Conference on Youth and the Community, "Memo to Pasadena, Altadena," May 12, 1952, Community Planning Council, "Report of Division Committee," May 1955, folder: Community Politics, box 34, MK-Huntington.

14. LACYC to Board of Police Commissioners, November 11, 1954, "Progress Report of the Teen Age Dance Subcommittee," November 23, 1955, folder BIII-7c-cc, box 34, Metropolitan Recreation and Youth Services Council, "A Progress Report: 1950–1953," folder BIII-10-c, box

41, JAF-Huntington; *LAT*, February 6, 1955. Also see West Los Angeles Coordinating Council, "Report to California's Youth Committee," 1950, folder BIII-14-a-ff, box 60, JAF-Huntington; City of Pasadena, "Juvenile Delinquency Report to the U.S. Senate," August 5, 1958, folder: Pasadena, box 141, JD-NA. On interracial dances, see Anthony Macias, "Bringing Music to the People: Race, Urban Culture, and Municipal Politics in Postwar Los Angeles," *American Quarterly* 56, no. 3 (September 2004): 693–717.

15. Harold W. Kennedy to Los Angeles County Board of Supervisors, February 14, 1955, and attached letters from PTA and youth agency leaders, LACYC, Minutes, September 21, 1955, folder BIII-7c-cc, box 34, JAF-Huntington; *LAT*, April 15, July 14, 1954, March 27, 1955. Walter Creighton (CBNE) quoted in *LAT*, October 20, 1954.

16. CYA, "An Outline of a Community Program for the Prevention of Juvenile Delinquency," August 1953, folder 61, box 89, EGB-Bancroft; LACYC, Minutes, January 20, 1954, folder BIII-7c-cc, box 34, JAF-Huntington; *LAT*, November 18, 1953, March 27, 1955.

17. Los Angeles County Juvenile Court four-part series in *LAT*, May 8–11, 1955; "Juvenile Crime" in Orange County, two-part series in *LAT*, September 4, 11, 1955. On racial trends, see Bureau of Criminal Statistics, *Delinquency and Probation in California, 1954* (State of California, Department of Justice, 1955), 40–42.

18. U.S. Children's Bureau, *Some Facts about Juvenile Delinquency* (Washington, GPO: 1953); also see "Juvenile Delinquency Issue," *The Child* 17, no. 4 (December 1952). The data in these reports is from 1951; in 1953, juvenile courts processed around 435,000 minors, of an estimated 1.25 million detained by the police but handled informally. See *Juvenile Delinquency: Interim Report of the Committee on the Judiciary*, March 10, 1955, 5.

19. Frederic Wertham, *Seduction of the Innocent* (New York: Rinehart & Co, 1954); Wertham, "What Parents Don't Know about Comic Books," *LHJ*, November 1953, 50–53, 214–20; Wertham, "The Comics . . . Very Funny!" *Saturday Review of Literature*, May 29, 1948, 6–7, 27–29; Testimony of Frederic Wertham, "Juvenile Delinquency (Comic Books)," *Hearings before the Subcommittee to Investigate Juvenile Delinquency, Committee on the Judiciary*, U.S. Senate, April 21, 1954 (Washington: GPO, 1954), 79–97. On New York, see *Report of the New York State Legislative Committee to Study the Publication of Comics*, March 1952, March 1954, 1955, in box 32, JD-NA. On grassroots anticomics activism, also see Andrea Friedman, "Sadists and Sissies: Anti-Pornography Campaigns in Cold War America," *Gender and History* 15, no. 2 (August 2003), 201–27.

20. NBC Radio, *Special Report*, May 3, 1954, folder: Correspondence-General-Comic Books (1), box 167, JD-NA; Wertham, "Comic Books—Blueprints for Delinquency," *RD*, May 1954, 24–29. The "silent generation" phrase first appeared in "People: The Younger Generation," *Time*, November 5, 1951, 46–52.

21. Letters from parents and civic groups in multiple folders: Correspondence-General-Comic Books, box 167, JD-NA; Senator Robert C. Hendrickson quoted in "Juvenile Delinquency (Comic Books)," *Hearings*, 1.

22. Drawn from around one thousand youth letters addressed to the Subcommittee to Investigate Juvenile Delinquency in folder: Correspondence: Pro-Comic Letters, box 169, JD-NA, and related materials in the general correspondence folders in box 167. Quotations and direct references from Maspeth (NY) group letter, September 26, 1954, Elmont (NY) group letter, October 25, 1954, N. L. Pullings letter, December 13, 1954, Barbara Flake letter, November 5, 1954, Barry Chevin letter, November 28, 1954, Stephen Hochman letter, September 3, 1954, Charles

Schuler Perryman letter, June 8, 1954, ibid. On the comic industry's editorials, see E.C. Comics, "A Special Editorial," n.d. [1954], E.C. Fan-Addict Club Bulletin, June 1954, ibid. On dismissal of youth protests, see Robert Hendrickson to Mario Levi, September 29, 1954, ibid.

23. *Comic Books and Juvenile Delinquency: Interim Report of the Subcommittee to Investigate Juvenile Delinquency*, March 1955 (Washington: GPO, 1955), quotations 7, 17; Comics Code Authority, "What Do You Know about This Comics Seal of Approval," n.d. [1955], loose materials, box 211, JD-NA. Also see Amy Kiste Nyberg, *Seal of Approval: The History of the Comics Code* (Oxford: University Press of Mississippi, 1998); David Hadju, *The Ten-Cent Plague: The Great Comic-Book Scare and How It Changed America* (New York: Farrar, Straus and Giroux, 2008).

24. *Television and Juvenile Delinquency: Interim Report of the Subcommittee to Investigate Juvenile Delinquency*, 1955 (Washington, GPO, 1955), quotation 38; *Motion Pictures and Juvenile Delinquency: Interim Report of the Subcommittee to Investigate Juvenile Delinquency*, April 1956 (Washington, GPO, 1956), quotations 19, 7; "Juvenile Delinquency (Motion Pictures)," *Hearings before the Subcommittee to Investigate Juvenile Delinquency, Committee on the Judiciary*, U.S. Senate, June 15–18, 1955 (Washington: GPO, 1955), quotations 126, 128.

25. *Rebel Without a Cause* (Warner Bros., 1955, dir. Nicholas Ray). On the film, also see Margot Henriksen, *Dr. Strangelove's America: Society and Culture in the Atomic Age* (Berkeley: University of California Press, 1997), 162–66; Leerom Medovi, *Rebels: Youth and the Cold War Origins of Identity* (Durham: Duke University Press, 1995), 177–91.

26. Studio documentary included as extra feature of *Rebel Without a Cause: Special Edition* (Burbank, CA: Warner Home Video, 2005).

27. Geoffrey M. Shurlock to J. L. Warner, March 22, 1955, Shurlock to Warner, March 31, 1955, *Rebel Without a Cause*, History of Cinema, series 1, MPCC-AMPAS; House of Representatives, *Switchblade Knives*, Report No. 1945, June 23, 1958; "An Act to Prohibit the Introduction, or Manufacture for Introduction, into Interstate Commerce of Switchblade Knives," Public Law 85–623, August 12, 1958.

28. "What to Do About Juvenile Crime," *Life*, March 15, 1954, 24; *Gang Boy* (Sid Davis Productions, 1954), https://archive.org/details/gang_boy. On hot rod clubs, see LACYC, Minutes, January 20, 1954, folder BIII-7c-cc, box 34, JAF-Huntington.

29. *Juvenile Delinquency: Interim Report of the Committee on the Judiciary*, March 10, 1955, quotations 88, 44; J. Edgar Hoover, "You Can Help Stop Juvenile Crime," *American Magazine*, January 1955, 1–4. On the investigation of the Four Aces "gang" in suburban Maryland, see Ernest A. Mitler, "Memo of Interview with Robert Kluver," August 3, 1956, folder: Four Aces, box 182, JD-NA; *Baltimore Sun*, August 4, 1956.

30. Harrison Salisbury, *The Shook-Up Generation* (New York: Harper & Brothers, 1958), 104–17.

31. Los Angeles County Probation Department, *Special Report*, June 1956, *Annual Report*, 1956–1957, folder BIII-7-d, box 35, JAF-Huntington. For discretionary policy, also see Bureau of Criminal Statistics, *Delinquency and Probation in California, 1956* (Sacramento: Department of Youth Authority, 1957), 16–19 (quotation 18); LACYC Monthly Bulletin, November 1954, folder 22, box 84, EGB-Bancroft. On suburbs, also see Ray Nortvedt (LACYC) to Ford, November 23, 1955, folder BIII-7c-cc, box 34, JAF-Huntington.

32. CYA, "Crusade for Youth," 1956, folder 4, box 75, Governor's Advisory Committee on Children and Youth, "The Age of Conflict," February 1956, folder 14, box 74, Knight-CSA;

Knight, Address to Governor's Conference on Children and Youth, April 4, 1956, folder 4, box 125, GJK-Stanford.

33. Citizens' Advisory Committee on Crime Prevention, "Recommendations to the Attorney General Following Its Study on Juvenile Violence," November 5, 1957, folder 21, Edmund G. Brown, Press Release, March 24, 1958, folder 20, box 84, Brown, "The Problem of Juvenile Violence," 1958, folder 33, box 87, EGB-Bancroft.

34. Data compiled from the annual reports of the Bureau of Criminal Statistics, *Delinquency and Probation in California*, 1954–1964 (Sacramento: California Youth Authority, 1955–1965).

35. Bureau of Criminal Statistics, *Delinquency and Probation in California, 1957* (Sacramento: California Youth Authority, 1958), 27, 10 (quotations). Also see Bureau of Criminal Statistics, *Delinquency and Probation in California, 1956* (Sacramento: California Youth Authority, 1957), 17–19. For a similar critique, see Mabel A. Elliott, "Perspective on the American Crime Problem," *Social Problems* 5, no. 3 (Winter 1957): 183–93.

36. See figure 2.3; based on the 1957–1963 volumes of Bureau of Criminal Statistics, *Delinquency and Probation in California* (Sacramento: California Youth Authority, 1958–1964). On the adjudication process, also see Bureau of Criminal Statistics, *Crime in California, 1958* (Sacramento: Department of Justice, 1959), 96–99.

37. Hoover, "Where Does Discipline Begin?" *This Week Magazine*, November 9, 1958, 1–4; FBI, *Uniform Crime Reports for the United States, 1959* (Washington: GPO, 1960), 16–17.

38. Youth Research Institute survey in *LAT*, January 9, 1955; quotation in Jhan and June Robbins, "We're Raising a Great Crop of Kids," *This Week Magazine*, published in *LAT*, February 27, 1955, K7–K9.

39. Robert Wallace, "Crime in the U.S.," *Life*, September 9, 1957, 47–70; FBI, *Uniform Crime Reports, 1959*. Also see Sam Castan, "Teen-Age Murder Weapons," *Look*, November 10, 1959, 66a–66e (a feature on "teen-age terror" and the "frightening wave of juvenile savagery" in urban areas).

40. Jean Libman Block, "Conduct Code for Teen-Agers," *AW*, February 17, 1957, 13–15, in folder 62, box 89, EGB-Bancroft.

41. "Juvenile Delinquency," *Hearings before the Subcommittee to Investigate Juvenile Delinquency, Committee on the Judiciary*, U.S. Senate, Part 9, March 9–10, 1961 (Washington: GPO, 1961), Dodd quotations 1481, 1482; *Juvenile Delinquency: Report of the Subcommittee to Investigate Juvenile Delinquency*, April 18, 1961 (Washington: GPO, 1961), quotations 2, 3; Dodd, "Investigation of Juvenile Delinquency," *CQ*, January 3, 1961, folder 4557, box 192, series III, TJD-UConn. On Mexico, also see Dodd, Press Release, February 10, 1961, folder 4562, ibid.

42. Thomas J. Dodd, "Statement Introducing a Bill to Regulate the Manufacture and Distribution of Habit-Forming Barbiturates and Amphetamine Drugs," August 23, 1961, folder 4633, Dodd, "Statement on the Illegal Use of Dangerous Drugs," August 24, 1961, Dodd, Press Release, August 24, 1961, folder 4634, box 193, series III, TJD-UConn; Dodd, "Remarks before the White House Conference on Narcotics," September 28, 1962, F3717:200, SCN-CSA.

43. "The New Addicts," *Newsweek*, August 13, 1962, 42–43; Helen McGill Hughes, ed., *The Fantastic Lodge: The Autobiography of a Girl Drug Addict* (Boston: Houghton Mifflin, 1961), quotation viii. Also see media coverage of suburban dope rings in New Jersey and New York reported in Dodd, "Statement Introducing a Bill to Regulate the Manufacture and Distribution of Habit-Forming Barbiturates and Amphetamine Drugs."

44. "Juvenile Delinquency: Narcotic and Dangerous Drug Abuse in the State of California," Part 12, *Hearings before the Subcommittee to Investigate Juvenile Delinquency, Committee on the Judiciary*, U.S. Senate, August 6–7, 1962 (Washington: GPO, 1963), Brown quotation 2794; Dodd, Press Release, August 23, 1962, folder 4767, box 195, series III, TJD-UConn; LACNDDC, *Darkness on Your Doorstep: A Report to Parents on Juvenile Narcotics Addiction*, 1963, folder 17, box 444, EGB-Bancroft.

45. Brown, Press Release, August 6, 1962, folder: Governor Edmund G. Brown, box 70, JD-NA; CDOJ, Press Release, January 31, 1963, San Diego Police Department, "Border Inspection Station Report," 1963, folder 1, box 623, EGB-Bancroft; "Juvenile Delinquency: Narcotic and Dangerous Drug Abuse in the State of California," *Hearings*, Brown quotation 2795.

46. CYA, "Use of Dangerous Drugs by Juveniles in California," June 1963, folder 4, box 623, California Interdepartmental Committee on Narcotics, "California Faces the Drug Abuse Problem," June 1963, folder 17, box 444, EGB-Bancroft; Bureau of Criminal Statistics, *Drug Arrests and Dispositions in California, 1962* (Sacramento: CDOJ, 1963).

47. California State Board of Pharmacy to Assembly Committee on Criminal Procedure, November 7, 1963, David L. Klein/Endo Laboratories, "Percodan: A Rejoinder," 1963, folder 1, box 623, "Kick Pills" series in *Valley Times*, February/March 1964, folder 2, box 637, EGB-Bancroft. Letters from parents in folder 3, box 623, folders 2–3, box 637, EGB-Bancroft.

48. "Background Material Leading to White House Conference," September 1962, folder: Background Material, John F. Kennedy to Stanley Mosk, October 6, 1960, "Planning Confidential" File for White House Conference on Narcotics, n.d. [1962], folder: Conference Planning, John F. Kennedy, "Remarks to White House Conference on Narcotic and Drug Abuse," September 27, 1962, folder: Remarks of the President, box 3, DFM-Kennedy; Committee to Re-Elect Governor Brown, "The War against Narcotics," 1962, folder 9, box 575, EGB-Bancroft.

49. Edmund G. Brown, Statement to White House Conference on Narcotic and Drug Abuse, September 27, 1962, folder: California/Governor Brown, box 24, Attorney General Stanley Mosk, "Narcotics: A California Summary," September 1962, folder: California Publications, box 23, "Transcript of Proceedings: Panel No. 1," September 27, 1962, 27–38 (Mosk quotation 28), folder: Transcript of Proceedings #1, "Progress Report of an Ad Hoc Panel on Drug Abuse," September 7, 1962, folder: Progress Report, box 3, DFM-Kennedy. On the ineffectiveness of California's civil commitment program, see LACNDDC, "Legislative Recommendations," November 1964, and other reports in F3717:322, LACNDDC-CSA.

50. Joint Committee of the ABA and the AMA on Narcotic Drugs, *Drug Addiction: Crime or Disease?* (Bloomington: Indiana University Press, 1961), quotations 162, 165; Benjamin DeMott, "The Great Narcotics Muddle" *HM*, March 1962, 46–54; John Kobler, "The Narcotic Dilemma: Crime or Disease?" *SEP*, September 8, 1962, 64–70 (King quotation).

51. Robert F. Kennedy, "Address to White House Conference on Narcotic and Drug Abuse," September 28, 1962, folder: Remarks of the Attorney General, box 3, Stanley Mosk, "Transcript of Proceedings for Panel on Civil Commitments and Parole, White House Conference on Narcotic and Drug Abuse," September 27, 1962, folder: Panel 4 Statements, box 4, DFM-Kennedy; *Robinson v. California*, 370 U.S. 660 (1962).

52. *Drug Addiction: Crime or Disease?*, quotation 163; "Progress Report of an Ad Hoc Panel on Drug Abuse"; Nelson A. Rockefeller, Statement to the White House Conference on Narcotics, September 26, 1962, folder: Panel 2 Statements, box 4, DFM-Kennedy.

53. Walter Dunbar and Richard A. McGee, "As Others See It: California's Program of Treatment and Control for Narcotic Addicts," February 2, 1965, folder 23, box 531, EGB-Bancroft; Alfred R. Lindesmith, "Comments on 'The Progress Report of an Ad Hoc Panel on Drug Abuse,'" October 9, 1962, folder: Post Conference Correspondence, box 5, Isidor Chein, "The Use of Narcotics as a Personal and Social Problem," UCLA Conference on Narcotics, April 1963, folder: UCLA, box 21, DFM-Kennedy.

54. "A Tunnel Back into the Human Race," *Life*, March 9, 1962, 54–67. Also see Walker Winslow, "Experiment for Addicts," *The Nation*, April 29, 1961. Synanon's own literature emphasized its openness to everyone regardless of race or class; Synanon Foundation pamphlet, n.d. [c. 1962], box 13, folder White House Conference on Narcotics, WFT-Hoover. Also see Lewis Yablonsky, *The Tunnel Back: Synanon* (New York: Macmillan Co., 1964); Clark, *Recovery Revolution*, 17–74. Synanon actually had a high failure rate, estimated at 85 percent; see Schneider, *Smack*, 172–73.

55. "Juvenile Delinquency: Narcotic and Dangerous Drug Abuse in the State of California," *Hearings*, 2778–79, 2802 (quotation); Dodd, "A Study in Heroism," September 6, 1962, folder: Synanon, box 21, DFM-Kennedy; *NYT*, November 16, 1964.

56. John F. Kennedy, "Executive Order 10940: Establishing the President's Committee on Juvenile Delinquency and Youth Crime," May 11, 1961, folder: President's Committee, box 13, DFM-Kennedy; Kennedy, "Letter to the Speaker of the House of Representatives Concerning Measures to Combat Juvenile Delinquency," May 11, 1961, APP, https://www.presidency.ucsb.edu/node/234956 (quotation), Kennedy, "Remarks Upon Signing the Juvenile Delinquency and Youth Offenses Control Act," September 22, 1961, APP, https://www.presidency.ucsb.edu/node/235667.

57. Abraham Ribicoff, "Juvenile Delinquency: The Scope of the Problem," July 10, 1961, "Summary of Activities: President's Committee on Juvenile Delinquency and Youth Crime," n.d. [late 1961], folder: President's Committee, box 13, DFM-Kennedy; Robert F. Kennedy, "Statement before the Subcommittee on Education of the U.S. House of Representatives," July 12, 1961, folder: 7/12/1961–7/15/1961, box 253, RFK-Kennedy.

58. Leonard S. Cottrell quoted in Minutes of Demonstration Projects Panel, January 8–9, 1962; Richard A. Cloward quoted in Minutes of Citizens Advisory Council, January 3–4, 1963, folder: Minutes of Meetings, box 1, EC-Kennedy. Academic analysis in F. Ivan Nye, "Socioeconomic Status and Delinquent Behavior," *AJS* 63, no. 4 (January 1958): 381–89; England, "Theory of Middle Class Juvenile Delinquency," quotation 535; Hinton, *War on Poverty to the War on Crime*, 27–49.

59. England, "Theory of Middle Class Juvenile Delinquency"; Howard L. Myerhoff and Barbara G. Myerhoff, "Field Observations of Middle-Class 'Gangs,'" *Social Forces* 42, no. 3 (March 1964): 328–36 (quotations 333, 331, 332); Grace and Fred M. Hechinger, *Teen-Age Tyranny* (New York: William Morrow, 1963); Gerald J. Pine, "The Affluent Delinquent," *Phi Delta Kappan* 48, no. 4 (December 1966): 138–43; Vaz, ed., *Middle-Class Juvenile Delinquency*; Herbert J. Gans, *The Levittowners: Ways of Life and Politics in a New Suburban Community* (New York: Pantheon, 1967), 206–16. For a distillation of the prior consensus, see Richard E. Gordon, Katherine K. Gordon, and Max Gunther, *The Split-Level Trap* (New York: Bernard Geis/Random House, 1960).

60. Samuel Grafton, "The Tense Generation," *Look*, August 27, 1963, 17–22; Joseph Lelyveld, "The Paradoxical Case of the Affluent Delinquent," *NYT Magazine*, October 4, 1964, 13, 106–10.

On sexual "delinquency" among white middle-class females, also see Mary Louise Allen, "What Can We Do about America's *Unwed* Teen-Age Mothers?" *McCall's*, November 1963, 40–51, 214–15.

61. Bill Davidson, "Teen-Age Drinking," *SEP*, April 10, 1965, 23–27; Connecticut Department of Mental Health, "Teen-Age Alcohol Use," 1964, box 1 (loose materials), TAUSC-CSL.

62. *LAT*, April 15, 1954, April 14, June 15, 22, 1958, June 26, 1960, April 30, 1961, June 7, 11, October 15, 1961, September 4, 1962, June 5, 24, September 3, 1963, September 8, 1964.

63. *DR*, June 25, July 9, August 6, September 24, October 8, 15, 22, November 5, 12, 19, 1964; "The Drinking Problem," *Time*, October 2, 1964; "The Night of the Teen-Ager," *Time*, October 16, 1964, "Darien's Dolce Vita," *Time*, November 27, 1964; *NYT*, July 4, 9, 1965.

64. *DR*, October 1, 8, 22, 29, November 12, 24, 1964; Richard King to Gov. John Dempsey, October 1, 1964, folder: Darien, box A-247, Dempsey-CSL.

65. *NEIRAD*, May 1963, November 1964, February 1965, May 1966, Darien High School NEIRAD Archive, http://neirad.darienps.net/archive.php; *DR*, December 17, 1964.

66. "Message from Governor John Dempsey," April 1963, folder: Teenage Drinking (P-R), Dempsey to Paul Balboni, April 1, 1966, folder: Teenage Drinking (A-B), *Report of the Teenage Liquor Law Commission*, March 1965, folder: Teenage Drinking, box A-301, Dempsey-CSL; *NYT*, December 1, 1964. On New Jersey and the national context, see "Death's Silent Partner" series, *Ridgewood Sunday News*, November 22–December 27, 1964, folder: Teenage Drinking (P-R), ibid.; Davidson, "Teen-Age Drinking"; "Teen-Age Drinking" series, *CSM*, October 26–November 8, 1960.

67. Constituent letters to Governor Dempsey in 10 folders labeled Teenage Drinking, box A-301, Dempsey-CSL. Quotations from Wallace C. Mayorga Jr. to Dempsey, March 1, 1965, Peggy Dickinson to Dempsey, April 7, 1965, ibid. Proceedings of Conference on Educational Involvement in Teenage Alcohol Use, December 5, 1966, box 1, TAUSC-CSL.

68. Synanon documentary and related materials in "A WNHC-TV Campaign against Drug Addiction," 1964, folder: Drugs, box A-250, *Report of Narcotic Advisory Council*, 1963, *Report of Narcotic Advisory Council*, 1965, folder: NAC, box A-276, Dempsey-CSL; *NYT*, January 17, November 22, 1965. Also see Schneider, *Smack*, 172–73.

69. Robert P. Goldman, "Dope Invades the Suburbs," *SEP*, April 4, 1964, 19–25.

70. Dodd, "Statement on Introduction of a Bill to Control the Distribution of Habit-Forming Barbiturates and Amphetamine Drugs," January 9, 1963, folder 4810, Dodd, Press Release, February 7, 1963, folder 4822, box 195, series III, TJD-UConn.

71. Genevieve H. Millet, "Teenagers and the Dope Hazard," *PM*, May 1964, 46–47, 82–84; Bill Davidson, "The Thrill-Pill Menace," *SEP*, December 4, 1965, 23–27. Also see Joe Phipps and Robert Robinson, "Sleeping Pills and Pep Pills—Handle with Extreme Caution!" *RD*, November 1963, 103–7.

72. Dodd, "Statement Regarding the Consideration of the Drug Abuse Control Amendments of 1965," June 23, 1965, Lyndon B. Johnson, "Remarks at Signing Ceremony of the Drug Abuse Control Amendments Act of 1965," July 15, 1965, folder: Drug Abuse Control Amendments, box 19, DFM-Kennedy; Committee on Labor and Public Welfare, U.S. Senate, *Drug Abuse Control Amendments of 1965*, Report No. 337, June 21, 1965; Davidson, "Thrill Pill Menace."

73. J. Edgar Hoover, "The Faith to Be Free," December 7, 1961, "Keys to Freedom," November 16, 1963, folder: FBI, box 21, MK-Huntington. On "colored gangs," see Hinton, *War on Poverty to the War on Crime*, 83–84.

74. Lyndon B. Johnson, "Special Message to the Congress on Law Enforcement and the Administration of Justice," March 8, 1965, APP, https://www.presidency.ucsb.edu/node/242223; Hinton, *War on Poverty to the War on Crime*, 11–26, 63–133 (quotation 12).

75. On media coverage, see *LAT*, August 14–16, 1965; CBS-TV, "Watts—Riot or Revolt?" (December 1965), https://www.c-span.org/video/?327579-1/reel-america-watts-riot-revolt-1965. On suburban response, see extensive correspondence in folders 2–3, box 317, series 6.6.1, KH-Huntington; *Anarchy: Los Angeles* (Los Angeles: Kimtex Corp., 1965).

76. Kenneth Hahn, Statement on Watts Riot to Los Angeles County Board of Supervisors, August 12, 1965, Statement to McCone Commission, September 30, 1965, Mrs. Charles E. Brown to Hahn, August 18, 1965, folder 2, box 317, series 6.6.1, KH-Huntington; Governor's Commission on the Los Angeles Riots, *Violence in the City: An End or a Beginning?* (State of California, December 2, 1965); HoSang, *Racial Propositions*, 53–90.

77. Ponchitta Pierce, "Crime in the Suburbs," *Ebony*, August 1965, 167–72; "The Year of the Rebel . . . and the Riots," 30–31, "A City Stripped of Its Illusions," 29, 34, *Los Angeles*, September 1965, folder 9, box 317, series 6.6.1, KH-Huntington.

78. CBS Reports, *16 in Webster Groves*; Dan W. Dodson, "The Effects of Suburban Living," in *Children and Youth in the 1960s* (White House Conference on Children and Youth, 1960), 13–20; Peter Wyden, "Suburbia's Coddled Kids," *SEP*, October 8, 1960, 34–35, 44–46; George Gallup and Evan Hill, "Youth: The Cool Generation," *SEP*, December 23–30, 1961, 63–80. On suburban deprivation, also see Celia Spalter Deschin, "A Community Self-Portrait: The Five Towns" (National Council of Jewish Women: Adelphia University, 1965); Alice Miel with Edwin Kiester Jr., *The Shortchanged Children of Suburbia* (American Jewish Committee: Institute of Human Relations Press, 1967).

79. SDS, *The Port Huron Statement*, 1962, JAL-UM; James Miller, *Democracy Is in the Streets: From Port Huron to the Siege of Chicago* (New York: Simon & Schuster, 1987); Mario Savio, "An End to History," December 1964, Free Speech Movement Archives, http://www.fsm-a.org/stacks/endhistorysavio.html. Also see W. J. Rorabaugh, *Berkeley at War: The 1960s* (New York: Oxford University Press, 1989).

80. "The Inheritor," *Time*, January 6, 1967, 18–23. On alienation, also see Kenneth Keniston, *The Uncommitted: Alienated Youth in American Society*, rev. ed. (New York: Dell Publishing, 1965).

81. Richard Goldstein, "Drugs on the Campus," *SEP*, May 21, 1966, 40–62, and "Drugs on the Campus: Part Two," *SEP*, June 4, 1966, 34–44, published in book form as Richard Goldstein, *1 in 7: Drugs on Campus* (New York: Walker, 1966).

82. Richard H. Blum et al., *Students and Drugs* (San Francisco: Jossey-Bass, 1970), 15–18; Edward A. Suchman, "The 'Hang-Loose' Ethic and the Spirit of Drug Use," *Journal of Health and Social Behavior* 9, no. 2 (June 1968): 140–55; Lillian L. Imperi, Herbert D. Kleber, and James S. Davie, "Use of Hallucinogenic Drugs on Campus," *JAMA* 204, no. 12 (June 17, 1968): 1021–24.

83. John Corry, "Drugs a Growing Campus Problem," *NYT*, March 21, 1966; Jack Shepherd, "Drugs on the Campus: Potheads in Missouri," *Look*, August 8, 1967, 17; J. L. Simmons and Barry Winograd, *It's Happening: A Portrait of the Youth Scene Today* (Santa Barbara, CA: Marc-Laird Publications, 1966), 91.

84. Shepherd, "Drugs on the Campus: Potheads in Missouri"; Shepherd, "Drugs: A Personal LSD Experience," *Look*, August 8, 1967, 23; Albert Rosenfeld, "Marijuana: Millions of Turned-on Users," *Life*, July 7, 1967, 16–23.

85. Simmons and Winograd, *It's Happening*, 1–30, 85–104 (quotation 96); Suchman, "The 'Hang-Loose' Ethic," 140–55; Erich Goode, "Multiple Drug Use among Marijuana Smokers," *Social Problems* 17, no. 1 (Summer 1969): 48–64; Goode, *The Marijuana Smokers* (New York: Basic Books, 1970).

86. James T. Carey, *The College Drug Scene* (Englewood Cliffs, NJ: Prentice-Hall, 1968), quotations 8, 14–15, 2.

87. Goldstein, "Drugs on the Campus: Part Two," 42.

88. "Psychiatry: An Epidemic of Acid Heads," *Time*, March 11, 1966, 44–46; "Drugs: The Dangers of LSD," *Time*, April 22, 1966, 52; Albert Rosenfeld, "The Spread and Perils of LSD," *Life*, March 25, 1966, 28–30; Bill Davidson, "The Hidden Evils of LSD," *SEP*, August 12, 1967, 19–23; Barry Farrell, "Scientists, Theologians, Mystics Swept Up in a Psychic Revolution," *Life*, March 25, 1966, 30–33.

89. Sidney Cohen, "Uncanny Power of the Hallucinogens," *The Drug Takers* (New York: Time-Life Books, 1965), 90–91, 98–105, 123 (quotation 91); Cohen, *The Beyond Within: The LSD Story* (New York: Atheneum, 1964); Bernard Weinraub, "LSD: A Fascinating Drug and a Growing Problem," *NYT*, April 26, 1966, 26; Davidson, "Hidden Evils of LSD"; Rosenfeld, "Spread and Perils of LSD"; Goldstein, "Drugs on the Campus"; *NYT*, March 21, 1966. On the impact, see David Sanford, "LSD Crackdown," *TNR*, March 16, 1968, 11–12; Blum, *Students and Drugs*, 301–2.

90. Stevens, *Storming Heaven*, esp. xv ("mystic religious experience"), 272–88; Brecher, *Licit and Illicit Drugs*, chapters 50–51; Michael Pollan, *How to Change Your Mind* (New York: Penguin Press, 2018). Sidney Cohen stepped back, partially, from some of his earlier sensationalistic warnings in *The Drug Dilemma*, 2nd ed. (New York: McGraw-Hill, 1969, 1976), 10–21.

91. Stanley Yolles (NIMH director) in "Organization and Coordination of Federal Drug Research and Regulatory Programs: LSD," *Hearings before the Subcommittee on Executive Reorganization, Committee on Government Operations*, U.S. Senate, May 24, 1966 (Washington: GPO, 1966), 38; CRS, *LSD and the Control of Its Abuse*, Report 254 ED, December 21, 1967.

92. Testimony of James L. Goddard, "LSD and Marijuana Use on College Campuses," *Hearings before a Special Subcommittee of the Committee on the Judiciary*, U.S. Senate, May 23, 1966 (Washington: GPO, 1966), 320–53; Testimony of Walter H. Bowart, Paula Sherwood, and Eve Babitz, June 15, 1966, ibid., 543–68. Also see William C. Selover, "Senators Press Campaign for Crackdown on LSD," *CSM*, May 25, 1966, 1, 3.

93. Testimony of Bowart, Sherwood, and Babitz, June 15, 1966, "LSD and Marijuana Use on College Campuses," *Hearings*, 543–68.

94. Testimony of Sidney Cohen, May 26, 1966, "Organization and Coordination of Federal Drug Research and Regulatory Programs: LSD," *Hearings*, 144–58; CRS, *LSD and the Control of Its Abuse*; *LAT*, May 31, 1966. Also see Cohen, "Uncanny Power of the Hallucinogens," 90–91, 98–105, 123; Stevens, *Storming Heaven*, 272–88; Arthur Schlesinger Jr., "Our Angry Undergraduates," *SEP*, September 21, 1968, 23–27, 66–72.

95. Lyndon B. Johnson, "Special Message to the Congress on Crime and Law Enforcement: 'To Insure the Public Safety,'" February 7, 1968, APP, https://www.presidency.ucsb.edu/node/236741; Testimony of John Finlator, "Increased Controls over Hallucinogens and Other Dangerous Drugs," *Hearings before the Subcommittee on Public Health and Welfare, Committee on Interstate and Foreign Commerce*, House of Representatives, February 26, 1968 (Washington: GPO, 1968), 67–71; Sanford, "LSD Crackdown."

96. Johnson, "Statement by the President Upon Signing Bill Relating to Traffic in or Possession of Drugs such as LSD," October 25, 1968, APP, https://www.presidency.ucsb.edu/node/236893; Public Law 90–639, "An Act to Amend the Federal Food, Drug, and Cosmetic Act to Increase the Penalties for Unlawful Acts involving Lysergic Acid Diethylamide (LSD)," October 24, 1968; Hinton, *War on Poverty to the War on Crime*, 96–133.

97. Johnson, "Special Message to Congress Transmitting Reorganization Plan 1 of 1968 Relating to Narcotics and Drug Abuse Control," February 7, 1968, APP, https://www.presidency.ucsb.edu/node/236668; Frydl, *Drug Wars in America*, 356–58; Musto and Korsmeyer, *Quest for Drug Control*, esp. 21–37.

98. *NYT*, October 19, 1967; Sanford, "LSD Crackdown"; Musto and Korsmeyer, *Quest for Drug Control*, 26–27; "Increased Controls over Hallucinogens and other Dangerous Drugs," *Hearings*.

99. "Increased Controls over Hallucinogens and other Dangerous Drugs," *Hearings*, esp. 172–82 for quotations and data. Helen H. Nowlis, "A Report to NAPSA," February 26, 1968, reproduced in ibid., 215–217.

100. *NYT*, January 18–19, 25, March 11, 1968, May 13–15, 1969. Letters to Governor Nelson Rockefeller in reel 76, subseries 3, series 37, NAR-Rockefeller; quotations from Lorraine Hopler to Rockefeller, February 17, 1968, Robert Penner to Rockefeller, February 5, 1968, C. Dan Pangakos to Rockefeller, February 8, 1968, Edward C. Wendol to Rockefeller, January 21, 1968, Richard A. Rosenberg to Rockefeller, February 8, 1968.

101. *CT*, March 15, 1970; David Sanford, "Pot Bust at Cornell," *TNR*, April 15, 1967, 17–20.

102. "Student Freedom or Bust," May 1968, "Freedom: It's Happening," May 1968, "The Third Day, Police Brutality," June 1968, "The Mark at the Door," August 1968, Microfilm Reel 37, Michigan State University: Demonstrations; Administration Building, Part 1: Leftist Politics and Anti-War Movements, The American Radicalism Collection, Michigan State University, http://tinyurl.galegroup.com/tinyurl/8Dhcd1. On Wisconsin, see *WP*, October 2, 1968.

103. Berkeley Police Department, "Report on Incidence of Drug Use and Arrests in the South Campus Area and the City of Berkeley," September 16, 1969, reproduced in "Narcotics Legislation," *Hearings before the Subcommittee to Investigate Juvenile Delinquency, Committee on the Judiciary*, U.S. Senate (Washington: GPO, 1969), 1112–37. On the adjudication of arrested youth, also see chapter 3.

104. Charles Hollander/U.S. National Student Association, Press Release, December 18, 1968, Alan Reitman, National Student Association Memorandum, January 15, 1969, Reitman to National Student Association, March 18, 1969, folder 6, box 1091, subgroup 2, ACLU-Princeton; *NYT*, December 2, 1968; *WP*, December 19, 1968.

105. UC Berkeley Survey Research Center, "Public Reactions to the Student Protest Movement," January 1966, folder 8, box 96, series 4, DEM-UCSC; Constructive Action, *The Berkeley Revolution* [pamphlet and film], 1965, Truth about Berkeley Committee, "Berkeley," 1965, folder: Universities-Riots, box 6, MK-Huntington; *LAT*, May 16, 1965.

106. Letters about UC-Berkeley in folders 4–5, box 568, EGB-Bancroft. Watts references in Charles Schwieso to Gov. Brown, April 1, 1966, folder 4, Henry Harrison to Brown, May 22, 1966, folder 24, box 568, ibid. On the election, see McGirr, *Suburban Warriors*, 187–216; Matthew Dallek, *The Right Moment: Ronald Reagan's First Victory and the Decisive Turning Point in American Politics* (New York: Oxford University Press, 2004), quotations 195, 247.

107. "Man and Woman of the Year: The Middle Americans," *Time*, January 5, 1970, 10–17; Lassiter, *Silent Majority*, esp. 232–37, 301–4.

108. George E. Franklin Jr., "Enough Is Enough," n.d. [late 1960s], Fed-Up Citizen, "I Am a Sick American," n.d. [late 1960s], folder: Patriotism (2), box 12, Americanism Educational League, "You Remember the Real America," n.d. [c. 1970], folder: Americanism Educational League, box 16, MK-Huntington; Davidson Charlton Wysor, "My Declaration of War," June 1968, folder 5, box 26, TM-OSA.

109. J. Edgar Hoover, "A Timely Message," *FBI Law Enforcement Bulletin*, September 1, 1968, folder: SDS, box 6, MK-Huntington; C. D. Brennan to W. C. Sullivan, "Counterintelligence Program-Internal Security-Disruption of the New Left," May 9, 1968, FBI Director to SAC Albany, July 5, 1968, reproduced in Ward Churchill and Jim Vander Wall, *The COINTELPRO Papers: Documents from the FBI's Secret Wars against Domestic Dissent* (Boston: South End Press, 1990), 177–78, 183–84; T. Edward Mosher, "Inside the Revolutionary Left," *RD*, September 1971, 53–57.

110. Governor Ronald Reagan, "Campus Disorders" Press Release, March 3, 1969, Statement on Campus Disorders, March 17, 1969, folder: Campus Disturbances, box GO75, series II, Governor's Office Files, RRGP-Reagan; Fire and Police Association of Los Angeles, "Public Higher Education in California: Some Causes of Student Revolt," 1968, folder: FLPA, box 28, MK-Huntington.

111. Senator Thomas Dodd/Senate Internal Security Subcommittee, "The New Left," October 9, 1968, folder 3685, box 140, series III, TJD-UConn; Testimony of Marjorie King, March 31, 1970, "Extent of Subversion in the 'New Left,'" *Hearings*, Part 3, 187–217 (quotations 199, 217).

112. Mark Kleiman, "High School Reform: Toward a Student Movement" (Chicago: Students for a Democratic Society, June 1967), JAL-UM. Kleiman originally drafted this document in 1965 as a sophomore, and SDS published a revised version in 1967.

113. Testimony of Marjorie King, "Extent of Subversion in the 'New Left,'" *Hearings*, Part 3, 188; ibid., Part 4, June 10, 1970. Also see Gael Graham, "Flaunting the Freak Flag: *Kerr v. Schmidt* and the Great Hair Debate in American High Schools, 1965–1975" *Journal of American History* 91, no. 2 (September 2004), 522–43.

114. *Inside ACLU*, October 20, 1969, April 20, 1970, folder 20, box 9, TCLU-UTA; ACLU hair code litigation documents in folder: Long Hair Problems, box 228, ACLUSC-UCLA.

115. David Romano, "I Saw America in the Streets," 3–12, and Michael Marqusee, "Turn Left at Scarsdale," 13–23, in *The High School Revolutionaries*, ed. Marc Libarle and Tom Seligson (New York: Random House, 1970). Also see Diane Divoky, ed., *How Old Will You Be in 1984: Expressions of Student Outrage from the High School Free Press* (New York: Avon Books, 1969); Gael Graham, *Young Activists: American High School Students in the Age of Protest* (DeKalb, IL: Northern Illinois University Press, 2006).

116. James Mills and Bill Eppridge, "John and Karen, Two Lives Lost to Heroin" and "The World of Needle Park," *Life*, February 26, 1965, 66–92. On the agenda, see Barbara Baker Burroughs, "Bill Eppridge: A Personal Reflection on the Photographer in a Tumultuous Time," *Digital Journalist*, June 2008, http://digitaljournalist.org/issue0806/bill-eppridge-a-personal reflection on the photographer in a tumultuous time.html.

117. James Mills and Bill Eppridge, "Drug Addiction Part II: 'I Told Them Not to Go Home,'" *Life*, March 5, 1965, 92–102; Mills, "Realities We Must Face—But Won't," *Life*, March 5, 1965,

105–18. On the media portrayals of white urban heroin use during this era, also see Schneider, *Smack*, 142–58.

118. Johnson, "Special Message to the Congress on Law Enforcement and the Administration of Justice," March 8, 1965.

119. *The Drug Takers* (New York: Time-Life Books, 1965), quotation 4; James Mills, *The Panic in Needle Park* (New York: Farrar, Straus and Giroux, 1965); *The Panic in Needle Park* (20th Century-Fox, dir. Jerry Schatzberg, 1971); *Synanon* (Columbia Pictures, dir. Richard Quine, 1965); Martin Arnold, "Narcotics a Growing Problem of Affluent Youth," *NYT*, January 4, 1964, 1, 24.

120. U.S. House of Representatives, *Narcotic Addict Rehabilitation*, Report No. 2316, October 19, 1966 (Washington: GPO, 1966).

121. Loudon Wainwright, "The Strange New Love Land of the Hippies," *Life*, March 31, 1967, 15–16.

122. "The Hippies," *Time*, July 7, 1967, 18–22; William Hedgepeth, "Inside the Hippie Revolution," *Look*, August 22, 1967, 58–64.

123. James R. Allen and Louis Jolyon West, "Flight from Violence: Hippies and the Green Rebellion," *AJP* 125, no. 3 (September 1968): 120–26; Harry R. Brickman, "The Psychedelic 'Hip Scene': Return of the Death Instinct," *AJP* 125, no. 6 (December 1968): 78–84; Kenneth Keniston, "Heads and Seekers: Drugs on Campus, Counter-Cultures and American Society," *American Scholar* 38, no. 1 (Winter 1968–69): 97–112.

124. KBIX Reports, *The Maze: Haight/Ashbury* (1967), BATA-SFSU, https://diva.sfsu.edu/collections/sfbatv/bundles/189371; KBIX Reports, *The Maze: Etched in Acid* (1967), BATA-SFSU, https://diva.sfsu.edu/collections/sfbatv/bundles/189388.

125. Joan Didion, "The Hippie Generation," *SEP*, September 23, 1967, 25–31, 88–94; republished in Didion, *Slouching Towards Bethlehem* (New York: Farrar, Straus and Giroux, 1968).

126. John Luce and Wayne Miller, "A Young Doctor's Crusade," *Look*, August 8, 1967, 23–28; Jane Whitbread, "Runaways," *Look*, July 25, 1967, 26–32; "Youth: The Runaways," *Time*, September 15, 1967, 46–49; "Runaway Kids," *Life*, November 3, 1967, 18–29.

127. Drawn from coverage in *NYT*, October 9–20, 1967. Also see "Speed Kills," *Time*, October 20, 1967, 23; "Runaway Kids," *Life*, November 3, 1967, 18–29.

128. The Beatles, "She's Leaving Home," *Sgt. Pepper's Lonely Hearts Club Band* (1967); Joshua Kaufman, James R. Allen, and Louis Jolyon West, "Runaways, Hippies, and Marihuana," *AJP* 126, no. 5 (November 1969): 163–66.

129. David A. Noebel, "The New Pagans: The Hippie Cult," *Christian Crusade* (October 1967), reprinted by Network of Patriotic Letter Writers, folder: Network of Patriotic Letter Writers, box 17, *The Educator* (January 1970), folder: Sex Education (2), box 6, Ambassador College Research Department, *Hippies, Hypocrisy, and "Happiness"* (Pasadena, CA, 1968), folder: Drugs (1), box 21, MK-Huntington.

130. Henry Gross, ed., *The Flower People* (New York: Ballantine, 1968), quotation viii; interview with "Carol," ibid., 1–7.

131. Kaufman, Allen, and West, "Runaways, Hippies, and Marihuana"; J. Fred E. Shick, David E. Smith, and Frederick H. Meyers, "Use of Marijuana in the Haight-Ashbury Subculture," in *The New Social Drug: Cultural, Medical, and Legal Perspectives on Marijuana* (Englewood Cliffs, NJ: Prentice-Hall, 1970), ed. Smith, 41–62. Subsequent public health studies found that

heroin addiction in the Haight-Ashbury peaked in 1969–1970 and again in 1973–1974; that the addicted population consisted almost exclusively of adults, not teenagers, most from working-class backgrounds; and that the incidence of heroin use was statistically inflated because addicts from throughout the Bay Area sought the nonpunitive services of the Haight-Ashbury Free Medical Clinic. See John A. Newmeyer, "Further Notes on the Heroin Epidemic in the San Francisco Bay Area," 1975, folder: San Francisco Poly-Drug Project, box 5, PGB-Carter.

132. KBIX Reports, *The Maze: Etched in Acid* (1967), BATA-SFSU, https://diva.sfsu.edu/collections/sfbatv/bundles/189388; KRON-TV Interview of "Sandra," summer 1967, reproduced in *American Experience: Summer of Love* (Arlington, VA: Public Broadcasting Service, 2007).

133. Larry Beggs, "The Haight-Ashbury Scene and Our Response," n.d. [spring 1967], folder 11, Beggs, "Shelter/Counsel/Love at Huckleberry House," *Youth*, January 14, 1968, 2–13, folder 16, "Huckleberry's for Runaways" brochure, 1968, folder 2, Beggs, "The Runaway as a Contemporary Severance Ritual," 1976, Beggs, "Huckleberry House and the Summer of Love," October 12, 1997, folder 5, box 2, LB-SFPL. Also see *WSJ*, August 11, 1969 (final quotation); KQED-TV, "Huckleberry House and Runaways" segment, May 22, 1968, BATA-SFSU, https://diva.sfsu.edu/collections/sfbatv/bundles/189472.

134. "Huckleberry's for Runaways" brochure, 1968, folder 2, Youth Advocates, Inc., "History of Huck's," 1974, folder 9, box 2, LB-SFPL; Testimony of Chief Thomas J. Cahill, "Crime in America—Illicit and Dangerous Drugs," *Hearings before the Select Committee on Crime*, House of Representatives, October 27, 1969 (Washington: GPO, 1970), 428–45. Also see Michael E. Brown, "The Condemnation and Persecution of Hippies," *Trans-Action*, September 1969, 33–46; Agee, *Streets of San Francisco*, 213–45.

135. "Runaways," *BB*, October 20–26, 1967, 6, "House Bust Considered Betrayal," *BB*, October 27–November 2, 1967, 4; *SFE*, October 24, 1967; *SFC*, October 24, 1967; Larry Beggs, "What's Happening at Huckleberry House," March 1, 1970, folder 9, box 2, LB-SFPL.

136. Larry Beggs, *Huckleberry's for Runaways* (New York: Ballantine, 1969). Summary drawn from letters (anonymized by archival policy) from 1968–1969 in folders 1–3, box 1, LB-SFPL.

137. Larry Beggs, "What's Happening at Huckleberry House," March 1, 1970, Youth Advocates, Inc., "Youth: From Huckleberry's for Runaways to Youth Advocates," 1974, folder 9, Beggs, "The Runaway as a Contemporary Severance Ritual," 1976, folder 5, box 2, LB-SFPL; Edward L. Beggs, *Open House: A Successful New Community Treatment Approach for Young Suburban Addicts* (New York: Ballantine, 1973). On the model, see Frances A. Koestler, *Runaway Teenagers* (Public Affairs Pamphlet No. 522, 1977), folder 17, box 2, LB-SFPL.

138. Testimony of Reverend Thomas Murphy, "Drug Abuse in the Washington Area," *Hearings before the Committee on the District of Columbia*, U.S. Senate, March 26, 1969 (Washington: GPO, 1969), 131–34; Testimony of Stephen M. Brown, ibid., 179–91; Testimony of Paul Rosenberg, "Drug Abuse," *Hearings before the Select Subcommittee on Education, Committee on Education and Labor*, House of Representatives, August 20, 1969 (Washington: GPO, 1970), 584–90.

139. Barbara Katz, "Teen-Age Runaway Cases Triple," *LAT*, August 3, 1969. Also see *LAT*, April 14, July 6, September 10, 1968. On the litigation against "antihippie" ordinances, see Goluboff, *Vagrant Nation*, 221–57.

140. *BB*, September 29-October 5, 1967, 2; *LAT*, March 6, April 8, May 3, June 7, 1970, December 5, 1971.

141. Koestler, "Runaway Teenagers"; Lillian Ambrosino, *Runaways* (Boston: Beacon Press, 1971); Bibi Wein, *The Runaway Generation* (New York: David McKay Co., 1970). The most definitive statistical report is Tim Brennan, *The Incidence and Nature of Runaway Behavior* (Washington: Department of Health, Education, and Welfare, 1975), ERIC-DOE, https://files.eric.ed.gov/fulltext/ED117597.pdf. Also see FBI, *Uniform Crime Reports*, 1964–1974. The FBI estimated that reported runaway arrests were only about 75 percent of the actual nationwide total.

142. CYA, *Report on Crime: The Runaway Youth*, December 7, 1973, folder: Runaway Youth, box 20, Governor's Office Files, RRGP-Reagan; Allen Breed (CYA director) April 1971 memo quoted in Mary Lou Schram, "Run Away Where?" *California Living Magazine*, December 10, 1978, 7–10.

143. Testimony of William Treanor, Becky Lovelace, and Lyonelle Norris, "Runaway Youth," *Hearings before the Subcommittee to Investigate Juvenile Delinquency, Committee on the Judiciary*, U.S. Senate, January 13, 1972 (Washington: GPO, 1972), 7–19 (Bayh quotation 5–6); Hinton, *War on Poverty to the War on Crime*, 218–49. Also see Staller, *Runaways*, esp. 125–71; Schram, "Run Away Where?" On crime control in California, see Kohler-Hausmann, *Getting Tough*, 207–87.

144. "Increased Controls over Hallucinogens and other Dangerous Drugs," *Hearings*; Nixon, "Remarks at the Opening Session of the Governors' Conference."

145. Anonymous, *Go Ask Alice: A Real Diary* (New York: Avon Books, 1971); *Go Ask Alice* (ABC-TV, January 24, 1973); *Born Innocent* (NBC-TV, September 10, 1974); Julie Sorel, *Dawn: Portrait of a Teenage Runaway* (New York: Ballantine, 1976); *Dawn: Portrait of a Teenage Runaway* (NBC-TV, September 27, 1976). On the genre, see Elana Levine, *Wallowing in Sex: The New Sexual Culture of 1970s Television* (Durham: Duke University Press, 2007). Sharon Tate in *LAT*, December 4, 1969.

Chapter 3. Generation Gap

1. Roland H. Berg, "Drugs: The Mounting Menace of Abuse," *Look*, August 8, 1967, 12–13. On the theme of mainstream drug dependence, also see Leslie H. Farber, "Ours Is an Addicted Society," *NYT Magazine*, December 11, 1966, 43, 102–10.

2. Henry L. Giordano/Bureau of Narcotics and Dangerous Drugs, *The Dangers of Marihuana: Facts You Should Know: An Educational Message on Marihuana Abuse and Control* (Washington: GPO, 1968).

3. "Pop Drugs: The High as a Way of Life," *Time*, September 26, 1969, 68–78. Also see "The Family: Pot and Parents," *Time*, August 30, 1968, 44–45.

4. Very little scholarship exists on the discretion exercised by criminal justice systems in the suburbs and regarding white middle-class youth during this era. For a pioneering study of how police reform in San Francisco resulted in new forms of racial and spatial discretion toward white bohemians versus nonwhite residents, see Agee, *Streets of San Francisco*. For insight into how spatial proximity to urban centers operated in heroin markets, see Schneider, *Smack*, esp. 142–58. On law enforcement discretion during this period more generally, see Goluboff, *Vagrant Nation*. Michelle Alexander highlights recent trends in police and prosecutorial discretion that produced stark racial disparities in drug war enforcement against white suburban youth versus African American urban communities in *New Jim Crow*, esp. 58–136.

5. Calculated or drawn from the "Arrest Data" sections of the FBI's annual *Uniform Crime Reports*, 1964–1972; National Commission on Marihuana and Drug Abuse, *Marihuana: A Signal of Misunderstanding: First Report* (Washington: GPO, March 1972), 106–12. On the national war on crime, see Hinton, *War on Poverty to the War on Crime*; Flamm, *Law and Order*. On the politicization and distortion of crime data, also see Muhammad, *Condemnation of Blackness*.

6. LACNDDC, Minutes, February 25, 1967, F3717:322, LACNDDC-CSA; Jess Stearn, *The Seekers: Drugs and the New Generation* (Garden City, NY: Doubleday, 1969), 150–52.

7. Robert M. Carter et al., *Middle-Class Delinquency: An Experiment in Community Control: A Report to the President's Committee on Juvenile Delinquency and Youth Development on the Contra Costa County Demonstration Project* (Berkeley: University of California Regents, April 1968), quotations 1, 4, 9, 10, 27.

8. Carter, *Middle-Class Delinquency: An Experiment in Community Control*, 19–23, 90. Also see Carter, "Delinquency in the Upper and Middle Classes," *General Practice* 37, no. 3 (March 1968), 122–29; Vaz, ed., *Middle-Class Juvenile Delinquency*; Loth, *Crime in the Suburbs*. On federal policy, see Hinton, *War on Poverty to the War on Crime*, esp. 27–133.

9. G. Thomas Gitchoff, *Kids, Cops, and Kilos: A Study of Contemporary Suburban Youth* (San Diego: Malter-Westerfield Publishing Co, 1969), 59–69; Carter, "Foreword," in ibid., v–xiv; Carter, *Middle-Class Delinquency: An Experiment in Community Control*, 60.

10. Gitchoff, *Kids, Cops, and Kilos*, quotations 61, 73, 84, 106. The concept of the "hang-loose ethic" originated in Simmons and Winograd, *It's Happening*.

11. Carter, *Middle-Class Delinquency: An Experiment in Community Control*, 51; Interviews with Roni Rotholz, "David," and "Sam" in Gitchoff, *Kids, Cops, and Kilos*, 39–43, 86–92, 128–37.

12. Richard H. Blum and Associates, *Students and Drugs: Drugs II: College and High School Observations* (San Francisco, Jossey-Bass, Inc.: 1969), 320–48 (quotations 346–47).

13. Blum, *Students and Drugs: Drugs II*, 320–48 (quotations 338, 341–44).

14. Juvenile Justice Commission of San Mateo County, *Narcotics Inquiry Report for San Mateo County* (Redwood City, CA: San Mateo County, 1967), quotations 1, 3, 6, 7.

15. Juvenile Justice Commission of San Mateo County, *Narcotics Inquiry Report*, quotations 5, 25, 18–19, 36, 58.

16. San Mateo County Department of Public Health and Welfare, *Summary Report: Surveys of Student Drug Use, San Mateo County, California*, March 1977, RJR-UCSF, https://industrydocuments.library.ucsf.edu/tobacco/docs/tggv0093; Geoffrey Richard Wagner Smith, "Possession of Marijuana in San Mateo County: Some Social Costs of Criminalization," *Stanford Law Review* 22, no. 1 (November 1969): 101–28 (quotation 121).

17. San Mateo County Department of Public Health and Welfare, *Summary Report: Surveys of Student Drug Use*.

18. John Kaplan, "Marijuana Project: Foreword," *UCLA Law Review* 15 (1967–1968): 1501–06; Smith, "Possession of Marijuana in San Mateo County," 122–25.

19. Lloyd Johnston, *Drugs and American Youth: A Report from the Youth in Transition Project* (Ann Arbor: University of Michigan Institute for Social Research, 1973), 28–41, 98–151, 176–227 (quotations 31, 188, 225).

20. Nelson A. Rockefeller, Remarks to the Westchester Junior League Conference, October 3, 1967, "Youth in Westchester: Problems and Challenges," October 3, 1967, folder 2056,

box 53, series 33, Rockefeller, "War on Crime and Narcotics Addiction: A Campaign for Human Renewal," February 23, 1966, folder 498, box 44, subseries 3, series 10, NAR-Rockefeller. For a similar warning, see Rockefeller, Remarks at Breakfast Meeting on Narcotics Program, February 15, 1967, folder 1483, box 50, series 33, NAR-Rockefeller.

21. Joseph Persico to Nancy Shea, July 20, 1967, folder 2056, C. Richard Samson to Shea, September 15, 1967, William J. O'Brien to Persico, September 28, 1967, Persico Loose Notes, n.d. [1967], folder 2057, box 53, series 33, NAR-Rockefeller.

22. J'n Mullens, Letter to the Editor, *EVO* 2, no. 18 (August 5–17, 1967): 4, Douglas C. Hart, Letter to the Editor, *EVO* 2, no. 14 (June 15-July 1, 1967): 14, H.S.K., Letter to the Editor, *EVO* 2, no. 16 (July 13–July 30, 1967): 14, JAL-UM. Also see Rockefeller, Remarks to the Westchester Junior League Conference, October 3, 1967; Whitbread, "Runaways," *Look*, July 25, 1967; "Youth: The Runaways," *Time*, September 15, 1967; "Runaway Kids," *Life*, November 3, 1967.

23. Interview with "Randy," in Gross, *Flower People*, 49–68 (quotations 61, 52); interview with "Carol," ibid., 1–7 (quotation 2).

24. John Kifner, "The Drug Scene: Many Students Now Regard Marijuana as Part of Growing Up," *NYT*, January 11, 1968, 18. Also see *NYT*, October 19, 1967, January 8, 1968; Keniston, *The Uncommitted*.

25. *NYT*, May 8, October 15, 1966, May 7, November 30, 1967, January 27, November 30, 1969, August 23, 1970. On absorption, see Carter, "Delinquency in the Upper and Middle Classes."

26. Edwin Diamond, "The Drug Scene in East Egg," *NYT Magazine*, May 17, 1970, 29, 87, 90, 95–98, 104; *NYT*, May 7, November 30, 1967.

27. *NYT*, February 2, 9, 1968, May 14, June 28, 1970. For a contemporary analysis equating teenage pot smoking and adult consumption of alcohol, see Nechama Tec, *The Grass Is Green in Suburbia: A Sociological Study of Adolescent Usage of Illicit Drugs* (Roslyn Heights, NY: Libra Publishers, 1974), 4–8. On the licit/illicit market construction, see Courtwright, *Dark Paradise*; Tone, *Age of Anxiety*; Rasmussen, *On Speed*.

28. Suffolk County Police Department Narcotic Squad, "In Service Training Manual," January 1, 1968, Melvin J. O'Klock to Rockefeller, October 16, 1968, Hicksville Petition to Rockefeller, February 19, 1968, George Wilson to Rockefeller, n.d. [January 1970], reel 76, subseries 3, series 37, NAR-Rockefeller.

29. Mary A. Harnett to Rockefeller, January 2, 1970, Isabel M. Brown to Rockefeller, January 29, 1970, reel 76, subseries 3, series 37, NAR-Rockefeller; *NYT*, March 7, 1971.

30. EM [anonymized] to Rockefeller, November 23, 1969, Lucille Costello to Rockefeller, February 2, 1970, Francis J. Donovan to Rockefeller, February 18, 1970, reel 76, subseries 3, series 37, NAR-Rockefeller.

31. L. L. to Rockefeller, January 26, 1970, reel 76, subseries 3, series 37, Transcript of Utica Drug Abuse Forum, August 26, 1970, folder 345, box 32, subseries 1, series 21, NAR-Rockefeller, quotations 39, 56, 60, 78–80.

32. Nassau County Probation Department, *Drug Abuse in Suburbia: Third Interim Report*, August 1971, reel 62, subseries 4, series 37, NAR-Rockefeller.

33. Nassau County Probation Department, *Drug Abuse in Suburbia: Third Interim Report*, 75–150.

34. Nassau County Probation Department, *Drug Abuse in Suburbia: Third Interim Report*, quotations 4, 2, 10, 14–15, 43.

35. Nassau County Probation Department, *Drug Abuse in Suburbia: Final Report*, August 1978, NCJRS, https://www.ncjrs.gov/pdffiles1/Digitization/52204NCJRS.pdf, quotation 62.

36. "Report of Narcotic Advisory Council," January 25, 1967, folder: Narcotic Advisory Council, box A-267, Dempsey-CSL; Judge Samuel J. Tedesco, "Statement to Senate Subcommittee to Investigate Juvenile Delinquency," September 18, 1969, folder 6536, box 243, series IV, Mrs. Robert A. Haggerty to Thomas J. Dodd, September 30, 1969, folder 3692, box 140, series II, TJD-UConn.

37. Leonard A. Schine to John Dempsey, October 21, 1969, folder: Drug Abuse, box A-250, Dempsey-CSL; *NYT*, September 30, 1967, July 16, 1969; Educational Resources, Inc., "A Drug Prevention Program," n.d. [1969], folder 4245, box 170, series III, TJD-UConn. Fairfield County teenagers quoted in Will Oursler, *Marijuana: The Facts, The Truth* (New York: Paul S. Eriksson, Inc., 1968), 178–88.

38. Peter L. Costas Testimony, "Narcotics Legislation," *Hearings before the Subcommittee to Investigate Juvenile Delinquency, Committee on the Judiciary*, U.S. Senate, October 20, 1969 (Washington: GPO, 1969), 703–29 (quotation 710); Connecticut Drug Advisory Council, "Report to Governor Dempsey," n.d. [1969], reproduced in "Narcotics Legislation," *Hearings*, 729–32.

39. Statement of Governor John Dempsey, September 18, 1969, reproduced in "Narcotics Legislation," *Hearings*, 713; Connecticut Drug Advisory Council, *Report to Governor Dempsey*, January 30, 1970, folder: Drug Advisory Council, box A-250, Dempsey-CSL.

40. Tec, *Grass Is Green in Suburbia*, quotations 211, 60. On the "drug subculture" connection, see Goode, *Marijuana Smokers*, 180–207.

41. Tec, *Grass Is Green in Suburbia*, quotations 224, 194, 71, 223, 218.

42. *NVS*, October 10, 1967, March 29, 1968, *Vienna Globe*, January 15, 1970 (Horan quotation), Drugs folder, VF-FCPL.

43. "Drug Abuse in the Washington Area," *Hearings before the Committee on the District of Columbia*, U.S. Senate, March 26, 1969 (Washington: GPO, 1969), 156; *WP*, September 28, October 5–6, 1967, March 3, May 30, November 20, 1968; *Fairfax City Times*, November 2, 1967, Marijuana folder, VF-FCPL.

44. Meredith Platt, "The Modern Dope Pusher Doesn't Look the Part," *WP*, July 4, 1968, E1, E3; Platt, "Does Your Child Take Dope?" *WP*, June 13, 1968, F1, F8; Platt, "When a Teen-Ager Gets in Trouble the Whole Family Needs Help," *WP*, June 27, 1968, F1, F3.

45. John Bechtel (juvenile police officer in Montgomery County) quoted in "Drug Abuse in the Washington Area," *Hearings*, 150; *NVS*, October 10, 1967, Drugs folder, VF-FCPL; Testimony of Mayor Thomas Eastham, "Crime in America—In the Nation's Capital," *Hearings before the Select Committee on Crime*, House of Representatives, February 27, 1970 (Washington: GPO, 1970), 319–29 (quotation 324).

46. *Fairfax Herald*, May 15, 1970, *NVS*, June 19, 1969, Drugs folder, VF-FCPL; *WP*, April 10, 1969. On residential treatment, see Platt, "When a Teen-Ager Gets in Trouble."

47. Lucy Post Frisbee, "Child's Use of Drugs Can Shatter Parents' World," *Vienna Globe*, November 14, 1968, *Fairfax Sentinel*, December 31, 1970, *NVS*, June 19, 1969 (teenage response), Drugs folder, VF-FCPL; Simon L. Auster, "Some Observations on Adolescent Drug Use," *Educational Research* 27, no. 3 (December 1969): 281–86.

48. Testimony of Robert F. Horan Jr., March 26, 1969, "Drug Abuse in the Washington Area," *Hearings*, 155–64 (quotations 161, 163); Horan, "Remarks at Symposium on Adolescent Drug Use," October 23, 1969, *NVS*, March 29, 1968, Drugs folder, VF-FCPL; Meredith Platt, "Suburban Family Copes with Children on Drugs," *WP*, June 20, 1968, F1, F4-F5. Law enforcement data in "Drug Abuse in the Washington Area," *Hearings*, 147–50, 162.

49. *WP*, February 16, 18, 1969.

50. "Drug Abuse in the Washington Area," *Hearings*, 144–55 (quotations 79–80, 143 148); Testimony of John Ingersoll, March 25, 1969, ibid., 82–103 (quotations 82, 88); Testimony of Robert F. Horan Jr., March 26, 1969, ibid., 155–64 (quotation 163).

51. Testimony of Reverend Thomas Murphy, March 26, 1969, "Drug Abuse in the Washington Area," *Hearings*, 131–34; Testimony of Stephen M. Brown, ibid., 179–91 (quotations 180, 182); Testimony of Mr. X, ibid., 207–10.

52. Testimony of Jane Sachs and Dave Burton, March 26, 1969, "Drug Abuse in the Washington Area," *Hearings*, 194–95; "Crime in America—In the Nation's Capital," *Hearings*, 285, 308–14.

53. Testimony of Robert Shephard, February 27, 1970, "Crime in America—In the Nation's Capital," *Hearings*, 314–18.

54. "Drugs in Suburbia: Children of Affluence, Bored and Disillusioned, Turn to Pot and Pills," *WSJ*, November 12, 1970, 1, 28; "Drugs in Suburbia: Alarmed Towns Mount Attacks on Use of Pot, Pills by Young People," *WSJ*, November 18, 1970, 1, 33.

55. Fairfax County, "Drug Abuse Program," May 11, 1970, Fairfax County, News Release, May 12, 1970, "Crossroads House: Haven for Drug Addicts," n.d. [c. 1973], Drug Treatment Programs folder, *Drug Abuse: A Special Report to Citizens of Fairfax*, April 1973, Fairfax League of Women Voters, "Drugs: Problem, Law, Treatment," April 1973, *Fairfax Sentinel*, December 31, 1970, Drugs folder, VF-FCPL.

56. *LAT*, August 14, 1967; Mike Davis, "Riot Nights on Sunset Strip," *Labour/Le Travail* 59 (Spring 2007): 199–214.

57. Los Angeles County District Attorney's Office, "The Law As It Affects Juveniles and Adults," n.d. [late 1960s], reproduced in "Drug Abuse," *Hearings before the Select Subcommittee on Education, Committee on Education and Labor*, House of Representatives, August 20, 1969 (Washington: GPO, 1970), 655–56; Testimony of Frank Augusta, ibid., 557–62. Arrest data in Bureau of Criminal Statistics, *Crime and Delinquency in California, 1972: Drug Arrests and Dispositions* (Sacramento: CDOJ, August 1973), 4–12.

58. Kenneth Hahn, Press Release, January 24, 1967, folder 2B, box 55, series 1.43.2.11, LAC Board of Supervisors, Motion, March 22, 1966, folder 1a, box 212A, series 1.24.2.1, KH-Huntington.

59. "Drug Abuse," *Hearings*, 649; *LAT*, January 1, 1967.

60. Allan S. Morton et al., "Marijuana Laws: An Empirical Study of Enforcement and Administration in Los Angeles County," *UCLA Law Review* 15 (1967–1968): 1507–85 (quotations 1534, 1538, 1536, 1531, 1541); LACNDDC Minutes, February 25, 1967, F3717:322, LACNDDC-CSA.

61. Morton, "Marijuana Laws," quotations 1562, 1561, 1564, 1567. Studies of general marijuana disposition trends in California during the mid-1960s confirmed that prosecutors and judges reserved the toughest charges and sentences to those with prior criminal records, disproportionately the working-class, poor, and racial minority populations that lived in heavily policed areas in general. See Stanley E. Grupp, "Prior Criminal Record and Adult Marijuana Arrest Dispositions," *Journal of Criminal Law, Criminology, and Police Science* 62, no. 1 (1971): 74–79.

62. *LAT*, December 6, 1966, June 7, 9, December 16, 1967.

63. Leon L. Kaplan, "Drug Abuse Education and Control in the Los Angeles City Unified School District," June 1969, reproduced in "Drugs in our Schools," *Hearings before the Select Committee on Crime*, House of Representatives, December 8–9, 1972 (Washington: GPO, 1973), 2148–76; *LAT*, January 24, 1967, June 3, 1969; *The Mod Squad* (ABC-TV, 1968–1973).

64. Irvine Helbing to George W. Norene, August 7, 1968, Barry Rumbles, "Report on 19 Students Expelled from the Pasadena Schools in the Year 1968," folder 4, box 2, LVLM-PHL; *LAT*, August 26, 1968, March 29, April 3, 1969.

65. Michael Brown, "Stability and Change in Drug Use Patterns among High School Students, 1968–1971," folder: Drugs in High Schools, box 225, ACLUSC-UCLA; *LAT*, January 22, 1969, March 22, 1969.

66. *LAT*, June 13, 1969. On the larger patterns of police misconduct in drug enforcement in California, see Smith, "Possession of Marijuana in San Mateo County," 101–28. On stop-and-frisk as racial profiling policy, see Felker-Kantor, *Policing Los Angeles*; Alexander B. Elkins, "Battle for the Corner: Urban Policing and Rioting in the United States, 1943–1971," (PhD dissertation, Temple University, 2017).

67. *LAT*, June 13, November 17, 1969.

68. Bureau of Criminal Statistics, *Drug Arrests and Dispositions in California, 1967* (Sacramento: CDOJ, 1968); Michael R. Aldrich, Tod H. Mikuriya, and Gordon S. Brownell, *Preliminary Report: Fiscal Costs of California Marijuana Law Enforcement, 1960–1984* (Berkeley: Medi-Comp Press, 1986), chapter 1; National Governors' Conference Center for Policy Research and Analysis, *Marijuana: A Study of State Policies and Penalties* (Washington: GPO, 1977), 141. Also see Walt Anderson, "The High Cost of Cannabis," *LAT West Magazine*, August 16, 1970, W8–W14.

69. "Narcotics: A Challenge to the South Bay," *South Bay Daily Breeze*, October 22–29, 1968, reprint in folder 1a, box 212A, series 1.24.2.1, KH-Huntington; *LAT*, March 17, August 18, 1968.

70. "Narcotics: A Challenge to the South Bay," *South Bay Daily Breeze*, October 22–29, 1968; *LAT*, July 11, August 18, December 29, 1968, January 12, May 30, July 6, 1969, November 30, 1970; Mel Knight, "Why Teens Turn to Drugs," *LAT*, November 13, 1970, H7.

71. Hahn, Press Release, November 20, 1968 (high schools), January 30, 1969 (border), folder 1a, box 212A, series 1.24.2.1, *Hahn Report*, September 19, 1969, folder 2B, box 55, series 1.43.2.11, KH-Huntington; Kaplan, "Drug Abuse Education and Control in the Los Angeles City Unified School District"; Los Angeles County District Attorney, *Young Citizens Council Speakers Manual*, n.d. [c. 1967], reproduced in "Drug Abuse," *Hearings*, 638–66. Also see Evelle J. Younger, "What Can Be Done?" n.d. [late 1960s], ibid., 663–64.

72. Mayor Sam Yorty, "Statement to the Senate Subcommittee on Juvenile Delinquency," August 25, 1969, folder 6530, box 242, series IV, TJD-UConn; Mayor's Citizens Narcotics Committee, "Report on Undercover LAPD at Schools," March 19, 1969, folder 2a, box 55, series 1.43.2.11, KH-Huntington; "Drug Abuse," *Hearings*, 603–19. Data in Bureau of Criminal Statistics, *Drug Arrests and Dispositions in California, 1969* (Sacramento: CDOJ, 1970), 9, 19.

73. Larry Diamond Testimony, August 20, 1969, "Drug Abuse," *Hearings*, 733–35; Lewis Yablonsky Testimony, ibid., 591–95; Paul Rosenberg Testimony, ibid., 584–90.

74. Sandy——[redacted] Testimony, August 20, 1969, "Drug Abuse," *Hearings*, [illegible]; Robert Eichberg Testimony, ibid., 570–84; Paul Rosenberg Testimony, ibid., 588; "The Dawn Program," December 1968, reproduced in ibid., 563–69.

75. Narcotics and Dangerous Drugs Committee, "The Outline for Development of the Los Angeles County Drug Abuse Plan, 1970–1971" December 1969, folder 11a, box 222, series 2.47, LACNDDC Report, December 1, 1971, folder 2B, box 55, series 1.43.2.11, KH-Huntington; *LAT*, December 27, 1969 (parts of this report not made public until *LAT*, September 9, 1971), February 4, 1970. Arrest and diversion data in Bureau of Criminal Statistics, *Drug Arrests and Dispositions in California, 1969*; *LAT*, August 28, 1970, June 12, 1972.

76. *LAT*, May 11, 1967, March 29, 1969; Blum, *Students and Drugs: Drugs II*, 336–37; Auster, "Some Observations on Adolescent Drug Use."

77. Patricia M. Wald and Annette Abrams, "Drug Education," in *Dealing with Drug Abuse: A Report to the Ford Foundation* (New York: Praeger Publishers, 1972), 123–72 (quotations 129, 123–24, 127, 131, 132).

78. *Narcotics: Pit of Despair* (California Narcotics Advisory Commission, 1967), Internet Archive, https://archive.org/details/0785_Narcotics_Pit_of_Despair_06_06_30_08. For criticism, see *LAT*, May 11, 1967, March 29, 1969. Youth reaction in interview with anonymous high school senior in Pleasant Hill, California, in Gitchoff, *Kids, Cops, and Kilos*, 107; Children's Bureau (HEW), *Youth Reports No. 2: Youth Reporters Discuss 'Problem' Drugs* (Washington, GPO: 1970), 29.

79. "Project DARE: A Service to the Community," n.d., "Preventive Action in the Battle with Drugs: Project DARE, Los Angeles, California," *Hospital and Community Psychiatry* 21, no. 10 (October 1970): 33–36, folder: Drugs (2), box 9, TM-OSA.

80. *Beyond LSD* (Film Associates, 1967), reproduced in *Classroom Scare Films, Volume 7: Drugs and Beyond* (Seattle: Something Weird Video, 2000). Also see Film Associates, "Beyond LSD: A Film for Concerned Adults and Teenagers," n.d. [c. 1967], "A Teen D.A.R.E.: Life Can Be Exciting without Drug Dreams," n.d. [late 1960s], folder: Drugs (2), box 9, TM-OSA.

81. "A Teen D.A.R.E.: Life Can Be Exciting without Drug Dreams," Project D.A.R.E., "Know the Facts about Drugs: You Decide!" n.d. [late 1960s], J. Thomas Ungerleider, "Listen, Teacher," *The Valuator* (Winter 1970), 23–28, Project D.A.R.E., "A Happening," n.d. [late 1960s], "Preventive Action in the Battle with Drugs: Project DARE, Los Angeles, California," folder: Drugs (2), box 9, TM-OSA.

82. Ungerleider, "Pot, Pills, Peer Pressure, and Pleasure," *Keeping Posted*, January 1971, 3–7, Ungerleider, "Listen, Teacher," folder: Drugs (2), box 9, TM-OSA. On happenings, see *LAT*, March 4, May 20, 1970; "Costa Mesa Happening," March 6, 1970, folder: Narcotics Program (1970), box GO 89, Legal Affairs Unit, Governor's Office Files, RRGP-Reagan.

83. *Drug Abuse: The Chemical Tomb* (Film Distributors International, 1969), Internet Archive, http://www.archive.org/details/DrugAbus1969. William Quinn of the California Medical Association, who also chaired the California Narcotics Advisory Commission, was the primary consultant for this film and for *Narcotics: Pit of Despair*.

84. *Marijuana* (Avanti Films/Film Associates, 1968).

85. *The People Next Door* (CBS Playhouse/Bailey Films, 1970); CBS, "A Guide for the Motion Picture *The People Next Door*," folder: Drugs and Drug Use, box 78, TM-OSA. Filming in *NYT*, February 17, 1970.

86. *The Seekers* (Benchmark Films/NACC, 1968); *Grooving* (Benchmark Films/NACC, 1970). On this antidrug curriculum, see "Education: Drug Misuse Weapon," in *The Attack on Narcotic Addiction and Drug Abuse* (NACC, Winter 1969), 13, folder 13, box 78, TM-OSA.

87. Transcript of Syracuse Drug Abuse Forum, September 17, 1970, folder 345, box 32, subseries 1, series 21, NAR-Rockefeller, quotations 17, 38; BNDD, *Public Speaking on Drug Abuse Prevention: A Handbook for the Law Enforcement Officer* (Washington: GPO, 1970).

88. National Clearinghouse for Mental Health Information, "Introduction," *Resource Book for Drug Abuse Education* (Washington: GPO, October 1969), 1; William H. McGlothin and Louis Jolyon West, "The Marihuana Problem: An Overview," ibid., 65–67; Stanley F. Yolles, "Prevention of Drug Abuse," ibid., 68–69; Winfield W. Salisbury and Frances R. Fertig, "The Myth of Alienation and Teen-Age Drug Use: Coming of Age in Mass Society," ibid., 83–86.

89. Time Education Program, *A Time Guide to Drugs and the Young* (1970), folder 4240, box 170, series III, TJD-UConn, quotations 20, 13, 10; Children's Bureau (HEW), *Youth Reporters Discuss 'Problem' Drugs*, quotations 1, 3, 37.

Chapter 4. Public Enemy Number One

1. Thomas J. Dodd, "New Hope for Young Drug Addicts," 1970, folder 4245, box 170, Dodd, "Narcotics and Drug Abuse," March 30, 1969, folder 5787, box 212, series III, Dodd, Press Release, April 18, 1969, "Brief Summary of Senator Dodd's Omnibus Narcotic and Dangerous Drug Control and Addict Rehabilitation Act of 1969," April 18, 1969, folder 6523, box 242, series IV, TJD-UConn. On the FBN, see Anslinger and Oursler, *The Murderers*.

2. *CR—Senate* (January 24, 1970), 1008. Michael Javen Fortner argues that scholars of law-and-order politics during the late 1960s and early 1970s have made the "black crime victim invisible" and that this category also drove the punitive shift in the war on drugs. His widely debated thesis is most applicable to the Rockefeller Drug Laws in New York (discussed in chapter 5). In national-level political debates during the Nixon era, public health liberals and African American community activists from Harlem and other urban areas portrayed heroin addicts as the victims of traffickers, and other inner-city residents as the victims of both, but they struggled to break through the predominant emphasis on the white middle-class victim. See Fortner, "The 'Silent Majority' in Black and White: Invisibility and Imprecision in the Historiography of Mass Incarceration," *Journal of Urban History* 40, no. 2 (March 2014): 252–82; Fortner, *Black Silent Majority*.

3. Calculated or drawn from the "Arrest Data" sections of the FBI's annual *Uniform Crime Reports*, 1964–1974. On New York City as the heroin capital, see Schneider, *Smack*. For the general scholarly literature and the prevalence of labeling the Rockefeller Drug Laws the epitome of American drug politics and policy before the 1980s, see the books cited in the notes below.

4. Scholarship that examines the balance between law enforcement and public health during the Nixon-era war on drugs, and the relationship between heroin and marijuana politics, includes Courtwright, *Dark Paradise*, esp. 161–74; Massing, *The Fix*, 85–131, Musto and Korsmeyer, *Quest for Drug Control*, 38–139; Baum, *Smoke and Mirrors*, 3–85.

5. In 1975, the Ford administration's "White Paper" concluded that the illicit use of amphetamines and barbiturates "probably ranks with heroin as a major social problem"; see Domestic Council Drug Abuse Task Force, "White Paper on Drug Abuse," September 1975 (Washington: GPO, 1975), 21–24. Internal studies by the Ford administration estimated that only one-fifth of heroin users were addicts (four hundred thousand out of two million), while about half of the seven to eight million combined amphetamine and barbiturate users "are in serious trouble";

see Musto and Korsmeyer, *Quest for Drug Control*, 175. During the 1970s, more emergency room admissions involved Valium and other tranquilizers than heroin, especially among women, and often in combination with alcohol; see Herzberg, *Happy Pills in America*, 122–49. On stimulants, also see Rasmussen, *On Speed*. For comparative analysis, see Brecher, *Licit and Illicit Drugs*.

6. On the politics of omnibus legislation, see David Courtwright, "The Controlled Substances Act: How a 'Big Tent' Reform Became a Punitive Drug Law," *Drug and Alcohol Dependence* 76, no. 1 (2004): 9–15. The disease model advanced by public health liberals in Congress, who favored medical treatment over incarceration of addicts, marginalized causal explanations centered on economic and racial inequality, as well as discriminatory policing and the extensive corruption of narcotics police. In the case of heroin in particular, both the medical treatment and the law enforcement approaches addressed the symptoms of drug abuse (and constantly conflated users and addicts) rather than indicting underlying causes such as unemployment, poverty, and racial segregation—an argument made most forcefully by Eric Schneider in *Smack*. The dominance of psychiatric and "culture of pathology" thinking in both the medical analysis and the law enforcement ideology, and the consensus framework through which public policy formation intermixed both approaches, resembles the conclusion of Khalil Muhammad that for racial liberals during the Progressive Era, "the statistical evidence of black criminality remained rooted in the concept of black inferiority or black pathology despite a shift in the social scientific discourse on the origins of race and crime. The shift from a racial biological frame to a racial cultural frame kept *race* at the heart of the discourse." Muhammad, *Condemnation of Blackness*, 9.

7. Alexander, *New Jim Crow*, esp. 40–57; Provine, *Unequal under Law*; Beckett, *Making Crime Pay*; Weaver, "Frontlash." On the war on drugs and crime as social control, also see Garland, *Culture of Control*; Simon, *Governing through Crime*. For a partisan-centered account of the war on crime that largely ignores drug politics, see Flamm, *Law and Order*.

8. Hinton, *War on Poverty to the War on Crime*; Murakawa, *First Civil Right*; Frydl, *Drug Wars in America*; Gottschalk, *Prison and the Gallows*; Kohler-Hausmann, *Getting Tough*.

9. ACLU, News Release, December 18, 1968, ACLU Due Process Committee to Board of Directors, September 26, 1968, ACLU Board of Directors Minutes, November 11, 1967, folder 16, U.S. National Student Association, Press Release, December 18, 1968, folder 6, box 1091, ACLU-Princeton. The Supreme Court first recognized a constitutional right to privacy in the marital contraception case *Griswold v. Connecticut*, 381 US 479 (1965).

10. Alan Reitman, National Student Association Memorandum, January 15, 1969, NSA Drug Studies Project, Press Statement, December 18, 1967, folder 6, ACLU of Washington, News Release, February 15, 1968, folder 16, box 1091, ACLU-Princeton; ACLU of Washington, "Policy Paper on Marijuana Law," 1968, folder: Marijuana, box 229, ACLUSC-UCLA.

11. ACLU Due Process Committee, "Revised Working Paper on Sale of Marijuana," April 23, 1969, Minutes, April 28, 1969, February 10, 1970, folder 16, box 1091, Lauren Selden to ACLU State Affiliates, "Marijuana Repeal Campaign," December 1, 1971, folder 10, box 1092, ACLU-Princeton. It is difficult to determine exactly when the national ACLU publicly stated its support for full legalization. Selden's memo cites a board decision in April 1970, but no ACLU witness articulated this position during testimony to Congress during the debate over the 1970 federal drug reform law, and neither newspaper archives nor the ACLU's annual reports contain a statement in favor of legalization of marijuana sale before 1972.

12. *Commonwealth v. Joseph D. Leis, et. al*, 355 Mass. 189 (1969). Trial court decision reprinted in *BG*, December 20, 1967. Oteri quoted in *BG*, October 1, 1967.

13. Complaint, "Marc Denner and Michael Melon v. Frank Petrucci, et. al," folder: Marijuana, box 229, ACLUSC-UCLA; *NYT*, August 29, 1969, December 22, 1970; *Denner v. Petrucci*, 441 F.2d 564 (1971); ACLU of Washington, Press Release, October 24, 1969, folder 14, Chris Young, "Marijuana Test Case," June 13, 1969, folder 15, box 1091, ACLU-Princeton; *State of Washington v. Williams*, 78 Wn.2d 459 (1970).

14. *WP*, May 25–26, 30, 1969; *Johnson v. Commonwealth of Virginia*, 211 Va. 815 (1971).

15. "Marijuana: The Law vs. 12 Million People," *Life*, October 31, 1969, 26–29, 32–33; Jane Howard, "For the Long-Distance Runner Who Got Caught—a 20-Year Sentence," *Life*, October 31, 1969, 30–31; Charles R. Warren Jr., to Phillip J. Hirschkop, August 26, 1969, folder 14, box 1091, ACLU-Princeton. On the response, see Edward Kennedy, "Marijuana, Narcotics, and the Drug Scene," *CR—Senate* (November 5, 1969), 33069–33071; "Pop Drugs: The High as a Way of Life," *Time*, September 26, 1969, 68–78; *WP*, January 3, 5, 1970; *CT*, March 15, 1970.

16. FBI, *Uniform Crime Reports*, 1968–1969. Conviction estimates in "Pop Drugs: The High as a Way of Life."

17. ACLU Pamphlet, *Marijuana*, n.d. [1972], folder 28, box 10, TCLU-UTA; Michael Aldrich (LeMar) to Martin Garbus, November 28, 1969, folder 14, box 1091, ACLU-Princeton; *People v. Sinclair*, 387 Mich. 91 (1972); "The Agitator," *Time*, March 13, 1972, 50; Joel Fort, "Pot: A Rational Approach," *Playboy*, October 1969, 131, et. seq. Appellate courts overturned the sentences of Sinclair and Lee Otis Johnson, the Texas activist, in 1972.

18. CBS Reports, *Marijuana* (Carousel Films, 1969).

19. "Marijuana: The Law vs. 12 Million People"; James L. Goddard, "Should It Be Legalized?" *Life*, October 31, 1969, 34; "Pop Drugs: The High as a Way of Life."

20. "Marihuana Thing," *JAMA* 204, no. 13 (June 24, 1968): 97–98; Council on Mental Health (AMA) and Committee on Problems of Drug Dependence (National Research Council), "Marihuana and Society," *JAMA* 204, no. 13 (June 24, 1968): 91–92.

21. *Leary v. United States*, 383 F.2d 851 (1967); *Leary v. United States*, 395 US 6 (1969); Brief of ACLU, *Leary v. United States*, October 1968, Brief of National Student Association, *Leary v. United States*, October 1968 (quotation 6), U.S. Supreme Court Records and Briefs; *LAT*, May 20, 1969 (Leary quotation). Also see Richard Nixon, "Special Message to the Congress on Control of Narcotics and Dangerous Drugs," July 14, 1969, folder: Drug Message-RN, box 77, EK-Nixon.

22. Nixon's Anaheim speech in *LAT*, September 17, 1968; *CT*, September 17, 1968. Also see Nixon, "Address Accepting the Presidential Nomination at the Republican National Convention," August 8, 1968, APP, https://www.presidency.ucsb.edu/node/256650; "Republican Party Platform of 1968," August 5, 1968, APP, https://www.presidency.ucsb.edu/node/273407.

23. David M. Kennedy and John N. Mitchell to Nixon, June 6, 1969, Special Presidential Task Force, "Narcotics, Marihuana and Dangerous Drugs: Findings and Recommendations," June 1969, folder 558, box 54, subseries 4, series 10, NAR-Rockefeller.

24. Nixon, Memorandum "Action Task Force: Narcotics, Marihuana and Dangerous Drugs," June 27, 1969, reproduced in Electronic Briefing Book on Operation Intercept, NSA GWU, http://nsarchive.gwu.edu/NSAEBB/NSAEBB86/intercept03.pdf; Special Presidential Task Force, "Narcotics, Marihuana and Dangerous Drugs," 12.

25. Dodd, Press Release, April 18, 1969, "Brief Summary of Senator Dodd's Omnibus Narcotic and Dangerous Drug Control and Addict Rehabilitation Act of 1969," April 18, 1969, Dodd, "Floor Statement on the Introduction of the Omnibus Narcotic and Dangerous Drug Control and Addict Rehabilitation Act of 1969," April 18, 1969, folder 6523, box 242, series IV, TJD-UConn. Also see President's Commission on Law Enforcement and Administration of Justice, *The Challenge of Crime in a Free Society* (Washington: GPO, February 1967), 211–31.

26. Dodd, "Opening Statement on the Narcotics Hearings," September 15, 1969, folder 4236, box 170, series III, TJD-UConn, 1–11. "New generation of criminals" quotation from Dodd, "Drug Abuse and the Prison System," September 28, 1969, folder 4237, box 170, series III, TJD-UConn. At no time during the hearings or subsequent debate did Dodd or his congressional allies mention that African Americans accounted for 22 percent of drug arrests nationwide in 1968, double the population share, or question whether racial disproportionality played any role in the criminal justice system; see FBI, *Uniform Crime Reports, 1968* (Washington: GPO, 1969), 120–22.

27. Nixon, "Special Message to the Congress on Control of Narcotics and Dangerous Drugs," July 14, 1969; S. 2637, Controlled Dangerous Substances Act of 1969, reprinted in "Narcotics Legislation," *Hearings before the Subcommittee to Investigate Juvenile Delinquency, Committee on the Judiciary*, U.S. Senate (Washington: GPO, 1969), 114–204; Attorney General John W. Mitchell to U.S. Senate, July 15, 1969, reprinted in ibid., 909–20. Also see Musto and Korsmeyer, *Quest for Drug Control*, 56–62.

28. John W. Mitchell to U.S. Senate, July 15, 1969, reprinted in "Narcotics Legislation," *Hearings*, 909–20; Stanley F. Yolles Statement, September 17, 1969, ibid., 275. On the internal debate, see *NYT*, July 28, 1969 (anonymous quotations); Musto and Korsmeyer, *Quest for Drug Control*, 56–59. On Yolles's resignation, see *WP*, March 25, 1972.

29. S. 2608, Comprehensive Narcotic Addiction and Drug Abuse Care Act of 1969 (July 14, 1969), Ralph Yarborough Testimony, "Narcotics Addiction and Drug Abuse," *Hearings before the Subcommittee on Alcoholism and Narcotics, Committee on Labor and Public Welfare*, U.S. Senate, August 7, 1969 (Washington: GPO, 1969), 45–79; Harold Hughes Opening Statement, August 6, 1969, ibid., 1–6; Berwyn F. Mattison/APHA to Dodd, September 30, 1969, reproduced in "Narcotics Legislation," *Hearings*, 950–52; Testimony of Henry Brill/AMA, September 18, 1969, ibid., 315–27.

30. *NYT*, July 15, 1969; "The Nixon Drug Law: A Crucial Fault," *Life*, September 5, 1969, 32; "A Common Sense Solution," *Ebony*, December 1969, 140.

31. Testimony of Richard Blum, August 7, 1969, "Narcotics Addiction and Drug Abuse," *Hearings*, 106–21; Testimony of Bard Grosse/National Student Association, ibid., 122–28; Aaron Grossman to Dodd, October 10, 1969, reproduced in "Narcotics Legislation," *Hearings*, 1047–1050.

32. John N. Mitchell, "Statement before the Subcommittee on Juvenile Delinquency on S. 2637," September 15, 1969, John E. Ingersoll, "Statement before the Subcommittee on Juvenile Delinquency on S. 2637," September 15, 1969, folder 6533, box 242, series IV, TJD-UConn; Attorney General John N. Mitchell, Image #U1644654-4, Corbis Images. From the President's Meeting Files, reproduced in Musto and Korsmeyer, *Quest for Drug Control*, 58–59: "The President argued on the political basis that it would be unwise for the Administration to appear to be reducing in any way the penalties for drug users or especially dope peddlers. It was generally agreed that any change in the sentences regarding penalties would be left up to the wisdom of

Congress. The Administration would not take responsibility for this by including it in any message or legislation." Also see *NYT*, October 19, 1969.

33. Dodd, Opening Remarks, September 15, 1969, "Narcotics Legislation," *Hearings*, 5; Yolles Statement, September 17, 1969, ibid., 266–87; Sidney Cohen, "Statement before the Subcommittee to Investigate Juvenile Delinquency on Control of Drug Abuse," September 17, 1969, folder 4237, box 170, series III, TJD-UConn, 1–18.

34. For pharmaceutical lobby and medical industry influence, see "Narcotics Legislation," *Hearings*, 315–26, 352–74, 418–29, 485–557, 617–61, 693–703, 734–908. On the politics of pharmaceutical drug regulation, also see Frydl, *Drug Wars in America*, esp. 353–61; Rasmussen, *On Speed*, 208–21; Herzberg, *Happy Pills in America*, 83–121. On Dodd, also see *CR—Senate* (January 23, 1970), 976–78, (January 24, 1970), 993–97.

35. Dodd, "Opening Statement on the Narcotics Hearings," September 15, 1969, folder 4236, box 170, series III, TJD-UConn; Deputy Attorney General Richard Kleindienst quoted in *LAT*, September 14, 1969. On Operation Intercept, also see *NYT*, September 9, 19, October 5, 1969; Brecher, *Licit and Illicit Drugs*, 434–50. Commissioner of Customs Myles Ambrose later labeled Operation Intercept a form of "shock treatment for the Mexicans." See PBS *Frontline*, interview with Myles Ambrose, 2000, http://www.pbs.org/wgbh/pages/frontline/shows/drugs/interviews/ambrose.html.

36. Testimony of John E. Ingersoll, October 20, 1969, "Narcotics Legislation," *Hearings*, 663–83 (Dodd quoted at 678); *NYT*, October 19–21, 1969; Jeff Donfeld to Egil Krogh, "Themes for Attorney General Mitchell," November 19, 1969, folder: Narcotics Education, box 77, EK-Nixon.

37. "Compromise Provisions between S. 1895 and S. 2637," November 3, 1969, Dodd Office Memorandum, November 3, 1969, folder 6540, box 243, series IV, Dodd Staff Report on Subcommittee Hearings, 1969, folder 4232, Committee on the Judiciary, "The Controlled Dangerous Substances Act of 1969," December 16, 1969, folder 4243, box 170, series III, TJD-UConn. On HEW, see Testimony of Assistant Secretary Roger Egeberg, October 20, 1969, "Narcotics Legislation," *Hearings*, 683–93.

38. Field Research Corporation, "The California Poll: Majority of California Public 'Uptight' about Marijuana," May 21, 1969, folder LP311:1894, box 57, MPF-CSA; George H. Gallup, *The Gallup Poll: Public Opinion, 1935–1971* (New York: Random House, 1972), 1174–75; Gallup Organization, "Gallup Poll # 1969-0789: Nixon/Vietnam/Marijuana/Birth Control," October 2–7, 1969, Dataset Collections, RC-CU, http://ropercenter.cornell.edu/polls/dataset-collections/; *LAT*, May 26, October 26, 1969; *NYT*, October 23, 1969; Gallup, *The Gallup Poll: Public Opinion, 1935–1971*, 2246–47.

39. Art Linkletter, "The Drug Society," October 23, 1969, folder: Narcotics Education, box 77, EK-Nixon; "Remarks at a Bipartisan Leadership Meeting on Narcotics and Dangerous Drugs," October 23, 1969, APP, https://www.presidency.ucsb.edu/node/239877; *LAT*, October 5–6, 1969, *NYT*, October 24, 1969.

40. "Remarks at a Bipartisan Leadership Meeting on Narcotics and Dangerous Drugs," October 23, 1969; H. R. Haldeman, *The Haldeman Diaries: Inside the Nixon White House* (New York: G. P. Putnam's Sons, 1994), 102.

41. Jeff Donfeld, "Governors' Conference: Summary of Agenda Proposals," n.d. [late 1969], folder: Governors' Conference, box 77, "Suggested Remarks at Opening of Governor's

Conference," undated draft (probably by Jeff Donfeld, possibly by Patrick Buchanan), folder: Narcotics Education, box 77, EK-Nixon.

42. Richard Nixon, Spiro Agnew, and Art Linkletter, "Remarks to the Conference of Governors," December 3, 1969, folder: Drugs, box A-250, Dempsey-CSL. On the arrest of Agnew's daughter, see *LAFP*, September 5, 1969; Timothy Miller, *The Hippies and American Values* (Knoxville: University of Tennessee Press, 1991), 4.

43. John N. Mitchell and John Ingersoll, "Remarks to the Conference of Governors," December 3, 1969, folder: Drugs, box A-250, Dempsey-CSL; *NYT*, December 4, 1969.

44. S. 3246 debate in *CR—Senate* (January 23, 1970), 972–980, (January 24, 1970), 993–1012, (January 26, 1970), 1159–1185, (January 27, 1970), 1303–1341, (January 28, 1970), 1637–1691. Quotations 1169, 1011, 1669, 1183.

45. *CR—Senate* (January 27, 1970), 1303–1336, (January 28, 1970), 1637–1647. Ervin quotation in *CR—Senate* (January 26, 1970), 1159. First Hughes quotation in *CR—Senate* (January 23, 1970), 973. Dodd and Hughes exchange in *CR—Senate* (January 27, 1970), 1329–1330.

46. *CR—Senate* (January 27, 1970), 1322; *CR—Senate* (January 28, 1970), 1647–1662. The floor vote was 82–0, but fourteen of the absent senators sent word that they would have voted "yea" if present.

47. Committee for Effective Drug Abuse Legislation, Press Release, February 13, 1970, reproduced in "Drug Abuse Control Amendments-1970," Part 1, *Hearings before the Subcommittee on Public Health and Welfare, Committee on Interstate and Foreign Commerce*, House of Representatives (Washington: GPO, 1970), 426–30. Five members of the Committee for Effective Drug Abuse Legislation testified: Neil L. Chayet, Henry Brill (also representing the AMA), Jerome H. Jaffe, Jonathan O. Cole, Daniel X. Freedman (also representing the American Psychiatric Association), in ibid., February 17–20, 1970, 231–55, 275–86, 310–27, 429–37. Dodd and Mansfield in *CR—Senate* (January 28, 1970), 1689–1690.

48. Statement of Charles H. Wilson, February 3, 1970, "Drug Abuse Control Amendments-1970," *Hearings*, Part 1, 69–73; Statement of Lionel Van Deerlin, ibid., 62–64; Testimony of John E. Ingersoll, ibid., 79–170 (quotation 127); Statement of Richard T. Hanna, February 17, 1970, ibid., 208–13; Statement of Lawrence Speiser (Director of ACLU of Washington, DC), February 18, 1970, ibid., 297–310.

49. Select Committee on Crime, U.S. House of Representatives, *Marihuana: First Report by the Select Committee on Crime* (Washington: GPO, 1970), quotations 2, 86, 63, 94.

50. Statement of John N. Mitchell, "Controlled Dangerous Substances, Narcotics and Drug Control Laws," *Hearings before the Committee on Ways and Means*, House of Representatives, July 20, 1970 (Washington: GPO, 1970), 199–204 (quotation 203); Testimony of Roger O. Egeberg, Bertram S. Brown, Sidney Cohen, and Nancy Wolff, ibid., 269–97 (quotation 282); "Statements on Behalf of the Committee for Effective Drug Abuse Legislation" (Jonathan O. Cole, Roger Meyer, Arnold Mandell, Neil Chayet), July 23, 1970, ibid., 307–415, 420–27; Chayet, "Summary of Key Provisions of H.R. 18583," ibid., 415–20; Statement and Testimony of Hope Eastman/ACLU, July 22, 1970, ibid., 376–95 (quotation 378); Statement of Mrs. Edward F. Ryan/National Congress of Parents and Teachers, July 27, 1970, ibid., 449–52.

51. H.R. 18583, Comprehensive Drug Abuse Prevention and Control Act of 1970, and floor debate in *CR—House* (September 23, 1970), 33296–33319, (September 24, 1970), 33603–33667 (Linkletter at 33306; LaVarre at 33605).

52. *CR—House* (October 14, 1970), 36651–36655; *CR—Senate* (October 14, 1970), 36880–36885; Committee on Labor and Public Welfare, U.S. Senate, "Review of Substitute Amendment to Title 1 of H.R. 18583: Comprehensive Drug Abuse Prevention and Control Act of 1970" (Washington: GPO, 1970), quotations 5, 6; *CR—Senate* (October 6, 1970), 35052–35086, (October 7, 1970), 35475–35559 (Dodd quotation 35489). On the reconciliation process, also see House of Representatives, *Conference Report to Accompany H.R. 18583*, Report No. 91–1603, October 13, 1970. Dodd in *CR—Senate* (October 6, 1970), 35052–35055.

53. Nixon, "Remarks on Signing the Comprehensive Drug Abuse Prevention and Control Act of 1970," October 27, 1970, APP, https://www.presidency.ucsb.edu/node/240103; *NYT*, October 28, 1970.

54. Statement of John N. Mitchell, February 3, 1970, "Drug Abuse Control Amendments-1970," *Hearings*, Part 1, 79–82; Senate Committee on Labor and Public Welfare, "Review of Substitute Amendment to Title 1 of H.R. 18583"; Gallup Organization, "Gallup Poll # 1969–0789: Nixon/Vietnam/Marijuana/Birth Control," October 2–7, 1969.

55. Nixon, "Statement by the President," March 11, 1970, White House, "Drug Abuse Program Fact Sheet," March 11, 1970, folder: Drugs, box A-250, Dempsey-CSL; *NYT*, March 12, 1970. For "ghetto problem" quotation, see Jeff Donfeld to Egil Krogh, September 29, 1970, folder: Ad Hoc Committee–Drug Abuse, box 10, EK-Nixon. To assuage liberal critics, the administration also modified the Law Enforcement Assistance Administration funding guidelines to allow cities to use federal block grants for treatment centers and not just police crackdowns.

56. Jeb Magruder to John Ehrlichman, n.d. [1970], folder: Follow-Up Drug Conference, Jeff Donfeld to Egil Krogh and Jeb Magruder, March 12, 1970, folder: TV Writers Meeting, *Broadcasting* (April 13, 1970), Krogh to Eugene Rossides, July 2, 1970, folder: Proposed TV series–Drugs, box 77, EK-Nixon; *NYT*, June 23, 1970; Nixon, "Remarks to Athletes Attending a White House Sponsored Conference on Drug Abuse," February 3, 1972, APP, https://www.presidency.ucsb.edu/node/255510. Also see Wald and Abrams, "Drug Education," in *Dealing with Drug Abuse*, 114–15. The White House demanded formal approval over programming that featured federal drug enforcement agencies to insure their depiction "in a favorable light," based on the model of the FBI's longstanding arrangement with Hollywood.

57. Commissioner of Education James E. Allen Jr. to Head of State Education Departments, March 24, 1970, National Governors' Conference Memo, March 27, 1970, White House, "Drug Abuse Program Fact Sheet," March 11, 1970, folder: Drugs, box A-250, Dempsey-CSL; National Clearinghouse for Drug Abuse Information/National Institute of Mental Health, *A Federal Source Book: Answers to the Most Frequently Asked Questions about Drug Abuse* (Washington: GPO, 1970), quotations 2, 3, 8, 10, 11.

58. BNDD, *Teen-Age Booby Trap* (Washington, DC: Commercial Comics, 1970); BNDD, "An Invitation to Sponsor 'Teen-Age Booby Trap,'" 1970, folder: Drugs, box A-250, Dempsey-CSL; *What If They Call Me "Chicken"?* (Washington, DC: Commercial Comics, 1970), folder: Malcolm Alter and Steve Jacobs (2), box 11, CET-Reagan.

59. Committee on Labor and Public Welfare, U.S. Senate, *Federal Drug Abuse and Drug Dependence Prevention, Treatment, and Rehabilitation Act of 1970*, Report No. 91–1341, October 14, 1970.

60. "The Drug Scene: What Every Parent and Teenager Should Know" series, *BG*, November 2, 1969, reprinted at the request of Senator Edward Kennedy in *CR—Senate* (November 5,

1969), 33071–33081. Also see *BG*, January 19, 1970 ("Use of Heroin Is Spreading into Middle Class Suburbia"), February 20, 1970 ("Heroin Seen Pushing into Colleges, Suburbs"), August 1, 1971 ("Heroin Knows No Bounds—It's Everyone's Problem Now"). Additional stories in *LAT*, September 13, 1970; *WP* February 16, 1969; *NYT*, February 16, March 9, 1970.

61. W. B. Rood, "Today's Heroin Addicts: Younger, Wealthier," *LAT*, September 13, 1970; "Dead Youth's Letter of Warning about Drugs," n.d. [c. 1970], folder: Drugs (2), box 4, TM-OSA. Data in Shick, Smith, and Meyers, "Use of Marijuana in the Haight-Ashbury Subculture," 41–62.

62. Robert Levengood, Paul Lowinger, and Kenneth Schooff, "Heroin Addiction in the Suburbs: An Epidemiologic Study," *AJPH* 63, no. 3 (March 1973): 209–14 (quotation 213); Beggs, *Open House: A Successful New Community Treatment Approach for Suburban Addicts.*

63. For four of many examples, see suburban Boston in "Federal Drug Abuse and Drug Dependence Prevention," *Hearings before the Special Subcommittee on Alcoholism and Narcotics, Committee on Labor and Public Welfare*, U.S. Senate, April 10–11, 1970 (Washington: GPO, 1970); suburban Maryland and Virginia in "Crime in America—In the Nation's Capital," *Hearings*, February 27–28, 1970, esp. 166–71, 286–92; suburban DC in "Narcotics Addiction and Drug Abuse," *Hearings before the Special Subcommittee on Alcoholism and Narcotics, Committee on Labor and Public Welfare*, U.S. Senate, August 6–8, 1969 (Washington: GPO, 1969), esp. 135–42; suburban Los Angeles in "Drug Abuse," *Hearings*, August 20, 1969. On heroin addiction rates, see Musto and Korsmeyer, *Quest for Drug Control*, 175.

64. *Fairfield County Courier*, November 7, 1969, HOL [anonymized] to John Dempsey (first quotation) and other letters from suburban Hartford parents in folder: Drug Abuse-10 State Conference, RF [anonymized] to Dempsey, November 21 and 29, 1969 (second quotation), folder: Drugs (Special Act 202), Connecticut Department of Corrections report, January 5, 1970, folder: Drug Advisory Council, box A-250, Dempsey-CSL. Also see letter-writing campaign by Naugatuck parents and students in folder: Naugatuck Narcotics Problem, box A-277, Dempsey-CSL. On heroin and Vietnam soldiers, see Schneider, *Smack*, 159–81. On the role of drug use among GIs in Vietnam in shaping the Nixon administration's drug policies, also see PBS *Frontline* interview with Egil "Bud" Krogh Jr., 2000, http://www.pbs.org/wgbh/pages/frontline/shows/drugs/interviews/krogh.html.

65. "Blacks Declare War on Dope," *Ebony*, June 1970, 31–40; Rockefeller in *NYT*, September 19, 1970; Testimony of Edna Eagan/Parents Foundation Against Drug Abuse, July 26, 1969, "Drug Abuse," *Hearings*, 431–38; Edna Eagan, "Drug Abuse," republished in *CR—House* (April 8, 1970), 10939. Officials in the John Lindsay mayoral administration and the state narcotics commission conceded the accuracy of the critique that they paid the most attention to the white heroin crisis; see *NYT*, March 9, 1970. On the African American antinarcotics movement in Harlem, see Fortner, *Black Silent Majority*. On NYPD narcotics corruption, see Schneider, *Smack*, 116–41.

66. Stanley Church/March on Drugs to Nelson A. Rockefeller, July 30, 1970, reel 76, subseries 3, series 37, Rockefeller, "Speech at Kick-Off of Drug-Out Day Parade," August 14, 1970, folder 3128, box 77, series 33, NAR-Rockefeller; *NYT*, March 27, August 10, 15, 1970.

67. Hugh Morrow to Nelson A. Rockefeller, July 30, 1970, August 10, 1970, folder 339, New York State Health Department, "Direct Deaths Due to Drug Abuse," n.d. [1973], folder 342, box 32, subseries 1, series 21, NAR-Rockefeller. Debunking in Brecher, *Licit and Illicit Drugs*, 101–14.

68. For the distorted data that circulated nationally, see the New York section of chapter 5 and also NACC, "The Cost of Addict Crime in New York State" and "Arrests of Admitted Addicts," n.d. [1971], folder 1837, box 9, series 25, NAR-Rockefeller. Of the many methodological flaws in the compilation of the addict crime data, the two most basic involved the attribution of causation to the drug itself for any law violation by any arrested person who admitted being a heroin user, and the direct extrapolation of data drawn from the arrested group to the entire estimated heroin-using population. For additional examples, see NYPD, Press Release, April 24, 1969, folder 284, box 27, subseries 4, series 10, New York State Department of Corrections, "Felony Arrests of Narcotics Users," 1971, folder 343, box 32, subseries 1, series 21, NAR-Rockefeller. For internal studies that contradicted this hype, see Carl D. Chambers/NACC, *An Assessment of Drug Use in the General Population: Special Report No. 1: Drug Use in New York State*, May 1971, folder 338, box 31, subseries 1, series 21, NACC, "Crimes Committed by Drug Users," n.d. [1972], folder 341, box 32, subseries 1, series 21, NAR-Rockefeller. On the general distortion of heroin addiction and crime data in the late 1960s and early 1970s, see Drug Abuse Council, *A Perspective on 'Get Tough' Drug Laws* (Washington: Drug Abuse Council, 1973); Domestic Council Drug Abuse Task Force, "White Paper on Drug Abuse," 1975; Courtwright, *Dark Paradise*, 165–74; David J. Bellis, *Heroin and Politicians: The Failure of Public Policy to Control Addiction in America* (Westport, CT: Greenwood Press, 1981), 18–37.

69. Testimony of Claude Pepper, July 21, 1970, "Controlled Dangerous Substances, Narcotics and Drug Control Laws," *Hearings*, 316–44; Select Committee on Crime, House of Representatives, *Heroin and Heroin Paraphernalia: Second Report by the Select Committee on Crime* (Washington: GPO, 1971), quotations 39, 10.

70. Egil Krogh to Jeff Donfeld and Geoff Shepard, February 17, 1971, Donfeld to Krogh, February 17, 1971, folder: Law and Order–Drugs, box 29, EK-Nixon; Senate Committee on Labor and Public Welfare, "Federal Drug Abuse and Drug Dependence Prevention, Treatment, and Rehabilitation Act of 1970," *Hearings*, quotation 5.

71. "Excerpt of Remarks of the President to the White House Conference on Drug Abuse for Religious Leaders," March 26, 1971, George Bell to H. R. Haldeman, October 1, 1970, folder: Presidential Meeting with Religious Leaders, box 23, CWC-Nixon; *BAA*, May 29, 1971; CRS, *Federal Programs Relating to the Control of Drug Abuse*, Report 72–272 ED, December 7, 1972. The Congressional Black Caucus also did not mention the FBI crime data showing drug arrests of African Americans at more than double the population share (see fig. 4.1).

72. FBI, *Uniform Crime Reports, 1971* (Washington: GPO, 1972), 34. Usage data compares the accepted estimate of 150,000 to 250,000 heroin addicts to the estimated 24 million Americans who had experimented with marijuana, including 8 million current users, as compiled by the National Commission on Marihuana and Drug Abuse, *Marijuana: A Signal of Misunderstanding*, 7.

73. President's Drug Abuse Program, Minutes of Steering Group Meeting, June 10, 1971, folder: President's Drug Abuse Program, box 52, "Summary, Narcotics Meeting," June 3, 1971, folder: Summary of President's Remarks, box 32, EK-Nixon; "The President's News Conference," June 1, 1971, APP, https://www.presidency.ucsb.edu/node/240177. On legal pharmaceuticals, see Herzberg, *White Market Drugs*.

74. Nixon, "Special Message to the Congress on Drug Abuse Prevention and Control," June 17, 1971, APP, https://www.presidency.ucsb.edu/node/240245; Nixon, "Remarks about

an Intensified Program for Drug Abuse Prevention and Control," June 17, 1971, APP, https://www.presidency.ucsb.edu/node/240238; "Mission Statement: Special Action Office for Drug Abuse Prevention," June 15, 1971, folder: Special Action Office for Drug Abuse Prevention, box 31, EK-Nixon.

75. CRS, *Drug Abuse Office and Treatment Act of 1972: Summary of Major Provisions*, Report 72-150 ED, June 29, 1972; Committee on Government Operations, U.S. Senate, *Drug Abuse Office and Treatment Act of 1971*, Report No. 92–486, November 17, 1971 (Washington: GPO, 1971); "Drug Abuse Prevention and Control," *Hearings before the Committee on Government Operations*, U.S. Senate, July 7–9, 15–16, 30, 1971 (Washington: GPO, 1971), Ribicoff quotations 4–5, Zinberg 351–65; "Drug Abuse, Prevention, Treatment, and Rehabilitation, 1971," *Hearings before the Subcommittee on Alcoholism and Narcotics, Committee on Labor and Public Welfare*, U.S. Senate, August 2–5, 1971 (Washington: GPO, 1971), Hughes quotation 72. Four years later, the Ford administration's "White Paper" acknowledged that a majority of current heroin users were not addicts; Domestic Council Drug Abuse Task Force, "White Paper on Drug Abuse," 1975. Also see Baum, *Smoke and Mirrors*, 13–71.

76. Nixon, "Statement about the Drug Abuse Office and Treatment Act of 1972," March 21, 1972, APP, https://www.presidency.ucsb.edu/node/255218; Senate debate over the Drug Abuse Office and Treatment Act in *CR—Senate* (December 2, 1971), 44049–44113 (Kennedy quotation 44103); Ribicoff in Senate Committee on Government Operations, *Drug Abuse Office and Treatment Act of 1971*, 3; PBS *Frontline*, interview with Jerome Jaffe, 2000, http://www.pbs.org/wgbh/pages/frontline/shows/drugs/interviews/jaffe.html. Also see "Evaluating the Federal Effort to Control Drug Abuse," Part 3, *Hearings before the Committee on Government Operations*, House of Representatives, June 18, 1973 (Washington: GPO, 1973), 644–46; Bellis, *Heroin and Politicians*.

77. Nixon, "Statement on Establishing the Office for Drug Abuse Law Enforcement," January 28, 1972, Krogh, Memo for the President's File, February 1, 1972, folder: Drug Prosecution Program, box 1, GCS-Nixon; Testimony of John D. Ehrlichman, "Federal Drug Enforcement," *Hearings before the Permanent Subcommittee on Investigations, Committee on Government Operations*, U.S. Senate, July 27, 1976, (Washington: GPO, 1976), 794–95. ODALE director's quotation in PBS *Frontline*, interview with Myles Ambrose, 2000, http://www.pbs.org/wgbh/pages/frontline/shows/drugs/interviews/ambrose.html.

78. Myles J. Ambrose, "A War We Intend to Win" (Address to the International Narcotics Conference), October 9, 1972, folder 12, box 1092, ACLU-Princeton. "Marijuana dealers" quotation in "Search and Destroy: The War on Drugs," *Time*, September 4, 1972, 22–31. "Remarkable success" quotation in PBS *Frontline*, interview with Myles Ambrose; PBS *Frontline*, interview with Egil "Bud" Krogh Jr. Also see Hinton, *War on Poverty to the War on Crime*, 183–85, 202–9.

79. "Reorganization Plan No. 2 of 1973," *Hearings before the Subcommittee on Reorganization, Research, and International Organizations, Committee on Government Operations*, U.S. Senate, May 18, 1973 (Washington: GPO, 1974), 445–560 (Percy quotations 446–447). For a sampling of media features on the Collinsville victims, see *NYT*, April 29, 1973 (Ambrose quotation); *CT*, May 5, 1973; *LAT*, October 30, 1973. Washington in *CD*, August 16, 1973. A *New York Times* investigation confirmed a pattern of civil liberties abuses and mistaken raids by ODALE, mainly in low-income and nonwhite areas and involving incidents that did not receive much if any media coverage; *NYT*, June 25, 1973.

80. Nixon, "Message to the Congress Transmitting Reorganization Plan 2 of 1973 Establishing the Drug Enforcement Administration," March 28, 1973, APP, https://www.presidency.ucsb.edu/node/256311; CRS, *Control of Drug Abuse: Summary of Principal Legislative Activity in the 93rd Congress*, Report 74–230 ED, December 3, 1974. Also see Musto and Korsmeyer, *Quest for Drug Control*, 119–39.

81. Response Analysis Corporation/National Commission on Marihuana and Drug Abuse, "Public Attitudes toward Marijuana: A Nationwide Study of Beliefs, Information and Experiences," January 1972, in *Marihuana: A Signal of Misunderstanding: The Technical Papers of the First Report of the National Commission on Marihuana and Drug Abuse*, vol. 2 (Washington: GPO, 1972), 855–1119 (data from 885, 911, 916).

82. Oval Office Conversation No. 500–17, May 17, 1971, with Nixon and Art Linkletter, Oval Office Conversation No. 568–3, September 9, 1971, with Nixon, Raymond Shafer, Jerome Jaffe, and Egil Krogh, reproduced in Common Sense for Drug Policy Research Report, "Nixon Tapes Show Roots of Marijuana Prohibition: Misinformation, Culture Wars, and Prejudice," March 2002, http://www.csdp.org/research/nixonpot.txt.

83. Oval Office Conversation No. 690–11, March 21, 1972, with Nixon and H. R. Haldeman, reproduced in Common Sense for Drug Policy Research Report, March 2002.

84. Shafer quoted in Oval Office Conversation No. 568–3, September 9, 1971, with Nixon, Raymond Shafer, Jerome Jaffe, and Egil Krogh, reproduced in Common Sense for Drug Policy Research Report, March 2002. Hughes proposed the unsuccessful amendment to lower marijuana penalties even further in the 1970 legislation; *NYT*, January 29, 1970. In Nixon's bipartisan leadership briefing on the drug law, Javits asked why marijuana should not be legalized and regulated like alcohol; see "Remarks at a Bipartisan Leadership Meeting on Narcotics and Dangerous Drugs," October 23, 1969.

85. Egil Krogh to Nixon, September 8, 1971, "Interim Summary of the Commission's Research Report," n.d. [September 1971], folder 16, CMDA-Nixon; Oval Office Conversation No. 498–5, May 13, 1971, with Nixon, H. R. Haldeman, and John Ehrlichman, Oval Office Conversation No. 568–3, September 9, 1971, with Nixon, Raymond Shafer, Jerome Jaffe, and Egil Krogh, reproduced in Common Sense for Drug Policy Research Report, March 2002; *NYT*, May 20, 1971.

86. *Marihuana: A Signal of Misunderstanding*, quotations iii, 6–9. For a parallel argument that the "culture of narcissism" interpretation in the 1970s reflected racial fears that white middle-class Americans were adopting a "ghetto mentality," see Zaretsky, *No Direction Home*, 183–221.

87. *Marihuana: A Signal of Misunderstanding*, quotations 134, 142, 95, 102. On the secret meetings, see *WP*, February 20, 1972, and pp. 92–93 of the report for the quotation.

88. David Parker to Charles Colson and Egil Krogh, March 10, 1972, Krogh to Nixon, March 20, 1972, "The President's Schedule," March 21, 1972, folder 16, CMDA-Nixon; transcript of Nixon press conference in *NYT*, March 25, 1972.

89. Geoff Shepard to David Parker, February 23, 1973, folder 18, Michael R. Sonnenreich to Egil Krogh, April 7, 1972, folder 16, CMDA-Nixon.

90. Bob Haldeman to John Ehrlichman, March 21, 1972, Draft, "Presidential TV Address on the War against Drug Abuse," May 3, 1972, folder: Drug Speech File, box 1, "Proposed Presidential Remarks: Drug Abuse Fight," April 4, 1972, folder: Narcotics Fireside Chat, box 3, GCS-Nixon. Nixon's New York remarks in *NYT*, March 21, 1972.

91. Nixon, "Statement about Drug Abuse Law Enforcement," September 22, 1972, APP, https://www.presidency.ucsb.edu/node/254999; Nixon, "Campaign Statement about Crime and Drug Abuse," October 28, 1972, APP, https://www.presidency.ucsb.edu/node/255436; George McGovern, Press Release, September 18, 1972, Geoff Shepard to Richard Harkness, Memo on "Senator McGovern and Drugs," July 31, 1972, folder: McGovern–Drugs, box 15, EK-Nixon; "Society: Loosening Up," *Time*, June 26, 1972, 19. Also see NORML, "Presidential Candidates Survey on Marijuana," March 2, 1972, folder 4, box 3, TCLU-UTA.

92. Nixon, "Campaign Statement about Crime and Drug Abuse," October 28, 1972; Nixon, "Radio Address on Crime and Drug Abuse," October 15, 1972, APP, https://www.presidency.ucsb.edu/node/255210; "Republican Party Platform of 1972," August 21, 1972, APP, https://www.presidency.ucsb.edu/node/273411; "Democratic Party Platform of 1972," July 10, 1972, APP, https://www.presidency.ucsb.edu/node/273248. Also see Flamm, *Law and Order*, 162–78. Data in FBI, *Uniform Crime Reports, 1972* (Washington: GPO, 1973), 34.

93. Nixon, "Radio Address on Law Enforcement and Drug Abuse Prevention," March 10, 1973, Bill Baroody to David Gergen, March 9, 1973, folder: Radio: Crime and Drugs, box 33, DG-Nixon. Heroin Trafficking Act proposed in Nixon, "State of the Union Message to the Congress on Law Enforcement and Drug Abuse Prevention," March 14, 1973, APP, https://www.presidency.ucsb.edu/node/256237. For the planning, see Geoffrey Shepard Memo to John Ehrlichman, March 31, 1972, folder: Legislative Proposals, box 2, GCS-Nixon.

94. *NYT*, March 11, 1973; CRS, *Control of Drug Abuse: Summary of Principal Legislative Activity in the 93rd Congress*, Report 74-230 ED, December 3, 1974.

95. National Commission on Marihuana and Drug Abuse, *Drug Use in America: Problem in Perspective* (Washington: GPO, 1973), quotations 3, 27, 399, 398. On Shafer's complaint that the commission had been "cast aside in a cavalier manner," see Geoff Shepard to John D. Ehrlichman, March 16, 1973, folder 18, CMDA-Nixon. Budget in CRS, *Federal Programs Relating to the Control of Drug Abuse*; CRS, *Control of Drug Abuse*. Arrest data in FBI, *Uniform Crime Reports, 1973* (Washington: GPO, 1974), 34, 121–22.

Chapter 5. Impossible Criminals

1. *In re Dorian C. Jones*, 35 Cal. App. 3d 531 (1973); RPW [anonymized] to Birch Bayh, February 28, 1975, reproduced in "Marijuana Decriminalization," *Hearing before the Subcommittee to Investigate Juvenile Delinquency, Committee on the Judiciary*, U.S. Senate, May 14, 1975, (Washington: GPO, 1977), 239.

2. Statement of John N. Mitchell, February 3, 1970, "Drug Abuse Control Amendments—1970," *Hearings*, Part 1, 79–82; Statement of John E. Ingersoll, ibid., 82–89.

3. Harris Survey, "Alcohol Believed More Harmful than Marijuana," February 28, 1974, reproduced in "Marijuana Decriminalization," *Hearing*, Supplement 1, 1932–33; George H. Gallup, *The Gallup Poll: Public Opinion, 1972–1977*, vol. 2 (Wilmington: Scholarly Resources Inc., 1978), 1063–86.

4. Michael Aldrich (head of LeMar International) to Martin Garbus, November 28, 1969, folder 14, box 1091, ACLU-Princeton.

5. See HoSang, *Racial Propositions*, for an argument that "political whiteness" is a hegemonic, consensus ideology through which "even self-identified liberal groups played an active role in

reproducing its normative assumptions, constraining the boundaries of acceptable racial justice campaigns in the future" (22) and where "no large gulf existed between so-called racial liberalism and racial conservatism" (86).

6. Lester Grinspoon, *Marihuana Reconsidered* (Cambridge: Harvard University Press, 1971); John Kaplan, *Marijuana: The New Prohibition* (New York: Thomas Y. Crowell Co., 1970); Richard J. Bonnie and Charles H. Whitebread II, *The Marijuana Conviction: A History of Marijuana Prohibition in the United States* (Charlottesville: University of Virginia Press, 1974). Subsequent journalism and scholarship has reproduced this tendency to discuss marijuana and heroin as separate historical issues. See Anderson, *High in America*; Eric Schlosser, *Reefer Madness: Sex, Drugs, and Cheap Labor in the American Black Market* (Boston: Houghton Mifflin, 2003); Rudolph J. Gerber, *Legalizing Marijuana: Drug Policy Reform and Prohibition Politics* (Westport, CT: Praeger, 2004).

7. Prohibition of alcohol in the 1920s also represented a mass state intervention in the white middle-class recreational drug market but did not involve anywhere near the scale of arrests and compulsory rehabilitation programs.

8. NORML, "Statement in Support of the Need to Reform Marijuana Laws," 1971, NORML advertisement, "Pot Shot," 1971, folder 15, box 1092, ACLU-Princeton; NORML advertisement, "Pot Luck," 1971, folder 28, box 10, TCLU-UTA; NORML, *The Leaflet* (November 1971), *The Leaflet* (January–February 1972), folder: Marijuana: Repeal Prop., box 229, ACLUSC-UCLA; Patrick Anderson, "The Pot Lobby," *NYT Magazine*, January 21, 1973, 8–9, 65, 70–72, 86. Also see Anderson, *High in America*.

9. NORML, "Critique of the Report of the National Commission on Marihuana and Drug Abuse," n.d. [Spring 1972], Lester Grinspoon, "A Critique of 'Marihuana—A Signal of Misunderstanding,'" n.d. [Spring 1972], NORML Press Release, February 9, 1972, folder 15, box 1092, ACLU-Princeton; NORML pamphlet, n.d. [1972], reprinting George Chun, "Marijuana: A Realistic Approach," *California Medicine* 114, no. 4 (April 1971), NORML pamphlet, n.d. [1972], reprinting Norman Q. Brill, "The Marijuana Problem," *California Medicine* 114, no. 4 (April 1971), NORML, Text of PSA #2, n.d. [1972], folder 28, box 10, TCLU-UTA.

10. NORML Press Release, "Petition Filed with Department of Justice to Decriminalize Marijuana," May 19, 1972, folder 15, box 1092, ACLU-Princeton. On the Nixon administration's response, see Donald E. Miller to Egil Krogh, August 1972, folder: Goals and Objectives SAODAP, box 2, GCS-Nixon. The American Public Health Association cosigned the NORML reclassification petition.

11. Amorphia, Position Statement, n.d. [1971], folder 7, Aldrich, "Notes on Structuring Legal Sale of Marijuana to Minimize Abuse," August 15, 1971, folder 9, Blair Newman, "The Prospects and Potentials of Legalized Marijuana: Playboy Corporation vs. The People," 1972, folder 11, Aldrich to "Friends of Weed," March 18, 1972, folder 5, CMI Press Release, March 22, 1972, folder 14, Amorphia Press Release, June 19, 1972, folder 7, Newman, Amorphia Memo, October 5, 1972, folder 1, Amorphia, "Background Perspective," March 25, 1973, folder 7, box 21, JLS-UM; Anderson, "Pot Lobby," 70. On Amorphia's national agenda, see Aldrich, "New Morning," January 23, 1973, folder 1, box 21, JLS-UM.

12. Lauren Selden to ACLU State Affiliates, "Marijuana Repeal Campaign," December 1, 1971 (and enclosures), folder 10, ACLU, "Marijuana Repeal Campaign: Legislative Manual," January 1972, folder 14, box 1092, ACLU-Princeton; ACLU Pamphlet, *Marijuana*, n.d. [1972],

folder 28, box 10, TCLU-UTA. Also see *ACLU Annual Report, 7/71–6/72* (New York: ACLU, 1972), 25–26.

13. ACLU, "Position Paper on Criminal Sanctions for Illicit Drug Use," May 3, 1971, folder 14, NORML, "Statement in Support of the Need to Reform Marijuana Laws," 1971, folder 15, box 1092, ACLU-Princeton; Kaplan, *Marijuana: The New Prohibition*; Grinspoon, *Marihuana Reconsidered*, quotations 328, 339, 333, 371.

14. ACLU Pamphlet, *Marijuana*, n.d. [1972], folder 28, box 10, TCLU-UTA; Chun, "Marijuana: A Realistic Approach." Also see Grinspoon, *Marihuana Reconsidered*, 323–71 (quotation 359).

15. Drug Abuse Survey Project, *Dealing with Drug Abuse: A Report to the Ford Foundation* (New York: Praeger Publishers, 1972), esp. 3–38; Brecher, *Licit and Illicit Drugs*, esp. 521–39.

16. S. 3517 and Javits/Hughes remarks in *CR—Senate* (April 20, 1972), 13734–13735. Background in *CR—Senate* (January 24, 1970), 1008, (January 28, 1970), 1653. Also see Oval Office Conversation No. 500–17, May 18, 1971, with Richard Nixon and Art Linkletter, reproduced in Common Sense for Drug Policy Research Report, March 2002.

17. S. 746 and Javits/Hughes remarks in *CR—Senate* (February 2, 1973), 3156–3157; Jacob K. Javits, Press Release, October 29, 1971, folder 14, box 1092, ACLU-Princeton. On Prohibition of alcohol, see Lerner, *Dry Manhattan*.

18. BNDD, *Drug-Taking in Youth* (Washington: GPO, 1971); BNDD, "Comments on the First Report of the National Commission on Marihuana and Drug Abuse," n.d. [spring 1972], reproduced in "Marijuana Decriminalization," *Hearing*, Supplement 1, 1303–13; Donald E. Miller (BNDD chief counsel), "Marihuana: The Law and Its Enforcement," *Drug Abuse Law Review* 1 (1971), reproduced in ibid., 959–78; Testimony of Donald Miller/DEA, May 14, 1975, ibid., 10–41, 166 (quotation).

19. George H. Gallup, *The Gallup Poll: Public Opinion, 1972–1977*, vol. 1 (Wilmington: Scholarly Resources Inc., 1978), 22–25, 98–99, 372–73.

20. Bertram S. Brown, Statement before the Commission on Marihuana and Drug Abuse, May 17, 1971, folder 105849-001-0421, NCMDA-NA; Brown Testimony, June 13, 1973, "Evaluating the Federal Effort to Control Drug Abuse," *Hearings*, Part 3, 556–642; *WP*, May 18, 1971. White House response in Haldeman, *Haldeman Diaries*, 288, 291; Nixon quotation in Oval Office Conversation No. 500–17, May 18, 1971, with Richard Nixon and Art Linkletter, reproduced in Common Sense for Drug Policy Research Report, March 2002.

21. Testimony of Jerome H. Jaffe, "Marihuana Research and Legal Controls, 1974," *Hearings before the Subcommittee on Alcoholism and Narcotics, Committee on Labor and Public Welfare*, U.S. Senate, November 19, 1974 (Washington: GPO, 1974), 66–76; ABA, Marijuana Resolution, August 1973, and "Recommendation: Section of Individual Rights and Responsibilities, Report to the House of Delegates," May 12, 1973, reproduced in ibid., 194–209; *WP*, August 9, 1973; AMA in *NYT*, June 20–21, 1972. On NORML's role, see Keith Stroup, Memo: "ABA's Proposed Position on Marijuana," June 15, 1973, folder 20, box 1092, ACLU-Princeton.

22. FBI, *Uniform Crime Reports*, 1969–1974; "Marijuana Decriminalization," *Hearing*, Supplement 1, 1375.

23. "Marihuana Research and Legal Controls, 1974," *Hearings*, Javits quotation 2; Testimony of Robert L. DuPont, November 19, 1974, ibid., 5–66 (quotations 13, 28); Testimony of R. Keith Stroup, ibid., 100–129 (quotation 103).

24. NORML, "Statements on Position and Policy," December 5, 1975, reproduced in "Marijuana Decriminalization," *Hearing*, 80–81.

25. FBI, *Uniform Crime Reports*, 1969–1977.

26. The DEA cited data from the LAPD that 85 percent of marijuana arrests resulted from "incidental" stops and then presumed the similarity of enforcement patterns nationwide. See "Marijuana Decriminalization," *Hearing*, 160–63. Evidence presented later in this chapter strongly indicates that the LAPD statistics were exaggerated, perhaps because law enforcement did not want to reveal the funneling of federal LEAA funds in the war on drugs toward marijuana arrests rather than heroin markets, a conclusion also reached by Patricia G. Erickson, "Questioning the Conventional Wisdom: A Comment on the Marijuana Arrest Studies," *Journal of Drug Issues* 11, no. 4 (Fall 1981): 389–97. In another forum, congressional liberals accused Nixon's ODALE agency and local law enforcement funded by the LEAA of "making the easy arrests" and meeting quotas by taking the easy path of busting "users of marijuana rather than traffickers of hard drugs." See "Evaluating the Federal Effort to Control Drug Abuse," *Hearings*, Part 2, 259.

27. FBI, *Uniform Crime Reports, 1976* (Washington: GPO, 1977), 173. Southern California marijuana arrest data calculated from California State Office of Narcotics and Drug Abuse, *A First Report of the Impact of California's New Marijuana Law, SB 95* (Sacramento: State of California, 1977), NCJRS, https://www.ojp.gov/pdffiles1/Digitization/45532NCJRS.pdf, 21–24. On the intensification of stop-and-frisk policing and racial discrimination in urban crime control policies in the 1970s, see Hinton, *War on Poverty to the War on Crime.*

28. An analysis of marijuana possession arrests compared to estimated rates of marijuana use in the early 1970s illuminates other general patterns in law enforcement in two specific locations, Cook County, Illinois (including Chicago) and the metropolitan Washington, DC, area (including the Maryland and Virginia suburbs). In Cook County, Black residents were more than twice as likely as white residents to be arrested on marijuana charges, males five times as likely as females, blue-collar workers eight times as likely as white-collar workers, students more than twice as likely as white-collar workers, and the under-twenty-five age category five times as likely as over-twenty-five pot smokers. In metropolitan Washington, Black residents were slightly less likely than white residents to be arrested for marijuana possession, males almost five times as likely as females, blue-collar workers fifteen times as likely as white-collar workers, students twice as likely as white-collar workers, and the under-twenty-five category only somewhat more likely than over-twenty-five pot smokers. See Weldon T. Johnson, Robert E. Petersen, and L. Edward Wells, "Arrest Probabilities for Marijuana Users as Indicators of Selective Law Enforcement," *AJS* 83, no. 3 (November 1977): 681–99.

29. State drug laws in "The Legal Status of Marihuana," *Marihuana: A Signal of Misunderstanding: The Technical Papers*, vol. 1, 552–56. New Jersey in William T. Cahill, "Drug Abuse: Problem of the Decade!" April 27, 1970, loose materials, box 8, TM-OSA. Illinois in Richard B. Ogilvie, "Special Message on Drug Abuse," April 15, 1971, folder: Meeting with President, box 32, EK-Nixon. Florida in Governor's Task Force on Narcotics, Dangerous Drugs, and Alcohol Abuse, *Drug Abuse in Florida* (May 1970), folder: Drug Alert (3), box 4, TM-OSA; *WSJ*, June 15, 1971 (quotation).

30. "The Legal Status of Marihuana," *Marihuana: A Signal of Misunderstanding: The Technical Papers*, vol. 1, 548–68; *Marihuana: A Signal of Misunderstanding*, 172.

31. "Marihuana Research and Legal Controls, 1974," *Hearings*, 12; on local centers, see "Evaluating the Federal Effort to Control Drug Abuse," *Hearings*, Part 2, 468–500.

32. Joel M. Gora to Benson Wolman, August 23, 1971, folder 10, box 1092, ACLU-Princeton; NORML, *The Leaflet* (September–December 1976), reproduced in "Marijuana Decriminalization," *Hearing*, 1097–1108.

33. Keith Stroup, Memo: "Sample Legislation," June 15, 1973, folder 20, box 1092, ACLU-Princeton; *ACLU Annual Report, 7/71–6/72*, 25–26; Dallas case in *Rener v. Beto*, 447 F.2d 20 (1971). Litigants achieved success in a few state courts, without establishing a federal precedent. In 1971, the Illinois Supreme Court invalidated the mandatory-minimum ten-year provision for sale of any amount of marijuana in the state's Narcotic Drug Act; *People v. McCabe*, 49 Ill. 2d 338 (1971).

34. *People v. Lorentzen*, 387 Mich. 167 (1972); *People v. Sinclair*, 387 Mich. 91 (1972); *NORML v. Guste*, 380 F. Supp. 404 (E.D. La. 1974); William G. Milliken, "Special Message to the Legislature on Alcohol and Drug Abuse," March 4, 1971, folder: Drugs 1971–1973 (2), box 1222, WGM-UM; 1971 law in *Marihuana: A Signal of Misunderstanding: The Technical Papers*, vol. 1, 554, 561. Appellate documents in "Marijuana Decriminalization," *Hearing*, Supplement 1, 2253–2296.

35. *Trevino v. State of Texas*, 380 S.W.2d 118 (1963); TCLU, Memorandum to Board of Directors, July 28, 1969, folder 7, box 7, Griffin Smith Jr., "Marijuana and the Criminal Law," in *Marijuana in Texas: A Report to the Senate Interim Drug Study Committee*, March 1972, folder 27, box 10, TCLU-UTA. Population estimates from Campbell Gibson and Kay Jung, "Historical Census Statistics on Population Totals by Race, 1790 to 1990, and by Hispanic Origin, 1970 to 1990, for the United States, Regions, Divisions, and States" (Washington, U.S. Census Bureau, September 2002).

36. *DTH*, December 10–12, 1967 (three-part series on runaways), folder: Delinquency-1960s, *DTH*, August 3, 1968, folder: Drugs-LSD, *DTH*, April 8, 1969, March 3, 1969, *DMN*, March 21, 1970, folder: Drugs-Juveniles, Dallas Crime Commission, "Whose Court is the Ball in Now?" in *DMN*, December 20, 1968, *DTH*, December 15, 1968, *DMN*, April 18, 1969, folder: Greater Dallas Crime Commission, 1960–1969, VF-DPL.

37. *WP*, November 29, 1970; Betty Andujar to Mrs. Lovick Hightower, February 12, 1973, folder 11, box 17, BA-UTA.

38. Crawford C. Martin, Speech at Texas A&M, June 11, 1969, folder 1, box 11, *Austin American*, December 4, 1972, clipping in folder 28, box 10, TCLU-UTA.

39. Robert B. White, Harold A. Goolishian, and Ernest S. Barratt, "Adolescents and the Drug Problem," November 6, 1970, folder 12, box 17, BA-UTA.

40. J. Alan Holman, "The Extent of Marijuana Use in Texas," *Marijuana in Texas: A Report to the Senate Interim Drug Study Committee*, 1–19 (quotation 6), folder 27, box 1, George Beto, Statement to Senate Interim Drug Study Committee, April 10, 1972, folder 27, box 10, Senate Interim Drug Study Committee, *Final Report*, January 1973, folder 4, box 3, TCLU-UTA; *LAT*, April 14, 1972.

41. NORML, *The Leaflet* (February–March 1973); *Demolli v. State of Texas*, 478 S.W.2d 554 (1972); Frank Allan Demolli to Andujar, April 6, 1973, folder 10, box 17, State Program on Drug Abuse, "Texas Drug Scene," March 1973, folder 11, box 11, BA-UTA. For the background on the Demolli case, see Anderson, *High in America*, 111–17, 124–25. Extreme cases in *LAT*, April 14, 1972. Also see Richard Cowan editorial in *Fort Worth Star-Telegram*, February 5, 1973, folder 12,

box 17, BA-UTA; Cowan, "American Conservatives Should Revise Their Position on Marijuana," *National Review* (December 8, 1972), 1344–46.

42. Andujar to Mrs. Lovick Hightower, February 12, 1973, Andujar to Charles W. Ferguson, February 12, 1973, folder 11, box 17, BA-UTA. On the "concerned parent" trope, also see Mr. and Mrs. Frank Keith to Andujar, April 5, 1973, folder 10, box 17, ibid., and other letters in this folder.

43. Mrs. W. J. Woolridge to Andujar, May 10, 1973, Mimi Ross to Andujar, April 15, 1973, JG [anonymized] to Andujar, March 1973, Mrs. WHB [anonymized] to Andujar, April 12, 1973, B. D. Rutherford to Andujar, April 3, 1973, folder 10, box 17, BA-UTA.

44. Katie Allen to Andujar, March 22, 1973, Mrs. Lars Bergman to Andujar, April 2, 1973, L. Lee Lankford to Andujar, May 10, 1973, JWM [anonymized] to Andujar, February 21, 1973, folder 10, Mrs. W. H. Shires to Andujar, February 3, 1973, Thomas T. Barnhouse to Andujar, January 24, 1973, folder 11, box 17, BA-UTA.

45. Ronald G. Young to Chris Miller, April 1973, Miller to James D. Wilmeth, March 22, 1973, Carmen Glazner to Chris Miller, May 16, 1973, folder 6, box 10, CM-UTA; Patrick Stout to Andujar, April 4, 1973, folder 10, box 17, Rev. John D. Craig to Governor Dolph Briscoe and Andujar, April 27, 1973, folder 11, box 11, BA-UTA.

46. *Fort Worth Star-Telegram*, January 18, 1973, folder 12, box 17, Andujar to Kenneth Ryker, April 30, 1973, folder 10, box 17, BA-UTA.

47. Texas Controlled Substances Act, H.B. No. 447, 63rd Legislature (1973); National Governors' Conference Center for Policy Research and Analysis, *Marijuana: A Study of State Policies and Penalties* (Washington: GPO, 1977), 176–82; State Program on Drug Abuse, "Texas Drug Scene," February 1973, folder 12, box 17, BA-UTA. On the politics of the 1973 law, see Griffin Smith Jr., "How the New Drug Law Was Made," *Texas Monthly* (September 1973); Paul Danaceau, "Pot Luck in Texas: Changing a Marijuana Law" (Drug Abuse Council: September 1974), reproduced in "Marijuana Decriminalization," *Hearing*, Supplement 1, 1836–1908. In a case involving Frank Demolli, the Texas Court of Criminal Appeals overturned a provision of the 1973 law that would have allowed resentencing of marijuana prisoners under the new, more lenient penalty structure; *NYT*, September 6, October 11, 1973.

48. *Marijuana: A Study of State Policies and Penalties*, 176–185. Comparison with California trends calculated from California State Office of Narcotics and Drug Abuse, *A First Report of the Impact of California's New Marijuana Law, SB 95*, 21–24. On police and prosecutorial support for marijuana reform, also see Danaceau, "Pot Luck in Texas," 24, 63.

49. Dallas Police Department, *Drug Abuse Research Project: Final Evaluation*, October 15, 1974, NCJRS, https://www.ojp.gov/pdffiles1/Digitization/36493NCJRS.pdf. The Dallas Police Department did not evaluate Mexican Americans separately in the 1974 report, based on the small sample size, but stated that narcotics agents were "well aware of the Mexican American involvement in the Dallas drug scene." Statewide data in Texas Department of Community Affairs, *Drug Abuse in Texas: The Problem and the State's Response*, 1980, NCJRS, https://www.ojp.gov/pdffiles1/Digitization/69425NCJRS.pdf; Gibson and Jung, "Historical Census Statistics on Population Totals by Race, 1790 to 1990, and by Hispanic Origin, 1970 to 1990."

50. Kenneth D. Gaver, "Narcotics in Oregon: The Problem, Present Approaches, and Recommendations," June 19, 1968, Tom McCall to Melvin H. Larson, March 4, 1968, folder: Drugs (1968), box 26, Gaver, "Man and Marihuana (Cannabis)," *Alcohol and Drug Section* (1967), Mental Health Division, Oregon State Board of Control, folder: Drugs, box 4, TM-OSA.

51. Charles Davis (Oregon ACLU) to McCall, April 14, 1969, McCall to Davis, June 27, 1969, folder: Drugs (May–August), box 78, TM-OSA. Provisions of the 1969 law in Portland City Club Foundation, "Oregon Report on Legal Sanctions for Marijuana," April 14, 1972, reproduced in "Marijuana Decriminalization," *Hearing*, Supplement 1, 1727–1738.

52. John F. Sevy to McCall, April 30, 1967, ML [anonymized] to McCall, February 28, 1968, folder: Drugs, box 26, "A Statistical Study of Criminal Drug Litigation in the Circuit Court for Lane County, Oregon, 1966–1970," March 3, 1971, folder: Drugs, box 4, TM-OSA.

53. Wayne Buhlinger to McCall, February 2, 1971, McCall to Buhlinger, February 10, 1971, Buhlinger to McCall, March 9, 1971, McCall to Buhlinger, March 12, 1971, Buhlinger to McCall, June 17, 1971, folder: Drugs, box 4, TM-OSA.

54. Loren Sicks to McCall, July 9, 1970, folder: Drugs (1), box 3, Angela M. Schneider to McCall, August 27, 1969, folder: Drugs (September–December), box 78, Robert E. McIntyre to McCall, November 29, 1969, folder: Drug Alert (1), box 4, Mrs. LP [anonymized] to McCall, February 28, 1972, folder: Drugs, box 9, TM-OSA.

55. Help Kids, Inc., "Petition for Official Action on Drug Control," April 16, 1969, folder: Drugs (January–April), box 78, Anita E. Russel to McCall, October 23, 1968, folder 12, box 26, Harriet [unreadable] to McCall, November 15, 1969, folder: Drugs (September–December), box 78, Eric James Canon to McCall, November 11, 1969, McCall to Canon, February 18, 1970, Canon to McCall, March 18, 1970, Canon to McCall, July 1, 1970, Canon to McCall, July 2, 1970, folder: Drugs (4), box 3, TM-OSA.

56. McCall, "Statement on Attacking Drug Abuse in Oregon," December 5, 1969, folder: Drugs (September–December), box 78, TM-OSA. On "alienated youth," see Oregon Crime Control Coordinating Council, Minutes, August 23, 1968, folder: Crime Control Coordinating Council, box 26, ibid. On Operation Drug Alert and Kiwanis International, also see *WSJ*, October 22, 1970. Studies in Norman B. Henderson, "Summary of Marijuana Questionnaire for Five Schools in the Portland Area," n.d. [late 1960s], folder: Drugs (2), box 4, Cathy Bowen, "Reaction Formation," 1969, folder: Drugs (Sept-Dec), box 78, TM-OSA.

57. Alcohol and Drug Division, Oregon Mental Health Division, "Report of Statewide Drug Forum," November 14, 1969, loose materials, box 8, Marvin M. Young to McCall (youth quotation), November 21, 1969, folder: Drug Alert (1), box 4, TM-OSA.

58. McCall, "Dear Oregonian" letter, October 31, 1969, folder: Drugs (September–December), box 78, McCall, Speech at the Western Institute of Drug Problems, August 17, 1970, Kenneth D. Gaver, "What's Happening in Oregon Today," September 23, 1970, folder: Drug Alert (2), GE [anonymized] to McCall, March 11, 1970, folder: Drugs, box 4, McCall to Mrs. DL [anonymized], December 16, 1971, McCall to DW [anonymized], September 8, 1972, folder: Drugs (3), box 9, TM-OSA. Other heroin-related letters in folder: Drugs (3), box 3, folder: Drugs, box 9, TM-OSA.

59. McCall, "Statement before the National Commission on Marihuana and Drug Abuse," June 14, 1971, folder: Drugs (2), box 4, TM-OSA.

60. McCall, Opening Remarks to the Western Institute of Drug Problems, August 9, 1971, Edward M. Scott, "A Comparison between Two Groups of Parents," printed in *Drug Abuse—Now*, 2–7, 152–165, box 8 loose materials, TM-OSA. Also see Edward M. Scott, *The Adolescent Gap: Research Findings on Drug Using and Non-Drug Using Teens* (Charles C. Thomas, Springfield, IL: 1973).

61. MLH to McCall, June 29, 1971, Mrs. DGL to McCall, December 16, 1971, folder: Drugs (3), box 4, TC to McCall, November 12, 1971, folder: Drugs, box 9, TM-OSA [names anonymized].

62. MELO: *Marijuana Education for Legalization in Oregon*, Flier, 1972, Allan Hytowitz/MELO to McCall, June 21, 1972, folder: Drugs (2), box 9, TM-OSA; *Marihuana: A Signal of Misunderstanding: The Technical Papers*, vol. 1, 555.

63. Wayne Mayo to McCall, June 27, 1973, Anonymous to McCall, June 29, 1973, folder: Correspondence, A-W, January 1973–December 1973, box 8, TM-OSA.

64. *Marijuana: A Study of State Policies and Penalties*, 98–104; *LAT*, September 9, 1973; McCall to Anne Washer, August 9, 1973, folder: Correspondence, A-W, January 1973–December 1973, box 8, McCall to Mr. and Mrs. H. S. Thompson, December 18, 1973, folder: Drugs (1), box 8, TM-OSA. Opposition in Ruth Caldwell to McCall, July 22, 1973, Betty L. Tomminger to McCall, July 23, 1973, Rita S. Brehm to McCall, August 7, 1973, folder: Correspondence, A-W, January 1973–December 1973, box 8, Mr. and Mrs. Paul Beresford to McCall, October 3, 1973, folder: Drugs (1), box 8, TM-OSA. For the celebratory Oregon view, see Baum, *Smoke and Mirrors*, 76–91; Anderson, *High in America*, esp. 120–23.

65. Testimony of J. Pat Horton, November 19, 1974, "Marihuana Research and Legal Controls, 1974," *Hearings*, 129–34 (quotation 131), Horton Testimony, May 14, 1975, "Marijuana Decriminalization," *Hearing*, 96–99; *NYT*, December 18, 1973 (Portland quotation).

66. Drug Abuse Council, "Marijuana Survey: State of Oregon," December 15, 1974, folder: Drug Abuse, box 11, Stuart Eizenstat's Subject Files, CMCC-Carter; Drug Abuse Council, "Survey of Marijuana Use and Attitudes: State of Oregon," December 1, 1975, reproduced in "Marijuana Decriminalization," *Hearing*, 105–8; Stroup, "Legislation Action Memo," August 15, 1975, in ibid., 1389–1396; NORML, *Special Report: A Compilation of State Citation Laws for Marijuana Offenses*, August 15, 1975, in ibid., 1397–1403.

67. Office of the Governor, Press Release, February 23, 1970, folder: Narcotics Program, 1970, box GO 79, Legal Affairs Unit, Governor's Office Files, RRGP-Reagan.

68. NIDA, *Drug Users and the Criminal Justice System* (Washington: GPO, June 1977), 28–29; Bureau of Criminal Statistics, *Crime and Delinquency in California, 1972: Drug Arrests and Dispositions* (Sacramento: CDOJ, August 1973). Additional arrest data and cost estimates in California Senate Select Committee on Control of Marijuana, *Marijuana: Beyond Misunderstanding* (Sacramento, May 1974), 117, and Michael R. Aldrich, et. al, "Costs of California Marijuana Law Enforcement: A Preliminary Study," February 13, 1974, Appendix IV.A, ibid.

69. Bureau of Criminal Statistics, *Crime and Delinquency in California, 1972: Drug Arrests and Dispositions*; Aldrich, "Costs of California Marijuana Law Enforcement: A Preliminary Study," 1974.

70. Aldrich, "Costs of California Marijuana Law Enforcement: A Preliminary Study," 1974; T. Mike Walker and Geoffrey Link, "Lawyers for Legal Pot," n.d. [1972], folder: Marijuana Repeal Prop, box 229, ACLUSC-UCLA; San Francisco Committee on Crime, *Eleventh Report on Dangerous Drugs and Narcotics*, July 19, 1971, folder 10, box 1092, ACLU-Princeton.

71. LAPD, *Victimless Crimes: A Research Project* (Los Angeles: Los Angeles Police Department, May 1972); *LAT*, March 23, 1972. Data in Bureau of Criminal Statistics, *Crime and Delinquency in California, 1972: Drug Arrests and Dispositions*, 7, 11. On the LAPD as a right wing political institution, see Felker-Kantor, *Policing Los Angeles*.

72. Aldrich, "Dimensions of Change: Amorphia and How We Grew," January 1973, folder 9, Aldrich to "Friends of Weed," March 18, 1972, folder 5, CMI, "Yes on 19 or Bust!" 1972, "Proposition

19 Position Paper," 1972, folder 13, box 21, JLS-UM; *LAT*, February 12, 1971 (Newman quotation). Aldrich started the first college chapter of LeMar, the early marijuana legalization network, as a graduate student at SUNY–Buffalo in the late 1960s and ultimately became the head of LeMar International, which he merged into Amorphia after moving to California.

73. Amorphia to "Dear Friends," October 9, 1972, folder 6, CMI, Press Release, April 12, 1972, folder 14, Aldrich, "Confidential Report: Amorphia Participation in CMI," December 16, 1972, folder 1, box 21, JLS-UM. On the initial, abandoned petition, see California Alliance to Legalize Marijuana, "Initiative Measure to be Submitted Directly to the Electors," December 1971, folder: Marijuana Repeal Prop, box 229, ACLUSC-UCLA.

74. CMI, "Argument in Favor of Proposition 19," 1972, folder 13, box 21, CMI, "It's Time to Change the Law: Vote Yes 19," 1972, folder 17, CMI, "Marijuana Enforcement in California," 1972, folder 13, box 21, JLS-UM; Robert Ashford (director of Yes on 19), "Should Californians Decriminalize Marijuana Use?" *LAT*, November 2, 1972. Critique in HoSang, *Racial Propositions*. In a retrospective, Aldrich observed that Amorphia had compromised too much in supporting CMI's "straight middle-class education drive, . . . perhaps to its discredit." Aldrich, "Confidential Notes on Keith Stroup," January 22, 1973, folder 6, box 21, JLS-UM.

75. Amorphia, Press Release, June 19, 1972, folder 7, Aldrich, "Notes on Structuring Legal Sale of Marijuana to Minimize Abuse," August 15, 1971, folder 9, CMI, "Proposition 19 Speakers' Handbook," 1972, folder 16, Amorphia, "Jocks for Joynts," July 17, 1972, Mothers for Marijuana, "Vote Yes on Nineteen," 1972, folder 13, Blair Newman, "The Prospects and Potentials of Legalized Marijuana: Playboy Corporation vs. The People," 1972, folder 11, Amorphia Directors to New York Times Magazine, February 8, 1973, folder 3, Aldrich, "Confidential Report: Amorphia Participation in CMI," December 16, 1972, folder 1, box 21, JLS-UM; *LAT*, July 10, 1972. Stroup quoted in Anderson, "Pot Lobby," 8. There is no evidence that Playboy had a conspiracy or even a business plan to corporatize the marijuana market, as Amorphia alleged.

76. Gordon Brownell to Supporters of Marijuana Law Reform, December 7, 1972, folder 5, Citizens Opposing the Marijuana Initiative, Press Release, September 12, 1972, folder 14, box 21, JLS-UM; James E. Sills/Citizens Opposing the Marijuana Initiative, "No, for Medical, Social Good," *LAT*, November 2, 1972; NORML, *The Leaflet* (February–March 1973), folder 25, box 80, NDI-WSU. Results in *LAT*, November 8, 1972.

77. CMI, "Statement of Recommended Principles and Guidelines for the Next Initiative Campaign," n.d. [Spring 1973], folder 13, Blair Newman, "Program Planning Beyond the Election," September 22, 1972, folder 2, Amorphia, "The Cannabis Co-Op: A Non-Profit National Organization to End Marijuana Prohibition," January 23, 1973, folder 1, Gordon Brownell to John and Leni Sinclair, April 30, 1973, folder 3, *Amorphia Report* (October–November 1973), *Amorphia Report* (May 1974), folder 7, box 21, JLS-UM; *LAT*, May 8, 1973, June 16, 1974.

78. *LAT*, April 21, 28, August 3, December 1–2, 29–30, 1972, January 21, 1973, June 16, September 1, 28, 1974.

79. Bureau of Criminal Statistics, *Drug Diversion 1000 P.C. in California: 1974* (Sacramento: CDOJ, 1976), NCJRS, https://www.ojp.gov/pdffiles1/Digitization/37312NCJRS.pdf; *LAT*, January 1, 1973 (quotation by a San Fernando Valley probation officer).

80. California Senate Select Committee on Control of Marijuana, *Marijuana: Beyond Misunderstanding*, 1974, quotations 7, 5, 32, 9 (judge), 26–30 (UCLA study), 6. Aldrich and other Amorphia officers compiled the arrest and cost data for the Moscone report; see Aldrich, "Costs of California Marijuana Law Enforcement: A Preliminary Study," 1974.

81. Chief Daryl F. Gates, "In Defense of Undercover Policemen at School," December 23, 1974, folder 1, box 697, ACLU-Princeton; Morton Dorman to Kenneth Hahn, December 12, 1974, folder 6, box 235, series 6.4.2, KH-Huntington; ACLU of Southern California, "LAPD Raps Students Rights; Protection by ACLU," *Open Forum* (February 1975), 1–2, "No Police in Schools without Court Order," *Open Forum* (July 1976), 1–2, ESL-UCB; *LAT*, December 4–7, 9, 11, 13, 18, 20–21, 1974, May 29, June 22, 1975. Statewide arrest data in Bureau of Criminal Statistics, *Crime and Delinquency in California, 1976* (Sacramento: CDOJ, 1977), 20, 23.

82. ACLU of Southern California, "Police Entrapment in Drug Bust Case Ruled Illegal," *Open Forum* (July 1977), 1, ESL-UCB; *LAT*, December 31, 1974, May 30, June 22, 1975. "Hardcore Delinquents" series in *LAT*, December 3, 1974, January 26, May 18, 1975. In 1976, the state legislature passed a law transferring juveniles ages sixteen and seventeen to adult courts for the felony crimes of murder, arson, rape, armed robbery, kidnapping, aggravated assault, and some firearms violations. See Bureau of Criminal Statistics, *Crime and Delinquency in California, 1978: Part II: Dispositions, Correction, Probation* (Sacramento: CDOJ, 1979), 33–46.

83. George R. Moscone, Press Release, December 9, 1974, folder: Marijuana, box B-3–4, JB-USC; *LAT*, March 1, December 10, 1974.

84. Reagan in *LAT*, December 5, 1974; Deukmejian in *LAT*, March 20, 1975; Ed M. Davis to Edmund G. Brown Jr., April 10, 1975, folder: Marijuana, box B-3-4, JB-USC; *LAT*, March 13, March 22, May 1, 1975. On Oregon, see George R. Moscone, "Information Packet on Senate Bill 95," March 31, 1975, folder: Marijuana, box B-3–4, JB-USC; Drug Abuse Council, "Marijuana Survey: State of Oregon," 1974.

85. Drug Abuse Council, "Marijuana Survey: State of California," March 8, 1975, folder: Narcotics Enforcement, box E-26–7, JB-USC.

86. Orange County Petition to Governor Edmund G. Brown Jr., November 18, 1974, BSB to Brown, January 6, 1975, DD to Brown, April 29, 1975, SLP to Brown, February 3, 1975, CC to Brown, February 3, 1975, folder: Bureau of Narcotics Enforcement, box E-26–7, JB-USC [correspondents anonymized]. Davis quoted in *LAT*, April 29, 1975. On NORML, see Gordon Brownell to Don Solem, "Thoughts on Strategy," December 20, 1974, Brownell to Attorney General Evelle J. Younger, January 13, 1975, folder: Marijuana, box B-3–4, JB-USC.

87. DJM to Brown, March 11, 1975, RL and MB to Brown, n.d. [December 1974], SMD to Brown, April 21, 1975, GA to Brown, February 2, 1975, DH to Brown, December 19, 1974, SRH to Brown, May 1, 1975, and other letters in folder: Bureau of Narcotics Enforcement, box E-26–7, JB-USC [correspondents anonymized].

88. George R. Moscone, "Information Packet on Senate Bill 95," March 31, 1975, NORML, "Special Report: Senate Passes SB 95," April 4, 1975, folder: Marijuana, box B-3–4, JB-USC; *Marijuana: A Study of State Policies and Penalties*, 98–100, 140–46. Also see *LAT*, February 11, 1975 (Moscone quotation), July 10, 1975 (Brown quotation).

89. *LAT*, December 13, 23, 26, 1975; LAPD Administrative Narcotics Division, "Opiate Overdose Deaths and Addict Population," September 1976, F3717:1559, LACNDDC-CSA.

90. Bureau of Criminal Statistics, *Crime and Delinquency in California, 1976* (Sacramento: CDOJ, 1977); Bureau of Criminal Statistics, *Crime and Delinquency in California, 1978: Part II*; California State Office of Narcotics and Drug Abuse, *A First Report of the Impact of California's New Marijuana Law, SB 95*, quotation 1. It is impossible to identify the proportion of "incidental" marijuana arrests and those arising from deliberate drug-related investigations with anywhere

close to precision. This conclusion is in part an inference from the statistical data published by the California Department of Justice, the recognition that the LEAA provided tens of millions of dollars to local agencies for drug enforcement initiatives, and the archival evidence that law enforcement in Los Angeles County dedicated enormous resources to drug operations and particularly to marijuana investigations. Police also arrested many teenagers and young adults, especially racial minorities and visible white "hippies," through race-based and age-based stop-and-frisk tactics and profiling in traffic stops that the "incidental" claim includes. In a broader national assessment that includes Los Angeles County, Patricia G. Erickson makes the same argument that police data purporting to demonstrate that most marijuana arrests were "incidental" and "fortuitous" is disingenuous, in part because more than one-third occurred indoors and generally inside private homes, which almost always involved informants (arrestees who turned in others in exchange for dropped charges or plea bargains). See Erickson, "Questioning the Conventional Wisdom: A Comment on the Marijuana Arrest Studies," *Journal of Drug Issues* 11, no. 4 (Fall 1981): 389–97. On stop-and-frisk and racial profiling, also see Felker-Kantor, *Policing Los Angeles*.

91. Alan Robbins, Press Release, January 23, September 26, 1975, Evelle J. Younger, Press Release, January 23, 1975 (quotation), folder: SB 268, box SAR 1/1, AR-CSUN; *LAT*, September 27, 1975; California State Office of Narcotics and Drug Abuse, *A First Report of the Impact of California's New Marijuana Law, SB 95*, quotation 15. On Brown's law-and-order positioning, see Kohler-Hausmann, *Getting Tough*, 250–87.

92. NORML, "Special Report: Maine, Colorado, and California End Jail Penalties," July 21, 1975, reproduced in "Marijuana Decriminalization," *Hearing*, Supplement 1, 1384–1385; HEW/Field Research Corporation poll, conducted during November 1976, included in Stroup to NORML Special Mailing List, February 9, 1977, folder: Memoranda 9/3/76–2/8/77, box 20, PGB-Carter. Law enforcement officials in California disputed this study and insisted without evidence that decriminalization had led to significantly higher rates of marijuana use in the state; see California Attorney General Evelle J. Younger to Jimmy Carter, August 4, 1977, folder: Memoranda 8-1-77-8-31-77, box 22, PGB-Carter. On marijuana interdiction, see Bureau of Criminal Statistics, *Controlled Substances Seized in California, 1978* (Sacramento: CDOJ, 1979), NCJRS, https://www.ojp.gov/pdffiles1/Digitization/63161NCJRS.pdf.

93. Letters written in 1978 to Governor Jerry Brown, without names included here since many were from minors, in folder: Narcotics Enforcement, box F-31–7, JB-USC.

94. *Marijuana: A Study of State Policies and Penalties*, 83–111. On Ohio, see *Downey v. Perini*, 518 F.2d 1288 (1975); NORML, "Ohio Decriminalizes Marijuana," August 22, 1975, folder: Marijuana, box B-3–4, JB-USC.

95. Nelson A. Rockefeller, Press Release, July 27, 1970, Rockefeller, "Youthful Drug Abuse: Model Community Program," July 29, 1970, folder 3104, box 77, Rockefeller, "White Paper: An Action Plan to End Drug Abuse," October 1970, folder 3339, box 81, series 33, NAR-Rockefeller. On the forums as "first class public relations" with Rockefeller as the "star of the show," see Hugh Morrow to Rockefeller, July 30, 1970, August 10, 1970, folder 339, box 32, subseries 1, series 21, NAR-Rockefeller. On pressure from Black activists, see Citizens Organized Against Drug Abuse, "Proposal: An All-Out Effort to Eliminate the Sale and Use of Heroin in a Large Section of Harlem," April 10, 1970, folder 3872, box 140, subseries 11, series 34, Alton G. Marshall to Rockefeller, July 31, 1970, folder 3110, box 77, series 33, NAR-Rockefeller; *NYT*, August 5, 1970; Fortner, *Black Silent Majority*.

96. Hollis. S. Ingraham (Commissioner of Health) to Alton G. Marshall, July 20, 1970, Donald R. Lee (state NAACP chair) to Rockefeller, August 13, 1970, reel 76, subseries 3, series 37, NAR-Rockefeller.

97. Rockefeller, Speech to Governor's Meeting on Drug Abuse (Latham), July 30, 1970, Rockefeller, "Youthful Drug Abuse: Model Community Program," July 29, 1970, Rockefeller, Loose Notes on Albany Meeting, July 30, 1970, Joe Persico to Rockefeller, July 31, 1970, folder 3104, box 77, series 33, NAR-Rockefeller. Persico, the head speechwriter, told the governor, "I am truly sorry we missed the mark so badly on the first one."

98. Rockefeller, Speech to Governor's Meeting on Drug Abuse (Valhalla), July 31, 1970, folder 3104, box 77, series 33, Transcript of Syracuse Drug Abuse Forum, September 17, 1970 (quotations 17–18, 38), Transcript of Utica Drug Abuse Forum, August 26, 1970, folder 345, box 32, subseries 1, series 21, Lois J. Wilson to Rockefeller, July 30, 1970, reel 75, subseries 3, series 37, NAR-Rockefeller.

99. Rockefeller for Governor, Press Release, October 28, 1970, folder 339, box 32, subseries 1, series 21, Rockefeller, "White Paper: An Action Plan to End Drug Abuse," October 1970, folder 3339, box 81, series 33, Robert R. Douglass and Alton G. Marshall to Rockefeller, November 11, 1969, Douglass to Rockefeller, January 16, 1970, folder 283, box 27, subseries 4, series 10, NAR-Rockefeller; Lawyers Committee for Reform of Marijuana Laws, "Dear Colleague" Letter, December 17, 1971, folder 9, box 1092, ACLU-Princeton.

100. Rockefeller, "Message to the Legislature," February 9, 1970, Joe Persico to Robert R. Douglass, January 30, 1970, folder 283, box 27, subseries 4, series 10, Rockefeller to Chester R. Hardt, August 27, 1970, folder 340, box 32, subseries 1, series 21, NAR-Rockefeller. Temporary State Commission to Evaluate the Drug Laws, *Marihuana: Interim Report*, 1971, in folder 1626, box 72, subseries 3, series 25, NAR-Rockefeller (quotations 9, 46, 40, 66). On hardliners' strategy, see Robert R. Douglass, "Realignment of Some of our Dangerous Drug Laws," October 27, 1969, folder 1626, box 72, subseries 3, series 25, NAR-Rockefeller.

101. Temporary State Commission to Evaluate the Drug Laws, *Marihuana: Interim Report*, recommendations 10–12; Nassau County Probation Department, *Drug Abuse in Suburbia: Third Interim Report*, August 1971, reel 62, subseries 4, series 37, NAR-Rockefeller, 75–150. On the soft drugs promise, see Nelson A. Rockefeller, "Narcotics and Drug Abuse," September 24, 1970, folder 3339, box 81, series 33, NAR-Rockefeller.

102. Suffolk County Mental Health Board to Henry Brill (NACC), October 30, 1970, CG [anonymized], Letter to *Catskill Daily Mail*, October 3, 1970, forwarded to Rockefeller, October 14, 1970, reel 75, subseries 3, series 37, NAR-Rockefeller. Because of the pre-1972 classification of marijuana as a narcotic, court-ordered addiction examinations were mandatory under New York's civil commitment law, which one judge from Nassau County labeled a "gross waste of time and money" involving "thousands of futile examinations." See Francis J. Donavan to Rockefeller, February 18, 1970, reel 76, subseries 3, series 37, NAR-Rockefeller.

103. Temporary State Commission to Evaluate the Drug Laws, *Marihuana: Interim Report*, 9–10, 67–93; *Marijuana: A Study of State Policies and Penalties*, 98; Nassau County Probation Department, *Drug Abuse in Suburbia: Final Report*, August 1978, 28. Letters summarized here, from 1970–1971, can be found on reels 75–76, subseries 3, series 37, NAR-Rockefeller. Quotation from Yvonne Jones to Rockefeller, August 21, 1970, folder 339, box 32, subseries 1, series 21, NAR-Rockefeller.

104. Ramon Diaz (East Harlem Protestant Parish) to Rockefeller, November 11, 1970, Diaz to T. N. Hurd, February 26, 1971, Andrew J. Di Paola (Glen Cove Mayor) to Rockefeller, January 26, 1971, Sadie E. Scott (Five Towns Community Center) to Rockefeller, March 10, 1971, reel 61, subseries 4, series 37, NAR-Rockefeller.

105. Lawyers Committee for Reform of Marijuana Laws, "Dear Colleague" Letter, December 17, 1971, folder 9, box 1092, ACLU-Princeton; David Michaels, reform coalition leader, quoted in Temporary State Commission to Evaluate the Drug Laws, *Marihuana: Interim Report*, 91; Carl D. Chambers/NACC, *An Assessment of Drug Use in the General Population: Special Report No. 1: Drug Use in New York State*, May 1971, Rockefeller, Press Release, June 24, 1971, folder 338, box 31, subseries 1, series 21, NAR-Rockefeller. Milton Luger, the director of the NACC, did inform Governor Rockefeller that the political discussion of heroin addiction revolved around "monstrous misconceptions." See Luger to Rockefeller, June 21, 1971, ibid.

106. Rockefeller, "Message to the Legislature," January 3, 1973, 16–24, Rockefeller, "Special Message-Drugs," January 10, 1973, Rockefeller, "Testimony at Joint Hearing before Senate and Assembly Code Committees," January 30, 1973, folder 1837, box 89, series 25, NAR-Rockefeller; Paul Good, "My Son—Perhaps Yours," *NYT*, January 29, 1973, 29.

107. Rockefeller Transcript, "News Conference with the Reverend Oberia D. Dempsey, the Reverend Earl B. Moore, Mr. Glester Hinds, Dr. George Weldon Murray, Dr. Robert William Baird," January 22, 1973, folder 1837, box 89, series 25, NAR-Rockefeller. On the debate, see Fortner, *Black Silent Majority*; Donna Murch, "Who's to Blame for Mass Incarceration?" *Boston Review* (October 6, 2015); Fortner, "The Historical Method and the Noble Lie," *Boston Review* (October 23, 2015). By "no question," I mean that the Rockefeller archives and the newspaper records clearly reveal that the most organized and visible support for tough punishment for narcotics "pushers" and addict-criminals in the years before and immediately after the governor made his proposal came from Harlem and other nonwhite areas of New York City. I read all the letters sent to the governor that are available in the Rockefeller Center Archives, on the multiple "crime" and "narcotics" microform reels, and expression of pressure from presumably white correspondents for punitive laws against heroin pushers was sporadic and minimal in the suburbs and somewhat more evident from working-class white residents of urban neighborhoods. The vocal demands of nonwhite antidrug activists (and desperate African American and Puerto Rican parents who wrote the governor) does not mean that most Black residents of New York City took a conservative turn in the early 1970s or did not also support structural and social welfare solutions for crime and drug addiction, but rather that they dealt with the reality of their immediate lives and neighborhoods. None of this should be unexpected, given that relatively few white suburban youth used heroin and that the open-air markets that served the entire metropolitan region were based in Harlem and other nonwhite urban neighborhoods. These markets flourished, despite the state and national wars on drugs, not only because of the demonstrated historical impossibility of eradicating the underground circulation of prohibited substances through supply-side controls, but also as a consequence of the extensive corruption of the NYPD and especially its narcotics units, a reality underappreciated by all sides of the scholarly debate about the Rockefeller Drug Laws. On extensive police corruption in New York City and the spatial concentration of heroin markets in nonwhite areas, see Schneider, *Smack*.

108. Rockefeller, "Questions and Answers Transcript following Testimony at Joint Hearings," January 30, 1973 (quotations 63, 65, 68), NACC, "The Cost of Addict Crime in New York

State," included in Rockefeller, "Special Message—Drugs," January 10, 1973, folder 1837, box 89, series 25, NAR-Rockefeller. Although this document lists the NACC as the author, it seems probable from the archival context that Rockefeller's political advisors selectively compiled the data for inclusion with the bill sent to the legislature and then attributed the commission for credibility. For contradictory, much better documented internal data, see Carl D. Chambers/NACC, *An Assessment of Drug Use in the General Population: Special Report No. 1: Drug Use in New York State*, May 1971, folder 338, box 31, subseries 1, series 21, NAR-Rockefeller. Also see the conclusion that "the high percentage of violent crimes (street crimes) frequently attributed to narcotics addicts is actually unsupported by reliable evidence," in NACC, "Crimes Committed by Drug Users," n.d. [1972], folder 341, box 32, ibid. The Drug Abuse Council pointed out the discrepancy with the data in the FBI *Uniform Crime Reports* and estimated that 30 to 40 percent of heroin purchases involved money obtained through crimes against property or persons. See Drug Abuse Council, *A Perspective on "Get Tough" Drug Laws*, 1.

109. Rockefeller, "Drug Statement" (on bill signing), May 8, 1973, folder 1838, Rockefeller, "Questions and Answers" Transcript, January 30, 1973, Rockefeller, Press Release: "Drug Modifications," April 13, 1973, folder 1837, box 89, series 25, Temporary State Commission to Evaluate the Drug Laws, Memorandum, n.d. [early 1973], folder 845, box 70, subseries 4, series 10, NAR-Rockefeller. On the hashish/marijuana shift, also see Aldrich, Memo on Rockefeller Laws, January 10, 1973, folder 5, David Michaels, "Governor Rockefeller's New New York Drug Law—A Commentary," *Amorphia Report* (October–November 1973), 1, 3, folder 7, box 21, JLS-UM; *NYT*, January 9, 15, 1973.

110. For the discussion about suburban housewives and college LSD users, see Rockefeller, "Questions and Answers" Transcript, January 30, 1973, esp. 1–4, 26–32, folder 1837, box 89, series 25, "Supplemental Questions (and Possible Answers) Posed by Assemblyman DiCarlo," n.d. [January 1973], folder 846, box 70, subseries 4, series 10, "Statement by Mayor John V. Lindsay," January 9, 1973, Lindsay Administration, "Governor's Annual Message Proposals on Narcotics Trafficking," January 9, 1973, folder 341, box 32, subseries 1, series 21, NAR-Rockefeller. On pressure from suburban legislators, also see M. Wilson to Hugh Morrow, February 16, 1973, folder 354, box 34, subseries 1, series 21, NAR-Rockefeller.

111. New York State Drug Abuse Program, "Schedule of Drug Offenses and Penalties under New York State Penal Law (Article 220)," folder 346, box 33, subseries 1, series 21, NAR-Rockefeller; New York Civil Liberties Union, Legislative Memorandum #23, March 7, 1973, folder 23, box 1092, ACLU-Princeton; David Michaels, "Governor Rockefeller's New New York Drug Law—A Commentary." Advertisements containing the penalty schedule ran in the *New York Times*, *New York Amsterdam News*, and other newspapers; see folder 348, box 33, subseries 1, series 21, NAR-Rockefeller.

112. Senator Jacob K. Javits, Press Release, January 7, 1973, folder 341, box 32, subseries 1, series 21, NAR-Rockefeller. Also see Julilly Kohler-Hausmann, "'The Attila the Hun Law': New York's Rockefeller Drug Laws and the Making of a Punitive State," *Journal of Social History* 44, no. 1 (Fall 2010): 71–95 (quotation 73); Kohler-Hausmann, *Getting Tough*, 29–120.

113. Harvard Hollenberg (Temporary State Commission to Evaluate the Drug Laws) to William C. Dumino, January 5, 1973, folder 846, Temporary State Commission to Evaluate the Drug Laws, Memorandum, n.d. [early 1973], John F. O'Mara (President of State District Attorneys Association), Testimony before the Senate and Assembly Code Committee, February 6,

1973, folder 845, box 70, subseries 4, series 10, NAR-Rockefeller; NYPD officer quoted in *NYT*, May 13, 1973.

114. New York State Drug Abuse Commission, "New York State Drug Abuse Program," n.d. [1973], folder 346, Matthew Mansfield, "Drug Abuse Program—General Directions and Organization," June 21, 1973, folder 347, Wells, Rich, Greene, Inc., "Presentation for N.Y. State Drug Abuse Program," January 4, 1974, Hugh Morrow to Rockefeller, May 18, 1973, Morrow to Rockefeller, October 5, 1973, Joe Persico to Morrow, August 2, 1974, folder 346, box 33, subseries 1, series 21, NAR-Rockefeller.

115. Joint Committee on New York Drug Law Evaluation, "Final Report," June 1977, republished as *The Nation's Toughest Drug Law: Evaluating the New York Experience* (Washington: Department of Justice, March 1978). The Joint Committee consisted of the Drug Abuse Council and the Bar Association of New York City. Also see Mason B. Williams, "How the Rockefeller Laws Hit the Streets: Drug Policing and the Politics of State Competence in New York City, 1973–1989," *Modern American History* 4, no. 1 (March 2021): 67–90.

116. Helena Gaviola to Rockefeller, January 26, 1973, Alan Berliner to Rockefeller, November 18, 1973, Bruce Burroughs to Rockefeller, November 15, 1973, Marilyn L. Monive to Rockefeller, November 1973, Patrick Weirs to Rockefeller, August 31, 1973, Mary-Jo Briguglio to Rockefeller, August 6, 1973, Russell Boris to Rockefeller, July 31, 1973, reel 61, subseries 4, series 37, NAR-Rockefeller.

117. Nassau County Probation Department, *Drug Abuse in Suburbia: Final Report*, August 1978, quotations 43, 103.

118. *NYT*, January 29, 1975, January 8, November 15, 1976, February 3, 1977; *NYAN*, January 17, 1976, February 12, 1977; *New York Post*, July 14, 1975, compiled in "Marijuana Decriminalization," *Hearing*, Supplement 1, 1703–4. On state data, also see *NYT*, February 3, 1977.

119. *NYT*, July 28–30, 1977. Carey quoted in NORML, Press Release, July 1, 1977, folder: Memoranda 7/14/77–7/31/77, box 22, PGB-Carter.

120. Drug Abuse Council, *A Perspective on "Get Tough" Drug Laws*; also see Joint Committee on New York Drug Law Evaluation, *Nation's Toughest Drug Law*.

121. Ari Rosmarin, "The Phantom Defense: The Unavailability of the Entrapment Defense in New York City's 'Plain View' Marijuana Arrests," *Journal of Law and Policy* 21, no. 1 (2012): 189–242; Ryan S. King and Marc Mauer, "The War on Marijuana: The Transformation of the War on Drugs in the 1990s," *Harm Reduction Journal* 3, no. 6 (2006); Harry G. Levine and Deborah Peterson Small, *Marijuana Arrest Crusade: Racial Bias and Police Policy in New York City, 1997–2007* (New York: New York Civil Liberties Union, April 2008).

Chapter 6. Parent Power

1. *An American Family* (New York: Educational Broadcasting System, 1973). Coverage in "An American Family," *Newsweek*, January 15, 1973, 68; "The Broken Family: Divorce U.S. Style," *Newsweek*, March 12, 1973, 47–57; Anne Roiphe, "Things Are Keen but Could Be Keener," *NYT Magazine*, February 18, 1973, 8–9, 43–53; Abigail McCarthy, "An American Family and the Family of Man," *Atlantic Monthly*, July 1973, 72–76; *LAT*, January 7, 1973 ("weed-smoking bash" quotation). Also see Jeffrey Ruoff, *An American Family: A Televised Life* (Minneapolis: University of Minnesota Press, 2002).

2. Lloyd D. Johnston, Jerald G. Bachman, and Patrick M. O'Malley, *Highlights from Drugs and the Class of '78: Behaviors, Attitudes, and Recent National Trends* (Rockville, MD: NIDA, 1979), 6, 10, 15–16, 34; Johnston, "Characteristics of the Daily Marijuana User," in *Treating the Marijuana Dependent Person* (New York: American Council on Marijuana, 1981), 12–15; NIDA, *Marijuana Research Findings: 1976* (Washington: GPO, 1977), 5–9. The data on twelve- and thirteen-year-olds came from the widely publicized, comprehensive survey of adolescent drug use in San Mateo County Department of Public Health and Welfare, *Summary Report: Surveys of Student Drug Use, San Mateo County, California*, March 1977.

3. Marsha Keith Schuchard to Jimmy and Rosalynn Carter, February 28, 1978, folder 1/20/77–8/31/78, box HE-12, WHCF-JC.

4. "Special Meeting to Organize a National Federation," April 3, 1980, folder: PRIDE (5–6), OA 16999, series II, DIM-Reagan. On the concept of "moral entrepreneurs," see Becker, *Outsiders*. For an application of the concept to the DEA and the news media in the 1970s and 1980s, see Jenkins, *Synthetic Panics*, esp. 11–23 and 183–97. Many accounts of the role of the "parents' movement" in the war on drugs have been written by journalists and/or marijuana legalization advocates and generally mischaracterize (and sometimes ridicule) Schuchard and other activists as political conservatives and religious zealots. See Schlosser, *Reefer Madness*, 23–24; Arnold S. Trebach, *The Great Drug War: And Radical Proposals That Could Make America Safe Again* (New York: Macmillan, 1987), esp. 117–46, which classifies the NFP as a movement of "hatred" and "theological dogma." For more balanced snapshots in journalistic histories of the war on drugs, see Baum, *Smoke and Mirrors*, 88–90, 99–103, 118–21; Anderson, *High in America*, 300–311; Massing, *The Fix*, 143–54. A number of ideological conservatives and Republican activists did join the NFP in the early-to-mid 1980s, as discussed in chapter 7, when the confederation expanded exponentially across the nation, but this did not significantly alter its nonpartisan agenda and bipartisan support among Washington politicians. Tom Adams, the director of NIDA's Pyramid Project (which provided federal support for grassroots drug prevention organizations) compared the NFP to Mothers Against Drunk Driving, Lois Gibbs's anti–toxic waste crusade, and other parent-led citizens' movements in *Grass Roots: How Ordinary People Are Changing America* (New York: Citadel Press, 1991). On the victims' rights movement and the broader politics of protecting vulnerable children in the 1970s, see Jenkins, *Decade of Nightmares*. Jenkins evaluates the antimarijuana "parents' movement" as mainstream "populist activism" rather than right-wing conservatism; see 126–29, 204 (quotation).

5. "Opening Comments by Keith Schuchard," International PRIDE Conference on Youth and Drug Abuse, April 9, 1983, Robert DuPont Speech, April 9, 1983, folder: PRIDE–International Conference, OA 13748, series III, CET-Reagan; Transcript of PBS interview with Robert DuPont, 2000, http://www.pbs.org/wgbh/pages/frontline/shows/drugs/interviews/dupont.html.

6. Hillary Rodham Clinton, *It Takes a Village: And Other Lessons Children Teach Us* (New York: Simon and Schuster, 1996). On "political whiteness," see HoSang, *Racial Propositions*. On the mainstream "crisis of the American family" in the 1970s, see Zaretsky, *No Direction Home*; Self, *All in the Family*; Renfro, *Stranger Danger*; Chappell, *War on Welfare*, esp. 159–68. Most of these books and many others, excepting Chappell, adopt the "right turn" or "conservative triumph" narrative as the endpoint of the 1970s-era family crisis. For a critique, see Lassiter, "Inventing Family Values," *Rightward Bound*. My analysis here differs in arguing that the causes, participants,

and policy consequences of the "family crisis" in general, and the antimarijuana movement in particular, extend across the political spectrum and fit into a persisting framework of white middle-class victimization and privilege more than a liberal-conservative, Republican-Democrat, or right-left paradigm. On the persistence of crisis rhetoric surrounding the mythical "American family," see Stephanie Coontz, *The Way We Never Were: American Families and the Nostalgia Trap* (New York: Basic Books, 1992).

7. "Parent Power," interview with Marsha Manatt (Marsha Schuchard), n.d., "Final Comment by Keith Schuchard," International PRIDE Conference on Youth and Drug Abuse, April 9, 1983, folder: PRIDE–International Conference, OA 13748, series III, CET-Reagan.

8. I appreciate many of the insights of the "moral panic" literature, and pay close attention to the political and cultural construction of crises and epidemics, but am emphasizing a different causal sequence that focuses on social movements, interest group politics, and state formation. The ability of a highly organized group of activists to convince government bureaucrats and politicians to adopt specific policies or sound general alarms often operates through discourses of moral panic, usually accompanied by similar tropes and hype in media coverage, but this does not mean that anywhere near a majority of the people these advocates claim to be representing are participants in a moral panic on the ground. For pioneering work on moral panics, see Cohen, *Folk Devils and Moral Panics*; Hall, *Policing the Crisis*. The most sophisticated historical application of the sociological literature on moral panic to this period of American history is Jenkins, *Moral Panic*; also see Jenkins, *Decade of Nightmares*; Jenkins, *Synthetic Panics*.

9. Jerald G. Bachman, Lloyd D. Johnston, and Patrick M. O'Malley, "Smoking, Drinking, and Drug Use among American High School Students: Correlates and Trends, 1975–1979," *AJPH* 71, no. 1 (January 1981): 59–69. Additional data on youth attitudes about drugs, discussed below, can be found in the "Monitoring the Future" surveys funded by NIDA and published annually starting in 1978.

10. Sue Rusche quoted/paraphrased in Massing, *The Fix*, 310. Arrest data is from the FBI's *Uniform Crime Reports*, as recounted below. The FBI did not report national totals of marijuana arrests by race, but general trends in drug arrests and studies of specific states and localities revealed the increasing focus of marijuana arrests on African Americans in particular and non-white urban youth in general, especially by the early-to-mid 1980s, as part of broken-windows and stop-and-frisk policing. See Jamie Fellner, "Race, Drugs, and Law Enforcement in the United States," *Stanford Law and Policy Review* 20, no. 2 (2009): 257–92; Human Rights Watch, *Decades of Disparity: Drug Arrests and Race in the United States*, March 2009, https://www.hrw.org/sites/default/files/reports/us0309web_1.pdf. On the self-fulfilling perception of drug markets, Black criminality, and racially targeted policing from the 1960s through the 1980s, see Hinton, *War on Poverty to the War on Crime*.

11. HEW, *Marihuana and Health: Second Annual Report to Congress* (Washington: GPO: May 1972), quotation 132; Testimony of Robert L. DuPont, November 19, 1974, "Marihuana Research and Legal Controls, 1974," *Hearings*, 5–42; "Marihuana-Hashish Epidemic and its Impact on United States Security," *Hearings before the Subcommittee to Investigate the Administration of the Internal Security Act, Committee on the Judiciary*, U.S. Senate, May 9, 16–17, 20–21, June 13, 1974 (Washington: GPO, 1974), quotations vi, xi, xii.

12. Testimony of Keith Stroup, November 20, 1974, "Marihuana Research and Legal Controls, 1974," *Hearings*, 100–129 (quotation 101); NORML, "Marijuana Study Challenged,"

March 8, 1974, reproduced in ibid., 109–20; Testimony of Thomas E. Bryant (Drug Abuse Council), November 19, 1974, ibid., 76–91. Also see Drug Abuse Survey Project, *Dealing with Drug Abuse*, 32–33.

13. S. 1450, "Marijuana Control Act of 1975," reproduced in "Marijuana Decriminalization," *Hearing*, lxxxiii–lxxxv; Bayh and Hart quotations in ibid., 2, 6–7; Testimony of Keith Stroup, May 14, 1975, ibid., 49–96; NORML, "Questions and Answers about Marijuana Decriminalization," March 27, 1975, reproduced in "Marijuana Decriminalization," *Hearing*, Supplement 1, 1367–1379; NORML, "Legislative Action Memo," August 15, 1975, ibid., 1389–1396; Harris Survey, "Alcohol Believed More Harmful than Marijuana," February 28, 1974, ibid., 1932–1933. The decriminalization bill secured only three additional co-sponsors in the Senate (Alan Cranston, D-CA; Gaylord Nelson, D-WI; Edward Brooke, R-MA).

14. Domestic Council Drug Abuse Task Force, "White Paper on Drug Abuse," 1975, quotations 35, 3, 2, 25, 27, 33. The "White Paper" did observe that chronic narcotics addicts represented "only a small percentage of those who have ever used heroin," 19. Also see Musto and Korsmeyer, *Quest for Drug Control*, 140–81 (drug abuse data on 175).

15. Gerald Ford, "Special Message to the Congress on Drug Abuse," April 27, 1976, APP, https://www.presidency.ucsb.edu/node/257419; Charles B. Rangel (cosigned by 84 House members) to Gerald Ford, November 18, 1975, folder 1975/12/22-Drug Abuse Meeting, box 54, JMC-Ford; Musto and Korsmeyer, *Quest for Drug Control*, 170–71. On Bayh, see "Marijuana Decriminalization," *Hearing*, esp. 173–97.

16. Richard Parsons, Memo: "Marihuana" (Ford statement), February 13, 1976, folder: Drug Abuse–Trip to Miami, box 11, White House "Drug Abuse Meeting" Files, April 7, 1976, folder: Drug Abuse–Meeting with the President, box 11, JMC-Ford. DEA and interdiction debate in "The Global Connection: Heroin Entrepreneurs," volume 1, *Hearings before the Subcommittee to Investigate Juvenile Delinquency, Committee on the Judiciary*, U.S. Senate, July 28, August 5, 1976 (Washington: GPO, 1976), Bensinger quotation 43, Bayh quotation 1, DuPont quotations 273, 271. On NORML, see Robert L. DuPont, "Changing Perspectives on the Marihuana Controversy," November 15, 1974, reproduced in "Marihuana Research and Legal Controls, 1974," *Hearings*, 43–65; NORML, "Statements on Position and Policy," December 5, 1975, reproduced in "Marijuana Decriminalization," *Hearing*, 80–81.

17. "Information on President's Position on Marijuana," March 7, 1977, folder: Drug Abuse, box 188, SEE-Carter (includes compilation of news articles, especially Associate Press wire story of September 3, 1976); "Carter Endorses Decriminalization," *HT*, May 1976, reproduced in "Marijuana Decriminalization," *Hearing*, Supplement 1, 1463–66; Larry A. Schott, "Election '76: Carter and Ford on Marijuana," *The Leaflet* (September–December 1976), ibid., 1097–1108; Peter G. Bourne to Hamilton Jordan, February 2, 1977, folder: Memoranda 2/1/77–2/28/77, box 20, PGB-Carter; *NYT*, September 8, 1974, August 11, 1975, March 20, April 30, 1976; *WP*, May 3, 1976. Carter also confirmed that the U.S. Navy discharged his son Jack in 1970 for smoking marijuana. See *NYT*, January 19, 1977.

18. Bourne, Memorandum to the President: "Monthly Drug Report #1," March 3, 1977, folder: ODAP, box 28, Bourne, Speech to U.S. Regional Narcotics Conference, April 14, 1977, folder: Speeches by Dr. Bourne, box 43, National Association of State Drug Abuse Program Coordinators, *Special Report on Peter Bourne and ODAP*, February 15, 1977, folder: NASDAPC, box 41, Bourne to Stroup, February 11, 1978, folder: Correspondence 2/1/78–2/28/78, box 9,

PGB-Carter; Bourne, "Statement on Drug Abuse," March 22, 1974, Bourne, "It Is Time to Reexamine our National Narcotics Policy," May 16, 1975, folder: Drug Abuse, box 11, Stuart Eizenstat's Subject Files, CMCC-Carter; *WP*, December 12, 1976, May 14, 1977.

19. Bourne to Jimmy Carter, February 26, 1977, Bourne, Memorandum to the President: "Monthly Drug Report #2," April 7, 1977, folder: ODAP, box 28, Bourne Testimony to House Select Committee on Narcotics Abuse and Control, March 14, 1977, folder: Congressional Hearings on Decriminalization of Marijuana, box 32, PGB-Carter; Joe Onek to Stu Eizenstat, "Marijuana Decriminalization," March 5, 1977, folder: Drug Abuse (Narcotic), box 188, SEE-Carter.

20. Bourne, Memorandum to the President: "Drug Policy Message," April 25, 1977, Memorandum to the President: "Monthly Drug Report #6," September 12, 1977, folder: OPAP, box 28, PGB-Carter; Stu Eizenstat to Carter, Message on Drug Abuse, July 7, 1977, folder: ODAP Drug Policy Message (4), box 247, SEE-Carter.

21. Draft Message on Drug Abuse (with Carter's handwritten comments), folder: Drug Abuse (Narcotic), box 188, Eizenstat to Carter, Message on Drug Abuse, July 7, 1977, Eizenstat and Bourne to Carter, Presidential Message on Drug Abuse, July 29, 1977, folder: ODAP Drug Policy Message (4), box 247, SEE-Carter.

22. "Remarks of the President on the President's Message on Drug Abuse," August 2, 1977, folder: Drugs, box 16, AMG-Carter; Carter, "President's Message on Drug Abuse," August 2, 1977, folder: ODAP Drug Policy Message (3), box 247, SEE-Carter.

23. NIDA, *Marijuana Research Findings: 1976*, 4–6; Gallup, *The Gallup Poll: Public Opinion, 1972–1977*, Volume 2, 1063–1086.

24. Lassiter, "Inventing Family Values"; Zaretsky, *No Direction Home*; Jenkins, *Decade of Nightmares*; Self, *All in the Family*; Coontz, *Way We Never Were*.

25. "The American Family: Future Uncertain," *Time*, December 28, 1970, 34–39; "The Broken Family: Divorce U.S. Style," *Newsweek*, March 12, 1973, 47–57; Christopher Lasch, *The Culture of Narcissism: American Life in an Age of Diminishing Expectations* (New York: W. W. Norton, 1979); White House Conference on Families, *Listening to America's Families: Action for the 80's* (Washington: GPO, 1980).

26. Urie Bronfenbrenner, "The Calamitous Decline of the American Family," *WP*, January 2, 1977, C1, C3; Kenneth Keniston, "Children as Victims: The Emptying Family," *NYT*, February 18, 1976, 31; Keniston, "Heads and Seekers."

27. Renfro, *Stranger Danger* ("endangered childhood" quotation at 7); Jenkins, *Moral Panic*, 118–63; Jenkins, *Decade of Nightmares*, esp. 108–51. On SLAM, see *LAT*, April 3, July 24, 1980, December 3, 1981, April 21, September 23, 1982. On MADD, see chapter 7.

28. Gordon Brownell (NORML) to Peter Bourne, September 6, 1977, folder: Correspondence 7/7/77–11/1/77, box 6, NORML Packet from Stroup to Midge Castanza (Assistant to the President), July 15, 1977, folder: Memoranda 7/14/77–7/31/77, box 22, PGB-Carter; Testimony of Keith Stroup, "Decriminalization of Marihuana," *Hearings before the Select Committee on Narcotics Abuse and Control*, House of Representatives, March 15, 1977 (Washington: GPO, 1977), 333–63; Eileen Brennan, "If Lobbyist Keith Stroup Has His Way, Lighting Up a Joint Will No Longer Be a Crime," *People*, June 19, 1978, 40–42.

29. Joyce Nalepka to Peter Bourne, July 12, 1978, folder: Correspondence 7/6/78–8/18/78, box 28, Craig and Barbara Boyan to Bourne, August 27, 1977, and September 1, 1977, folder:

Correspondence "Bo" 1977–78, box 13, Sydney U. Barnes to Bourne, folder: Correspondence "Ba" 1977–78, box 12, PGB-Carter.

30. Marsha Keith Schuchard to Jimmy and Rosalynn Carter, February 28, 1978, folder 1/20/77–8/31/78, box HE-12, WHCF-Carter. Also see Baum, *Smoke and Mirrors,* 88–90, 99–100.

31. Schuchard to Jimmy and Rosalynn Carter, February 28, 1978, Schuchard to Joseph Califano, June 27, 1978, "How You Can Get Rich!" advertisement, *High Times,* December 1977, folder 1/20/77–8/31/78, box HE-12, WHCF-Carter.

32. Marsha Manatt, *Parents, Peers, and Pot II: Parents in Action* (Rockville, MD: NIDA, 1983), 3–5; Program of Fourth Annual Southeast Drug Conference "The Family versus the Drug Culture," May 25–27, 1978, folder: Drug Abuse (2), box 18, JMJO-Carter; PBS interview with Robert DuPont, 2000; on the NORML conference, also see Anderson, *High in America,* 151, 311–14. Schuchard wrote NIDA publications under her surname prior to marriage, "Marsha Manatt."

33. Schuchard, "The Family versus the Drug Culture," May 25, 1978, folder: Drug Abuse (4), box 19, JMJO-Carter.

34. Schuchard, "Family versus the Drug Culture."

35. NIDA, *Marijuana Research Findings: 1976,* quotations v, 10–11; Bachman, Johnston, and O'Malley, "Smoking, Drinking, and Drug Use among American High School Students: Correlates and Trends, 1975–1979"; Schuchard, "Family versus the Drug Culture."

36. San Mateo Department of Public Health and Welfare, *Summary Report: Surveys of Student Drug Use, San Mateo County, California,* March 1977. About twice as many middle-school students drank alcohol as smoked marijuana, around one-sixth of the high school students had taken both LSD and amphetamines, and heroin use was miniscule in San Mateo County. Also see NIDA, *Marijuana Research Findings: 1976,* 5–9. Arrests calculated from data in *Marijuana: A Study of State Policies and Penalties,* 155–157; California State Office of Narcotics and Drug Abuse, *A First Report of the Impact of California's New Marijuana Law, SB 95,* 23.

37. "Background Information on P.R.I.D.E.," folder: PRIDE 11/3/83, OA 13748, series III, CET-Reagan; PRIDE, "Starting a Parents Group," n.d., folder: PRIDE (2), box 4, OA 15003, DAPO-Reagan.

38. Sue Rusche, *How to Form a Families in Action Group in Your Community* (Decatur, GA: DeKalb Families in Action, 1979); biographical information from Baum, *Smoke and Mirrors,* 101–2. Also see Sue Rusche, "Countering the Drug Culture," *Synergist* 11, no. 1 (Spring 1982): 34–36.

39. Rusche, *How to Form a Families in Action Group,* 11; Schuchard, "Family versus the Drug Culture"; Manatt, *Parents, Peers, and Pot II,* 8–20, 153–56.

40. Rusche, *How to Form a Families in Action Group.* On the paraphernalia laws, see *Associated Press,* December 1, 1980; *CSM,* December 17, 1980; articles compiled in "National Families in Action: A Guide to Publications," http://nationalfamilies.org/publications/index.html.

41. Lloyd D. Johnston, "A Review and Analysis of Recent Changes in Marijuana Use by American Young People," *Marijuana: The National Impact on Education* (New York: American Council on Marijuana, 1982), 8–13 (quotation 8); HHS News, "Report Shows Dramatic Increase in Use of Marijuana and Cocaine," June 20, 1980, folder LP311:1898, box 58, MPF-CSA.

42. Lloyd D. Johnston, Jerald G. Bachman, and Patrick M. O'Malley, *Highlights from Drug Use among American High School Students, 1975–1977* (Rockville, MD: NIDA, 1978), 7–33;

Johnston, Bachman, and O'Malley, *Highlights from Drugs and the Class of '78*, 6–10, 33–34. On race, see Johnston, "Characteristics of the Daily Marijuana User," 12–15.

43. Johnston, Bachman, and O'Malley, *Highlights from Drugs and the Class of '78*, 38–57 (quotation 48).

44. Thomas J. Gleaton and Marsha Schuchard to Patricia Yarham, July 25, 1978, Watson to Gleaton and Schuchard, August 4, 1978, Jimmy Carter to Sue Rusche, April 28, 1978, folder 1/20/77–8/31/78, box HE-12, WHCF-Carter; Bourne quotation in PBS Frontline, interview with Peter Bourne, 2000, http://www.pbs.org/wgbh/pages/frontline/shows/drugs/interviews/bourne.html.

45. *National Organization for the Reform of Marijuana Laws v. Department of State, et al.*, Civil No. 78–0428, U.S. District Court for the District of Columbia, folder: ODAP, Peter Bourne to Loraine Hendricks, July 11, 1978, folder: Correspondence 7/1/78–7/12/78, box 12, Montana NORML to Mazie F. Pope, July 13, 1978, folder: Correspondence 7/6/78–8/18/78, box 28, PGB-Carter; Anderson, *High in America*, 203–82; *NYT*, April 18, 1978. Anti-paraquat form letters in folder: Correspondence 3/15/78–3/31/78, box 10, also Frank C. Branchini to Bourne, March 11, 1978, folder: Correspondence Bra-Bri 1977–78, box 13, PGB-Carter. On the congressional ban, see Stuart Eizenstat and Lee Dogoloff to Griffin Bell, August 9, 1979, folder: Drug Policy (1), box 189, SEE-Carter.

46. *NYT*, July 21–22, 1978; Anderson, *High in America*, 10–23, 275–83; Jimmy Carter to Senior Staff, July 24, 1978, folder: 6/1/78–1/20/81, box HE-10, WHCF-Carter. Anderson reports Bourne's use of cocaine at the party as fact, verified by multiple witnesses, while Bourne maintained that Stroup had "fabricated" the story as revenge for the paraquat policy; see "Interview with Peter Bourne," *Newservice*, July/August 1983, 36–39, 54–58.

47. Lee Dogoloff, "Weekly Drug Report," September 22, 1978, folder: Drug Policy, box 19, JMJO-Carter; Gleaton and Schuchard to Patricia Yarham, July 25, 1978, folder 1/20/77–8/31/78, Gleaton to Jack Watson, December 8, 1978, folder: 9/1/78–1/20/81, box HE-12, WHCF-Carter; Bourne interview, PBS. Also see Interview with Lee Dogoloff, Drug Abuse Policy Section, Domestic Policy Staff, November 26, 1980, Interview with Bob Angarola, Domestic Policy Staff, November 26, 1980, EIP-Carter. Dogoloff did not mention marijuana in a major 1977 drug policy speech; see "Toward a Coherent System of Narcotics Addiction," n.d. [1977], folder: Memoranda 7/14/77–7/31/77, box 22, PGB-Carter. For more on Carter's family agenda, see Self, *All in the Family*, esp. 310–38; J. Brooks Flippen, *Jimmy Carter, the Politics of Family, and the Rise of the Religious Right* (Athens: University of Georgia Press, 2011).

48. Dogoloff, Speech to National Conference of Program Coordinators in State Departments of Education, September 20, 1978, folder: Drug Policy, box 19, JMJO-Carter; Dogoloff Interview; Gleaton to Jack Watson, December 8, 1978, folder: 9/1/78–1/20/81, box HE-12, WHCF-Carter.

49. Transcript of Peter Bensinger on "Issues and Answers," ABC-TV, n.d. [July 1977], folder: DEA (1), Bensinger, "Statement before the Senate Subcommittee on Juvenile Delinquency," February 10, 1978, folder: DEA (3), box 16, AMG-Carter; *NYT*, December 28, 1978, October 9, 1979; Joel Kotkin and Dorothy J. Samuels, "Reefer Sadness: Feds Crack Down on Dope," *VV*, February 12, 1979; "The Colombian Connection: How a Billion-Dollar Network Smuggles Pot and Coke into the U.S.," *Time*, January 29, 1979, 22–29.

50. Dogoloff, "Summary of the Principals Retreat," April 5, 1979, Charles O'Keeffe to Eizenstat, January 29, 1979, folder: Drug Abuse (2), box 18, JMJO-Carter; Bensinger to Dogoloff, July 6, 1979, DEA, "National Five Year Goals for the Reduction in the Illicit Traffic and Abuse of Controlled Substances," 1979 folder: Drug Policy (1), box 189, SEE-Carter. Bensinger also insisted that marijuana should continue to be classified as a Schedule 1 drug (highly dangerous without medical benefit), as with heroin. The Senate passed a watered-down version of marijuana decriminalization (with little debate), restricting the civil infraction fine to amounts less than thirty grams and potential jail time for anything above that weight, as part of omnibus crime legislation sponsored by Senator Edward Kennedy that shifted from indeterminate to fixed sentencing for many federal offenses, which leading House Democrats opposed. See CRS, *Proposed Changes in Marihuana Controls, 95th Congress, Comparative Analysis*, Report 78–36 ED, February 21, 1978; "Senate-Passed Criminal Code Dies in House," *CQ Almanac 1978* (Washington: CQ, 1979), 165–173.

51. Dogoloff, Statement to Senate Committee on Narcotics and Drug Abuse Control, July 10, 1979, folder: Drug Abuse (1), box 18, JMJO-Carter; Dogoloff, "Visit to Naples, Florida, August 15, 1979," August 31, 1979, folder: 7/1/79–9/30/79, box HE-12, WHCF-Carter.

52. Bourne, "Cocaine Policy Paper" Rough Draft, July 28, 1977, folder: Cocaine Policy Paper, box 32, PGB-Carter; "The Colombian Connection," *Time*, January 29, 1979, 22–29; Johnston, Bachman, and O'Malley, *Highlights from Drugs and the Class of '78*, 10, 19. Carter mentioned cocaine seven times between 1977 and 1980, according to the documents compiled by the *American Presidency Project*, usually in a multidrug list that focused on the threat of either marijuana or heroin.

53. Robin de Silva, "The Young American and the Flight toward Drugs," *WP*, July 3, 1977, H1, H5-H7; also see *WP*, June 11, 1977, May 26, 1978, June 8, 1978 ("drug pushers"), July 9, 1978 ("fast surpassing"), August 25, 1978 ("unsuspecting"), December 28, 1978; "Use of PCP Soaring Here," *Fairfax Journal*, n.d. [1977], Drugs folder, VF-FCPL; Schuchard to Jimmy and Rosalynn Carter, February 28, 1978, folder 1/20/77–8/31/78, box HE-12, WHCF-Carter. For a critical analysis of media hype in the PCP "epidemic," see Jenkins, *Synthetic Panics*, 54–75. For NIDA's more sober analysis, which also highlighted the PCP incursion into the suburbs, see *PCP Phencyclidine Abuse: An Appraisal* (Rockville, MD: NIDA, August 1978). On the federal response, Dogoloff, Statement to Senate Committee on Narcotics and Drug Abuse Control, July 10, 1979, folder: Drug Abuse (1), box 18, JMJO-Carter; *WP*, April 4, June 8, August 24, 1978.

54. City of Lakewood, California, "Analysis of Resolution Pertaining to the Control of Drug Paraphernalia," n.d. [1980], "Q&A: A Primer on the Issue of Drug Paraphernalia Control," n.d. [1980], folder: Drug Paraphernalia, box 23, CET-Reagan; *NYT*, August 10, 1980. On the campaign against head shops, also see Joshua Clark Davis, "The Business of Getting High: Head Shops, Countercultural Capitalism, and the Marijuana Legalization Movement," *The Sixties: A Journal of History, Politics, and Culture* 8, no. 1 (2015): 27–49.

55. "Drug Paraphernalia and Youth," *Hearing before the Subcommittee on Criminal Justice, Committee on the Judiciary*, U.S. Senate, November 16, 1969 (Washington: GPO, 1980), quotations 8, 13, 47, 58.

56. Testimony of Patricia Burch, November 16, 1979, "Drug Paraphernalia and Youth," *Hearing*, 51–58; Testimony of Joyce Nalepka, ibid., 110–13; *WT*, January 6, 1980.

57. Sen. Charles Matthias, Press Release, November 14, 1979, folder: Drug Paraphernalia Hearings, box 5, subseries 5, series 1, CMM-JHU; "Drug Paraphernalia and Youth," *Hearing*,

85–92, 110–13; Dogoloff, Statement to Senate Committee on Narcotics and Drug Abuse Control, July 10, 1979, folder: Drug Abuse (1), box 18, JMJO-Carter; *WP*, October 5, November 15, 21, 1979. Also see Musto and Korsmeyer, *Quest for Drug Control*, 187.

58. Thomas Regnier, "'Civilizing' Drug Paraphernalia Policy: Preserving Our Free Speech and Due Process Rights while Protecting Children," *NYU Journal of Legislation and Public Policy* 14, no. 1 (2001): 115–62; Kerry Murphy Healey, *State and Federal Experience with Drug Paraphernalia Laws* (Washington: National Institute of Justice, February 1988); *CSM*, December 17, 1980. Dogoloff quoted in *NYT*, August 10, 1980.

59. Dogoloff Interview. On the strategy of appealing to federal policymakers as parents, also see Massing, *The Fix*, 149–50.

60. Strategy Council on Drug Abuse, "Federal Strategy for Drug Abuse and Drug Traffic Prevention, 1979," folder: ODAP Drug Policy Message (1), box 247, SEE-Carter; Dogoloff to Eizenstat, "1979 Drug Abuse Campaign," February 5, 1979, Dogoloff to Carter, April 2, 1979, folder: 2/1/79–4/30/79, Dogoloff to Public Service Directors, April 16, 1979, folder: 5/1/79–6/30/79, box HE-11, Dogoloff to Eizenstat, September 5, 1980, folder: 5/15/80–1/20–81, box HE-12, WHCF-Carter; "Reefer Madness," *New Republic*, October 6, 1979, 7–10.

61. Dogoloff, "1979 Drug Abuse Campaign"; Eizenstat and Dogoloff, "Presidential Event—Adolescent Drug Abuse Prevention," n.d. [1980], folder: Drug Policy (1), box 189, SEE-Carter; Dogoloff Interview; White House Conference on Families, *Listening to American Families*. On the regional conferences, also see *NYT*, October 23, 1980. On liberal political culture and "permissiveness," see Zaretsky, *No Direction Home*, esp. 183–221.

62. "Justifiable criticism" handwritten by Stuart Eizenstat on a letter to HEW Secretary Joseph A. Califano, May 3, 1979, folder: 5/1/79–6/30/79, box HE-11, SEE-Carter. Also see Dogoloff to Eizenstat, April 20, 1979, folder: 5/1/79–6/30/79, box HE-11, ibid. On Nalepka, see Dogoloff, "Coalition for Concern about Marijuana Use in Youth Meeting, October 4, 1979," November 28, 1979, folder: 10/1/79–5/15/80, box HE-12, ibid.; Dogoloff Interview; Minutes of NIDA Liaison Committee Meeting, April 23, 1981, folder: PRIDE (2–5), OA 16999, series II, DIM-Reagan.

63. Testimony of Norman Zinberg, "Health Consequences of Marijuana Abuse: Recent Findings," *Hearings before the Select Committee on Narcotics Abuse and Control*, House of Representatives, July 17, 1979 (Washington: GPO, 1979), 10–16, 24–52; *NYT*, October 9, 1979. On Zinberg, also see Marsha Schuchard to Jimmy and Rosalynn Carter, February 28, 1978, folder 1/20/77–8/31/78, box HE-12, WHCF-Carter.

64. Gabriel G. Nahas, *Marijuana—Deceptive Weed* (New York: Raven Publishers, 1973, rev. ed. 1975), Nahas, *Keep Off the Grass* (New York: Reader's Digest Press, 1976), quotations 93, 85; Testimony of Gabriel G. Nahas, July 17, 1979, "Health Consequences of Marijuana Abuse: Recent Findings," *Hearings*, 6–10, 24–84; Testimony of William Pollin, July 19, 1979, ibid., 89–156 (quotation 91). On Nahas's links to the parents' movement, see Minutes of NIDA Liaison Committee Meeting, April 23, 1981. Criticism in NORML Press Release, "Marijuana Study Challenged," March 8, 1974 (including reviews from *JAMA* and *New England Journal of Medicine*), reproduced in appendix of California Senate Select Committee on Control of Marijuana, *Marijuana: Beyond Misunderstanding*.

65. Select Committee on Narcotics Abuse and Control, House of Representatives, *Considerations for and against the Reduction of Federal Penalties for Possession of Small Amounts of*

Marihuana for Personal Use (Washington: GPO, 1977), quotation 6; "Health Consequences of Marijuana Abuse: Recent Findings," *Hearings*, quotations 1, 46.

66. Testimony of William Pollin, "Oversight Hearings on Federal Drug Strategy—1979," *Hearings before the Select Committee on Narcotics Abuse and Control*, House of Representatives, July 10, 1979 (Washington: GPO, 1979), 440–71 (quotation 470); Testimony of Jesse Jackson, June 12, 1979, ibid., 145–63 (quotations 147, 157); Charles Rangel's exchange with DEA director Peter Bensinger, June 21, 1979, ibid., 386–96. Data from FBI, *Uniform Crime Reports*, 1975–1980.

67. *Reading, Writing, and Reefer* (NBC News: April 17, 1979). The rhetoric of "guinea pigs in a national experiment" mirrored one of the most common tropes deployed by the white antibusing movement during the 1970s. See, for one such example of many, Thomas J. Sugrue, *Sweet Land of Liberty: The Forgotten Struggle for Civil Rights in the North* (New York: Random House, 2008), 483.

68. *Reading, Writing, and Reefer*. On the Atlanta connection, see Rusche, *How to Form a Families in Action Group*, 4.

69. *Stoned* (ABC Afterschool Special: Learning Corporation of America, 1980). On Cohen and LSD, see chapter 2.

70. Peggy Mann, "Marijuana Alert I: Brain and Sex Damage," *RD*, December 1979, 3–8; Walter X. Lehmann, "Enemy of Youth," *RD*, December 1979, 8–10; Mann, "Marijuana Alert II: More of the Grim Story," *RD*, November 1980, 11–17; Mann, "Marijuana: The Myth of Harmlessness Goes Up in Smoke," *SEP*, July/August 1980, reprint. Also see Mann, "Marijuana and Driving: The Sobering Truth," *RD*, May 1979, 18–22; Mann, "The Case against Marijuana Smoking," *WP*, July 30, 1978, B1–B2; Mann, "The Case against Marijuana," *Family Circle*, February 20, 1979, reprint; Mann, "Do You Know Where Your Children Are? (And What They're Into?)", *LHJ*, October 1979, reprint. Letter reproduced in "Health Consequences of Marihuana Use," *Hearings before the Subcommittee on Criminal Justice, Committee on the Judiciary*, U.S. Senate, January 16–17, 1980 (Washington: GPO, 1980), 222.

71. Peggy Mann and Betsy Houlton, *Twelve Is Too Old* (New York: Doubleday, 1980; Woodmere Press, 1987), quotations 66, 99, 76, 101–2.

72. Mann and Houlton, *Twelve Is Too Old*, quotations 118, 119, 120, 129. DuPont quotation from back cover of 1987 edition. On Library of Congress designation, see 1987 edition and *WP*, Jan, 15, 1985.

73. *For Parents Only: What Kids Think about Marijuana* (Vision Associates Production for the Drug Prevention Agencies of the Federal Government, 1980); Eizenstat and Dogoloff, "Dear Congressman" Letter, February 29, 1980, folder: Drug Abuse Prevention, box 106, SEE-Carter.

74. *For Parents Only*; NIDA, *For Parents Only* discussion guidebook (Washington: DHHS, 1980). On the distribution, see "Background Information on P.R.I.D.E.," folder: PRIDE 11/3/83, OA 13748, series III, DAPO-Reagan.

75. Marsha Manatt, *Parents, Peers, and Pot* (Rockville, MD: NIDA, 1979), iii–ix (Pollin's foreword), 1–21. Distribution total in "Background Information on P.R.I.D.E." Many drug experts at NIDA considered *Parents, Peers, and Pot* to be full of exaggerated and unscientific claims and opposed its publication; see Massing, *The Fix*, 152–53.

76. Manatt, *Parents, Peers, and Pot*, 1–21.

77. Ibid., 22–56.

78. Ibid., 34–79.

79. "Health Consequences of Marihuana Use," *Hearings*, January 16–17, 1980, Mathias quotation 2; Grinspoon quotations 21, 26; Sue Rusche quotations 218, 221; Joyce Nalepka quotation 202. Surveys in Gallup Poll, "Opposition to Legalization of Marijuana Unchanged," June 1980, Field Institute, "The California Poll: Majority Favors Considerable Relaxation of Marijuana Laws and Penalties," April 4, 1979, folder LP311:1894, box 57, MPF-CSA.

80. PRIDE Press Release, "National Federation of Parents for Drug Free Youth Formed," April 4, 1980, NFP Press Release, May 8, 1980, "List of Attendees, Sixth Annual Southeast Drug Conference," n.d. [April 1980], folder: PRIDE (2–5), Minutes, "Special Meeting to Organize a National Federation," April 3, 1980, "PRIDE's Role in Formation and Early Assistance to NFP," July 11, 1983, folder: PRIDE (5–6), OA 16999, series II, DIM-Reagan; NFP, "Federation Formed to Unite Parents Groups Nationwide," May 1980, folder: Marijuana Pamphlets, OA 12590, RLW-Reagan.

81. Peggy Mann, "The Parent War against Pot," *WP Outlook*, January 6, 1980, B1, B4; Mann, "Parents Organizing against Marijuana Traffic," *LAT*, November 27, 1980, L1–L3; Mann, "Marijuana: Part 2," *Scouting*, October 1981, 31–32, 73–77. On the Naples Informed Parents connection to PRIDE, see Manatt, *Parents, Peers, and Pot II*, 27–40. Also see "Conference Newsletter: Florida's First Informed Parents Conference," November 6–8, 1981, folder: Sarasota County Informed Parents, box 5, OA 15003, DAPO-Reagan.

82. NFP, Executive Board and Board of Directors, n.d. [1980], folder: NFP (1), box 4, OA 15003, DAPO-Reagan; "List of Attendees, Sixth Annual Southeast Drug Conference," n.d. [April 1980], folder: PRIDE (2–5), OA 16999, series II, DIM-Reagan; Manatt, *Parents, Peers, and Pot II*, 73–88.

83. Testimony of Joann Lundgren, "Comprehensive Alcohol and Drug Abuse Amendments of 1981," *Hearings before the Subcommittee on Alcoholism and Drug Abuse, Committee on Labor and Human Resources*, U.S. Senate, March 30, 1981 (Washington: GPO, 1981), 202–7; Manatt, *Parents, Peers, and Pot II*, 132–46; Californians for Drug-Free Youth Newsletter, Summer 1983, folder: California, box 13, CET-Reagan; *LAT*, November 16, 1980, September 22, December 16, 1982.

84. Mann, "Marijuana: Part 2," *Scouting*, October 1981, 76; *LAT*, May 9, 1980; Gleaton, "Statement before the Subcommittee on Alcoholism and Drug Abuse," March 30, 1981, folder: PRIDE (2–5), OA 16999, series II, DIM-Reagan; Manatt, *Parents, Peers, and Pot II*, 37.

85. Elizabeth Coleman Brynner, "New Parental Push against Marijuana," *NYT Magazine*, February 10, 1980, 9, 38, 51–52; Mann, "Marijuana: The Myth of Harmlessness"; Mann, "Putting a Match to the Marijuana Myth," *SEP*, September 1980, reprint; Mann, "Marijuana: Part 1: What It Is, What It Does, and What It's Doing to Our Kids," *Scouting*, September 1981, 31–34 (second quotation); Mann, "Marijuana: Part 2," *Scouting*, October 1981, 31–32, 73–77.

86. NFP, Minutes of Board of Directors Meeting, November 8, 1980, April 1, 1981, folder: PRIDE (2–5), OA 16999, series II, DIM-Reagan; NFP Newsletter, Fall 1981, folder: Senate Subcommittee on Alcohol and Drug Abuse (1 of 2), OA 12587, RLW-Reagan; PRIDE, Program for Seventh Annual Southeast Drug Conference, April 2–4, 1981, folder: Committees of Correspondence (2), box 3, OA 15003, DAPO-Reagan. On Pettigrew's group, see *WP*, May 1, October 12, 1982; Manatt, *Parents, Peers, and Pot II*, 104–15.

87. NFP membership application in NFP Newsletter, Fall 1981; PRIDE's statement of philosophy in PRIDE, "Starting a Parents Group," n.d. [1977], folder: PRIDE (2), box 4, OA 15003, DAPO-Reagan; Testimony of Marsha Keith Schuchard, "Examination of the Health and Educational Effects of Marijuana on Youth," *Hearing before the Subcommittee on Alcoholism and Drug Abuse, Committee on Labor and Human Resources*, U.S. Senate, October 21, 1981, 115–27 (quotation 116); Joann Lundgren Testimony, March 30, 1981, "Comprehensive Alcohol and Drug Abuse Amendments of 1981," *Hearings*, 206; Schuchard, "Family versus the Drug Culture"; Manatt, *Parents, Peers, and Pot*. Many of the parent activists who would soon found the NFP attacked NORML, head shops, rock music, and other alleged causes of teenage pot smoking in the January 1980 "Health Consequences of Marihuana Use," *Hearings*, 186–313.

88. Jack H. Watson Jr. to Stanley Meyer, July 25, 1980, folder: 9/1/78–1/20/81, Eizenstat and Dogoloff to Phil Wise, May 15, 1980, folder: 10/1/79–5/15/80, box HE-12, WHCF-Carter; Jimmy Carter, "The State of the Union Annual Message to the Congress," January 16, 1981, APP, https://www.presidency.ucsb.edu/node/250760.

89. Minutes of NIDA Liaison Committee Meeting, April 23, 1981; Dogoloff Interview.

90. Lloyd D. Johnston, Jerald G. Bachman, and Patrick M. O'Malley, *Highlights from Student Drug Use in America, 1975–1981* (Rockville, MD: NIDA, 1981).

91. Johnston, Bachman, and O'Malley, *Highlights from Student Drug Use in America, 1975–1981*, quotation 12; Johnston, "Characteristics of the Daily Marijuana User," 12 (second quotation).

Chapter 7. Zero Tolerance

1. John Heyn and Jeffrey Krulik, *Heavy Metal Parking Lot* (Pirate Video, 1986), rereleased with outtakes in 2007 by Film Baby Studio; Penny Phillips to Ronald Reagan, April 14, 1983, Phillips, "PANDAA Rock Concert Committee Meets with Capital Centre Management," November 1982, Phillips, "A Rock Concert at the Capital Centre," November 1982, PANDAA Newsletter, March 1983, folder: PANDAA, OA 13748, CET-Reagan. On Maryland's drinking age, see *WP*, January 29, 1982.

2. "1980 Republican Platform Text," *CQ Almanac 1980*, 36th ed., 91-B–121-B (Washington: CQ, 1981); Transcript of Reagan News Conference, March 6, 1981, folder: President Reagan's News Conference, OA 9432, CET-Reagan; NFP Newsletter, Fall 1981, folder: Senate Subcommittee on Alcohol and Drug Abuse (1 of 2), OA 12587, RLW-Reagan; Ronald Reagan, Marijuana Statement at Campaign Event, 1980, https://www.youtube.com/watch?v=VxHBx6H-xFo, also reproduced in *Grass*, dir. Ron Mann (Sphinx Productions, 2000). For the 1970 quotation, see Office of the Governor, Press Release, February 23, 1970, folder: Narcotics Program, 1970, box GO 79, Legal Affairs Unit, Governor's Office Files, RRGP-Reagan.

3. Alexander, *New Jim Crow*, quotations 49, 53; Provine, *Unequal under Law*; Beckett, *Making Crime Pay*; Garland, *Culture of Control*; Western, *Punishment and Inequality in America*; Reeves and Campbell, *Cracked Coverage*; Reinarman and Levine, eds., *Crack in America*.

4. Tonry, *Malign Neglect*. Michael Massing argues that the Reagan administration redirected federal public health resources and attention to the suburban marijuana "crisis" so comprehensively that, rather than exploiting racial backlash about urban drug users, the White House "ignored every warning sign" about crack. Instead the Reagan administration policed nonwhite

drug users in urban centers primarily and at times exclusively through militarized crime control initiatives. See Massing, *The Fix*, 177–90 (quotation 190).

5. Katherine Beckett, "Setting the Public Agenda: 'Street Crime' and Drug Use in American Politics," *Social Problems* 41, no. 3 (August 1994): 425–47; Weaver, "Frontlash"; Alexander, *New Jim Crow*, 48–49; and other books cited above.

6. On zero tolerance and privatization, see Alexandra M. Lord, *Condom Nation: The U.S. Government's Sex Education Campaign from World War I to the Internet* (Baltimore: Johns Hopkins University Press, 2010); Harvey B. Feigenbaum, Jeffrey Henig, and Chris Hamnett, *Shrinking the State: The Political Underpinnings of Privatization* (Cambridge: Cambridge University Press, 1999); Renfro, *Stranger Danger*. On "political whiteness," see HoSang, *Racial Propositions*. On the victims' rights movement, see Gottschalk, *Prison and the Gallows*, 115–64.

7. MADD has received little scholarly attention, and generally not as part of the victims' rights movement. For accounts of the organization, see Barron H. Lerner, *One for the Road: Drunk Driving since 1900* (Baltimore: Johns Hopkins University Press, 2011); Adams, *Grass Roots*, esp. 98–99, 190–96, 230–42.

8. George L. Kelling and James Q. Wilson, "Broken Windows: The Police and Neighborhood Safety," *The Atlantic*, March 1982; Fellner, "Race, Drugs, and Law Enforcement in the United States."

9. Data from "Persons Arrested" sections of FBI, *Uniform Crime Reports*, 1978–1989. On the general context, see the books cited above.

10. Lynn Norment, "Charles Rangel: The Front-Line General in the War on Drugs," *Ebony*, March 1989, 128–34; Ronald Reagan and Nancy Reagan, "Speech to the Nation on the Campaign against Drug Abuse," September 14, 1986, https://millercenter.org/the-presidency/presidential-speeches/september-14-1986-speech-nation-campaign-against-drug-abuse (video version).

11. Bill Barton, "President's Message," NFP Newsletter, Fall 1981; NFP, Minutes of Board of Directors Meeting, November 8, 1980, folder: PRIDE (2–5), OA 16999, series II, DIM-Reagan; Testimony of Marsha Keith Schuchard, October 21, 1981, "Examination of the Health and Educational Effects of Marijuana on Youth," *Hearing*, quotations 124, 115; *WSJ*, March 26, 1982. Middle America quotation in Hilary DeVries, "Parents Band Together to Push Back Drug Tide," *CSM*, May 4, 1982.

12. Joyce Nalepka to NFP Board Members, July 13, 1981, Robert L. DuPont, "A Fresh Perspective for the War on Drugs," July 2, 1981, folder: Parents for Drug-Free Youth, box 4, OA 15003, DAPO-Reagan. Also see Massing, *The Fix*, 158–60.

13. Schuchard Testimony, October 21, 1981, "Examination of the Health and Educational Effects of Marijuana on Youth," *Hearing*, 115, 120–24; Thomas J. Gleaton, "Statement before the Subcommittee on Alcoholism and Drug Abuse," March 30, 1981; Carla Lowe to President Reagan, November 9, 1981, folder: Polls/Surveys-General, OA 13748, CET-Reagan; Pat Burch and Susan Silverman to Richard S. Schweiker, October 28, 1982, folder: NFP Youth (1), box 4, OA 15003, DAPO-Reagan.

14. NFP Press Release, October 21, 1981, folder: Senate Subcommittee on Alcohol and Drug Abuse (1), OA 12587, RLW-Reagan; Minutes of NIDA Liaison Committee Meeting, April 23, 1981; Testimony of William Pollin, October 21, 1981, "Examination of the Health and Educational Effects of Marijuana on Youth," *Hearing*, 5–35; Schuchard Testimony, ibid., 115–32.

15. Testimony of Donald Ian MacDonald, October 21, 1981, "Examination of the Health and Educational Effects of Marijuana on Youth," *Hearing*, 75–80, 95–100; Andy MacDonald, "Hooked on Drugs: What It's Really Like, *Families*, November 1981, 37–40.

16. NFP Press Release, October 21, 1981; Testimony of Ingrid L. Latner, October 21, 1981, "Examination of the Health and Educational Effects of Marijuana on Youth," *Hearing*, 81–93; Schuchard Testimony, ibid. 115–32; Nalepka to NFP Board Members, July 13, 1981, NFP, "Warning!" (LSD flier), folder: Parents for Drug-Free Youth, box 4, Gleaton, "PRIDE: Community-School Plan for Drug Abuse Prevention," 1981, folder: PRIDE (2), OA 15003, DAPO-Reagan; Andy MacDonald, "Hooked on Drugs"; Manatt, *Parents, Peers, and Pot II*, 13–24.

17. Carlton E. Turner, "Statement to Permanent Subcommittee on Investigations, U.S. Senate," November 18, 1981, folder: Drug Policy Documents (3), OA 19057, DIM-Reagan; Turner, Memorandum for Oversight Working Group, December 1, 1981, folder: Working Group on Drug Abuse, OA 12590, RLW-Reagan. Quotation from Turner, "Briefing Remarks: The Chemical People," March 21, 1983, folder: Chemical People (4), box 15, CET-Reagan.

18. "Federal Drug Strategy—1981," *Hearing before the Select Committee on Narcotics Abuse and Control*, House of Representatives, November 19, 1981 (Washington: GPO, 1982), quotations 1, 2, 4, 10.

19. DAPO, "The Reagan Administration's Five-Point Plan to Prevent and Control Drug Abuse in the United States," March 31, 1982, folder: 094400–094899, box 14, OPD-Reagan; Ronald Reagan, "Remarks on Signing Executive Order 12368, Concerning Federal Drug Abuse Policy Functions," June 24, 1982, APP, https://www.presidency.ucsb.edu/node/245538.

20. Ronald Reagan, Remarks to the International Association of Chiefs of Police, September 28, 1981, folder: Drug Policy Documents (5), OA 19057, DIM-Reagan.

21. Select Committee on Narcotics Abuse and Control, U.S. House of Representatives, *Annual Report, Part II: Recommendations for a Comprehensive Program to Control the Worldwide Problem of Drug Abuse*, 1981, 13–17, 46–48, folder: Select Committee on Narcotics Abuse and Control, OA 12587, RLW-Reagan.

22. Nancy Reagan, Press Release, April 2, 1981, folder: PRIDE (2–5), OA 16999, series II, DIM-Reagan; Ann Wrobleski to Mrs. Reagan, March 24, 1981, "Briefing Outline Mrs. Reagan/Drug Program," n.d. [1981], "Background Memorandum Mrs. Reagan/Drug Project," n.d. [1981], folder: Drugs/Alcohol, Mrs. Reagan, OA 11221, MEB-Reagan; "Draft: Background Memorandum Mrs. Reagan/Drug Project," July 29, 1981, folder: Mrs. Reagan's Report, OA 9432, CET-Reagan. On negative publicity, see Peter McGrath, "The World of Nancy Reagan," *Newsweek*, December 21, 1981; *WP*, February 17, 1982.

23. Carlton Turner to Ann Wrobleski, August 11, 1981 (quotations), Turner, "Internal Memo Regarding Meeting with Mrs. Reagan-July 15, 1981" July 20, 1981, folder: Mrs. Reagan's Report, OA 9432, CET-Turner; *WP*, July 14, 1981.

24. Dodie Kazanjian to Michael Deaver, "Mrs. Reagan Press Kit: Drug/Alcohol Abuse," November 5, 1981, folder: Drugs/Alcohol, Mrs. Reagan, OA 11221, MEB-Reagan; Memo to Ann Wrobleski, "Drug Q&A for AMA and Good Morning America," November 9, 1981, folder: ACM Conference, box 434, OMR-Reagan; NFP Newsletter, Fall 1981; *WP*, November 10, 1981.

25. Ann Wrobleski, "Drug Initiatives, January/June 1982," June 14, 1982, folder: Mrs. Reagan's Drug Program, OA 16995, RLW-Reagan; Nancy Reagan, Speech to PTA Conference, March 1, 1982, folder: Nancy Reagan: PTA Conference, box 434, OMR-Reagan; Nancy Reagan,

"Remarks at the Governors' Wives Luncheon," February 22, 1982, folder: March 1985–July 1986 (7), box 2, CET-Reagan; *Chicago Sun-Times*, February 21, 1982; *WP*, February 17, 1982. On Texas War on Drugs, see Manatt, *Parents, Peers, and Pot II*, 116–129.

26. Nancy Reagan, "Remarks to PRIDE Conference," April 2, 1982, folder: Nancy Reagan PRIDE Conference in Atlanta, box 434, OMR-Reagan; PRIDE, "National Parent Conference on Youth and Drugs," April 1–3, 1982, folder: PRIDE (2), box 4, OA 15003, DAPO-Reagan; Ann Wrobleski, "Drug Initiatives: June/November," June 15, 1982, folder: Mrs. Reagan's Drug Program, OA 16995, RLW-Reagan; *WP*, April 24, 1982.

27. "White House Drug Use Briefing Stresses Prevention," *ACTION Update* (April 1982), folder: White House Briefing, OA 12590, RLW-Reagan; Nancy Reagan, "White House Drug Conference Opening Remarks," March 18, 1982, folder: Nancy Reagan: WH Drug Conference, box 434, OMR-Reagan; *NYT*, March 23, 1982; "Nancy Reagan Says Drugs Hurt Childhood Innocence," *UPI*, March 23, 1982. On corporate funding, see Ann Wrobleski, "Drug Initiatives, January/June 1982."

28. "White House Drug Use Briefing Stresses Prevention," *ACTION Update* (April 1982), "From 'Little House' to the White House" wire story, April 20, 1982, folder: White House Briefing, OA 12590, RLW-Reagan; Melissa Gilbert, *Prairie Tale: A Memoir* (New York: Simon and Schuster, 2009), 121–35 (quotation 123); SD to Nancy Reagan, May 5, 1982, LW to Nancy Reagan, December 1982, KMH to Ronald Reagan, June 29, 1982, folder: Delightful Kiddie Letters, box 18, LS to Mrs. Reagan, November 1983, folder: Chemical People Letters, box 15, CET-Reagan [names anonymized].

29. DAPO, *1984 National Strategy for Prevention of Drug Abuse and Drug Trafficking* (Washington: GPO, 1984), 37; ACTION, "Summary of Accomplishments in Reducing Drug Use, January 1981 through June 1982," folder: Awareness–Presidential Meetings (1), OA 12590, Carlton Turner, "Response to U.S. Senate Questions," n.d. [October 1981], folder: Senate Subcommittee on Alcohol and Drug Abuse, "Action Drug Prevention Program Progress Report," September 1984, folder: Drug Strategy Accomplishments Requested by VP, OA 12587, RLW-Reagan. On the ineffectiveness of zero-tolerance programs, see Earl Wysong, Richard Aniskiewicz, and David Wright, "Truth and DARE: Tracking Drug Education to Graduation and as Symbolic Politics," *Social Problems* 41, no. 3 (August 1994): 448–72. On the broader privatization agenda, see Paul Mokrzycki Renfro, "Keeping Children Safe Is Good for Business: The Enterprise of Child Safety in the Age of Reagan," *Enterprise and Society* 17, no. 1 (March 2016): 151–87.

30. Thomas W. Pauken/ACTION, "The Good News Report," #5 and #6, n.d. [1982], Pauken, "Straight, Inc.—A Drug Treatment Center," March 11, 1982, folder: White House Briefing on Drug Use and the Family, OA 12590, RLW-Reagan. Also see the suburban Virginia gateway story recited in Pauken, Testimony to Select Committee on Narcotics Abuse and Control, October 4, 1983, folder: ACTION Tom Pauken (2), box 5, CET-Reagan.

31. Michael Demarest, "Cocaine: Middle Class High," *Time*, July 6, 1981, 56–63; NBC-TV, "Pleasure Drugs—The Great American High" Transcript, April 20, 1982, folder: NBC White Paper, OA 9433, NBC-TV, "Cocaine: One Man's Poison" Script, 1983, folder: Cocaine: One Man's Poison, OA9434, CET-Reagan. Data in Lloyd D. Johnston, Patrick M. O'Malley, and Jerald G. Bachman, *Highlights from Drugs and American High School Students, 1975–1983* (Rockville, MD: NIDA, 1984).

32. Linda Hall to Thomas Pauken, November 8, 1982, folder: ACTION (Thomas Pauken 5/24/82), Mahmoud Baptiste to James Rosebush, February 9, 1982, Pauken to Baptiste, February 11, 1982, folder: ACTION (Thomas Pauken 1), box 5, Carlton Turner to Ed Harper, September 8, 1982, folder: 096881–097899, box 15, CET-Reagan; Turner to Ed Harper, January 17, 1983, folder: 117800–119999, box 16, Turner to Edward Meese, November 1, 1983, folder: 181800–183230, box 20, OPD-Reagan; ACTION, "Summary of Accomplishments in Reducing Drug Use, January 1981 through June 1982," folder: Awareness–Presidential Meetings (1), OA 12590, RLW-Reagan; *LAT*, March 24, 1982.

33. Ronald Reagan, "Remarks on Signing Executive Order 12368," June 24, 1982; William French Smith to C. Everett Koop, February 8, 1982, folder: Surgeon General Koop, OA 13694, CET-Reagan; Koop, "Statement," included as preface to *Marijuana and Health: Ninth Report to the U.S. Congress* (Washington: DHHS, 1982), iii–iv. Meetings during 1982–1983 with NFP leaders described in Carlton Turner's memos to Ed Harper in multiple folders in boxes 14, 16, and 18, OPD-Reagan.

34. "Information Paper: Domestic Marijuana Eradication," November 1, 1982, folder: 097901–099999, box 15, U.S. Coast Guard to Carlton Turner, "Monthly Drug Abuse Summary," April 1982, White House Oversight Working Group, "Monthly Report: DEA," April 1982, Turner to Ed Harper, May 18, 1982, folder: 072000–072178, box 13, DAPO, "Cannabis Eradication and the Paraquat Issue," July 16, 1982, folder: 089500–090599, box 14, DAPO, "Fact Sheet," July 19, 1982, folder: 094400–094899, box 14, OPD-Reagan; "Aid Bill Gives President Broader Authority," *CQ Almanac 1981*, 37th ed., 161–84 (Washington: CQ, 1982). Also see Massing, *The Fix*, 164–65.

35. Turner, "Communications Themes: The President's Campaign Against Drug Abuse," May 7, 1982, folder: 072000–072178, box 13, OPD-Reagan; NFP Newsletter, Fall 1981; NFP, Minutes of Board of Directors Meeting, April 1, 1981, folder: PRIDE (2–5), OA 16999, series II, DIM-Reagan.

36. Radio Address of the President and the First Lady, October 2, 1982, "Fact Sheet: President Reagan's Campaign Against Drug Abuse," October 5, 1982, folder: CCWG–Drug Abuse Health Issues, OA 12590, RLW-Reagan. On the Carter precedent, see "Federal Response to Drug Trafficking in the Southeast United States: Review of 1979 Activities," January 1980, folder: Drug Policy Documents (3), OA 19057, DIM-Reagan.

37. Joseph R. Biden Jr., "Controlling Crime: A National and International Necessity," November 15, 1982, folder: 109675–112529, box 16, OPD-Reagan. For Reagan officials, see remarks by Carlton Turner and Associate Attorney General Rudolph Giuliani in "Press Briefing," October 5, 1982, folder: 097901-099999, box 15, ibid. Democratic prosecutors in New York City accused the White House of ignoring heroin and "making too much of marijuana"; see Turner to Ed Harper, September 28, 1982, folder: 096881–097899, ibid.

38. "Federal Drug Strategy—1983," *Hearings before the Select Committee on Narcotics Abuse and Control*, House of Representatives, November 1–2, 1983 (Washington: GPO, 1984), Statement of Carlton Turner, 50–55, Statement of Charles Rangel, 49; "Reagan Vetoes Package of Anti-Crime Bills," *CQ Almanac 1982*, 38th ed., 419–21, "Presidential Veto Message: Reagan Vetoes Anti-Crime Bill," 35-E-36-E (Washington: CQ, 1983).

39. Joyce Nalepka to Ronald Reagan, August 3, 1982, folder: Parents for Drug-Free Youth (3), Mary Jacobson to Carlton Turner, November 4, 1982, folder: Parents for Drug-Free Youth (1),

box 4, OA 15003, DAPO-Reagan; Nancy Reagan, Remarks to NFP Conference, October 11, 1982, folder: Nancy Reagan: NFP Conference, box 435, OMR-Reagan; *NYT*, October 12, 1982.

40. *Epidemic: America Fights Back* (MTI Teleprograms/Gannett Co., 1983); also see *Epidemic! Kids, Drugs and Alcohol* (MTI Teleprograms/Gannett Co., 1982); PRIDE Newsletter, Spring 1982, folder: Buddy Gleaton (2), OA 13748, CET-Reagan. For Reagan's 1984 advertisements, see *The Living Room Candidate*, http://www.livingroomcandidate.org/commercials/1984/prouder-stronger-better.

41. *Epidemic: America Fights Back*; NFP, "1983 Conference Update," Nalepka to Reagan, August 3, 1982, folder: Parents for Drug-Free Youth (3), box 4, OA 15003, DAPO-Reagan.

42. Mary Jacobson, "A Message from our President," NFP Newsletter, 1983, folder: Chemical People (1), box 14, Carlton Turner to Samuel Chilcote, April 15, 1983, Turner to William Corbett, February 18, 1983, folder: Deglamorization of Drugs (2), OA 9434, CET-Reagan; Turner to Ed Harper, October 26, 1982, folder: 097901–099999, box 15, OPD-Reagan.

43. "Action Drug Prevention Program Progress Report," September 1984, folder: Drug Strategy Accomplishments, OA 12587, RLW-Reagan; "Pharmacists Against Drug Abuse Program Announced in Washington," PRIDE Newsletter, June 1983, folder: Buddy Gleaton, OA 13748, CET-Reagan; *BG*, November 16, 1982 (including quotation by Jack O'Brien of McNeil Pharmaceutical). For Michael Landon's public service commercial, see https://www.youtube.com/watch?v=Gv7_B0j_xeM. On network television, Carlton Turner, "Communications Themes: The President's Campaign Against Drug Abuse," May 7, 1982, folder: 072000–072178, box 13, OPD-Reagan; "The Reporter," *Diff'rent Strokes* (NBC-TV), aired March 19, 1983.

44. NFP Newsletter, 1983, WQED/Pittsburgh, "The Chemical People: A Landmark Public Television Event," 1983, Joyce Nalepka to William Pollin, June 1, 1984, folder: Chemical People (1), box 14, Lloyd Kaiser to Robert Kramer, June 14, 1984, folder: Chemical People Letters, Carlton Turner, "Briefing Remarks: The Chemical People," March 21, 1983, folder: Chemical People (4), box 15, CET-Reagan.

45. *The Chemical People: The Chemical Society* (WQED Pittsburgh/MTI Teleprograms, 1983); Nancy Reagan, "Remarks at Chemical People Luncheon," March 21, 1983, folder: Nancy Reagan Chemical People Luncheon, box 435, OMR-Reagan; Nancy Reagan and Michael Landon, "An Appeal to Americans," October 27, 1983, ID#37984, Moving Images Related to Drugs and Drug Enforcement, DEA-NA, https://catalog.archives.gov/id/37984.

46. *The Chemical People: The Chemical Society.*

47. *The Chemical People, Program 2: Community Answers* (WQED Pittsburgh/MTI Teleprograms, 1983).

48. *The Chemical People, Program 2: Community Answers.*

49. Lloyd W. Singer to Lloyd Kaiser, November 6, 1983, folder: Chemical People II (3), Carla Lowe to California PBS Affiliate Stations, April 25, 1983, folder: Chemical People (3), box 15, CET-Reagan; *BG*, November 2, 1983; *LAT*, October 27, November 4, 1983; *SDT*, May 29, 1984.

50. "The Chemical People: Teacher/Leader Guide," 1983, folder: Chemical People, box 14, CET-Reagan; *LAT*, November 4, 1983, February 8, July 15, November 29, 1984; *Allentown Morning Call*, January 18, 1984; *NYT*, December 30, 1984.

51. *LAT*, August 28, 1983, February 19, 1984; "Narcotics Trafficking and Abuse in the Los Angeles Area," *Hearing before the Select Committee on Narcotics Abuse and Control*, House of Representatives, October 31, 1986 (Washington: GPO, 1987), quotation 24; Bureau of Justice

Assistance, *Implementing Project DARE: Drug Abuse Resistance Education*, June 1988, NCJRS, https://www.ojp.gov/pdffiles1/Digitization/115417NCJRS.pdf. For a sampling of academic critique, see Wysong, Aniskiewicz, and Wright, "Truth and DARE"; Christopher L. Ringwalt et al., "Past and Future Directions of the D.A.R.E. Program: An Evaluation Review," *National Institute of Justice Research in Brief* (September 1994), NCJRS, https://www.ojp.gov/pdffiles1/Digitization/152055NCJRS.pdf; Dennis P. Rosenbaum, "Just Say No to D.A.R.E.," *Criminology and Public Policy* 6, no. 4 (November 2007): 815–24.

52. ODAP, "Update on Drug Abuse Prevention Campaign—Trends Improving," April 28, 1983, Weekly Reader, "Pressure to Try Drugs, Alcohol Starts in Early Grades," April 25, 1983, Nancy Reagan, "Dear School Principal," April 1983, Nancy Reagan, "Dear Friend," April 1983, "The New Teen Titans" Teacher's Guide, New Teen Titans Poster, Certificate of Heroism, folder: Awareness–Presidential Meetings (2), OA 12590, Keebler Company, Press Release, April 25, 1983, folder: Drug Abuse Prevention Comic Books Teen Titans (1), OA 16996, RLW-Reagan.

53. *The New Teen Titans: Plague!* (New York: DC Comics, 1983), *The New Teen Titans: Problem Child* (New York: DC Comics, 1983), folder: Drug Abuse Prevention Comic Books Teen Titans (3), OA 16996, RLW-Reagan.

54. *The New Teen Titans: Battle!* (New York: DC Comics, 1983), folder: Drug Abuse Prevention Comic Books Teen Titans (3), OA 16996, RLW-Reagan.

55. Matthew King to Carlton Turner, May 5, 1983 (quotation), William W. Norin to Patrick McKelvey, July 28, 1983, folder: Drug Abuse Prevention Comic Books Teen Titans (2), OA 16996, RLW-Reagan. Positive feedback in folder: Drug Abuse Prevention Comic Books Teen Titans (5), ibid.

56. Carlton Turner Testimony, November 1, 1983, "Federal Drug Strategy—1983," *Hearings*, 50–55; William Pollin Testimony, ibid., 64–70; Thomas Pauken Testimony, ibid., 77–92; Charles Rangel comments in ibid., 8, 89–90.

57. Ronald Reagan, "Remarks on Signing the National Drug Abuse Education and Prevention Week Proclamation," September 21, 1984, APP, https://www.presidency.ucsb.edu/node/261592. "Retribution" quotation from Reagan, "Remarks Announcing Federal Initiatives against Drug Trafficking and Organized Crime," October 14, 1982, APP, https://www.presidency.ucsb.edu/node/246317.

58. Statement of Joyce Nalepka, November 2, 1983, "Federal Drug Strategy—1983," *Hearings*, 393–401; Interview with Peter Bourne, *Newservice* (July/August 1983), 37–38.

59. Lloyd D. Johnston, Patrick M. O'Malley, Jerald G. Bachman, and John E. Schulenberg, *Monitoring the Future: National Survey Results on Drug Use, 1975–2006*, vol. I (Bethseda, MD: NIDA, 2006), 199.

60. Lloyd D. Johnston, Patrick M. O'Malley, and Jerald G. Bachman, *National Trends in Drug Use and Related Factors among American High School Students and Young Adults, 1975–1986* (Rockville, MD: NIDA, 1987). Also see Nancy S. Tobler, "Meta-Analysis of 142 Adolescent Drug Prevention Programs: Quantitative Outcome Results of Program Participants Compared to a Control or Comparison Group," *Journal of Drug Issues* 16, no. 4 (1986): 537–67; Robert L. Bangert-Drowns, "The Effects of School-Based Substance Abuse Education—A Meta-Analysis," *Journal of Drug Education* 18, no. 3 (1988): 243–64; Wysong, Aniskiewicz, and Wright, "Truth and DARE."

61. National Commission on Excellence in Education, *A Nation at Risk: The Imperative for Educational Reform* (Washington: GPO, 1983); media coverage in *The Bottom Line in Education: 1980 to the Present* (Stone Lantern Films, 2000).

62. Renfro, *Stranger Danger*; Jenkins, *Moral Panic* (quotation 143).

63. Phyllis and David York, with Ted Wachtel, *ToughLove* (Garden City, NY: Doubleday, 1982), quotations 24, 6, 120; ToughLove, "How to Start Your ToughLove Parent Support Group," n.d. [early 1980s], folder: ToughLove, box 1, OA 15002, DAPO-Reagan. Quotation from book advertisement in *NYT*, October 10, 1982.

64. Ann Landers, "Giving Kids 'Tough' Love," *Family Circle*, November 3, 1981, 34, 104–6. This article and other ToughLove materials collected by Reagan White House's DAPO staff and found in folder: ToughLove, box 1, OA 15002, DAPO-Reagan.

65. Jude Johnston, "ToughLove: Parents Helping Each Other Out," *Guidepost*, December 17, 1981, 1; Elise Piquet, "ToughLove: A New Way of Dealing with Problem Teens," *Families*, February 1982, 43–46; Molly Moore, "Tough Love: Parents Apply Firm Hand with Wayward Children," *WP*, September 17, 1981, VA1; *ToughLove Notes* (Fall–Winter 1981), folder: ToughLove, box 1, OA 15002, DAPO-Reagan.

66. Straight, Inc., "The Dream for Every Parent," n.d. [early 1980s], Straight, Inc., *Epidemic*, No. 1, n.d. [early 1980s], folder: STRAIGHT (1), James E. Hartz to Carlton Turner, February 19, 1982, folder: STRAIGHT (2), Turner to Hartz, May 18, 1982, folder: STRAIGHT (3), box 1, OA 15002, DAPO-Reagan.

67. Andy MacDonald, "Hooked on Drugs"; Bettinita Harris, "Inside Straight" series, *St. Petersburg Independent*, July 26–29, 1982.

68. Harris, "Inside Straight" series, *St. Petersburg Independent*, July 26–29, 1982; Straight, Inc., *Epidemic*, No. 1; Testimony of Donald Ian MacDonald, October 21, 1981, "Examination of the Health and Educational Effects of Marijuana on Youth," *Hearing*, 76.

69. *Collins v. Straight, Inc.*, 748 F.2d 916 (1984); "Report on Class Action Suit against Straight, Inc.," n.d. [1982], Andrew I. Malcolm and Barbara E. Malcolm, "An Examination of Straight Incorporated," September 5, 1981, folder: Straight (1), Richard A. Hayman to Carlton Turner, September 25, 1981, folder: Straight (3), box 1, OA 15002, DAPO-Reagan; *WP*, July 28, August 24, December 2, 8, 1982, January 2, May 10–11, 13, 25, June 8, 1983. Also see Nancy Reagan, "Let's Get Kids Off Drugs," *LHJ*, January 1983.

70. "Getting Straight," *20/20*, ABC-TV, 1983, http://www.youtube.com/watch?v=EccdPYsyrjQ; "Straight, Inc," *60 Minutes*, CBS-TV, January 1984; [Redacted] to Van Gordon Saulter (CBS President), January 26, 1984, "Letters to the Readers from Straight Parents," *St. Petersburg Times*, May 15, 1983, folder: STRAIGHT (1), box 1, OA 15002, DAPO-Reagan.

71. Beth Polson and Miller Newton, *Not My Kid: A Family's Guide to Kids and Drugs* (New York: Arbor House, 1984), quotations 5, 10, 97, 16, 135, 174 (and jacket copy). Newton left Straight to open a similar for-profit residential treatment center in Bergen County, New Jersey, in 1984. State regulators shut the facility down in 1998, one year before a $4.5 million malpractice settlement in a lawsuit by a female committed at age fourteen by her parents and held there for six years (with allegations of systematic physical and psychological abuse). See Tim O'Brien, "Closure for a Quack Victim," *New Jersey Law Journal*, January 24, 2000, https://www.fornits.com/anonanon/articles/200003/20000320-10.htm.

72. *Not My Kid* (ITC Entertainment, 1985), first aired on CBS-TV and produced by Beth Polson; also see *WP*, January 15, 1985.

73. PANDAA Newsletter, November 1981, November 1982, January 1983, March 1983, folder: PANDAA, OA 13748, CET-Reagan.

74. PANDAA Newsletter, November 1982, January 1983, March 1983, Penny Phillips, "PANDAA Rock Concert Committee Meets with Capital Centre Management," November 1982, Phillips, "A Rock Concert at the Capital Centre," November 1982, folder: PANDAA, OA 13748, CET-Reagan; *Fairfax Journal*, December 1, 1983, August 10, 1984, Drugs folder, VF-FCPL.

75. PANDAA Newsletter, November 1981, November 1982, January 1983, March 1983, folder: PANDAA, OA 13748, CET-Reagan; Fairfax County Police Department, *A Parent's Guide to Drug Abuse*, 1983, folder: Drug Treatment Programs, VF-FCPL; Fairfax County Task Force on Drunk Driving, *Final Report*, 1982, Virginia Room, Fairfax County Public Library; Tobias quoted in *WP*, April 2, 1987. On school policies, also see *WP*, December 2, 1983, March 7, 1984, April 2, 1987; *Alexandria Gazette*, August 16, 1983, Schools-Students-Drug Use folder, VF-FCPL; *WP*, October 20, 1983, June 19, 1987.

76. Families Action Newsletter, May/June 1982, folder: Families Action Newsletter, Florida Informed Parents Newsletter, February 1984, folder: Florida Informed Parents, OA 15688, Houston Informed Parents, Inc. Newsletter, February 1983, folder: Houston Informed Parents, OA 13696, CET-Reagan; Texas War on Drugs Committee, Statement on H.B. 393, n.d. [1983], folder: Texans' War on Drugs, box 4, OA 15003, DAPO-Reagan; *LAT*, December 16, 1982, December 15, 1983, January 15, 26, July 14, 1984; *San Diego Union*, January 7, 1984.

77. PBS Frontline, *Stopping Drugs, Part II* (Documentary Consortium, PBS Video, 1987).

78. Robert DuPont, *Getting Tough on Gateway Drugs: A Guide for the Family* (Washington, DC: American Psychiatric Press, 1984), quotations 241, 229; Donald Ian MacDonald, *Drugs, Drinking, and Adolescents* (Chicago: Year Book Medical Publishers, 1984), quotations 2, 71.

79. National Research Council, *Alcohol and Public Policy: Beyond the Shadow of Prohibition* (Washington: National Academy Press, 1981), 76–78; Ruth C. Engs, "Responsibility and Alcohol: Teaching Responsible Decisions about Alcohol and Its Use for Those Who Choose to Drink," in *Youth and Alcohol Abuse: Readings and Resources*, ed. Carla Martindell Felsted (Phoenix: Oryx Press, 1986), 93–100 (quotation 97); Millree Williams and Jill Vejnoska, "Alcohol and Youth: State Prevention Approaches," in ibid., 101–17; NIAAA, "Talking to Your Teenager about Drinking and Driving," n.d. [early 1980s], folder: Presidential Commission on Drunk Driving (4), box 23, DIM-Reagan. On state trends in the 1970s, also see NTSB, "Facts on Youthful Drinking and Driving," 1983, reproduced in "Prohibit the Sale of Alcoholic Beverages to Persons under 21 Years of Age," *Hearings before the Subcommittee on Commerce, Transportation, and Tourism, Committee on Energy and Commerce*, House of Representatives, October 4, 19, 1983 (Washington: GPO, 1984), 488–91.

80. DAPO, "The Reagan Administration's Five-Point Plan to Prevent and Control Drug Abuse in the United States," March 31, 1982, folder: 094400–094899, box 14, Carlton Turner to Ed Harper, November 2, 1982, folder: 107001–109674, box 16, OPD-Reagan; *Drugs and Drug Abuse Education Newsletter* (November 1982), Thomas Gleaton to Turner, December 13, 1982, folder: Buddy Gleaton (2), OA 13748, CET-Reagan.

81. NFP, "Resolution: No 'Responsible Use,'" November 1982, folder: PRIDE (4–6), PRIDE, "Position Paper on the Issue of Responsible Alcohol Use by Adolescents," 1983, folder: PRIDE

(1–5), OA 16999, series II, DIM-Reagan; NFP, "What Parents Must Learn about Teens and Alcohol," 1982, folder: Drugs (1), box 21, MK-Huntington.

82. American Business Men's Research Foundation, "Monday Morning Report," June 23, 1980, Robert L. Hammond to Phyllis Scheps, May 17, 1982, "Court Decision Answers Questions on Drinking Age," December 1978, reproduced in "Prohibit the Sale of Alcoholic Beverages to Persons under 21 Years of Age," *Hearings*, 497–506.

83. Peter L. Amico, "How to Raise the Legal Drinking Age: The New Jersey Story," April 1983, reproduced in "Prohibit the Sale of Alcoholic Beverages to Persons under 21 Years of Age," *Hearings*, 469–491; Lee B. Laskin, "A Report on the Drinking Age Issue: The Need for a Return to the 21-Year-Old Limit," May 10, 1982, ibid., 512–46.

84. Anne Arundel County Drug and Alcohol Program, *Families in Action Newsletter* (October 1982), folder: Families Action Newsletter, OA 15688, CET-Reagan; NFP, "What Parents Must Learn about Teens and Alcohol," 1982; Peggy Mann, *Arrive Alive: How to Keep Drunk and Pot-High Drivers off the Highway* (New York: Woodmere Press, 1983), 107–9.

85. Laskin, "Report on the Drinking Age Issue"; NTSB, Safety Recommendation H-82–18, July 22, 1982, reproduced in "Prohibit the Sale of Alcoholic Beverages to Persons under 21 Years of Age," *Hearings*, 431–33. On "drugged driving," see Testimony of Peggy Mann, "Alcohol, Drugs, and Driving," *Hearing before the Subcommittee on Alcoholism and Drug Abuse, Committee on Labor and Human Resources*, U.S. Senate, August 5, 1982 (Washington: GPO, 1982), 19–45; Mann, "Marijuana and Driving: The Sobering Truth," *RD*, May 1979, 22–26; Mann, *Arrive Alive*.

86. "Federal Legislation to Combat Drunk Driving Including National Driver Register," *Hearing before the Subcommittee on Surface Transportation, Committee on Commerce, Science, and Transportation*, U.S. Senate, March 3, 1982 (Washington: GPO, 1982); NTSB, "Information on Raising the Drinking Age," 1983, reproduced in "Prohibit the Sale of Alcoholic Beverages to Persons under 21 Years of Age," *Hearings*, 434–35.

87. Candy Lightner and Nancy Hathaway, *Giving Sorrow Words: How to Cope with Grief and Get On with Your Life* (New York: Warner Books, 1990), quotations 1, 9; *CT*, May 10, 1981; Testimony of Candy Lightner, March 3, 1982, "Federal Legislation to Combat Drunk Driving Including National Driver Register," *Hearing*, 69–71. On Lightner and MADD, also see Lerner, *One for the Road*.

88. Governor Jerry Brown, Press Release, December 30, 1980, *Sacramento Union*, August 27, 1980, *Sacramento Bee*, August 27, 1980, folder: Drunken Drivers, box C-11–7, Governor's Task Force on Alcohol, Drugs and Traffic Safety, *Task Force Report: Alcohol, Drugs and Traffic Safety* (Sacramento, June 1981), Governor's Office, "Enrolled Bill Report: AB 541," September 25, 1981, folder: Drunk Driving, box A-5–3, JB-USC; *LAT*, October 2, 1980 (Lightner quotation), February 6, 1982. On "responsible use," see MADD, *That's Why We're MADD*, n.d. [early 1980s], MADD, *9 Things You Can Do To Help MADD*, n.d. [early 1980s], folder: Promotional Materials, box 2, MADD-UM; *LAT*, June 11, 1981 (quotation).

89. MADD Organization Handbook, 1984, folder: MADD National Policies and Guidelines, box 1, MADD-UM; *LAT*, October 2, 1980, June 11, November 3, 1981; *WP*, March 22, 1981. Also see Lerner, *One for the Road*, 64–92.

90. Ronald Reagan, "Remarks on Signing Executive Order 12358, Establishing Presidential Commission on Drunk Driving," April 14, 1982, APP, https://www.presidency.ucsb.edu/node/245010; Carlton Turner to Martin Anderson, December 29, 1981, White House Press Release,

May 18, 1982, folder: Presidential Commission on Drunk Driving (1), box 23, DIM-Reagan; Presidential Commission on Drunk Driving, *An Interim Report to the Nation*, December 13, 1982 (Washington: GPO, 1982).

91. *What is S.A.D.D.?* pamphlet, 1982, Wayland High School S.A.D.D., "Drinking-Drive Contract," folder: SADD, OA 9435, series III, CET-Reagan; *BG*, April 27, 1982, January 6, 1983; Testimony of Robert Anastas (SADD executive director), August 5, 1982, "Alcohol, Drugs, and Driving," *Hearing*, 83–106, 114–15 (quotation 86). Also see "The SADD Movement" in Sandy Golden, *Driving the Drunk Off the Road: A Handbook for Action* (Washington, DC: Acropolis Books, 1983), 21–38. Material on local SADD chapters from *CT*, December 15, 1982; *LAT*, May 23, 1983; *BG*, April 17, 1983; *WP*, January 14, 1982, May 25, 1983.

92. Testimony of Charles L. Short, August 5, 1982, "Alcohol, Drugs, and Driving," *Hearing*, 106–9; NHTSA, "Idea Sampler: To Promote Observance of National Drunk and Drugged Driver Awareness Week" (Washington: Department of Transportation, 1983); *LAT*, September 19, 1983, May 29, 1985.

93. HHS News, Press Release, October 4, 1982, folder: CCWG–Drug Abuse Health Issues, OA 12590, RLW-Reagan; Testimony of Phyllis Scheps, "Measures to Combat Drunk Driving," *Hearing before the Subcommittee on Surface Transportation, Committee on Commerce, Science, and Transportation*, U.S. Senate, June 14, 1984 (Washington: GPO, 1984), 29–31; Nancy J. Granat to Peter K. Vaslov, November 30, 1983, folder: Parents Groups–Misc. Info, OA 13748, Carlton Turner to Ben Elliott, August 3, 1984, folder: Memos August 1984–May 1985 (2), box 4, CET-Reagan. On MADD's support, see *MADD National Newsletter* (Spring 1983), folder: National Clippings and Pamphlets, box 1, LEL-UM; Testimony of Candy Lightner, "National Minimum Drinking Age," *Hearing before the Subcommittee on Alcoholism and Drug Abuse, Committee on Labor and Human Resources*, U.S. Senate, June 19, 1984 (Washington: GPO, 1984), 33–41.

94. MADD, Press Release, January 26, 1983, folder: National Board General 1983 (1), box 1, LEL-UM; *Mothers Against Drunk Driving: The Candy Lightner Story* (NBC, March 14, 1983); NBC, *Mothers Against Drunk Driving: The Candy Lightner Story* Viewer's Guide, 1983, folder: National Clippings and Pamphlets, box 1, LEL-Bentley; James B. Jacobs, *Drunk Driving: An American Dilemma* (Chicago: University of Chicago Press, 1989), xv–xvi.

95. Testimony of Candy Lightner, October 4, 1983, "Prohibit the Sale of Alcoholic Beverages to Persons under 21 Years of Age," *Hearings*, 10–12, 64–72; Lightner Testimony, June 19, 1984, "National Minimum Drinking Age," *Hearing*, 33–41; Presidential Commission on Drunk Driving, *Final Report*, November 1983 (Washington: GPO, 1983), quotation 2; *NBC Nightly News*, December 13, 1983.

96. Testimony of Michael M. Birkley, October 4, 1983, "Prohibit the Sale of Alcoholic Beverages to Persons under 21 Years of Age," *Hearings*, 143–74, 199–204; Birkley, "Death and the Legal Drinking Age: A Tri-State Study," April 1983, reproduced in ibid., 58–63. Lightner's "very biased" comment in ibid., 65. Also see Birkley Testimony, June 19, 1984, "National Minimum Drinking Age," *Hearing*, 79–100. For additional studies, see "Measures to Combat Drunk Driving," *Hearing*, 41–87.

97. Testimony of Katherine Ozer, October 19, 1983, "Prohibit the Sale of Alcoholic Beverages to Persons under 21 Years of Age," *Hearings*, 417–25; Testimony of Celeste Bergman, June 19, 1984, "National Minimum Drinking Age," *Hearing*, 100–9; Bergman, "Raising the Drinking Age Is Not the Answer," *WP*, June 23, 1984, A13.

98. "Measures to Combat Drunk Driving," *Hearing*; "National Minimum Drinking Age," *Hearing*, Lautenberg quotation 19; *WP*, June 14, 1984; Ronald Reagan, "Remarks at River Dell High School in Oradell, New Jersey," June 20, 1984, APP, https://www.presidency.ucsb.edu/node/260820; Reagan, "Remarks on Signing a National Minimum Drinking Age Bill," July 17, 1984, APP, https://www.presidency.ucsb.edu/node/261306. Also see Gallup Poll, "21-Year National Drinking Age Law Backed by Large Majority of Public," January 27, 1983, reproduced in "Prohibit the Sale of Alcoholic Beverages to Persons under 21 Years of Age," *Hearings*, 557.

99. "Implementation of the National Minimum Drinking Age Act," *Hearing before the Subcommittee on Surface Transportation, Committee on Public Works and Transportation*, House of Representatives, October 1, 1992 (Washington: GPO, 1992); Lloyd D. Johnston, Patrick M. O'Malley, and Jerald G. Bachman, *Drug Use among High School Seniors, College Students, and Young Adults, 1975–1990* (Rockville, MD: NIDA, 1991), 51–90 (of vol. 1), 139–68 (of vol. 2).

100. Doris Aiken (Remove Intoxicated Drivers) to Ronald Reagan, July 30, 1984, folder: Memos August 1984-May 1985 (2), box 4, Sue Rusche, "An Alternative to the SADD Contract," October 8, 1984, folder: Parents Groups–Sue Rusche (1), OA 13748, CET-Reagan; Testimony of William Orr/SADD, June 14, 1984, "Measures to Combat Drunk Driving," *Hearing*, 21–24. Also see "Implementation of the National Minimum Drinking Age Act," *Hearing*. On Lightner, see Norma Phillips, Memo to MADD Chapters, October 11, 1985, and related materials in folder: National Board General 1985 (3), box 1, LEL-UM; Lerner, *One for the Road*, 136.

101. NFP, "Operation Prom/Graduation: Saving the Fun, Saving Lives," 1986, folder: Outreach Operation Program Graduation, box 2, MADD-UM; Phyllis Scheps and Arlene Rothenberg (New Jersey NFP) to NFP Board of Directors, State Networkers, Legislative Liaisons, January 26, 1986, folder: PRIDE (5–6), OA 16999, series II, DIM-Reagan; Micky Sadoff, *Get MADD Again, America!* (Irving, Texas: MADD, 1991).

102. PRIDE, "Position Paper on the Issue of Responsible Alcohol Use by Adolescents," 1983, folder: PRIDE (1–5), "Consensus resulting from NFP/PRIDE Meeting held on December 5, 1983, Chicago, Illinois," included in Mary Jacobson to Thomas Gleaton, April 2, 1986, folder: PRIDE (4–6), OA 16999, series II, DIM-Reagan; Marsha Schuchard, "Can Parents Teach Adolescents How to Drink Responsibly in the Home?" PRIDE Newsletter, June 1984, 6, folder: PRIDE (1), box 4, OA 15003, DAPO-Reagan.

103. *Epidemic: Deadliest Weapon in America* (MTI Teleprograms/Gannett Co., 1985); Thomas Gleaton and Marsha Schuchard to NFP Board of Directors and State Networkers, December 9, 1985, Scheps and Rothenberg to NFP Board of Directors, State Networkers, Legislative Liaisons, January 26, 1986, Collin Siedor to Gleaton, March 14, 1986, folder: PRIDE (5–6), NFP to Coronet/MTI Film & Video, November 7, 1985, Shirley Coletti (NFP chair) to Gleaton, n.d. [April 1986], Gleaton and Schuchard to NFP Board of Directors, May 26, 1986, folder: PRIDE (4–6), OA 16999, series II, DIM-Reagan.

104. *Generation at Risk: The Chemical People II* (PBS: WQED Pittsburgh, 1986). On the broader context, see Males, *Scapegoat Generation*; Jenkins, *Decade of Nightmares*, Jenkins, *Moral Panic*; Renfro, *Stranger Danger*.

105. Adams, *Grass Roots*, 242–63; "First Lady Greets Anti-Drug Youth," *ADAMHA News* (March 1985), 1, 4–5. The "Just Say No" movement later experienced a schism over the Reagan White House's favoritism toward the sponsor Procter & Gamble, whose stated goal was to "build the business" (quoted in Adams, *Grass Roots*, 244).

106. "Fact Sheet: Keebler Company Drug Awareness Campaign," folder: Keebler, box 2, OA 15002, DAPO-Reagan; Carlton Turner Memo, "The Keebler Company 'I Believe In Me' Film," April 17, 1986, folder March 1985–July 1986 (5), Nancy Reagan, "The Drug Abuse Epidemic," March 1985, folder March 1985–July 1986 (6), box 2, ACTION PSA Scripts, 1986, folder: ACTION (1), box 5, CET-Reagan.

107. Ronald Reagan, "Remarks Announcing the Campaign Against Drug Abuse and a Question-and-Answer Session with Reporters," August 4, 1986, *Public Papers of the Presidents of the United States: Ronald Reagan, 1986* (Washington: GPO, 1989), 1045–50. The six-point plan came largely from DAPO; see Carlton Turner, "Memorandum for the Domestic Policy Council: Drug Abuse Policy Opportunities," July 14, 1986, folder: March 1985–July 1986 (1), box 2, CET-Reagan. On the PMRC, see Riismandel, *Neighborhood of Fear*, esp. 142–75.

108. "Come on America . . . Join the Club: Just Say No," 1986, "Just Say No Foundation Highlights," August 20, 1986, September 30, 1986, folder: Just Say No Foundation, box 4, OA 15003, DAPO-Reagan. On Hollywood films, also see PBS Frontline, *Stopping Drugs, Part II.*

109. Craig Reinarman and Harry G. Levine, "The Crack Attack: Politics and Media in the Crack Scare," *Crack in America*, 18–51; Reeves and Campbell, *Cracked Coverage*. Data in Johnston, O'Malley, and Bachman, *National Trends in Drug Use and Related Factors among American High School Students and Young Adults, 1975–1986*, 16, 36. Headline in Michael Massing, "Crack's Destructive Sprint Across America," *NYT Magazine*, October 1, 1989, 38–41, 58–60.

110. *NYT*, November 17, 29, 1985; *LAT*, December 4, 1985; Tom Morganthau, "Kids and Cocaine," *Newsweek*, March 17, 1986, 58–65 (the subtitle tagline is from the cover).

111. Morganthau, "Kids and Cocaine"; Terry E. Johnson, "Tale of Three Addictions," *Newsweek*, March 17, 1986, 60–62; Morganthau, "Crack and Crime," *Newsweek*, June 16, 1986, 16–22; Jacob V. Lamar Jr., "Crack: A Cheap and Deadly Cocaine Is a Spreading Menace," *Time*, June 2, 1986, 16–18; Lamar, "Today's Native Sons," *Time*, December 1, 1986, 26–29; "'I Am a Coke Addict': What Happens When Nice Guys Get Hooked," *Life*, October 1, 1986, cover image.

112. Carlton Turner Memo, "Review of Staff Meeting Remarks" (drug talking points for President Reagan), June 5, 1986, folder: March 1985-July 1986 (7), box 2, CET-Reagan.

113. *NYT*, July 24, 1986; Jack McCallum, "The Cruelest Thing Ever," *Sports Illustrated*, June 30, 1968, 20–27.

114. Carlton Turner, "Memorandum for the Domestic Policy Council: Drug Abuse Policy Opportunities," July 14, 1986, folder: March 1985–July 1986 (1), box 2, Turner to Donald T. Regan, Memo Re: "House Democrats' Drug Strategy," August 4, 1986, Secretary of Education William J. Bennett to Regan, June 18, 1986, folder: Misc. Papers (1), box 1, CET-Reagan; Massing, *The Fix*, esp. 175–90. The White House archives indicate that the Reagan administration's public health disinterest in nonwhite urban crack users paralleled its "malign neglect" of homosexual men during the early years of the AIDS crisis, as neither of these groups consisted of constituents who mattered to executive branch policymakers, except as criminal threats. See Tonry, *Malign Neglect*; Randy Shilts, *And the Band Played On: Politics, People, and the AIDS Epidemic* (New York: St. Martin's Press, 1987).

115. "Crack Cocaine," *Hearing before the Permanent Subcommittee on Investigations, Committee on Governmental Affairs*, U.S. Senate, July 15, 1986 (Washington: GPO, 1986), quotation 4; Carlton Turner, Memorandum: "Administration's Drug Initiative," July 24, 1986, folder: March 1985–July 1986 (2), box 2, Turner-Reagan. Also see Provine, *Unequal under Law*, 107–15.

116. "The Crack Cocaine Crisis," *Joint Hearing before the Select Committee on Narcotics Abuse and Control and the Select Committee on Children, Youth, and Families*, House of Representatives, July 15, 1986 (Washington: GPO, 1987), quotation 1; Lee Ann Bonanno and Janet Bonanno at 12–24.

117. "Trafficking and Abuse of Crack in New York City," *Hearing before the Select Committee on Narcotics Abuse and Control*, House of Representatives, July 18, 1986 (Washington: GPO, 1987); Opening Statement of Charles B. Rangel, "The Federal War on Drugs: Past, Present, and Future," *Hearing before the Select Committee on Narcotics Abuse and Control*, House of Representatives, October 3, 1986 (Washington: GPO, 1987), 53–64 (additional quotation 1).

118. Ronald Reagan and Nancy Reagan, "Speech to the Nation on the Campaign Against Drug Abuse," September 14, 1986, Miller Center-Presidential Speeches, https://millercenter.org/the-presidency/presidential-speeches/september-14-1986-speech-nation-campaign-against-drug-abuse. Also see Ronald Reagan, "Remarks at the National Conference on Alcohol and Drug Abuse Prevention in Arlington, Virginia," August 6, 1986, Ronald Reagan Presidential Library, https://www.reaganlibrary.gov/archives/speech/remarks-national-conference-alcohol-and-drug-abuse-prevention-arlington-virginia.

119. Anti-Drug Abuse Act of 1986, Public Law 99–570, October 27, 1986; DOJ, *Handbook on the Anti-Drug Abuse Act of 1986*, March 1987, NCJRS, https://www.ojp.gov/pdffiles1/Photocopy/157817NCJRS.pdf. The final vote was 97–2 in the Senate and 392–16 in the House; see https://www.congress.gov/bill/99th-congress/house-bill/5484.

120. Reinarman and Levine, "Crack Attack"; Reeves and Campbell, *Cracked Coverage*; Provine, *Unequal under Law*, esp. 91–119; Deborah J. Vagins and Jesselyn McCurdy, *Cracks in the System: Twenty Years of the Unjust Federal Crack Cocaine Law* (ACLU, March 2006).

121. White House Press Release, "Fact Sheet: The Crusade for a Drug-Free Nation," January 25, 1988, folder: CDFA (2), White House Office of Public Affairs, "The Reagan Record on the National Crusade for a Drug-Free America," June 6, 1988, folder: CDFA (4), "Working Paper: Focus on the User," February 12, 1988, folder: CDFA (1), box 2, MacDonald, "Where Do We Go from Here," April 22, 1988, folder: Correspondence September 1987–November 1988 (2), box 14, OA 16758, DIM-Reagan. Also see MacDonald, *Drugs, Drinking, and Adolescents*.

122. "Working Paper: Focus on the User," February 12, 1988, folder: CDFA (1), box 2, DIM-Reagan. On white suburban markets, see Scott Jacques and Richard Wright, *Code of the Suburb: Inside the World of Young Middle-Class Drug Dealers* (Chicago: University of Chicago Press, 2015); N. Curcione, "Suburban Snowmen: Facilitating Factors in the Careers of Middle-Class Coke Dealers," *Deviant Behavior* 18, no. 3 (1997): 233–53.

123. DAPO, "Media Executives Drug Abuse Prevention Briefing," March 7, 1988, MacDonald, "Address Media Executives on Drug Abuse," March 7, 1988, folder: Media Executives, OA 16995, RLW-Reagan; *21 Jump Street* (Fox-TV, 1987), episodes 1 and 2.

124. Anti-Drug Abuse Act of 1988, Public Law 100–690, November 18, 1988; CRS, *Anti-Drug Abuse Act of 1988: Highlights of Enacted Bill*, Report 88-707 GOV, November 16, 1988; Office of the President, "Statement of Administration Policy: H.R. 5210," August 30, 1988, DAPO, "House Drug Bill—Talking Points—Shaw Amendment," August 1988, folder: Legislation, Anti-Drug Abuse Act of 1988 (4), box 4, DIM-Reagan; Provine, *Unequal under Law*, 115–17; Reinarman and Levine, "Crack Attack," 39–40.

125. Jamie Fellner, *Punishment and Prejudice: Racial Disparities in the War on Drugs* (Human Rights Watch, May 2000); Fellner, "Race, Drugs, and Law Enforcement in the United States";

Human Rights Watch, *Targeting Blacks: Drug Law Enforcement and Race in the United States* (New York: Human Rights Watch, 2008); Vagins and McCurdy, *Cracks in the System*; Alexander, *New Jim Crow*, esp. 95–136; Tonry, *Malign Neglect*; Ira Glasser and Loren Siegel, "'When Constitutional Rights Seem Too Extravagant to Endure': The Crack Scare's Impact on Civil Rights and Liberties," *Crack in America*, 229–48. Data from FBI, *Uniform Crime Reports*, 1984–1994.

126. Jacob V. Lamar, "Kids Who Sell Crack," *Time*, May 9, 1988, 20–33; CDOJ, "A Confidential Publication for Law Enforcement: Crips & Bloods Street Gangs," 1988, NCJRS, https://www.ojp.gov/pdffiles1/Digitization/146790NCJRS.pdf; Davis, *City of Quartz*, 267–322.

127. Massing, "Crack's Destructive Sprint Across America"; Andrew H. Malcolm, "Crack, Bane of Inner City, Is Now Gripping Suburbs," *NYT*, October 1, 1989, A1, A24; Malcolm, "Affluent Addicts' Road Back Begins in a Climb Past Denial," *NYT*, October 2, 1989, A1, B10.

128. *Crack U.S.A.: County Under Siege*, dir. Vince DiPersio and Bill Guttenbag (HBO, 1989).

Epilogue

1. *Plano Star Courier*, October 10, 1997, July 23, 1998; "Our Town: Plano, Texas, Deals with Heroin Epidemic amongst Teenagers," *Dateline NBC*, January 14, 1998 (for "clean-cut teenagers" and "bright future" quotations); "Heroin in Suburbia: It Can't Happen Here," *ABC World News Sunday*, January 18, 1998; "Heroin Traffickers Target Texas Suburb," *CNN Today*, July 22, 1998; "Drug Crisis in America: Who's to Blame for the Influx of Illegal Narcotics?," *CNN Talkback Live*, July 22, 1998; "Suburban Heroin," *CNN & Company*, July 23, 1998. For more critical investigations, see Mike Gray, "Texas Heroin Massacre," *Rolling Stone*, May 27, 1999, 32–36; Pamela Colloff, "Teenage Wasteland," *Texas Monthly*, January 1999, 102–9, 133–34, 178–79.

2. Violent Crime Control and Law Enforcement Act of 1994, Public Law 103–322, September 13, 1994; CRS, *Crime Control: Summary of the Violent Crime Control and Law Enforcement Act of 1994*, Report 94–910 S, November 11, 1994; William J. Clinton, "Remarks on Signing the Violent Crime Control and Law Enforcement Act of 1994," September 13, 1994, APP, https://www.presidency.ucsb.edu/node/218677; Sheryl Gay Stolberg and Anstead W. Herndon, "'Lock the S.O.B.s Up': Joe Biden and the Era of Mass Incarceration," *NYT*, June 25, 2019. Also see John J. DiIulio Jr., "The Coming of the Super-Predators," *Weekly Standard*, November 27, 1995, 23–28; William J. Bennett, John J. DiIulio Jr., and John P. Walters, *Body Count: Moral Poverty . . . and How to Win America's War against Crime and Drugs* (New York: Simon & Schuster, 1996); White House Office of Public Affairs, "The Reagan Record on the National Crusade for a Drug-Free America," June 6, 1988, folder: CDFA (4), box 2, OA 16758, DIM-Reagan. On interdiction, see Michael Shifter, "Plan Colombia: A Retrospective," *Americas Quarterly* 6, no. 3 (Summer 2012): 36–42; Suzanna Reiss, "Beyond Supply and Demand: Obama's Drug Wars in Latin America," *NACLA Report on the Americas* 43, no. 1 (January/February 2010): 27–31.

3. "Effectiveness of the National Youth Anti-Drug Media Campaign," *Hearing before the Subcommittee on Criminal Justice, Drug Policy, and Human Resources, Committee on Government Reform*, House of Representatives, July 11, 2000 (Washington: GPO, 2001), including Barry R. McCaffrey testimony at 13–78; Bennett, DiIulio, and Walters, *Body Count*, 137–90; Lee Fang, "The Anti-Pot Lobby's Big Bankroll," *The Nation*, July 21, 2014, 12–16.

4. White House, *National Drug Control Strategy: Progress in the War on Drugs, 1989–1992*, January 1993, NCJRS, https://www.ojp.gov/pdffiles1/ondcp/140556.pdf; Baum, *Smoke and*

Mirrors, 262–328; Lloyd D. Johnston, Patrick M. O'Malley, and Jerald G. Bachman, *National Survey Results on Drug Use from the Monitoring the Future Survey, 1975–1995*, vol. 1 (Rockville, MD: NIDA, 1996), esp. 7–13.

5. McCaffrey quoted in *CNN Sunday Morning*, December 21, 1997; NIDA, Summary of the National Conference on Marijuana Use: Prevention, Treatment, and Research, July 1995, NIDA Archives, https://archives.drugabuse.gov/sites/default/files/mjconf.pdf; NIDA, "Marijuana: Facts for Teens," NIH Publication No. 10-4037 (DHHS, 1995, rev. 1998); NIDA, "Marijuana: Facts Parents Need to Know," NIH Publication No. 10-4036 (DHHS, 1995, rev. 1998). On the Bush administration, see Scott Burns/White House Office of National Drug Control Policy, "An Open Letter to America's Prosecutors," November 1, 2002, reproduced https://norml.org/wp-content/uploads/pdf_files/whitehouse_fax.pdf; White House, *National Drug Control Strategy: 2009 Annual Report*, January 2009, NCJRS, https://www.ojp.gov/pdffiles1/ondcp/2009ndcs.pdf.

6. ACLU, *The War on Marijuana in Black and White* (New York: ACLU, June 2013). Final quotation in Baum, *Smoke and Mirrors*, 332.

7. Andrew Cohen, "How White Users Made Heroin a Public Health Problem," *The Atlantic*, August 12, 2015, https://www.theatlantic.com/politics/archive/2015/08/crack-heroin-and-race/401015/. For historical context, see Donna Murch, "How Race Made the Opioid Crisis," *Boston Review*, August 27, 2019, http://bostonreview.net/forum/donna-murch-how-race-made-opioid-crisis. On methamphetamine, which also spread illicitly because of the pharmaceutical industry's resistance to regulatory controls, see Jenkins, *Synthetic Panics*, 29–53, 132–59; Jonah Engle, "Merchants of Meth: How Big Pharma Keeps the Cooks in Business," *Mother Jones*, July/August 2013, 28–39.

8. White House, *National Drug Control Strategy 2010*, May 2010, NCJRS, https://www.ojp.gov/pdffiles1/ondcp/ndcs2010.pdf, 30, 33; Barack Obama, "Remarks at a Community Forum on Prescription Drug Abuse and Heroin Use in Charleston, West Virginia," October 21, 2015, APP, https://www.presidency.ucsb.edu/node/311449; Randal C. Archibold, "In Heartland Death, Traces of Heroin's Spread," *NYT*, May 30, 2009 (part of "War without Borders" series, March–December 2009); Sam Quinones, *Dreamland: The True Tale of America's Opiate Epidemic* (New York: Bloomsbury, 2015). On northern Mexico, see Charles Bowden, *Murder City: Ciudad Juárez and the Global Economy's New Killing Fields* (New York: Nation Books, 2010); David A. Shirk, "The Drug War in Mexico: Countering a Shared Threat" (New York: Council on Foreign Relations, March 2011).

9. R. Gil Kerlikowske (Obama drug czar) quoted in *LAT*, October 21, 2010; DEA, "The DEA Position on Marijuana," January 2011, updated April 2013, NCJRS, https://www.ncjrs.gov/App/Publications/abstract.aspx?ID=254295; Deborah S. Hasin et al., "Medical Marijuana Laws and Adolescent Marijuana Use in the USA from 1991 to 2014: Results from Annual, Repeated Cross-Sectional Surveys," *Lancet Psychology* 2, no. 7 (July 2015): 601–8; "David Simon, Creator of The Wire, Says New U.S. Drug Laws Help Only 'White, Middle-Class Kids,'" *The Guardian*, May 25, 2013; Jelani Cobb, "The Home Front," *New Yorker*, August 29, 2016, 25–26. Data from "State Policy" tracker, Marijuana Policy Project, https://www.mpp.org/states/.

10. White House, *National Drug Control Strategy 2010*, quotations iii, 2, 10; Biden quotation in *CNN Newsroom*, September 3, 2020; R. Gil Kerlikowske, "Remarks at the George Washington University Conference on 'Hemispheric Security: Emerging Issues,'" February 28, 2011,

https://obamawhitehouse.archives.gov/ondcp/news-releases-remarks/remarks-by-gil-kerlikowske-at-the-george-washington-university-conference; Joseph R. Biden Jr., "A Proclamation on Granting Pardon for the Offense of Simple Possession of Marijuana," October 6, 2022, https://www.whitehouse.gov/briefing-room/presidential-actions/2022/10/06/granting-pardon-for-the-offense-of-simple-possession-of-marijuana/. Also see Matthew D. Lassiter, "'Tough and Smart': The Resilience of the War on Drugs during the Obama Administration," *The Presidency of Barack Obama: A First Historical Assessment*, ed. Julian Zelizer (Princeton University Press, 2018), 162–78.

11. Human Rights Watch, *Nation Behind Bars: A Human Rights Solution*, 2014, https://www.hrw.org/sites/default/files/related_material/2014_US_Nation_Behind_Bars_0.pdf; Human Rights Watch and ACLU, *Every 25 Seconds: The Human Toll of Criminalizing Drug Use in the United States*, October 2016, https://www.hrw.org/report/2016/10/12/every-25-seconds/human-toll-criminalizing-drug-use-united-states; Global Commission on Drug Policy, *War on Drugs*, June 2011, http://www.globalcommissionondrugs.org/wp-content/themes/gcdp_v1/pdf/Global_Commission_Report_English.pdf.

INDEX

www.ingramcontent.com/pod-product-compliance
Lightning Source LLC
Chambersburg PA
CBHW032336280326
41935CB00008B/355

* 9 7 8 0 6 9 1 2 4 8 9 4 3 *